THE COMPLETE BOOK OF
HOME
REMODELING

THE COMPLETE BOOK OF
HOME REMODELING

ROBERT SCHARFF

McGRAW-HILL BOOK COMPANY

NEW YORK   SAN FRANCISCO   ST. LOUIS

AUCKLAND   NEW DELHI
DÜSSELDORF   PANAMA
JOHANNESBURG   PARIS
KUALA LUMPUR   SÃO PAULO
LONDON   SINGAPORE
MEXICO   SYDNEY
MONTREAL   TOKYO
            TORONTO

Library of Congress Cataloging in Publication Data

Scharff, Robert.
    The complete book of home remodeling.

    Includes index.
    1.   Dwellings—Remodeling—Amateur's manuals.
I. Title.
TH4816.S27   643′.7   74-23670
ISBN 0−07−055167−7

1234567890   VHVH   784321098765

The editors for this book were Leonard Josephson and
Tobia L. Worth, the designer was Edward J. Fox, and
the production supervisor was Stephen J. Boldish.
It was set in Melior by The Clarinda Company.

It was printed and bound by Von Hoffmann, Press, Inc.

Dedicated to my wife Mary
for her untiring assistance and inspiration

CONTENTS

PREFACE

This book was written for the homeowner who wishes to remodel and improve his home, either by doing it himself or by hiring a professional contractor. In other words, it covers *everything* one needs to know in order to remodel both the interior and exterior of an existing house. It features methods of improving a house with the creation of additional living space, by adding rooms in such areas as the basement, attic, or garage. There is also a chapter on how to expand your home.

It is not necessary to break down the subject matter any further in the Preface; the extent of the range of information can be found in the Contents, Index, and, of course, the text itself. This book is not a treatise on remodeling; rather it is intended to tell the remodeler how to plan a job and how to go about completing the project.

ACKNOWLEDGMENTS

The compilation of this volume required the help of many people. For their technical help as well as for many of the illustrations, I wish to thank the following associations and manufacturers: Air-Conditioning and Refrigeration Institute; American Society of Heating, Refrigeration, and Air Conditioning Engineers; American Standard, Inc.; Armstrong Cork Company; Bird & Son; Brick Institute of America; Cedar Closet Association; Certain-Teed Products Corporation; Connor Forest Industries, Inc.; Decro-Wall Corporation; Dura-a-Flex Inc.; E. J. Bruce Company; Formica Corporation; General Tire & Rubber Company; Georgia-Pacific Corporation; Homasote Company; Home Ventilating Institute; Kohler Company; Marsh Wall Products, Inc.; Masonite Corporation; Miami-Carey Manufacturing Company; Mineral Fiber Products Bureau; Modernfold Industries, Inc.: Montgomery Ward Company; Mutschler Inc.; Ozite Corporation; Pemko Manufacturing Company; Pennsylvania State Extension Service; Portland Cement Association; PPG Industries, Inc.; Rockwell Manufacturing Company; Roxbury Carpet Company; St. Charles Manufacturing Company; Stewart Industries,

Inc.; Thomas Industries, Inc.; Tibbals Flooring Corporation; Tile Council of America; United States Gypsum Company; United States Plywood Corporation; Vega Industries Inc.; Viking Sauna Company; Vistron Corporation; Wallcovering Industry Bureau; Wasco Products, Inc.; Western Wood Products Association; Westinghouse Electric Corporation; and Wood-Mosaic Corporation.

I would like to especially thank the following for their specific help and assistance in the chapters mentioned: the Small Homes Council of the University of Illinois for the material on lumber and plywood as well as the tables that appear in Chapter 2; the United States Department of Agriculture (Forest Service) for use of information and illustrations from their Handbook No. 73 — *Wood-Frame House Construction* by L. O. Anderson — found in Chapters 2, 3, 4, 7, and 15; Sears, Roebuck and Company for permission to use data and illustrations from several of their excellent instruction publications that are used in Chapters 5, 6, and 7; the Lau Blower Company for the technical data that appears in Chapter 7; the Anderson Corporation for the window and sliding glass door material that was used for Chapter 8; Asphalt Roof Manufacturers Association for the information on replacing a roof which can be found in Chapter 8; Benjamin Moore & Company and the National Paint & Coating Association for the tables and data that appear in Chapter 9; the Tappan Company and their Quaker Maid Kitchens Division for their assistance (which included attending their kitchen design school) in preparing Chapter 10; the Maytag Company for a major portion of the information on laundries given in Chapter 10; the Eljer Plumbingware Division of the Wallace-Murray Corporation for the technical data that appear in Chapter 11; and the California Redwood Association for much of the deck and garden structure building information that can be found in Chapter 16. I would also like to thank Morton Waters and Arnold B. Romney of *Family Handyman* magazine for their assistance on various phases of the book. Finally, I wish to thank my typist, Janet Just, and my artist, Mary Puschak, for their help in the completion of this book. Complete credits for the use of many illustrations that appear in the book can be found on page 483.

To the others who, inadvertently, may have been omitted from the above thank you's, please accept my deep apologies for such omissions.

ROBERT SCHARFF

THE COMPLETE BOOK OF
HOME
REMODELING

Chapter 1

THE BUSINESS SIDE OF REMODELING A HOME

Chapter 1

The urge for self-improvement is strong in each one of us and, we like to think, finds its most satisfying expression in the modernized home. Here are a few of the many reasons for wanting to remodel: need for more space, increase in decorative beauty, and better living qualities. Of course, one of the major points to keep in mind while planning a remodeling job is the increase in value or resale price of your home.

Just about anywhere in the country a well-maintained home in an attractive neighborhood should bring an appreciably higher price today than when it was originally purchased. This holds true even if you have made no improvements on either the house or the land since you purchased the property. However, most people have made changes in the house they bought in line with their family's own needs, and in most cases these improvements also add to the value of the house when it is placed on the market.

At the same time you cannot expect a dollar-for-dollar return on every improvement made. For example, changes that you make to add to the convenience or comfort of your family may not be so highly thought of by every prospective buyer. A recreation room converted from basement space, however, or a family room added on to the original house represents an important addition, and the homeowner who has made this improvement should expect that better than 70 to 80 percent of his cost can be recovered in the selling price.

Regional difference will also affect the "return" value of the improvement. A case in point is the outdoor patio, practically taken for granted in Southern states where the climate makes it a useful addition to family living space nearly all year long. In contrast, a patio area in New England, Michigan, or Minnesota, even though it may enhance the overall appearance of the plot and settling of the house, can be put to full use only from late spring to early fall. In this case, perhaps no more than half the cost can be added to the asking price of the house.

Additions which real estate experts point out as having a high percentage of recovery are a second bathroom in a three- or four-bedroom house; a lavatory addition on the ground floor of a two-story house; a third bedroom to what was formerly a two-bedroom house (if the third bedroom is of comparable size to the others); and a fully modernized kitchen. But do not expect to recapture very much of the cost of landscaping and other cosmetic changes. Tastes differ, and the flocked wallpaper for which you paid $18 a roll may strike another person as a terrible waste of money. Other prospects may not be impressed by wall-to-wall carpeting, and the same may be true of expensive and unusual lighting fixtures. A new exterior paint job may make the house look more attractive, but the cost should be considered a normal maintenance expense.

There are, of course, times when remodeling a home is not advisable. One of the first questions you should ask yourself is: "Will the remodeling costs added to the present value of my home price it right out of the market?" It is poor business sense to "overimprove" your home and place it in a significantly higher price bracket than the houses in the neighborhood—unless, of course, you plan to remain in the area indefinitely. For instance, if the houses in the neighborhood (including yours) are presently valued at about $25,000 and the remodeling project you propose would cost $10,000, it is very possible that you may never see this extra expense of renovation when selling the house in the years ahead. While it is always possible for the values in the area to increase over the years, you must consider things as they now stand. The only exception to this principle is when you have an older house than those around you and it has a lower market value. In such a case, you can increase its value by remodeling and bringing it up to the standards of the neighborhood.

Condition of the house. Another very important factor to be determined is whether the house is structurally sound enough to warrant the expense of renovation. If you are presently living in the house, you will probably know most of its faults. But if you are planning to purchase an old house and then remodel it, you must determine its condition. This is not an easy task for the average layman. And for this reason it is wise to consult someone who knows construction, even if you have to pay him a fee. But whether you do this or not, you can get a rough idea of the building's condition by asking yourself the following dozen questions:

1. Is the house plumb and true? Or does it lean or sag overall or in parts? Stand off at a distance and eye it critically. Look for a sag in the ridgeline, a leaning of the house at the corners; and for dips in window and sill lines. Remember that for every hump or sag there must be at least one split or rotted framing member. The costs of these types of repairs are usually quite high, and the repairs are difficult to do because extensive tearing out of floors or walls is often required.

2. How good is the roof? Look for split, broken, or buckled shingles; for bare patches where mineral particles have washed off asphalt roofing; and for worn-out butts and fungus on wood shingles. If possible, climb up under the roof and see if you can spot any pinpoints of light shining through.

3. Is the old wood porch (if there is one) in sound condition? Because it is exposed to the elements and because the space underneath may not be adequately ventilated, the porch may be rotting out, and this is dangerous. Rebuilding it can be quite a job.

The Business Side of Remodeling a Home

4. Is paint blistering and peeling on outside wood walls? Condensation may be to blame (although sometimes it is just a bad paint job). You may be in for frequent repainting jobs, or, worse, you may find that the wood in the outside walls is rotting.

5. How good is the foundation? Is it straight, or does it sag or bow? Is there any sign of moisture or dampness in the basement? Is the basement floor heaved or cracked? All faults of this type require extensive work to repair.

6. Are the exposed wood sills, joists, girders, and posts sound? Are they well joined and free from termites or rot? The only way you can tell is to poke an ice pick or knife into them. If the blade sinks in easily (as though you were piercing a sponge), the wood is rotten or under attack by termites, and will need to be replaced.

7. Is the wiring adequate? Check whether there are three wires leading from the utility pole into the house (an indication that you can run 240-volt appliances as well as the 120-volt ones). Then have the local utility company check the adequacy of the service entrance and the fuse boxes or circuit breakers.

8. Is the furnace in good condition? If the unit is old, it is wise to have it inspected by a heating contractor. If recent improvements have been made in heating or plumbing installations, check to make certain that the framing members have not been too seriously cut and weakened to make room for soil pipes or new heating ducts. If so, repairs will have to be made to provide sufficient support, especially under load-bearing walls.

9. Does water flow in a steady, strong stream from all faucets and toilets? If not, the pipes are clogged. Even if the flow is good, the pipes may be corroded, about to give way. Look for leaks in the basement.

10. Are floors sagging in the middle or running downhill? This may not be serious, although it is usually annoying. The condition is generally caused by the natural settling of the house that occurs soon after it is built. On the other hand, there is the possibility that some of the old beams and structural members are slowly giving out, in which case they will have to be replaced or shored up. Also, do the floors squeak as you walk across them? They may even feel unusually bouncy. It is not too difficult to fix this, but it is a nuisance. Certain types of old floors may require extensive refinishing.

11. Are the interior walls and partitions solid and straight? Do doors and windows work easily, and are they tight-fitting? Are the walls around tubs and showers sound and waterproof? Tile walls will last much longer than plaster, but even tiles may be in bad shape if the mortar has fallen out of the joints.

12. Are hazards built into the house? Some of the more obvious ones are doors that swing into a hall, a door that opens directly onto a flight of stairs, narrow stair treads, steps at odd places, too little headroom on stairs, and a stairway without a railing. Such built-in hazards can be very expensive and difficult to overcome.

There are other things you should look for when judging an old house—the condition of gutters and leaders, fireplace, hot-water heater, and so on—but if the house can pass the 12-question test with flying colors, it is structurally worth remodeling.

FINANCING HOME IMPROVEMENTS

Of utmost importance in the business side of remodeling a home is financing. Most people have home improvement ideas that usually are bigger than their budget. But there is really no mystery to turning remodeling and modernization dreams into reality. The key is easy monthly-payment financing.

Few of us have enough money to finance a major home remodeling job without some kind of financial assistance. And even if we do, there are often many sound reasons for not disturbing a family's savings account. As we have already stated, money put into remodeling is an investment. The increased value of the home after remodeling often exceeds the cost of remodeling.

"Pay-as-you-go" financing is usually feasible only for small-scale home improvements. On larger projects, "pay-as-you-go" tends to drag the job out, resulting in inconvenience and perhaps additional costs. Where major alterations, remodeling, and additions involve a large expenditure or many crafts—such as plumbing, electrical work, carpentry, paneling, flooring, paving, roofing, re-siding, or painting—easy monthly-payment financing is often the best, and only, answer.

It is much simpler to finance home improvements than to finance a new home, no matter what the national money situation might be. A home improvement loan offers a greater number of alternatives and is usually more economical, too, because the homeowner need not sacrifice his equity in his present home or a low interest rate on his present mortgage.

Improvement loan plans. Banks and savings and loan associations are the principal sources of home improvement financing, but do not overlook other possibilities. Here are some of the more common home improvement financing plans:

1. FHA Property Improvement Loan (Title I). Under this plan you may borrow up to $5,000 and take up to five years to pay. To qualify, your improvements must be "built-in," or become a permanent structural part of the property. The loans are obtained by application, and when they are approved by the

lender, a note is signed. Frequently, the contractor will handle the application, and the homeowner just signs the necessary paper. While inspection is not usually required, the lender may spot-check to make certain that the job is being done as outlined in the agreement. Contrary to what some persons think, the Federal Housing Administration (FHA) does not lend money to homeowners. Loans are made by lending institutions. The FHA merely insures the loan; that is, the government guarantees the lender that it will get its money if the borrower defaults. The loan application must be made to the lender, such as a bank or savings and loan association. Since not all lending institutions handle Title I loans, a telephone check with the nearest FHA office will give you the information you need.

2. FHA Section 203 (h or k) Loan (Title II). This program was devised for improving older homes in locations outside urban renewal areas (Section 203k) and in locations inside certified urban renewal areas (Section 203h). If your house is over 10 years old, financing can be obtained to make major improvements costing up to $10,000. The loan is secured by a second mortgage for a period of up to twenty years, and it is not discounted. With this type of FHA loan, some specifications and drawings are necessary and must be presented to both the lending institution and the regional FHA office. There are three inspections required: the first, before construction; the second, during construction; and the third on completion.

3. Conventional bank improvement loan. This type of loan is frequently more flexible than FHA loans in terms of purpose, amount available, and terms, and you may include improvements such as appliances that are not built in. In addition to savings and commercial institutions, many savings and loan associations offer this kind of loan. As a rule, however, the interest rates on conventional bank improvement loans are higher than the FHA types since the lending institution does not have the governmental guarantee. But some banks and savings and loan associations, because of the competitive aspect, may give equally suitable terms, especially if you have an excellent credit rating.

4. Refinancing existing mortgage. The necessity for the project may justify replacing or retiring your present mortgage with a new one large enough to pay off the remainder of the old loan and cover the cost of the improvement. But, refinancing an existing mortgage usually entails a new appraisal, as well as closing costs. It is almost always issued at current interest rates, which may be higher than the original mortgage. In the case of a major or extensive improvement job, refinancing may be the only answer. Refinancing may be accomplished under either conventional or FHA auspices. Under FHA Section 203b, mortgage financing is available up to $30,000, with up to thirty years to pay back the money borrowed.

5. Open-end mortgage. Some mortgages include an open-end clause which permits you to "add on" an additional obligation without affecting the rate of the original loan. It is available through the holder of the first mortgage. Except for its tie to the original mortgage an open-end loan is much like a second mortgage. As a rule, it is easier to get and usually less costly than a second mortgage, and closing costs are lower than when refinancing. Interest rates on the open-end portion of the mortgage may be the same as for the original mortgage or set at current rates. Generally, the lending institution will give you an option of paying back the loan by increasing the size of your monthly payments or by continuing the same payment and lengthening the period of the loan.

6. New mortgage. If you have no mortgage indebtedness on your house, it is possible to obtain one on the property to make improvements. A prospective purchaser of an older house that requires considerable improvements can usually save money by combining the cost of the house with the cost of modernization in the mortgage.

7. Finance company loan. Available through finance companies, such a loan can be secured by other personal property such as furniture or automobiles. Occasionally, it can be secured by a signature note.

8. Credit union loan. If you are a credit union member, you can usually take out a moderate-size loan without too much difficulty. Interest rates on such loans are normally very low.

9. Dealer credit and installation loan. You can often receive credit for the purchasing of building materials from your local dealer. Many are members of charge plans or have their own credit programs. In some cases, the dealer sells the amount you owe him, known as "commercial paper," to a bank or finance company, and you, in turn, make payments to them. There are generally few restrictions placed on what you buy with your loan. If you are dealing with a remodeling contractor, he can help arrange financing for both materials and labor.

10. Passbook loan. If you have a savings account with a bank, you can usually get a "passbook" loan, using your savings as collateral. Interest rates are usually at preferred rates.

11. Life insurance policy loan. Generally, you can borrow up to 95 percent of the accumulated cash value of your life insurance policy. This type of loan is available at low interest rates, and there are no restrictions on how you use the loan or how long you take to pay it back. But borrowing against the cash value of your policy, no matter what the reason, is a calculated risk, because if you should die before the loan is paid back, the amount your

family receives will be reduced by the size of the unpaid portion of the loan.

12. Collateral loan. Stocks, bonds, and other similar securities can often be used as collateral to obtain a loan from a commercial bank.

The availability and terms of any of these loan plans vary according to the geographic location. Even FHA practices differ with the regional office.

Cost of credit. Obviously, the lower the amount you must borrow, the lower the total interest costs you will have to pay. The prevailing practice among most lending institutions is to "discount" the interest on short-term home improvement loans, including FHA loans. Do not confuse "discount rate" with the "simple interest rate" applicable to long-term loans. On an installment-type loan the effective rate is about double the discount rate. The interest is computed on the full amount of the loan, even though the borrower does not actually have full use of the money over the period of the loan. Generally speaking, the length of a loan period, rather than the interest rate, is the major factor in determining how much interest you will have to pay.

Borrowing can also reduce improvement costs. You may be able to save by having the entire job done at one time. And with construction costs rising steadily over the last three decades, you may be able to protect yourself against future price increases in an inflationary economy by doing the job now.

The most important reason of all for borrowing is that it enables you to make an improvement on your home that your family can enjoy now and that will increase the home's value in the future, an improvement that might not be possible without financing.

How to get the loan you need. You get a loan by making an application to a lender, such as a bank or savings and loan association, stating the purpose of the loan and the amount you need and providing additional information that will satisfy the lender that the loan is a good risk. But first, be sure your financial house is in order. Your past credit record is like a fingerprint. It identifies you as a good or poor credit risk, or somewhere in between.

Consolidate or clear up your outstanding debts. If you owe money to creditors, or have a lot of unsettled charge accounts, pay these off first. If you have a major outstanding debt, such as monthly car payments, it will affect the amount of money you will be able to borrow.

Deal with a lender who knows you—where you have a savings or checking account, or where you have financed a car or paid off some other loan. It is an ironic fact of economic life that a person who has always paid for his purchases in cash may have difficulty getting a loan approved, because borrowing is one of the best ways to establish credit.

As was stated earlier, do not try to "overimprove" your home. In some locations an improvement of $10,000 on a $25,000 house is likely to be considered an "overimprovement" by the lender. Spending $10,000 would not make it a $35,000 house if it is located in a neighborhood of $25,000 houses. Except in unusual circumstances, the application will be turned down.

To obtain most loans, a detailed description (plans and specifications) of the proposed improvement, plus a realistic estimate of the cost, is needed before the lending institution can act on your application. When planning, keep your project and your ambitions within your budget. As a rule, your monthly payments for shelter, including a mortgage and home improvement loan payments, should not exceed one-quarter of your monthly income. If the cost is too much for you to handle, trim your home improvement program down to something you can afford.

BEFORE STARTING THE REMODELING

Armed with the decision to make a home improvement and the money required to do the job, you must make up your mind whether you are going to do all the work yourself, act as general contractor, or hire a general contractor.

Doing the work yourself. There is not any job that a *competent* do-it-yourselfer cannot tackle. In fact, many so-called amateur improvement projects are superior to professional jobs because the amateur is doing the work on his own home. Yet, keep in mind that the professional craftsman plies his trade every day, and is bound to known "tricks" of his craft (even if he sometimes does not apply them well). If you plan to do the home improvement work yourself, take the time to learn as many of these tricks as you can before you begin the job. While books such as this one can tell you what to do and how to do it, you are, nonetheless, undertaking an unfamiliar job, and you will be learning as you go along. Therefore, before you start to do any remodeling project, ask yourself these four questions and answer them honestly:

1. Are you starting the job before you have acquired the necessary skill for the remodeling task? Skills can be learned (after all, the professionals had to learn them), but they require practice. For instance, practice sweating short lengths of copper tubing into fittings before you take on a real plumbing job. Also work with hand and power tools until you know how to use them properly. Frequently, it is wise to enroll in an adult education shop course to learn some of the skills of remodeling.

2. Is it legal for you to do the work? Many cities and towns have local ordinances requiring all plumbing and electrical work to be performed by

licensed contractors. In many incorporated municipalities, plumbing, electrical work, heating systems, and sometimes major carpentry must be inspected by local inspectors. Therefore be sure to obtain a copy of the local building code. All too frequently an enthusiastic remodeler will take his self-made renovation plans to a lending institution only to find that these plans are worthless because they do not meet the local ordinances.

3. Will the job put your house out of commission for too long a time? Remodeling a kitchen usually means eating out for a few days, but consider the strain of having to eat out for two weeks or more as the job drags on. This has often happened because of poor planning. Then again, repairs to a heating system can be spread over weeks or months in the summer, when the system is not in use, but the heat can be shut off only for a few hours in the winter.

4. Will you really save money by doing it yourself? This question can be skipped by anyone who works around the house chiefly for the fun of it. But for those who work out of deference to their financial situation, it may be the most important question of all. In theory, it is true that the bigger the job, the more you will save doing it yourself. It may also be true that putting in a weekend of overtime on your regular job might pay you enough to have someone else do the job. In some cases, you may even come out slightly ahead financially.

Of course, if you do not have all the necessary skills for a major remodeling job, you may wish to do part of the work yourself. You can hire help for work on the foundation, framing, and roofing, reserving for yourself the wiring and plumbing installations, interior and exterior finishing operations, and other minor tasks. The five major trades involved in a major remodeling job are carpentry, masonry, plumbing, heating, and electrical work. The following list indicates what must be considered in undertaking each of them.

1. Carpentry is usually the easiest of the trades for the average person to master. Most of us have used some woodworking tools at various times in our lives. Thus, with the possible exception of fine cabinetry, which requires a great deal of practice and patience, you should have little difficulty in turning out successful carpentry work. This is true only if you have done careful planning, the key to all renovation tasks. For instance, any job that requires opening a portion of the house to the weather can cause problems. It's true that plastic sheets and other materials may close the opening temporarily. But be honest with yourself. How long is "temporarily" going to be? Frequently, it is a good idea to hire help to do the rough work quickly and then finish the job yourself at a more leisurely pace once the improvement is under roof and thus protected against the elements. Also avoid any so-

called dangerous jobs such as installing a new roof on a steep slope. While the work is not overly hard, the risk is not always worth the money you are able to save.

2. Masonry work, especially on small jobs such as building a patio or walkway, some brick steps or a barbecue, usually is not too difficult. Care, patience, and a little common sense are the important ingredients in such work. Bigger jobs, such as laying a foundation for an addition or facing your house with bricks, require more skill and practice. For this reason, it would be wise to first undertake one of the simpler masonry jobs described in Chapter 16 before attempting the more difficult ones detailed in Chapters 2 and 15.

3. Plumbing remodeling work, as stated earlier in the chapter, may require the services of a licensed contractor in your locality. However, in recent years, thanks to new materials and techniques, many areas are relaxing their plumbing codes to let the homeowner do his own work, as long as it is inspected by a building inspector. Therefore, before you start any plumbing job, check with your local building officials. The new materials—copper and plastic and water supply tubing—are fairly easy to work with. However, in many cases, it is wise to leave the installation of drain pipe to a professional. Unless the system is properly installed, there is danger of sewer gas leaking into the house. Drain pipe is also rather difficult to handle.

4. Heating work of any appreciable size, such as installing a new furnace, is generally best left to a heating contractor or plumber. You must remember that a furnace is a container for an extremely hot fire. The burner, flue, and all automatic controls require expert handling for the sake of efficient operation and safety. In addition, the costs, unlike those for most remodeling jobs, are in materials and equipment. Labor is generally the smallest part of the expense. However, there are many things that the average handyman can do to remodel his home's climate. These are described in Chapter 7.

5. Electrical work, like plumbing, may have to be done by a qualified contractor—by law. If your electrical code permits you to do the work, electrical work can be learned fairly easily by the confirmed do-it-yourselfer. While there are some jobs for which it is best to hire a professional electrician (see Chapter 5), you can perform the vast majority yourself. A power cutoff while you rework wiring is no problem as long as you work fairly rapidly. However, a delay of six hours or more can start a thaw in your freezer and spoilage in the refrigerator. Therefore, before you begin a major electrical remodeling job, learn how to hook up temporary circuits to keep your home functioning.

If you feel confident in all five trades, you are ready to do any major home remodeling job yourself.

The Business Side of Remodeling a Home

Hiring a general contractor. The easiest, and the most expensive, way to undertake a renovation job is to hire a general remodeling contractor. He assumes the responsibility of constructing the project and is in charge of all building operations.

When you work with a general contractor, be businesslike about it. Before selecting a contractor obtain two or three bids. These will be a rough estimate as a rule. Beware of the contractor whose estimate is far below the others; he is attempting to "low ball" you with a too-attractive bid and will re-estimate the job (perhaps at a higher figure than the others) after you are involved with him. Or he might do the work for his original price but use inferior materials. Also stay away from special prices, special deals, or special offers. Since the general contractor must be competent in his work, in his financial affairs, and in his business relationships, rate all contractors whom you are considering according to the following criteria:

1. Reputation in general. Your bank or lending institution, the Better Business Bureau, or the local Chamber of Commerce can help you here. The latter two know of complaints registered against a specific contractor, while a financial institution will know his general reputation.

2. Recommendations. Talk with people for whom he has worked to find out if he completes his jobs satisfactorily for the price he has agreed upon and within a reasonable time. Remember that a contractor will never give you an unsatisfied customer as a reference. The five recommendations that he gives you may cover up 50 unsatisfactory jobs.

3. Financial resources; credit. Your bank or local credit bureau can tell you whether the contractor has had financial trouble and how he pays bills.

4. Experience and competence. Years in business and work done should be considered when selecting a contractor.

5. Relations with subcontractors and material men. Subcontractors and material suppliers may also be able to give you information about the contractor's reputation. But since they do regular business with the general contractor, any negative comments naturally will be guarded. Collectively, the subcontractors (electrician, plumber, painter, and roofer, among others) do a large share of the remodeling work on any house. It is, therefore, a good idea to check on the type of subcontractors your general contractor hires. What is the quality of their work?

6. Membership in trade associations. In areas where such trade associations exist, this is one of your best checkpoints, as these associations have been formed by contractors to uphold honest, ethical practices. The National Established Repair, Service & Improvement Contractors Association (NER-SICA) is the only national association of home improvement and remodeling contractors, but there are also many fine associations that have been organized on local levels.

Once you have decided upon a general contractor, put your agreement with him in writing. There should be a clear understanding of the plans and specifications. (The plans consist of all drawings in connection with the work; the specifications consist of a description of all materials, their quality, and installation or application.) Actually, the contractor is responsible only for the materials and construction of the project as described in the specifications and drawings.

The specifications should include a description of all materials used, including brand names, quality markings, and model numbers where applicable. Check carefully. Items omitted become "extras"; the owner pays for them over and above the contract. In addition to materials, the specifications describe the work to be done by listing all the necessary building operations under major classifications, such as concrete, masonry, carpentry, finishes, furnishings, mechanical, and electrical. As you read further in this book, you will understand better this portion of the specifications.

All business arrangements relating to the actual construction as well as such matters as rights, responsibilities, and method of payment should be put in writing.

As a rule, the contractor maintains all liability insurance, including workmen's compensation, bodily or personal injury, and property damage, while the owners are responsible for all property insurance, including fire, extended coverage, vandalism, and malicious mischief. The contractor is usually responsible for securing and paying for all permits; fees; and licenses required for the work, and his work must comply with all laws, ordinances, rules, and regulations of any public authority. The contractor must also provide and pay for all labor, water, power, equipment, tools, and scaffolding necessary during the remodeling job. If requested, he should be in a position to furnish a surety bond guaranteeing completion of the contract.

Fees and payments. The usual arrangements for payment are as follows:

1. Lump sum (most common). The contractor agrees to construct the project for a fixed sum, which includes all costs and the contractor's profit. The owner pays this sum, plus any "extras" due to changes or omissions.

2. Cost-plus. The contractor is paid the actual cost of materials and labor plus a fixed fee (or fixed percentage of costs, usually 10 to 15 percent, for his overhead and profit). This method does not place an upper limit on the cost of the project.

3. Maximum total. The maximum total cost of the project is agreed upon by the owner and the contractor. This includes the contractor's fees. Any

saving in total cost is divided between the owner and the contractor.

The usual schedules for making payments are:

1. Partial payment. This plan is the most commonly used. Payments are made monthly, based on the amount of work completed and materials delivered to the site.

2. On completion. The contractor receives the entire amount upon completion of the remodeling project. Few contractors will accept this method on a project which extends over a period of several months.

In each of the above methods, a percentage (usually 10 percent) of the value of the work completed is retained by the owner. This retained amount is due upon the final acceptance of the project by the owner.

Changes and change orders. Probably more trouble and misunderstandings during remodeling construction are caused by changing the original plans and specifications than by any other act.

If changes are to be made during construction by either the owner or the contractor, or if extras are to be added, the instructions should be put in writing before the change is made. Have a written agreement on the cost of the change, whether an addition or deduction. Be sure that changes can be paid for from your cash or included in the loan.

Terminating the contract. Either the owner or the contractor may end a contract before the renovation project is completed under circumstances varying according to state statutes and terms of the contract. Written notice must be given.

Generally, the owner can terminate a contract if the contractor neglects to do the work properly or fails to perform any provision of the contract. The owner must, however, pay the contractor for work done, less damages.

The contractor may end a contract if the owner fails to pay him within a certain time after a payment is due or if work is stopped for any length of time by any public authority or by the owner.

Being your own remodeling general contractor. If you have the patience and have the time to supervise the various subcontractors needed in a given improvement job, and to cope with the headaches that may arise, you might save 10 to 25 percent of the total cost a general contractor would charge for the entire project. But keep in mind that, as most general contractors will tell you, the problems which come in remodeling projects are often unpredictable, and costs are easy to underestimate. For this reason, it could cost you more to be a homeowner-contractor.

If you decide to be your own general contractor, select your subcontractors by following the same basic procedure as just described for choosing general contractors. That is, select two or three for each trade for bids and then check them out most carefully. When you are your own general contractor, you must get the building permits and have adequate insurance as required by law. (Your insurance broker will be able to help you on this.) Be sure that each subcontractor has proper insurance, too; ask to see his insurance certificate, which covers items such as workmen's compensation, personal liability, and property damage. You must also draw up the remodeling plans and specifications yourself, or have them done for you. Each subcontractor must be provided with a set of these plans and specifications in order to bid on the job. Be sure to have a separate contract with each contractor. Never employ a craftsman yourself since you will be responsible for state and federal withholding taxes, unemployment benefits, and workman's compensation, for which there are endless forms to fill out. Actually, it is wise to have the contracts with the subs drawn up by your lawyer.

When you are your own general contractor, it is essential to establish a very firm work schedule. That is, you must plan to get the various subcontractors in and out with a minimum of confusion, waste of time, and duplication. If you are not careful, it is possible for one trade to be held up by another or for one craftsman to have to rip out the work of his colleague because of improper scheduling of the various subcontractors. Such errors can increase the cost of the job.

Before starting out as a general contractor for your remodeling job, acquaint yourself with the various trades and how the work should be done. This book will help you greatly in this matter. Also visit lumberyards and supply houses to become fully knowledgeable about the latest materials and application techniques. In other words, learn as much as possible about the various trades with which you will be dealing so that, in theory at least, you know what you are talking about in your discussions with the professionals. Since so many things may inadvertently go wrong when remodeling, you must make every possible effort to steer clear of the obvious errors. To help accomplish this, make certain to have well-drawn plans and well-written specifications, a minutely detailed work schedule, and the ability to make quick and intelligent decisions that affect the entire renovation.

When dealing directly with the subcontractors you can move at your own speed. You have to pay for work only as it is done. In addition, it is possible for you to do some of the work yourself at night, on weekends, or on vacations. When a subcontractor has completed his job, be sure to obtain a statement from him that specifies he has been paid in full for his work. This will protect you from a Mechanic's Lien, a legal claim filed against you to recover unpaid labor or material charges.

An architect and remodeling. A good architect can be most valuable, especially for a major remodeling

The Business Side of Remodeling a Home

project. The title "architect" is a legal one, indicating that a person has demonstrated his professional competence by examination and is registered, or licensed, by the state to practice architecture. The drawings necessary for construction purposes are also prepared by designers and draftsmen, who are not, however, licensed to practice architecture. The usual duties of the architect are to:

1. Analyze the family's living needs and relate these to the remodeling budget.

2. Visit the home to determine the various improvements needed or desired.

3. Draw preliminary sketches (general plan and appearance of the remodeling project).

4. Prepare preliminary estimates of costs.

5. Prepare working drawings and details (exact dimension drawings showing floor plans, exteriors, structural details, mechanical installations).

6. Prepare specifications.

7. Provide the necessary technical information for contracts relating to the work of the contractor and, in special cases, to the work of subcontractors.

8. Advise on the selection of the contractor or subcontractors. In competitive bidding, the architect analyzes the bids for the owner.

If the owner wishes to give the responsibility for the entire construction operation to the contractor, the architect concludes his services at this point. However, the usual procedure is to have the architect carry on the administration of the construction contract to the completion of the project. If he does this, then his further duties are to:

9. Observe construction to determine in general that the remodeling work is carried out according to the plans and specifications.

10. Examine requests from the contractor for changes or substitutions of materials; make written recommendations to the owner for the disposition of proposed changes; and issue written "change orders" for approved changes.

11. Check requests from the contractor for payments, and issue certificates for payment.

12. Make a final inspection.

13. Prepare a certificate for final payment when the renovation project is completed.

Many people hesitate to ask an architect about his services because they fear their inquiry will place them under obligation; however, no obligation is incurred until a contract is signed with the architect.

The fee for an architect who performs the duties mentioned above varies from 9 to 15 percent of the total cost, depending on the size and complexity of the project. When the architect performs only partial services, the fee is reduced. Services may also be provided on an hourly or negotiated basis. Additional reimbursable expenses may be due the architect. Any such expenses will be explained in the agreement between the owner and the architect.

The schedule of payments to the architect, as recommended by the American Institute of Architects, is as follows: (1) retainer, (2) at completion of design phase, (3) at completion of construction documents phase, (4) at completion of bidding or negotiation phase, and (5) monthly during the construction phase. This schedule is sometimes modified, depending on the size and complexity of the project.

If the owner decides not to remodel at any point during his dealings with the architect, this decision does not release him from paying the fees incurred up to that point. Incidentally, an architect should be selected with the same care used in choosing a contractor.

PLANNING YOUR REMODELING PROJECT

There are other business items involved in remodeling, such as making plans and preparing specifications, figuring out cost estimates, and obtaining building permits. Of course, if you hire an architect, he does all these things for you. Many remodeling general contractors will provide such service, even making plans and drawing up specifications. However, if you are going to do the remodeling yourself, or farm out some or all of the work to subcontractors, you will have to take care of these items. In the upcoming chapters of this book, the necessary information for drawing up plans, writing up specifications, and figuring out reasonable estimates is given. There are also valuable data on how to deal with your local building departments.

Before you start the actual drawing of plans, schedule planning sessions whenever possible with the other members of your family so that you can take advantage of their ideas. Work out ideas in rough sketch form and do not be afraid to change and/or improve. Remember that planning is the biggest single factor involved in any remodeling project.

When planning to remodel, you can get plenty of fresh ideas by visiting lumberyard showrooms and building supply houses, writing to manufacturers for their literature, leafing through the pages of home and decorating magazines, reading books such as this one, and inspecting the many new model homes. You actually have at your disposal thousands of dollars worth of interior design arrangements and architectural ideas when you visit new model homes. But when planning, try to start off with a rather firm idea of the final appearance you are attempting to achieve. From this point, work backward to figure out how this effect can be had. Some of your ideas, of course, may have to be scaled down and others discarded completely, but it is best to start with the ultimate goal and work down.

Before going into the actual "how to" of making your remodeling project a reality, let us bring up one more point of business—updating your insurance to safeguard your investment. Too many people stop thinking about their home improvement project after the last brick is laid or the last nail driven into a wall. What you may not realize is that even before the project is started you should notify your insurance company of your plans in order to avoid falling into what is known as the homeowner's coverage insurance gap. All too often a policyholder may put a $5,000 or $6,000 addition onto his home and not tell his insurance company. The oversight can be costly in two ways. First, if the home is destroyed by fire, it will not be covered for the full loss. And, second, if the home is not covered for at least 80 percent of its replacement value, the policyholder will lose out on a special feature included in the homeowner's policy: Waiver of the usual deduction for depreciation when the amount of insurance on the home is kept above the 80 percent level.

Not only is it important to make sure that a home is adequately covered when an addition is put on, but periodically it may be necessary to increase the amount of coverage in order to counteract the crippling effects of inflation. For instance, a home bought 20 years ago for $15,500 probably would cost twice that amount to replace today, considering the rise in construction costs. Therefore, whenever there is a major change in your home, such as substantial remodeling or a room addition, have the family's insurance agent visit your home so he can accurately assess your insurance needs.

Chapter 2

THE BASICS OF REMODELING

Before you can hope to start any remodeling project, you must have a nodding acquaintance with basics of remodeling: a knowledge of the basic materials used and the basic techniques employed.

LUMBER

A good basic knowledge of the characteristics and types of woods is invaluable in any form of carpentry work, especially remodeling. Actually, lumber should be selected to serve the particular purpose for which it is to be used. Buying lumber of insufficient strength and quality for your job can be wasteful and even dangerous; buying a better grade than is needed is extravagant.

Lumber is graded according to quality and strength. While this grading is of great help to the purchaser, the many species of wood and the several grades of quality complicate the task of buying lumber. In addition to knowing and appreciating the physical properties and the limitations of lumber, prospective home remodelers find that an understanding of lumber merchandising terms is helpful. Many persons describe their needs in words which, to a dealer, mean quality in excess of the grade actually needed. For instance, if a home remodeler who needs a set of shelves in the basement merely states that he wants a "good-looking board," this may mean to the dealer a top-grade board. Actually, one of the lower grades could serve just as well at less cost.

Classifications of lumber. Wood is classified as *softwood* or *hardwood* for convenience only. These terms have no reference to the softness or hardness of the wood. For instance, Douglas fir, a softwood, is much harder than poplar, which is a hardwood.

Softwood comes from cone-bearing trees, trees with scale-like or needle-like leaves such as fir, pine, redwood, spruce, and cedar. Hardwood comes from non-cone-bearing trees, trees that have broad leaves, such as oak, maple, birch, and elm.

Quality of lumber. Lumber comes from many species of trees, all of which have certain characteristics such as growth rings and grain. These vary from species to species and determine the suitability of particular woods for particular uses.

Of all the demands placed on wood in home remodeling, strength is the most important. The strength required of each piece of lumber depends not only on the purpose it is to serve but also on the way the load (or stress) is distributed on the piece, and the length of time the piece must support the load. In turn, the strength of each piece of lumber itself depends on (1) the kind and quality of wood, (2) the way the piece is loaded in relation to the direction of its grain, and (3) its size.

Quality and strength of wood are affected by grain, by defects, and indirectly by moisture content.

Grain. Grain, the arrangement of fibers or cells in the wood, is sometimes the basis for selecting lumber. Boards chosen for beauty often have fibers arranged in a wavy or curly pattern. In some woods, the fibers form a pronounced pattern due to differences in the size of the cells.

For strength, boards should have a grain that is straight; that is, the wood fibers should run neatly parallel to the sides of the board.

When the fibers deviate from the parallel, the board is said to have cross grain. A small amount of cross grain is generally acceptable. Cross grain is the result of (1) the fibers following a spiral pattern in the tree's growth or (2) the sawmill operator not sawing the board parallel to the bark surface.

The grain pattern (Figure 2–1) varies according to the way the board is sawed—flat-sawed or quarter-sawed (vertical grained). Flat-sawed boards are more apt to warp or shrink than quarter-sawed boards and, thus, are less desirable for some uses.

Hardwoods are porous woods. Those woods with large pores (cell openings), such as oak, are called open-grained woods. Woods that have smaller pores scattered over the surface of the annual growth rings are close-grained woods. Walnut, gum, and maple are examples.

Defects. Because knots, checks, splits, shakes, and pitch pockets weaken a piece of lumber, the number and size of these defects (Figure 2–2) are specified for the various grades.

1. A knot is a part of a branch which has become incorporated into the body of a tree. Although the knot itself is as strong as the rest of the wood,

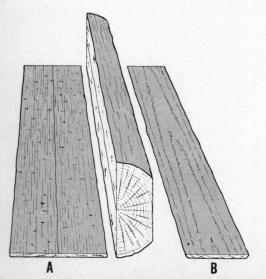

Figure 2–1. Two methods of board cutting: (A) flat-sawed; (B) quarter-sawed.

the cross grain which develops around the knot weakens the lumber. Furthermore, when the lumber is being dried, checks and cracks often develop in this irregular grain. Knots can be tight or loose. Loose knots, formed when the wood grows around a dead branch, are apt to fall out when the log is cut into lumber. Round knots are produced when the limb is crosscut; spike knots are produced when the limb is sawed lengthwise.

2. Checks and splits are separations of the wood along the grain. A split extends through lumber; a check does not. Checks and splits usually develop as a result of unequal shrinkage in a piece of lumber. How much they weaken lumber depends on (1) their size and (2) where they are located in the piece. Small checks from drying have little effect on strength.

3. Shakes differ from splits in that a shake is a separation *between* two growth rings; a split usually runs *across* growth rings.

4. Pitch pockets are openings which contain solid or liquid pitch. They are found in pine, spruce, Douglas fir, tamarack, and western larch.

Moisture content. The amount of moisture in wood affects its performance. As wood dries, it shrinks; when dry wood gets wet, it swells. Lumber that is excessively moist over a long period of time is likely to rot.

Do not use freshly cut or green lumber for remodeling work. Although it costs less than lumber that has been dried, it is usually more expensive in the end because of difficulties resulting from shrinkage—nail-popping, warping, checking, and cracking of walls.

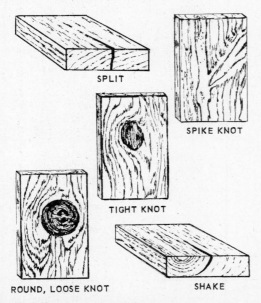

Figure 2-2. Common lumber defects.

SPLIT

SPIKE KNOT

TIGHT KNOT

ROUND, LOOSE KNOT

SHAKE

Lumber should be dried to about the same moisture content it will have when it is put into use—about 10 percent. Problems can be expected if the moisture content exceeds 20 percent. Softwood lumber now is classified by the American Softwood Lumber Standard as either "dry" or "green"; dry lumber has been seasoned to a maximum moisture content of 19 percent or less. Electric moisture meters can be used to check moisture content if the dryness of the lumber is questionable.

1. Common methods of seasoning lumber are as follows:

(a) Air-drying. Wood is stacked and allowed to season out of doors. This method is impracticable in cold, damp weather; in hot, dry weather, the green lumber may warp or check since shrinkage is difficult to control.

(b) Kiln-drying. Lumber is placed in a large "oven" where the rate of seasoning is controlled by adjusting humidity, air temperature, and air circulation. Kiln-drying is more expensive than air-drying, but the lumber can be dried faster and to a lower moisture content by the former method.

Lumber dried to the same moisture content by either method will give equal satisfaction, if it does not warp or check in drying.

Regardless of how it is dried, lumber will pick up or lose moisture until it reaches a balance with the moisture content of the air. Paint does not prevent wood from absorbing moisture as the finishes do not completely seal the wood. Paint does slow the rate of moisture absorption and the subsequent drying of wood as atmospheric conditions change.

2. Storing lumber. To avoid warping, staining, and other possible ill effects, lumber delivered to a job should be stored in a dry place and stacked as it is in lumberyards. If the lumber must be stored out of doors, put it on a level foundation off the ground. Protect it from rain and ground moisture with tarpaulins or moisture-resistant coverings. Interior millwork and flooring should not be delivered until they can be stored inside the enclosed building.

3. Wood flooring. When a house is heated, wood-finish flooring is apt to shrink. To avoid excessive shrinkage, the flooring should be stacked inside the house for a week or more before it is laid so that it reaches a balance with the moisture content of the air inside the house. Plaster should be dry before bringing in flooring; otherwise the flooring will absorb moisture given off by the plaster. These suggestions also apply to paneling.

Decay and stain. When the moisture in wood is excessive (20 percent or more), the wood is susceptible to decay, blue stain, or mold. Decay is caused by fungi, small plant organisms which feed on wood until it becomes soft and punky. Even though this wood may appear to be sound, it loses some of its strength.

Fungi require favorable temperatures, air, and

Table 2—1. *Wood preservatives*

Preservative	Toxicity	Odor	Color	Paintability	Soil contact	Permeability
Creosote	+++	+	+	+	+++	+++
Penta	+++	++	+++	+++	+++	+++
Water-soluble preservatives*	+++	+++	++	+++	++	++

*Containing chrome-copper-arsenic or fluor-chrome-arsenate-phenol.
+=usable
++=better
+++=best

water to remain active. There is no such thing as "dry rot" since the so-called dry-rot fungi can carry moisture several yards into dry wood.

Certain woods, such as cedar, cypress, and redwood, are more resistant to decay and insect attack than others because the heartwood contains chemicals which are poisonous to fungi. Sapwood is generally not as resistant to decay as heartwood but absorbs wood preservatives better.

Chemical preservatives, which poison the food supply of the fungi and give wood resistance to insect attack, are frequently used to treat the more susceptible woods. Methods of applying preservatives are pressure treatment (most effective), hot-cold bath, cold-soaking, and brush or spray (least effective). The most common chemicals used as wood preservatives, and their ratings according to various characteristics, are given in Table 2—1.

Some fungi do not rot the wood but cause only stain or mold which affects the wood's appearance. Wood which is blue-stained can be painted, or if the stain is not too deep, it can be planed to restore its original appearance.

BUYING LUMBER

Lumber is priced and sold by the board-foot unit — that is, a piece which is nominally 1 inch thick by 12 inches wide by 1 foot long. Moldings are usually sold by the lineal foot. To determine the board-foot volume of a piece of lumber, use the following equation:

Nominal thickness (in.) × Nominal width (in.) × Length (ft) ÷ 12

A 2 × 4 that is 12 feet long contains 8 board feet:

$$\frac{2 \times 4 \times 12}{12} = 8$$

Sawmills cut softwood lumber in lengths ranging from 4 to 24 feet in multiples of one foot. Standard lengths of hardwood lumber range from 4 to 16 feet in multiples of one foot. Table 2—2 shows the lengths commonly stocked by retail dealers. To get a 9-foot length, you usually pay for a 10-foot length. Some lumber dealers permit you to

Table 2—2. *Board-foot content*

Size (inches)	Length (feet)							
	8	10	12	14	16	18	20	22
1 × 2	1½	1⅔	2	2⅓	2⅔	3	3⅓	3⅔
1 × 3	2	2½	3	3½	4	4½	5	5½
1 × 4	2¾	3⅓	4	4⅔	5⅓	6	6⅔	7⅓
1 × 5	3⅓	4⅙	5	5⅚	6⅔	7½	8⅓	9⅙
1 × 6	4	5	6	7	8	9	10	11
1 × 8	5⅓	6⅔	8	9⅓	10⅔	12	13⅓	14⅔
1 × 10	6⅔	8⅓	10	11⅔	13½	15	16⅔	18⅓
1 × 12	8	10	12	14	16	18	20	22
1 × 14	9⅓	11⅔	14	16⅓	18⅔	21	23⅓	25⅔
1 × 16	20⅔	13⅓	16	18⅔	21⅓	24	26⅔	29⅓
2 × 4	5⅓	6⅔	8	9⅓	10⅔	12	13⅓	14⅔
2 × 6	8	10	12	14	16	18	20	22
2 × 8	10⅔	13⅓	16	18⅔	21⅓	24	26⅔	29⅓
2 × 10	13⅓	16⅔	20	23½	26⅔	30	33⅓	36⅔
2 × 12	16	20	24	28	32	36	40	44
4 × 4	10⅔	13⅓	16	18⅔	21⅓	24	26⅔	29⅓
4 × 6	16	20	24	28	32	36	40	44
4 × 8	21⅓	26⅔	32	37⅓	42⅔	48	53⅓	58⅔
4 × 10	26⅔	33⅓	40	46⅔	53⅓	60	66⅔	73⅓
4 × 12	32	40	48	56	64	72	80	88
4 × 14	37⅓	46⅔	56	65⅓	74⅔	84	93⅓	102⅔
4 × 16	42⅔	53⅓	64	74⅔	85⅓	96	106⅔	117⅓
6 × 6	24	30	36	42	48	54	60	66
6 × 8	32	40	48	56	64	72	80	88

select a few boards from a given grade, but there is often an extra charge for such selection.

Size of lumber. The thickness and width of softwood lumber depend upon whether the pieces are rough-sawed or planed smooth, green or dry. Dimensions of milled lumber are nearly always scant since the wood must be seasoned and dressed (planed) after it is cut from the log. For instance, a green, rough-sawed board 1 inch thick is actually ¾-inch thick if dry and dressed; it is 25/32-inch thick if it is green (above 19 percent moisture content) and dressed. If the lumber is grade-marked, the stamp will indicate whether the piece was green or dry when it was dressed to size.

Table 2—3

Thicknesses			Face widths		
Actual (inches)			Actual (inches)		
Nominal size*	Minimum dry†	Dressed green	Nominal size	Minimum dry†	Dressed green
1	¾	25/32	2	1½	1⁹/16
1¼	1	1¹/32	3	2½	2⁹/16
1½	1¼	1⁹/32	4	3½	3⁹/16
2	1½	1⁹/16	5	4½	4⅝
2½	2	2¹/16	6	5½	5⅝
3	2½	2⁹/16	7	6½	6⅝
3½	3	3¹/16	8	7¼	7½
4	3½	3⁹/16	9	8¼	8½
			10	9¼	9½
			11	10¼	10½
			12	11¼	11½

*Thickness sometimes is expressed as 4/4, 5/4, etc.
†Dry lumber has been seasoned to a moisture content of 19 percent or less.

Table 2–3 shows nominal and actual sizes for commonly used softwood boards and dimension lumber as standardized by the American Softwood Lumber Standard. Hardwood lumber is generally sold rough-sawed; nominal and actual size are about the same.

In buying lumber you should always specify the nominal thickness and width that represent the actual dimensions needed.

Types of lumber. Softwood logs are sawed into yard lumber, structure lumber, and factory and shop lumber.

Yard lumber. This lumber is of grades, sizes, and patterns used for ordinary construction and general building purposes. It is less than 5 inches thick. Yard lumber is further classified into *dimension lumber*, *common boards*, and *finish lumber*. Dimension lumber is nominally 2 to 5 inches thick.

Table 2–4. Lumber use

Wood Use and Paintability Ratings: +++ = Best; ++ = Better; + = Usable

Color of Paneling: D = Dark; M = Medium; L = Light

USES, MINIMUM GRADES AND CHARACTERISTICS OF WOOD SPECIES	SOFTWOODS													HARDWOODS[1]					
	CEDAR, WEST. RED	CYPRESS	FIR, DOUGLAS	FIR, WHITE	HEMLOCK, EASTERN	HEMLOCK, WESTERN	LARCH, WESTERN	PINE, PONDEROSA	PINE, SO. YELLOW	PINE, WHITE (WEST. AND EAST.), SUGAR	REDWOOD	SPRUCE, WESTERN	YELLOW POPLAR	ASH, WHITE OAK	BEECH	BIRCH, HARD MAPLE	CHERRY, WALNUT	ELM	RED OAK, SYCAMORE (quartered)
Sills Std. or No. 2 Dimension[2]	+++	+++	++	+	+	+	++	+	++	+	+++	+	++						
Joists, rafters, trusses No. 2 SLF or SJF	+	++	+++	++	++	++	+++	+	+++	+	++	++	++						
Studs Stud	+	+++	+++	++	++	++	+++	++	+++	++	+++	++	++						
Plates Std. or No. 2 Dimension	+	++	+++	++	++	++	+++	+	+++	+	++	++	++						
Sheathing (wall and roof) Standard	+++	+++	++[3]	+++	+++	+++	++	+++	++[3]	+++	+++	+++	+++						
Siding	+++	+++	+	+	+	++	+	++	+	+++	+++	++	++						
Flooring Subflooring: Standard	++	+++	+++	++	++	++	+++	++	+++	++	+++	++	+++						
Finish: (See your dealer for grades)			++						++					+++					
Porch:[4]			+++						+++			+++							
Millwork	+	+++	++	+	+	+	++	+++	++	+++	+++	+	+++						
Shelving Finish: Const. Rough: Utility	++	+++	++	++	++	++	++	+++	++	+++	+++	++	+++						
Gates. fence boards	++	+++	+++	+	+	+	+++	++	+++	++	+++	+	++						
Posts for fences[2]	+++	+++	++	+	++	+	++	+	++	+	+++	+	+						
Interior Paneling Freedom from warping	+++	++	++	++	++	++	++	+++	++	+++	+++	+++	++	++	+	++	+++	+	++
Amount of grain pattern	++	+++	+++	++	++	++	+++	+	+++	+	++	+	+	+++	++	++	++	+++	+++
Natural heartwood color	D	M	M	L	M	L	M	L	L	L	D	L	M	L	M	M	D	M	M
PAINTABILITY[5] (Exterior)	+++	+++	+	++	+	++	+	++	+	++	+++	++	++						

[1] See your dealer for recommended grades of hardwoods.
[2] Use heartwood for woods rated +++ use pressure-treated woods for species rated ++ and +.
[3] Plywood recommended.
[4] Use pressure-treated lumber.
[5] Paintability rating depends on the use of high quality material and the method of application.

Table 2–5. *Selecting lumber*

TYPES	GRADE	GRADE DESCRIPTION	USES
BOARDS		**Graded on Appearance**	
Thickness: 1″, 1¼″, 1½″¹ *Width:* 4″, 6″, 8″, 10″, 12″	Select Merchantable	Suitable for use without waste; grade characteristics (knots, splits, cross grain, etc.) permitted are minor.	Trim, cabinet work; paneling, shelving or where lumber with finest appearance is important.
Stock length: two-foot multiples from 6 to 20′	Construction	Characteristics are limited to assure serviceability.	Subfloors, sheathing, siding.
	Standard	Graded to assure high degree of service.	Used along with construction for general construction.
	Utility	Based on utility instead of appearance.	Sheathing, roof boards, subfloor; low-cost general construction.
	Economy	All characteristics which do not interfere with use of full-length piece are permitted.	Temporary construction.
	or may be designated No. 1, No. 2, No. 3, etc.		
DIMENSION²		**Graded on Strength and Stiffness**	
Thickness: 2–4″ *Stock length:* two-foot multiples from 6 to 20′	*Select Structural	Bending strength of piece is more important than stiffness. Graded full length. Bending strength is 67% of clear, straight-grained wood.	Trusses, house framing.
Structural Light Framing	*No. 1	Bending strength is 55% of clear straight grain.	Construction.
Width: 2–4″	*No. 2	Bending strength is 45% of clear straight grain.	Construction.
Light Framing	*No. 3	Bending strength is 26% of clear straight grain.	Construction.
	Construction	Provides for general (nonstructural) framing; allows larger knots and more cross grain than Structural Light Framing.	General use where utility and appearance are more important than strength.
	Standard	Lowest quality accepted in FHA-insured construction.	
	Utility		
	Economy	Admits all characteristics found in lumber except broken ends.	
Stud			
Width: 2–4″	Stud	Limited to lengths 10 feet and shorter.	For studs in load-bearing walls.
Structural Joists and Planks	*Select Structural	Stiffness more important than bending strength.	Floor and ceiling joists, decking.
Width: 6″ and wider Always stress rated	*No. 1, 2, 3		
Appearance Framing			
Width: 2″ and wider	*Appearance	Exposed uses where knotty lumber of high strength and finest appearance is needed. Equivalent to No. 1 Structural Light Framing or No. 1 Structural Joists and Planks.	Trusses, ceiling beams, columns.
TIMBERS			
Thickness: Generally 5″ and more	*Select Structural	Have very high strength and finest appearance.	For heavy construction, exposed framing.
Width: Generally 5″ and more	*Construction Standard	For members stressed in bending. Ranked slightly below Select Structural grade.	
Stock length: 6′ to 20′	Utility	Not stress rated, but suitable for general construction.	
Beams and Stringers *Thickness:* sometimes includes 2 to 4″ *Width:* Usually at least 2″ more than thickness	*or may be designated No. 1, No. 2, No. 3, etc.*		
Post and Timbers			
Width: Sometimes limited to not more than 2″ greater than the thickness	*Select Structural *Construction Standard Utility	Graded for strength as a column. Highest strength and appearance.	For heavy construction, exposed framing.
Square Edge and Sound	No. 1 Timbers No. 2 Timbers No. 3 Timbers	Not stress rated.	For use where heavy or large sizes are needed, but where strength and appearance are not of prime importance.

*Stress rated. Consult "Working Stresses for Joists and Rafters" published by National Forest Products Association.
¹See size chart, page 14, for actual dimensions. ²See individual grades for width dimensions.

It is uniform in size, and is used for light-frame construction; i.e., joists, rafters, studs. Dimension lumber does not carry the stress rating stamped on structural lumber. Common boards (or merely "boards") are less than 2 inches nominal thickness. They have square edges and commonly are planed on both sides and edges. Boards are for general use, such as shelving, siding, or rustic paneling. Finish lumber is 4 inches or less in thickness. It is of select quality. Defects in even the lowest grades normally can be hidden with a coat of paint.

Structural lumber. This lumber is 2 or more inches in nominal thickness and width. It is used for joists and planks, beams and stringers, and posts and timbers. With the exception of joists and planks, structural lumber is at least 5 inches thick or wide, nominal. Structural lumber is stress rated; the grade mark stamped on the piece will show the kind of wood, its strength value, and the grading agency.

Factory and shop lumber. This lumber is graded according to the amount of each piece that is suitable for cuttings for doors, sashes, foundry patterns, or general cut-up purposes.

Pattern lumber. This lumber is special-purpose lumber machined from common boards of finish lumber. The most used are moldings, flooring, dressed-and-matched (D&M) lumber, shiplap, and various sidings.

Grades of lumber. To indicate quality, lumber is inspected and assigned to grades. The poorest-quality piece permitted in each grade is specified by the grading rules. As assurance to the purchaser, many manufacturers of softwood lumber stamp the grade on the end or face of the piece.

Softwood. The grades of this lumber are based on a standard developed by the United States Department of Commerce. Since each lumber-manufacturing association has its own interpretation of the national grading system, grading terms and standards vary. In the end, the grade of a single piece of lumber is based either on the judgment of the grader as to how the piece will be used, or on a machine that rates its bending strength and stiffness.

Hardwood. This lumber is graded by the National Hardwood Lumber Association rules. The grading process measures the percentage of usable material in each piece. The five basic grades are Firsts and Seconds (FAS), Selects, No. 1 Common, No. 2 Common, and No. 3 Common.

Tables 2–4 and 2–5 give the grades of softwood lumber most commonly used for home construction. When classified by size, pieces of softwood lumber that have been planed to a nominal thickness of less than 2 inches, and are 2 inches or more wide, are called boards. Pieces that have been planed to a nominal thickness of 2 to 4 inches, are more than 2 inches wide, and which are intended for use as joists, planks, rafters, studs, etc., are classified as dimension lumber. Timbers are usually 5 inches or more in the least dimension. Timbers are further classified as beams and stringers, posts and timbers, or square edge and sound.

Because there are several interpretations of the American Softwood Lumber Standard, the grades are given here in general terms. For details on a specific wood, write to the lumber manufacturing association whose grade rules include the species.

Guide for selecting lumber. To order lumber, determine the requirements of your job. Write down the thickness, width, and length of each piece needed, and the number of pieces of each size. Check the chart here to determine the minimum grade recommended and the kinds of woods that are best for each purpose. Better grades than those suggested may be used, but little is gained in efficiency for the added cost. Where several species have the same rating, choose the cheapest. The species listed are the ones commonly used in house construction. All may not be available in your locality. Paintability is not considered in the grading of lumber. However, since some woods hold paint better than others, the chart includes a paintability rating when exterior paint is to be used.

PLYWOOD

Plywood is made of an odd number of thin sheets of wood glued together with the grain of the adjacent layers perpendicular. The grain of the two outside plies must be parallel to provide stability. This gives the panel nearly equalized strength and minimizes dimensional changes. The thin layers of wood, called plies, usually are "peeled" from a log as veneer. In some instances the veneer is sliced from the log. The veneer is cut into various lengths, dried, selected or graded, then glued together to make a sheet or panel of plywood.

Both softwood and hardwood plywoods are available. Softwood plywood is extensively used in building construction; hardwood plywood is used for cabinetwork and furniture; both are used for paneling. Softwood and hardwood plywood are classified by grade and type. Grade is determined by the quality or condition of the separate plies and the appearance of the face plies; type refers to the durability of the adhesive bond between the plies.

Softwood plywood. Softwood plywood is manufactured from several species of wood, of which Douglas fir is the most common. Some of the other species used in significant quantity include: Southern yellow pine, Western larch, Western hemlock, Sitka spruce, commercial white firs, Alaska and Port Orford cedar, and California redwood.

Size. Plywood is most readily available in sheets or panels 4 feet wide by 8 feet long. Lengths up to 16 feet are available, but not always stocked. Widths range from 24 to 60 inches, with 48 inches being most common.

Thickness. Plywood is manufactured in thicknesses of $1/4$ inch to $1\frac{1}{8}$ inches. A special $1/8$-inch plywood is also available for model making and similar uses. There always will be an odd number of plies, the minimum number being three. Table 2–6 lists the number of plies for some standard plywood thicknesses.

Table 2–6

Number of plies	Plywood thickness (inches)		
3	$1/4$	$5/16$	$3/8$
5	$1/2$	$5/8$	$3/4$
7	$7/8$	to	$1\frac{1}{8}$

Types. Two types of softwood plywood are available: *exterior* (waterproof) and *interior* (moisture-resistant); within each type there are several grades.

Exterior-type plywood is used when the wood will come into contact with excessive moisture and water, such as in boats, outdoor fences, combination sheathing and siding for houses, and outdoor furniture. This type of plywood is manufactured with phenolic or resorcinol-type adhesives, which are insoluble in water.

Interior-type plywood can be used in protected areas, such as wall and roof sheathing, interior wall paneling, and cabinets. Interior plywood is assembled with a protein-type adhesive such as casein, soybean, or blood-based products. Also, some synthetic adhesives are becoming more widely used in the production of interior-type plywood. These adhesives are not waterproof and tend to deteriorate or dissolve from contact with excessive moisture. Therefore, interior-type plywood should not be used where it will be exposed to excessive moisture or high humidity. If it is used as subflooring, care must be taken to keep water around sinks and bathroom facilities from coming in contact with the plywood. If used as roof sheathing, it must be protected from the weather. Some types of construction leave the outer edges exposed to rain. Currently, structural grades are produced with exterior-type adhesives.

Grades. The presence or absence of defects in the face or surface plies determines the grade of the plywood. The quality of the veneer is graded N (best), A, B, C, and D (poorest). N grade is a special-order veneer for use as a natural finish. In A-A grade plywood, for instance, both faces are of A quality; in C-D grade, one face is of C quality and the other of D quality. Only minor surface defects and limited patches are permitted in Grade A quality, and the face must be sanded. Grade B allows some appearance defects and permits more patching than Grade A as long as the surface is sanded smooth. Grades C and D permit knots, knotholes, and some splits, with larger defects permitted in the D grade. Some manufacturers produce a C-grade plywood that is plugged. A special grade of plywood, which usually has the second ply repaired, is used for underlayment. Only plywood bearing the "Underlayment" grade stamp should be used for that purpose.

The interior plies may be of any grade, although D is commonly used for the inner plies of the interior type. C is the lowest-grade veneer permitted for exterior type, and defects in the inner plies of marine plywood for boat hulls must be patched and repaired.

The end use of the plywood will determine the selection of the proper grade. Grade A-A might be selected where appearance is a factor, and it is desirable that both outer plies be free of unrepaired

Table 2–7. Some common grades and uses of Douglas fir plywood

Interior type (nonwaterproof adhesives)			
Grade	Thickness (4' × 8' panels)		
	3 plies	5 plies	
A-A	1/4", 3/8"	1/2", 5/8", 3/4"	Appearance important for both sides; furniture, cabinet doors, partitions.
A-B	1/4", 3/8"	1/2", 5/8", 3/4"	Appearance on one side not so important; cabinets, display counters.
A-D	1/4", 3/8"	1/2", 5/8", 3/4"	Wall paneling, displays, built-ins, counter tops, table-tops.
B-D	1/4", 3/8"	1/2", 5/8", 3/4"	Backing for interior finish materials.
C-D	5/16", 3/8"	1/2", 5/8", 3/4"	Wall, roof, sheathing, short-period construction barricades, nail-glued truss gussets, shipping cases.
C-D (plugged)	1/4", 3/8"	1/2", 5/8", 3/4"	Sheathing where a solid face is required.
Interior underlayment	1/4", 3/8"	1/2", 5/8", 3/4"	Underlayment for resilient floor material. 1/2-inch and thicker used as combination subfloor and underlayment.
C-D (C face repaired)*		7 plies – 1 1/8"	Combination subfloor and underlayment for floor systems designed with supports 4' on center. May be purchased with tongue and groove edges.
C-D (with exterior-type glue)	3/8"	1/2"	Subfloor, wall and roof sheathing, truss gussets.

Exterior type (waterproof adhesives)			
	3 plies	5 plies	7 plies
A-A	1/4", 3/8"	1/2", 5/8", 3/4"	7/8", 1"	Outdoor furniture, boats, signs, fences; appearance important for both sides.
A-B	1/4", 3/8"	1/2", 5/8", 3/4"	1"	Most uses as for A-A grade; side not so important from appearance standpoint.
A-C	1/4", 3/8"	1/2", 5/8", 3/4"	1"	Exposed uses, combinations (sheathing-siding), soffits, signs, one side appearance important.
C-C (repaired)*	1/4", 3/8"	1/2", 5/8", 3/4"		Backing for wall finishes, base for thin flooring materials.
C-C (unsanded)	5/16", 3/8"	1/2", 5/8", 3/4"		Truss gussets, form buildings, combination sheathing and siding; rustic appearance.

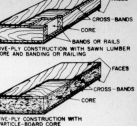

THREE-PLY CONSTRUCTION WITH VENEER CORE

FIVE-PLY CONSTRUCTION WITH VENEER CORE

FIVE-PLY CONSTRUCTION WITH SAWN LUMBER CORE AND BANDING OR RAILING

FIVE-PLY CONSTRUCTION WITH PARTICLE-BOARD CORE

Figure 2—3. Major types of plywood construction.

Table 2-7. Continued.

Exterior type (waterproof adhesives)

Marine plywood. No B plies or better throughout. No butted end-grain joints permitted in any ply. Boat-hull grade requires solid inner plies.	Hulls of racing boats and larger boats.

*One or both faces have been patched and touch-sanded.

---

hulls, or decorative use. the other end of the scale, is wall sheathing and subfloors

grades were added to the these are Standard, Structural Standard is designed for use sheathing, a substitute for C- manufactured using any of groups. Structural I and II are with exterior adhesives, and engineered applications, such as box beams, gusset plates for

some thirty species used in wood, a four-group classification. Species within each of the four properties, with the higher higher strength and stiffness designation is included in the iden-

defects, as for fences, boat
Grade C-D plywood, at the
often used for roof and wall
in frame construction.
A few years later
existing letter groups.
al I, and
al floor

er addition to the grading system is an ification index for use on construction panels. he index consists of two numbers, separated by a slash, which indicate the spacing of framing over which these panels are to be used. The number to the left of the slash indicates the maximum spacing of roof framing; the number on the right, the maximum spacing of floor framing members. Wall members are not included in the index numbering system.

Hardwood plywood. The species used in the face plies identifies hardwood plywood—that is, black walnut plywood would have one or both face plies of black walnut. Cherry, oak, birch, black walnut, maple, and gum among the native woods; mahogany, lauan, and teak in the imported category, are some of the more common species used in hardwood plywood. A major difference in the manufacture of softwood and hardwood plywood is the use of a solid "core" or extra-thick middle ply in some hardwood panels.

Veneer-core. Veneer-core plywood is manufactured with layers of wood veneer joined in the standard manner. It is intended for uses such as paneling, sheathing, and furniture parts, or when the plywood might be bent or curved.

Lumber-core. Lumber-core plywood contains a thick core made by edge-gluing several narrow strips of solid wood. This core forms the middle section to which veneer crossbands and face plies are glued. Lumber-core plywood is manufactured for specific uses such as tabletops, built-in cabinets, and fixtures and doors where butt hinges are specified.

Particleboard-core. In this plywood, the core is an aggregate of wood particles bonded together with a resin binder. Face veneers are usually glued directly to the core, although crossbanding is sometimes used. Particleboard-core plywood is used in manufacturing furniture and is particularly adaptable for table, desk, and cabinet tops. In most instances, particleboard-core plywood has greater dimensional stability than the other types.

Size. Hardwood plywood is most commonly sold in panels 4 by 8 feet, although it is usually possible to have plywood made in almost any desired size.

Thickness. Hardwood plywood is manufactured in 3, 5, 7, and 9 plies with thicknesses ranging from $\frac{1}{8}$ inch to 1 inch. Table 2—8 shows the most common thickness dimensions for the different number of plies.

Table 2—8

Number of plies	Plywood thickness (inches)			
3	$\frac{1}{8}$	$\frac{3}{16}$	$\frac{1}{4}$	
5	$\frac{1}{4}$	$\frac{3}{8}$	$\frac{1}{2}$	$\frac{5}{8}$
7	$\frac{5}{8}$	$\frac{3}{4}$		
9	$\frac{3}{4}$	1		

Types. The following four types of hardwood plywood are available:

1. Type I is manufactured with waterproof adhesives and is used in areas where it would come in contact with water.

2. Type II is manufactured with water-resistant adhesives and is used in areas where it would not ordinarily be subjected to contact with water. However, it can be used in areas of continued dampness and excessive humidity.

3. Type III is manufactured with moisture-re-

sistant adhesives and is intended for use in areas where it will not come in contact with any water. It can be subjected to some dampness and excessive humidity.

4. Technical has the same adhesive specifications as Type I but varies in thickness and arrangement of plies.

Grades. Hardwood plywood is manufactured in six specific grades. As in softwood plywood, each face must be specified.

1. Specialty grade (SP). This is a plywood made to order to meet the specific requirements of a particular buyer. Plywood of this grade usually entails special matching of the face veneers.

2. Premium grade (#1). The veneer on the face is fabricated for matched joints, and contrast in color and grain is avoided.

3. Good grade (#1). The veneer on the face is fabricated to avoid sharp contrasts in color and grain.

4. Sound grade (#2). The veneer on the face is not matched for color or grain. Some defects are permissible, but face is free of open defects and is sanded and smooth. It is usually used for surfaces to be painted.

5. Utility grade (#3). Tight knots, discoloration, stain, wormholes, mineral streaks, and some slight splits are permitted in this grade. Decay is not permitted.

6. Backing grade (#4). This grade permits larger defects. Grain and color are not matched, and the veneer is used primarily as the concealed face. Defects must not affect strength or serviceability of the panel made from it. At the manufacturer's option, this face can be of some species other than the exposed face.

OTHER LUMBERYARD MATERIALS

There are several other basic sheet materials of which you should have knowledge. For instance, there is hardboard, which comes in standard or tempered form. It is commonly supplied in 1/8- and 1/4-inch thick sheets of 4-by-8-foot-size. It may be used for both interior and exterior covering material. As with plywood or medium hardboard, the high-density hardboard in the thicker types can be applied vertically with batten strips, or horizontally as a lap siding. In perforated form, both types of hardboard are used as soffit material under cornice overhangs to ventilate attic spaces. In untreated form, high-density hardboard of special grade is also used as an underlayment for resilient flooring materials. Hardboards can be obtained with decorative laminated surfaces that provide a pleasing appearance as interior paneling. Medium hardboards are generally available in nominal 7/16- and 1/2-inch thicknesses in 4-foot-wide sheets or in the form of siding (see Chapter 8).

Interior insulating board inated paper board in 1/2- and be obtained in 4-by-8-foot side, or in paneled form for ing material. These materi tongued-and-grooved ceili 12 inches to 24 by 48 in tween 1/2 inch and 1 inch serve as a prefinished to provide acoustical qua board sheathing in 1/2- an available in 2-by-8-foot an 2-by-8-foot sheets are applie ally have shallow V or tongu The 4-by-8-foot sheets are squa vertically with perimeter nailif boards are made water-resistant asphalt coating or by impregnation sheathing can be found on page 49.

Particleboard, as previously sheet material made up of resin-bonded cles and is most often used as an under resilient flooring. It is also adaptable as material for interior walls or other uses wh not exposed to moisture. Particleboard is supplied in 4-by-8-foot sheets and in 3/8-inch ness for paneling, in 5/8-inch thickness for unde ment, and in block form for flooring. It is also u for cabinet and closet doors and as core stock f tabletops and other built-in furniture.

Plywood, particleboard, hardboard, and other sheet or panel materials are ordered in square-foot measurements. A piece of plywood 4 by 8 feet equals 32 square feet.

In storing panel material such as plywood, care should be taken to prevent damage from moisture and rain. If necessary, plywood and other sheet items that are to be kept for only a few days before use can be stored outside if a good protective covering, such as polyethylene film, tarpaulin, or other waterproof material, is applied. The panel material stack should be loosely wrapped to prevent moisture condensation under the cover. Plywood and other similar materials to be stored for a long period should be stacked flat inside a dry, covered storage area.

Interior finish and millwork include doorjambs and doors; casing, base, base shoe, stool, apron, and other trim and moldings; stair parts; and various cabinets, fireplace mantels, and other manufactured units. Such interior trim as casing and base is stocked in most retail lumberyards in several patterns and at least one species of wood.

FASTENING TECHNIQUES

In remodeling work, where structural details, parts, and elements are moved or new ones added, proper fasteners are more important than when entirely

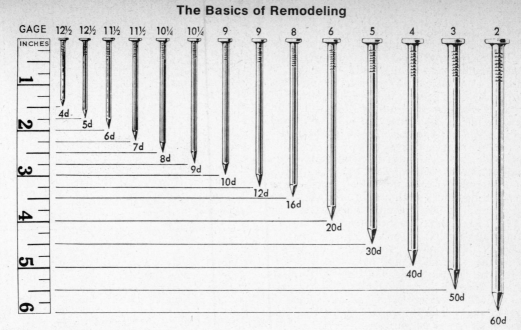

Figure 2—4. Sizes of common wire nails.

Table 2—9. Common nails

Size*	Length	Diameter gauge number	Diameter of head (inches)	Approximate number per pound
2d	1	15	11/64	830
3d	1¼	14	13/64	528
4d	1½	12½	¼	316
5d	1¾	12½	¼	271
6d	2	11½	17/64	168
7d	2¼	11½	17/64	150
8d	2½	10¼	9/32	106
9d	2¾	10¼	9/32	96
10d	3	9	5/16	69
12d	3¼	9	5/16	63
16d	3½	8	11/32	49
20d	4	6	13/32	31
30d	4½	5	7/16	24
40d	5	4	15/32	18
50d	5½	3	½	14
60d	6	2	17/32	11

Finishing nails

Size*	Length (inches)	Diameter gauge number	Diameter of head gauge number	Approximate number per pound
2d	1	16½	13½	1,351
3d	1¼	15½	12½	807
4d	1½	15	12	584
5d	1¾	15	12	500
6d	2	13	10	309
8d	2½	12½	9½	189
10d	3	11½	8½	121
16d	3½	11	8	90
20d	4	10	7	62

*The nail industry still clings to the penny system to indicate the length of the most commonly used nails, ranging in length from 1 to 6 inches. The symbol for penny is *d*.

new houses are being built. Unless fasteners are used in ample quantities and according to proper sizes and placement, serious cracks and other difficulties will occur.

Nailing. The length, diameter, head size, and approximate number to a pound of the various penny sizes of common nails and finishing nails are shown in Table 2—9.

As a rule, fastenings are the weakest link in all forms of construction and in all materials; therefore the resistance offered by the wood to the withdrawal of nails is important. Usually, the denser and harder the wood, the greater is the inherent nail-holding ability, assuming the wood does not split.

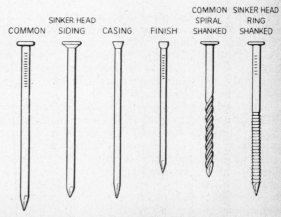

Figure 2—5. Nails commonly used in remodeling work.

The size, quantity, and placement of nails have a marked effect on the strength of a joint. Thus, more nails are required in woods of medium holding power than in woods of high holding power.

The resistance of nails to withdrawal increases almost directly with their diameter; if the diameter of the nail is doubled, the holding strength is doubled, providing the nail does not split the wood when it is driven. The lateral resistance of nails increases as the diameter increases.

The nail most generally used in wood-frame construction is the common nail. However, galvanized and aluminum nails are used extensively in applying siding and exterior trim because these nails resist rusting. The galvanized nail is slightly better than the common bright nail in retaining its withdrawal resistance.

Superior withdrawal resistance has been shown by the deformed-shank nail, which is produced in two general forms, the ring- or annular-groove and the spiral-groove shanks. The annular-groove nail is outstanding in its resistance to withdrawal loads and is commonly used in construction of pole-type buildings.

Interior carpentry uses the small-headed finish nail, which can be set and puttied over. That is, where the nailhead must not show or must be inconspicuous, it is driven well below the surface with a nail set. The hole in the wood over the nailhead can then be filled flush with the surface, with putty, plastic wood, or sawdust mixed with glue. Nail sets are made in several sizes, usually $1/32$-, $2/32$-, and $4/32$-inch, the size being indicated by the diameter of the small end of the tapered shank. The end of a nail set is often "cupped" or hollowed, which prevents it from "walking" or slipping on the nail. Use a nail set of a size which will not enlarge the hole made by the head of the nail.

The moisture content of the wood at the time of nailing is extremely important for good nail holding. If plain-shank nails are driven into wet wood, they will lose about three-fourths of their full holding ability when the wood becomes dry. This loss of holding power is so great that siding, barn boards, or fence pickets are likely to become loose when plain-shank nails are driven into green wood that subsequently dries. Thus the most important rule in obtaining good joints and high nail-holding ability is to use well-seasoned wood.

The splitting of wood by nails greatly reduces their holding ability. Even if the wood is split only slightly around the nail, considerable holding strength is lost. Because of hardness and texture characteristics, some woods split more in nailing than do others. The heavy, dense woods, such as maple, oak, and hickory, split more in nailing than do the lightweight woods, such as basswood, spruce, and balsam and white fir.

Predrilling is a good practice when working

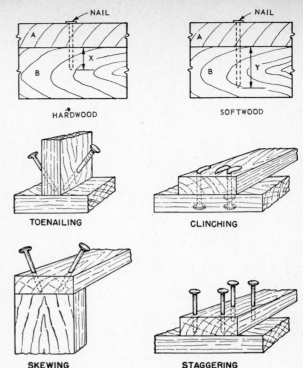

Figure 2–6. *(top)* Nail penetration into hardwood and softwood; *(bottom)* methods of nailing.

with dense woods; especially when large-diameter nails are used. The drilled hole should be about 75 percent of the nail diameter. Woods without a uniform texture, like Southern yellow pine and Douglas fir, split more than do such uniform-textured woods such as Northern and Idaho white pine, sugar pine, or ponderosa pine. In addition to predrilling, the most common means taken to reduce splitting is the use of small-diameter nails. The number of small nails must be increased to maintain the same gross holding strength as with larger nails. Slightly blunt-pointed nails have less tendency to split wood than do sharp-pointed nails. Too much blunting, however, results in a loss of holding ability.

There is a simple rule to follow when selecting nail lengths for both rough (framing) and finish (trim, cabinets) carpentry. The rule applies to hardwoods and softwoods. Figure 2–6 (top) shows the rule graphically. Suppose that pieces A and B are to be nailed together. In the case of hardwoods, the nail penetration, X, into the bottom piece should be one-half the length of the nail. For softwoods, the penetration, Y, into the bottom piece should be two-thirds the length of the nail. Thus, the thickness of the top piece determines the required nail length.

In order to increase their holding power, com-

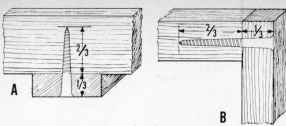

Figure 2—7. Typical screw joints for wood: (A) side grain fastened to side grain; (B) side grain fastened to end grain.

Table 2—10. Body and lead holes for wood screws

Screw gauge	Diameter (in decimals)	Body hole drill number	Lead hole drill number	Counter-sink drill number
0	.058	53	unnecessary	32
1	.071	49	unnecessary	20
2	.084	44	56	16
3	.097	40	56	4
4	.111	33	52	B
5	.124	1/8	52	F
6	.137	28	47	L
7	.150	24	47	O
8	.163	19	42	S
9	.177	15	42	T
10	.190	10	42	X
11	.202	5	38	7/16
12	.215	7/32	38	29/64
14	.242	D	31	33/64
16	.269	1	28	37/64
18	.294	19/64	23	41/64

mon nails used in rough carpentry work should be clinched. In other words, if a portion of a nail extends out beyond the surface of wood, that portion may be bent over. If common nails are clinched, they will have about 45 percent greater holding power than a corresponding nonclinched nail. The clinched portion of a nail should be at least 1/4 inch long. Longer clinched portions do not provide much more holding power. Clinching should be done perpendicular to the grain of wood.

When plywood is used, the size nail to use depends on the thickness. For 3/4-inch use 6d. For 5/8-inch use 6d or 8d. For 1/2-inch use 4d or 6d. For 3/8-inch use 3d or 4d. For 1/4-inch use 3/4- or 1-inch brads, or 3d nails. These are all finish. If you want something heavier, use a casing nail. A 6-inch spacing is about right for most work. Further information on fastening plywood panels may be found in Chapter 3.

Screwing. Screws have much greater holding power than nails. An added advantage to using screws is that work held together by them is easily taken apart and put together again without damaging the pieces. But screws take longer to install and are generally used only in finish carpentry work.

If a screw is driven in without first boring a pilot hole for the threaded part, the wood may split and in some instances the screwhead may be twisted off. (A little soap rubbed into the threads of a wood screw makes it easier to drive.) Bore holes for small screws with a small brad awl; for large screws use bits or twist drills. If the wood is soft (pine, spruce, basswood, tulip), bore the hole only about half as deep as the threaded part of the screw. If the wood is hard (oak, maple, birch), the hole must be almost as deep as the screw.

If the screw is large or if it is a brass screw, bore a pilot hole slightly smaller in diameter than the threaded part of the screw and then enlarge the hole at the top with a second drill the same diameter as the unthreaded portion of the screw.

Screws are sometimes set below the surface of the wood and concealed by a wooden plug. Plugs can be cut with a tool called a plug cutter, which fits into an ordinary brace. Plugs should be cut from

the same kind of wood as that in which they are to be inserted, and the grain should match as closely as possible. They should be cut so that the grain runs across the plug, not lengthwise.

First bore a hole at least 3/8-inch deep with an auger bit the same size as the wooden plug. Then bore the proper pilot and clearance holes. Drive the screw in as far as it will go with a screwdriver. Select a suitable plug, put some glue on its sides, and insert it in the hole, with the grain on the end of the plug running in the same direction as the grain on the surface of the work. Drive the plug in as far as it will go. When the glue has dried, use a chisel or a plane to pare the plug off level with the surface. Wood screws are sized according to diameter and length. The length is indicated in inches or fractions thereof; the diameter is indicated by a number. The smallest diameter is #0, and the largest common size is #24. The most generally used sizes are #3 to #16.

For 3/4-inch plywood, use #8 screws, 1 1/2 inches long, and predrill a 5/32-inch hole. For 5/8-inch plywood, use #8 screws, 1 1/4 inches long, and predrill a 5/32-inch hole. For 1/2-inch plywood, use #6 screws 1 1/4 inches long, and predrill a 1/8-inch hole. For

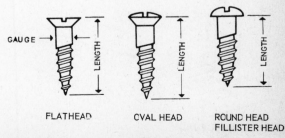

Figure 2—8. Method of measuring common screws.

$^{3}/_{8}$-inch plywood, use #6 screws, 1 inch long, and predrill a $^{1}/_{8}$-inch hole. For $^{1}/_{4}$-inch plywood, use #4 screws, $^{3}/_{4}$-inch long, and predrill a $^{7}/_{64}$-inch hole.

The method of measuring screws is shown in Figure 2–8. The length of a flathead wood screw is the overall length, but the length of round- and fillister-head screws is measured from the point to the underside of the head. The length of an ovalhead screw is measured from the point to the edge of the head.

Standards for screws have been established by cooperation between the manufacturers and the United States Bureau of Standards so that standard screws of all screw manufacturers are alike. The standard diameters are given in Table 2–11.

Table 2–11. Standard wood screw diameters

| Number | Diameter | | |
	Basic	Maximum	Minimum
0	.006	.064	.053
1	.073	.077	.066
2	.086	.090	.079
3	.099	.103	.092
4	.112	.116	.105
5	.125	.129	.118
6	.138	.142	.131
7	.151	.155	.144
8	.164	.168	.157
9	.177	.181	.170
10	.190	.194	.183
11	.203	.207	.196
12	.216	.220	.209
14	.242	.246	.235
16	.268	.272	.261
18	.294	.298	.287
20	.320	.324	.313
24	.372	.376	.365

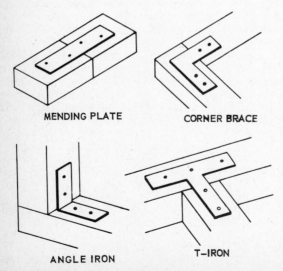

MENDING PLATE CORNER BRACE

ANGLE IRON T–IRON

Figure 2–9. Common types of mending plates.

Using mending plates. Metal fasteners, generally called mending plates and angle irons, can be used to reinforce wood joints. Available in many shapes and sizes, they can be set either into the wood or on its face. A mending plate recessed into the wood has more holding power than one placed on the surface. As shown in Figure 2–9, one half is first centered on one member of a joint and screwed in place. The second member of the joint is then held tightly against the first, and the other half of the fastener is screwed fast.

Wall fasteners. There are various methods of fastening materials to walls and ceilings, the type of fastener depending on the construction of the wall.

Lead expansion plugs. These are most frequently used for masonry walls, especially when heavy objects must be hung. There are two basic types. In one the lead plug is inserted in a drilled hole, and a screw or lag bolt is driven into the plug which is expanded by the screw and holds fast. The second type requires that the plug be set in the predrilled hole, the screw put in place, and the lead plug expanded by a hollow pipe driven against the plug with a hammer. While the latter type has greater holding power, the former is easier to install and is the most popular.

When making a hole in a masonry wall, use a star drill or three-edged impact drill of the same size as the selected lead plug. Drill the hole deep enough so the selected screw or bolt will not touch the bottom of the hole and the plug can be countersunk into the wall. In this way the screw can be drawn flush with the wall. When making the hole, rotate the drill slightly after each light tap with a hammer. Make sure the drill is held straight; if driven at an angle it will only enlarge the hole and the plug will not fit properly. Once the hole is made the lead plug is inserted and is held tightly in place when it is expanded by a screw or lag bolt. If the plug turns in the hole, or threatens to fall through a bottomless hole such as may occur in cavity construction, turn the screw into the plug a twist or two before inserting it into the hole. If you have drilled the hole too big, use the next larger size plug. Also make sure that the hole is deep enough so the selected screw or bolt will not touch the bottom of the hole.

Pin rivets. These are hammer-driven fasteners used on masonry or concrete walls. The predrilled hole should be made the same diameter as the shank of the rivet and about $^{1}/_{8}$ inch deeper. The rivet is pushed through the work into the hole, all the way. The rivet is then expanded and held in the wall by hitting its head with a hammer.

Nail shields. These are also used in masonry walls. A hole the same diameter as the shield must first be drilled in the wall. The shield is then inserted and the nail is hammered through the workpiece into the shield. This fastener gets its holding power

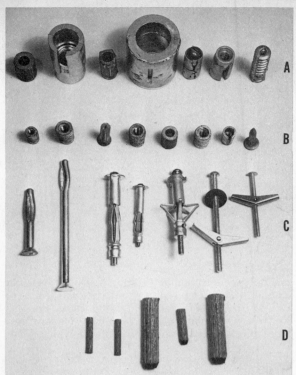

Figure 2—10. Commonly employed wall fastening methods: (A) lead expanding bolts; (B) calking; (C) drive pins, expansion anchors, and toggle bolts; (D) fiber rawl plugs.

from the shield rather than the nail, and it can support heavier loads than the pin rivet.

One-piece drive pins. This is another fastener used on a masonry surface. It comes with round and countersunk heads (furring strips to masonry, for example), tie-wire head and stud-type styles. The predrilled hole in the masonry may be as deep as you like, as long as the pin does not touch the bottom. When it is hammer-driven, it is extremely resistant to withdrawal, and has more tensile strength than conventional bolts.

Fiber plugs. On plaster walls, as well as those of masonry, the fiber plug is frequently employed. It works on the same principle as the lead plug. That is, the fiber plug is inserted in a drilled hole and a screw is driven into the plug, which is expanded by the screw and secured fast. The plug size for interior plaster walls is about $5/32$ to $1/4$ inch and about an inch long, while for exterior masonry walls and basement foundation, sizes up to 3 inches in length are common.

Plastic anchors. This is one of the most economical of all wall fasteners. When a screw is inserted into this anchor, it snaps apart behind hollow walls, or expands in solid walls, for a firm grip. A

lip prevents the anchor from slipping through and covers the raw edges of the hole. The hole should be the same diameter as the shank of the fastener. Lead screw anchors are used in the same manner and will hold heavier loads, but they are more expensive.

Toggle bolts and expansion anchors. When something is to be fastened to a surface of dry-wall construction, a hole is drilled first and then either a *toggle bolt* or one of the *expansion anchors,* such as Mollies, are pushed through. A toggle bolt requires an oversize hole to admit the wings, which spring open inside the wall. The piece to be fastened to the wall must be placed on the bolt before it is inserted into the wall. Once in the wall, if the bolt is withdrawn, the wings will drop off behind the wall. A Molly expands inside a hollow wall and grips the back of the wall. Unlike the toggle bolt, it has a sleeve which remains in the wall and permits withdrawing and replacing the bolt. It has a lip which covers the edges of the hole. Unless this fastener is correctly sized for the wall thickness, it will not work. Insert a bent wire into the wall to determine the thickness of the wall.

Pin rivets, drive pins, and nail shields are designed to carry fairly heavy loads in masonry or concrete walls. Expansion anchors and toggle bolts can be used only on hollow wall construction. Lead expansion plugs, plastic and lead anchors, and fiber plugs can be used on both solid and hollow wall construction. Remember that the holding power of a hollow-wall fastener depends basically on the strength of the wall material; plaster is stronger than dry wall. As a rule, these fasteners can withstand a maximum of a few hundred pounds. On the other hand, some solid wall fasteners are able to withstand up to a few thousand pounds' pull. Actually, the holding power of a fastener in a solid masonry or concrete wall depends to a great extent on the tightness and strength of the fastener employed.

To find out if a wall is hollow or not, tap it lightly and listen for echoes or a hollow sound. As a last resort, drill a few holes spaced about 8 inches apart in an inconspicuous spot. If you can drill to a depth of 2 inches without going through the material, the wall can be considered solid.

Joist hangers. In remodeling work you are apt to encounter several situations where joists cannot be supported in the conventional manner. In such cases, steel joist hangers, such as shown in Figure 2—11, may be used to great advantage. The A part of the illustration shows a hanger for fastening ceiling joists to beams. This hanger is especially helpful when it is impossible to put the joists on top of the beam. The B part of the illustration shows how hangers may be used to fasten floor joists to beams. The C part of the illustration shows how hangers may be used to fasten new posts or columns to

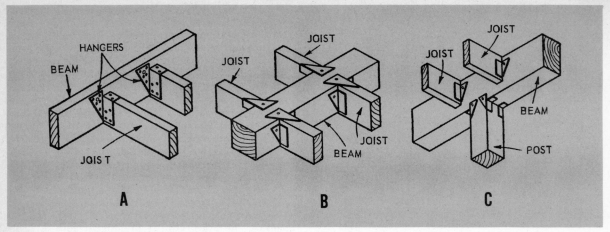

Figure 2—11. Three arrangements of joist hangers.

beams where added support is required. Also shown are somewhat different types of hangers for fastening smaller joists to beams.

Gluing. Glue is the neatest, most durable, and strongest wood fastener when properly used. However, it is used only in finished carpentry projects such as cabinets and built-ins. In all cases, the adhesive should be mixed and applied according to the manufacturer's instructions.

CONCRETE

The strength and durability of concrete vary with the kinds of cement and aggregates used, and the amount of water added. The type of mix—cement, water, and aggregates—is determined by the quality of concrete needed for a particular job. A knowledge of the several components of concrete is necessary in home improvement.

Types of cement. Portland cement is an extremely fine powder manufactured in a cement plant. Portland cement, when mixed with water, forms a paste. This paste binds materials such as sand and gravel or crushed stone (aggregate) into concrete.

The quality of the paste determines the strength and durability of the finished concrete; too much mixing water makes the paste thin and weak. For example, concrete made with a mix containing 6 gallons of water per bag of cement will be about 40 percent stronger than the same concrete mix made with 8 gallons of water per bag of cement.

Water for mixing should be clean and free of oil, acid, and other foreign substances. Usually drinking water may be used for making concrete.

Fine aggregate consists of sand; coarse aggregate consists of gravel, crushed stone, or air-cooled slag. Good, sound aggregate is necessary for making quality concrete. Loam, clay, dirt, and vegetable matter are detrimental to concrete, and aggregate containing these materials should not be used.

Mortar is a mixture of mortar sand, masonry cement, and water. Mortar is used for laying concrete blocks, bricks, and stones, and for plaster and stucco coats.

Various types of cements are manufactured for every use. Normal portland cement is gray. If white concrete is needed or desired, as in flower pots, lawn ornaments, or other decorative work, use white portland cement.

High-early-strength cement hardens more quickly than normal portland cement and is used where high strength is needed in a shorter time. It is also often used in cold-weather concreting.

Air-entraining portland cement contains an agent which forms billions of microscopic air bubbles in concrete. When hardened, air-entrained concrete virtually eliminates scaling due to freezing and thawing. It also resists scaling due to deicing salts. All concrete exposed to freezing and thawing or deicing salts should be air-entrained concrete.

Concrete. Table 2–12 gives the approximate amounts of materials needed for various size batches of concrete. It may be necessary to vary the amounts of aggregates slightly, depending on their characteristics.

The amount of concrete needed can be quickly found for any square or rectangular areas by using this formula:

Width (ft) × length (ft) × thickness (ft) = cubic yard

Mixing concrete. Make a trial mix using the amounts of materials shown in Table 2–12. If this mix does not give satisfactory workability, vary the amounts of aggregate used. Do not vary the amounts of cement and water.

All concrete should be mixed thoroughly until it is uniform in appearance (Figure 2–12). Add some of the mixing water, then the gravel and cement, then sand and the balance of the mixing water. Each piece of aggregate should be completely coated with cement paste.

When hand mixing small jobs, mix the dry materials (cement and aggregates) in a container or on a suitable hard surface. Make a depression in the pile and add some of the mixing water. Continue mixing and add the remainder of the measured amount of water. The mix should be workable. If the mix is too dry, reduce the amount of sand and gravel in the next batch; if too wet, add more aggregate. Never change the ratio of water and cement.

Pre-mixed cement. Two things are common to all pre-mixes: all parts of the mix are correctly proportioned, and all contain cement, which acts as a binder when water is added. But sharp distinctions can be made between them in terms of content and, most importantly, by function.

1. Sand mix contains cement and sand and is good for repairs and projects where up to a 2-inch thickness of mix will do.

2. Concrete mix (also called gravel mix) contains cement, sand, and gravel and is for use on jobs where extra strength, more than a 2-inch thickness of mix, is required.

3. Mortar mix is a mixture of sand, cement, and lime, its distinguishing content characteristic and reason for its plasticity and easy workability. This workability makes it most useful for joints between bricks, stones, cinder blocks, and concrete blocks. You can also use it for pointing masonry joints.

4. Waterproof mix is used as a top coat on surfaces subject to a lot of water. Use it also to repair a below-grade crack in the foundation to prevent moisture penetration. Waterproof pre-mixes contain cement, sand, and a waterproofing compound such as polyvinyl acetate. If you cannot buy the pre-mix, you can easily make your own by adding waterproofing compound to a bag of sand mix. Instructions for mixing are on the compound's container.

When using pre-mixed cement, be sure to follow the instructions on the bag concerning amounts of water to be added.

Ready-mixed concrete. For larger jobs consider using ready-mixed concrete; this eliminates the work of mixing and proportioning. It is as easy to order as ready-mixed concrete; just remember the numbers 6-6-6. These stand for 6 bags of cement per cubic yard, 6 gallons of water per bag of cement, and 6 percent entrained air.

You should be prepared when the concrete arrives. Be sure that all ground preparations have been completed, that forms are coated with light form oil, and that equipment and sufficient help are on hand.

Working with concrete. Concrete should not be placed on frozen earth, mud, or earth covered with standing water. If the supporting earth is extremely dry, it should be dampened to prevent absorption of the mixing water in the concrete. Chutes are recommended when the concrete is dropped more than 3 or 4 feet.

Striking off concrete. After the concrete is placed, it is struck off with a straightedge, usually a 2×4. The stakes holding the forms should be cut off even with the top of the forms to permit continuous movement of the strike-off board. One to three strike-off passes should be sufficient. A trowel or spade can be worked along the face of the forms to give a smooth side surface to the concrete.

Finishing concrete. The type of finish depends upon the finishing tools used. A float gives a gritty texture. When a rougher texture is desired, the surface is floated and then broomed by dragging a stiff-bristle broom across the concrete. The stiffness of the bristles and the pressure applied determine the degree of roughness. Float and broomed finishes are recommended for sidewalks, driveways, and ramps. Steel-troweling gives a smooth finish that does not always provide sufficient footing. Floors, patios, and basement floors are a few places where a steel-trowel finish is often used.

After the concrete has been struck off, it is

Table 2–12. Materials needed for concrete

(A 1:2¼:3 mix = 1 part cement to 2¼ parts sand to 3 parts 1-inch maximum aggregate)

Concrete required (cubic feet)	Cement (pounds)	Maximum amount of water to use (gallons)	Sand (pounds)	Coarse aggregate (pounds)
1	24	1¼	52	78
3	71	3¾	156	233
5	118	6¼	260	389
6¾ (¼ cubic yard)	165	8	350	525
13½ (½ cubic yard)	294	16	700	1,050
27 (1 cubic yard)	588	32	1,400	2,100

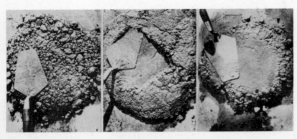

Figure 2–12. Concrete mixes: *(left to right)* too much gravel; not enough gravel; correct mixture.

Figure 2–13. Finishing concrete with a steel trowel. Note wood trowel at left.

floated with a light metal float. A float with a long handle is excellent for finishing flat slabs. A final floating with a hand float is often given. Brooming is usually done after floating. Steel-troweling (Figure 2–13) is also done after floating. The proper time to begin steel-troweling is critical. Premature troweling causes a mixture of water, cement, and fine sand to work to the surface, resulting in poorer wearability and surface crazing. Troweling should be done after water sheen has disappeared. Do not sprinkle water or dry cement on the surface.

An edging tool used between the concrete and the form will produce a smooth, rounded edge that will resist breaking and chipping. The edging tool should be used early, while the concrete is still plastic.

Curing concrete. After finishing, the concrete must be cured. Up to 50 percent more strength can be developed if fresh concrete is properly cured. Curing is one of the most inexpensive ways to ensure a long-lasting, satisfactory job.

Plastic sheeting or waterproof paper placed over the concrete soon after finishing is an economical method of curing. Sand, straw, burlap, and other materials that are kept continuously wet for at least six days may be used to cure the fresh concrete. Forms left in place for several days will also help cure concrete.

BRICK AND STONEMASONRY

Only a few tools are required in masonry work. The trowel is used to handle the mortar (made of cement and other ingredients) that is placed between the stones or bricks to bond them together. The brick hammer is used for breaking bricks and squaring them to fit odd spaces. A chisel or cold chisel may also be used to cut bricks and to cut holes or open cracks in masonry for repair. A level, plumb bob and line, and rule or tape measure are necessary to assure that the structure will be straight, square, and of the proper dimensions. A 10- to 12-foot-long straight edge, made of seasoned wood, enables the bricklayer to lay the different courses or layers of brick straight and true. Joint finishers are usually made of steel and are so shaped as to permit quick and easy smoothing and compacting of the mortar in the joints between the bricks. A mortar box of a size adequate to mix the amount of mortar required (4 by 6 feet with sides 10 inches high is a good average size), plus a shovel and hoe, are required to mix mortar.

Bricks. A simple, natural product of clay and water, brick was man's first manufactured building block. Archeologists uncovering ancient cities have found brick walls more than 9,000 years old. While other materials have been invented, brick still is in use in home construction because it is unsurpassed for sheer beauty and ruggedness.

Brick types. Bricks fall into four general classes:

1. Common bricks. Unselected brick, 8 by 2¼ by 3¾ inches in size, is not specially treated for color or texture. This is the cheapest type available and is used where appearance is not a primary concern. Used common bricks, as their name implies, are bricks that have been used in construction work and have been reclaimed. They are popular today as a decorative surface.

2. Face bricks. This type of brick is made especially for facing purposes and is usually treated to produce various surface colors and textures. It is more expensive than common brick.

3. Ornamental bricks. Bricks of this type have a salt-glazed or ceramic surface that is glossy and smooth. They are the most expensive type and are generally used for decorative purposes in commercial structures.

4. Fire bricks. Made of refractory clay to resist very high temperatures, this brick is used mostly for lining fireplaces and chimneys. Common brick cannot withstand high temperatures in such applications and would soon crumble.

Bricklaying. Bricks are laid on a foundation—a footing (see page 32) or a subwall—which must be smooth and level so that the layers or courses of brick will be level and have a pleasing appearance. The first step in a bricklaying job is to lay out, without mortar, the first layer of bricks on the foundation, starting at one corner and progressing entirely around the foundation. This procedure is called "chasing out the bond" and permits planning the job so that the bricks will come out evenly at every corner. The term bond in this instance does not refer to the bonding of the different materials but to the arrangement of the bricks in the wall. Different arrangements can be made to produce varied patterns.

As the first layer of bricks is laid out, space for mortar should be left between the bricks. Then, if the bricks do not come out evenly when a corner is reached, the mortar spaces or joints can be readjusted slightly so the last brick just fits, with equal spaces being left between all bricks. These spaces or joints between the bricks, called the "cross joints," are normally 3/8-inch wide; in some brickwork they are as much as 5/8-inch wide. After all the bricks have been properly placed on the foundation, their positions should be carefully marked on the foundation so that they can be laid with mortar in the same positions. When this is done, the mortar can be prepared and the bricklaying job begun.

Preparing the mortar. The most commonly used mortar is made from cement, sand, hydrated lime, and water. The lime reduces the speed with which the mortar sets and prevents shrinkage of the mortar as it sets so that cracks are less apt to develop in the joints. The sand must be clean and must not contain any pebbles. For the average remodeling job it is best to purchase ready-mixed mortar, which requires only the addition of water. This material is sold by the bag and simplifies the mixing job. Sufficient water is added to obtain a workable mixture, which should be fairly stiff but soft enough to flow when subjected to pressure. For filling in behind stonework, back of retaining walls, or between the tile liners and bricks of chimneys, thin mortar, called "grout," is used. It is prepared by adding extra water to the mortar. Grout is thin enough to flow into the spaces and fill them completely.

If it is desired to mix the mortar on the job rather than use ready-mixed mortar, the following will make enough mortar to lay 1,000 bricks with 3/8-inch joints: 6 cubic feet of cement (6 sacks), 18 cubic feet of sand, 50 to 60 pounds of hydrated lime, and the proper amount of water.

After the mortar is mixed, it begins to set, and if some time is allowed to go by, it may become so stiff that it is difficult to use. The addition of more water and the further mixing of the mortar temper it so that it again becomes workable. However, such tempering naturally weakens the mortar and is not recommended. The best procedure is to mix mortar in smaller batches so that it can be quickly used up.

Laying the brick. After the mortar is ready, the first course of bricks already in position on the foundation is laid. The first brick at a corner is removed, a bed of mortar is placed on the foundation with a trowel, and the brick is replaced in the exactly correct position. Sufficient mortar must be used to fill completely the space between the brick and the foundation, and the brick must be tapped down or settled into the mortar bed so that the thickness of the mortar or the joint will match the thickness of the joints between adjacent bricks. Excess mortar that oozes out of the joint should be scraped off the outside edge with a trowel and then used for the cross joint between the first and second bricks. The second brick is picked up off the foundation and "buttered" on the end facing the first brick; the mortar bed is placed on the foundation, and the second brick is laid. After the first layer or course of bricks is laid in this fashion, the second layer is started and work proceeds in the same manner. It is not necessary to chase out the bond or lay out the second or subsequent course of bricks. Good judgment in placing the second layer is all that is required.

Often more than one brick is taken off the foundation at a time, and a mortar bed sufficient for several bricks is applied. Laying several bricks at a time in this manner speeds up the work. However, work must proceed rapidly when bricks are laid in this manner; otherwise the mortar in the bed will be partly set before the last brick is laid.

For any extensive brickwork it is necessary to use leads and lines to assure true alignment of each course of bricks. Frequent use of the level and the straightedge also assures good alignment. The leads consist of several layers of brick laid up at the corners. These leads are carefully laid up absolutely square and level and serve as guides for the intervening wall between the corners. Lines are

Figure 2–14. Important steps in the making of a brick wall: *(left to right)* checking the wall with a level; buttering the end of a brick; striking off the joint.

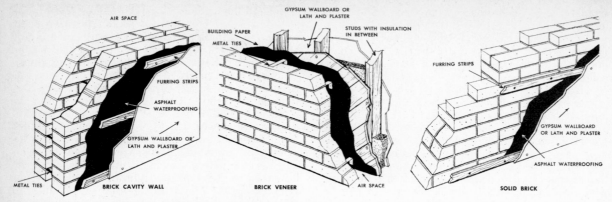

Figure 2–15. Three types of brick wall used in residential construction.

stretched between the leads, and each course of bricks is laid to a line. The line is attached to nails or special clamps fastened into the bricks so that the line will just touch the upper outside edge of the bricks as they are laid between the corners. The line must be stretched taut so that it does not sag. If the distance is too great, one or more additional leads must be laid up at intermediate places along the wall to serve as supports for the line.

Types of brickwork walls. There are many different kinds of brick walls, but only three (Figure 2–15) are used in residential construction.

The most common brick wall used in house construction is a "veneered" wall. It consists of a single layer of facing brick laid up outside the wall sheathing material and separated from it by a layer of build felt or paper. The structural wall itself is framed in the conventional manner with wood studs (see page 44), and the bricks act only as an exterior finishing material. The bricks are attached to the frame wall by metal strips, called "ties," which are nailed to the sheathing and embedded in the mortar between bricks. A sufficient number of these ties must be employed to assure good integration of the brick veneer facing and the framework.

The second type of brick wall used in houses is a solid masonry wall. With this type of wall there is no wood frame behind the bricks. Instead, the bricks, and usually a "back up" of hollow masonry units or bricks, provide both enclosure and structural system. Furring strips are then fastened to the masonry units, and the interior finished wall material is applied over the furring strips. With solid masonry construction, waterproofing is most important since both the bricks and mortar will readily absorb moisture. Thus, if water should seep through the wall, the interior finish would be damaged unless proper precautions are taken. This usually includes a coating or two of hot tar on the inside surface of the solid brick wall.

The third type of brick wall is known as a "cav-ity" wall. This is a wall in which a space is left between an outer and an inner width of brick. The space, usually about 2 inches wide, may be filled with insulation or be left as a dead air space. In the latter case, the dead air space blocks the passage of water through the wall and also provides some insulation. Cavity wall construction is often used when it is desirable to have an exposed brick interior wall.

Types of bonds. The process of putting bricks together for a structurally sound and aesthetically pleasing wall is known as "bonding." The pattern itself is called a "bond." Actually, bonding involves various arrangements of "stretcher" and "header" bricks. A stretcher is a brick laid lengthwise along the face of a wall with its side showing. A header is laid at a right angle to the face of a wall with only the end of the brick showing. The number of brick bonds is almost infinite, but nearly all of them derive from the following four basic patterns (Figure 2–16), which date back many centuries:

1. Running bond. This is the most common and simplest brick bond. It consists of stretchers only. The bricks in each course or row are lapped halfway over the bricks in the course below. The running bond lends itself to rapid construction and presents a uniform and balanced appearance throughout the wall.

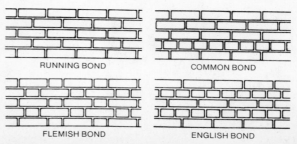

Figure 2–16. Four common brick bonds.

2. Common bond. The common bond is an often used variation of the running bond. In it, a course of headers is placed at regular intervals among the stretcher courses. The header course gives additional strength to the wall and emphasizes the horizontal pattern of the stretcher courses.

3. Flemish bond. This bond is formed by alternating headers and stretchers in each course of bricks. The headers in one course are centered over the stretchers in the course below. The Flemish bond produces a handsome pattern of crosses and is easily adaptable to many decorative variations.

4. English bond. The English bond is composed of alternating courses of stretchers and headers. The headers are centered on the stretchers and the joints of the preceding course. This produces a wall which is very strong, and the clean, distinct pattern of its mortar joints presents a pleasing visual effect.

Contemporary modifications of these traditional bonds include omitting headers or stretchers to form perforated walls or screens, and the recession or projection of some units to create strong light-and-shadow effects.

Types of joints. Mortar joints add to both the beauty and efficiency of a wall. There are a number of ways to treat joints, any one of which can add to the appearance of a wall. In addition, striking the joint properly helps the brick units bond together and helps seal the wall against moisture. The following six basic joints (Figure 2–17) are most commonly used:

1. Concave joint. Created through the use of a rounded jointing tool.

2. V-shaped joint. Created with a V-shaped tool.

3. Weathered joint. Made by inclining the joint so that it sheds water readily.

4. Struck joint. Another inclined joint, but the reverse of the weathered joint.

5. Raked joint. Made by removing some of the mortar with a square-edged tool. The struck and raked joints are decorative but invite water seepage because water tends to collect in the joint.

6. Flush joint. This is the simplest joint, made by holding the edge of the trowel flat against the

Figure 2–18. Steps in laying a concrete block foundation.

brick and striking off the excess mortar, leaving the mortar flush with the face of the brick. A variation is the squeezed joint, made by merely leaving the excess mortar which is squeezed out as the brick is tapped down into place. Some judgment is required when this joint is used to avoid applying too heavy a bed of mortar, since this would make the squeezed-out part too bulky. The most effective joints in terms of their ability to resist moisture are the concave, V-shaped, and weathered joints.

Stonemasonry. In many respects stonemasonry and brickmasonry are similar. However, stonemasonry is a more specialized trade and requires considerable judgment in laying out a job. Stones of many types are used in homes, varying from rough, irregular, random-sized native stone to precisely cut limestone to be laid up in a definite pattern. The general rules applying to bricklaying also apply to stonemasonry. Quite often stone is used only as a facing material and is placed over a brick, concrete, or concrete block wall. More on stonemasonry may be found on page 88.

Concrete or cinder blocks. For a great deal of remodeling work, such as adding one or more rooms to your home, concrete or cinder blocks are possibly the easiest way to obtain the necessary foundation walls. These materials are laid in much the same manner as bricks. The blocks are hollow and usually measure 8 by 8 by 16 inches. They are laid on a foundation or a footing, as in the case of bricks with mortar joints. The first course of blocks should be laid out and the width of the joints adjusted so that the corner blocks just fit to provide the proper length of wall. Leads must be built and lines stretched, as in bricklaying, to assure straight and level walls.

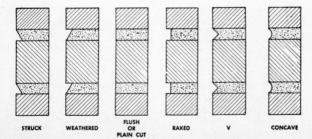

| STRUCK | WEATHERED | FLUSH OR PLAIN CUT | RAKED | V | CONCAVE |

Figure 2–17. The most popular brick mortar joints.

Chapter 2

HOME CONSTRUCTION

If you know how your home is built, you can do a faster and better improvement or remodeling job. Of course, houses differ greatly in size, shape, and style, personal preferences and regional conditions accounting for the wide variations. But whatever the variations, except in the case of some factory-built houses, which frequently employ novel erection techniques, most homes follow essentially the same construction procedures. There are two basic methods of building a house, constructing the frame of masonry or of wood. The latter is the most common.

A knowledge of construction procedures described here is essential for most remodeling work, especially when making an addition to your home as described in Chapter 15. It is important to keep in mind that the construction techniques detailed in the succeeding pages are relatively standard throughout the country in modern home building. But departures from standard practice are common; some of them are relatively unimportant, others quite fundamental. Before making major renovations or alterations you should find out how your home is constructed. An exact knowledge of what is hidden in the walls and how it was put there will prevent costly and irksome mistakes. The information can be obtained in several ways: From blueprints, if they are available; if blueprints are not

at hand, a building contractor or an architect may be consulted. Also in this book there are many tips on how to find what is under the skin of your home.

Foundation. Every structure needs a foundation. The function of a foundation is to provide a level and uniformly distributed support for the house. The foundation must be strong enough to support and distribute the load of the house, and sufficiently level to prevent the walls from cracking and the doors and windows from sticking. The foundation also helps to prevent cold air and dampness from entering the house. There are two basic structural members of a foundation: the footings and walls or piers.

Footings. The footings act as the base of the foundation and transmit the superimposed load to the soil. The type and size of footings are usually determined by the soil condition, and in cold climates the footings must be far enough below ground level to be protected from frost action. Local codes usually establish this depth, which is often 4 feet or more in northern sections of the United States and Canada.

Well-designed footings are important in preventing settling or cracks in the wall. One of the most popular methods of determining the footing size, generally used with most normal soils, is based on the proposed foundation wall thickness. The footing thickness or depth should be equal to the wall thickness of the foundation. Footings should project beyond each side of the wall one-half the wall thickness (Figure 2–19A). This is a general rule, of course, as the footing-bearing area should be designed for the load capacity of the soil. Local regulations often relate to these needs. This also applies to column and fireplace footings. If soil is of low load-bearing capacity, wider reinforced footings may be required. The following are a few rules that apply to footing design and construction:

1. Footings must be at least 6 inches thick, with 8 inches or more preferable.

2. If footing excavation is too deep, fill with concrete—never replace the dirt.

3. Use formboards for footings where soil conditions prevent sharply cut trenches.

4. Place footings below the frostline.

5. Reinforce footings with steel rods where they cross pipe trenches.

6. Use key slot for better resistance to water entry at wall location.

7. In freezing weather, cover with straw or supply heat.

Footings for piers, posts, or columns (Figure 2–19B) are generally square and include a pedestal on which the member will bear. A protruding steel pin is ordinarily set in the pedestal to anchor a wood post. Bolts for the bottom plate of steel posts are usually set when the pedestal is poured. At other times, steel posts are set directly on the footing and

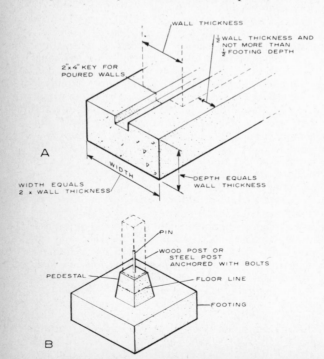

Figure 2–19. Concrete footing: (A) wall footing; (B) post footing.

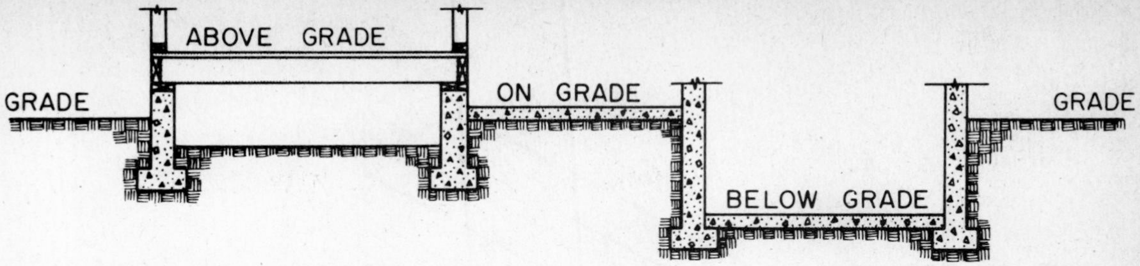

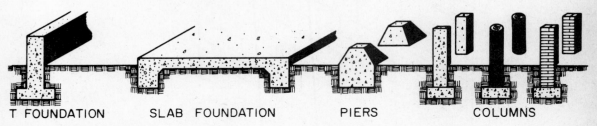

Figure 2–20. Foundation positions.

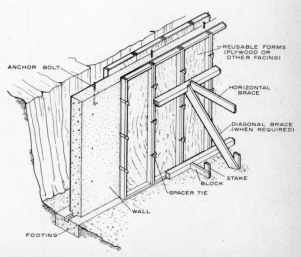

Figure 2–21. Types of foundation.

the concrete floor is poured around them.

Pier or column footings vary in size depending on the allowable soil pressure and the spacing of the piers, posts, or columns. Common sizes are 24 by 24 by 12 inches and 30 by 30 by 12 inches. The pedestal is sometimes poured after the footing. The minimum height should be about 3 inches above the finish basement floor and 12 inches above finish grade in crawl-space areas. Footings for fireplaces, furnaces, and chimneys are ordinarily poured at the same time as other footings.

Foundation walls and piers. Foundation walls form an enclosure for basements or crawl spaces and carry wall, floor, roof, and other building loads. The two types of walls most commonly used are poured concrete and concrete block.

Wall thicknesses and types of construction are ordinarily controlled by local building regulations. Thicknesses of poured concrete basement walls may vary from 8 to 10 inches, and concrete block walls from 8 to 12 inches, depending on story heights and length of unsupported walls.

Clear wall height, in most cases, should be no less than 7 feet from the top of the finish basement floor to the bottom of the joists; greater clearance is usually desirable to provide adequate headroom under girders, pipes, and ducts. Today the trend is to pour 8-foot-high walls above the footings, which provide a clearance of 7 feet 8 inches from the top of the finish concrete floor to the bottom of the joists. Concrete block walls, 11 courses above the footings with 4-inch solid cap block, will produce about a 7-foot-4-inch height to the joists from the basement floor.

Poured concrete walls. Poured concrete walls (Figure 2–22) require forming that must be tight and also be braced and tied to withstand the forces of the pouring operation and the fluid concrete. Poured concrete walls should be double-formed (formwork constructed for each wall face). Reusable forms are used in the majority of poured walls and they can usually be rented from contractor supply houses. Panels may consist of wood framing with plywood facings and are fastened together with clips or other ties. The formwork should be plumb,

Figure 2–22. Forming for poured concrete walls.

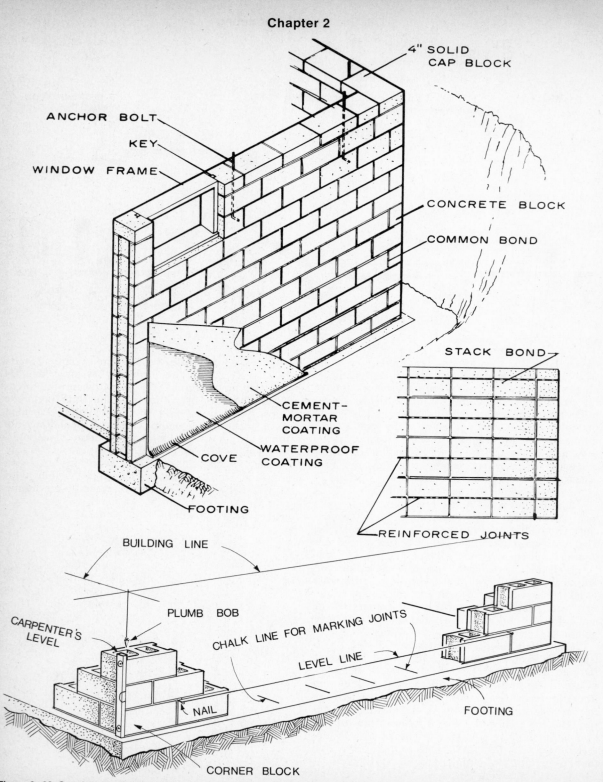

ANCHOR BOLT

KEY

WINDOW FRAME

4" SOLID CAP BLOCK

CONCRETE BLOCK

COMMON BOND

CEMENT-MORTAR COATING

WATERPROOF COATING

COVE

FOOTING

STACK BOND

REINFORCED JOINTS

BUILDING LINE

PLUMB BOB

CARPENTER'S LEVEL

CHALK LINE FOR MARKING JOINTS

LEVEL LINE

NAIL

FOOTING

CORNER BLOCK

Figure 2—23. Concrete block wall: *(bottom)* laying up wall; *(top)* details of a completed wall.

straight, and braced sufficiently to withstand the pouring operations.

Frames for cellar windows, doors, and other openings are set in place as the forming is erected, along with forms for the beam pockets, which are located to support the ends of the floor beam. Reusable forms usually require little bracing other than horizontal members and sufficient blocking and bracing to keep them in place during pouring operations. Level marks of some type, such as nails along the form, should be used to assure a level foundation top. This will provide a good level sill plate and floor framing.

When the foundation is being laid, concrete should be poured continuously without interruption and constantly puddled to remove any air pockets. The material should be worked under window frames and other blocking. Anchor bolts for the sill plate should be placed while the concrete is still plastic. Concrete, of course, should always be protected when temperatures are below freezing. Forms should not be removed until the concrete has hardened and acquired sufficient strength to support loads imposed during early construction. At least two days (and preferably longer) are required when temperatures are well above freezing, and perhaps a week when outside temperatures are below freezing.

Poured concrete walls can be dampproofed with one heavy cold or hot coat of tar or asphalt. It should be applied to the outside from the footings to the finish gradeline. Such coatings are usually sufficient to make a wall watertight against ordinary seepage (such as may occur after a rainstorm), but should not be applied until the surface of the concrete has dried enough to assure good adhesion. In poorly drained soils, a membrane (such as described for concrete block walls) may be necessary.

Concrete block walls. Concrete blocks, as previously stated, are available in various sizes and forms, but those generally used are 8, 10, and 12 inches wide. Modular blocks allow for the thickness and width of the mortar joint, so are usually about $7\frac{5}{8}$ inches high by $15\frac{5}{8}$ inches long. This results in blocks which measure 8 inches high and 16 inches long from centerline to centerline of the mortar joints.

Concrete block walls require no formwork. Block courses start at the footing and are laid up with about $\frac{3}{8}$-inch mortar joints, usually in a common bond (see page 30). Joints are tooled smooth to resist water seepage. Full bedding of mortar should be used on all contact surfaces of the blocks. When pilasters (column-like projections) are required by building codes or to strengthen a wall, they are placed on the interior side of the wall and terminated at the bottom of the beam or girder supported. Basement door and window frames should be set with keys for rigidity and to prevent air leakage

(Figure 2–23). Block walls are often capped with 4 inches of solid masonry or concrete reinforced with wire mesh. Anchor bolts for sills are usually placed through the top two rows of blocks and the top cap. They should be anchored with a large plate washer at the bottom, and the block openings filled solidly with mortar or concrete.

Freshly laid block walls must be protected in temperatures below freezing. Freezing of the mortar before it has set will often result in low adhesion, low strength, and joint failure.

To provide a tight, waterproof joint between the footing and wall, an elastic calking compound is often used. The wall is waterproofed by applying a coating of cement-mortar over the block with a cove formed at the juncture with the footing. When the mortar is dry, a coating of asphalt or other waterproofing will normally assure a dry basement.

For added protection when wet soil conditions may be encountered, a waterproof membrane of roofing felt or other material can be mopped on, with shingle-style laps of 4 to 6 inches, over the cement-mortar coating. Hot tar or hot asphalt is commonly used over the membrane. This covering will prevent leaks if minor cracks develop in the blocks or joints between the blocks.

Crawl-space foundation. In many areas of the country, crawl-space construction is often used in preference to that of a full basement or a concrete slab. This is especially true when just making an addition. But the success of such a foundation depends on three things: (a) a good soil cover, (b) a small amount of ventilation, and (c) sufficient insulation to reduce heat loss. These details will be covered in later chapters.

One of the primary advantages of the crawl space over the full basement is, of course, the reduced cost. Little or no excavation or grading is required except for the footings and walls. In mild climates, the footings are located only slightly below the finish grade. However, in the Northern states where frost penetrates deeply, the footing is often located 4 or more feet below the finish grade. This, of course, requires more masonry work and increases the cost. The footings should always be poured over undisturbed soil and never over fill,

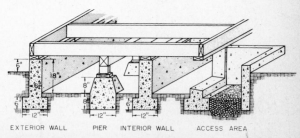

EXTERIOR WALL   PIER   INTERIOR WALL   ACCESS AREA

Figure 2–24. Typical crawl-space foundation construction.

unless special piers and grade beams are used.

The construction of a masonry wall for a crawl space is much the same as for a full basement, except that no excavation is required within the walls. Waterproofing and drain tile are normally not required for this type of construction. Footing size and wall thicknesses vary somewhat by location and soil conditions. A common minimum thickness for walls in single-story frame houses is 8 inches for hollow concrete block and 6 inches for poured concrete. The minimum footing thickness is 6 inches, and the width is 12 inches for concrete block and 10 inches for the poured foundation wall for crawl-space homes. However, in well-constructed houses it is common practice to use 8-inch walls and 16-by-8-inch footings.

Poured concrete or concrete block piers are of-ten used to support floor beams in crawl-space houses. They should extend at least 12 inches above the groundline. The minimum size for a concrete block pier should be 8 by 16 inches with a 16-by-24-by-8-inch footing. A solid cap block is used as a top course. Poured concrete piers should be at least 10 by 10 inches in size with a 20-by-20-by-8-inch footing. Unreinforced concrete piers should be no greater in height than 10 times their least dimension. Concrete block piers should be no higher than four times the least dimension. The spacing of piers should not exceed 8 feet on center under exterior wall beams and interior girders set at right angles to the floor joists, and 12 feet on center under exterior wall beams set parallel to the floor joists. Exterior wall piers should not extend above grade more than four times their least dimension unless supported laterally by masonry or concrete walls. For wall footing sizes, the sizes of the pier footings are based on the load and the capacity of the soil.

Concrete floor slabs on the ground. One common type of floor construction for basementless houses is a concrete slab over a suitable foundation. Sloping ground or low areas are usually not ideal for slab-on-ground construction because structural and drainage problems would add to costs and problems. Split-level houses often have a portion of the foundation designed for a grade slab. In such use, the slope of the lot is taken into account and the objectionable features of a sloping ground become an advantage.

The finish flooring for concrete floor slabs on the ground was originally asphalt tile laid in mastic directly on the slab. These concrete floors did not prove satisfactory in a number of instances, and considerable prejudice has been built up against this method of construction. The common complaints are that the floors are cold and uncomfortable and that condensation sometimes collects on the floor, near the walls in cold weather, and elsewhere during warm, humid weather. Some of these undesirable features of concrete floors on the ground apply to both warm and cold climates, and others only to cold climates.

Improvements in methods of construction based on past experience and research have materially reduced the common faults of the slab floor but consequently increased their cost.

Floors are cold principally because of loss of heat through the floor and the foundation walls, with most loss occurring around the exterior walls. Suitable insulation around the perimeter of the house will help to reduce the heat loss. Radiant floor heating systems are effective in preventing cold floors and floor condensation problems. Peripheral warm-air heating ducts are also effective in this respect. Vapor barriers over a gravel fill under the floor slab prevent soil moisture from rising through the slab.

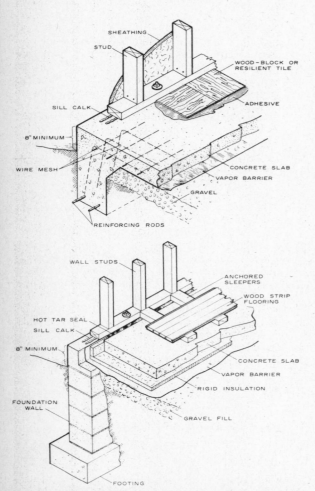

Figure 2–25. *(top)* Combined slab and foundation. *(bottom)* Independent concrete floor slab and wall. Concrete block is used over poured footing, which is at frost line. In addition, rigid insulation may be located along the inside of the block wall.

The following basic requirements should be met in the construction of concrete floor slabs to provide a satisfactory floor:

1. Establish finish floor level high enough above the natural ground level so that finish grade around the house can be sloped away for good drainage. Top of slab should be no less than 8 inches above the ground, and the siding no less than 6 inches.

2. Top soil should be removed and sewer and water lines installed, then covered with 4 to 6 inches of gravel or crushed rock well tamped in place.

3. A vapor barrier consisting of a heavy plastic film, such as 6-mil polyethylene, asphalt-laminated duplex sheet, or 45-pound or heavier roofing, with a minimum of ½-perm rating should be used under the concrete slab. Joints should be lapped at least 4 inches and sealed. The barrier should be strong enough to resist puncturing during placing of the concrete.

4. A permanent, waterproof, nonabsorptive type of rigid insulation should be installed around the perimeter of the wall. Insulation may extend down on the inside of the wall vertically or under the slab edge horizontally.

5. The slab should be reinforced with 6-by-6-inch #10 wire mesh or other effective reinforcing. The concrete slab should be at least 4 inches thick.

6. After leveling and screeding, the surface should be floated with wood or metal floats while the concrete is still plastic. If a smooth dense surface is needed for the installation of wood or resilient tile with adhesives, the surface should be steel troweled.

Floor framing. The floor framing in a wood-frame house consists specifically of the posts, beams, sill plates, joists, and subfloor. When these are assembled properly on a foundation, they form a level anchored platform for the rest of the house. The posts and center beams of wood or steel, which support the inside ends of the joists, are sometimes replaced with a wood-frame or masonry wall when the basement area is divided into rooms. Wood-frame houses may also be constructed upon a concrete floor slab or over a crawl-space area with floor framing similar to that used for a full basement.

One of the important factors in the design of a wood floor system is to equalize shrinkage and expansion of the wood framing at the outside walls and at the center beam. This is usually accomplished by using about the same total depth of wood at the center beam as is used for the outside framing. Thus, as beams and joists approach moisture equilibrium or the moisture content they reach in service, there are only small differences in the amount of shrinkage. This will minimize wall cracks and prevent sticking doors and other inconveniences caused by uneven shrinkage. If there is a total of 12 inches of wood at the foundation wall (including joists and sill plate), this should be balanced with about 12 inches of wood at the center beam.

Recommended nailing practices. Of primary consideration, as previously mentioned in this chapter, in the construction of a house is the method used to fasten the various wood members together. These connections are most commonly made with nails, but on occasion metal straps, lag screws, bolts, and adhesives may be used.

Proper fastening of frame members and covering materials provides the rigidity and strength to resist severe windstorms and other hazards. Good nailing is also important from the standpoint of normal performance of wood parts. For example, proper fastening of intersecting walls usually reduces wall cracking at the inside corners. The schedule in Table 2–13 outlines good nailing practices for the framing and sheathing of a well-constructed wood-frame house.

Table 2–13

Joining	Nailing method	Number	Size	Placement
Header to joist	End-nail	3	16d	
Joist to sill or girder	Toenail	2	10d or	
		3	8d	
Header and stringer joist to sill	Toenail		10d	16 inches on center
Bridging to joist	Toenail each end	2	8d	
Ledger strip to beam, 2 inches thick		3	16d	At each joist
Subfloor, boards				
1 × 6 inches and smaller		2	8d	To each joist
1 × 8 inches		3	8d	To each joist
Subfloor, plywood				
At edges			8d	6 inches on center
At intermediate joists			8d	8 inches on center

(cont'd)

Table 2–13 (continued)

Joining	Nailing method	Nails		
		Number	Size	Placement
Subfloor (2 × 6 inches, T&G) to joist or girder	Blind-nail (casing) and face-nail	2	16d	
Soleplate to stud, horizontal assembly	End-nail	2	16d	At each stud
Top plate to stud	End-nail	2	16d	
Stud to soleplate	Toenail	4	8d	
Soleplate to joist or blocking	Face-nail		16d	16 inches on center
Doubled studs	Face-nail, stagger		10d	16 inches on center
End stud of intersecting wall to exterior wall stud	Face-nail		16d	16 inches on center
Upper top plate to lower top plate	Face-nail		16d	16 inches on center
Upper top plate, laps and intersections	Face-nail	2	16d	
Continuous header, two pieces, each edge			12d	12 inches on center
Ceiling joist to top wall plates	Toenail	3	8d	
Ceiling joist laps at partition	Face-nail	4	16d	
Rafter to top plate	Toenail	2	8d	
Rafter to ceiling joist	Face-nail	5	10d	
Rafter to valley or hip rafter	Toenail	3	10d	
Ridge board to rafter	End-nail	3	10d	
Rafter to rafter through ridge board	Toenail	4	8d	
	Edge-nail	1	10d	
Collar beam to rafter				
2-inch member	Face-nail	2	12d	
1-inch member	Face-nail	3	8d	
1-inch diagonal let-in brace to each stud and plate (four nails at top)		2	8d	
Built-up corner studs				
Studs to blocking	Face-nail	2	10d	Each side
Intersecting stud to corner studs	Face-nail		16d	12 inches on center
Built-up girders and beams, three or more members	Face-nail		20d	32 inches on center, each side
Wall sheathing				
1 × 8 inches or less, horizontal	Face-nail	2	8d	At each stud
1 × 6 inches or greater, diagonal	Face-nail	3	8d	At each stud
Wall sheathing, vertically applied plywood:				
3/8-inch and less thick	Face-nail		6d	6-inch edge
1/2-inch and over thick	Face-nail		8d	12 inches intermediate
Wall sheathing, vertically applied fiberboard				
1/2-inch thick	Face-nail			1 1/2-inch roofing nail
25/32-inch thick	Face-nail			1 3/4-inch roofing nail (3 inches edge and 6 inches intermediate)

Table 2–13 (continued)

| | | Nails | | |
Joining	Nailing method	Num-ber	Size	Placement
Roof sheathing, boards, 4-, 6-, 8-inch width	Face-nail	2	8*d*	At each rafter
Roof sheathing, plywood ³/₈-inch and less thick	Face-nail		6*d*	6 inches edge and 12 inches intermediate
¹/₂-inch and over thick	Face-nail		8*d*	

Posts and girders. Wood or steel posts are generally used in the basement to support wood girders or steel beams. Masonry piers might also be used for this purpose and are commonly employed in crawl-space houses. The round steel post can be used to support both wood girders and steel beams and is normally supplied with a steel bearing plate at each end. Secure anchoring to the girder or beam is important (Figure 2–26).

Wood posts should be solid and not less than 6 by 6 inches in size for freestanding use in a basement. When combined with a framed wall, they may be 4 to 6 inches to conform to the depth of the studs. Wood posts should be squared at both ends and securely fastened to the girder (Figure 2–27). The bottom of the post should rest on and be pinned to a masonry pedestal 2 to 3 inches above

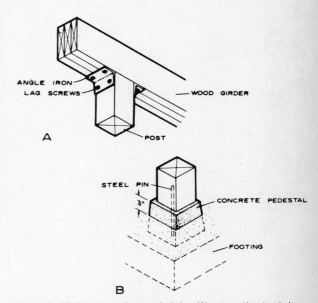

Figure 2–27. Wood post for wood girder: (A) connection to girder; (B) connection to base.

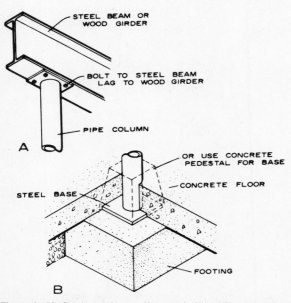

Figure 2–26. Steel post for wood or steel girder: (A) connection to beam; (B) base plate mounted on and anchored to a concrete pedestal.

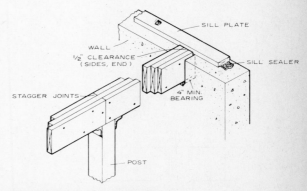

Figure 2–28. Built-up wood girder.

the finish floor. In moist or wet conditions it is good practice to treat the bottom end of the post or use a moisture-proof covering over the pedestal.

Both wood girders and steel beams are used in present-day house construction. The standard I-beam and wide flange beam are the most commonly used steel beam shapes. Wood girders are of two types, solid and built up. The built-up beam is preferred because it can be made up from drier dimension material and is more stable.

The built-up girder (Figure 2–28) is usually made up of two or more pieces of 2-inch dimension lumber spiked together, the ends of the pieces joining over a supporting post. A two-piece girder may be nailed from one side with 10d nails, two at the end of each piece and others driven stagger fashion 16 inches apart. A three-piece girder is nailed from each side with 20d nails, two near each end of each piece and others driven stagger fashion 32 inches apart.

Ends of wood girders should bear at least 4 inches on the masonry walls or pilasters. When wood is untreated, a ½-inch air space should be provided at each end and at each side of wood girders framing into masonry. In termite-infested areas, these pockets should be lined with metal. The top of the girder should be level with the top of the sill plates on the foundation walls, unless ledger strips are used. If steel plates are used under ends of girders, they should be of full bearing size.

Girder-joist installation. Perhaps the simplest method of floor-joist framing is one where the joists bear directly on the wood girder or steel beam, in which case the top of the beam coincides with the top of the anchored sill. This method is used when basement heights provide adequate headroom below the girder. However, when wood girders are used in this manner, the main disadvantage is that shrinkage is usually greater at the girder than at the foundation.

For more uniform shrinkage at the inner beam and the outer wall, and to provide greater headroom, joist hangers or a supporting ledger strip is commonly used. Depending on sizes of joists and wood girders, joists may be supported on the ledger strip in several ways (Figure 2–29). Each provides

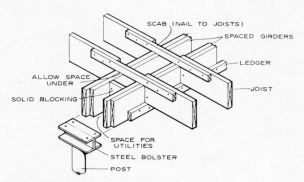

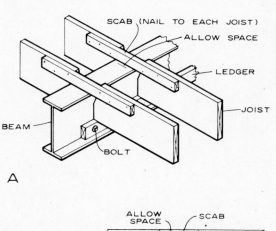

Figure 2–30. Spaced wood girder.

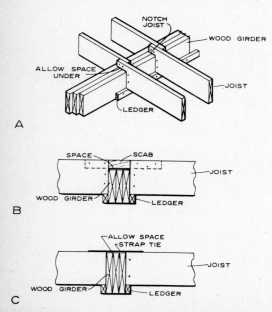

Figure 2–29. Ledger on center wood girder: (A) notched joist; (B) scab tie between joists; (C) flush joist.

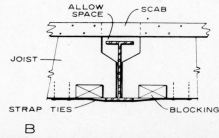

Figure 2–31. Steel beam and joist: (A) bearing on ledger; (B) bearing on flange.

about the same depth of wood subject to shrinkage at the outer wall and at the center wood girder. A continuous horizontal tie between exterior walls is obtained by nailing notched joists together (Figure 2–29A). Joists must always bear on the ledgers. In Figure 2–29B the connecting scab at each pair of joists provides this tie and also a nailing area for the subfloor. A steel strap is used to tie the joists together when the tops of the beam and the joists are level (Figure 2–29C). It is important that a small space be allowed above the beam to provide for shrinkage of the joists.

When a space is required for heat ducts in a partition supported on the girder, a spaced wood girder is sometimes necessary (Figure 2–30). Solid blocking is used at intervals between the two members. A single post support for a spaced girder usually requires a bolster, preferably metal, with sufficient span to support the two members.

Joists may be arranged with a steel beam generally the same way as illustrated for a wood beam. Perhaps the most common methods, depending on joist sizes, are:

1. The joists rest directly on the top of the beam.

2. The joists rest on a wood ledger or steel angle iron, which is bolted to the web (Figure 2–31A).

3. The joists bear directly on the flange of the beam (Figure 2–31B). In the third method, wood blocking is required between the joists near the beam flange to prevent overturning.

Wood sill construction. The two general types of wood sill construction used over the foundation wall conform to either platform or balloon framing. The box sill is commonly used in platform construction. It consists of a 2-inch or thicker plate anchored to the foundation wall over a sill sealer, which provides support and fastening for the joists and header at the ends of the joists (Figure 2–32). Some houses are constructed without benefit of an anchored sill plate, although this is not entirely desirable. The floor framing should then be anchored with metal strapping installed during pouring operations.

Balloon-frame construction uses a nominal 2-inch or thicker wood sill upon which the joists rest. The studs also bear on this member and are nailed to both the floor joists and the sill. The subfloor is laid diagonally or at right angles to the joists, and a firestop added between the studs at the floorline (Figure 2–33). When a diagonal subfloor is used, a nailing member is normally required between joists and studs at the wall lines. Because there is less potential shrinkage in exterior walls with balloon framing than in the platform type, balloon framing is usually preferred over the platform type in full two-story brick or stone veneer houses.

Floor joists. Floor joists are selected primarily to meet strength and stiffness requirements. Other

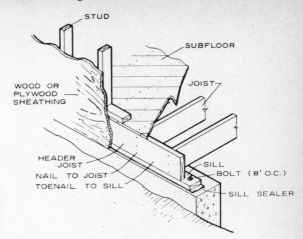

Figure 2–32. Platform construction.

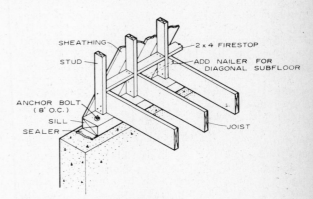

Figure 2–33. Sill for balloon framing.

desirable qualities for floor joists are good nail-holding ability and freedom from warp.

Wood floor joists are generally of 2-inch (nominal) thickness and of 8-, 10-, or 12-inch (nominal) depth. The size depends upon the loading, length of span, spacing between joists, and the species and grade of lumber used. As previously mentioned, grades in species vary a great deal. For example, the grades generally used for joists are "Standard" for Douglas fir, "No. 2 or No. 2KD" for Southern pine, and comparable grades for other species.

Span tables for floor joists, which are published by the Federal Housing Administration, or local building codes can be used as guidelines. These tables and codes often give only the minimum sizes, and it is wise when working on your own home to use the next larger size than that listed in the tables. The data given on page 421 are also good guides for most remodeling work.

Joist installation. After the sill plates have been anchored to the foundation walls or piers, the

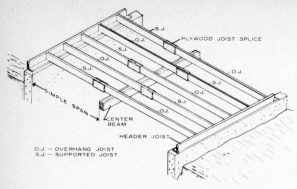

Figure 2—34. "In-line" joist system. Alternate extension of joists over the center support with plywood gusset joint allows the use of a smaller joist size.

joists are located according to the house design. (Sixteen-inch center-to-center spacing is most commonly used.)

Any joists having a slight bow edgewise should be so placed that the crown is on top. A crowned joist will tend to straighten out when subfloor and normal floor loads are applied. The largest edge knots should be placed on top, since knots on the upper side of a joist are on the compression side of the member and will have less effect on strength.

The header joist is fastened by nailing into the end of each joist with three 16d nails. In addition, the header joist and the stringer joists parallel to the exterior walls in platform construction are toe-nailed to the sill with 10d nails spaced 16 inches on center. Each joist should be toenailed to the sill and center beam with two 10d or three or four 8d nails, then nailed to each other with three or four 16d nails when they lap over the center beam. If a nominal 2-inch scab is used across butt-ended joists, it should be nailed to each joist with at least three 16d nails at each side of the joint.

The "in-line" joist splice is sometimes used in framing for floor and ceiling joists. This system normally allows the use of a one-size-smaller joist when center supports are present. Briefly, it consists of uneven-length joists; the long overhanging joist is cantilevered over the center support, then spliced to the supported joist (Figure 2–34). Overhang joists are alternated. Depending on the span, species, and joist size, the overhang varies between about 1 foot 10 inches and 2 feet 10 inches. Plywood splice plates are used on each side of the end joints.

It is good practice to double joists under all parallel bearing partition walls; if spacing is required for heat ducts, solid blocking is used between the joists.

Bridging. Cross-bridging between wood joists has often been used in house construction, but research by several laboratories has questioned the benefits of bridging in relation to its cost, especially in normal house construction. Even with tight-fitting, well-installed bridging, there is no significant ability to transfer loads after subfloor and finish floor are installed. However, some building codes require the use of cross-bridging or solid bridging.

Solid bridging is often used between joists to provide a more rigid base for partitions located above joist spaces. Well-fitted solid bridging securely nailed to the joists will aid in supporting partitions above them. Load-bearing partitions should be supported by doubled joists.

Subfloor. Subflooring is used over the floor joists to form a working platform and base for finish flooring. It usually consists of (a) square-edge or tongued-and-grooved boards no wider than 8 inches and not less than ¾ inch thick or (b) plywood ½ to ¾ inch thick, depending on species, type of finish floor, and spacing of joists.

Subflooring boards may be applied either diagonally (most common) or at right angles to the joists. When subflooring is placed at right angles to the joists, the finish floor should be laid at right angles to the subflooring. Diagonal subflooring permits finish flooring to be laid either parallel or at right angles (most common) to the joists. End joints of the boards should always be made directly over the joists. Subfloor is nailed to each joist with two 8d nails for widths under 8 inches and three 8d nails for 8-inch widths.

The joist spacing should not exceed 16 inches on center when finish flooring is laid parallel to the joists, or where parquet finish flooring is used, nor exceed 24 inches on center when finish flooring at least ²⁵/₃₂ inch thick is at right angles to the joists. Where balloon framing is used, blocking should be installed between ends of joists at the wall for nailing the ends of diagonal subfloor boards.

Plywood should be installed with the grain direction of the outer plies at right angles to the joists and be staggered so that end joints in adjacent panels break over different joists. Plywood should be nailed to the joist at each bearing with 8d common or 7d threaded nails for plywood ½-inch to ¾-inch thick. Space nails 6 inches apart along all edges and 10 inches along intermediate members. When plywood serves as both subfloor and underlayment, nails may be spaced 6 to 7 inches apart at all joists and blocking. Use 8d or 9d common nails or 7d or 8d threaded nails.

For the best performance, plywood should not be laid up with tight joints whether used on the interior or exterior. The following spacings are recommended by the American Plywood Association on the basis of field experience (under wet or humid conditions spacing should be doubled):

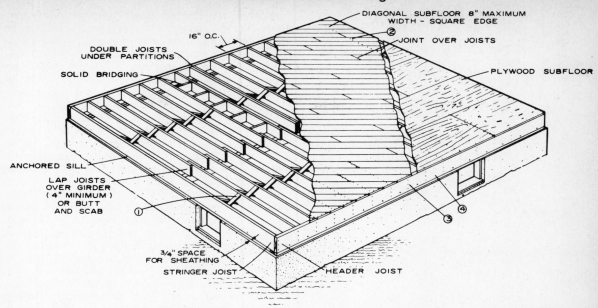

Figure 2—35. Floor framing: (1) nailing bridging to joists; (2) nailing board subfloor to joists; (3) nailing header to joists; (4) toe-nailing to sill. Bridging is often omitted in small residential construction.

Plywood location and use	Spacing Edges (inch)	Ends (inch)
Underlayment or interior wall lining	$\frac{1}{32}$	$\frac{1}{32}$
Panel sidings and combination subfloor underlayment	$\frac{1}{16}$	$\frac{1}{16}$
Roof sheathing, subflooring, and wall sheathing	$\frac{1}{8}$	$\frac{1}{16}$

Wall framing. The term "wall framing" includes primarily the vertical studs and horizontal members (soleplates, top plates, and window and door headers) or exterior and interior walls that support ceilings, upper floors, and the roof. The wall framing also serves as a nailing base for wall covering materials.

The wall framing members used in conventional construction are generally nominal 2-by-4-inch studs spaced 16 inches on center. Depending on thickness of covering material and the purpose of the wall, 24-inch spacing might be considered (see page 411). Top plates and soleplates are also nominal 2 by 4 inches in size. Headers over doors or windows in load-bearing walls consist of doubled 2-by-6-inch and deeper members, depending on span of the opening. Ceiling height for the first floor is 8 feet under most conditions. It is common practice to rough-frame the wall (subfloor to top of upper plate) to a height of 8 feet $1\frac{1}{2}$ inches. In plat-form construction, precut studs are often supplied to a length of 7 feet $8\frac{5}{8}$ inches for plate thickness of $1\frac{5}{8}$ inches. When dimension material is $1\frac{1}{2}$ inches thick, precut studs would be 7 feet 9 inches long. This height allows the use of 8-foot-high dry-wall sheets and still provides clearance for floor and ceiling finish or for plaster grounds at the floor line. Second-floor ceiling heights should not be less than 7 feet 6 inches in the clear, except for the portion under sloping ceilings. One-half of the floor area, however, should have at least a 7-foot-6-inch clearance.

As with floor construction, two general types of wall framing are commonly used, platform construction and balloon-frame construction. The platform method is more often used because of its simplicity.

Platform construction. The wall framing in platform construction is erected above the subfloor, which extends to all edges of the structure. A combination of platform construction for the first floor sidewalls and full-length studs for end walls extending to end rafters of the gable ends is commonly used in single-story houses.

One common method of framing is the horizontal assembly (on the subfloor) or "tilt-up" of wall sections. This system involves laying out precut studs, window and door headers, cripple studs (short-length studs), and windowsills. Top plates and soleplates are then nailed to all vertical mem-

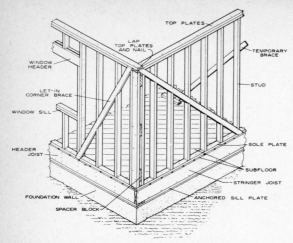

Figure 2–36. Wall framing used with platform construction.

When all exterior walls have been erected, plumbed, and braced, the remaining nailing is completed. Soleplates are nailed to the floor joists and headers or stringers (through the subfloor), corner braces (when used) are nailed to studs and plates, door and window headers are fastened to adjoining studs, and corner studs are nailed together (Figure 2–36).

Several arrangements of studs at outside corners can be used in framing the walls of a house. Blocking between two corner studs is used to provide a nailing edge for interior finish (Figure 2–37). Interior walls should be well fastened to all exterior walls they intersect. This intersection should also provide nailing surfaces for the dry-wall finish. This may be accomplished by doubling the outside studs at the interior wall line (Figure 2–38A). Another method used when the interior wall joins the exterior wall between studs is shown in Figure 2–38B.

Short sections of 2-by-4-inch blocking are used between studs to support and provide backing for a 1-by-6-inch nailer. A 2-by-6-inch vertical member might also be used. The same general arrangement of members is used at the intersection or crossing of interior walls. Nailing surfaces must be provided in some form or another at all interior corners.

After all walls are erected, a second top plate is

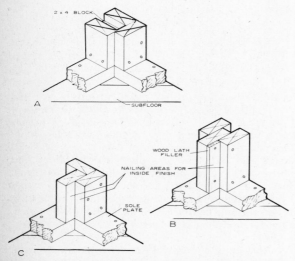

Figure 2–37. Examples of corner stud assembly: (A) standard outside corner; (B) special corner with lath filler; (C) special corner without lath filler.

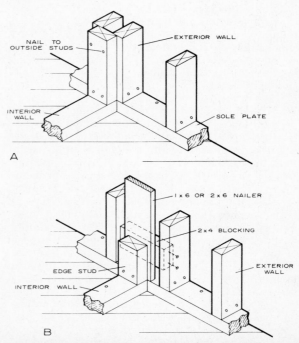

Figure 2–38. Intersection of interior wall with exterior wall: (A) with doubled studs on outside wall; (B) with partition between outside studs.

bers and adjoining studs to headers and sills with 16*d* nails. Let-in corner bracing should be provided when required. The entire section is then erected, plumbed, and braced.

A variation of this system involves fastening the studs only at the top plate and, when the wall is erected, toenailing studs to the soleplates, which have been previously nailed to the floor. Corner studs and headers are usually nailed together beforehand to form a single unit. The complete finished walls with windows and door units in place and most of the siding installed can also be fabricated in this manner.

The Basics of Remodeling

added that laps the first at corners and wall intersections. This gives an additional tie to the framed walls. These top plates can also be partly fastened in place when the wall is in a horizontal position. Top plates are nailed together with 16d nails spaced 16 inches apart and with two nails at each wall intersection. Walls are normally plumbed and aligned before the top plate is added. By using 1-by-6-by-1-by-8-inch temporary braces on the studs between intersecting partitions, a straight wall is assured. These braces are nailed to the studs at the top of the wall and to a 2-by-4-inch block fastened to the subfloor or joists. The temporary bracing is left in place until the ceiling and the roof framing are completed and sheathing is applied to the outside walls.

Balloon construction. As decribed earlier in this chapter, the main difference between platform and balloon framing is at the floor lines. The balloon wall studs extend from the sill of the first floor to the top plate or end rafter of the second floor, whereas the platform-framed wall is complete for each floor.

In balloon-frame construction, both the wall studs and the floor joists rest on the anchored sill (Figure 2–39). The studs and joists are toenailed to the sill with 8d nails and nailed to each other with at least three 10d nails. The ends of the second-floor joists bear on a 1-by-4-inch ribbon that has been let into the studs. In addition, the joists are nailed with four 10d nails to the studs at these connections. The end joists parallel to the exterior on both the first and second floors are also nailed to each stud.

In most areas, building codes require that firestops be used in balloon framing to prevent the

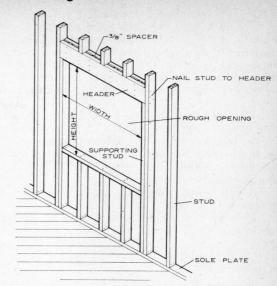

Figure 2—40. Headers for windows and door openings.

spread of fire through the open wall passages. These firestops are ordinarily of 2-by-4-inch blocking placed between the studs or as required by local regulations.

Window and door framing. The members used to span over window and door openings are called headers or lintels. As the span of the opening increases, it is necessary to increase the depth of these members to support the ceiling and roof loads. A header is made up of two 2-inch members, usually spaced with ⅜-inch lath or wood strips, all of which are nailed together. They are supported at the ends by the inner studs of the double-stud joint at exterior walls and interior bearing walls. Two headers of species normally used for floor joists are usually appropriate for these openings in normal light-frame construction. The following sizes might be used as a guide for headers:

Maximum span (feet)	Header size (inches)
3½	2 × 6
5	2 × 8
6½	2 × 10
8	2 × 12

For other than normal light-frame construction, independent designs may be necessary. Wider openings often require trussed headers, which may also need special design.

Location of the studs, headers, and sills around window openings should conform to the rough opening sizes recommended by the manufacturers of the millwork. The framing height to the bottom

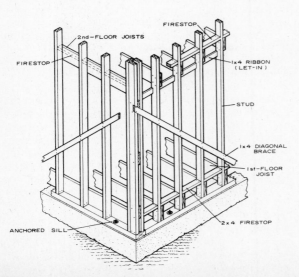

Figure 2—39. Wall framing used in balloon construction.

of the window and door headers should be based on the door heights, normally 6 feet 8 inches for the main floor. Thus, to allow for the thickness and clearance of the head jambs of window and door frames and the finish floor, the bottoms of the headers are usually located 6 feet 10 inches to 6 feet 11 inches above the subfloor, depending on the type of finish floor used.

Rough opening sizes for exterior door and window frames might vary slightly among manufacturers, but the following allowances should be made for the stiles and rails, thickness of jambs, and thickness and slope of the sill:

Double-hung window (single unit)

Rough opening width = total glass width plus 6 inches

Rough opening height = total glass height plus 10 inches

For example, the following tabulation illustrates several glass and rough opening sizes for double-hung windows:

Window glass size (each sash)		Rough frame opening	
Width (inches)	Height (inches)	Width (inches)	Height (inches)
24 ×	16	30 ×	42
28 ×	20	34 ×	50
32 ×	24	38 ×	58
36 ×	24	42 ×	58

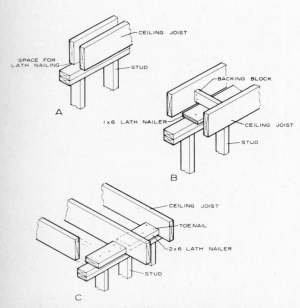

Figure 2–41. Horizontal lath nailers at the ceiling: (A) with ceiling joists over stud wall; (B) lath or panel nailer between ceiling joists; (C) stud wall at right angle to joist.

Casement window (one pair—two sash)

Rough opening width = total glass width plus 11¼ inches

Rough opening height = total glass height plus 6⅜ inches

Doors

Rough opening width = door width plus 2½ inches

Rough opening height = door height plus 3 inches

Interior walls. The interior walls in a house with conventional joist and rafter roof construction are normally placed so that they serve as bearing walls for the ceiling joists as well as room dividers. Walls located parallel to the direction of the joists are commonly non-load bearing. Studs are a nominal 2 by 4 inches in size for load-bearing walls but can be 2 by 3 inches in size for non-load-bearing walls. However, most contractors use 2 × 4's throughout. Spacing of the studs is usually controlled by the thickness of the covering material. For example, 24-inch stud spacing will require ½-inch gypsum board for dry wall interior covering.

The interior walls are assembled and erected in the same manner as exterior walls, with a single bottom (sole) plate and double top plates. The upper top plate is used to tie intersecting and crossing walls to each other. A single framing stud can be used at each side of a door opening in non-load-bearing partitions. The studs must be doubled for load-bearing walls.

Additional information on framing interior walls can be found in Chapters 12 and 13.

Lath nailers. During the framing of walls and ceilings it is necessary to provide for both vertical and horizontal fastening of dry wall at all inside corners. Figures 2–37 and 2–38 illustrate corner and intersecting wall construction and show methods of providing lath or panel nailers at these areas.

Horizontal lath or panel nailers at the junction of wall and ceiling framing may be provided in several ways, as shown in Figure 2–41. For instance, A shows doubled ceiling joists above the wall, spaced so that a nailing surface is provided by each joist. In B the parallel wall is located between two ceiling joists. A 1-by-6-inch lath or panel nailer is placed on and nailed to the top plates with backing blocks spaced on 3- to 4-foot centers. A 2-by-6-inch member might also be used here in place of the 1 by 6.

When the partition wall is at a right angle to the ceiling joists, one method of providing lath or panel nailers is to let in 2-by-6-inch blocks between the joists (C). They are nailed directly to the top plate and toenailed to the ceiling joists.

Ceiling framing. After exterior and interior walls are plumbed and braced and top plates added, ceiling joists can be positioned and nailed in place. They are normally placed across the width of the house, as are the rafters. The partitions of the house are usually located so that ceiling joists of even lengths (10, 12, 14, and 16 feet or longer) can be used without waste to span from exterior walls to load-bearing interior walls. The sizes of the joists depend on the span, wood species, spacing between joists, and the load on the second floor or attic. The correct sizes for various conditions can be found in the FHA joist tables or are designated by local building requirements.

Ceiling joists are used to support ceiling finishes. They often act as floor joists for second and attic floors and as ties between exterior walls and interior partitions. Since ceiling joists also serve as tension members to resist the thrust of the rafters of pitched roofs, they must be securely nailed to the plate at outer and inner walls. They are also nailed together, directly or with wood or metal cleats, where they cross or join at the load-bearing partition (Figure 2–42A) and to the rafter at the exterior walls (Figure 2–42B). They should be toenailed at each wall.

Post and beam framing. In contemporary houses, exposed beams are often a part of the interior design and may also replace interior and exterior load-bearing walls. With post and beam construction, exterior walls can become fully glazed panels between posts, requiring no other support. Areas below interior beams within the house can remain open or can be closed in with wardrobes, cabinets, or light curtain walls.

This type of construction, while not adaptable to many styles of architecture, is simple and straightforward. However, design of the house should take into account the need for shear or racking resistance of the exterior walls. This is usually accomplished by solid masonry walls or fully sheathed frame walls between open glazed areas.

Roofs of such houses are often either flat or low-pitched, and may have a conventional rafter-joist combination or consist of thick wood decking spanning between beams. The need for a well-insulated roof often dictates the type of construction that might be used.

The connection of the supporting posts at the floor plate and beam is important to provide uplift resistance. Figure 2–43 shows connections at the soleplate and at the beam for solid or spaced members. The solid post and beam are fastened together with metal angles nailed to the top plate and to the soleplate as well as the roof beam (A). The spaced beam and post are fastened together with a 3/8-inch or thicker plywood cleat extending between and nailed to the spaced members (B). A wall header member between beams can be fastened with joist hangers.

Continuous headers are often used with spaced posts in the construction of framed walls or porches requiring large glazed openings. The beams should be well fastened and reinforced at the corners with lag screws or metal straps.

In low-pitch or flat roof construction for a post and beam system, wood or fiberboard decking is often used. Wood decking, depending on thickness, is frequently used for beam spacings up to 10 or

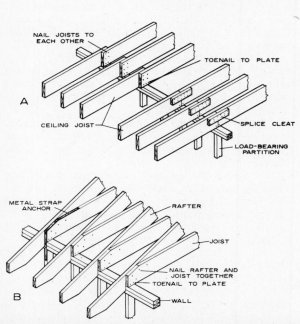

Figure 2–42. Ceiling joist connections: (A) at center partition with joists lapped or butted; (B) at outside wall.

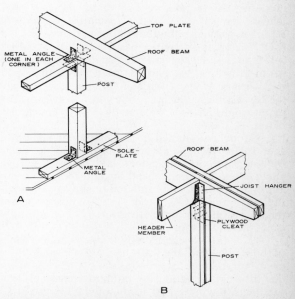

Figure 2–43. Post and beam connections: (A) solid post and beam; (B) spaced post and beam.

more feet. However, for the longer spans, special application instructions are required. Depending on the type, 2- to 3-inch-thick fiberboard decking normally is limited to a beam or purlin spacing of 4 feet.

Tongued-and-grooved solid wood decking, 3 by 6 and 4 by 6 inches in size, should be toenailed and face-nailed directly to the beams and edge-nailed to each other with long nails used in predrilled holes. Thinner decking is usually square-end-trimmed to provide a good fit. If additional insulation is required for the roof, fiberboard or an expanded foamed plastic in sheet form is fastened to the decking before the built-up or similar type of roof is installed. The moisture content of the decking should be near its in-service condition to prevent joints from opening later as the wood dries.

Roof framing. The architectural style of a house often determines the type of roof and roof slope that are appropriate. As was just stated, contemporary design may have a flat or slightly pitched roof, a rambler or ranch type an intermediate slope, and a Cape Cod cottage a steep slope. Generally, however, the two basic types may be called flat or pitched, defined as (a) flat or slightly pitched roofs in which roof and ceiling supports are furnished by one type of member, and (b) pitched roofs where both ceiling joists and rafters or trusses are required.

The slope of the roof is generally expressed as the number of inches of vertical rise in 12 inches of horizontal run. The rise is given first, for example, 4 in 12.

A further consideration in choosing a roof slope is the type of roofing to be used. However, modern methods and roofing materials offer great leeway in this choice. For example, a built-up roof is usually specified for flat or very low-pitched roofs, but with different types of asphalt or coal-tar pitch and aggregate surfacing materials, slopes of up to 2 in 12 are sometimes used. Also, in sloped roofs, where wood or asphalt shingles might be selected, doubling the underlay and decreasing the exposure distance of the shingles will allow slopes of 4 in 12 and less.

Flat or low-pitched roofs, sometimes known as shed roofs, can take a number of forms. Roof joists for flat roofs are commonly laid level or with a slight pitch, with roof sheathing and roofing on top and with the underside utilized to support the ceiling. Sometimes a slight roof slope may be provided for roof drainage by tapering the joist or adding a cant strip to the top.

The house design usually includes an overhang of the roof beyond the wall. Insulation is sometimes used in a manner to provide for an airway just under the roof sheathing to minimize condensation problems in winter. Flat or low-pitched roofs of this type require larger members than do steeper

pitched roofs because they carry both roof and ceiling loads.

The use of solid wood decking often eliminates the need for joists. Roof decking used between beams serves as: (a) supporting members, (b) interior finish, and (c) roof sheathing. It also provides a moderate amount of insulation. In cold climates, rigid insulating materials are used over the decking to further reduce heat loss.

When overhang is involved on all sides of the flat roof, lookout rafters are ordinarily used. Lookout rafters are nailed to a doubled header and toenailed to the wallplate. The distance from the doubled header to the wall line is usually twice the length of the overhang. Rafter ends may be finished with a nailing header that serves for fastening soffit and facia boards. Care should be taken to provide some type of ventilation at such areas.

Gable roof. Perhaps the simplest form of the pitched roof, where both rafters and ceiling joists are required because of the attic space formed, is the gable roof. All rafters are cut to the same length and pattern, and erection is relatively simple, each pair being fastened at the top to a ridge board. The ridge board is usually a 1-by-8-inch member for 2-by-6-inch rafters and provides support and a nailing area for the rafter ends.

A variation of the gable roof, used for Cape Cod or similar styles, includes the use of shed and gable dormers. Basically, this is done in a one-story house because the majority of the rafters rest on the first-floor plate. Space and light are provided on the second floor by the shed and gable dormers for bedrooms and bath. Roof slopes for this style may vary from 9 in 12 to 12 in 12 to provide the needed headroom.

A third style in roof designs is the hip roof. Center rafters are tied to the ridge board, while hip rafters supply the support for the shorter jack rafters. Cornice lines are carried around the perimeter of the building.

While these roof types are the most common, there are also such forms as the mansard and the A-frame (where wall and roof members are the same members).

In normal pitched-roof construction, the ceiling joists are nailed in place after the interior and the exterior wall framing are complete. Rafters should not be erected until ceiling joists are fastened in place, as the thrust of the rafters will otherwise tend to push out the exterior walls.

Rafters are usually precut to length with the proper angle cut at the ridge and eave, and with notches provided for the top plates (Figure 2–44A). Rafters are erected in pairs. Studs for gable end walls are cut to fit and nailed to the end rafter and the top plate of the end wall soleplate (Figure 2–44B). With a gable (rake) overhang, a fly rafter is

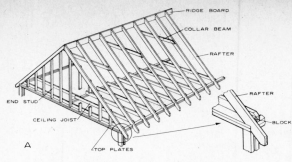

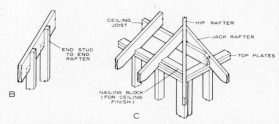

Figure 2—44. Ceiling and roof framing: (A) overall view of gable roof framing; (B) connection of gable and studs to end rafter; (C) detail of corner of hip roof.

used beyond the end rafter and is fastened with blocking and by the sheathing.

Hip roofs, like gable roofs, are framed at the center section of a rectangular house. The ends are framed with hip rafters, which extend from each outside corner of the wall to the ridge board at a 45 degree angle. Jack rafters extend from the top plates to the hip rafters (Figure 2–44C).

When roof spans are long and slopes are flat, it is common practice to use collar beams between opposing rafters. Steeper slopes and shorter spans may also require collar beams, but only on every

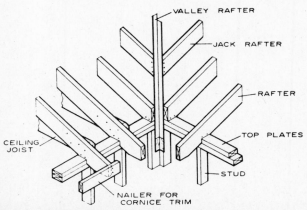

Figure 2—45. Framing at a valley.

third rafter. Collar beams may be 1-by-6-inch material. In 1½-story houses, 2-by-4-inch members or larger are used at each pair of rafters, which also serve as ceiling joists for the finished rooms.

Valleys. The valley is the internal angle formed by the junction of two sloping sides of a roof. The key member of valley construction is the valley rafter. In the intersection of two equal-size roof sections, the valley rafter is doubled (Figure 2–45) to carry the roof load, and is 2 inches deeper than the common rafter to provide full contact with jack rafters. Jack rafters are nailed to the ridge and toenailed to the valley rafter with three 10d nails.

Dormers. In construction of small gable dormers, the rafters at each side are doubled and the side studs and the short valley rafter rest on these members. Side studs may also be carried past the rafter and bear on a soleplate nailed to the floor framing and subfloor. This same type of framing may be used for the sidewalls of shed dormers. The valley rafter is also tied to the roof framing at the roof by a header. More on the construction of dormers may be found in Chapter 12.

Sheathing. Wall sheathing is the outside covering used over the wall framework of studs, plates, and window and door headers, while roof sheathing is the covering over the rafters.

Wall sheathing. The most common types of wall sheathing are: boards, plywood, structural insulating board, and gypsum sheathing.

Wood sheathing is usually of nominal 1-inch boards in a shiplay, a tongued-and-grooved, or a square-edge pattern. Widths commonly used are 6, 8, and 10 inches. It may be applied horizontally or diagonally. The boards should be nailed at each stud crossing with two nails for the 6- and 8-inch widths and three nails for the 10- and 12-inch widths. When diagonal sheathing is used, one more nail can be used at each stud; for example, three nails for 8-inch sheathing. Joints should be placed over the center of studs unless end-matched (tongued-and-grooved) boards are used.

Plywood used for sheathing should be 4 by 8 feet or longer and applied vertically with perimeter nailing to eliminate the need for corner bracing. Use 6d nails for plywood ⅜-inch or less in thickness. Use 8d nails for plywood ½-inch or more in thickness. Spacing should be a minimum of 6 inches at all edges and 12 inches at intermediate framing members. Plywood may also be applied horizontally, but since it is not as efficient from the standpoint of rigidity and strength, it normally requires diagonal bracing.

The three common types of *insulating board* (structural fiberboards) used for sheathing include regular density, intermediate density, and nail-base. Insulating board sheathings are coated or impregnated with asphalt or given other treatment to pro-

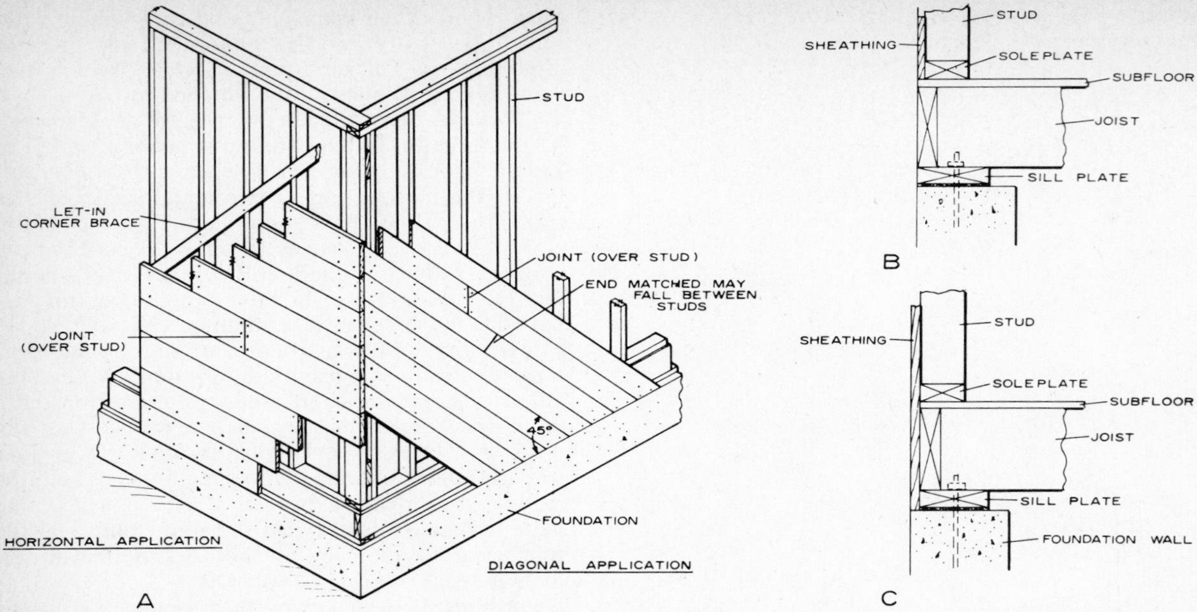

Figure 2—46. Application of wood sheathing: (A) horizontal and diagonal; (B) started at subfloor; (C) started at foundation wall.

vide a water-resistant product. Regular-density sheathing is manufactured in ½- and ²⁵/₃₂-inch thicknesses and in 2-by-8-foot, 4-by-8-foot, and 4-by-9-foot sizes. Intermediate-density and nail-base sheathing are denser products than regular-density. They are regularly manufactured only in ½-inch thickness and in 4-by-8-foot and 4-by-9-foot sizes. While 2-by-8-foot sheets with matched edges are used horizon-

tally, 4-by-8-foot and longer sheets are usually installed with the long dimension vertical.

Corner bracing is required on horizontally applied sheets and usually on applications of ½-inch regular-density sheathing applied vertically. Additional corner bracing is usually not required for regular-density nail-base sheathing when properly applied with long edges vertical. Naturally, fas-

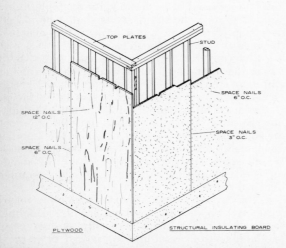

Figure 2—47. Vertical application of plywood or structural insulating board sheathing.

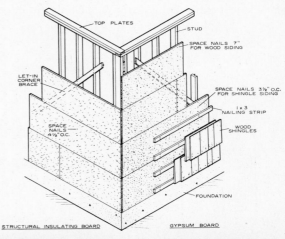

Figure 2—48. Horizontal application of 2-by-8-foot structural insulating board or gypsum sheathing.

tenings must be adequate around the perimeter and at intermediate studs, and adequately fastened (nails, staples, or other fastening system). Nail-base sheathing permits shingles to be applied directly to it as siding, if annular grooved nails are employed.

Gypsum sheathing is ½ inch thick, 2 by 8 feet in size, and is applied horizontally for stud spacing of 24 inches or less. It is composed of treated gypsum filler faced on two sides with water-resistant paper, often having one edge grooved and the other with a matched V edge.

Sheathing paper should be used behind a masonry veneer finish and over wood sheathing. It should be installed horizontally starting at the bottom of the wall. Succeeding layers should lap about 4 inches. Ordinarily, it is not used over plywood, fiberboard, or other sheet materials that are water-resistant. However, 8-inch or wider strips of sheathing paper should be used around window and door openings to minimize air infiltration.

Roof sheathing. Roof sheathing usually consists of nominal 1-inch lumber or plywood. In some types of flat or low-pitched roofs with post and beam construction, wood roof planking or fiberboard roof decking might be used.

Board sheathing to be used under such roofing as asphalt shingles, metal-sheet roofing, or other materials that require continuous support, should be laid closed (without spacing). Wood shingles can also be used over such sheathing. Boards should be matched, shiplapped, or square-edged with joints made over the center of rafters. Not more than two adjacent boards should have joints over the same support. It is preferable to use boards no wider than 6 or 8 inches to minimize problems which can be caused by shrinkage. Boards should have a minimum thickness of ¾-inch for rafter spacing of 16

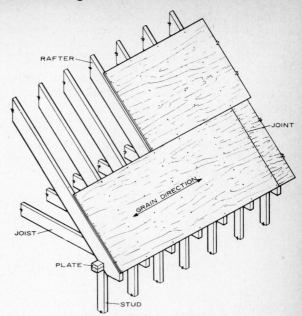

Figure 2—50. Application of plywood roof sheathing.

to 24 inches, and be nailed with two 8*d* common or 7*d* threaded nails for each board at each bearing.

When *plywood roof sheathing* is used, it should be laid with the face grain perpendicular to the rafters. Standard sheathing grade plywood is commonly specified, but where damp conditions occur it is desirable to use a standard sheathing grade with exterior glueline. End joints are made over the center of the rafters and should be staggered by at least one rafter 16 or 24 inches, or more. For wood shingles or shakes and for asphalt shingles, 5/16-inch-thick plywood is considered to be a minimum thickness for 16-inch spacing of rafters. It should be nailed at each bearing, 6 inches on center along all edges and 12 inches on center, 6*d* nails along intermediate members. A 6*d* common nail or 5*d* threaded nail should be used for 5/16- and 3/8-inch plywood, and 8*d* common or 7*d* threaded nail for greater thicknesses. Unless plywood has an exterior glueline, raw edges should not be exposed to the weather at the gable end or at the cornice, but should be protected by the trim. Allow a ⅛-inch edge spacing and 1/16-inch end spacing between sheets when installing.

Plank roof decking, consisting of 2-inch and thicker tongued-and-grooved wood planking, is commonly used in flat or low-pitched roofs in post and beam construction. Common sizes are nominal 2-by-6-inch, 3-by-6-inch, and 4-by-6-inch V-grooved members, the thicker planking being suitable for spans up to 10 or 12 feet. Maximum span for 2-inch

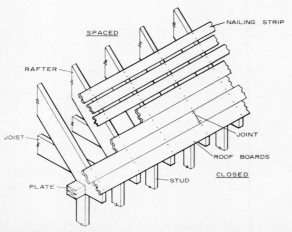

Figure 2—49. Installation of closed and spaced types of board roof sheathing.

planking is 8 feet when continuous over two supports, and 6 feet over single spans, in grades and species commonly used for this purpose. Special load requirements may reduce these allowable spans. Roof decking can serve both as an interior ceiling finish and as a base for roofing. Heat loss is greatly reduced by adding fiberboard or other rigid insulation over the wood decking.

Fiberboard roof decking is used the same way as wood decking, except that supports are spaced much closer together. Planking is usually supplied in 2-by-8-foot sheets with tongued-and-grooved edges. Thicknesses of the plank and spacing of supports ordinarily comply with the following specifications:

Minimum thickness (inches)	Maximum joist spacing (inches)
1½	24
2	32
3	48

Manufacturers of some types of roof decking recommend the use of 1⅞-inch thickness for 48-inch spacing of supports. Nails used to fasten the fiberboard to the wood members are corrosion resistant and spaced not more than 5 inches on center. They should be long enough to penetrate the joist or beam at least 1½ inches. A built-up roof is normally used for flat and low-pitched roofs having wood or fiberboard decking.

Once the structure is framed and sheathed, it is ready for the finish work. The exterior finishing remodeling details, including the application of roofing materials, are given in Chapters 8 and 15, while the interior techniques are covered in Chapters 3 and 4. Specific remodeling projects and uses of the basics of remodeling discussed in this chapter can be found in Chapters 10 through 16.

THE BUILDING CODE

A building code is a collection of laws listed in book or pamphlet form for a given community. It outlines restrictions that will maintain minimum standards set by the building department of the community for safeguarding life and health. These laws help to control design, construction, materials, location of the building, use of the structure by the occupants, quality of materials, and use of materials. To stay within the law, you must observe the code. Thus, before you start any remodeling project or alteration job, check with your local building official to find out about any special code regulations or restrictions in your area. Sometimes there are height limits or property line setback restrictions to be considered. Property lines should also be carefully checked. Precautions like these may save you a costly rebuilding job later.

One of the major advantages of the building codes is that they allow an amateur home craftsman to remodel his own home by supplying all the engineering information necessary to do the job. While a building department does not give architectural advice, it makes sure that the alteration conforms to the safety and good construction standards of the local code. From this standpoint the building department can solve many of your problems. Remember, though, that the building code requirements are minimal and your planned use of, let us say, an overhead storage space may dictate somewhat stronger construction.

Once your plans have been approved by the building department, a building permit will be issued. This permit ensures the appearance of an inspector to inspect the work and be sure that it is done in accordance with the building code. More on the electrical and plumbing parts of the building codes is given in Chapters 5 and 6.

MAKING PLANS

Plans of the remodeling project are required by the building department before a permit is issued. The bank or lending institution will also want a set of plans.

For most remodeling jobs, a floor plan is needed. This is a drawing of the outline and partitions of a building as you would see them if the house were cut (sectioned) horizontally about four feet above the floor line. There are many types of floor plans, ranging from very simple sketches to completely dimensioned detailed floor-plan working drawings.

Dimensions show the width and length of the building or alteration; they show the location of doors and windows and the position of stairs, fireplaces, etc. Dimensioning architectural drawings can be done in many ways and for many reasons. Because a building that may be 50 feet long must be drawn on a sheet that is only a few feet long, a small scale (usually ¼″ = 1′0″) must be used. For small areas such as a basement room or a kitchen, a larger scale (usually ½″ = 1′0″) may be employed.

Preliminary or rough floor plans can be drawn on graph paper. This paper can be secured at stationery stores, or lines could be drawn on plain paper. For the purpose of drawing rough floor plans, consider that each such square represents one square foot. Tack a piece of such graph paper down on a drafting board, and begin drawing the plans for your remodeling project.

While some building departments will accept rough, but scaled, drawings to issue a permit, most lending institutions, especially on larger loans, require complete working drawings. If you cannot or do not wish to make such drawings, you can usually take your scaled graph-paper drawing to a professional architectural draftsman and he will make the necessary plans. While the fee for this service is not generally too high, it will depend as a rule on how much the draftsman must contribute technically, and how large the plans are. If you wish to learn more about making plans, it is suggested that you read either or both of the following books: *Architecture Drafting and Design* by Donald E. Hepler and Paul I. Wallach; *Blueprint Reading for Home Builders* by J. Ralph Dalzell.

Specifications. Specifications are written instructions describing the basic requirements for construction of a building. They describe sizes, types, and quality of building materials. The methods of construction, fabrication, or installation are also spelled out explicitly. In addition, information that cannot be conveniently included in the drawings, such as the legal responsibilities, methods of purchasing materials, and insurance requirements, is included in the specifications.

If you are hiring a contractor, specifications tell him, "These are the materials you must use, this is how you must use them, and these are the conditions under which you undertake this job." In other words, specifications help to guarantee you that the contractor will deliver the job as specified. They also help ensure that that project be done according to standards that the building laws require. Specifications are used frequently by banks and federal agencies in appraising a remodeling proposal.

Since many specifications are similar, the use of a fill-in form is the easiest way to prepare them. The fill-in forms include all the major classifications contained in most remodeling specifications; you add the exact size and type of material required. These forms are available at most drafting supply stores. Some banks and other lending agencies also furnish these printed forms for making specifications.

Estimating the cost. Once you have the drawings and specifications completed, estimates for the costs of material and labor (if you do not plan to do the work yourself) can be obtained. When making building lists, be sure to include even the smallest item. From nails to electric radiators, everything should be named and described to make quantity, quality, and type clear. Such a careful itemizing does more than just aid in determining the cost of your remodeling project. It minimizes chances of overlooking some of the important items that a professional craftsman would automatically include when ordering materials.

Once the building list has been drawn up, lumberyards, hardware stores, and other building supply dealers will help you in making your remodeling cost estimates. Cost estimating and shopping are most important and should be carefully done before undertaking any remodeling project.

When making your selection of products for the remodeling project, do so with care. Sometimes the more expensive items may prove to be more economical than less costly ones over a period of time. As a rule, the costlier materials will last longer and give you years of trouble-free service. However, this is not always true; therefore be inquisitive. Ask questions and try to learn as much as possible about the material or product. Determine how much it costs, how it can be applied, what colors are available, is it durable, etc. Most important of all, do you like it and do you and your family really want to live with it?

Chapter 3

CEILINGS AND WALLS

Figure 3–1. Four popular ceiling applications: *(top left)* 12-by-12-inch tiles; *(top right)* "invisible seam" tile treatment; *(bottom left)* 4-by-4-foot panel grid treatment; *(bottom right)* random strip panels.

Seventy percent of what you see when you enter a room is walls and ceiling. There are hundreds of materials that may be used to cover them. In this chapter we will take a look at the more popular ones, starting first with the ceiling, which in new construction is installed first.

CEILINGS

While many of the products described later in the chapter as "wall materials"—plywood, hardboard, gypsum wallboard—may be used on ceilings, the most popular for remodeling are ceiling tiles, often called "acoustical" or sound-conditioning tile. There are three popular ways to tile a ceiling: (1) fasten the tiles directly to the ceiling or to furring strips nailed directly across it; (2) install a grid system directly to the exposed beams; and (3) suspend the new ceiling from a grid which will drop it below the existing one. The first is the one most often employed for installing a new ceiling in an existing room. If the old ceiling is in fairly good condition, the new ceiling can be fastened directly to it with adhesive. But if the ceiling is in poor shape, furring must be used. The use of grids, either fastened directly to the beams or suspended below them, offers many interesting ceiling treatments including the so-called invisible seam arrangement, as shown in Figure 3–1.

The materials available for ceiling coverages (Figure 3–1) generally range in size from 12-by-12-inch tiles all the way up to large 4-by-10-foot panels. However, the most popular sizes for direct application are the 12-by-12-inch and 12-by-24-inch varieties, while for suspended ceilings the 2-by-2-foot and 2-by-4-foot units are usually used.

Planning the job. Whatever method of application you choose for ceiling tiles, utmost care should be given to measuring and laying out your ceiling area. Measure the length of each wall at the height of your new ceiling and mark it on your plan. For ease, use grid or graph paper. Let each square represent a square foot of your ceiling area. For example, if both long walls are 15 feet 6 inches, lightly draw a straight line midway between the fifteenth and sixteenth squares. If both short walls are 12 feet 4 inches, lightly draw a straight line one-third of the way past the twelfth square. Write down measurements where indicated. Once your room dimensions are charted on your plan, measure and mark the positions of lighting fixtures, alcoves, columns, ducts, or any other items which will require special cutting or additional materials. Also measure and mark areas to be left uncovered, such as skylights, attic doors, recessed lighting units, and vents.

Since balance makes for best appearance, plan your ceiling so that border tiles or suspended panels are of equal width or length and more than half their original measurement on opposite sides of the ceiling. This is easily accomplished by shifting tile or suspended panels by one-half their width (or length) in either direction. When 12-by-12-inch ceiling tile is used, for example, a room measuring 15 feet 6 inches long will take 14 rows of 12-inch tiles plus border tiles at opposite walls trimmed uniformly to 9 inches (Figure 3–2). A room 12 feet 4 inches wide will take 11 rows of 12-inch tiles plus border tiles along opposite walls trimmed uniformly to 8 inches.This means that the corner tiles for a room measuring 15 feet 6 inches by 12 feet 4 inches would be trimmed to measure 9 inches by 8 inches. The total number of tiles required are:

		Example
1. Whole tiles	$14 \times 11 =$	154
2. $8'' \times 12''$ border tiles (short walls)	$11 \times 2 =$	22
3. $9'' \times 12''$ border tiles (long walls)	$14 \times 2 =$	28
4. $9'' \times 8''$ corner tiles	$1 \times 4 =$	4
5. Add "alibi" or extra tiles		10
Total quantity of tiles		218

Add any tiles required for special alcoves or vertical application over boxed ductwork. Subtract tiles eliminated by skylights, columns, large, recessed lighting fixtures, and attic doors. If your room is irregular in shape, plan to arrange your tiles for the best appearance in the largest ceiling area. If you plan to install a recessed lighting fixture between joists, make allowances for it on your plan. Ceiling tiles can be applied in a basic grid pattern or offset to form an ashlar pattern. Both can be planned with the help of your grid.

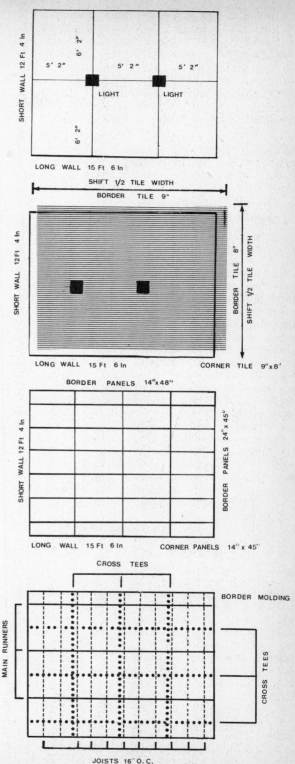

Figure 3–2. Steps in planning a ceiling tile job.

If 2-by-4-foot suspended panel tiles are used, the same 15 foot 6 inch by 12 foot 4 inch ceiling with joists running between the long walls will take two complete panel lengths and border panels trimmed uniformly to 45 inches (parallel to long wall); plus five complete panels (widthwise) and border panels trimmed uniformly to 14 inches. The corner panels would be trimmed to 14 by 45 inches. The total number of suspended panels required are:

		Example
1.	Whole panels*	$2 \times 5 = 10$
2.	24″ × 45″ border panels (short walls)	$2 \times 5 = 10$
3.	14″ × 48″ border panels (long walls)	$2 \times 2 = 4$
4.	14″ × 45″ corner panels	$1 \times 4 = 4$
5.	Add "alibi" or extra panels	3
	Total quantity of panels	31

*May include luminous panels for lighting.

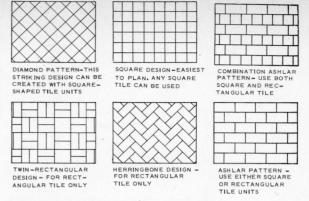

Figure 3–3. Popular ceiling tile pattern layouts.

Plan your suspended ceiling so that main runners are placed at right angles to ceiling joists and at 4-foot intervals. If joists are covered, locate by tapping lightly on existing ceilings. Using your room layout plan, draw lines perpendicular to the direction of joists (parallel to long wall) to represent position of main runners, spaced 4 feet on centers. Draw lines for cross tees between main runners and at 4-foot intervals parallel to the joists (if the long edges of panels are to run parallel to joists). Note: To arrange the long edges of panels parallel to joists, revise your drawing and border panel measurements to fit. Here, all cross tees will parallel joists between main runners, and they will be spaced 2 feet apart. Once your suspended ceiling system is determined, it will be helpful to stretch reference strings between walls to indicate positions of main runners and cross tees. Once your plan is complete, add up the quantity of grid system materials you require, as follows:

1. Wall angle molding (add up wall lengths) _____ feet _____ inches.

2. Main runners (according to plan) quantity _____ length each _____.

3. Cross tees (according to plan) quantity (4-foot) _____ quantity (2-foot) _____.

After selecting the tile, you will usually be guided in the method of installation by the condition of the ceiling, plus your own preference. There are three common methods of installing ceiling tiles: (1) nailing and stapling; (2) cementing; and (3) mechanical suspension.

Nailing or stapling ceiling tiles. Nailing or stapling are generally the best methods to use when applying ceiling tiles to a badly cracked or broken plaster ceiling or over exposed ceiling joists. A framework of wood furring strips must first be nailed up to provide a firm and even base for the finished tile ceiling. That is, apply 1-by-3-inch wood furring strips at right angles to ceiling joists or rafters. If present ceiling conceals location, sound for joists by tapping on the ceiling to determine their location. Nail the furring strips to the joists using two 8d nails at each joist crossing.

The first furring strip is applied flush where the wall and ceiling meet. The location of the second furring strip is determined by the width of the border tile that you decided on in planning your ceiling layout. Space this second strip so that the stapling edge of the border tile will be centered on it. Work across the ceiling from the second strip, installing furring strips parallel to it on 12-inch centers for 12-by-12-inch and 12-by-24-inch tiles. The next to the last strip will be the same distance from the wall as the second strip, and the last strip is nailed flush against the wall. Furring strips must be level to provide a smooth, even base for your new ceiling. Check them with a straightedge and shim, if necessary, to insure evenness. Snap a chalk line down the center of the second furring strip and across other strips at 90 degrees to serve as a guide in applying the tiles.

Start the installation at the corner of the room. Cut the border tiles to the size previously determined. Make sure that the stapling edges of the tiles face into the center of the room. Apply the first tile, placing the stapling edge on the chalk line marked on the furring strip, staple it in place and face the nail at the wall. Provide a small space between the first tile and the wall to allow for possible movement. If 12-by-24-inch tiles are used, apply them with their long dimension parallel to the furring.

With the first tile in place, apply additional border and full tiles. Always be sure tongue-and-groove edges fit together snugly, but do not force. Work across the room, installing two border tiles at a time and filling in with full-sized tiles in the numerical order shown, keeping the stapling edges out. Make sure that joints in both directions are continuous and straight.

To install tiles with joints broken in a staggered

Figure 3—4. Three methods of applying tiles: *(left to right)* staples; nailer clips; nails.

pattern (ashlar pattern), the application is the same as described, but alternate rows are started with a half tile. Application is easy as tiles need be exactly aligned in one direction only. This method should not be used with designs which carry through from one tile to the next.

Use two staples in each flange of each 12-inch tile; and for 16-inch and 24-inch tiles, use four staples in one flange and one in the other. Nails can be substituted for staples if you prefer, or if you do not have or cannot rent a stapling gun. However, nailing is slower and more difficult, and may result in damaged edges from badly aimed blows.

Ceiling tiles can be cut easily to fit around lighting fixtures. Use a coping saw, working with the finished face of the tile up to prevent damage to the surface. In many cases pipes or electrical cables directly under the joists can be concealed easily by doubling-up on the furring. Nail the first furring strips parallel with the pipes, the second layer of strips at right angles to the first.

Lowering a ceiling with furring strips. To lower a ceiling that is too high with furring strips, first determine your desired new ceiling height. At a point 1¼ inches above the new height, mark a level line around the perimeter of your room. (This 1¼ inches allows for the approximately ¾-inch thickness of furring strip and ½-inch thickness of tile.) Fasten 1-by-3-inch furring strips on the present ceiling at right angles to the ceiling joists or rafters. Locate the first strip approximately 32 to 36 inches from the wall, spacing additional strips at the same interval parallel to the first strip. On both sidewalls paralleling these furring strips, attach 1-by-3-inch wood furring strips. Align the bottom of these strips carefully with the guideline previously marked around the perimeter of the room.

Next, cut the hanger sections from 1-by-3-inch furring. These hanger sections should be slightly longer than the distance from the present ceiling to

the bottom of the wall guideline. Nail these hangers vertically along the ceiling furring at approximately 32-inch intervals. Stretch a line from one wall guideline to the opposite wall guideline and snap a chalk line across all the hangers. Nail the furring strips flat against the hanger sections, lining the bottom of the strip accurately with the chalk line on the hanger. Cut off the bottom of the hanger extending below this point. Additional hangers should be installed so that a hanger section appears every 24 inches.

Your ceiling is now ready for the installation of the furring strips to the hanger sections according to the instructions described earlier. The first strip is nailed flush at the wall, the second strip's position is determined by the border tile width, and the parallel strips are positioned across the room on 12-inch centers. Use two 8*d* nails at each nailing point to assure a firm hold. Apply the ceiling tiles following the steps given on page 58.

Cementing ceiling tile. When using an adhesive to cement tiles, you start the work in the center of the room rather than in a corner. To determine the exact

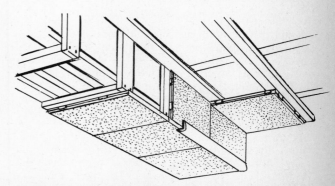

Figure 3—5. Method of dropping a ceiling around heating ducts and floor beams.

will not be divided in equal quarters, but the borders will be equal for each pair of edges.

When installing an ashlar tile arrangement, snap the center lines as just mentioned. Then snap another line the short way of the room, spaced half a tile away from the first. Set the first tile as before; but stagger the next one.

To make the work easier, use a plank over two sawhorses. Arrange a box or bench with two piles of the tile, back side up. Then work a small quantity of adhesive well into the back of the tile with a putty knife in six spots for 24-inch tiles, four spots for 12-inch tiles. Then apply additional adhesive until each spot is about the size of a golf ball. Keep adhesive spots about 2½ inches from the tile edge.

With the cement still in ball shapes, line up the tile for application by placing it lightly against the old ceiling about 1½ inches from the adjacent tile. Then simply slip the tile into position with gradually increasing pressure. If the surface of the old ceiling should be slightly uneven, increase the thickness of the adhesive to make the finished tile surface level. (Do not pull the tile away from the base to make it level. Rather, remove it and add more adhesive.)

In any tile installation, when the tiles are in place, you can finish off the room nicely with one of a number of attractive cove moldings. Use 3d to 6d finishing nails to apply such molding, nailing it into wall studs whenever possible in preference to nailing through the tile into furring strips or joists. More details on the installation of molding are given later in this chapter.

Figure 3—6. Cementing ceiling tile: *(top)* Apply tile cement at each corner of the back of the tile with a putty knife. Cement spots should be about the size of a walnut and be kept about 1 inch from the edge of the tile. New plaster must be thoroughly dry. Wallpaper should be removed. Gypsum lath ³/₈ inch thick is satisfactory for cement application. Nail lath to supports on 16-inch centers. *(bottom)* After the cement has been applied, the tile should be placed on the ceiling about 1½ inches from the adjacent tile and slid into its proper position.

center of the room, measure along the sides to locate the center lines and then snap a chalk line between the midpoints of each wall. Checking against the paper layout, determine the border widths. Should you be unable to achieve the proper arrangement of tiles (a poor border layout) snap secondary guidelines half a tile width to one side of the center lines. The first tile will then be set with its corner at the intersection of the guiding chalk lines. By starting the installation in this way, you can work the four equal quarters of the room individually. Of course, if the room is square, the borders will be even. However, when the secondary chalk lines are snapped as just described, the room

Figure 3—7. One type of lighting fixture may simply be inserted in place of a tile during the installation of the ceiling. The secret of installing this fixture is its adapter plate, which may be integrated with the tongue-and-groove tiles that surround it. Attached to furring strips with four wood screws, the plate serves as the base to which the other parts are added to form a complete fixture.

Figure 3—8. Method of installing a wood-grain acoustical strip ceiling: (A) Nail 1-by-3-inch furring strips perpendicular to the joists at 12-inch intervals. (B) Check each strip with a carpenter's level. Correct high spots by wedging thin strips of wood between furring strips and joists. (C) Install the first strip in the right corner of the room and work from right to left. Staple through the flange of each board where it crosses each furring strip. A full piece of ceiling plank requires five staples. (D) After the first row of board has been installed, the first piece of board for the next row should be cut 12 inches so that the end joint falls on the furring strip 3 feet from the wall. The first board of the third row should be cut 24 inches so that the joint falls on the furring strip 2 feet from the wall. Staggering the end joints of the planks in this fashion produces a random effect.

Mechanical suspension. There are several grid mechanical suspension or grid systems presently available, but all involve five basic elements: (1) attaching level wall angle moldings to the walls at the desired ceiling height; (2) attaching a suspension wire to the joists at 4-foot intervals; (3) suspending main runners from suspension wires at 4-foot intervals perpendicular to the joists; (4) applying cross tees between the main runners and at the borders; and (5) slipping the 2-by-4-foot suspended ceiling panels into place. The method of figuring the amounts of these materials needed is given on page 57.

To install the mechanical suspension grid system, determine the desired new ceiling height (at least 3 inches below pipes, conduits, etc; 5 inches below fluorescent lamps) and snap a level chalk line on all walls at this height. Check the level of your lines carefully with a carpenter's level.

Once the wall lines have been determined, attach the wall angle moldings with 4d common nails spaced no more than 24 inches on centers. Make sure that the bottom of the molding is in line with the level chalk line. Then mark the end joists at 4-foot intervals as determined in the ceiling plan. Stretch a chalk line between these points at opposite ends of the room and mark the intermediate joists. Attach 12-gauge galvanized wires to the end joists at these marks and at intervals no greater than 4 feet. Stretch a taut line 1 inch above the lower surface of the wall angle moldings and bend wires sharply along this line. Next cut the main runners at the starting end so that all slots where the cross tees intersect will be accurately placed according to your plan. *This is important.* Attach wires to the main runners with one end resting on the wall angle molding. Join the main runners by inserting the end tab in the slots of its companion runners and bend tabs.

To install the cross tees, insert the end tabs in the previously aligned slots in the main runner (or in the slots of the other cross tees), according to your layout. At the edges of the ceiling, cut the cross tees $1/16$ inch scant of the distance to the wall. The cut end rests on the wall angle molding.

When installing ceiling panels, insert them through the openings in the grid and drop them in place. To avoid marring the panel surface, handle the panels by their edges as much as possible. Where there is a need to secure the panels into the grid, the hold-down tabs in the 4-foot cross tees may be bent into position with a screwdriver. Cut the panels face-up, with a fine-tooth saw or fiberboard

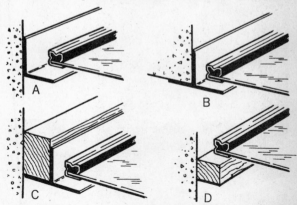

Figure 3—9. One of the following types of wall bracketing can be used to support the suspension grid frame on the diffuser panels: (A) The simplest and quickest to install is a metal L section that is mounted to the wall for the panels to rest on. (B) This method is used where a soffit is provided, creating a cavity. The luminous ceiling is installed flush to the rest of the ceiling area. (C) This method of edge mounting can be used where a soffit is not provided and a custom-finished appearance is desired. (D) The most economical method of installation requires only a wood molding trim strip mounted on the wall at the proper distance from the existing ceiling.

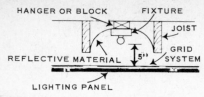

Figure 3–10. Points to be considered when a lighting fixture is installed in a grid ceiling.

knife to fit the border rows at the ends and sides of the room.

It is possible to install translucent plastic sheets in a grid system in place of standard textured and patterned acoustical fiberboard ceiling tiles or panels. There are a number of different kinds of translucent panels suitable for this on the market, ranging from an egg-crate or louvered style to plain white frosted ones. These translucent materials also may be used as "luminous grid ceiling panels." That is, they are used in conjunction with fluorescent lamps placed above the panels. Complete grid lighting units are available. Frequently the lighting units can be wired into your present ceiling fixture if there is one. Otherwise you will have to wire it in as described in Chapter 6.

Fluorescent lighting over translucent panels normally provides more even distribution of light than incandescent bulbs. Fluorescent tubes emit the light intensity over a larger area more evenly, whereas incandescent bulbs can produce a "hot spot" with very little light reaching the edges of the lighting panels. Incandescent light may also raise the panel temperature to over 120 degrees F, which may cause sagging of the panels. The number of tubes and their distance above each panel determine the desired light level. For most situations, two 40-watt tubes will be adequate. Three tubes may be required over visual-task areas, e.g., workshop, office, kitchen. Where large luminous ceiling areas require a critical placement of tubes for a shadowless ceiling, butt or stagger tubes. (Fluorescent tubes emit light from the sides only. The space between ends will produce darkened areas on panels.) It is recommended that approximately 5 inches of clearance be allowed between lighting panels and tubes for the best appearance. Hot spots are possible if the lights are too close, and light may be lost if the tubes are too far from the panel. To maximize lighting efficiency use a reflective surface at the sides of the fixture, as shown in Figure 3–10. This will improve lighting efficiency by directing more light to the back of the lighting panel. Commercial lighting reflectors, aluminum foil, or white-painted hardboard will adequately reflect light down into the room.

If surface-mounted or hanging fixtures are de-

Figure 3–11. Method of installing a drop-grid ceiling: (A) Nail molding to the wall at the desired ceiling height to provide support for the panels at the perimeter of the room. (B) Attach hanger wires to the joists at 4-foot intervals. (C) Fasten the main runners of the metal framework to the hanger wires. (D) Snap the cross tees into place between the main runners. (E) Lay the ceiling panels into the grid formed by the main runners and the cross tees. (F) The completed job.

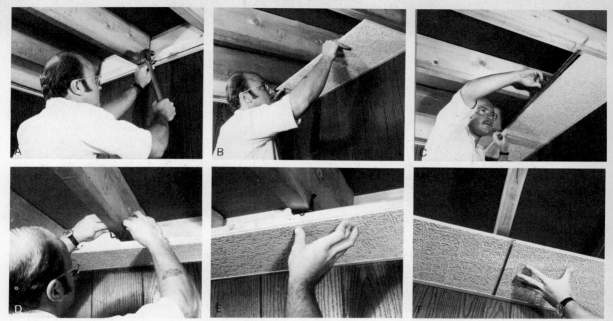

Figure 3–12. Direct attachment method of installing the invisible grid system: (A) Starting in a corner of the room, nail the metal wall molding in place 1⅜ inches below the joist level. (B) After the molding has been applied, lay the first tile into place as shown. Note that the tile is always installed perpendicular to the joists. (C) Slide a 4-foot cross tee into the kerf on the leading edge of the tile. Note how the tee provides support without being visible. (D) Each cross tee should be supported by at least one joist clip.

Merely slide the clip onto any convenient joist by spreading the legs as shown; then pull it down slightly to set the metal teeth into the wood. (E) Push up on the tile until the cross tee engages the joist clip. This completes the installation of the first 1-by-4-foot tile. (F) Continue the process with succeeding tiles, working one row at a time across the room. Note how the tiles butt tightly together to form a clean, unbroken surface.

sired, refer to your fixture manufacturer's instructions for detailed mounting instructions.

Grid system on exposed beams. Where minimum loss of ceiling height is important under an exposed joist ceiling, use special beam hanger clips. The new ceiling can be as close as 1⅛ inches to the existing ceiling, assuming there are no pipes, lights, or other obstructions. However, panel removal is not possible in this grid system.

After the wall angle molding has been installed, slide the hanger clips onto the top flange of main runners, one hanger for every 4 feet. Level the main runner with the wall angle molding as previously described. Then fasten the hanger to the beams as directed by manufacturers of the clips. Start the application at one end of the room and install the ceiling panels and cross tees as you work across the room.

Invisible grid system. This system provides the same flexibility as a standard grid system, but the grid is hidden. The square-cut edges and random embossed designs of the tiles or panels allow them to be installed in any position, without worrying about where the seams fall. This means you do not have to cut wasteful border tiles, and the leftover piece from each row can be used to start the next row. The grid components snap together easily and are adjustable to provide a built-in allowance for error.

While both the suspension type and direct installation grid arrangements may be employed with this system, the major difference is that the cross tee supports the edges of the tiles and remains invisible, as shown in Figure 3–12. That is, slide the cross tee into the slot above the tongue of the tiles. Continue across the room, inserting tiles and cross tees. Place the wall springs between the edge of the last tile and the wall, to hold the tile tight.

The invisible grid system allows the use of either recessed or surface-mounted lighting. Attach extra hanger wire to the main runners supporting the lighting fixture. Surface-mounted lights require a 2-by-4-inch piece of lumber to hold the junction box, while specially designed 1-by-4-foot and 2-by-4-foot recessed light fixtures simply rest on the runners for fast, easy installation (Figure 3–13). After the lighting fixtures are secure, install the tiles around them.

To make an access panel for plumbing and electrical boxes, simply trim off the tongue edge

Figure 3–13. One of the specially designed recessed light fixtures for a grid system. Heating elements that fit in this manner are also available.

plus the flange from the two short ends. The flange on the long side opposite the tongue is left. Install this tile as usual by inserting the long flange edge into the preceding row. When the tile is in position, locate the holes in the cross tee by pushing the nails through the tile. Remove the nails, and insert the screws into the holes. Tighten until the tile is level and the screws are countersunk into the tile face. If

Figure 3–14. Solutions for difficult ceiling problems: (A) making a frame to hide ducts; (B) covering the bottom side of ducts with ceiling panels; (C) cutting a panel to fit a pipe; (D) fitting it around a post.

you like, you can paint the screwheads white. Quick access is possible by simply removing the screws.

As is mentioned later in this chapter, the grids can be covered with false wood-beamed arrangements. These add beauty to any ceiling design. Also, as we stated earlier, many other materials may be used for a ceiling. As we will see later in the chapter, installing larger ceiling panels requires either a helper or props. Make two T-head props, from 1 × 4's, about 1 inch longer than the distance from the floor or scaffold to the ceiling. With the face of the panel down, lift it and wedge it into position with the props. The panels should be forced tightly together except when an open-joint design is desired. Many different panel-joint treatments are possible with standard wood moldings.

False ceiling beams. Beamed ceilings are an old favorite in Early American design. Today ready-made, ready-to-install beams are available at most lumber dealers for this purpose. They are made of solid lumber, plywood, polyurethane plastic foam, or metal. The number of beams and patterns employed depends on the size of the room and personal preference. Some room ceilings will appear best with the beams running in one direction only, while others look fine with crossing beams.

Solid wood beams are available. They are milled to fit over furring strips, which have already been nailed to the ceiling joist. If the furring, which is normally 2 × 2's, can not be fastened to the joists, expanded anchors or toggle bolts may be used. The beams may then be nailed or screwed to the furring strips. (The use of screws allows removal of the beams whenever it becomes necessary to paint the ceiling.) For corner installation, two furring strips are used, but one side of the beam must be cut to permit it to be attached to the furring strip. For crossing patterns, simply run furring strips at right angles to one another. Gaps should be left between the furring strips and any surface they meet, regardless of whether it is another furring strip, wall, or ceiling. All nails or screws should be set below the surface and touched up with the proper colored putty sticks. Excess putty can be wiped off with a water-moistened rag.

Another popular fake beam is made with three pieces of lumber—hardboard or plywood butted, rabbeted, or mitered to form a U-shaped cross section (Figure 3–16). Most of the fake beams come flat and assemble with glue to make a U-shaped channel. This channel is fitted over a furring strip, which has previously been installed on the ceiling, and fastened with brads. Set their heads below the surface and touch them up with colored putty sticks.

Most solid lumber and U-shaped channel beams come stained, but not otherwise finished. To protect the wood, it is wise to apply a coat or two of varnish or shellac to the beams.

Figure 3—15. Types of false ceiling beams: *(left)* solid lumber; *(center)* plywood; *(top right)* polyurethane plastic foam; *(bottom right)* metal.

U-shaped polyurethane foam beams are available in replicas of a variety of woods—walnut, oak, and maple, to name a few. They come in lengths of from 8 to 20 feet and in several widths and thicknesses. Some are solid, while others are channeled so that you can run concealed wiring through them. They can be cut with an ordinary handsaw. The plastic beams may be installed with adhesive or fastened to the ceiling by means of anchor plates. Manufacturers provide the instructions for both. Incidentally, while most foam beams come already finished, you purchase some in a raw stage and then apply a special stain to simulate the effect you desire.

When installing a suspended panel ceiling, you can purchase metal grids that are covered with lithographed paper patterns which simulate wood. Some of these are quite attractive.

The number of beams used depends on the size of the room and the pattern desired. Some ceilings look best with the beams running in one direction only, while others are more attractive with

A B C D

Figure 3—16. Plywood beams can be made of ¼-inch plywood or purchased in kit form. Although the photographs show the assembly of the kit type, the same procedure would be followed in making one's own plywood beams. (A) When assembled, the plywood beam components form a U channel, which is nailed to previously installed standard 1-by-6-inch nailer strips. (B) With the cloth tape hinge serving as a "third hand" beam, components are fastened at miter cuts by nailing 12 inches on center with 1-inch finish nails. The tape is then stripped off and discarded. (C) The completed beams may be left in natural fir finish, stained, or painted. (D) In the final stage of installation, the beam is raised to the ceiling and placed with open end over previously installed 1-by-6-inch nailer strips. The beam is nailed to strips 16 inches on center with 1-inch finish nails. Solid wood beams can be made in the same manner as plywood ones.

crossing beams. Let your room and personal preference dictate the choice.

DRY-WALL CONSTRUCTION AND FINISH

There are two basic types of wall construction, dry-wall and lath-and-plaster. Though lath-and-plaster finish is still employed to a very limited degree in home construction, the use of dry-wall materials is the most popular today. Dry-wall finish, as the name implies, is a material that requires little, if any, water for application. More specifically, dry-wall finish includes plywood, hardboard, insulation board (fiberboard), gypsum wallboard, or similar sheet material, as well as wood paneling in various thicknesses and forms.

The use of thin sheet materials such as gypsum or plywood requires that studs and ceiling joists have good alignment to provide a smooth, even surface. Wood sheathing or furring will often correct misaligned studs on exterior walls. A "strong back" provides for aligning of ceiling joists of unfinished attics and can be used at the center of the span when ceiling joists are uneven. Table 3–1 lists thicknesses of wood materials commonly used for interior covering.

Table 3–1. *Minimum thicknesses for plywood, insulation board, and wood paneling*

Framing spaced (inches)	Thickness (inches)		
	Plywood	Insulation board	Wood paneling
16	$1/4$	$1/2$	$3/8$
20	$3/8$	$3/4$	$1/2$
24	$3/8$	$3/4$	$5/6$

Solid-wood paneling. Various types and patterns of woods are available for application on walls to obtain the desired decorative effects. For informal treatment, knotty pine, redwood, whitepocket Douglas fir, sound wormy chestnut, and pecky cypress, finished natural or stained and varnished, may be used to cover one or more sides of a room. In addition, there are such desirable hardwoods as red oak, pecan, elm, walnut, white oak, and cherry also available for wall paneling. Most types of paneling come in thicknesses from $3/8$-inch to $3/4$-inch; widths vary from 4 to 8 inches, lengths from 3 to 10 feet.

When planning a wood-paneled room remember that if you wish to accent a wall, use boards of random widths; subdue it by the use of equal-width boards. Small rooms can be given the illusion of increased size by applying the paneling horizontally. Of course, paneling can be applied vertically, horizontally, diagonally, or in combined directions (Figure 3–17).

To estimate quantities of board paneling, measure and multiply the areas to be paneled. Deduct for major openings only. Then add 10 to 20 percent for waste in fitting, lap of boards, if any, and the difference of rough width from finished width.

Solid wood is subject to shrinkage and swelling, even though kiln-dried. After delivery, therefore, stack the lumber inside the house at a temperature as close to room temperature as possible. The paneling should never be stored where it will be exposed to weather or to excessive moisture. The building or room in which the wood planking is to be installed should be completely closed in and dry before installation begins. Masonry and other work involving moisture should be completed and dried. A moisture barrier such as polyethylene plastic sheeting (4 mils thick) should be provided behind paneling where any danger of moisture penetration exists. This is a requirement on outside walls and on all concrete or masonry walls. Also, if you intend to install paneling over a masonry wall that is often damp, it is a good idea to apply a wood preservative containing pentachlorophenol to the back of each

Figure 3–17. Three methods of installing solid wood paneling: *(left to right)* horizontally; vertically; diagonally.

Figure 3—18. Patterns of board arrangement: *(left to right)* channel rustic pattern; shiplap pattern; tongue-and-groove pattern.

panel. This will protect the paneling against moisture, mildew, fungus, and termites and other insects.

Before doing any installation, lay out the boards on the floor adjacent to the installation wall. Arrange the most attractive combination of widths, lengths, grain patterns, and shades of color. Then install the boards in the selected sequence. Use shorter pieces at the top and bottom of the wall area, where more than two pieces are required for wall height. Stagger the end joints to form a pleasing pattern on the wall, and avoid positioning two or more end joints near each other. Vary the widths to enhance the random effect. For best contrast, use narrow planks adjacent to wider ones. Figure 3—18 illustrates three patterns of panel arrangements. The channel rustic patterns provide strong vertical accents with bold shadow lines, while the bevel-edged tongue-and-groove and shiplap patterns offer the more subtle V-groove effect. Where no accent line at all is desired, square-edged adaptations are used to create tight, flush joints. Most patterns may be installed either vertically or horizontally; the choice is yours.

Installation techniques. For most vertical applications over plaster or similar walls, 1 × 2 or 1 × 3 furring strips installed (nailed or glued) horizontally at 16- or 24-inch centers are recommended. Where the wall is uneven or wavy, wooden wedges or shims should be used behind the furring strips to bring them into an even line. Starting at one corner the first piece of paneling should be plumbed vertically with a level. This may necessitate trimming the corner edge if the wall corner is not plumb. Succeeding panels are then applied by blind-nailing (through the tongue of the panel) or are face-

Figure 3—19. Methods of installing solid wood paneling against a masonry wall: *(top left)* Three furring strips usually are provided, at top, center, and bottom. Use a wide strip at floor level for fastening baseboard. *(top right)* The baseboard must be surface-nailed. For a professional job, drive the nails well into the wood with a nail set; use a filler to hide the holes. *(bottom left)* Nail paneling to furring strips at tongued edge so that the groove of the next panel will hide the nails. Use a grooved block to hammer paneling into place. *(bottom right)* Paneling around a basement window.

nailed to the furring strips. Use 8d nails for ¾-inch boards when face-nailing, 6d for blind-nailing. Use proportionately smaller nails for thinner panelings. If face-nailing is used, set the nails ¹⁄₃₂-inch below the surface and fill the resulting holes with colored filler or stick putty.

When solid wood paneling is to be applied horizontally on an existing wall that is reasonably sound and true, furring strips are not usually required. Once the trim has been removed and the studs located, the boards are nailed through the existing wall material into the studs. If the old wall surface is masonry or in poor condition or not true, furring strips should be installed as for vertical solid paneling except that strips should run vertically rather than horizontally (Figure 3–19). Shim the strips to obtain a true nailing surface. Inside corners are formed by butting the panel units flush with the other walls. If random widths are employed, boards on adjacent walls should be well matched and accurately aligned. When nailing the boards, be sure to install them so that the tongue edge is out. This will permit you to blind-nail through their tongues. Drive the nails in at an angle so they come out the back of each board behind the tongue. The nail heads, of course, will be hidden in the groove of the next board. At the top of the wall, be sure to leave an expansion space of about ¼ inch. A molding will cover it.

To locate an outlet cutout on a panel, place the panel against the wall and, with a padded block over the approximate location of the outlet, tap it soundly with a hammer. The outlet box will indent the back side of the panel. Drill small pilot holes from the back (larger holes from finish side) and saw the outlet hole from the front side of the panel with a keyhole saw. After the cutout has been made and the panel board installed, advance the receptacles flush with the panel surface by replacing the holding screws with longer ones, slipping pieces of electrician's loom behind as backing. Be sure that the loom is cut long enough to compress properly as the screws are tightened.

Fit the solid paneling as closely as possible

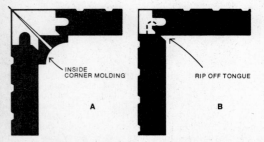

Figure 3–20. Finish inside corners by installing standard inside corner molding (A) or by butting planks (B). Use outside corner molding where required.

around the untrimmed door opening thickness. (The door, window, base, and ceiling should be removed before starting the job). Fur out window and door frames to equal the thickness of the furring strips plus thickness of the paneling. To give the job a finished look, use molding around windows and doors, along the floor and ceiling, and wherever else applicable.

In new work, wood paneling may be nailed to studs or furring in the same manner as plywood (page 71). A right-handed worker will prefer facing the tongues to the right and working from left to right, starting with a length nailed to a corner studding or furring. The boards that fill the space to the next stud are then laid out and cut to the proper length, the preceding one being used as a template to make sure that all are the same length. Each tongue should be fitted tightly into its groove by being rapped smartly with a hammer insulated by a tongued scrap of the wood. The boards between those anchored to studs can be secured to the top plate near the ceiling and to the shoe close to the floor. Warped lengths should be discarded. If possible, use only full-length pieces that extend from floor to ceiling, except where the wall is masked by bookshelves or other built-ins. Corners must be solid, which will usually require ripping at least one board for its full length to take off the tongue (Figure 3–20). The top of the paneling can be finished with a suitable cove or crown molding. For a top finish, see Chapter 10.

Adhesives for solid wood paneling. The ³⁄₈-inch solid board paneling may be applied directly over sound, even walls using a ceramic tile type of adhesive or mastic (see page 85). Ask your building supply dealer for advice concerning the type and brand available.

As in nailing, make sure the first panel is aligned vertically at the corner of the room. After fit is assured, use a putty knife to apply daubs of adhesive to the back of the panel. These should be about the size of a half dollar, at least ½ inch thick and spaced 18 inches apart near both edges of the panel. Place the panel in position and press it firmly to even out the adhesive and assure a tight bond. Succeeding panels are treated the same: placed close to the previous panel, pressed into place, and then slid tightly against it.

Plywood. The homeowner who is handy with tools can remodel a basement, living room, bedroom, kitchen, or attic with a minimum of money and labor by using plywood. Plywood panels come in finishes ranging from richly figured oak, mahogany, birch, and walnut to fir and pine, allowing a choice of decorative material to meet every taste and budget. They can be applied effectively to either traditional or modern interiors.

One outstanding advantage of plywood for interiors is the elimination of periodic redecorating and

Figure 3—21. Exterior siding materials such as wood shingles *(left)* can be used for interior applications. By employing such materials, it is possible to bring the outdoors in *(right)*. Shingles for interior application are almost the same as those for exterior use (see Chapter 8).

patching of cracks. Plywood walls are kickproof, punctureproof, and crackproof. The only upkeep required is an occasional waxing. The large sheets, 4 feet wide, 8 feet long, and ¼-inch thick, can be erected quickly and easily with ordinary hand tools.

Selection of a panel arrangement. The photographs in Figure 3—22 suggest a few interesting ways to arrange panels in architecturally and decoratively correct designs. Many of these can be used on all the walls in a room, others are intended to create a point of interest or contrast in one part of the room only. In the latter cases the rest of the

room may be paneled with full length plywood in natural finish, or with less expensive or lower grade plywood, painted or papered. Plywood panels can also be used in combination with painted or papered plaster, with glass, glass block, masonry, and other wall materials.

Figure 3—22. Designed plywood arrangements.

In choosing your panel arrangement, remember that it is best to start paneling at the openings, with vertical joints, and then divide the plain space in an orderly pattern, placing the panels in a reasonably balanced horizontal or vertical arrangement. Where the width of the wall is 10 feet or less, panels may be run horizontally in two or three pieces, with the openings cut out. Place vertical joints at each side of the top of doors and at the top and bottom of window openings. If the width of the door or window opening is more than 4 feet most designers do not hesitate to place panels horizontally. Remember, you can plan vertical arrangements to lend height and horizontal paneling to give breadth and sweep. Both can be combined in the same room with a pleasing effect. In certain woods, panels 9 or 10 feet long are available to solve special paneling problems.

A rough pencil drawing of walls to be paneled will help you design the best arrangement for the room. Always plan to let the joints between the panels follow the pattern set by the vertical joints at the openings. This helps to maintain a pleasing, symmetrical design.

Estimating the amount of plywood required. To estimate the number of panels required, measure the perimeter of the room. This is merely the total of the widths of each wall in the room. Use conversion Table 3–2 to figure the number of panels needed.

Table 3–2

Perimeter	Number of 4 × 8-foot panels needed
36 feet	9
40 feet	10
44 feet	11
48 feet	12
52 feet	13
56 feet	14
60 feet	15
64 feet	16
68 feet	17
72 feet	18
92 feet	23

For example, if your room walls measured 14 feet + 14 feet + 16 feet + 16 feet, this would equal 60 feet or 15 panels required. To allow for areas such as windows, doors, fireplaces, etc., use the following deductions:

Door	½ panel
Window	¼ panel
Fireplace	½ panel

Thus, the actual number of panels for this room would be 13 pieces (15 pieces minus 2 total deductions). If the perimeter of the room falls in between the figures in Table 3–1, use the next highest number to determine panels required. These figures are for rooms with 8-foot ceiling heights or less. For walls over 8 feet high, select a paneling which has V grooves and that will "stack," allowing panel grooves to line up perfectly from floor to ceiling.

For most wall paneling, ¼-inch plywood sheets are used. Of course, ⅜- and ¾-inch panels may be applied with good results, but they are more expensive. The latter thickness may be used as a partition without framing. For special designs, such as patterns made up of small panels—16- to 24-inch diamonds, squares, etc.—it is best to first sheathe the walls with ⁵⁄₁₆-inch Plyscord, then apply the finish panels as desired.

Erection of paneling in new construction. If you can, store the panels in the room for a few days before you start the job. Whether new or old, the studs should be straight, dry, plumb, and true to assure a smooth, flat wall surface. If new framing is being installed, use only #1 Common, thoroughly dry, straight framing lumber of uniform width and thickness. Framing should be erected on 16-inch centers (Figure 3–23). Where required, extra framing members should be installed to provide a nailing base for all edges of the panels. Where required, nail

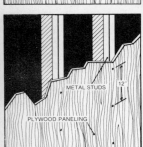

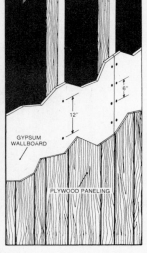

Figure 3–23. *(above)* Methods of erecting plywood panels in new construction. *(left)* Method of scribing irregularity in a wall.

cats (horizontal framing members) at 4-foot heights for additional support of panels for every panel edge and for every 4 feet of panel. If you are in doubt about the dryness of the framing lumber, apply fir sticks (¼ inch thick, 2½ inches wide, and 4 feet long), with the grain running the short way over the face of the framing members. For studs spaced 16 inches on centers, use ¼-inch plywood; for studs placed 24 inches or more on centers, apply ¾-inch panels.

Plan the sequence of panels about the room so that the natural color variations form a pleasing pattern in complementary tones or in direct contrast. Hold each panel against the wall to see how it looks before you nail it.

Here are three ways to start paneling, based on individual room problems:

1. For most interiors it is practical to start from one corner and work around the room.

2. If the wall or room has a fireplace or picture window, you should start paneling on each side (if fireplace or window goes to ceiling) or at the center (if fireplace or window does not go to ceiling), and work to the right or left around the room.

3. If all the panels are the same width and window or door units are balanced across a wall area, start at the center of the wall and work both ways.

Again, do not be concerned about the natural variations in color as they will enhance the appearance of the room, as long as there is some symmetry of arrangement.

There are several tricks for laying out panels to reduce cutting as well as to achieve a pleasing pattern of joints. To avoid intricate fitting around windows and doors, start full panels on each side of the openings. On plain walls, it is best to start at the center so that fractional panels will be the same at each end. You can keep all joints vertical, the simplest arrangement, or use the tops and bottoms of windows as guidelines for horizontal joints.

Be sure that the panels are square with the adjacent wall (at corners) and ceiling before nailing. If the panel is not square with the adjacent wall,

Figure 3—25. Applying plywood panels with nails: (A) Panels are set in place so that they line up with the furring strips behind the plywood sheet. (B) Nails should be driven at an angle into the panel. The finishing nailheads should be driven below the surface with a nail set. (C) Cutouts for electrical outlets and switches should be made before panels are installed. Uneven matching wall surfaces should be scribed with a compass. (D) Nails can be covered with matching stick putty. (E) Matching prefinished moldings can be nailed into place to complete the job.

scribe it to the corner. Keep the bottom of each wall panel about ¼ inch above the floor to allow space for the lever used to pry the panel tightly against the ceiling. As the panels go up, keep checking them for plumbness. Shim out the studs or fill hollows of the framing. Keep a level handy for truing up and down (vertical position). Molding will take care of the irregular meeting with floor and ceiling. When nailing, start along one edge of the panel and work across the width so as to avoid bulges.

When cutting plywood with a handsaw, or on a table saw, plywood should be cut with the good face up. If you are using a portable electric handsaw, either circular or sabre, cut the plywood with the good face down. If you are using a radial saw, cut the plywood with the good face up for cross cuts and miters, and down for ripping. With a hand-

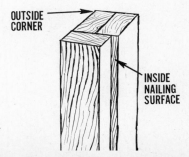

Figure 3—24. Forming a corner to fasten plywood.

OUTSIDE CORNER

INSIDE NAILING SURFACE

saw, or on a table saw, permit only the teeth of the blade to protrude through the work. For smooth cuts, use blades that have teeth with no set and that are hollow ground. Special small-toothed blades are available for cutting plywood.

Installing with adhesive. The application of plywood with panel adhesive is widely employed by homecraftsmen. Its use largely eliminates the need for brads or nails and the resulting concealment of their heads. Generally, the adhesive comes ready to use in a tube with a plastic nozzle. This tube fits into almost any calking gun, and the panel adhesive comes out of the nozzle as a heavy bead. If the wall is in good condition, smooth and true, the adhesive can be applied directly to the back of the panel all around the edges in intermittent beads about 3 inches long and spaced about 3 inches apart. Keep the adhesive at least ¼ inch from the edges of the panel and be sure that it is continuous at the corners and around openings for electrical outlets and switches. Additional adhesive should be applied to the back of the panel in horizontal lines of intermittent beads spaced approximately 16 inches apart. Once the adhesive is applied, the panel may be pressed against the wall. It may be moved as much as is required for satisfactory adjustment. To make this easier, drive three or four small finishing nails about half their length through the panel near the top edge. The panel can then be pulled away from the wall at the bottom with the nails acting as a hinge. After any adjustment has been made, a paddle block should be used to keep the panel pressed back on the wall, and then the nails are driven home. (These will be covered by a molding.)

A rubber mallet or a hammer and padded block should be used on the face of the panel to assure good adhesion between panel and wall.

This adhesive also may be used on furring strips and open studs. It is applied directly to each furring strip or stud in continuous or intermittent beads. Panels are then applied by the same method as just described above. But never apply adhesives on plaster walls in poor condition, with flaking paint or wallpaper that is not tightly glued. If the plaster seems hard and firm and does not crumble when you drive a nail into it, it is probably safe for adhesives. The flaking paint or loose wallpaper problem can usually be solved as detailed in Chapter 9.

Prefinished plywood may also be installed with contact cement. After each panel has been cut to the proper size, mark off the points of contact between the studs and the back of the panel. Next coat the back of the panel at these points with contact adhesive; then coat the studs with the cement, too. When the cement is tacky (check manufacturer's instructions for the right degree), apply the panel to the studs. There can be no second guesses, for the cement grabs. To avoid errors, you can place a paper buffer between panel and studs; slide it out after the panel is aligned. Then press the panel to the wall and tap it at all adhesive points with a rubber mallet or hammer and wood block. Nail it with 4d finish nails to the plate and sill to reinforce the cement bond at these weak points. The nail holes will be covered by the moldings.

A word of caution about prefinished panels: handle them with care. Should the surface scratch,

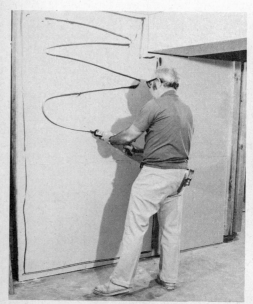

Figure 3–26. Adhesives for plywood panels can be applied to the wall as shown *(left)* or to furring as in Figure 3–31. In either case, once the adhesive has been applied, the panel can be carefully applied *(right)*.

repair it according to the instructions in Chapter 9. To avoid soiling the panels, apply the finish to the trim and molding before installation. Most of the larger companies make hardwood moldings that will harmonize with their various species of plywood. Some sell moldings that are already finished to match, while others sell special stains that will enable you to blend the trim in with the finished wall later on. Some companies also make veneered metal moldings with a matching wood facing to conceal exposed plywood edges and to finish off inside or outside corners.

Erection over old plaster and dry wall. Where existing walls are in good condition, you can put the panels right over the old surface and nail through it into the studs. On plaster walls, you can locate the studs by tapping (they give a solid sound; the spaces in between, a hollow one) and by test poking with a nail or small drill. You can also locate studs by following the placement of nails in the baseboards. On dry walls (wallboard and plasterboard), you can usually find the studs by prying off the baseboard molding and noting the points where the panels have been nailed on. When nailing, make sure to go through the wall material into the studs beneath with small finishing nails or brads, which will be countersunk, and into the plate and sill with heavier nails where moldings will cover the area.

On walls that are badly out of line or where the plaster is cracked, you may have to put up a light framework of 1-by-2-inch furring strips to cover the irregularities and insure a true vertical surface. Be sure to level with shims. One-quarter-inch three-ply fir-plywood strips 2½ inches wide are ideal for this purpose, except in cases where paneling is used with recess joints. With such joints it is proper to use strips that match the face of a hardwood panel. Apply the furring horizontally across the studs, nailing it into the studs. Then fit on vertical furring wherever it is required to provide a nailing surface behind all panel edges. Shim all the furring plumb and true and nail through the plaster into the studs every 16 inches with 8d cut-steel nails or resin-coated nails.

Installing plywood wall planks. Plywood plank panels are 8 feet long by 16¼ inches wide and they go up without furring strips—over wallpaper, plaster, sheathing, or bare studs. These are grooved on the long edges in a special design that makes the installation of plank paneling the quickest of all plywood walls. The material is held by special clips that you nail into the wall or studs. Follow the manufacturer's directions.

Hardboard. Hardboard specially manufactured for use as prefinished paneling is specifically treated for resistance to stains, scrubbing, and moisture. It is also highly resistant to dents, mars, and scuffs. In most cases, the material is prefinished in wood grains such as walnut, cherry, birch, oak, teak, and

Figure 3—27. Examples of the many different patterns in which prefinished hardboard is manufactured.

Figure 3–28. Installing a hardboard wainscot (partial wall): (A) Measure a level line around the room. (B) Nail molding and finishing strip in place at proper height. (C) Hold prefinished panels in place with clips. (D) Install clips as shown. The clips serve a twofold purpose: they build in uniform spacing and expansion room, and they help support the panels while the adhesive takes hold. Planks and random planks should never be forced tightly together.

pecan, and in a variety of shades. It may be smooth-surfaced or random-grooved. In addition there are the decorative and work-saving plastic-surfaced hardboards which resist water, stains, and household chemicals exceptionally well. A typical surface consists of baked-on plastic. Most hardboard is sufficiently dense and moisture-resistant for use in bathrooms, kitchens, and laundry rooms. The variety of finishes and sizes is extensive. Finishes include rich-looking wood grains, exceptional marble reproductions, plain colors, speckled colors, simulated tile, lace prints, wallpaper textures, and murals. Vinyl-clad panels are also available in decorative and wood-grain finishes.

Use $^3/_{16}$- $^1/_4$- and $^5/_{16}$-inch hardboards over open framing. All panel edges should be backed. Studs or framing members should be spaced no more than 16 inches on center. Use $^1/_4$-inch or $^5/_{16}$-inch board thicknesses for structural wall members. Hardboards $^1/_8$ and $^3/_{16}$ inch thick should be applied over solid backing. Quarter-inch-thick boards may be applied directly over studding or stripping not over 16 inches on center.

To prepare the old wall for the board remove all wallpaper or scaly paint or dirt. Then remove such fixtures as the lavatory, toilet tank, and wall-hung accessories. Next mark an accurate starting point for your panel (Figure 3–28). For a wainscot effect this line is usually 48 inches above the floor. In floor-to-ceiling work, use a level to establish the horizontal joints and a plumb bob to mark the location of the vertical joints.

First cut to size the metal molding used with panel boards. Use a hacksaw and miter box, and file off rough edges after cutting. The molding has

wide flanges through which nails are driven; panels conceal nailheads. Where moldings meet in a corner, flanges must be cut back so they do not overlap. With planning, you can make a decorative feature out of the molding lines.

To apply panel boards, start with an inside corner molding. Leave $^1/_4$ inch between the top of the strip and the guideline for the cap strip, if one is to be used. Make holes in the flange with a steel punch, then nail the molding in place with 4d fin-

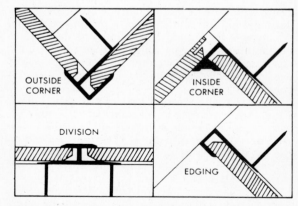

Figure 3–29. Installing concealed hardboard fastening moldings: Metal single-flange outside and inside corner moldings are applied after a plank on one wall has been fitted to the corner. Allow approximately $^1/_8$-inch expansion space at the corner. Nail through molding flanges with rock-lath nails. Fit panels to allow $^1/_8$-inch expansion space in the molding channel. Nail edge moldings in place before installing the first panel. Moldings are available in bright metal, wood-grained, and color-matching finishes.

ishing nails. In "wet" areas such as bathrooms, caulk the joints between the table and wall with a proof compound, and nail the metal molding in place while the caulking is still soft.

Cut the panel boards with a fine-tooth saw held at a low angle, keeping the finished surface face up. Sand the rough edges. Try the panel for size, lining it up with a guide line. To get added protection against buckling of the boards with expansion, bevel the edges that fit into moldings. Trim each edge down with a plane or sandpaper until it moves freely into the molding. Bevel on the back side with an ordinary plane held at a 45-degree angle. Then apply the adhesive to the back of the panel, not to the wall. Lay the panel on a padded support and spread the adhesive with a notched spreader (Fig. 3–30). Remove any adhesive that gets on the face of the sheet with a solvent designated by the manufacturer. Long panel boards can be sprung into place after you apply the adhesive. Slip one end of the panel into its molding strip, then bow out the center until the other end slips into the next molding. Then press the panel into place, kneading and pressing at every point several times until a firm bond with the wall is made. To install a piece of panel board that is too short to spring into place between moldings, insert one side in the attached corner molding (after the adhesive is spread on the back), fit the second molding over the exposed edge, and push the panel into place. Only the exposed flange of outside molding is nailed down.

Cap molding for a wainscot may be installed at any time after the panels are in place. Cut the molding, miter the corners, and fasten it with small fin-

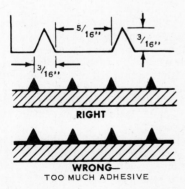

Figure 3–30. To apply hardboard adhesive, use a comb spreader made from hardboard and cut as shown at top. Place the panel face-down on a padded surface to protect the face, and apply adhesive to the back of the panel in accordance with the instructions on the container. Leave no adhesive between the ridges. For quicker bonding it is sometimes desirable to utilize a cohesive technique, applying a thin, solid layer of adhesive to the wall, allowing it to dry, and then applying a combed-on layer to the plank as illustrated. Be sure to remove any excess adhesive immediately with mineral spirits.

ishing nails. Countersink the nailheads, fill the holes with plastic wood, and touch them up with paint. Caulk this molding, too. If the paneling runs to the ceiling, use a division molding at this point, then put a crown molding at the ceiling line.

When installing plastic-finished hardboard panels in new construction, nail 1-by-3-inch furring strips horizontally on 16-inch centers and vertically on 48-inch centers for $1/4$-inch and $5/16$-inch boards. To bring out the face of the strips to a level plane, shim the furring with ordinary shingles driven between wall and strip. Nail the shingles in place. When furring over masonry, apply the strips with masonry nails and anchor them with nails and mastic, or stud driver. Arrange the hardboard panels around the room in the desired sequence, standing them against the wall. Do not slide the panels over each other.

Always begin the job in a corner, and make sure the panel is plumb. Start by nailing a temporary 1×2 level starter strip of wood in place at the bottom of wall, and rest the panels on this strip during installation. Mark a plumb line the desired distance from the corner to locate the first vertical joint. To compensate for unevenness or lack of plumb in the adjoining wall, place the first panel in perfectly plumb position so that the distance between the panel and the wall area to be scribed can be spanned by your scribing compass. Rule a scribing line with a china marking pencil, and cut the panel with a coping saw if an uneven cut is required.

Before fastening a panel to the wall, make sure each panel is plumb by using a level of sufficient length to give you an accurate reading. The slightest irregularity in fit between panels can cause them to get out of plumb. It is easy to adjust panels if each one is plumbed. Use color-matched, annular-thread or ring-groove hardboard nails, driven perpendicular to the panel surface 6 inches on center to blend with the panels, or use adhesive for nail-free installation. Another method is to use countersink 3d finish nails and fill the hole with matching putty.

The panels should be in only moderate contact with each other. They should never be butted tightly together. V-grooved panels are beveled at the edges, and when lightly butted they form a full-depth groove. Other hardboards adapt to a variety of joint treatments: rounded edges; bull-nose wooden inserts; wood, plastic, or metal moldings; battens; and lap joints. For hardboards that are patterned so that the edges blend into the overall pattern of the board when they are butted together, leave a space between panels the thickness of a matchbook cover. Where joints are exposed, a beveled or rounded edge may be used. Inside corners may be covered with cove molding or gently butted. Actually, to give the job a finished look, use moldings around windows and doors, in corners, along baseboards,

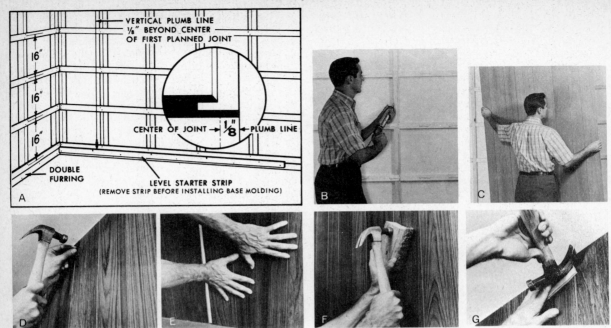

Figure 3-31. Applying hardboard on furring in new or old construction: (A) Nail 1-by-2-inch furring strips horizontally into old wall at stud locations, spaced 16 inches apart. Apply vertical furring where panel edges are to be bound. (Furring may be attached vertically with a cartridge-type adhesive, if desired.) (B) After making sure that all surfaces to which adhesive is to be applied are clean and dry, apply ⅛-inch-thick continuous ribbon to furring or other surfaces to which panel edges are to be bonded. Apply intermittent ribbon (3-inch bead—6 inches open space) to intermediate furring. Adhesive and room temperatures should be between 60 and 100°F during application. (C) Move panel into position over furring strips and immediately press into position. (D) Install two nails at top of the panel to maintain its position, leaving the heads exposed for subsequent easy removal. (E) With uniform hand pressure, press the panels firmly into contact with the adhesive bead. (F) After fifteen to twenty minutes, reapply pressure to all areas to be bonded, using a padded block of wood and a hammer or mallet. A final set is thus provided. (G) Carefully remove the nails, protecting the panel surface with a scrap of carpeting. When installing base, follow the procedure shown in D. If prefinished plastic moldings are not used, a wood molding can be stained or painted to harmonize or contrast with the paneling.

and, where applicable, over joints. A number of manufacturers have simplified the job with prefinished casings, baseboards, inside and outside corner moldings, cove moldings, and shoe moldings to match prefinished panels.

Perforated hardboard. Perforated hardboard is a very versatile material. In addition to being a most attractive wall material, perforated hardboard may be a permanent solution to the problem of using your walls for more than just places to hang pretty pictures (Figure 3-32). There are a wide variety of fixtures available at most hardware stores that make it possible to use walls for many different purposes. Just a few ideas are shown here and on other pages in this book.

When applying perforated hardboard over studding, cut the panels into widths that equal a multiple of the center-to-center stud spacing. On a wall where 2-by-4-inch studs are located on 16-inch centers, for instance, cut the hardboard to widths of 16, 32, 48 inches, etc. Try to plan the width and placement so that you will not have narrow pieces at the wall ends. Since no furring is required over bare studs, place the perforated panels so that the edges fall on stud center lines and nail them directly to each stud, using 3d finishing nails spaced about 8 inches apart. Countersink the nail heads and fill the holes with plastic wood or wood putty. As an alternate method, panels may also be glued to studs, using contact or panel adhesive. Install them as directed on page 74.

When perforated hardboard is applied over an existing wall surface, the installation of furring is necessary since the holes in the paneling must have space behind them so that the fixtures can be inserted. If you plan to panel an entire wall this way, it is a good idea to place a row of 1-by-2-inch strips along the bottom of the wall, end to end, after removing the old baseboard. Repeat the process at the ceiling. Then, nail vertical furring at the edges of the wall from floor to ceiling. Finally, placing them horizontally again, nail the strips from end to end 2, 4, and 6 feet above the floor. Once the furring strips have been applied, the perforated panels can be fas-

Figure 3–32. Home applications of perforated hardboard.

tened in the same way to the studs, except that the strips are glued or nailed.

If you plan to cover only a portion of the wall with perforated hardboard, a frame of furring strips should be nailed to the wall studs in the size and shape of the panel. If the framed area is larger than 2 feet in either direction, additional strips will be required. This extra furring inside the frame need not be spaced exactly; the important thing is that perforated panel be supported at intervals of approximately 2 feet. The panels may be fastened to furring by nails, adhesive, or both.

When cutting a panel make sure that the saw blade does not pass through a row of perforations, since the resulting edge is most difficult to conceal. Incidentally, there are two other methods of making a joint, in addition to butting the two sides together (Figure 3–33). The first is to nail a molding over the joint. The second is to plane a 45-degree bevel along the meeting edges before the panels are in-

stalled. The groove that results wherever the panels meet can then be filled with wood putty or spackle and sanded smooth before finishing with paint. This will result in an invisible joint.

Insulation board or fiberboard. Insulation board or fiberboard is available in the form of planks and sheets. The plank is 8, 12, or 16 inches wide by 8, 10, 12, or 14 feet long. The sheet is 4 or 8 feet wide by 6, 7, 8, 9, 10, 12, or 14 feet long. Both are usually prefinished by the manufacturer; therefore, when in-

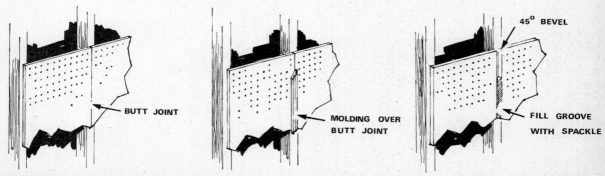

Figure 3–33. Methods of installing perforated hardboard.

Figure 3—34. Installation of large sheets of insulation board on ceilings *(top)* and walls *(bottom)*. Hidden clips are used.

stalling be sure not to dirty them more than necessary. They can be used very successfully in finishing off an attic because of their insulating value, plus their ease of handling. They are low-cost and can be painted or left natural.

For vertical application of planks, nail 1-by-3-inch furring strips horizontally on wall studs. For a ½-inch-thick plank, space the strips 9 inches on centers up to shoulder height and 12 inches on centers above this height. For a ¾-inch plank, space the strips 12 inches on centers up to shoulder height and 16 inches on centers above this height. Determine the position of the planks first to ensure proper arrangement of joints around the door and window openings, and at corners.

In horizontal application, the framing should be furred horizontally with 1-by-3-inch strips. Space the strips to conform to the width of the plank so that there is a nailing base at every joint. If a 12- or 16-inch-width plank is used, it is advisable to put an extra furring strip back of the center of each plank up to a height of about 5 feet.

A plank may be applied to gypsum wallboard or plaster that is sound, reasonably level, and dry. Use adhesive and supplementary nailing along the joints. Space the nails approximately 16 inches on centers. The backing must be such as to hold the nails securely. If the plaster is not sound, apply a nailing base of furring strip. A plank may be applied to plywood or other continuous wood backing without the use of adhesives, since nails along it will give sufficient security. Masonry surfaces such as concrete, whether plastered or unplastered, should be furred, with no adhesive used.

Nail through the thickest part of the tongue of the plank and as close to the bevel as possible, with heads flush. For a ½-inch plank use 1-inch #17 flathead brads, spaced to match the furring or, for application to continuous backing, spaced 12 inches on center. For a ¾-inch plank, use 1¼-inch #17 flathead brads. For face nailing at wall and ceiling junctures use 1¼-inch #16 brads or finishing nails, for a ½-inch plank; for a ¾-inch plank, use 1¾-inch nails. Start the wall application of a plank in one corner of a room, face-nailing it at wall junctures. The tongue edge of each plank should always be the leading edge, to permit nailing. The exposed nailheads should later be covered with a suitable molding, unless inconspicuous finish nails are used. Edges of a ceiling application of a plank should be nailed in the same manner. Instead of nails, ⁹⁄₁₆-inch cement-coated staples may be used, placed as close to the bevel as possible.

Where adhesive is to be used on continuous surfaces covered with calcimine or cold-water paints, it is advisable to remove the paint. Loose or chipped paint should be scraped off, and grease or dirt should be removed with a strong washing-soda solution followed by clear-water sponging. Let the surface dry thoroughly. Apply 2- to 3-inch spots of adhesive at about 12-inch intervals along the edges of the plank, and also down the center if the plank is as much as 12 or 16 inches wide; or apply ribbons of adhesive 2 to 3 inches wide along the edges, with an intermediate ribbon in the center of a 12- or 16-inch-wide plank. Drive nails through the thickest part of the tongue as close to bevel as possible, with heads flush.

For sheets, the framing members (studs, joists, or furring strips) should be spaced 16 inches on centers for ½-inch board. For ¾- or 1-inch-thick panels, space furring 16 or 24 inches on centers. Over a rough or irregular surface, or a masonry or poor plaster surface, install strips that are properly shimmed. On gypsum or plaster, provide furring strips, preferably 1 by 3 inches, spaced not more than 16 inches on centers and accurately shimmed to a true level plane. The board may be applied to plywood or other continuous wood backing by nailing. Masonry surfaces, such as concrete, whether plastered or unplastered, should be furred.

Nail the boards to intermediate framing members first, spacing nails 6 inches apart; then along the edges, space the nails 3 inches apart and $\frac{3}{8}$ inch in from the edge. Along edges or on intermediate bearings, for a $\frac{1}{2}$-inch board, use $1\frac{1}{4}$-inch galvanized finishing nails, cadmium-plated needle-point #17 gauge nails with $\frac{3}{32}$-inch flatheads, or #16 gauge brads; for a 1-inch board, use $1\frac{3}{4}$-inch nails. Drive the finishing nails or brads at an angle and set the heads flush with a nail set to avoid hammer marks on the board. Drive flathead nails straight and flush. Do not set any type of nail below the surface.

Where nails are to be covered (with battens, moldings, plastic paint, or wall covering), use $1\frac{1}{2}$-inch galvanized shingle nails, galvanized roofing nails, or box nails for square-edge $\frac{1}{2}$-inch board, driving the heads slightly below the surface; for a 1-inch board, use 2-inch nails.

To clean the finished wall, you can remove dust by brushing lightly with a whisk broom or clean rag, or by vacuum cleaning with a brush attachment. Smudges may be removed with an art gum eraser. If you desire to paint rather than use the finish of the manufacturer, whether you use plank or board, see page 326.

Gypsum wallboard. Gypsum wallboard—also called plasterboard, sheetrock, gypsum-board, wallboard—is low cost, durable, and easy to handle when installing. This wallboard is a sheet of material composed of a gypsum filler faced with paper. Sheets are normally 4 feet wide and 8 feet in length, but can be obtained in lengths up to 16 feet. The edges along the length are usually tapered, although some types are tapered on all edges. This allows for a filled and taped joint. This material may also be obtained with a foil back, which serves as a vapor barrier on exterior walls. It is also available with vinyl or other prefinished or predecorated surfaces. In new construction, a $\frac{1}{2}$-inch thickness is recommended for single-layer application. In laminated two-ply applications, two $\frac{3}{8}$-inch-thick sheets are used. The $\frac{3}{8}$-inch thickness, while considered minimum for 16-inch stud spacing in single-layer applications, is normally specified for repair and remodeling work. Table 3–3 lists maximum member spacing for the various thicknesses of gypsum wallboard.

Figure 3–35. Burlap-finished installation board makes an attractive basement room.

When the single-layer system is used, the 4-foot wide gypsum sheets are applied vertically or horizontally on the walls after the ceiling has been covered. Vertical application covers three stud spaces when studs are spaced 16 inches on center, and two when spacing is 24 inches. Edges should be centered on studs, and only moderate contact should be made between edges of the sheet.

Gypsum wallboard is generally available in four basic sizes, 4×8, 4×10, 4×12, and 4×14, and in two thicknesses, $\frac{3}{8}$ and $\frac{1}{2}$ inch. The $\frac{5}{8}$-inch thickness is usually a special order and the larger panels are slightly higher priced. But it is wise to always order the largest size panel you can use; the difference in price, if any, is worth it because the panel covers a larger area with less time and total effort and greatly reduces the number of joints that must be taped to complete the job. While smaller boards are much easier for one man to handle, this should not be the prime consideration. If, for instance, the room to be wallboarded is 14 by 21 feet, it would be better to use one 4 by 12 panel and one 4 by 10 panel rather than three 4 by 8 panels. Not only would there be a smaller amount of waste, there would be one less joint to tape. In such a case, the little extra cost of the large sheets and the effort needed to handle them would be justified in the time saved and neatness of the finished job.

Preparation and installation. The horizontal method of application is best adapted to rooms in which full-length sheets can be used, as it minimizes the number of vertical joints. Also, plan to work from the top of the room down, i.e., the ceiling and/or top half of the walls, in that order. On walls, this approach provides a better joint, and panels already installed are less likely to be marred by other panels being handled. Where joints are neces-

Table 3–3. Gypsum wallboard thickness (single layer)

Installed long direction of sheet	Minimum thickness (inch)	Maximum spacing of supports (on center; inches)	
		Walls	Ceilings
Parallel to framing members	3/8	16	16
	1/2	24	16
	5/8	24	16
Right angle to framing members	3/8	16	16
	1/2	24	24
	5/8	24	24

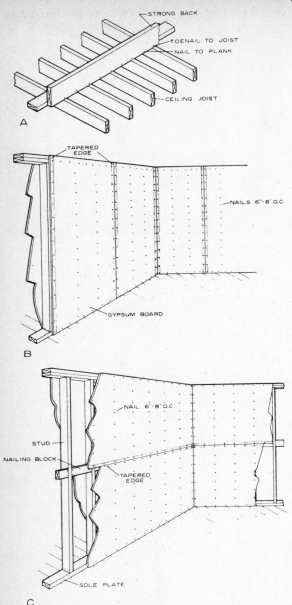

Figure 3—36. Application of gypsum board finish: (A) strong back; (B) vertical application; (C) horizontal application.

proved method of wallboard manufacturers) and (2) a method of adhesive in combination with nailed edges only (used primarily with the decorative or finished type of gypsum wall). Actually, there is another method, which is a combination of these two. That is, the laminated two-ply application of wallboard includes an undercourse of $3/8$-inch material applied vertically and nailed in place. The finish $3/8$-inch sheet is applied horizontally, usually in room-size lengths, with an adhesive. This adhesive either is applied in ribbons or is spread with a notched trowel. The manufacturer's recommendations should be followed in all respects.

Of the two basic systems noted, the full nailing is the preferred one. Fivepenny cement-coated cooler-type nails ($1^5/8$ inches long) should be used with $1/2$-inch gypsum, and fourpenny ($1^3/8$ inches long) with the $3/8$-inch-thick material. (Use sixpenny nails in applying gypsum board over old walls.) Ring-shank nails, about $1/8$ inch shorter, can also be used. Some manufacturers often recommend the use of special screws to reduce "bulging" of the surface ("nail-pops" caused by the drying out of the frame members). If the moisture content of the framing members is less than 15 percent when gypsum board is applied, "nail-pops" will be greatly reduced. It is good practice when framing members have a high moisture content to allow them to approach moisture equilibrium before the application of the gypsum board. Nails should be spaced 6 to 8 inches for sidewalls and 5 to 7 inches for ceiling application. The minimum edge distance is $3/8$ inch. Incidentally, always nail from the center of the panel outward for a snug fit. Use the convex face of the hammer to dimple the nailheads slightly below the surface so that they can be concealed with joint plaster (Figure 3–37). (A nail set should *not* be used.) But do not drive them so deep that you break

Figure 3—37. Start nailing gypsum board from the center out. *(left)* The nail should be set with a crowned hammer. *(right)* The "dimple" required to finish over the board.

sary, they should be made at windows or doors. End joints over openings should be on studs. When ceiling heights are over 8 feet 3 inches, or when this horizontal method results in more waste or joint treatment, the vertical method of application should be used.

Two basic methods are presently employed for the installation of gypsum wallboard panels: (1) overall nailing according to a set pattern (the apthe paper covering. With predecorated gypsum board you should use color-matched nails, which can be purchased with the wall material.

Ceilings of gypsum board go up first, of course. While it is easier for two people to work on a ceiling, one can easily install it by temporarily nailing 1-by-2-inch wood strips below the ceiling level, forming a shelf on which to rest the edge and/or end of the wallboard. Nail from the center of the panel toward the ends and edges.

Adhesive installation. When installing predecorated gypsum wallboards, as previously stated, you can make use of adhesive; the procedure to follow is almost exactly the same as for other adhesive applications for plywood and other finished panels (described earlier in the chapter). That is, the adhesive material is applied directly on studs with a standard caulking gun. But unlike some adhesives, this is not a contact type and therefore permits you to shift the panel if a placement demonstrates the need for correction.

After the adhesive has dried for about 15 minutes, put the panel in a vertical position, drive one 1¼-inch (5d) nail every 8 inches along the ceiling edge and along the floor edge of the panel. (If you do not plan to use a molding along these edges, be sure to use color-matching nails.) Then impact the panel with the heel of your hand over all the studs to be sure there is proper contact. This step is extremely important and should be done thoroughly.

When applying the next panel, be sure that the adhesive does not come up into the joint. To avoid this, place the second panel overlapping the first, then slide the second panel into position. Nail and impact as above.

Predecorated or finished gypsum boards are frequently used to cover existing plaster or wallboard surfaces. The boards may be installed by either overall nailing or adhesive and nails. With the former method, start in a corner and drive the color-matched nails through the panel, through the existing wall surface, and into the studs. Place the first nails in the middle area of the panel, then work toward the edges. Nail every 8 inches along each stud. If the wall is cracked or uneven, horizontal furring should be applied and panels nailed to it.

When using the adhesive and nails, apply the adhesive to the horizontal furring and nail the panel along the ceiling and floor strip every 12 inches. If the walls are in good condition and the surface is even, the laminated two-ply application of wallboard described earlier can be used.

Fitting odd pieces, cutting openings. The scoring and snapping method of making straight cuts in gypsum wallboard is fast, accurate, and much cleaner than sawing. First, score the paper covering on one side with a sharp knife (a linoleum knife is good for this job) guided by a straightedge. It is easy to break the gypsum core after you have

scored the surface paper. Pull the sheet forward until the scored line is over the edge of the sheet below. Then grasp the edge firmly and snap downward. The gypsum core will break cleanly, leaving the waste piece hinged by the covering material on the back. Reach under the sheet and score the underside of the break with the knife, then snap the waste piece upward sharply to complete the separation. Avoid tearing the paper away from the core; it might tear into the section to be used. If it is necessary, smooth the newly cut edge with fine sandpaper and light strokes, keeping the sanding block square with the edge.

Before cutting a piece of gypsum wallboard to fit a space, measure carefully, especially for pieces around windows, heating registers, and electrical outlets. When cutting openings for electrical and heating outlets, first pierce the corners of the open-

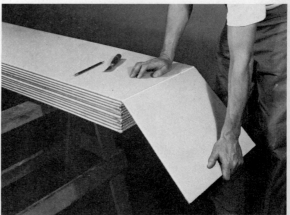

Figure 3-38. *(top)* Using a sharp knife, cut the face paper and edges and snap the boards as shown, breaking the core. Cut the back paper from the reverse side, and snap forward for a clean break. *(bottom)* When cutting an opening in a gypsum board wall, use a keyhole saw and start the cut by puncturing the wall with the saw tip.

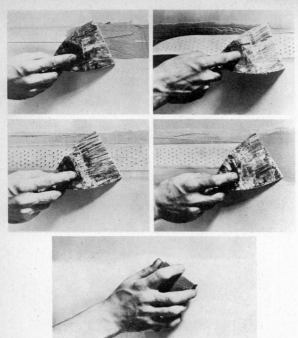

Figure 3–39. How to tape a seam: *(top left)* Ready-mixed joint compound is easy to use. The material, which has the consistency of heavy cream, is applied with a broad knife. The channel between the wallboard edges is filled. *(top right* and *center left)* The perforated tape is embedded in the compound directly over the joint. Smooth the compound around and over the tape to level the surface. Spot nailheads with the compound. *(center right)* A second coat of bedding compound is applied after the first coat has dried for at least twenty-four hours. Apply thinly and feather out 3 to 4 inches on each side of the joint. Allow to dry for twenty-four hours. *(bottom)* A final coat is applied very thinly and feathered out about 8 to 10 inches on each side of the channel. Finish by sanding the cement smooth. Avoid heavy pressure that might scuff the surface.

ing with a drill. Then cut through both the front and back paper with knife and punch out the core. Cutouts for electrical switches and outlets can be made with a keyhole saw. To locate the exact position, hold the gypsum board panel in place. Then, using a wood block to protect the board, tap around

the outlet with a hammer. The indentation on the back of the board is your guide for cutting.

Arches are easy to construct. First cut a strip of wallboard to the width of the arch and score the back paper at 1-inch intervals. Then break the core at the scorings. Nail the wallboard to the framing with nails spaced in alternate segments. Sand the edges flush with the wall surface.

Windows and doors in new constructions can be cut out after the gypsum board is applied. The cutouts are made with a saw (using the door or window frame as a guide). The scraps or cuttings from openings are saved, to be used in the small corner areas and for wall ends. If you are budgeting your job closely, you may prefer to economize with scrap usage around corner windows and doors and over windows, even though the piecing process takes longer to accomplish. Where the sash is already in place, of course, cutouts for doors and windows must be made beforehand.

Taping joints and plastering nailheads. With your room completely walled, you can now begin the final stages of the installation, which consist of taping and cementing joints, filling hammer-head dimples, and smoothing over any possible surface irregularities. Joint cement, "spackle," is used to apply the tape over the tapered edge joints and to smooth and level the surface. It comes in powder form and is mixed with water to a soft putty consistency so that it can be easily spread with a trowel or putty knife. It can also be obtained in premixed form. The general procedure (Figure 3–39) for taping is as follows:

1. Use a wide (5-inch) spackling knife and spread the cement in the tapered edges, starting at the top of the wall.

2. Press the tape into the recess with the putty knife until the joint cement is forced through the perforations.

3. Cover the tape with additional cement, feathering the outer edges.

4. Allow the cement to dry, sand the joint lightly, and then apply the second coat, feathering the edges. A steel trowel is sometimes used in applying the second coat. For best results, a third

Figure 3–40. Methods of holding gypsum board panels for ceiling work.

coat may be applied, feathering beyond the second coat.

5. After the joint cement is dry, sand smooth the area. (An electric hand vibrating sander works well.)

6. For hiding hammer indentations, fill them with joint cement and sand them smooth when the cement is dry. Repeat the process with a second coat when necessary.

Interior corners between walls and ceilings may also be concealed with some type of molding. When moldings are used, taping this joint is not necessary. Wallboard corner beads at exterior corners will prevent damage to the gypsum board. They are fastened in place and covered with the joint cement.

The gypsum wallboard, unless of the decorative type, is either painted or wallpapered as described in Chapter 9 to complete the job.

Figure 3—41. Ceramic tile may be used for both walls and floors.

LATH AND PLASTER

Lath and plaster interior wall finish have dropped in popularity in recent years, especially with home handymen. Plaster is much more difficult to apply than dry wall and, because it is a wet material, it requires drying time before other work can be started. For these reasons, we have not included lath and plaster techniques in this book.

OTHER WALL-COVERING MATERIALS

In addition to the so-called standard wall covering—wallboards, plywood, planks, hardboard—there is a wide range of other materials that can be used, including many types of tiles, glass, imitation and real stone, wallpaper, fabrics, and paints. (The last three items are covered in Chapter 9.)

Ceramic tiles. There are many types of ceramic tiles, including glazed wall tiles, ceramic mosaics, quarry tiles, and specialty tiles, and they are available in a wide range of designs and colors. Actually, tiles range in size from small 1-inch-square mosaics to impressive 12-inch squares, and are available in high or low relief designs with colorful glazes or multicolored patterns. There are also handsome contoured tiles. Along with hexagons, octagons, and rectangles, there are curvilinear shapes inspired by historic Moorish designs, houses in Normandy, and villas in Florence. Many of these are quarry tiles which are now offered in a large range of natural colors as well as durable glazes. Because of the many practical and decorative virtues uniquely its own, tile has a place in any room in your home.

In the past, tile could be installed only by highly skilled craftsmen since the only setting material available was cement, which is difficult to work with and requires the experience of the professional. Today, as a result of the development of new setting techniques and materials, it is possible to install your own tile.

To estimate the number of tiles required, add the length and width of a room, multiply by 2, then multiply this answer by the height of the wall to cover. This will give you the square footage of the area to be tiled. For example, for an 8 by 12 room, add 8 and 12 (20) and multiply by 2 (40). If the wall is to be tiled up to 5 feet in height, multiply 40 by 5. This gives a total of 200 square feet to be tiled. If you plan to use common 4¼-inch square tiles, then eight will cover a square foot of surface; thus 200 times 8, or 1600, tiles are needed. The factor of 8 already takes into account waste and allowances for doors and windows. It is always a good idea to get a little more than you actually require in case of accidental breakage and for future replacement should a tile become cracked. You must remember that tiles, even the same color and made by the same manufacturer, are made according to dye lot and shade. Make sure all of your tiles are the same shade and dye lot number.

There are many special trim shapes in glazed ceramics, allowing you to make both outside and inside corners, tub enclosures, tile wainscot borders, and even countertop and windowsill edge pieces. Take a rough sketch of your room along with you to your dealer so he can help you specify these special shapes. These are generally sold by the lineal foot.

Before installing the tile, make sure that surfaces are plumb, sound, and free of old materials that might later loosen and cause the new tiles to fall out. That is, loose plaster must be removed and the holes refilled with sound material. If you are tiling over old tile, any loose tiles must be reglued or removed and their holes filled with spackle. Decora-

Figure 3–42. Techniques of installing tile: *(top left)* The mastic is applied with a notched trowel. *(top center)* Each tile is pressed into the mastic. A tab, or stub, on each tile keeps the tiles equidistant. *(top right)* The rows of tiles should be kept level. *(middle left)* The easiest way to cut ceramic tile is to use a tile-cutting machine rented from a dealer. *(middle right)* Steel nippers are used for cutting tiles so that they fit around pipes. *(bottom left)* The grout can be applied with a sponge or with a sponge-coated float. *(bottom center)* The dried grout remaining on the tile surface can be removed with a damp cloth or sponge. *(bottom right)* Seams at edges of tubs, countertops, and similar installations should be filled with a sealer.

tive wood wall paneling is often installed with a minimum of fasteners because an unblemished surface is desirable. Be sure that these panels are nailed down securely before applying tile over them. The bond between the tile and the wall is only as strong as the surface of the wall. For this reason, the surface must be clean and prepared for adhesive. Be sure to remove all traces of wax, oils, loose paints, and anything else that would get between the adhesive and the wall. You can apply tile over a sound coat of paint as long as it is clean and you have roughed up the surface with sandpaper. You cannot, however, successfully apply tile over wallpaper. It may hold for a little while, but you run the risk of having a whole wall collapse—in one magnificent sheet perhaps—at some point.

Wet areas, such as tub enclosures, shower stalls, laundry floors, or other surfaces that come in constant contact with water, pose some special problems. Water will not penetrate the tiles themselves, but it will penetrate the grout, in very small but accumulative amounts, and pass into the surface behind the tile. If the backing surface is affected by moisture, the bond between the adhesive and the surface will begin to fail, eventually freeing the tiles. The grout will also begin to fail, opening small cracks that allow more and more moisture in. Surprisingly enough, neither exterior-grade nor marine plywood nor cement-asbestos board is appropriate for wet areas. Although these materials are not damaged by moisture, they do swell and "move" when wet, physically disturbing the bond between the wall and tile. Conventional wallboard or plaster simply fail in the presence of moisture.

If an existing wall composed of any of these materials is to form a wet wall in your renovation, it must be covered by a surface which will provide a durable support. Water-resistant gypsum wallboard is a suitable surface for wet wall areas, and, of course, previously tiled surfaces, properly prepared, are ideal. If you intend to install tile yourself in wet areas, your local supplier can guide and counsel you in the appropriate methods and techniques.

A tile installation involves three basic steps: (1) applying the adhesive properly; (2) applying the tile; and (3) filling in the spaces between the tiles with a material called grout.

Most adhesives are applied to the wall with a trowel with a notched edge (Figure 3–42). It leaves a deposit of adhesive that looks very much like a plowed field, and because of the carefully controlled size of the notches, it leaves just the right amount of adhesive. If you use the trowel carefully, it will be hard to get too much or too little adhesive on the mounting surface. Be sure not to leave any bare spots. For easy working conditions, apply the adhesive to a surface of about 10 to 15 square feet at a time.

The tiles themselves are designed to eliminate some of the careful measuring and precise positioning that an attractive tile job calls for. The smaller mosaic tiles are furnished on a foot-square sheet of paper or scrim, which holds each tile in the right position. You need only locate each sheet on the wall or floor relative to its neighboring sheet. The larger glazed tiles are applied individually. Almost all commercial ceramic tiles have built-in spacing tabs on each edge, which are later hidden by the grout. Handmade porcelain and ceramic tiles, however, do not have these handy spacers. To apply these tiles, simply insert two 6d nails between tiles to give them uniform joints. Leave the nails in until the adhesive hardens and the tiles are firmly in place.

In tiling the wall, in any room but the bathroom, begin your tiling at the floor line. If you are using a special baseboard shape, install it all around the room before installing the regular tiles above it. Be careful not to get adhesive on the walls above the baseboard as it will harden before you get back to that area with your regular tiles and will be difficult to remove. If you are planning to use ceramic tiles on the floor (see page 126), this work is done first.

Draw a center vertical line on the longest wall.

Since the wall is almost certainly not exactly the width of a certain number of uncut tiles, the last tiles on each end will have to be cut to fit. Measure from the center line to one end of the wall. If the last partial tile is more than one half the width of a whole tile, begin your installation at the center line with the line at a tile joint. If the last tile is less than half a tile, begin at the center by placing a tile directly over the center line. Spacing this way will prevent an unsightly small fraction of tile at each corner. Work in areas 3 or 4 feet square so you will not have exposed adhesive on the wall for any length of time. Finish each wall to the ceiling before beginning the next.

When setting the tiles in the adhesive, press them firmly in place, using a slight turning motion. Fill the bottom row first. Leave one tile off the end of each additional horizontal row until you have reached the top of the "staircase." Check to see if both vertical and horizontal lines are straight with a level. If not, the number of tiles needing adjustment will be fewer than if the same number of full rows had been set. If they are level, though, keep adding tiles in the same "staircase" manner, frequently checking with the level. A little extra care spent on the junctions where the tiles come together will greatly enhance the finished work.

To cut tiles (Figure 3–43), first mark the glazed surface with a pencil or sharp crayon. If there are ridges on the back of the piece, mark parallel to, not across them. Using another tile as a straightedge, scratch along the indicated cut with a steel wheel glass cutter. Now place a finishing nail on the tile, face up, keeping it in line with the cut. Then exert pressure on both sides of the tile at the same time to make the break. Smooth any rough edges with a Carborundum stone. Some home handymen quickly develop a knack of giving one edge of the marked tile a sharp blow, which will cause it to break at the indicated place. Professional tile cutters are some-

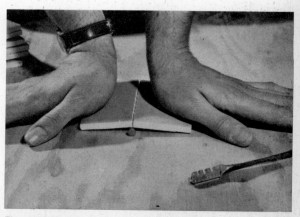

Figure 3—43. An easy method of cutting a tile.

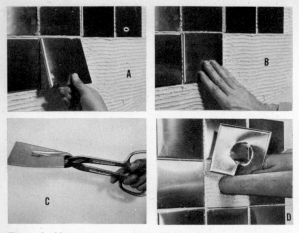

Figure 3—44. Installing metal tile: (A) Metal tiles are applied with a mastic adhesive. When grouting is planned, leave 1/8 inch between the tiles. (B) Slide the tile into final position with a firm diagonal motion to ensure a good contact with the mastic. (C) Cut the tile with a tinner's shears. If necessary, the edges may be smoothed with a metal file. (D) Slit a cutout to fit around a pipe. The tile is bent to slide over the pipe and snaps back flat.

times loaned or rented by tile dealers. This device is simply a big glass cutter in a frame to hold the tile securely. Simply draw the cutter across the tile, press the handle to make a clean break, and the tile is ready to install.

The shaped cuts, to fit the tile around plumbing, light fixtures, and such, can be made with a glass cutter, then nibbled away with a tile nipper. Take small bites, not large ones. By far the easiest method is the use of a "rod saw," a small abrasive rod that mounts in a hacksaw frame. Use it as you would a coping saw with plywood.

When tiling a bath you begin a bit differently. Find the lowest corner of the tub in its recess. From that corner, measure 1/4 inch plus the width of one tile up the wall, then mark the place. With a level, draw a horizontal line from this point all around the room. This line will be your reference line for the whole job, and you will begin by tiling *up* from it. While most adhesives will hold the unsupported tile firmly enough, you may feel a little safer if you tack a furring strip at the line to set the tiles on. When the wall above the line is complete, remove the furring strip, then add the course of tiles *below* the line (remember the 1/4 inch plus the width of one tile you skipped). As you work from the low corner of the tub toward the high corner (the difference probably will not be more than a 1/4 inch or so), you must maintain that 1/4-inch space by trimming small amounts off the bottom of the tiles with a tile nipper. That space is kept to insure adequate room for sealing between the tub and the wall. When the tub

enclosure is complete, go on to the other walls, but start at your reference line so the horizontal lines throughout the room will be uniform. In a bath installed this way, do not expect the tiles at the baseboard or floor to come out even. You will almost certainly have to trim them to fit.

As soon as all the tiles are in place, remove any spots of adhesive with thinner or solvent. Let the job set for a day and it is ready for grouting, or filling the spaces between tiles. Always wear rubber or plastic gloves. Most grouts are caustic and could cause problems for your hands, especially around the fingernails. Latex grouts are generally considered to be superior to regular grouts because they will "give" a little and are not as likely to crack when they dry. Many of the modern grouts come premixed and are available in a wide range of colors.

One of the easiest ways to apply grout to the tile joints is with a sponge, sponge float, or small squeegee (a smaller version of the kind used to wash windows). Using upward and sideward strokes, force the grout into the joints. Make sure all joints are completely filled and any air pockets have been eliminated. Grout only about 25 or 30 square feet at a time. A sponge doubled in half works well to grout corners and other areas where the squeegee cannot work. A few minutes after the grout has been applied, a thin film will appear over the entire tiled surface. Wipe it off lightly with a damp sponge, frequently rinsing the sponge out in clean water. Repeat this process until all the joints have been grouted. Then to smooth and harden the joints, strike them with a toothbrush handle or the head of a medium-sized nail. Although the nail does the best job, especially on grout that has already started to harden, care must be taken not to damage the remaining grout or to scratch the tile surface. Permit the tile grout to dry completely, usually about 48 hours, before using.

Plastic and metal tile. While plastic tiles cost about one-fifth less than ceramic tiles and in most cases will serve the same purpose, this wall material has never been too popular. The main reason is that it requires about the same amount of work to install as ceramic, but the finished job does not have the same beauty. On the other hand, metal tiles—copper, stainless steel, and aluminum—do have beauty, but their high cost usually limits their use to the grease-catching walls of kitchens.

The 4 1/4-inch square plastic and metal tiles can be bought in easy-to-use, peel-and-stick form as well as in the mastic-set type. The latter kind are installed in the same manner as ceramic tiles except that not all metal or plastic tiles require a grout filler in the joints. There is a mastic material, which can be applied to the joints and smoothed with the fingers to fill the joints, that can be used if desired or recommended for the type of tiles you wish to use. Certain plastic tiles make use of a plastic grout strip that is inserted in the joints and held in place with the adhesive that also holds the tile.

Cork tiles. Cork tiles in sizes ranging from 12 by 12 inches to 12 by 36 inches and in colors from light tan to dark brown are available for wall use. (Large panels — 4 by 8 feet — are also available and these are installed like fiberboard — page 77.) They are all about ½ inch thick.

Before starting any cork job, make sure that the wall or walls to be covered are clean, sound, and whole. After any necessary repairs have been made, remove the cap molding from the baseboard so the cork will be able to rest on it directly.

To tell if the wall is really square, measure exactly 4 feet up the wall from the top of the center of the baseboard. Run a horizontal line across the wall, using a level. Measure the height from the baseboard at each end as well as in the middle. Do the same from the ceiling. If there are any uneven areas, the cork tiles can be trimmed to fit by using a razor blade.

Cork tiles that already have an adhesive affixed to their backs are now available. To install these self-stick types, peel off the protective paper and press them into place. Set the first row of tiles along the wall's center line, starting at one end and working your way across. The next rows or courses above and below may overlap like brickwork, if you desire. Once the first courses are in place, line up the next tiles on the ones already in place.

Some cork tiles are set in adhesive. To install these, spread the adhesive in a wide swath, about 4 feet, using a serrated trowel. The tiles are then pressed into the adhesive and the work proceeds in the same manner as for the self-stick types.

If you plan to cover only a portion of the wall, it is wise to use a piece of quarter-round ½-inch molding to reinforce the edge since the cork can become ragged and crumbly without its edge protection.

Simulated brick and stonework. For interior use, simulated plastic bricks and stones are inexpensive, easy to install, and, in most cases, look like the real thing. But in addition to their decorative value, these textured wall surfaces can be installed without having to add bracing to the floor or a step to the foundation, which would be necessary with ordinary brick or stone because of the weight.

Imitation bricks and stones are made of various plastic materials; styrene, urethane, and rigid vinyl are the most common. Some are fire resistant and may be used as fascias for fireplaces. All false bricks and stones are highly durable and come in a wide variety of colors and styles (Figure 3–45). Some are sold in sheet form, while others are installed individually. They can even be obtained already applied to ¼- and ¾-inch plywood. Select whatever brand appears the most realistic to you.

Figure 3–45. Plastic brick and stone effects.

Some types can be used for both interior and exterior use.

When the stones and bricks are set individually, a mastic that is indistinguishable from real portland cement mortar is employed (Figure 3–46). This mastic is usually available in white, gray, tan,

Figure 3–46. The mortar for bricks and stonework usually comes in a tube. It is applied as shown.

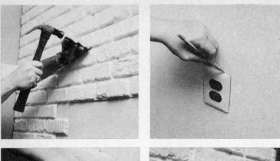

Figure 3–47. Steps in applying "sheet" bricks: *(top left)* The brick sheets are nailed in place with special nails furnished by the manufacturer. *(top right* and *bottom left)* All cuts are marked, and the cuts are made with a saber saw or a coping saw. *(bottom right)* The mortar is applied with a caulking gun to complete the job.

methods of installing his simulated bricks and stonework, a step-by-step procedure is not given here. Be sure to follow the maker's instructions exactly. In all cases the simulated material should be applied only to a surface that is dry and clean. Remove any loose pieces of wallpaper or paint and level any bumps or hollows with patching plaster or by sanding so the simulated material will have a flat surface to which it can adhere. If the wall surface is paint, it is usually wise to roughen the surface with a medium-grit sandpaper, scratching through the paint to the subsurface material. On the other hand, if the surface is new plaster or plasterboard, it should be given a prime coat of paint. Whatever wall surface you are working with, place a drop cloth or newspaper below the wall surface to catch any mastic mortar that is dropped. If the installation is to extend to the ceiling, use the top of the wall as a starting reference line. From the top of the wall, draw a vertical line down the wall on each side of the area to be covered. Use either a carpenter's level or a plumb line to make sure the lines are vertical. If the installation is to run the entire width of the wall, the room corners can serve as the vertical lines. Incidentally, most manufacturers of imitation brick and stone supply L-shaped pieces for inside and outside corners; they give the finished "masonry" work a more realistic appearance.

Quarried stone. Lightweight, natural quarried stone that is held in place by special clips can be applied over almost any surface, including wood or plywood, brick or cement block, on either interior or exterior surfaces. Each piece of the stone is 1 inch thick and is grooved at top and bottom to receive the heavy-duty wall anchors secured with special steel tie pins (Figure 3–48). No special foundation or floor reinforcement is necessary because a steel starter strip supports the bottom row of stone. A hammer and level are the basic tools needed to install the stone, which is furnished in random lengths from 8 to 24 inches in modular

or black, and it keeps the lightweight bricks and stones from slumping. Many of these imitation products employ the self-stick principle. That is, you just peel off the protective paper on the back and press the bricks or stones into place. Once they are in place, the mastic is worked into the space between them. When setting bricks and some stone patterns, check frequently to make certain that the rows are level and that the spacing between them is relatively uniform. Some stone patterns look best if installed in a random pattern.

Since each manufacturer has slightly different

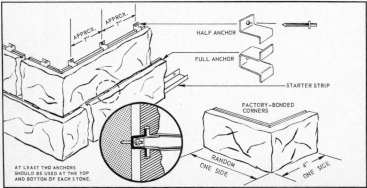

Figure 3–48. Applying real stone veneer with clips.

Figure 3—49. A mirrored wall makes any room appear larger.

heights of 4 and 8 inches. Factory-bonded corners are also available. After the stone is applied, any mortar can be used to fill the joints.

Mirrored walls. While virtually everyone knows about the "looking glass" function and average decorative uses of mirrors, many homeowners overlook the total potential of mirrors as remodeling design tools. Properly employed, mirrors are capable of expanding space, multiplying beauty, camouflaging structural flaws, and in many other ways supplying a unique visual element that offers almost magical solutions to various "knotty" design problems.

Basically, the feeling of depth that a mirror supplies gives a feeling of space where no space exists. In problem rooms this means walls can be visually moved outward, ceilings pushed upward, and space generally manipulated at will. If an area tends to be too long and narrow, a mirrored side wall visually broadens the corridor. If a room is short

and boxy, a mirrored end wall extends the depth. And in low rooms, there is no better way to raise the roof, visually, than to butt a mirror against the ceiling line.

Ordinarily, we think of a mirror's reflection as a doubling effect. In many cases, however, it is an even higher multiplier. By mirroring two adjacent walls of a small bath, for example, the apparent room dimensions are quadrupled, not doubled. While this technique should be used judiciously to avoid a busy or confused effect, it often can be worked to advantage in confined areas such as a bath or foyer.

In addition to multiplying space, mirrors also can create pleasant duplications of an important accessory. A decorative wall sconce, for example, when mounted on a mirror, becomes an unusual twin decorative device. A bell-shaped chandelier mounted flush on a mirrored ceiling becomes a

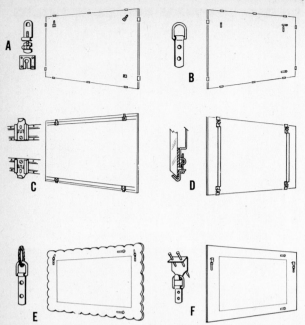

Figure 3–50. Installation of mirrors: (A) A venetian wall mirror is mounted on a hardboard back with two adjustable hangers and a swivel. The mirror may be hung in a vertical or a horizontal position. Leveling screws incorporated in the hanger assembly make it possible to level the mirror. (B) This mirror is mounted on a hardboard back with four steel strap hangers, which have been riveted to the back before assembly. Heavy picture hooks or wire is used for wall mounting. The mirror may be hung in a vertical or a horizontal position. (C) This backless mirror is intended for flush mounting. Two metal straps are affixed to the wall by screws or anchors. The bottom strap has permanent clips, allowing the mirror to slip into the proper groove. Top clips are adjustable and may be pressed tightly to the top of the mirror after mounting. (D) Two harness straps are attached to a mirror without a hardboard back. Adjustment screws are provided to secure the mirror. Two heavy brads or picture hooks that penetrate the wall at an angle are used to mount the mirror. (E and F) The backs of these framed mirrors are provided with steel strap hangers, which may be secured to the wall with heavy-duty picture wire and hooks or with a double brad hanger. Note that two separate loops of picture wire are used to avoid shearing the wire.

dazzling crystal globe. And in an instance such as this, the elegant effect of the crystal sphere is achieved at half the cost of the larger chandelier that the mirror implies is there.

A home remodeler who thinks of today's mirrors as merely clear silvered "looking glasses" is missing the full potential in color, pattern, texture, and styling variations modern production processes now make possible. If it appears that a clear mirror would be too bright or harsh for a certain installation, the designer may select a mirror made from a modern tinted plate glass. Unlike the colored glasses of the past, today's glasses, with their neutral gray and bronze hues, do not distort color values, providing a handsome muted effect while still reflecting the true colors of the room's decor. Improved production techniques also are responsible for a revival of the antique mirror. The smoky, shadowy effects possible today are startling in themselves, but these effects can be further heightened by applying a random veining in one or more of a variety of colors.

While there are countless accepted methods for installing all types of mirrors, this book shows nine commonly used installation techniques for standard and custom mirrors. The various styles of clips, brackets, and other mirror hardware shown here were developed in conjunction with and meet the standards developed by mirror manufacturers. By using any combination of hardware and installation methods, very good results may be obtained.

The mirror installer should always inspect the wall carefully before installation. Back-up wall surfaces must be smooth, firm, and thoroughly dry. In new construction or places of high humidity, a few minutes spent in sizing the wall with shellac or asphalt may save the cost of replacement. In addition, space should be provided between the mirror back and back-up wall for ventilation. Following installation, the face of the mirror should be cleaned with a mild liquid cleaner and soft cloth. Take care never to paint around the edges of mirrors or clean with acids or harsh cleaners.

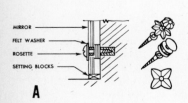
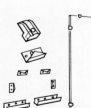
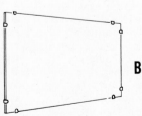

Figure 3–51. (A) Custom mirrors may be mounted with rosettes or buttons. Such hardware is sold complete with a special type of screw and flat washers. Three of the many available designs are shown here. The cross section shows the wall anchoring technique. (B) Custom mirrors may be mounted to the wall by plastic clips or metal channel clips or by a combination of clips and bottom molding. (C) The mounting of mirrors with mastic should be avoided if possible, but when many segments or blocks of mirrors are part of a design, this method may be required. The mirror manufacturer should be asked to recommend a brand of mastic. The diagram shows a pattern for applying mastic over 25 percent of the back surface. Mastic is available in cans, pails, or tubes. As a safety precaution, clips or molding should be used around the mirror perimeter.

Ceilings and Walls

Mirror tiles. Usually made in either 12-by-12-inch or 18-by-18-inch sizes, mirror tiles are available either plain or in a variety of colors and delicately etched patterns. They are installed by using adhesive or by a self-stick method. When installing self-stick tiles, the backing paper is taken off and the tile is pressed into place. Either type of mirror tile should be installed only over a clean, smooth, and sound surface. If the wall surface is extremely uneven, a sheet of hardboard or plywood can be nailed to the studs to provide a base for the tiles. Before applying the tiles, wipe the wall area with a clean, dry cloth, removing any oil, grease, or wax. Make sure the area is completely dry. Draw a level base line on the wall, or attach a straight-edged board temporarily to the wall studs to serve as a guide. When using the adhesive method, spread the mastic in ribbons over 25 percent of the back (not too close to the edge). Then place the tile against the wall slightly above and to the side of its permanent location and slide it into place, thus spreading the adhesive. Follow the same procedure with the second tile, leaving a slight space between the tiles. Small cardboard spacer strips are inserted between the tiles as needed to allow for any slight unevenness in the wall surface; then the second tile is butted tightly against the first one. Follow this procedure with all tiles, on horizontal as well as verti-

Figure 3—53. Two applications of glass blocks.

Figure 3—54. Popular three-dimensional plastic wall coverings.

Figure 3—52. Mirror tiles are an easy way to install a mirrored wall.

cal joints. It is best, if possible, to let each row of tiles dry overnight before applying the next row. After all the tiles are installed and the adhesive has dried thoroughly, the spacer strips are removed.

Glass blocks. Glass blocks are especially recommended to anyone who is planning to erect partitions, sectional partitions, or decorative panels between rooms where both light and privacy, combined with a certain amount of decoration, are desired. Glass blocks should not be used as a substitute for windows, but as a means of making remodeled basement rooms, attics, or other parts of the home lighter and brighter and of providing extra light at points in the home where ordinary windows are not practical (Figure 3–53).

Glass blocks are hollow and come 3⅞ inches thick, and 6, 8, or 12 inches square. They are available in a variety of colors and designs, such as intaglio units, sculptured glass modules, and light-diffusing types. Glass blocks can be laid with mortar by the method used for bricklaying, and this method should always be used where dampness is present. A new prefabricated system for erecting interior sections with strips of wood and wedges is also available. This permits easy erection and complete disassembly with salvage of all parts. Instructions for both types vary. You should, therefore, check the manufacturer's directions for laying the glass blocks you buy and follow them to the letter.

INTERIOR DOORS, FRAMES, AND TRIM

On remodeling additions, interior trim, doorframes, and doors are normally installed after the finish floor is in place. Cabinets, built-in bookcases, fireplace mantels, and other millwork units are also placed and secured at this time.

The decorative treatment for interior doors, trim, and other millwork may be paint or a natural

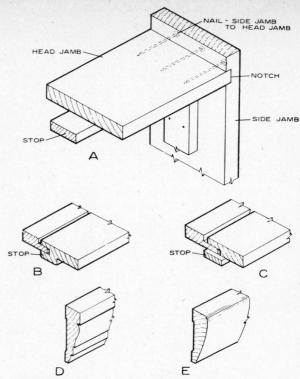

Figure 3–56. Interior door parts: (A) doorjambs and stops; (B) two-piece jamb; (C) three-piece jamb; (D) colonial casing; (E) ranch casing.

finish with stain, varnish, or other nonpigmented material. The paint or natural finish desired for the woodwork in various rooms often determines the type or species of wood to be used. Interior finish that is to be painted should be smooth, close-grained, and free from pitch streaks. Some species having these requirements in a high degree include ponderosa pine, Northern white pine, redwood, and spruce. When hardness and resistance to hard usage are additional requirements, species such as birch, gum, and yellow poplar are desirable.

For a natural finish treatment, a pleasing figure, hardness, and uniform color are usually desirable. Species with these requirements include ash, birch, cherry, maple, oak, and walnut. Some require staining for best appearance. Complete details on wood finishing can be found in Chapter 9.

Doors. In this chapter, we will concern ourselves with the interior door only. The installation of exterior doors is fully covered in Chapter 8.

Doorframes. Rough openings are usually framed out to be 3 inches more than the door height and 2½ inches more than the door width. This provides for the frame and its plumbing and leveling in the opening. Interior doorframes are made up

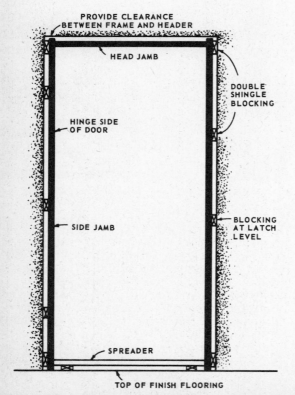

Figure 3–55. Doorframe in position with blocking and spreader.

of two side jambs and a head jamb and include stop moldings upon which the door closes. The most common of these jambs is the one-piece type (Figure 3–56A). Jambs may be obtained in standard 5¼-inch widths for plaster walls and 4⅝-inch widths for walls with ½-inch dry-wall finish. The two- and three-piece adjustable jambs are also standard types (Figure 3–56B and C). Their principal advantage is in being adaptable to a variety of wall thicknesses. Some manufacturers produce interior doorframes with the door fitted and prehung, ready for installing. Application of the casing completes the job. When used with two- or three-piece jambs, casings can even be installed at the factory.

Common minimum widths for single interior doors are: (a) bedrooms and other habitable rooms, 2 feet 6 inches; (b) bathrooms, 2 feet 4 inches; and (c) small closets and linen closets, 2 feet. These sizes vary a great deal, and sliding doors, folding door units, and similar types are often used for wardrobes and may be 6 feet or more in width. However, in most cases, the jamb, stop, and casing parts are used in some manner to frame and finish the opening.

Standard interior and exterior door heights are 6 feet 8 inches for first floors, but 6-foot 2-inch and 6-foot 4-inch doors are sometimes used on the upper floors.

Casing. Casing is the edge trim around interior door openings and is also used to finish the room side of windows and exterior door frames. Casing usually varies in width from 2¼ to 3½ inches, depending on the style. Casing may be obtained in thicknesses from ½ to ¾ inch, although ¹¹⁄₁₆ inch is standard in many of the narrow-line patterns. Figure 3–56D and E shows two common patterns.

Interior doors. The two general interior door types are the flush and the panel door. Novelty doors, such as the folding door unit, can be flush or louvered. Most standard interior doors are 1⅜ inches thick.

The flush interior door is usually made up with a hollow core of light framework of some type with thin plywood or hardboard (Figure 3–57A).

Plywood-faced flush doors may be obtained in gum, birch, oak, mahogany, and woods of other species, most of which are suitable for natural finish. Nonselected grades are usually painted, as are hardboard-faced doors.

The panel door consists of solid stiles (vertical side members), rails (cross pieces), and panel filters of various types. The five-cross panel and the colonial-type panel doors are perhaps the most common of this style (Figure 3–57B and C). The louvered door (Figure 3–57D) is also popular and is commonly used for closets because it provides some ventilation. Large openings for wardrobes are finished with sliding or folding doors, or with flush or louvered doors (Figure 3–57E). Such doors are usually 1⅛ inches thick.

Hinged doors should open or swing in the direction of natural entry, against a blank wall whenever possible, and should not be obstructed by other swinging doors. Doors should *never* be hinged to swing into a hallway.

Cutting the opening. If you wish to construct a new inside doorway, you must first make the opening in the wall. After selecting the position for the proposed door, you should determine the location of the studs. If possible, one side of the door should be located next to a stud. The width of the door will probably make it necessary to cut through at least two studs to the left or right. Using a plumb line, a long straightedge and level, or a mason's level, draw an outline of the door at least 5 inches more than the height and 4 inches more than the width of the door itself. This allowance provides for the thickness of the door frame, for the shims or wedges by which the frame is set true, for expansion and door-swinging clearance, and for the finish floor, if laid after the doorway is framed. If the finish floor is already laid, deduct its thickness from the height allowance.

When cutting through a plaster wall, cut along the outline with a cold chisel or an old wood chisel and hammer. To prevent jagged edges, a long board or scantling can be lightly nailed along each line before chiseling. The horizontal line for the header

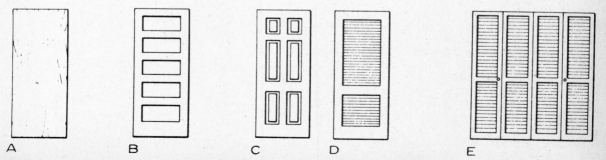

Figure 3–57. Interior doors: (A) flush; (B) panel (five-cross); (C) panel (colonial); (D) louvered; (E) folding (louvered).

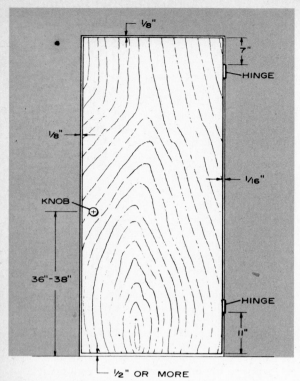

Figure 3–58. Door clearances.

with three sevenpenny or eightpenny coated nails. The assembled frames are then fastened in the rough openings by shingle wedges used between the side jamb and the stud. One jamb is plumbed and leveled using four or five sets of shingle wedges for the height of the frame. Two eightpenny finishing nails are used at each wedged area, one driven so that the doorstop will cover it. The opposite side jamb is now fastened in place with shingle wedges and finishing nails, using the first jamb as a guide in keeping a uniform width.

Casings are nailed to both the jamb and the framing studs or header, allowing about a ³⁄₁₆-inch edge distance from the face of the jamb. Finish or casing nails in 6d or 7d sizes, depending on the thickness of the casing, are used to nail into the stud. Fourpenny or 5d finishing nails or 1½-inch brads are used to fasten the thinner edge of the casing to the jamb. With hardwood, it is usually advisable to predrill to prevent splitting. Nails in the casing are located in pairs and spaced about 16 inches apart along the full height of the opening and at the head jamb.

Casing used with any form of molded shape must have a mitered joint at the corners. When casing is square-edged, a butt joint may be made at the junction of the side and head casing.

The door opening is now complete except for fitting and securing the hardware and nailing the stops in proper position. Interior doors are normally hung with two 3½-inch loose-pin butt hinges. The door is fitted into the opening with the clearances shown in Figure 3–58. The clearance and location of hinges, lock set, and doorknob may vary somewhat, but all must closely conform to good millwork standards. The edge of the lock stile should be beveled slightly to permit the door to clear the jamb when swung open. If the door is to swing across heavy carpeting, the bottom clearance may be slightly more.

In fitting doors, the stops are usually temporarily nailed in place until the door has been hung.

is chiseled along the nearest interval between laths. After large starting holes are bored at the upper corners, a coarse compass saw or power saber saw should be used, since it will bend less than the ordinary handsaw when cutting across the laths down the vertical lines chiseled in the plaster. These vertical lines are continued down through the baseboard, and at the baseboard a handsaw is used. The lath and plaster within the opening can now be removed. The exposed studs are sawed horizontally across a level at their tops and pulled loose from their floor plate. If the plate is above floor level, it too must be sawed flush with the floor level.

Dry walls (plasterboard, wallboard, and paneling) are handled in much the same manner, except that chiseling is not necessary.

Doorframe and trim installation. For both new and old work, Figure 3–59 shows the usual type of partition wall framing with the door opening made. Notice that a double header is installed at the top and that extra studs are set in at the sides. After preparing the opening, you are ready to install the doorframe.

When the frame and doors are not assembled and prefitted, the side jambs should be fabricated by nailing through the notch into the head jamb

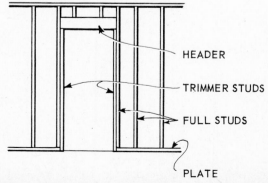

Figure 3–59. Rough framing for a door.

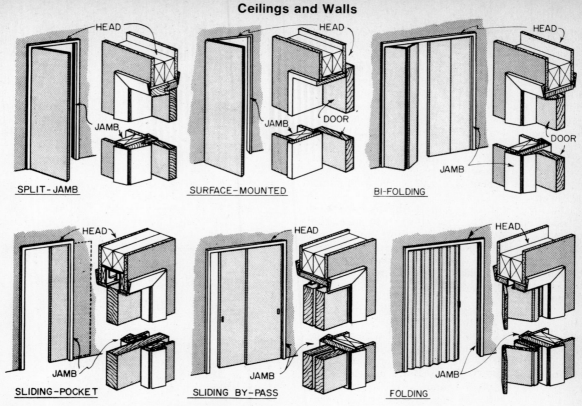

Figure 3–60. Framing methods for different types of interior doors.

Stops for doors in single-piece jambs are generally $^7/_{16}$ inch thick and may be $^3/_4$ inch to $2^1/_4$ inches wide. They are installed with a mitered joint at the junction of the side and head jambs. A 45-degree bevel cut at the bottom of the stop, about 1 to $1^1/_2$ inches above the finish floor, will eliminate a dirt pocket and make cleaning or refinishing of the floor easier. Some manufacturers supply prefitted door jambs and doors with the hinge slots routed and ready for installation. A similar door buck of sheet metal with formed stops and casing is also available.

Installation of door hardware. Hardware for doors may be obtained in a number of finishes, with brass, bronze, and nickel perhaps the most common. Door sets are usually classed as: (a) entry lock for exterior doors; (b) bathroom set (inside lock control with safety slot for opening from the outside); (c) bedroom lock (keyed lock); and (d) passage set (without lock).

The use of three hinges for hanging $1^3/_4$-inch exterior doors and two hinges for the lighter interior doors is common practice. There is some tendency for the exterior side to warp during the winter because of the difference in exposure on the opposite sides. The three hinges reduce this tendency. Three

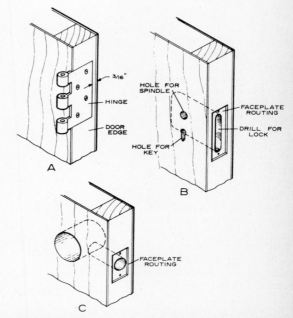

Figure 3–61. Installation of door hardware: (A) hinge; (B) mortise lock; (C) bored lock set.

hinges are also useful on doors that lead to unheated attics and for wider and heavier doors that may be used within the house.

Loose-pin butt hinges should be used and must be of the proper size for the door they support. For 1¾-inch-thick doors, use 4-by-4-inch butts; for 1⅜-inch doors, 3½- by-3½-inch butts. After the door is fitted to the framed opening, with the proper clearances, hinge halves are fitted to the door. They are routed into the door edge with about a ³⁄₁₆-inch back distance (Figure 3–61A). One hinge half should be set flush with the surface and fastened square with the edge of the door. Screws are included with each pair of hinges.

The door is now placed in the opening and blocked up at the bottom for proper clearance. The jamb is marked at the hinge locations, and the remaining hinge half is routed and fastened in place. The door is then positioned in the opening and the pins are slipped in place. If hinges have been installed correctly and the jambs are plumb, the door will swing freely.

Types of door locks differ with regard to installation, first cost, and the amount of labor required to set them. Lock sets are supplied with instructions for installation. Some types require drilling of the edge and face of the door and routing of the edge to accommodate the lock set and faceplate (Figure 3–61B). A more common bored type (Figure 3–61C) is much easier to install as it requires only one hole drilled in the edge and one in the face of the door. Boring jigs and faceplate markers

Figure 3–63. Steps required to hang a door.

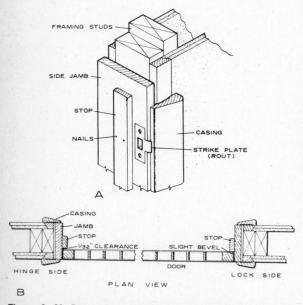

Figure 3–62. Door details (split-jamb): (A) installation of strike plate; (B) location of stops.

are available to provide accurate installation. The lock should be installed so that the doorknob is 36 to 38 inches above the floor line. Most sets come with paper templates marking the location of the lock and size of the holes to be drilled.

The strike plate is routed into the doorjamb

Figure 3—64. Installing a prehung door.

and holds the door in place by contact with the latch. To install the strike plate, mark the location of the latch on the doorjamb to determine the correct position of the strike plate. Rout out the marked outline with a chisel and also rout for the latch (Figure 3–62A). The strike plate should be flush with or slightly below the face of the doorjamb. When the door is latched, its face should be flush with the edge of the jamb.

The stops, which have been set temporarily during the fitting of the door and the installation of the hardware, may now be nailed in place permanently. Finish nails or brads, 1½ inches long, should be used. The stop at the lock side should be nailed first, and should be set tight against the door face when the door is latched. Space the nails 16 inches apart in pairs.

The stop behind the hinge side is nailed next, and a 1/32-inch clearance from the door face should be allowed to prevent scraping as the door is opened. The head-jamb stop is then nailed in place. Remember that when door and trim are painted, some of the clearances will be taken up.

Sliding doors. There are two basic arrangements for sliding doors: (1) by-pass installation, which is used primarily for large closets and (2) the recess installation, which slides in a wall pocket.

By-pass installation. Standard sliding door hardware for this type of installation is available at most lumberyards. The procedure for installation is as follows:

1. Sliding door and finished trim are added after the wall surfacing material has been put on. Using a piece of 1-inch stock, cut the jamb to the door width. Nail it in place.

2. Side doorjambs are nailed to the studs framing the door opening. Attach the sliding door track

with the screws provided so that the outside edge is 1½ inches from the edge of the top jamb.

3. Cut or buy two flush doors so that their combined width equals that of the closet plus 1 inch for overlap.

4. Attach the hanger to the doors with the screws provided (see Figure 3–66). A slot-type fin-

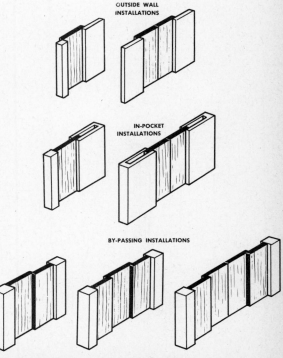

Figure 3—65. Sliding door arrangements.

Figure 3–66. Sliding door hardware.

ger pull or a round one similar to that used on cabinet doors is added to each door. Place the pull so that it is 48 inches from floor level.

5. Attach a strip guide to the rear of each door. After hanging the door in place, set the floor plate in place near the center of the closet opening.

6. Cut casing, a 1-by-4-inch or 1-by-6-inch or decorative trim, to frame the door opening, mitering the two corners just as you would for a standard door (see page 94). Nail the top casing to the jamb and through the wall material into the header so that the bottom edge is ¾ inch below the top of the door. Side casings are then attached. Use eight-penny finishing nails and countersink the heads below the surface of the wood.

Figure 3–67. In-pocket wall frame unit.

In-pocket installation. When the sliding doors are to be installed into a wall recess or pocket, the partition wall does not have to be made wider. If you buy packaged pocket door hardware at a lumberyard, the installation will be greatly simplified. The package includes metal studs with wood inserts, an overhead track from which to hang the door, and a pair of hangers with nylon rollers, which are screwed to the door and positioned so that the rollers ride in the track. Two pairs of metal studs take the place of the usual 2 × 4 wood studs. The metal studs are placed so that the sliding door rides between them in the recess or pocket in the wall. The wall material (shown in Figure 3–67) is nailed to the wooden inserts in the metal studs after the installation is completed. If you prefer not to buy the packaged material, you can build your own framing around the recess.

In either case, hang the door on the track. It is better to use adjustable door hangers as they make it easier to compensate for an uneven floor or door. While flush doors are most popular, you can use any type; but you must employ finger pulls, available in most hardware stores, set flush with the door surfaces. Also, set a recessed finger hold in the edge of the door 36 inches from the floor. A latch may be provided to lock the door. There are several types available; mounting instructions are supplied by the manufacturer.

Folding doors. There are two basic types of folding doors: (1) the bi-fold style and (2) the accordion style. Both are equally easy to install.

Bi-fold door installation. Bi-fold doors are available in either flush panel or louvered styles and come complete with all the hardware necessary for installation. It is important when determining the correct size of the doors required to know the type of hardware that will be used. For example, in the bi-fold hardware arrangement shown in Figure 3–68, the door size is determined by measuring the distance between jambs and subtracting 1 inch clearance. The doors should be 1½ inches shorter than the height of the opening.

While each manufacturer has a slightly different method of installing his hardware, the following description of installing a bi-fold door is more or less typical. First locate and install the pivot pins at the top of the doors and the pivot brackets and aligners at the bottom of the doors. Then mount the track across the top of the jamb. The doors are hung in place by inserting the pivot pins into the track and raising the doors until they slide into place over the bottom brackets. The height of the bottom brackets should be adjusted if there is insufficient clearance for slipping the doors into place. A wood molding strip is usually nailed at the top of the opening after the doors are installed to hide the door track from sight. Once all the adjustments have been made to the doors, care-

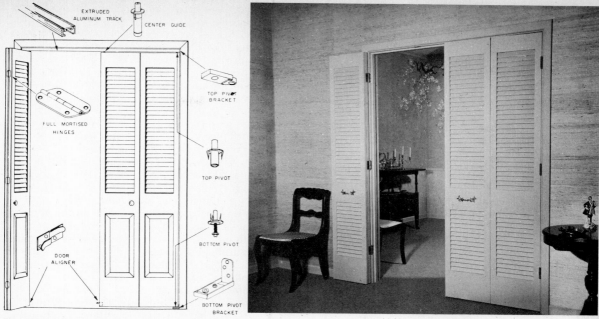

Figure 3—68. *(left)* Bi-fold hardware; *(right)* a bi-fold door in place.

fully retighten all the adjustment screws in order to guarantee permanent alignment and smooth action.

Installation of an accordion-style folding door. This type of door is available in wood, plastic, and cloth finish and blends well into any architectural style. To replace an old swinging-type door with a standard accordion-style folding door, use the following procedure:

1. After removing the old doors and hardware, pry off the doorstop on the sides and top, using a chisel. Then fill the holes and recesses left by the hinges with smoothed blocks of wood and wood filler.

2. Check the doorframe to make certain that it is square. If the frame is not square, measure the distance across the face of the doorjamb and cut three pieces of ½-inch lumber to the proper width to fit both sides and across the top. Shim them square, nail them with 1½-inch brads, and fill the gaps with wood filler.

3. Check the length of the overhead track. If it is too long, use a hacksaw to cut the track ⅛ inch less than the actual door opening. If there are any rough edges, file them smooth.

4. Position the track overhead and mark the location of the predrilled holes in the track. Drill pilot holes at these marked locations.

5. Slide the grooved door runners onto the track, making sure that each works freely and is secure. Place screws through the overhead track into the predrilled pilot holes in the doorframe and

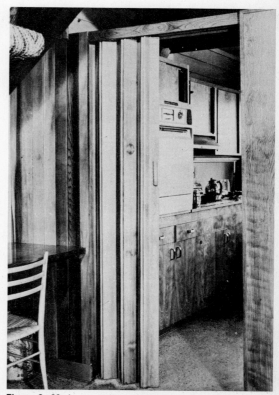

Figure 3—69. An accordion-style folding door in use.

Figure 3—70. Installing an accordion-style folding door.

the surfaces are finished later. This method eliminates the necessity of removing the old finish.

The simplest way to apply the covering material is to cut it slightly larger than the door, and, after application, carefully saw off the excess pieces and smooth down the edges to be flush with the edges of the door. When the door edges are rounded, so that there is a groove between the door and the covering, or if they are badly marred, it will be necessary to use facing strips. These are applied before the covering material is put on. First remove the door and rip ⅜ inch off its edges, all around. Then rip ⅜-inch stock to a width slightly greater than the thickness of the door and attach it to the edges with glue and finishing nails or screws. Miter the strips at the corners and plane them flush with the door on both sides. Spread glue on the edges of the facing strips and the covering material, and use screws to fasten the covering material down securely, countersinking the heads below the surface. When the glue is dry, plane the covering edges flush, and round the corners lightly with a fine sandpaper.

Before the door is rehung, the holes for the hardware may be drilled. When reinstalling the door, you will have to reset the hinges, lock striker plate, and stop strips to take care of the added thickness. The new surface may be either stained or painted. If hardwood plywood is used, the flush door may be finished to match the furniture in the room.

Hanging a mirror on a door. A full-length door mirror is useful for everyone. To overcome the problem of the added mirror weight, it is wise to locate a third hinge halfway between the present upper and lower hinges.

anchor the unit.

6. Fasten one edge of the sliding door to the doorframe by using screw-type nails. Then apply the latch to the other side of the door opening. It is a good idea to apply a light lubricant to the runners to make them slide more freely. The door is then ready for use.

Modernizing old doors. When old interior doors are badly scarred or so out of date that they will not harmonize with a modernized room, you can avoid the expense of replacing them by covering them with ¼-inch plywood or ⅛-inch hardboard.

In many cases it is possible to glue the plywood or hardboard directly to the door, provided the varnish or paint is entirely removed from the raised surfaces so that the adhesive will adhere. You can use a removing chemical and scraper, an electric paint remover, a blowtorch, or even repeated treatment with sandpaper. Wash all raised surfaces from which the paint has been removed with wood alcohol. Let the surfaces dry and then sand them smooth. Plywood or hardboard can also be fastened to the old door with finishing nails or flathead screws. The nail holes and screwheads can be filled when

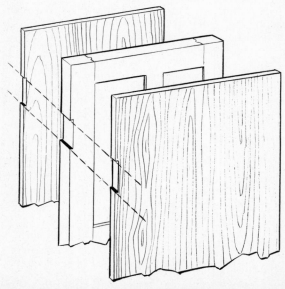

Figure 3—71. Covering an old door with ¼-inch plywood.

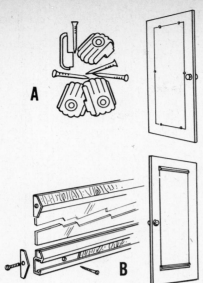

Figure 3—72. (A) The standard method of mounting door mirrors requires six plastic clips and screws, which are generally provided. The door may be removed from its hinges, if desired, and work performed on a flat plane. (B) Another method of mounting door mirrors employs metal channels top and bottom. The hardware is mounted and secured to the door by decorative plastic or metal molding, which conceals the screws.

The standard method of mounting door mirrors is with six plastic clips (shown in Figure 3–72) and screws, which are generally provided. The door may be removed from its hinges, if desired, and the work performed on a flat plane.

Another method of mounting door mirrors is by the use of metal channels top and bottom. Hardware is mounted and secured to the door by decorative plastic or metal molding that will conceal the screws. Where flush doors are involved, small expansion-type bolts should be used because most interior flush doors have hollow cores.

Where panel doors are involved, the central panel may be removed and the mirror installed to replace it. The wood panel is usually beveled and held in place with molding strips that can be pried up and out. If the panel is mortised in place, a saw cut all around will remove it and still leave a sufficient amount of the solid surface required for mirror mounting. Since most interior paneled doors are usually 1⅛ inches thick, a sheet of hardboard cut to the exact opening size may be used as backing support for the mirror. This backing piece should be held in place with a metal L-shaped molding drilled for 1-inch flathead screws. The mirror is then set in place on the opposite side (making sure the glass, too, is cut to the exact size of the opening, or the opening is enlarged to fit the mirror) and likewise held fast with similar metal molding.

Hardwood moldings may be substituted to contain the mirrors and backing, but when these are used it must be anticipated that the molding has but ⅜-inch bearing surfaces.

How to close up a doorway. Earlier in the chapter we described how to open a wall for a doorway. Now let us take a look at how to close up an undesirable door. The procedure is basically as follows:

1. Remove the door, hinges, and hardware. Using a chisel, carefully pry off the molding. As with any removal job, work carefully so that you can salvage as much of the trim and lumber as possible.

2. Using a nailer puller and wrecking bar, remove the doorframe. It may be necessary to use a hacksaw blade to cut off the nails holding the jamb to the studs. To prevent splitting the wood, pull out the complete doorframe as a unit. If the unit is stuck, tap it lightly with a hammer along all its edges. Should this not free it, look for unpulled nails. Once the frame is removed, pull up the door saddle.

3. Cut and nail into position 2×4's, flat side down, at both the top and bottom of the opening. A third stud should be located in the center of the opening and toenailed top and bottom.

4. To complete the project, apply the desired wall surfacing material to both sides of the opening framework. When nailing or gluing it in place, be sure to fasten it to all three upright studs and across the top and bottom. Install a piece of baseboard or other desired trim. After all cracks and nail holes have been filled, finish the wall as you wish.

Moldings. Moldings can work magic for the interior of one's home. In fact, molding details can set the theme of your home's decor. They can make a room traditional or modern, contemporary or period. With moldings you can give your home a whole new appearance without changing existing furniture. In addition, molding helps to conceal the room's architectural and carpentry faults. For instance, trim molding installed horizontally will make a short room look longer and lower, while a molding installed vertically will often make a low room appear higher. And when it comes to carpentry work, no one is perfect. Even the professional carpenter knows better than to hope for a precision fit each time he cuts a piece of paneling to fit against the ceiling or around a door or window. He relies on wood moldings to conceal what may even be a mild error of measurement behind a touch of elegance that adds richness and warmth to the entire room.

Here is a rundown of the more popular types of interior trim (Figure 3–73):

1. Baseboard protects the bottom of the wall from wear and tear and conceals irregularities at the wall-floor joint. Quarter-round or base shoe moldings may be used to complete the trim.

2. Casing is used to trim doors, windows, and

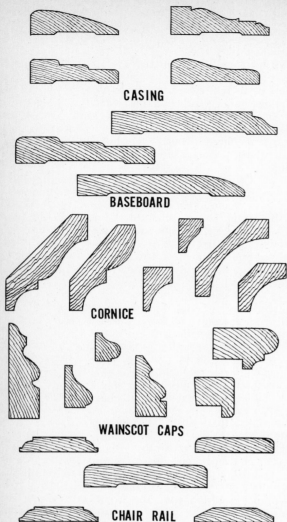

Figure 3-73. Moldings used as interior trim.

CASING

BASEBOARD

CORNICE

WAINSCOT CAPS

CHAIR RAIL

dining room. It is installed at a height appropriate to the furniture style.

There are also many other moldings—quarter-rounds, half-rounds, stops, screen moldings, balusters, and picture molds—that may be employed to add beauty to a room. Actually the variety of moldings that are available seems endless, as a look at the molding board of your lumber supply dealer will suggest. While there are vinyl-coated, plastic, or metal moldings available, most are made of wood. As has been said before, wood moldings are one of the least expensive ways to decorate a home.

Trim installation. The casing around the window frames on the interior of the house should have the same pattern as that used around the interior door frames. Other trim that is used for a double-hung window frame includes the sash stops, stool, and apron (Figure 3-74A). Another approach is to enclose the entire opening around the window with casing (Figure 3-74B). The stool is then a filler member between the bottom sash rail and the bottom casing.

The stool is the horizontal trim member that laps the windowsill and extends beyond the casing at the sides, with each end notched against the wall. The apron serves as a finish member below the stool. The window stool is the first piece of

other openings. It may also be used for chair rails, cabinet trim, and decorative purposes.

3. Cornice, whether of the crown or cove type, gives a rich appearance wherever two planes, such as a wall and ceiling, meet. It is also used for trimming exposed beams and, singly or in combination with other moldings, in decorative mantels and frames.

4. Wainscot caps are applied to the top of wainscoting. Some patterns have a wrap-around lip to conceal craftsmanship defects. Others may be used to cap decorative baseboards.

5. Chair rail protects the wall in areas subject to chair-back damage, such as the playroom and

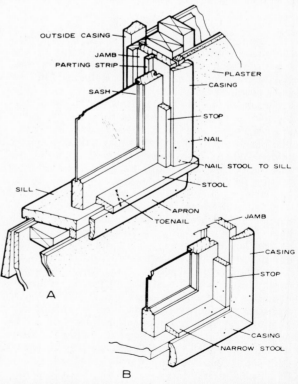

Figure 3-74. Installation of window trim: (A) with stool and apron; (B) enclosed with casing.

window trim to be installed and is notched and fitted against the edge of the jamb and the plaster line, with the outside edge being flush against the bottom rail of the window sash. The stool is blind-nailed at the ends so that the casing and the stop will cover the nailheads. Predrilling is usually necessary to prevent splitting. The stool should also be nailed at midpoint to the sill and to the apron with finishing nails. Face-nailing to the sill is sometimes substituted or supplemented with toenailing of the outer edge to the sill.

The casing is applied and nailed as described for doorframes, except that the inner edge is flush with the inner face of the jambs so that the stop will cover the joint between the jamb and casing. The window stops are then nailed to the jambs so that the window sash slides smoothly. Channel-type weather stripping often includes full-width metal subjambs into which the upper and lower sash slide, replacing the parting strip. Stops are located against these instead of the sash to provide a small amount of pressure. The apron is cut to a length equal to the outer width of the casing line. It is nailed to the windowsill and to the 2-by-4-inch framing sill below.

When casing is used to finish the bottom of the window frame as well as the sides and top, the narrow stool butts against the side window jamb. Casing is then mitered at the bottom corners and nailed as previously described.

Base and ceiling moldings. Base molding serves as a finish between the finished wall and floor. It is available in several widths and forms. Two-piece base consists of a baseboard topped with a small base cap (Figure 3–75A). When plaster is

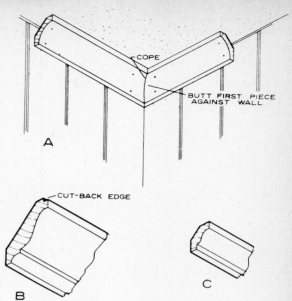

Figure 3–76. Ceiling moldings: (A) installation (inside corner); (B) crown molding; (C) small crown molding.

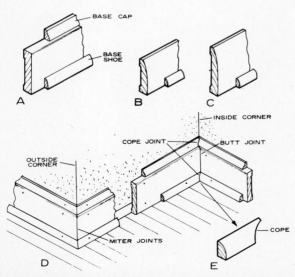

Figure 3–75. Base moldings: (A) square-edge base; (B) narrow ranch base; (C) wide ranch base; (D) installation; (E) cope.

not straight and true, the small base molding will conform more closely to the variations than will the wider base alone. A common size for this type of baseboard is $5/8$ inch by $3 1/4$ inches or wider. One-piece base varies in size from $7/16$ inch by $2 1/4$ inches to $1/2$ inch by $3 1/4$ inches and wider. Although a wood member is desirable at the junction of the wall and carpeting to serve as a protective "bumper," wood trim is sometimes eliminated entirely.

Most baseboards are finished with a base shoe, $1/2$ inch by $3/4$ inch in size (Figure 3–75B and C). A single-base molding without the shoe is sometimes placed at the wall-floor junction, especially where carpeting might be used.

Square-edged baseboard should be installed with a butt joint at inside corners and a mitered joint at outside corners. It should be nailed to each stud with two eightpenny finishing nails. Molded single-piece base, base moldings, and base shoe should have a coped joint at inside corners and a mitered joint at outside corners. A coped joint is one in which the first piece is square-cut against the plaster or base and the second molding coped. This is accomplished by sawing a 45-degree miter cut and, with a coping saw, trimming the molding along the inner line of the miter. The base shoe should be nailed into the subfloor with long slender nails and not into the baseboard itself. Thus, if there is a small amount of shrinkage of the joists, no opening will occur under the shoe.

Ceiling moldings are sometimes used at the

junction of wall and ceiling for an architectural effect or to terminate dry-wall paneling of gypsum board or wood (Figure 3–76A). As in the base moldings, inside corners should also be cope-jointed. This insures a tight joint and retains a good fit if there are minor moisture changes.

A cutback edge at the outside of the molding will partially conceal any unevenness of the plaster and make painting easier where there are color changes (Figure 3–76B). For gypsum dry-wall construction, a small simple molding might be desirable (Figure 3–76C). Finish nails should be driven into the upper wall plates and also into the ceiling joists for large moldings when possible.

Chapter 4

FLOORS AND STAIRS

Chapter 4

Floors, like walls, are found extensively in houses and are not easy to change. Whether applying a floor material to a new addition to your home or reconditioning a floor in an existing portion of the structure, you should choose the finished flooring most carefully and wisely.

The term "finished flooring" refers, of course, to the material used as the final wearing surface that is applied to a floor. Perhaps in its simplest form it might be paint over a concrete floor slab. One of the many resilient tile floorings applied directly to the slab would likely be an improvement from the standpoint of maintenance, but not necessarily from the comfort standpoint. In fact, numerous flooring materials now available may be used over a variety of floor systems. Each has a property that adapts it to a particular usage. Of the practical properties, perhaps durability and maintenance ease are the most important. However, initial cost, comfort, and beauty or appearance must also be considered. Specific service requirements may call for special properties, such as resistance to hard wear or comfort.

There is a wide selection of wood materials that may be used for flooring. Hardwoods and softwoods are available as strip flooring in a variety of widths and thicknesses and as random-width planks and block flooring. Linoleum, asphalt, rubber, cork, vinyl, and other materials in tile or sheet forms can also be used. Tile flooring is also available in particleboard, which is manufactured by combining small wood particles with resin under extremely high pressure. Ceramic tile and carpeting are used in many areas in ways not thought practical a few years ago. Plastic floor coverings, including the so-called seamless poured type used over concrete or stable wood subfloor, are another variation in the types of finishes available. Slate is also good as flooring material for entryways and other small areas in the home.

WOOD FLOORING

Softwood finish flooring costs less than most hardwood species and is often used to good advantage in bedroom and closet areas where traffic is light. It might also be selected to fit the interior decor. It is less dense than the hardwoods and less wear-resistant, and shows surface abrasions more readily. Softwoods most commonly used for flooring are Southern pine, Douglas fir, redwood, and Western hemlock. Table 4–1 lists the grades and gives descriptions of softwood strip flooring. Softwood flooring has tongue-and-groove edges and may be hollow-backed or grooved. Some types are also end-matched. Vertical-grain flooring generally has better wearing qualities than flat-grain flooring under hard usage.

Hardwoods most commonly used for flooring are red and white oak, beech, birch, maple, and pecan. The grades, types, and sizes of hardwood strip flooring are also given in Table 4–1. Manufacturers supply both prefinished and unfinished flooring.

Perhaps the most widely used pattern is a $^{25}/_{32}$-by-2¼-inch *strip flooring*. These strips are laid lengthwise in a room and normally at right angles to the floor joists. Some type of subfloor of diagonal boards or plywood is normally used under the finish floor. Strip flooring of this type is tongued-and-grooved and end-matched. Strips are random lengths and may vary from 2 to 16 feet or more. End-matched strip flooring in $^{25}/_{32}$-inch thickness is generally hollow backed (Figure 4–1A). The face is slightly wider than the bottom so that tight joints result when flooring is laid. The tongue fits tightly into the groove to prevent movement and floor squeaks. All of these details are designed to provide beautiful finished floors that require a minimum of maintenance.

Another matched pattern may be obtained in a

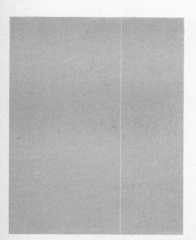

Table 4–1. *Grade and description of strip flooring of several species*

| Species | Grain orientation | Size (inches) | | First grade | Second grade | Third grade |
		Thickness	Width			
		SOFTWOODS				
Douglas fir	Edge grain	25/32	2 3/8 – 5 3/16	B and better	C	D
and hemlock	Flat grain	25/32	2 3/8 – 5 3/16	C and better	D	
Southern pine	Edge grain and Flat grain	5/16 – 1 5/16	1 3/4 – 5 7/16	B and better	C and better	D (and No. 2)
		HARDWOODS				
Oak	Edge grain	25/32	1½ – 3¼	Clear	Select	
	Flat grain	3/8	1½, 2	Clear	Select	No. 1 Common
		1/2	1½, 2			
Beech, birch, maple, and pecan*		25/32	1½ – 3¼			
		3/8	1½, 2	First grade	Second grade	
		1/2	1½, 2			

*Special grades in which uniformity of color is a requirement are available.

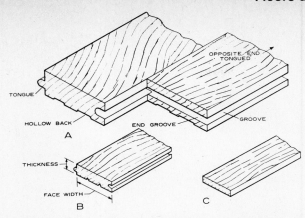

Figure 4–1. Types of strip flooring: (A) side-and-end—matched, 25/32 inch; (B) matched thin strips; (C) square-edged thin strips.

³⁄₈-by-2-inch size (Figure 4–1B). This is commonly used for remodeling work or when subfloor is edge-blocked or thick enough to provide very little deflection under loads.

Square-edged strip flooring (Figure 4–1C) might also be used occasionally. It is usually ³⁄₈ inch by 2 inches in size and is laid up over a substantial subfloor. Face-nailing is required for this type of flooring.

Wood-block flooring (Figure 4–2) is made in a number of patterns. Blocks may vary in size from 4 by 4 inches to 9 by 9 inches and larger. Thickness varies by type from 25/32 inch for laminated blocking or plywood block tile to ⅛-inch stabilized veneer. Solid wood tile is often made up of narrow strips of wood splined or keyed together in a number of ways. Edges of the thicker tile are tongued-and-grooved, but thinner sections of wood are usually square-edged. Plywood blocks may be ³⁄₈ inch and thicker and are usually tongued-and-grooved. Many block floors are factory-finished and require only waxing after installation. While stabilized veneer squares are still in the development stage, it is like-

ly that research will produce a low-cost wood tile that can even compete with some of the cheaper nonwood resilient tile now available.

Installation of wood strip flooring. The laying of wood strip flooring to a new addition to your home should be completed after the other interior wall and ceiling finish is completed, windows and exterior doors are in place, and most of the interior trim, except base, casing, and jambs, is applied, so that it will not be damaged by wetting or by construction activity.

Board subfloors should be clean and level and covered with a deadening felt or heavy building paper. This felt or paper will stop a certain amount of dust, will somewhat deaden sound, and, where a crawl space is used, will increase the warmth of the floor by preventing air infiltration. Since it is necessary to nail into the joists at a number of places, the location of the joists should be chalk-lined on the paper as a guide. Plywood subfloor does not normally require building paper.

Strip flooring should normally be laid crosswise to the floor joists (Figure 4–3). In conventional construction, the floor joists span the width of the building over a center supporting beam or wall. Thus, the finish flooring of the entire floor area of a rectangular house will be laid in the same direction. Flooring with L- or T-shaped plans will usually have a direction change at the wings, depending on joist direction. As joists usually span the short way in a living room, the flooring will be

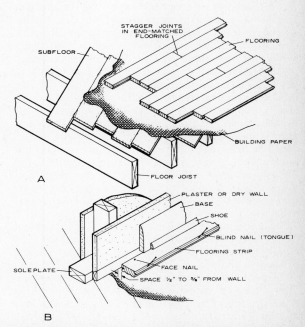

Figure 4–3. Application of strip flooring: (A) general application; (B) starting strip.

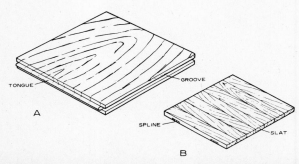

Figure 4–2. Wood-block flooring: (A) tongued-and-grooved; (B) square-edged, splined.

Figure 4—4. How to take the necessary measurements: *(left)* Walls may not be perfectly true at all points. Use a string as a guide in lining up the first course. Stretch the string between nails at opposite ends of the room at equal distances from the wall. Place a long piece of flooring with the groove edge nearest to the side wall and the groove end nearest to the end wall. Keep the piece at a uniform distance from the string, leaving an expansion space of about ½ inch from the wall. The space should be no larger than that to be covered by the shoe molding. The bottom edge of the baseboard comes just above floor level. Face-nail the flooring piece progressively at 10-inch intervals. Then toenail the tongue edge. *(center)* Whenever a piece must be cut to fill out a course, place it in reversed position for measuring. In this way you will ensure cutting off the tongue end (the groove end is needed for joining with the tongue end of the previous piece). *(right)* To fit flooring around jutting places like doorframes, place the strip flush against the frame. Measure the open space between the face edge of the previous piece and the groove edge of strip to be installed. Mark the strip accordingly on each side of the frame and saw out the piece. The flooring will fit snugly around the obstacle.

laid lengthwise to the room. This is desirable for appearance and also will reduce shrinkage and swelling effects on the flooring during seasonal changes.

Flooring should be delivered only during dry weather and stored in the warmest and driest place available in your house. Because of its low moisture content when kiln dried, wood flooring is highly subject to dampness and, until it is laid and completely finished, it is very important that it be kept dry at all times. This is especially so if the flooring is stored for any length of time prior to laying. It also is important that the building be heated if the flooring is laid during damp weather. If allowed to absorb moisture, a tightly laid floor will shrink when it dries out, leaving objectionable openings between the strips. In fact, moisture absorbed after delivery to the house site is one of the most common causes of open joints between flooring strips that appear after several months of the heating season.

Floor squeaks are usually caused by movement of one board against another. Such movement may occur because: (a) floor joists are too light, causing excessive deflection, (b) sleepers over concrete slabs are not held down tightly, (c) tongues are loose-fitting, or (d) nailing is poor. Adequate nailing is an important means of minimizing squeaks, and another is to apply the finish floors only after the joists have dried to 12 percent moisture content or less. A much better job results when it is possible

for you to nail the finish floor through the subfloor into the joists than if the finish floor is nailed *only* to the subfloor.

Various types of nails are used in nailing different thicknesses of flooring. For $^{25}/_{32}$-inch flooring, it is best to use eightpenny flooring nails; for ½-inch, sixpenny; and for $^3/_8$-inch fourpenny casing nails. (All the foregoing are blind-nailed.) For thinner square-edge flooring, it is best to use a 1½-inch

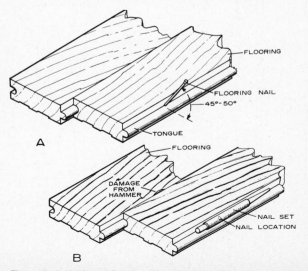

Figure 4—5. Nailing of flooring: (A) nail angle; (B) setting of nail.

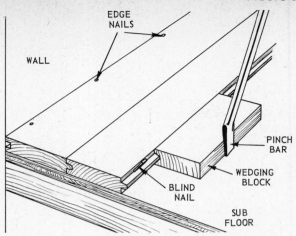

Figure 4-6. Lay each succeeding course by fitting the groove edges of flooring pieces into the tongue edges of the preceding course. Toenail, as illustrated here, but do not face-nail. For

$^{25}/_{32}$-inch-thick flooring one 7*d* or 8*d* flooring nail is nailed every 10 to 12 inches. Countersink the nails.

flooring brad and face-nail every 7 inches with two nails, one near each edge of the strip, into the subfloor. Other types of nails, such as the ring-shank and screw-shank type, have been developed in recent years for nailing of flooring. In using them, it is well for you to check with the floor manufacturer's recommendations as to size and diameter for specific uses. Flooring brads are also available with blunted points to prevent splitting of the tongue.

When nailing the first strip of flooring, place it ½ inch to ⅝ inch away from the wall (Figure 4-4). The space allows for expansion of the flooring when moisture content increases. The nail is driven straight down through the board at the groove edge. The nails should be driven into the joist and near enough to the edge so that they will be covered by the base or shoe molding. The first strip of flooring can also be nailed through the tongue. The nails should be driven into the tongue of the flooring at an angle of 45 to 50 degrees (Figure 4-5A). The nails should be driven not quite flush so as to prevent damaging the edge by the hammerhead. The nail can be set with the end of a large-size nail set or by laying the nail set flatwise against the flooring (Figure 4-5B). Nailing devices for both standard flooring and special nails are often used by flooring contractors. One blow of the hammer on the plunger drives and sets the nail.

To prevent splitting the flooring, it is sometimes desirable to predrill through the tongue, especially at the ends of the strip. For the second course of flooring from the wall, select pieces so that the butt joints will be well separated from those in the first course. Under normal conditions, each board should be driven up tightly. Crooked pieces may require wedging to force them into alignment or

may be cut and used at the ends of the course or in closets. To give a better appearance, do not group the joints too closely together. Joints in adjacent rows should be at least 6 inches apart. To effect this arrangement, lay out the pieces for the next few courses as you go along. Whenever it is necessary to cut a piece to fill out a course, place it in reversed position for measuring. In this way you will be more certain of cutting off the the tongue end. The groove end is needed for joining with the tongue end of the previous piece.

When you must fit around or under the casing of a doorway leading to an adjacent room or closet,

Figure 4-7. There is insufficient space to toenail the last two courses. Fit in the next-to-last course without nailing. Face-nail the last course, pulling it up tightly with a crowbar or a chisel. Protect the baseboard with cardboard. If shoe molding will not cover the remaining space, cut strips of flooring with a ripsaw and face-nail them in.

place the flooring strip against the doorframe. Then measure the open space between the face edge of the previous piece and the groove edge of the strip to be installed. Mark the strip accordingly on each side of the frame and saw out the piece. A pair of dividers or a compass is handy for marking strips when fitting flooring neatly around or under such an obstacle.

In completing the flooring, the last two courses usually cannot be toenailed because of insufficient space. Fit in the next-to-last course without nailing. Face-nail the last course, pulling it up tightly with a crowbar or chisel (Figure 4–7). Protect the baseboard with cardboard. If the shoe molding will not cover the remaining space, cut strips of flooring with a ripsaw and face-nail them in.

If you used prefinished flooring, all that remains is to add the base or shoe molding. If regular flooring was employed, the floor must be finished as described in Chapter 9.

Installation of wood flooring over concrete slabs. Installation of wood floor over concrete slabs is fully described in Chapter 12. As outlined there, one of the important factors in satisfactory performance is the use of a good vapor barrier under the slab to resist the movement of ground moisture and vapor. The vapor barrier is placed under the slab during construction. However, an alternate method must be used when the concrete is already in place (Figure 4–9).

Another system of preparing a base for wood

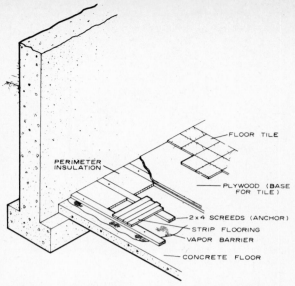

Figure 4–9. Basement floor details for existing construction.

flooring when there is no vapor barrier under the slab is shown in Figure 4–10. To resist decay, treated 1-by-4-inch furring strips are anchored to the existing slab, shimmed when necessary to provide a level base. Strips should be spaced no more than 16 inches on center. Spreading a good waterproof or water-vapor-resistant coating on the concrete before the treated strips are applied is recommended to aid in reducing moisture movement. A vapor barrier, such as a 4-mil polyethylene or similar membrane, is then laid over the anchored 1-by-4-inch wood strips and a second set of 1 × 4's is

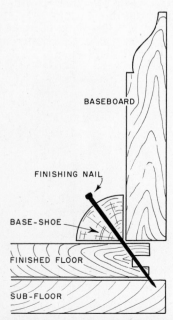

Figure 4–8. The simplest method of finishing the floor job with base-shoe molding.

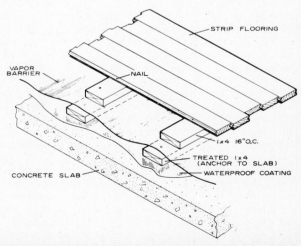

Figure 4–10. A base for wood flooring on a concrete slab without an underlying vapor barrier.

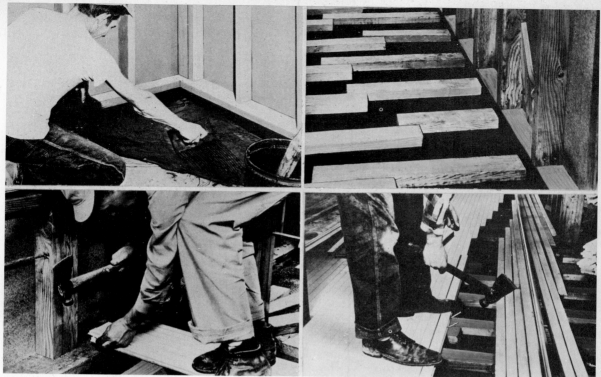

Figure 4–11. How to lay a wooden floor over concrete. *(top left)* The floor is first covered with a waterproof mastic, which is spread with a toothed trowel as in laying floor tiles. *(top right)* The short lengths of 2 × 4's (screeds) are pressed into the mastic, staggered and lapped several inches, the rows being 12 inches apart. Leave space between the screeds and the plate. *(bottom left)* If the wall is masonry, full-length 2 × 4's are laid against the wall to support the ends of the flooring. In the partition walls, make the plate and the screeds the same level. *(bottom right)* Nail the flooring boards over the screeds, nailing into each at every overlap. The screeds are thus tied together.

Figure 4–12. Floor preparation for laying parquet flooring: *(left)* The first step in the installation of wood flooring squares is the removal of base and shoe moldings. The moldings are pried loose carefully to avoid cracking or splintering, since they will be replaced after the floor has been finished. *(center)* If the wall paneling has been installed with too little space between the paneling and the original floor to allow for expansion and contraction of the new flooring, it may be necessary to trim the paneling at the bottom. *(right)* Two chalk lines are snapped from wall to opposite wall as that they cross to exact right angles. These working guidelines help to prevent misalignment of the new wood squares.

nailed to the first. Use 1½-inch-long nails spaced 12 to 16 inches apart in a staggered pattern.

When other types of finish floor, such as a resilient tile, are used, plywood is placed over the 1 × 4's as a base.

Wood and particleboard tile flooring. Wood and particleboard tile parquet flooring are applied, for the most part, with adhesive on a plywood or similar base. The exception is 25/32-inch wood-block floor, which has tongues on two edges and grooves on the other two edges. If the base is wood, these tiles are commonly nailed through the tongue into the subfloor. However, wood block may be applied on concrete slabs with an adhesive. Wood block or parquet flooring is installed by changing the grain direction of alternate blocks. This minimizes the effects of shrinking and swelling of the wood.

Wood-block floors can be laid over old wood floors, resilient tile, marble, terrazzo, and concrete. In all cases the old floor must be smooth, free from dust, and level. Holes, pockets, and low areas should be patched and filled in with patching cement. On an old wood or resilient floor, which is difficult to patch, it is best to lay down sheets of underlayment as described on page 117. On a con- crete floor, the surface must be dry and free from dust and powdering. If the concrete floor is in contact with earth below it, a vapor barrier of 2-mil polyethylene plastic sheeting must be used. Mastic cement is first spread over the concrete floor; then the polyethylene sheeting is laid on the mastic. Another coating of mastic goes over the plastic sheeting, and the squares are laid in this second coating.

The measuring techniques and methods of established work guidelines are fully discussed on page 120. In fact, the actual installation procedures of resilient floor tiles and those of wood are very similar.

One type of wood floor tile is made up of a number of narrow slats to form 4-by-4-inch and larger squares. Four or more of these squares, with alternating grain direction, form a block. Slats, squares, and blocks are held together with an easily removed membrane. Adhesive is spread on the concrete slab or underlayment with a notched trowel, and the blocks are installed immediately. The membrane is then removed, and the blocks are tamped in place for full adhesive contact. You should always heed the manufacturer's recommen-

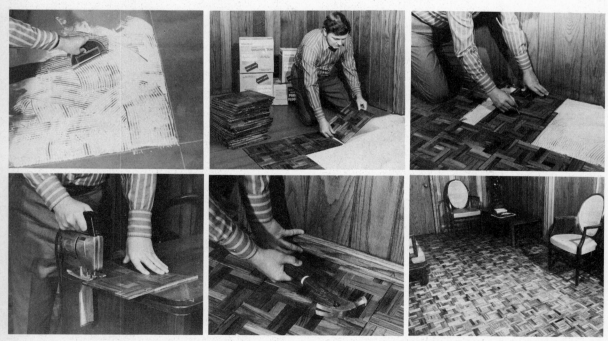

Figure 4–13. Applying wood squares with adhesive: *(top left)* A special mastic cement is applied to the floor at the point where the guidelines cross and divide the room into quarters. The trowel combs the cement into a series of ridges and valleys. *(top center)* The squares are laid carefully in the mastic snugly against each other. The first "tile" must be laid squarely where the lines cross to ensure the proper alignment of the rest. *(top right)* An overlapping full square is used to mark the last pieces for trimming, ⅜ inch being allowed at the wall for expansion. Trimmed pieces are used in the last row. A plastic sheet covers the mastic during marking. *(bottom left)* It is easiest to trim wood tile with a portable electric saber saw. *(bottom center)* Base molding in a matching wood grain is nailed on above the floor as a final step. Finishing nailheads will be counterset and the holes puttied. *(bottom right)* The completed job.

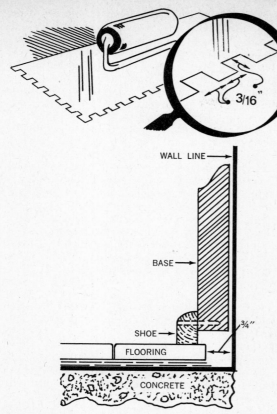

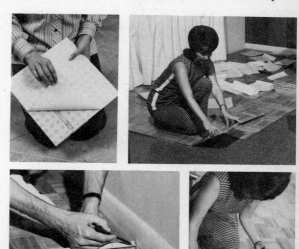

very complete; some even include instructions on the preparation of the base upon which the tile is to be laid. Particleboard tile should not be used over concrete.

Wood blocks are also available as self-sticking parquet squares (Figure 4–15). These pieces of wood are made up in a tile form and are held together by a special type of steel wire arrangement on the underside. Attached to the back of the square

Figure 4–14. *(top)* A typical notched trowel that leaves ³/₁₆-inch ridges and valleys in the mastic used as an adhesive for hardwood squares. Combing with the trowel prevents excessive use of the mastic. *(bottom)* Whether installed with mastic or by the self-sticking method, wood "tiles" must have room for expansion and contraction. The diagram depicts the best way to allow for floor movement without showing any gap at the base of the wall.

dations for choice of adhesive and method of application. Similar tiles made up of narrow strips of wood are fastened together with small rabbeted cleats, tape, or similar fastening methods. They, too, are normally applied with adhesive in accordance with the manufacturer's directions.

Plywood squares with tongue-and-groove edges are another popular form of wood tile. Installation is much the same as for the wood tile previously described. Usually, tile of this type is factory-finished.

A wood-base product used for finish floors is particleboard tile. It is commonly 9 by 9 by ³/₈ inch in size, with tongued-and-grooved edges. The back face is often marked with small saw kerfs to stabilize the tile and provide a better key for the adhesive. Manufacturer's directions concerning the type of adhesive and method of installation are usually

Figure 4–15. Applying self-sticking wood tiles: *(top left)* Lifting a special backing paper from this self-sticking tile shows plastic foam backing and adhesive dots that make the tile stick. *(top right)* A husband-and-wife team show how rapidly self-sticking tiles can be applied. Tongue-and-groove adhesive-backed squares are angled into place, then pressed down. *(center left)* A ³/₈-inch expansion space is left between the tiles and the wall or molding. Here only the quarter-round shoe molding strip has been removed. The base molding has been left on the wall. Matching-grained reducer strips are applied where the floor ends on an open area such as a doorway. *(center right and bottom left)* The wife applies double-faced tape to the underside of the doorway strip, while the husband sets it in place. Reducer strips can also be nailed or glued. *(bottom right)* The careful re-nailing of the shoe molding completes the job.

Chapter 4

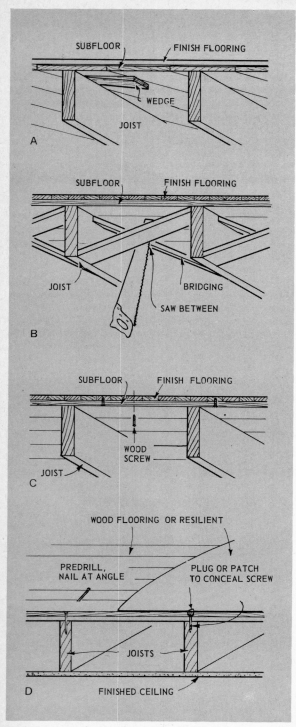

is a ⅛-inch layer of plastic foam that helps to reduce impact noise (the sound of footsteps). The back of the foam layer is covered with dots of pressure-sensitive or self-sticking adhesive, which are protected by a sheet of chemically treated paper that is peeled away just before installation. These squares also have tongues and grooves on all sides. When installing, be sure to insert the tile in your hands at an angle with the one on the floor and then, pressing forward to make tongues and grooves match, push it down to the floor. In this way you will make sure that the tiles will fit so closely that a hairline crack between the tiles will not be visible. Because of the tongue-and-groove system it is almost impossible to misalign the tiles, although you must be sure that you have the proper alternations of the parquet. The tiles at the end are trimmed with a jig-saber saw or coping saw. If you have to cut end tiles in an irregular pattern to make them fit around moldings or pipes, insert a fine-tooth narrow blade in the saber saw and follow the pencil lines traced on the tile. Where the tiles end at a doorway or another place where you must stop, you can use reducer strips of a matching wood which can be installed with fine nails or double-sided pressure-sensitive tape.

Reconditioning wood floors. Almost any wood floors can be given a new look if the floor boards are not structurally damaged. Often a complete refinishing job, such as is described on page 331, will remodel a floor. But if the floors squeak, sag, or are badly marred, the proper repairs must be made before the new finish is applied.

Squeaky floors. As subflooring dries out, it shrinks away from the floor joists and will creak when you walk on it. Whenever possible, this should be remedied from below the floor. Have someone stand on the creaking spot while you locate it in the basement. Then drive a wood shingle or wood wedge into the gap between the joists and the floorboards.

When the squeaks are caused by pieces of bridging rubbing together, simply run a saw between the pieces so that they do not touch.

Another cause of squeaks is loose flooring nails. If the subfloor is exposed, the best method for correcting this is to drive wood screws through predrilled holes in the subfloor into the floor while someone stands on the floor above. Use 2-inch screws if the finished floor is laid on sleepers and 1¼-inch screws if the finished floor is laid directly on the subfloor.

If a floor above a finished ceiling squeaks, the joists can be located by moving a magnet over the floor until it pulls, indicating a nail driven into a floor joist. Drill pilot holes at an angle through the finished flooring and drive small-headed spiral nails or finishing nails into the joist. Set the heads deeply and cover them over with wood putty. If the

Figure 4–16. Methods of correcting a squeaky floor: (A) a wood wedge; (B) cutting the wood bridging; (C) a wood screw driven from underneath; (D) repairing from above.

squeaks still persist, use 1¼-inch wood screws rather than nails. The heads can be countersunk and filled with wood plugs.

Sagging floors. Usually a well-built floor does not vibrate or show signs of sagging. However, as time goes by, certain spots loose their rigidity, which cause it to sag. This condition can be cured in one of the following ways:

1. As described in Chapter 2, one of the most common methods of supporting floor joists is to have one or more girders or beams running the length or width of the house. These girders, in turn, are supported by posts or columns. Frequently, when the posts begin to settle, this action causes the floor above the girder to become loose, vibrate, or sag. To correct, simply drive wood or metal wedges between the top of the post and the girder.

2. Where floors are not above a post or girder, the sag may be corrected by fastening a 2-by-4-inch or 2-by-6-inch brace between the joists snugly against the subfloor. The brace should be toenailed to the joists at each end. Then, to complete the job, drive small-headed spiral nails or finishing nails down through the floor from above into the brace. Countersink the nailheads and fill holes with wood putty.

3. If the brace method does not work, a post can be erected to support the weakened or sagging area. A 4 × 4 timber makes a good post, or you can purchase an adjustable jack post at most hardware dealers. In either case, place the post under the joist below the sagging area and raise it into position. Use a concrete block as a base, because the basement floor as a rule is not strong enough to carry the added weight. Should the basement floor begin to crack when the post is being lifted in place, stop the operation and chop a hole in the floor. Then dig down about 12 inches and pour concrete to provide a foundation for the support post.

4. When a floor above a finished ceiling is sagging, the only thing to do is tear out the ceiling to get at the joists and repair the sag. A new ceiling may be installed as described in Chapter 3.

Damaged portions. Damaged or rotted sections of flooring may be repaired by first removing the bad portion. This can be accomplished by drilling holes at each corner of the damaged piece and chiseling it out. Then cut a length of new flooring to the size of the piece to be removed and bevel one end. Also undercut the remaining portion of the damaged board to match the beveled portion of the replacement piece. After planing off the underside of the groove on the replacement piece, insert and nail the piece into place. If the new strip is thicker than the old, plane or sand it down flush.

RESILIENT FLOORING

Practicality, convenience, ease of application, and long wear are a few of the reasons why resilient flooring continues to be one of the most popular choices of homeowners everywhere. With the tremendous variety of materials, designs, and colors available, it is possible to create just about any floor scheme that strikes your fancy. For example, you can install a floor of all one color, or you can combine different colorings into a custom floor design that matches room requirements and individual taste. If your decorating taste leans to the natural look, you will find countless resilient materials that closely resemble the appearance of slate, brick, wood, terrazzo, marble, and stone. Many of these floors feature an embossed surface texture that adds a striking note to the design.

Types of resilient floors. Resilient floors are manufactured in two basic types: (a) sheet materials and (b) tiles. The latter are cemented in place to serve as a permanent floor. Sheet materials are also cemented in place, but in some cases can be installed loosely like rugs. Tiles generally come in 9- or 12-inch squares; sheet materials are available in continuous rolls up to 12 feet wide.

Tiles. Made of vinyl, asbestos fibers, and other components, resilient tiles are exceptionally dura-

Figure 4–17. Examples of available designs of resilient flooring.

ble and easy to keep clean. They lend themselves to a variety of customizing effects, since tiles of different colors and styles may be easily combined. In addition, most tile floors are ideal for do-it-yourself installation.

What kind of tile should you select? Asphalt tile, the first resilient tile, is the least expensive and can be installed at any grade level. It offers good durability, but compared to other types of resilient floors, it ranks low in resistance to grease and soil. For this reason, it is not recommended for kitchens. Most asphalt tiles are 1/8 inch in thickness.

Vinyl-asbestos tile is the most popular of all resilient tiles. It is inexpensive and can be installed anywhere, above, on, or below grade. Vinyl-asbestos tiles have exceptional durability and are easy to clean. They do not require waxing; they can be given a low sheen by buffing after the floor is mopped. Wear resistance is generally rated very good. These tiles are available in 1/16-, 3/32-, and 1/8-inch thicknesses.

Solid (or homogeneous) vinyl tiles that have a backing are the ultimate in the tile type of flooring. They rank as excellent in durability and have a surface that is smooth and nonporous. This makes upkeep easy and economical. You can use them on any grade level, and solid vinyl is available in many colors and patterns, and ranging in thickness from .080 gauge (thin) to 1/16 and 1/8 inch.

Rubber tile is one of the most resilient of all flooring materials, and it offers a great deal of comfort underfoot. Wear and soil resistance and upkeep maintenance are good. Today's rubber tile can be used in all areas of your home, but for some unknown reason, it has never become popular.

Cork, possibly the quietest of all floorings, is available as pure natural cork or combined with vinyl. The latter combination retains the beauty and warmth of cork while providing an added degree of cleaning ease. Vinyl cork has a higher degree of durability than natural cork.

Sheet flooring. The principal advantage of sheet flooring is seamlessness. Since it is installed in wide rolls, there are few seams in the finished floor. The result is a beautiful wall-to-wall sweep of color and design, a perfect setting for room furnishings. Some sheet floors can also be customized by combining two or more colors or styles. Sheet vinyls are resilient, therefore comfortable underfoot, and resistant to grease and alkalies as well. With special backing they can be used below, on, or above grade. Resistance to wear is generally very good. But the use of standard sheet vinyl flooring that is permanently installed with adhesive is not generally recommended for an amateur installer. It takes a skilled man to cut and fit it in place. This flooring comes in widths of over 6 feet and is rather heavy and awkward to handle. It is also fairly difficult to cut with an ordinary linoleum knife. Remember that if you make a wrong cut on a tile, not much is lost, but on sheet material, a bad cut can ruin considerable yardage. Flexible, lightweight cushioned vinyl flooring, on the other hand, is easy to cut, and easy to lay. Most cushioned vinyls come 6, 9, and 12 feet wide, which makes it possible to fit a room with a minimum of seams and waste.

Table 4–2. Guide to resilient flooring

Material	Backing	How installed	Where to install	Ease of installation	Ease of maintenance	Resilience and durability	Quiet
			Tile materials				
Asphalt	None	Adhesive	Anywhere	Fair	Difficult		Very poor
Vinyl asbestos	None	Adhesive	Anywhere	Easy	Very easy	Excellent	Poor
Vinyl	None	Adhesive	Anywhere	Easy	Easy	Good-excellent	Fair
			Sheet materials				
Rubber	None	Adhesive	Anywhere	Fair	Easy	Good	Good
Cork	None	Adhesive	On or above grade	Fair	Fair (with vinyl, good)	Good	Excellent
Inlaid Vinyl	Felt	Adhesive	Above grade	Fair	Easy	Good	Fair
	Foam and felt	Adhesive	Above grade	Difficult	Easy	Good	Good
	Asbestos	Adhesive	Anywhere	Very difficult	Easy	Excellent	Fair
	Foam	Adhesive	Anywhere	Very difficult	Easy	Excellent	Good
Printed Vinyl	Felt	Loose-lay	Above grade	Easy	Fair	Poor	Poor
	Felt	Adhesive	Above grade	Easy	Easy	Fair	Poor
	Foam and felt	Loose-lay	Above grade	Easy	Easy	Fair	Good
	Foam and asbestos	Adhesive or loose-lay	Anywhere	Fair-easy	Easy	Good	Good
	Foam	Loose-lay	Anywhere	Easy	Easy	Good	Good
Linoleum	Felt	Adhesive	Above grade	Very difficult	Very easy	Good	Fair

Linoleum, the oldest resilient flooring, is still very much with us because of its long-wearing qualities and low cost. It is, however, usually harder to maintain than most vinyl. It requires waxing on a regular basis to protect the surface from abrasion. The pattern range of modern linoleum, however, offers many striking colors that can dramatize and accent interiors.

Base for resilient floors. Putting down a base first makes the difference between a quickie job that probably will not last and the successful, long-lasting floor-covering installation. If the present flooring is perfectly smooth, level, and in good physical condition, the new resilient floor may be applied directly to it. Scrub the floor thoroughly to make sure that it is completely free of wax, paint, varnish, oil, or grease. Fill all the cracks and depressions with wood plastic or filler. Sand down any high spots and renail any loose boards of wood floors. Scaling concrete should be chipped out and patched with a concrete patch made especially for that purpose, patch that can be feathered at the edges.

It is wise, if there is any doubt in your mind regarding the condition of the old flooring, to install an underlayment. Also, in new work, resilient floors should not be installed directly over a board or plank subfloor. An underlayment grade of wood-based panels such as plywood, particleboard, and hardboard is widely used for suspended floor applications.

Four-by-8-foot plywood or particleboard panels, in a range of thickness from 3/8 to 3/4 inch, are generally selected for use in new construction. Four-by-4-foot or larger sheets of untempered hardboard, plywood, or particleboard of 1/4 or 3/8 inch thickness is used in remodeling work because of the floor thicknesses involved. The underlayment grade of particleboard is a standard product and is available from many producers. Manufacturer's instructions should be followed in the care and use of the product. Plywood underlayment is also a standard product and is available in interior types, exterior types, and interior types with an exterior glue line. The underlayment grade provides for a sanded panel with a C-ply or better face ply and a C-ply or better immediately under the face. This construction resists damage to the floor surface from con-

OVER WOOD SUBFLOOR

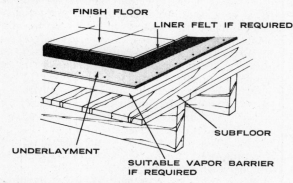

FINISH FLOOR
LINER FELT IF REQUIRED
SUBFLOOR
UNDERLAYMENT
SUITABLE VAPOR BARRIER IF REQUIRED

OVER OLD WOOD-FINISH FLOOR

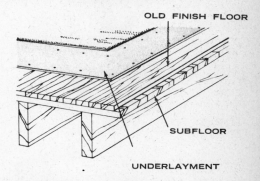

OLD FINISH FLOOR
SUBFLOOR
UNDERLAYMENT

OVER FILLER OR OLD TILE

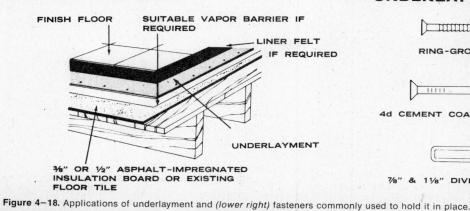

FINISH FLOOR
SUITABLE VAPOR BARRIER IF REQUIRED
LINER FELT IF REQUIRED
UNDERLAYMENT
3/8" OR 1/2" ASPHALT-IMPREGNATED INSULATION BOARD OR EXISTING FLOOR TILE

UNDERLAY FASTENERS

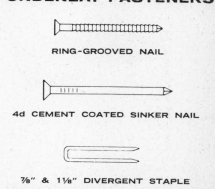

RING-GROOVED NAIL

4d CEMENT COATED SINKER NAIL

7/8" & 1 1/8" DIVERGENT STAPLE

Figure 4—18. Applications of underlayment and *(lower right)* fasteners commonly used to hold it in place.

Figure 4–19. Preparing a floor for resilient flooring: (A) The subfloor must be smooth to obtain a good finish job. Plane down any high spots and nail down all loose boards. (B) Allow a little less than $1/32$ inch (the thickness of a paper matchbook) between each 4-by-4-foot panel of underlayment or plywood to permit expansion. Stagger joints as shown. (C) Nail underlayment or plywood with coated or ring-groove nails at least every 4 inches on all edges and over the entire face of the panels. (D) If a great deal of underlayment must be laid, it may pay to rent a stapler for this purpose.

centrated loads such as chair legs and tables.

Generally, underlayment panels are separate and installed over structurally adequate subfloors. Combination subfloor-underlayment panels of plywood construction are finding increasing usage. Panels for this dual purpose use generally have tongue-and-groove or blocked edges and C-plugged or better faces to provide a smooth, even surface for the resilient floor covering.

When nailing the underlayment sheet, be sure of the following:

1. Always use cement-coated sinker nails, ring-grooved nails, or divergent chisel staples to fasten the underlayment to the old resilient floor surface or wood.

2. Never butt sheets of underlayment together. Leave about $1/32$ inch expansion space between them. The thickness of a dime is a good gauge for spacing the panels. Allow $1/8$ inch space between the wall or base and the underlayment.

3. Always stagger the seams to avoid the possibility of four corners meeting at one point. If possible, the direction of the continuous joints should be perpendicular to the direction of the boards in the subfloor.

4. If the nailing pattern is not already marked off by the manufacturer, nails should be spaced not more than 6 inches on center each way over the entire area of each panel and should not be closer than $3/8$ inch to the edge. Always start nailing at the center of a panel and work toward the edges. Nail the edges last. Drive the nailheads flush with the surface of the board; there is no need for countersinking the heads.

The thickness of the underlayment will vary somewhat, depending on the floors in the adjoining rooms. A new installation of tile in a kitchen area, for example, is usually made over a $5/8$-inch underlayment when finish floors in the adjoining living or dining areas are $25/32$-inch strip flooring. When thinner wood floors are used in adjoining rooms, adjustments are made in the thickness of the underlayment.

Concrete for resilient floors should be prepared with a good vapor barrier installed somewhere between the soil and the finish floor, preferably just under the slab. Concrete should be leveled carefully when a resilient floor is to be used directly on the slab, to minimize dips and waves.

Tile should not be laid on a concrete slab until it has completely dried. One method that may be used to determine dryness is to place a small square of polyethylene or other low-perm material on the slab overnight. If the underside is dry in the morning, the slab is usually considered dry enough for the installation of the tile.

In some cases, it may be wise to install both tile and sheet materials over lining felt (Figure 4–20). If you ever want to remove the flooring, you will be

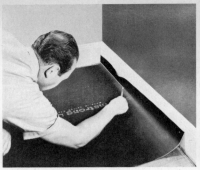 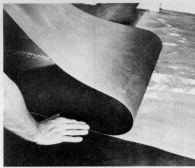 

Figure 4–20. Laying felt: *(left)* Start by laying oversize lengths of felt at one end. Crease with a pointed tool at the baseboards. *(center)* Lift back the felt and apply the paste with a trowel. *(right)*

Replace the felt before the paste dries. Press firmly with a cloth or use a rolling pin or linoleum roller.

glad you used felt. If you cement resilient flooring directly to wood or concrete, it is almost an impossible job to tear it up. When felt has been used, you just have to wet it and the floor comes right up. To apply felt, roll it out crosswise to the strip wood flooring, or over the underlayment. Then cut the felt to fit exactly from wall to wall. Succeeding widths of felt should butt at the edges, not overlap. Then roll back half of the felt and spread the proper adhesive on the first half of the subfloor. Begin spreading the paste at the middle of the floor and work toward the wall.

Roll the felt over the adhesive while the paste is wet. Roll it firmly with a linoleum roller or a kitchen rolling pin. Roll from the center to the edges, forcing out all the air pockets. The felt must stick securely to the floor. Then roll back the uncemented half of felt, apply paste to the other half of the subfloor and repeat the above procedure.

Installing floor tile. Laying the right kind of tile so that it looks neat and will stand up over the years requires careful planning. The various previously mentioned types are all layed in a similar fashion, but before any installation work can be started, you must determine the number of tiles needed and how they should be arranged.

How to figure number of tiles needed. Table 4–3 will aid you in figuring the number of tiles to complete an installation job. For instance, if you are working with a floor area which is 280 square feet (a 14-by-20-foot family room), and you want to use 9-by-9-inch tiles, the table indicates 356 tiles for 200 square feet and 143 tiles for 80 square feet, a total number of 499 tiles.

When ordering tiles, it is most important to consider the waste factors. In our example, the allowance for waste is 7 percent of the total number of tiles, or an extra 35 tiles. This would make a grand total of 534 tiles. Since tiles are usually boxed 80 to a carton, this would mean that we need over 6¾ cartons. Even if the dealer is willing to split a carton, it would be wise to take the seven full cartons. This will assure an adequate supply of tiles from the same lot and also allow for replacement if they are ever needed.

Laying out the pattern. As was stated earlier in this chapter, one of the major advantages of most tile materials is that they lend themselves to a variety of customizing effects. For instance, feature strips, from ½ inch to 3 inches wide, are available and can be employed to border a room or outline individual tiles, or they can be laid diagonally in a herringbone pattern; both solid and variegated colors are used. The use of insets is another way to give your floor an individual look. These are available in several different picture designs, and one is sure to

Table 4–3

Square feet	Number of tiles needed (inches)			Square feet	Number of tiles needed (inches)		
	9 × 9	12 × 12	9 × 18		9 × 9	12 × 12	9 × 18
1	2	1	1	60	107	60	54
2	4	2	2	70	125	70	63
3	6	3	3	80	143	80	72
4	8	4	4	90	160	90	80
5	9	5	5	100	178	100	90
6	11	6	6	200	356	200	178
7	13	7	7	300	534	300	267
8	15	8	8	400	712	400	356
9	16	9	8	500	890	500	445
10	18	10	9	600	1,068	600	534
20	36	20	18	700	1,246	700	623
30	54	30	27	800	1,424	800	712
40	72	40	36	900	1,602	900	801
50	89	50	45	1,000	1,780	1,000	890

Allowance for waste

1–50 square feet	14 percent
50–100 square feet	10 percent
100–200 square feet	8 percent
200–300 square feet	7 percent
300–1,000 square feet	5 percent
Over 1,000 square feet	3 percent

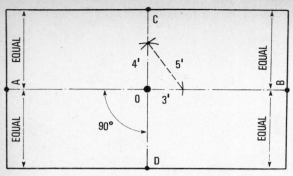

Figure 4–21. The right angle method of finding a center line.

Figure 4–22. Laying resilient tiles: (A) Measure the two opposite walls and find the center of each wall. Snap a chalk line on the floor between these points. (B) Locate the center of the chalk line. Using a carpenter's square or a tile, draw a line at right angles to the chalk line. (C) Lay a row of uncemented tiles along the chalk lines from the center, where the lines cross, to one side wall and one end wall. (D) If the last tile in step C is less than 2 or more than 8 inches from the wall, snap a new line 4½ inches closer to the wall. (E) Spread the adhesive with a trowel or brush (depending on the adhesive) and cover one-fourth of the room. Do not cover the chalk lines. (F) Starting at the center, place tiles in the adhesive. The first tiles must be flush with the lines. Do not slide the tiles into place. (G) The border tiles are less than full-size but can easily be cut to fit the space with a pair of ordinary household shears. (H) Solid-color strips can be used to create an unusual custom effect and enhance the decor of the room. (I) The installation of a cove base completes the job. Lengths of the base are cut to fit, cemented on the back, and pressed against the wall.

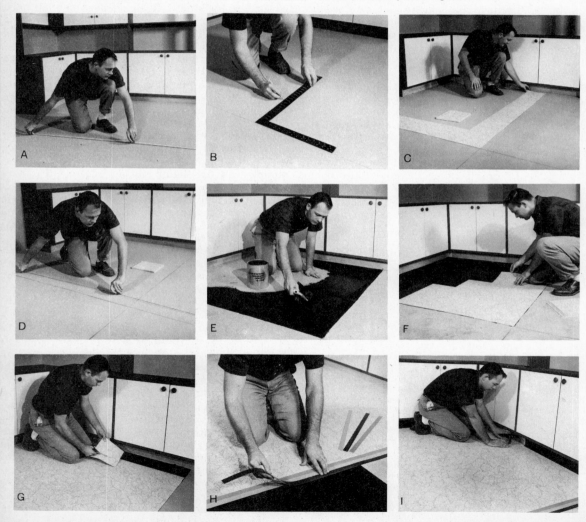

fit the theme of your room. You can also choose a standard three-letter monogram for your inset design. But, before laying out any pattern, you must mark the starting point, the center of the room. This can be accomplished as follows:

1. Measure along one wall to find the center point.

2. Locate the same center point at the opposite end of the room or as close to the center as you can get (disregard small alcoves, offsets, and other breaks).

3. Snap a line by rubbing chalk on string, holding the string taut on two center points. Then snap the string. This will mark a center line across the room.

4. Find the center point of the other two walls. (In all measuring, disregard bays, alcoves, and offsets).

5. Before snapping the crossline, be sure it is exactly at right angles to the first center line. This can be determined with a piece of tile or a large carpenter's square.

6. Snap this crossline onto the under floor. Now the main portion of the room (disregarding alcoves, etc.) is divided into quarters. To check right angles, make a 3 × 4 × 5 triangle as shown in Figure 4–21. If crosslines are truly at right angles, the three sides of each triangle must measure exactly 3 feet, 4 feet, and 5 feet as shown. If they do not, swing the string until these measurements are arrived at.

Before spreading the adhesive, lay a row of loose tiles along the chalk lines, starting at the center point and working out to one side wall and then to the other end wall. This determines the space left for the outside row of tiles (the border tiles). Measure the distance between the wall and the last tile. If the distance is less than 2 inches or more than 8 inches (for 9-inch-square tiles), move the center line parallel to, and 4½ inches closer to, that wall. This will prevent the peculiar look of tiles that are too small along either wall. If the central point is moved and either line is resnapped, check both lines again to be sure that they are at perfect right angles to one another.

Laying the tile. Spread a coat of the recommended cement or adhesive with a brush, roller, or trowel over one-quarter of the room, working from the walls out to the chalk lines. Spread the adhesive up close to, but do not cover, the chalk lines. When spreading the adhesive, remember that too much cement "bleeds" through between tiles and also forms a soft coating under the tile which permits heavy objects to dent the tile. Too little adhesive results in loose tiles, and possible cracking.

Lay the first tile carefully so that it fits exactly along the chalk marks. Place the field tile along the chalk lines in both directions, making sure that the first tiles are flush with the lines. Press each tile

Figure 4–23. Method of measuring a tile to fit a border.

into place, butting each tile tightly and neatly to the adjoining tile. Do not slide the tiles. This causes adhesive to ooze up between them. When installing marbleized patterns it is preferable to alternate the direction of veining in the adjacent tiles.

Once the first section is completed, spread the cement in the second quarter of the room and put down the tile in that quarter. Then do the third and fourth quarters. Whenever you start a new quarter, be sure the tiles along the chalk lines are tightly and accurately against these straight and squared lines.

To fit border tiles, lay a loose tile (A) squarely on the top of the last cemented tile nearest to the border space (Figure 4–23). Place another full tile (B), flush to the wall, on top of the middle tile (A). Then mark the middle tile (A) with a pencil along the edge of the top tile (B). Now cut the tile (A) along the mark just made; it should fit perfectly. Scissors can be used on vinyl and other soft tiles. A tile cutter, which usually can be rented from your tile supplier, will simplify the task for harder materials. For irregular surfaces, follow the same directions, but use a pair of dividers between the wall surface and tile to trace any irregular patterns.

There are some locations where the edge of the tiles will not be covered (as with base shoe molding around most of the room), and they must be scribed exactly. In such areas, place the tile in its true position relative to the position it will finally occupy. It must be parallel to the field tile (or already layed tile), but not necessarily to the wall, which might be irregular. Then scribe the lines perpendicular to the field and out from the wall with an extra tile or a steel square with one edge true to the field. Use dividers for marking the distance from the piece being fitted. Such a scribing procedure is usually necessary when fitting tiles exactly around the door trim.

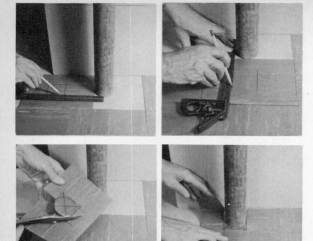

Figure 4—24. One way of fitting a tile around a pipe or a similar obstruction: Place the tile against the side of the pipe, mark the width, and repeat on the other side of the pipe. Draw a circle within the resulting square and cut out.

To fit tiles around pipes (Figure 4–24) or other obstructions, make a paper pattern to fit the space exactly. Then trace the outline onto the tile and cut it accordingly. For an intricate pattern, it may be necessary to heat the back of the tile over a floor or heat lamp to make it more pliable. Toilets and other large obstructions are best removed and tiled underneath. Be sure to disconnect the water when doing this.

By setting tiles carefully, you should be able to avoid excess cement coming up between the tiles. Some excess cement is bound to get onto the tile surface, however, and it should be removed immediately. Follow the directions on the cement container to wipe up the cement. Be careful not to allow solvent to run down between the tiles, as it will loosen them.

Do not wash or wax the floor for five to ten days after installation, until the tiles have become thoroughly bonded to the subfloor. Sweeping them with a soft broom or cleaning them with a damp cloth or mop is the only maintenance necessary during this period.

Waxing is not necessary with most resilient tile floor unless desired. Mopping and buffing will usually keep the floor looking new and attractive. But, if waxing is desired, be sure the floor is thoroughly cleaned. Apply a good floor wax in a very light coat. Apply the wax in straight motions (not sweeping or circular). For a higher shine, buff the floor by hand or use an electric polisher. Do not wax over dirty floors. Excessive wax produces areas where wax film is too thick and usually causes a floor to look discolored.

All resilient floor coverings will indent, more or less, if weight is applied to a small, concentrated area. Therefore, remove all small metal domes or buttons from furniture legs. Use broad, flat glides or cups. Replace hard, narrow rollers with soft wide rubber rollers.

Laying self-adhesive tiles. To make life simpler for the handyman, there are floor tiles available—usually of the vinyl-asbestos type—that come already prepared with adhesive. The key difference between these and conventional floor tiles is that there is no need to spread cement. Otherwise the measuring and layout techniques are the same.

The paper backing on self-adhesive tiles is removed only when you are actually ready to apply the tile (Figure 4–25). Start placing the tiles at the center point, following the chalk lines. Do not slide the tiles on the floor. Set them in place with their edges on the lines, then press them down firmly. Butt each tile squarely to the previous one. The corners should meet exactly. Do not apply pressure until you are sure the tile is correctly placed, because once applied, the adhesive makes the tile difficult to move. To fit the tiles around obstacles or at edges, cut the tiles as illustrated on this page, doing all cutting on the paper side of the tile.

Installing sheet resilient floor materials. There are two ways to install sheet resilient floor materials: (a) with adhesive and (b) by the loose-lay method. The latter is the easiest for the average home craftsman.

Loose-lay cushioned vinyl materials. As stated earlier, roll-sheet cushioned vinyl offers several advantages; but possibly the biggest is the fact that it does not require the use of an adhesive. The asbestos felt backing of this material "hugs" the floor and thus permits cushioned vinyl to be loose-laid.

Figure 4—25. Laying self-adhesive tiles is a simple job. Just peel off the protective paper on the back of the tile *(left)* and press into place *(right).*

Figure 4—26. Installing a loose-lay flooring. *(top left)* First remove the wood base or the shoe molding with a wrecking bar or a claw hammer. *(top center)* Measure and cut the sheet where it can be unrolled. Snap chalk lines 3 inches greater than the dimensions of the room. *(top right)* Line up the straight edge of the cut sheet with the longest and most regular wall. Let the material curve up the other three walls. *(bottom left)* Press the flooring firmly into place and trim waste with a knife or heavy scissors, allowing a $1/32$-inch clearance at the walls. *(bottom center)* At a doorway where the flooring meets hardwood, the edge of the sheet may be cemented or capped with a metal threshold. *(bottom right)* Replace the molding. Slip a piece of scrap sheet between the molding and the sheet. Nail the molding to the base, not to the floor. Then remove the scrap.

Cushioned vinyl can also be installed above or below grade and over smooth linoleum, concrete, or wood.

Some dealers will cut the material to your measurements, plus 3 inches oversize all around for safe clearance. If the dealer does not offer this cutting service, you will have to transfer your measurements to the sheet vinyl and cut 3 inches larger. Cutting may be done with a linoleum knife, shears, or utility knife.

After all the rough cuts are made, start laying the material at the longest and straightest wall, butting it—with the 3-inch allowance—against this wall, unrolling it across the room, and permitting the excess material to curve up the other three walls. You are now ready to cut around the perimeter of the room by pressing the material against the walls and various room projections and cutting with a linoleum or utility knife. A clearance gap of $1/8$ inch (slightly less at doorways) is left between the edge of the material and the baseboards to allow for expansion and contraction of the material and subfloor. This space, of course, will ultimately be covered by the molding. A clearance gap should also be allowed between the top of the sheet vinyl edges and what would be the bottom of the molding when it is installed, to allow the walls and subfloor to move without affecting the sheet material. With this in mind, when the shoe molding is installed, it should be nailed directly to the baseboard, not

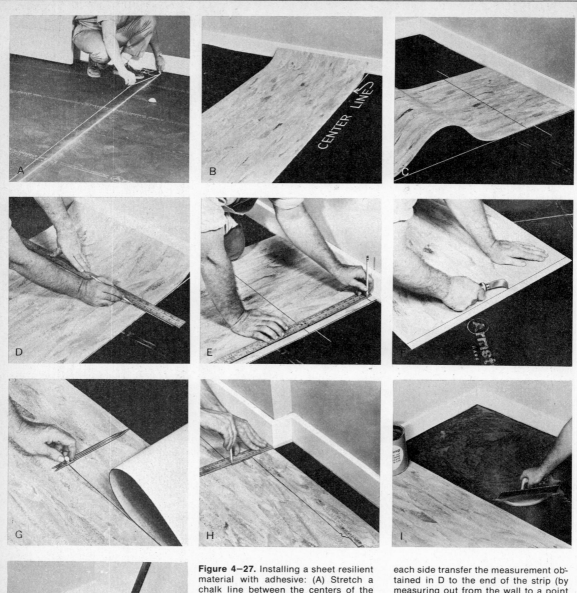

Figure 4–27. Installing a sheet resilient material with adhesive: (A) Stretch a chalk line between the centers of the opposite walls (or 12 inches off center, if necessary). (B) Lay the first strip to the center line, allowing the ends to flash up the wall. If one end has already been cut off square, butt it to the baseboard (the molding will cover the edge). (C) Slide the material back, keeping it straight along the center line, until the end touches the baseboard. Measure the distance between the line on the felt and the line on the material. (D) For accurate end trimming, lay a yardstick across the strip and draw a pencil line across the strip and onto the felt. (E) At each side transfer the measurement obtained in D to the end of the strip (by measuring out from the wall to a point on the strip). (F) The final cut can be made with a linoleum knife. (G) To mark overlapping strips, place a scriber point against the edge of the material. Then adjust the pointed thumbscrew to line up with the edge of the overlapping strip. (H) To accommodate irregularities in the wall, use a straightedge and draw lines straight out onto the material from surfaces perpendicular to the wall. (I) Fold back the material and trowel on paste. (J) Complete the job by rolling with a heavy roller such as a linoleum roller, which can usually be rented from a floor covering dealer.

through the sheet vinyl and into the subfloor. A thin sheet of cardboard, which will later be removed, should be placed between the bottom of the shoe molding and the top of the vinyl sheet while nailing to permit the proper clearance of approximately $\frac{1}{32}$ inch.

Frequently, the sheet material must be cut out to fit around doorjambs or other irregularities. This is sometimes quite a problem, particularly where the vinyl sheet is to be laid in a doorway. However, a piece of light cardboard or paper can be used as a template and cut out to fit the irregular space exactly. The cardboard or paper should be big enough to project out into the room after it has been cut and fitted into place. Then, with the sheet vinyl in place everywhere except in the irregular area into which it is to fit, put a few spots of glue on the edge of the paper or cardboard and unroll the material far enough for it to cover the glued part of the paper. When the vinyl sheet is rolled back, the paper will adhere to it and can be laid back on the vinyl. By using a knife to trim around the edges of the paper, you can cut out the sheet vinyl so that it fits the irregular space exactly.

An exposed edge of sheet vinyl, as for instance where the material ends in a doorway, can be protected by a metal strip. The metal strip is first nailed into place; the vinyl sheet is then laid on top of it and trimmed to fit under the curved metal edge. The curved edge can then be bent down, if not sufficiently bent, to form a permanent protection for the vinyl edge.

Use of adhesive. As previously stated, standard sheet flooring, either vinyl or linoleum, that is to be permanently installed with adhesive is best left to a professional craftsman. But if you believe that your skills are good enough to handle the job, here are some suggestions that might make the task a little easier.

The basic procedures of fitting and cutting described for installing loose-lay material are similar to those employed when using an adhesive. Because of the added weight, it is more difficult to make the cuts, especially when the material is inlaid. Some dealers will make rough cuts, about 3 inches oversize, to your measurements. The sheet flooring should be unrolled and left flat for a few hours in a warm room before it is laid. This makes it more pliable and easier to work. Since most standard sheet flooring comes with the backing—felt, rubber-foam, or asbestos—attached, it can be laid directly onto a properly prepared base (see page 117).

After the sheet material has been cut to an exact fit (allowance for expansion should be made at the walls as in the loose-lay method), it is laid with a special cement as directed by the manufacturer. Apply the cement evenly on the floor with a wide spreader over a few square feet at a time, and then press the material down firmly on it. Be sure that the entire surface is well covered with cement and that there are no bulges in the material where it has failed to adhere. Air bubbles under the sheet material are hard to remove after the linoleum is down; try to avoid them. As soon as all the sheet material has been cemented in place, it should be rolled down with a heavy roller, which usually can be rented from a flooring dealer. If nothing else is available, a regular garden roller can be used, provided it is clean and smooth. It is usually best to place weights on the seams to prevent their coming loose before the cement has fully dried.

RIGID FLOOR SURFACES

In special locations within the home, rigid floor materials such as ceramic tile, slate, flagstone, and brick may be used. In fact, ceramic tile is one of the oldest floor-covering materials; it dates back almost 7,000 years.

There are three types of ceramic tiles (Figure 4–28) in common use today: quarry tiles, ceramic

Figure 4–28. As shown here, ceramic tiles may be used in many areas other than bathrooms.

Figure 4–29. Steps in laying a ceramic tile floor: (A) Waterproof epoxy adhesive is applied with a trowel. Because the epoxy setup dries quickly, work in only a small area at a time. (B) Set the tile in the adhesive. (C) Tap the tile into place with a mallet. (D) Once all the tiles have been laid and the adhesive has dried, pour the grout on the tiles. (E) Spread the grout with a float. (F) Remove the excess grout. (G) Apply dry cement to the wet grout. (H) Clean up the cement to complete the job.

mosaics, and glazed tiles. The last are usually a little thinner than glazed wall tiles, but are made in various sizes and shapes and a variety of designs and colors. Some are so perfectly glazed that they form a monochromatic surface. Others have a softer, natural shade variation within each unit and from tile to tile. In addition, ceramic floors can be bright-glazed, matte-glazed, or unglazed. There are also extra-duty glazed floor tiles suitable for heavy-traffic areas.

Ceramic mosaics are available in 1-by-1- and 2-by-2-inch squares, and come with or without a glaze. In addition to the standard units, they may be had in a large assortment of colorful shapes. Mosaics are usually sold mounted in 1-by-1- and 1-by-2-foot sheets for easy installation.

Quarry tiles, which are also made from natural ceramic materials, are available in a variety of colors; the most common types are in shades of red, chocolate, and buff. They come in shapes ranging from square tiles to Spanish forms.

Slate tiles and flagstone are available in random shapes or can be purchased in geometric shapes, usually squares and rectangles. They may be had in green, red, purple, gray, and black. Because of cost, however, the use of slate and flagstone is usually limited to small, luxurious areas such as foyers and entryways.

Brick interior floors are becoming increasingly popular as a handsome and eye-catching element in a home. A wide selection of brick colors and sizes is available to the homeowner. Special bricks known as "pavers" are generally used in floors, patios, and walkways. Pavers are even more wear-resistant than standard bricks, and they are thinner, usually about 1½ inches thick. The thinner bricks reduce the floor's weight and are used where the added thickness is not needed. Standard bricks, however, may be used in any home.

Laying a ceramic tile floor. Ceramic floor tiles, which includes quarry tiles and pavers (unglazed floor units measuring 6 square inches or more in facial surface), are set very much the same way as wall tiles (see page 83). At one time it was thought that the only base on which floor tile could be laid was a heavy layer of concrete made of three parts sand and one part cement. This base was made about 3 inches thick and reinforced with wire mesh. Although some such construction is still desirable in public buildings where the floor must bear heavy traffic, the tendency in houses has been toward a less bulky and lighter construction. With the heavier construction, the floor joists are partly cut away, boards are fastened between the joists a couple of inches below the tops, waterproof building paper is laid on the boards, and concrete is poured on top of that. The tile is then laid on top of the concrete.

Today, ceramic floor tiles can be applied to almost any surface that is in good condition, firm, perfectly smooth, and free from moisture and foreign matter. It is usually a good idea to prime the floor surface with special ceramic tile primer before applying the adhesive or mastic. The tile adhesive, which may be of the same type as that used on the walls, is spread with a 1/8-inch steel trowel held at a slight angle. Spread the adhesive evenly, making an even pattern over the floor. Press the trowel firmly against the surface so that the proper amount of adhesive will be deposited through the notches in the trowel edge. Do not leave any bare spots. Also make certain there are no areas where the adhesive is too thick. Apply the adhesive in areas about 3 feet square so that you will not get too far ahead of the tile installation and let the surface of the adhesive lose its tackiness. Before applying the mastic, be sure all joints and fixture joints are calked to prevent any water seepage.

Mosaic floor tiles, as previously mentioned, come pasted onto paper sheets (Figure 4–30). When installing, press the sheets of tile on the floor, with the papered side uppermost. Let the tile set for an hour. Wet the paper slightly with a damp sponge and pull it off the tile. At this time, the adhesive will still be pliant so you can re-align individual tiles if necessary. With the small mosaics there is no need to determine a center line. Just begin with the rear wall, then work your way toward the other walls, completing the job at the door. Be sure to make the spaces between the sheets of tile equal to the space between the individual tiles, providing a uniform pattern throughout the floor. After the tiles are laid, if you must walk over the floor, do so on a board so that your weight will be more equally distributed. Incidentally the ceramic floor is always installed before the wall.

The floor, just like the wall, should be allowed to set for a full day before grouting. While commercial floor grout is available, it can be made by mixing one part waterproof portland cement and one part finely screened sand. A minimum amount of water should be used in mixing, just enough for workability. Spread this mixture over the floor and work it into the joints with a squeegee. The joints should be completely filled.

After the grout has set for about half an hour, wipe the surface with a sponge and then with a burlap cloth. If necessary, go over it several times until all traces of grout are gone. Then polish it with a dry cloth.

The floor must now be cured. Cover it and keep all traffic off it for about three days. If it is necessary to walk on it during that time, do so on boards.

Laying a brick floor. The brick floor may be laid in an endless variety of patterns. The basket weave, herringbone, and running bond are the most often used patterns (see page 464), but the actual number

Figure 4–30. Rubber-mounted or paperback ceramic tiles being installed: Small ceramic tile units firmly fused into a rubber grid combine the attractiveness and wearing qualities of ceramic with ease and economy of installation. The 9-by-9-inch rubber tile is laid in mastic like any floor tile and is easily fitted at the borders. An ordinary linoleum knife is used to cut through the rubber grid; tile nippers are employed to cut through the ceramic units.

is limited only by the imagination.

The brick may be laid on a concrete slab, tamped earth, or wood subfloor. When a wood subfloor is used, the space between floor joists should be reduced by about 25 percent to compensate for the additional weight. For instance, the rather standard spacing of 16 inches should be reduced to 12 inches. Before the brick is laid, the base floor or surface should be covered with two or three layers of heavy roofing felt to provide a vapor barrier between the base and the brick. When the brick is to be laid on a concrete or wood base, it may be placed directly on the felt vapor barrier.

In most floors, the brick is placed on the floor flat (the largest plane surface horizontal). For this, noncored bricks (without holes) are normally used. If the brick is placed on its edge, cored brick may be used.

The mortar (see page 29 for the proper mixture and method of setting) is placed on the floor and the bricks are set in it. Make sure that the bricks are level, the excess mortar is wiped away, and the joints are "tooled" for maximum hardness. After the mortar has hardened for several days, the brick surface should be cleaned with a commercial masonry cleaner according to directions.

Depending upon the type of bricks used, the surface may be a nonslip or relatively smooth one. In either case, no finishing is really necessary. If an extremely smooth surface is desired, the bricks may be sanded with a terrazzo grinder after the mortar joints have hardened for at least a week.

Normal sweeping or vacuuming and an occasional damp mopping is usually all the maintenance required for brick floors. If desired, interior brick floors may be waxed with a floor wax recommended by a wax manufacturer. Because some floor waxes discolor with age, brick floors should be sealed with a masonry sealer (a number are on the market) before being waxed. Sealing, even for unwaxed floors, will reduce the likelihood of staining from spilled liquids or cleaning solutions. Varnish and shellac are not recommended for brick floors because they do not stay in place, and their appearance deteriorates after a short time.

Laying a slate or flagstone floor. Slate or flagstone may be set in a bed of mortar on a concrete slab or in mastic or adhesive over a wood subfloor. The former is the cheaper method, but is not usually an advisable home craftsman's project. The setting of slates or flagstone in mastic is very similar to the method used for ceramic tiles or bricks, both in procedure and precautions.

Before actually laying the material, arrange the pieces, without mastic, in the way you wish them to be in the finished job. Number the pieces in the desired pattern with chalk. Slate or stone cutters usually can be rented from masonry supply dealers.

After the slates or stones have been cut to their

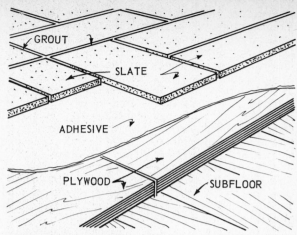

Figure 4—31. The necessary base for brick, slate, or flagstone.

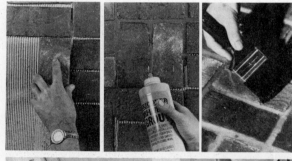

Figure 4—32. "Plastic" bricks similar to those described in Chapter 3 are available for both interior and exterior floors: *(top left)* To install bricks, apply a cement (mortar) coat as directed by the manufacturer. *(top center)* Once the bricks are in place, the grout can be applied by a tube. It can be finished off with a suitable mason's jointing tool or with the back of a metal spoon. *(top right)* After the grout and mortar have dried, a special sealer is applied. *(bottom)* The sealer gives the completed floor its beauty.

proper shapes, arranged in the desired pattern, and numbered, pick them up and then spread the adhesive on the subfloor to the thickness recommended on the container by the manufacturer (Figure 4–32). The slates or stones are set in the desired pattern in the adhesive. Tamp them with the handle of the trowel and carefully check to make sure they are level. If necessary add or remove a little adhesive until the slate or stone rests firm and level on the bed.

Allow the slates or stones to set for 24 hours before applying the grout. To prevent the grout from sticking to the top surface of the slates or stones, apply a thin coat of crude oil to these areas. Mix the grout as instructed on the container. The very soft mix can then be poured from a watering can with the sprinkler head removed. Pour the grout into all the spaces between the slates or stones and fill the cavities completely. Properly applied, the grout should be slightly above the surface of the material.

When the grout has begun to set, strike the joints with a grouting tool. Rub the tool back and forth over the joints to force the mortar into the joints. Remember that the finished joint should have a slightly concave appearance, with the sides level with the slate. The excess grout can easily be cleaned up with a piece of burlap, thanks to the oil layer on the surface of the slates or stones. To give the surface a finished look, apply one of the special oil finishes that are on the market for this purpose.

CARPETING

Carpeting many areas of a home from living room to kitchen and bath is becoming more popular as new carpeting materials are developed. The cost, however, may be considerably higher than a finished wood floor, and the life of the carpeting before replacement would be much less than that of the wood floor. Many wise home remodelers will install wood floors even though they expect to carpet the area. The resale value of the home is then retained even if the carpeting is removed. However, the advantage of carpeting in sound absorption and resistance to impact should be considered. If carpeting is to be used, subfloor can consist of 5/8-inch (minimum) tongued-and-grooved plywood (over 16-inch joist spacing). The top face of the plywood should be C-plugged grade or better. Mastic adhesives are also being used to advantage in applying plywood to floor joists. Plywood, particleboard, or other underlayments are also used for a carpet base when installed over a subfloor.

As for the carpet material itself, you have a choice of several types of synthetic fabrics, or natural wool. Table 4–4 compares some characteristics of wool and four major synthetic fabrics.

While a great deal of carpeting is sold on an installed basis, more and more installation is being done by the home craftsman. Carpet materials for the do-it-yourselfer are available in two forms: carpet tiles and roll carpeting. The former, usually in 12-by-12-inch squares, comes already backed with padding. The carpet tiles are installed in the same manner as resilient floor tiles (see page 122). There are also on the market self-adhesive carpet tiles as well as those that are installed without any adhesive at all. To lay this latter type, you put two strips of double-faced tape at right angles across the room, stick on a row of tiles both ways, then just lay the other carpet tiles in place with no adhesive at all. Their nonskid rubber backing holds them in place.

Roll carpeting can be laid in two ways: (a) with adhesive or (b) by using pressure-sensitive, double-faced tape or tackless stripping. When laying roll carpeting with adhesive, the same technique is followed as when installing resilient sheet material with cement (see page 122). The tackless stripping, available at most carpet dealers, consists of a 4-foot wooden strip with numerous fine spikes or points projecting at a 60 degree angle. The strips are nailed around the perimeter of the room, end to end, and 1/4 inch from the wall molding, with the spikes facing towards the wall. The spikes grip the backing of the carpet to hold it in place. The double-faced tape, available in several types, performs in much the same manner as the tackless stripping and for most carpet materials holds just as well and is much easier to work with.

Installing roll carpeting with tape. Before installing the carpet, check the floor area to make sure that it is clean, sound, smooth, dry, and warm (preferably about 70 degrees F, but definitely above 55 degrees F). Pressure-sensitive tapes will not bond readily to concrete floors or other floors that are dusty, cold, rough, or oily. Concrete should be vacuumed (or washed with water, then allowed to dry) before installing the double-faced carpet tape. Where there is existing floor molding, it is a good idea to remove the quarter-round molding before installing the carpet. The molding should be replaced after the installation is completed. It will help secure the edges of the carpet as well as give the installation a more professional appearance.

Table 4–4

	Wool	Acrylic	Nylon	Polyester	Polypropylene
Retains texture	Good	Good	Good	Good	Excellent
Durable	Good	Good	Excellent	Good	Excellent
Resilience	Good	Good	Good	Fair	Fair
Crushing recovery	Good	Fair	Good	Fair	Poor to fair
Fade resistance	Fair	Good	Fair	Good	Good
Cleaning	Excellent	Fair	Excellent	Good	Good
Spot and stain removal	Fair	Good	Fair	Good	Excellent
Static electricity	Poor in low humidity	Low	High	Poor in low humidity	Low

Figure 4–33. When using double-faced tape to install carpeting, be sure that the underflooring is clean so that no dirt or grease will impair the holding power of the tape at corners or seams. *(top left)* Start with the longest wall in the room, and butt the carpet carefully to the wall along its entire length. Trim the carpet with scissors to accommodate any irregularities at base of the wall. *(top center)* Bring the carpet carefully across the room to the facing wall. Keep it flat and smooth out any puckers. *(top right)* Where the carpet butts against the wall base, score heavily with the handle end of a scissors. Mark lightly along this line with white blackboard or tailor's chalk (the chalk brushes off easily), and cut the carpet with the scissors. Trim where necessary to accommodate wall irregularities. Do not cut the carpet short; it is preferable to allow a slight overage, fit the carpet to the wall, and cut it again.

The double-faced tape should be placed around the perimeter of the carpet in strategic or heavily trafficked areas. *(bottom left)* Where walls jut out, proceed as for a straight wall. Score, chalk, and cut, but cut only one wall edge at a time. Place the double-faced tape around all corners and juts, thus ensuring a tight bond of the foam backing with the floor. *(bottom center)* If the room is wider than the width of the carpet being used, take an additional strip of carpet and butt the seams together. *(bottom right)* To make a seam virtually invisible, use chalk to mark the seam line of the carpet on the floor. Lay the tape along this line (there should be about 1 inch of tape on either side of seam) and for a short distance along the wall across the seam to form a T. Then apply cement along both seam edges of the carpet. Replace the carpet on the floor and press down firmly.

Carpeting that is to be laid by the pressure-sensitive tape method comes self-padded or cushion-backed. That is, the padding material is already fastened or molded to the back of the carpet fibers. If the padding is not attached, tackless stripping should be used. Padding or backing is essential to any good carpet installation. The most used types of padding are felt (hair) and foam. Foam, either rubber or rebonded urethane, is the most popular today.

To install the cushion-backed carpeting, butt the carpet edge carefully against the longest unbroken wall of the room, trimming it with sturdy scissors or a utility knife to fit any irregularities, then roll the carpet across the room and smooth it out. Make relief cuts at room corners to allow the carpet to be flat on the floor. (If a corner or an offset is curved, a number of relief cuts will be necessary.)

To trim the excess carpeting, start at one wall, and fold back the carpet to expose the wall and floor joint. Using an ordinary soft chalk stick held at a 45-degree angle to the joint, make a chalk line by moving the point down the length of the joint. (Two lines will actually appear, one on the wall and one on the floor.) On wall surfaces that will not mark with chalk, such as ceramic tile or high-gloss enamel, apply a strip of 1-inch masking tape (not carpet tape) where the surface meets the floor. Make sure you remove the masking tape after the carpet is fitted. Also be sure to continue the chalk line around obstacles such as doorjambs and offsets. These chalk lines will serve as your trim lines. Carefully unfold the carpet, allowing the excess to run up the wall. Force the carpet into the wall-floor joint with firm finger pressure, and transfer the chalk lines onto the back of the carpet. Then fold the carpet back away from the joint, and make sure the two chalk lines are reproduced on the back. Make your trim cut on the line nearest to the edge of the carpet (the line made by the wall).

Unfold the carpet, and allow it to fall into position on the floor. The trimmed edge should just touch the wall or molding. If the fit is too tight at any point, carefully trim off the slight overcuts. Trim the excess from the other walls using the same technique. To trim around obstacles in an open area such as a support beam, toilet, or pipe, cut toward the obstacle from a convenient edge of the carpet. If necessary, rough-cut to allow 3 to 4 inches of excess around the object, and make relief cuts. Make chalk lines around the base of the obstacle, and follow the just-mentioned technique for trimming.

After the carpet has been cut to size, apply the double-faced tape flush with the wall around the entire perimeter of the room and at irregularly cut areas. Then press the carpet in place.

Seaming the carpet. Most cushion-backed carpeting comes in 12- and 15-foot widths. If your room is wider, it will be necessary to seam the carpet. To do this, unroll the first piece of carpet in the area. (Note the directional arrow or mark on the back. All pieces should have the arrow pointing in the same direction so the lay of the pile is uniform.) In some cases, particularly with shag carpet, it *may* be possible to butt one of the long sides of the first piece against a straight wall that has no doorways (with the short ends turned up the walls). If this is done and the fit along the wall is satisfactory, check the opposite edge of the carpet (seam edge) to make sure it is straight. Do this by stretching a line from one end of the seam edge to the other. If the seam edge is straight, proceed to the next step of the installation. If the seam edge is bowed or curves away from the line, the carpet cannot be installed properly by butting the first piece along the wall. Instead, it will be necessary to move the piece toward the wall until approximately 2 inches of the long side are uniformly turned up the wall rather than butted against it. The carpet will also have to be turned up any walls that have doorways in them. Make sure the main portion of the carpet is lying flat with no wrinkles or buckles.

Make a small pencil mark on the floor at each end of the carpet edge where the first seam will fall. Fold back the carpet, and strike a chalk line on the floor between the two pencil marks. Start 12 inches away from one end wall and apply the double-faced carpet tape along the chalk line, stopping 12 inches short of the other end wall. With the protective liner on the tape, press the tape down firmly. Apply a second strip of tape of the same length on the other side of the line. The chalk line should just be visible. Press the carpet down firmly.

Unfold the carpet to make sure the edge covers one tape strip completely and is against the chalk line along the entire length of the seam. If you are installing a shag carpet, brush all the shag pile up and away from the seam edge. Slowly pull off the protective liner from the tape strip beneath the carpet edge. As you pull off the tape liner, gently press the carpet down onto the exposed tape with the carpet edge against the chalk line. When the carpet edge completely covers the length of tape, walk on it to insure a good bond.

Roll out the second piece of carpet and butt it against the first piece at the seam edge. Make sure the directional arrow on the back is pointing in same direction as on the first piece. Rough-cut the carpet, if necessary, and allow the excess to run up the walls and into the doorways. Keep the second piece butted firmly against the seam edge and make the necessary relief cuts; do not trim. If you are installing shag carpet, brush back all the shag pile from both carpet edges, making sure you do not trap any tufts in the seam.

Beginning at one end, carefully remove the tape liner beneath the second piece of carpet, pulling the liner out through the seam. As you pull the liner out, butt the carpet firmly in place down onto the exposed tape and against the first piece. When the carpet edge completely covers the tape strip, walk on the seam to insure a good bond. Rub the seam lightly with your fingertips and free any pile that is pinched in the seam. Carefully trim any frayed pile from the surface of the seam with scissors. Also trim the excess from the wall edges of both pieces, using the chalk-line technique described earlier.

The next step is to tape the final 12 inches at both ends of the seam. Apply two strips of tape to the floor on both sides of the seam line. Complete the seam as described above. Repeat for the other end. *Note:* Follow this exact installation and seaming technique for subsequent pieces of carpet to be installed in the room. It will not be necessary, however, to strike a chalk line for the remaining seams. A pencil line drawn along the edge of the carpet will serve as the seam line.

To complete the installation, make a pencil line along the outside edge of the carpet in all doorways. Fold back the carpet edge and apply one strip of tape along the inside of the line. Unfold the edge, keeping the pile brushed up, and slowly peel off the liner while pressing the edge down onto the exposed tape. When the floor is completely covered, walk on the edge of the carpet for firm bond. For a finishing touch on exposed edges and doorways, use metal door trim or reducer strips, available at the dealer or any hardware store. Finally, replace or install the quarter-round molding around the room.
Installing roll carpeting with tackless stripping. The basic techniques of installing carpeting with tackless stripping and with pressure-sensitive tape are very similar. As already mentioned, the tackless strips are nailed to the floor around the perimeter of

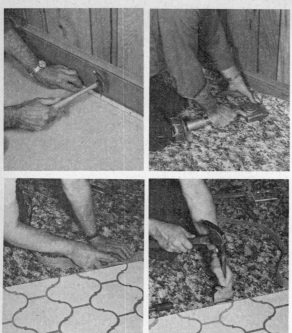

Figure 4–34. Installing roll carpeting with tackless stripping: *(top left)* The tackless strips are nailed to the floor around the perimeter of the room. *(top right)* A knee-kicker is used to stretch the carpet over the points of the tackless strips. *(bottom left)* The excess carpet is cut off. *(bottom right)* The edge is forced into place.

the room. Locate them a ¼ inch from the wall molding with the projecting points facing towards the wall. Then position the padding, tack it down, and trim off the excess so that the edge of the padding meets the edge of the strip farthest from the wall. Then cut the carpet to size as described on page 130.

Fasten the carpet along two walls with temporary tacking. Then, using a carpet stretcher, which usually can be rented from your carpet dealer, stretch the carpet taut over the spikes of the tackless strips along the two other walls. Bend the nose of the carpet stretcher downward to hook the carpet onto the spikes. Incidentally, the face of the stretcher, which is sometimes called a "knee-kicker," has adjustable needle-like teeth that are lengthened or shortened, according to the depth of the carpet pile, by a dial on its back. The teeth grip the carpet while you kick the cushioned end of the tool with your knee.

Remove the temporary tacking and restretch the carpet over the points of the tackless stripping. Trim the excess carpet, leaving a ⅜-inch overlap. Using a pointed hook, tuck the overlap into the channel between the strips and the wall molding.

Lift the carpet off the gripping spikes at points where too much has been trimmed and use the carpet stretcher to butt the carpet up against the wall molding. Protect the exposed edge of the carpet at a doorway by making use of metal door trim or reducer strips.

SEAMLESS PLASTIC FLOORING

Seamless flooring systems are colorful, decorative, and durable. There are a number of seamless systems on the market, and most contain three basic elements: a liquid plastic background base, plastic color chips, and a clear liquid plastic wear surface. The background and base coat is applied first, then alternate layers of the clear liquid and color chips. The chips become embedded in the clear plastic as several layers are built up, and then several more layers of the plastic are applied to seal and give gloss to the surface. All the coats are applied in a continuous flow without seams, leaving a sanitary, smooth, and easy-to-maintain finished surface.

Unlike other floor coverings, seamless flooring becomes a permanent part of the substrate. Most systems can be applied over existing worn floors such as wood, linoleum, concrete, ceramic tile, or vinyl. The condition of the existing floor and care in surface preparation are often more critical, however, than for an application over a new floor surface or subfloor of plywood and similar materials.

Seamless flooring is formulated to withstand extreme wear and abuse. Wear is normally limited to the top coat, which is easily retouched or restored simply by sanding the area and applying another glaze or wear coat. Since their introduction into the commercial and residential flooring field, seamless systems have proven highly satisfactory. Unsatisfactory installations usually can be traced directly to poor substrate preparation or failure to use a single manufacturer's complete system. The latter is extremely important since each component of the various systems—sealers, base coats, colored chips, or other decorative materials and wear coats—is formulated for compatibility with the others to give top performance.

Surface preparation. While surface preparation should always be in accordance with the manufacturer's recommendations for his particular seamless system, the basic rule is that all surfaces, new or old, must be in sound, stable, and clean condition to assure satisfactory results. Cracks should be patched, loose tiles should be replaced or sealed, existing flooring should be securely fastened to prevent movement after application, and all substrates should be thoroughly free of grease and dirt. The degree of surface preparation and method varies with each substrate, and often with each type of seamless flooring system.

If the original floor is badly worn and rough,

you should apply an underlayment as described earlier in this chapter to make the starting surface as smooth and level as possible. After installing underlayment, coat nailheads with shellac or a suitable primer to retard rust or oxidation. Fill, seal, or tape all cracks, joints, and other surface imperfections. Sand all filled areas smooth, vacuum, seal mill grade marks, and apply a seal or prime coat if recommended by the manufacturer.

Hard surfaces such as concrete and ceramic tile should, as a rule, receive an acid etching. Work with the acid very carefully and follow the manufacturer's recommendations completely. Failure of the floor to react to the acid etching indicates that there is a resistant contaminant on the concrete. Some curing compounds, oil and grease, asphalt and concrete-sealing compounds are extremely acid-resistant and must be removed by mechanical means, or by the use of a solvent. Old paint on concrete that is soft, chipped, or blistered must be removed, but some seamless systems can be applied over certain paint types if the concrete is in good condition and well bonded. Glossy finishes should be sanded until dulled. Remove wax, grease, and other materials as for old concrete. Keep in mind that some manufacturers do not recommend application over, on, or below grade concrete areas.

Because of chemical reaction, most manufacturers recommend that a bonding base of flat fiber glass strips be placed over asbestos and vinyl asbestos tiles. In putting down the fiber glass base a bonding liquid is first applied to the floor with a paint roller or brush in strips a little wider than the fiber glass material itself. Then, while the bonding liquid is still tacky, the precut fiber glass strips are laid in their proper position. Use a roller to press the fiber glass material into the bonding liquid and to remove any wrinkles. As you proceed across the room, each fiber glass strip is overlapped about an inch or so. Be sure to apply an extra coat of bonding liquid between the overlapped strips. When the fiber glass base is installed, it should be allowed to dry for about 4 hours.

Be certain your application tools and containers are clean. It is advisable to wear clean tennis shoes in the application area to avoid contamination of the clean, prepared surface. Remove the shoes when leaving the area or cover them with a plastic bag or similar material to avoid contamination of the shoes. Some manufacturers recommend wearing spiked shoes, such as golf shoes, when coating floors, before the base (chipping) coat has dried.

Have the following tools ready: (1) paint rollers, which are a popular means of applying many systems. A mohair (¼-inch nap) roller is recommended. (2) Notched trowels, paint brushes, or serrated rubber squeegees, which may be recommended by some manufacturers and can be used in place of rollers. Have cleaning solution for the tools handy. Some systems can be cleaned with soap and water before they are dry. Others require cleaning solutions or thinners.

Before applying any of the materials, make certain the room is well ventilated; it may be wise to use an exhaust or supplementary fan to remove solvent vapors. Also be sure to extinguish all pilot lights on stoves, water heaters, and heating systems. Do not permit any smoking in the area where the material is being applied.

Application of seamless floor. After the old floor has been properly prepared and the woodwork masked, apply the base or background coat. Base coats usually are available in black or white, and your choice will depend upon the effect you wish to achieve. A black base coat will as a rule make the color chips look darker, while on the white background they will appear lighter.

Spread the base chip coat with a paint roller (Figure 4–35) to which you can attach an extension handle in order to avoid stooping. Try to apply the base coat in consistent amounts all over. To apply, work on an area of approximately 3 by 8 feet. Once the base coat is applied, sprinkle the color chips into the wet plastic. If the base coat is not the chip-receiving coat, apply it and let it dry thoroughly. Then apply the manufacturer's recommended chip-receiving coat and, next, the decorative materials.

The technique of broadcasting the color chips is to toss them up and let them fall, almost as if they were snowflakes. (You can practice first on a clean floor, then sweep them up for use after applying the base plastic.) Do not skimp with the chips when creating your own color pattern. Be certain you have enough decorative materials or chips to create the pattern desired before you begin. To insure that the chips stick firmly into the clear liquid, it is a good idea to go over the area where the chips have been scattered with a clean roller. When proceeding across the floor, try to minimize the overlap between the different sections you work on. Balance the thickness of the overlapped areas with that of the rest of the floor. This may mean adding more liquid and chips between the overlaps as you go along. The best appearance is obtained when there is an even coverage. Apply enough color chips to leave the base coat beneath it barely visible. Excess decorative materials and chips can be easily removed with a clean broom or vacuum after the base coat has dried. Sand high areas where the chips have overlapped and are not firmly bonded. Vacuum thoroughly. If you discover any bare spots, apply a little more base plastic, sprinkle on the necessary chips, and go over the area again with the roller. Allow the base or chip-receiving coat to dry thoroughly before applying the finished plastic wear surface. Some coats dry in 4 to 6 hours;

Figure 4—35. *(left)* When applying a seamless plastic material, work in a small square area, about 2 to 3 square feet at a time. *(center)* As the base is applied, toss the vinyl chips at random in a selected pattern. *(right)* Apply the final coat as directed by the manufacturer. If desired, additional coats of the glaze can be applied to heavy-traffic areas. Each coat hardens in about an hour. The final coat should be left overnight (about twelve hours) before heavy furniture is put on it.

others must be left overnight to dry.

Some final coats can be applied as soon as the chip-receiving coat is hard enough to walk on; others require a longer, more thorough drying of the chip-receiving coat. Apply the final coat generously, if only one coat is recommended. Where more than one coat is recommended, apply a glaze or wear coat; allow it to dry according to manufacturer's directions; sand it if recommended; and then apply the second coat. Extra coats are often recommended if less texture is desired or to create a built-up, tougher surface. Use a roller to apply the final coat material.

The glaze, or wear coat, is a highly durable coating that resists abrasion and produces a long-lasting, easy-to-clean surface. Avoid traffic on this surface until it is completely dry, or as recommended by the manufacturer. If light traffic is essential, avoid tracking dirt over the area or scuffing the partially cured floor. Clean footwear is recommended. An important advantage of the poured floor lies in the fact that you can restore worn spots at a future time by simply applying more of the clear glaze or wear coat, thus giving the seamless floor an indefinite life.

STAIRS

The location, design, and installation of stairs are among the most important considerations in any remodeling job, whether partial or complete. Stairs should be beautiful, for that beauty adds one of the major ornamentations to a house. But just as important, stairways should be designed and constructed to afford safety and adequate headroom for the occupants as well as space for the passage of furniture. The two types of stairs commonly used in homes are: (1) the finished main stairs leading to the second floor or split-level floors and (2) the basement or service stairs leading to the basement or garage area. The main stairs are designed to provide easy ascent and descent and may be made a feature of the interior design. The service stairs to basement areas are usually somewhat steeper and are constructed of less expensive materials, although safety and convenience are still prime factors in their design.

Construction of stairs. Most finish and service stairs are constructed in place. The main stairs are assembled with prefabricated parts, which include housed stringers, treads, and risers, and are available in various types from most lumberyards. Basement stairs may be made simply of 2-by-12-inch carriages and plank treads. In split-level design or a midfloor outside entry, stairways are often completely finished with the walls, handrails, and appropriate moldings.

Wood species appropriate for main stairway components include oak, birch, maple, and similar hardwoods. Treads and risers for the basement or service stairways may be of Douglas fir, Southern pine, and similar species. A hardwood tread and a softwood or lower-grade hardwood riser may be combined to provide greater resistance to wear.

Types of stairways. The three general types of stairway runs most commonly used in house construction are the straight run (Figure 4—36A), the long "L" (Figure 4—36B), and the narrow "U" (Figure

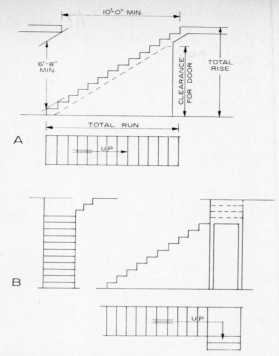

Figure 4–36. Common types of stair runs: (A) straight; (B) long "L."

4–37A). Another type is similar to the long "L," except that "winders" or "pie-shaped" treads (Figure 4–37B) are substituted for the landing. This type of stairway is not desirable and should be avoided whenever possible because it is obviously not as convenient or as safe as the long "L." It is used where the stair run is not sufficient for the more conventional stairway containing a landing. In such instances, the winders should be adjusted to replace the landings so that the width of the tread, 18 inches from the narrow end, will not be less than the tread width on the straight run (Figure 4–38A). Thus if the standard tread is 10 inches wide, the winder tread should be at least 10 inches wide at the 18-inch line. Frequently, in remodeling small and average-size homes in which stair space usually is limited, the two- or three-directional, open-string stair (so-called because one of the stringers is visible) with landings or winder treads often is best to use as it generally can be placed at the end of a room. In remodeling older homes it sometimes is necessary to use a single-directional, closed-string stairway (both stringers are closed in), especially in large rooms.

In planning the installation of stairs in a new location, which often is done in making alterations in old houses, obstacles that interfere with the placement of the stairwell may be encountered. These may be supporting main beams or joists,

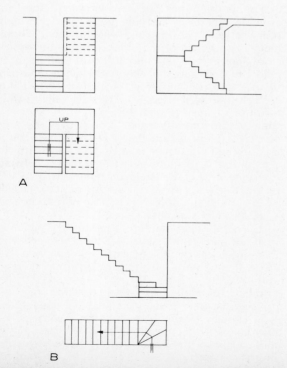

Figure 4–37. Space-saving stairs: (A) narrow "U"; (B) winder.

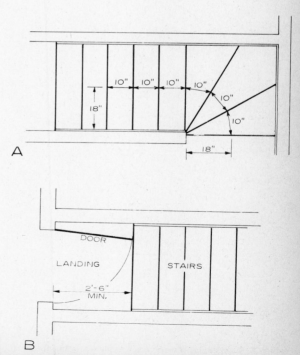

Figure 4–38. Stair layout: (A) winder treads; (B) landings.

chimneys, or other installations that cannot be moved. If the obstacle is at one end of the proposed opening, the loss in length sometimes can be compensated for by shifting the location of the stairs in the opposite direction. If this cannot be done, then winding steps or landings sometimes can be installed. Another solution to the lack of space is a spiral staircase, which requires as little as a 3½-foot diameter at both the top and landing floors. Spiral staircases are available in either wood or steel construction. The design of these prefabricated staircases is ornamental, with attractive hand railing and balusters. More details on spiral staircases are given later in this chapter.

Another basic rule in the layout of stairs concerns the landing at the top of the stairs when the door opens into the stairway, such as on stairs to the basement. This landing, as well as middle landings, should not be less than 2 feet 6 inches long (Figure 4–38B).

Sufficient headroom in any stairway is, of course, a primary requisite. For main stairways, clear vertical distance should not be less than 6 feet 8 inches (Figure 4–39A). Basement or service stairs should provide not less than a 6-foot 4-inch clearance.

The minimum tread width and riser height must also be considered. For closed stairs, a 9-inch tread width and an 8¼-inch riser height should be considered a minimum, even for basement stairways (Figure 4–39B). Risers with less height are always more desirable. The nosing projection should be at least 1⅛ inches; however, if the projection is too much greater, the stairs will be awkward and difficult to climb.

Ratio of riser to tread. There is a definite relation between the height of a riser and the width of a tread, and all stairs should be laid out to conform to well-established rules governing this relation. If the combination of run and rise is too great, there is undue strain on the leg muscles and heart of the climber; if the combination is too small, his foot may kick the riser at each step and an attempt to shorten the stride may be tiring. Experience has proved that a riser 7½ to 7¾ inches high with appropriate tread width combines both safety and comfort.

A rule of thumb that sets a good relation between the height of the riser and the width of the tread is: The tread width multiplied by the riser height in inches should be equal to 72 to 75. The stairs in Figure 4–39B would conform to this rule — 9 × 8¼ = 74¼. If the tread is 10 inches, however, the riser should be 7½ inches, which is more desirable for common stairways. Another rule sometimes used is: The tread width plus twice the riser height should equal about 25.

These desirable riser heights should be used to determine the number of steps between floors. For example, 14 risers are commonly used for main stairs between the first and second floors. The 8-foot ceiling height of the first floor plus the upper-story floor joists, subfloor, and finish floor result in a floor-to-floor height of about 105 inches. Fourteen divided into 105 is exactly 7½ inches, the height of each riser. Fifteen risers used for this height would result in a 7-inch riser height.

Stair widths and handrails. The width of the main stairs should be not less than 2 feet 8 inches clear of the handrail. However, many main stairs are designed with a distance of 3 feet 6 inches between the center line of the enclosing sidewalls. This will result in a stairway with a width of about 3 feet. With split-level entrance stairs, the minimum clear width is 2 feet 6 inches.

A continuous handrail should be used on at least one side of the stairway when there are more than three risers. When stairs are open on two sides, there should be protective railings on each side.

Framing for stairs. As was just stated, the stair opening, or well, should be cut wide enough and long enough to provide adequate headroom. Remember also that the dimensions of the opening must allow for the finish stringer, upper-floor nosing, and space for a rail. For example, the total finish allowance for the ordinary 36-inch, single-flight,

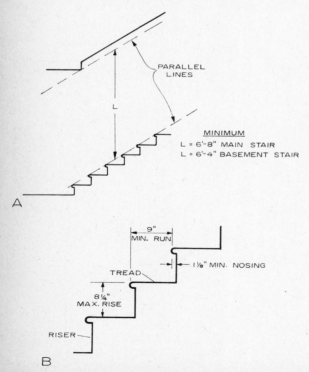

Figure 4–39. Stairway dimensions: (A) minimum headroom; (B) closed stair dimensions.

open-string stairway ordinarily would be about 5 inches. These figures are based on ⅝-inch thick dry wall and a standard 2⅜-inch-wide rail, plus 1 inch minimum finger room between the rail and the wall. Always check the walls of your stairwell with a level and straightedge to determine beforehand the allowances for out-of-plumb walls, corners, and other irregularities.

It is much easier to frame a stairway opening when its length is parallel to the joists. For basement stairways, the rough openings may be about 9 feet 6 inches long by 32 inches wide (two joists spaces). Openings in the second floor for the main stairs are usually a minimum of 10 feet long. Widths may be 3 feet or more. Depending on the short header required for one or both ends, the opening is usually framed as shown in Figure 4–40A when joists parallel the length of the opening.

When the length of the stair opening is perpendicular to the length of the joists, a long doubled header is required (Figure 4–40B). Under these conditions, the header, without a supporting wall be-

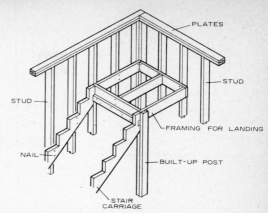

Figure 4–41. Framing for stair landing.

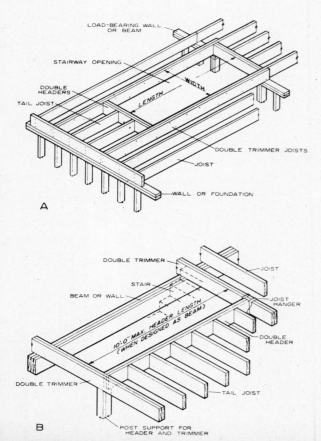

Figure 4–40. Framing for stairs: (A) length of opening parallel to joists; (B) length of opening perpendicular to joists.

neath, is usually limited to a 10-foot length. If there is a load-bearing wall under all or part of this opening, the framing is much simpler, for the joists will then bear on the top plate of the wall rather than being supported at the header by joist hangers or other means.

The framing for an L-shaped stairway is usually supported in the basement by a post at the corner of the opening or by a load-bearing wall beneath. When a similar stairway leads from the first to the second floor, the landing can be framed-out (Figure 4–41). The platform frame is nailed into the enclosing stud walls and provides a nailing area for the subfloor as well as a support for the stair carriages.

Stairway details. The following discussion gives pertinent information for installing basement stairs and main stairs.

Basement stairs. Stair carriages that carry the treads and support the loads on the stairs are made in two ways. Rough stair carriages commonly used for basement stairs are made from 2-by-12-inch planks. The effective depth below the tread and riser notches must be at least 3½ inches (Figure 4–42A). Such carriages are usually placed only at each side of the stairs; however, an intermediate carriage is required at the center of the stairs when the treads are 1 1/16 inches thick and the stairs are wider than 2 feet 6 inches. Three carriages are also required when the treads are 1⅝ inches thick and when the stairs are wider than 3 feet. The carriages are fastened to the joist header at the top of the stairway or rest on a supporting ledger nailed to the header (Figure 4–42B). Fire stops should be used at the top and bottom of all stairs.

Perhaps the simplest system is one in which the carriages are not cut out for the treads and risers. Rather, cleats are nailed to the side of the unnotched carriage and the treads are nailed to them. This design, however, is usually not as desirable as

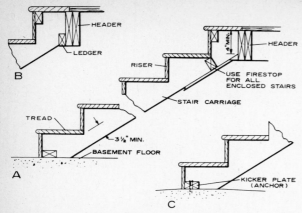

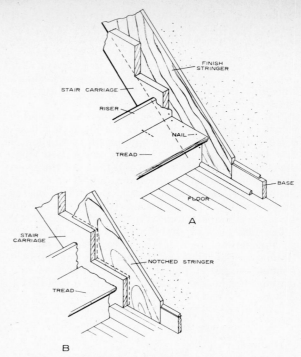

Figure 4–42. Basement stairs: (A) carriage details; (B) ledger for carriage; (C) kicker plate.

the notched carriage system when walls are present. Carriages can also be supported by walls located below them.

The bottom of the stair carriages may rest on and be anchored to the basement floor. Perhaps a better method is to use an anchored 2-by-4- or 2-by-6-inch treated kicker plate (Figure 4–42C).

Basement stair treads can consist of simple 1½-inch-thick plank treads without risers. However, from the standpoint of appearance and maintenance, the use of 1⅛-inch finished tread material and nominal 1-inch boards for risers is usually justified. Finishing nails fasten them to the plank carriages.

A somewhat more finished staircase for a fully enclosed stairway might be used from the main floor to the attic. It combines the rough notched carriage with a finished stringer along each side (Figure 4–43A). The finished stringer is fastened to the wall before the carriages are fastened. Treads and risers are cut to fit snugly between the stringers and are fastened to the rough carriage with finishing nails. This may be varied somewhat by nailing the rough carriage directly to the wall and notching the finished stringer to fit (Figure 4–43B). The treads and risers are installed as previously described.

Main stairway. An open main stairway with its railing and balusters ending in a newel post can be very decorative and pleasing in the traditional house interior. It can also be translated into a contemporary stairway design, which also results in a pleasing feature. The main stairway differs from the other types previously described because of: (a) the housed stringers that replace the rough plank carriage; (b) the routed and grooved treads and risers; (c) the decorative railing and balusters in open stairways; and (d) the wood species, most of which can be given a natural finish.

The supporting member of the finished main

Figure 4–43. Enclosed stairway details: (A) with full stringer; (B) with notched stringer.

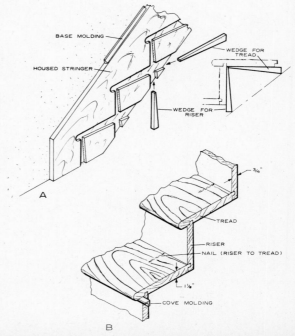

Figure 4–44. Main stair details: (A) housed stringer; (B) combination of treads and risers.

stairway is the housed stringer (Figure 4–44A). One is used on each side of the stairway and fastened to the finished walls. The stringers are routed to fit both the tread and riser. The stairs are assembled by means of hardwood wedges, which are spread with glue and driven under the ends of the treads and in back of the risers. Assembly is usually done from underneath and to the rear side of the stairway. In addition, nails are used to fasten the riser to the tread between the ends of the step (Figure 4–44B). When treads and risers are wedged and glued into housed stringers, the maximum allowable width is usually 3 feet 6 inches. For wider stairs, a notched carriage is used between the housed stringers.

When stairs are open on one side, a railing and balusters are commonly used. Balusters may be fastened to the end of the treads, which have a finished return (Figure 4–45). The balusters are also fastened to a railing that is terminated at a newel post. Balusters may be turned from doweled ends, which fit into drilled holes in the treads and railing. A stringer and appropriate moldings are used to complete the stairway trim.

When planning to remodel a steep staircase, you should keep in mind that the reason for such an arrangement was most likely to keep the stairwell to a minimum. For this reason, any change in the staircase opening will generally require a major change in the floor plan of that area. Walls may

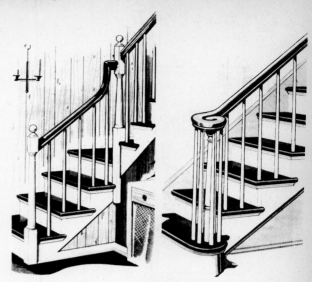

Figure 4–46. Two ready-made stairway designs.

have to be removed and closets taken out; but as a rule it is well worth the effort. If the stairwell can be expanded to either side, then a platform can be built near the center and the steps below that point can be run off at right angles to the existing flight. This is sometimes true of the totally enclosed stairway where one wall is simply a partition.

Remodeling by repairing stairs. Often stairs can be made livable by making simple repairs to them. For instance, a stair tread that squeaks as weight is applied and removed is loose; the noise results from the movement of the tread against other parts of the stair structure. The tread can usually be fastened down with finishing nails driven through it and into the riser under the front of the tread. The riser is the vertical board at the back of the step. In the best stair construction it is attached to the tread above by a tongue-and-groove joint. When nails are used to fasten the tread down to the riser, they can be driven in at angles or skewed to assure a better attachment. The nails should be driven under the surface of the wood with a nail set and the holes filled with crack filler or wood putty. It is also possible to eliminate many squeaks by removing the molding under the overhanging edge of the tread, driving thin wedges of wood into the joint between the tread and the riser, and replacing the molding.

A loosened handrail can be braced by simply tightening or replacing the wall bracket screws. They must, of course, be solidly anchored in a wall stud or used with heavy plugs, if the wall is masonry. At the top of the stairs, where the handrail end may be attached to the wall, a few long finishing nails can be used for reinforcement. If necessary, break out the wall surfacing and see to it that the

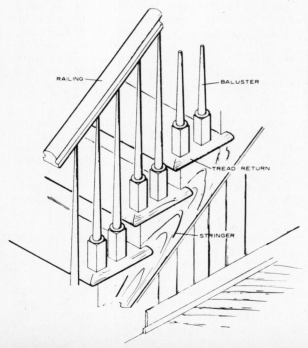

RAILING

BALUSTER

TREAD RETURN

STRINGER

Figure 4–45. Details of an open main stairway.

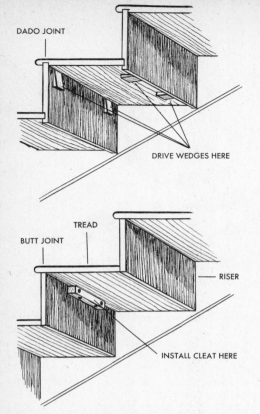

Figure 4—47. Two methods of removing squeaks from stairs.

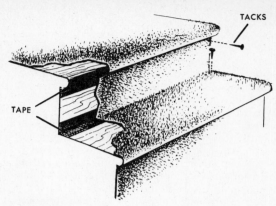

Figure 4—48. An easy method of carpeting stairs.

rail end is well seated against a solid support.

At the bottom of the stairs, where the rail posts are set into the steps, the peg may be loose. If so, an extra nail will help. Or, the newel post may be completely detached from the end frame. Correct this by working some glue into the back and tightening the post with screws, countersunk and plugged with matching grain.

Stairs can be refinished as described in Chapter 9.

Carpeting stairs. One of the quickest ways to remodel a staircase is to install carpeting. While stairways can be covered either with fitted carpeting or with strip carpeting, the former requires the services of an experienced carpet installer. On the other hand, strip carpeting, often called runners, can be installed by the average home craftsman.

Runners for stairway use come in standard widths of 18, 22½, 27, and 36 inches and are sold by the lineal yard. To find the amount of carpeting needed, measure in inches the depth of one tread and the height of one riser; add the two measurements together and multiply by the number of stairs; to this figure, add the length of any landings and divide the resulting amount by 36 to determine the number of lineal yards.

Both pressure-sensitive tape and tackless stripping can be used to hold the stair carpeting. When employing tape (Figure 4–48), place it on both sides of the intersection between the riser and tread, and over the tread nosing. Lift the carpet over the nosing of the first two stair treads and tuck it into the first stair where tread and riser meet. After making sure the carpet is secure, press it firmly against the nosings. Continue laying the carpet up the stairs, using the same method for each stair. Always remember that stair carpeting should be laid with the pile facing down the stairs for maximum wear resistance. Check the sweep of the pile by stroking it back and forth lengthwise. The smoother stroke is called the "lay" of the pile direction.

When fastening the carpet with tackless fittings, nail an angled strip to the treads and risers of each stair except the bottom one. Fit an underlay pad beneath each metal strip. Fix the end of the carpet, pile side facing down, to the back of the bottom tread with an angled strip and to the bottom of the first stair riser with a flat metal strip. Stretch the carpet over the tread nosings of the two bottom stairs. Keeping it taut, press the center into the first angled strip and smooth the carpet into the teeth, working from the center outwards.

Attic folding stairs. When attics are used primarily for storage and where space for a fixed stairway is not available, so-called disappearing stairs are often used and may be purchased ready to install (Figure 4–49). They operate through an opening in the ceiling of a hall and swing up into the attic space, out of the way, when not in use. The folding staircase

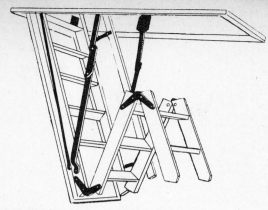

Figure 4—49. A typical folding attic stairway.

has a spring balance, and it can be lowered by pulling down a plywood panel in the ceiling with a short pole having a hook at one end. There are two basic styles of disappearing stairways: (1) the sliding ladder-type stairs, which are more solid underfoot, but require considerable overhead clearance in the attic; and (2) the jackknifed-type stairs, which fold up into two or three sections and unfold as they open into a single length; some models of these are quite rickety.

Before purchasing either type of disappearing stairway, check the required clearance or attic headroom and the floor space where the stairs will rest when they are in use. If you install the stairs too close to the wall, you will not be able to open them up properly. Where folding stairs are to be installed, the attic floor joists should be designed for limited floor loading.

To make the installation, outline the stairway's trapdoor dimensions on the ceiling below where the door is to be located. Drill 1-inch holes at the four corners of the rectangle and cut the opening. Remove a section of the joist as required and install the headers so the opening is framed out as for a normal stair opening. Then nail the stair frame in place. The stairway itself is installed by following the instructions furnished by the manufacturer. Make sure the stairs are plumb and square, and the opening mechanism is well balanced. Finish the installation by placing framing around the opening in the ceiling.

Spiral staircases. Prefabricated spiral staircases of either steel or wood are available, and require openings of only 3½, 4, 4½, and 5 feet in diameter. To determine the proper staircase size, after having selected the size of the opening, measure the finished floor-to-floor height of the staircase. Once

Figure 4—50. Two applications of a spiral staircase.

Table 4–5. *Finished floor to floor height*

Size, 3 feet 6 inches only		Size, 4 feet, 4 feet 6 inches, 5 feet	
Floor to floor (inches)	Number of treads	Floor to floor (inches)	Number of treads
81¼–90	9	82½–90¾	10
90¼–99	10	91 –99	11
99¼–108	11	99¼–107¼	12
108¼–117	12	107½–115½	13
117¼–126	13	115¾–123¾	14

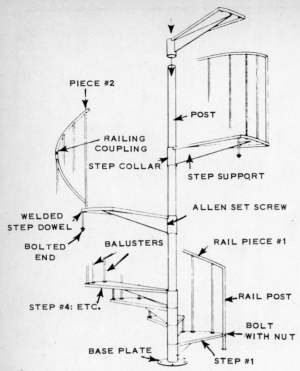

PIECE #2

POST

RAILING COUPLING

STEP COLLAR

STEP SUPPORT

ALLEN SET SCREW

WELDED STEP DOWEL

RAIL PIECE #1

BALUSTERS

BOLTED END

STEP #4: ETC.

RAIL POST

BOLT WITH NUT

BASE PLATE

STEP #1

Figure 4–51. Typical parts and installation of a spiral staircase.

this measurement is known, the number of treads can be determined (see Table 4–5).

When selecting either a left or right rotation of the stairs, consider the location of the platform and bottom step in relation to walls, doors, and hallways. Also give consideration to presenting the best view for the handrail and treads. The staircase well is framed as previously described.

The installation of a spiral staircase is simple (Figure 4–51), as indicated by the following typical instructions:

1. Stand the post up, align it to the exact position, and fasten the base plate.

2. Slide the step collars (Number 1 first) onto the post.

3. Position the steps to distribute the weight for balance. Then place the step dowels through outer holes in the lower steps and fasten them with nuts.

4. Install the handrail balusters in holes in the previously placed steps. Place the nuts, but leave them loose for railing adjustment.

5. Join the rail sections at the pipe coupling and tighten the set screw in the tapped hole. Then tighten the baluster nuts.

6. Fasten the floor joist to the top of the post support bracket and then tighten the allen-head set screw in the step collar to complete the job. If desired, the steps may be carpeted or tiled.

Chapter 5

REMODELING WITH ELECTRICITY

Modern living demands that your home have full housepower. By full housepower we mean, of course, that the wiring in a home is designed to carry sufficient electricity for all the lighting, appliances, and other equipment that a family uses, plus additional wiring for future growth. This means that an ample number of branch or wiring circuits provide for all the electrical needs; that the switches to control the lighting, and outlets to connect lamps and appliances, are placed where they are convenient to use; and that the installation meets both national and local minimum standards for safety. Codes and regulations give minimum standards. It is often desirable to design systems, select materials, and use installation methods of higher quality.

Low housepower is the direct opposite of full housepower. It means that the wiring is inadequate. There are several visible signs of low housepower:

1. Too few outlets are installed where needed. Octiplugs (devices that allow several appliances to be plugged into a single outlet) and extension cords are inconvenient and can be safety hazards.

2. Circuit breakers trip frequently or fuses blow often.

3. Lamps become dim when certain appliances such as the refrigerator begin operating.

4. Heating appliances operate slowly.

5. Television pictures shrink or wave when certain appliances are used.

6. Motor-driven appliances overheat frequently.

7. Only a few appliances can be operated at the same time.

There are some less visible signs that are also important. No appliance operates as efficiently on low housepower as it does with full housepower. Each light bulb gives less light and each appliance operates more slowly than it would with adequate housepower. Some appliances wear out more quickly as well. Low housepower is inconvenient and uneconomical. It is important, therefore, to plan for full housepower in both new and existing homes.

PLANNING YOUR ELECTRIC NEEDS

Electrical power in a home may be compared to a water system, such as a pipe with several faucets. As the first faucet is turned on, a stream of water rushes out with considerable pressure. As two or three more faucets are turned on, there is a noticeable drop in the pressure of the water coming from the first faucet. As more faucets are turned on, the water drops to a slow trickle from each faucet. This is because the pipe is limited in its water-carrying capacity; it cannot carry enough water to supply all faucets adequately.

Electrical circuits operate similarly. With an inadequate circuit, as more appliances are connected, the electrical power available to a given appliance is limited. In order to have enough power delivered to each appliance, it becomes necessary to operate only one or two at a time. The way to correct this problem is to have larger wires capable of delivering more electrical power to the appliances or to install more circuits so that appliances are fed from different circuits.

Low housepower is usually due to the wiring system in the home. Electric utility companies maintain and deliver as much power to a home as can be used under normal conditions. However, this power cannot enter the home and be put to use unless the wires are large enough to carry it. There is a practical limit to the size of the wire which can be distributed through a home. Therefore, more circuits (more wires) with fewer appliances on each circuit are used.

Estimating service needs. Table 5–1 lists electrical appliances together with their average demands for electric current. As we all know, lamp bulbs in a home require from 25 watts to 300 watts (the measurement used for current consumption). On the other hand, a heat-consuming device such as an electric clothes dryer demands about 5000 watts. Obviously, the thin wires used to convey current to your lights and television set (only 300 watts) are not going to carry as much as the dryer requires.

To determine the total service requirements for your home, take a paper and pencil and write down, for each room in the house and for each area outside the house, just how much wattage is being consumed at the present time. The amount of wattage each device requires is indicated clearly on it somewhere. It is shown on the large end of light bulbs, on the maker's nameplates of all motors, and on the plates of practically all heating devices. Also write down what you intend adding in any remodeling improvement or addition. The sum of the watts

Table 5–1. *Load requirements of household appliances*

Type of appliance	Typical watts	Usual voltage*	Size of wires	Fuse size recommended (amp)
Electric range	12,000	120/240	3 No. 6	50–60
Dishwasher	1200	120	2 No. 12	20
Refrigerator	300	120	2 No. 12	20
Home freezer	350	120	2 No. 12	20
Garbage disposer	300	120	2 No. 12	20
Automatic washer	700	120	2 No. 12	20
Automatic dryer	5000	120/240	3 No. 10	30
Rotary ironer	1650	120	2 No. 12	20
Water heater		Check with utility company		
Power workshop	1500	120	2 No. 12	20
Television	300	120	2 No. 12	20
20,000-Btu air conditioner	1200	120	2 No. 12	20
Heating plant	600	120	2 No. 12	15–20
Central air-conditioning system		Check with utility company		
Space heating		Check with utility company		

*Nominal voltages usually specified by manufacturers.

now being used by all present equipment and that required in the future is your total current need. Your home should be wired to handle this load.

To determine what load your present system will stand, cut off the power by pulling the lever of the main switch. (This step precedes *any* electrical work in the house. The fuse box or circuit breaker can then be opened safely.) It is a good idea to determine what circuits in the house are controlled by which fuse or circuit breaker. To do this, remove one fuse or throw one breaker, turn the main switch on, then check the house to discover which lights and outlets are not working. Indicate all these units on a chart near the fuse box. Add up all the electrical equipment that takes its current from this fuse. Repeat the step with each of the other circuits.

The size of the wires behind each of the fuses or circuit breakers will tell the wattage they can handle. You should have for each

No. 14 wire	a 15-amp fuse	1,750-watt capacity
No. 12 wire	a 20-amp fuse	2,300-watt capacity
No. 10 wire	a 30-amp fuse	2,600-watt capacity

If an older house has one or more 30-amp fuses, the electric service is limited to a few lights and a few plug-in type appliances. As soon as the 30-amp-per-line capacity is reached, or sooner, those lines have reached their maximum capacity. No more appliances can be plugged in; the house is outmoded electrically. The steps toward adequate wiring therefore include:

1. Bringing enough current to the house
2. Correct protection for the current with the right-type fuse or breaker
3. Sufficient branch lines with proper-size wires leading from them, each protected with the right-size fuse or breaker
4. Not overloading branch lines

Selecting the right service and circuits. The size of the service entrance wires determines the total amount of electricity the home can use at one time. From the service entrance, distribution to the various parts of the house must be made over adequate-size wires capable of handling the loads listed above, and protected with the correct amp-size fuses shown in connection with each wire size. Thus your electric service entrance installation is the heart of your system. It includes all wiring from power lines to service panel. With a proper installation, current is delivered to the panel at full voltage. Then, with up-to-date wiring in your home, current will flow to all outlets without loss, and lights and appliances will operate efficiently. Remember, if service wires are too light and the panel too small, you are in for future problems.

Electricity is delivered at pressures of about 120 volts and 240 volts. Major electrical appliances such as the electric range, water heater, clothes dryer, and large air conditioners are usually operated on a 240-volt system. As previously stated, the

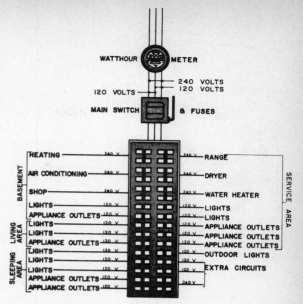

Figure 5—1. The branch circuit distribution panel.

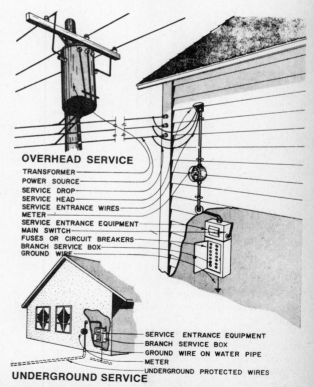

OVERHEAD SERVICE

TRANSFORMER
POWER SOURCE
SERVICE DROP
SERVICE HEAD
SERVICE ENTRANCE WIRES
METER
SERVICE ENTRANCE EQUIPMENT
MAIN SWITCH
FUSES OR CIRCUIT BREAKERS
BRANCH SERVICE BOX
GROUND WIRE

SERVICE ENTRANCE EQUIPMENT
BRANCH SERVICE BOX
GROUND WIRE ON WATER PIPE
METER
UNDERGROUND PROTECTED WIRES

UNDERGROUND SERVICE

Figure 5—2. Service entrance equipment.

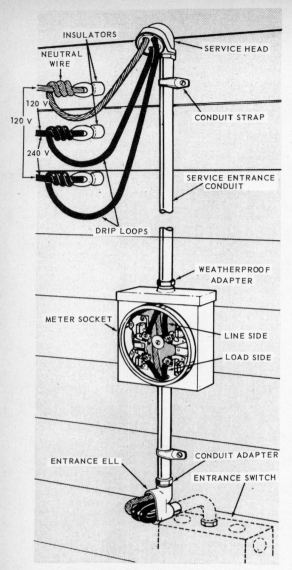

Figure 5–3. Service entrance using conduit.

central air conditioning together with lighting and the usual small appliances, you will need a 150-amp service as a minimum. With the addition of electric heating, a 200-amp service is necessary.

A 150-amp service provides sufficient electric capacity for lighting and portable appliances, including ironer, roaster, rotisserie, and refrigerator, 12,000-watt range, and 8,700-watt clothes dryer as well as for 5,000 watts (3 to 5 tons) of central or room air conditioning plus any of the appliances listed in Table 5 – 1, up to 5,500 watts. A 200-amp service provides the same capacity as the 150-amp service but will also handle electric house-heating equipment.

100-amp service. Number 2 or number 3 (type RHW insulation), 3-wire electric service with 100-amp service panel is minimum according to the National Electric Code for homes up to 3,000 square feet in floor area. In most areas, the minimum electric service for new homes is 100 amps for lights, roaster, ironer, refrigerator, and 8,000-watt range plus appliances listed in Table 5 – 1 up to a 10,000-watt total.

60-amp service. This service consists of number 8, 2-wire electric service (for 120 volts only) with a 30-amp service panel. Only a limited capacity for lighting and a few of the smaller appliances is provided; thus this service should never be used except temporarily or for one-room buildings. You would have to enlarge the service capacity before using any major electrical appliances.

Your local power company will decide where the electric service will enter your building. The service panel should be located near the room where the largest amount of current will be needed, usually the kitchen. The power company usually supplies the meter and sometimes furnishes and installs all wiring leading to the meter. Wiring beyond the meter is your responsibility. Wires should run as directly as possible from the electric service head down the wall to the meter and panel.

Electric service installation may be made with either (1) service cable or (2) rigid or thin-wall conduit. Which you use depends on state or local requirements, so check before you start. Service cable is the material most often used; it is armored or unarmored depending on locality. Its advantages are low material and installation costs. Conduit is steel pipe through which wires run.

Fuseless and fused panels. The circuit-breaker panel eliminates fuses. If a circuit is overloaded or shorted, the breaker automatically breaks the flow of current. Just flip the switch to restore service after the cause of the short has been corrected. A fuse-type panel may also be installed. It is less expensive, but the fuseless type is much more convenient and economical, because the circuit breakers are simply reset whenever overloads occur; they need not be replaced.

size of the service entrance should be based on current needed, now and in the future. In the older-style home, a 60-ampere electric service was sufficient. Today the size should be selected from the following guidance list for homes:

150- and 200-amp service. Number 1/0 or number 3/0 (type RHW insulation), 3-wire electric service with a 150- or 200-amp service panel respectively is preferred for modern wiring where full housepower is desired. In homes equipped with an electric range, water heater, high-speed dryer, or

Types of circuits. There are four basic types of circuits in the home: general-purpose, appliance, individual equipment, and communication.

General-purpose circuits are used to serve lights throughout the home and all convenience outlets except those in the kitchen, dining room, and laundry and utility room. Appliances generally connected to these circuits include television sets, radios, clocks, fans, heat and sun lamps, small air conditioners, and vacuum cleaners.

Appliance circuits serve all convenience outlets in the kitchen, dining room, and laundry and utility room. Equipment commonly connected to these circuits include the refrigerator, toaster, roaster, mixer, can opener, compactor, and hand iron.

Individual equipment circuits serve single appliances or items of equipment such as the range, food waste disposer, dishwasher, clothes dryer, water heater, and electric control on the heating plant.

Communication circuits serve the bells, chimes, intercom, built-in sound system, buzzers, security system, and so on.

The number of general-purpose circuits required varies with the size of the house. A good rule of thumb is to allow one 20-amp, 120-volt circuit for each 500 square feet of floor area, or one 15-amp, 120-volt circuit for not more than 375 square feet of floor space. Areas in the attic and basement that lend themselves to possible future use for living, that is, where it is practical to create finished rooms at some later date, should be included in the calculations.

The number of appliance circuits is also determined by the floor area of the house. A home containing up to 800 square feet should have three such circuits; from 800 to 1,500 square feet, there should be four circuits; from 1,500 to 3,000 square feet, there should be five circuits; and over 3,000 square feet, there should be six circuits.

The number of individual equipment circuits required is also based on the floor area of the home. Even though the equipment listed below may not be installed initially, it is desirable that the circuit provisions be made. Not less than four circuits are recommended in even the smallest house. These four circuits serve the cooking range, water heater, heating plant, and clothes washer. If the house measures between 1,000 and 1,500 square feet, circuits should be added for a clothes dryer and dishwasher. A larger home, containing up to 3,000 square feet, should have circuits for a food waste disposer and a bathroom heater. And the acme of electrification would include circuits for an air-conditioning unit and an electronic air cleaner. If you expect to use power tools drawing heavy loads, they should have their own separate circuit.

To get off to the right start, prepare your plans in accurate scale for every room in the house where electrical remodeling is to be done. Such plans help you determine exactly how much material will be needed and also serve as practical working guides when making the installation. That is, locate the exact position of all appliances and lighting fixtures on the plan. The exact position of switches and outlets to accommodate these appliances and fixtures should also be determined. Next, the electrical symbols representing the switches, outlets, and electrical devices should be drawn on the floor plan. A line is then drawn from each switch to the connecting fixture. While the *exact* position of each wire is determined when making the installation, you should indicate only the position of the fixture and the switch and the connecting line on the plan.

After your electrical plans have been completed, consult with the local power company. They will advise you on the type of electric service entrance to use, how much of the installation the power company will handle, and other electrical matters. In most localities, the local utility company will make the installation to the side of the house or yard pole.

Before starting the installation, find out whether you need a wiring permit. Securing the permit (if needed) should not be difficult, provided you have mastered the information in this chapter and acquainted yourself with the regulations of the National Electric Code so that your installation will pass inspection for safety. The National Electric Code is a book of regulations specifying correct installation methods and types of materials acceptable for various jobs. Your local power company can furnish a copy. In some communities local regulations sometimes supersede the National Code, so know what these local regulations are. Also be sure that materials you intend to use are approved by your power company.

SELECTING THE RIGHT WIRING MATERIALS

Modern wires and wiring devices have made the task of installing a proper electrical system in the home a great deal easier. When buying wiring materials, look for the Underwriters' tag or stamp to make sure that they meet minimum standards for safety and quality. Do not take chances with inferior materials that have not been listed by Underwriters.

Types of wire. There are three types of wiring you can use: armored; nonmetallic plastic sheathed; or thin-wall conduit, through which insulated wires are drawn.

Flexible armored cable. This type of wiring, commonly referred to as BX, can be supplied either in 2- or 3-wire types and with or without a lead sheath. The wires in BX, matched with a bare equipment ground wire, are initially twisted together. This grouping, totaling 3 or 4 wires with the

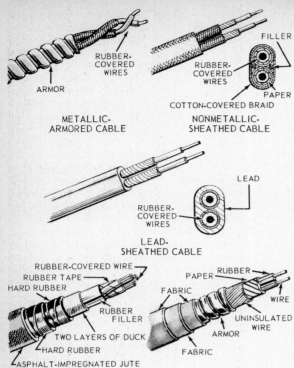

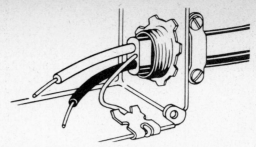

Figure 5—5. A three-wire nonmetallic-sheathed ground.

Figure 5—4. Multiconductor cables.

ground, is then wrapped in coated paper and a formed self-locking steel armor. The cable without a lead sheath is widely used for interior wiring under dry conditions. The lead sheath is required for installation in wet locations and through masonry or concrete building partitions where added protection for the copper conductor wires is required.

Nonmetallic cable. This type of wiring is available in two forms: one with a lighter-weight plastic jacket (designated as Type NM), which is popular for use inside the home; the other with a heavy plastic jacket (designated as Types NMC and UF) that many electrical codes now permit to be buried in the ground for running to the garage or other remote outdoor outlets, and which can be run through masonry. The plastic is impervious to moisture and most other corrosive effects, but should not be used in applications where it may be subject to physical wear or to mechanical abuse.

Plastic-covered cable can be obtained with two or more wires inside. It is also available with an extra ground wire inside, which is used to tie junction boxes together into a grounded system where this is needed (for instance, as the supply line to a garage). Actually, many local codes require

grounded boxes and nonmetallic cable with ground wire, similar to the plastic-sheathed cables described above. Figure 5–5 shows a simple installation of ground wire to outlet box. By using nonmetallic cable with a ground wire you have a continuous grounded system, which assures that the conductor will always be at ground potential, thus reducing the danger of shocks should some exposed metal be accidentally touched.

Conduit. There are two types of conduits: rigid and thin-wall. The former is much like water pipe, but with a smoother inside to protect the wires. Rigid conduits use threaded fittings. Thin-wall conduits are more economical, lighter, easier to cut or bend, and use compression-type fittings. Both are galvanized and may be used indoors or out, in damp or dry locations, and in masonry (except cinder concrete). Generally conduits are employed in new work only because it is difficult to install them in old structures. The most used sizes in home construction are ½-inch and ¾-inch conduits.

Once the conduit is installed, wires are "fished" through the pipes to every outlet as needed. For this, single-conductor insulated wires are generally used. As many wires as are needed can be fished through, up to the maximum number permitted in the size of conduit employed. Type T or Type TW conductors are the ones commonly used with conduits because they are prewaxed for ease in pulling through.

Wire size. The wire sizes are denoted by the use of the American Wire Gauge (AWG) standards. The largest gauge size is No. 0000. Wires larger than this are classified in size by their circular mil cross-sectional area. One circular mil is the area of a circle with a diameter of 1/1,000 of an inch. The most common wire sizes used in interior wiring are 14, 12, and 10, and are usually for house circuits.

The larger the number of the wire (Figure 5–6), the smaller its diameter, and the less capable it is of carrying heavy loads. While No. 14 is the smallest employed in actual house circuits, No. 18 and No. 16 are used as lamp cords and bell wire. No. 14 wire, capable of carrying 15 amps and 1,750 watts, is used for general lighting throughout the home

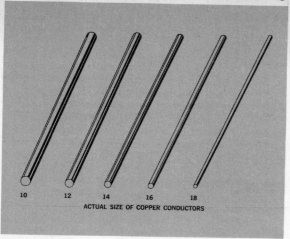

10   12   14   16   18
ACTUAL SIZE OF COPPER CONDUCTORS

Table 5—2. *Maximum wires in a box*

Box size (inches)	Deep boxes			
	Maximum number of wires			
	No. 14	No. 12	No. 10	No. 8
1½ × 3¼ octagonal	5	4	4	0
1½ × 4 octagonal	8	7	6	5
1½ × 4 square	11	10	9	7
1½ × 4¹¹/₁₆ square	16	14	12	10
2⅛ × 4¹¹/₁₆ square	20	18	14	12
2 × 1¾ × 2¾	5	4	4	0
2½ × 1¾ × 2¾	6	6	5	0
3 × 1¾ × 2¾	7	7	6	0
Shallow boxes (less than 1½ inches)				
3¼	4	4	3	0
4	6	6	4	0
4¹¹/₁₆	8	6	6	0

Figure 5—6. Wiring for general household use is available in 18-, 16-, 14-, 12-, and 10-gauge sizes. The larger the number of the wire, the smaller its diameter and its capacity for carrying heavy loads.

and for all convenience outlets except in the kitchen, dining area, and laundry. No. 12 wire, capable of carrying 20 amps and 2,300 watts, is used in the kitchen and dining area to service electric appliances such as refrigerators, freezers, broilers, blenders, and toasters. It is used in laundry areas for washing machines and gas dryers, but each should be on a separate circuit. No. 10 wire, rated at 30 amps and 3,500 watts, is designed for very heavy-drawing appliances, such as air conditioners, electric dryers, and washer-dryer combinations.

Wires are manufactured in both solid conductor or stranded. House circuits are usually wired with solid-conductor wire, while stranded wire — many small wires twisted together — is used primarily for extension cords. Heavy-service entrance wiring is stranded to be more flexible. Most wire conductors are still copper, but aluminum has become increasingly popular in the last few years because of its lower cost, greater availability over copper, and lighter weight. Since aluminum has slightly less current-carrying ability than copper, a next-larger wire size must be employed to carry the same load. Another consideration when using aluminum is that wiring devices, such as switches and receptacles, must be approved for aluminum wire. As a rule they are stamped "Al-Cu," the chemical terms for aluminum and copper. If they are not stamped, check with your electrical supplier. Many wiring devices are now made dual-metallic.

Electrical boxes. Outlet boxes provide a means of holding cable in position, a space for mounting such devices as switches and receptacles, protection for the device, and space for making splices and connections. Most electrical boxes are metal so

that they are part of the continuous grounded system. They are made in round, octagonal, and square shapes. They are available either with knockouts for connecting thin-wall conduit, with special clamps for nonmetallic plastic cable, or special clamps for flexible armored cable (BX). Their dimensions are fairly well standardized, regardless of manufacturer. Actually, their screw fittings on the front are standardized and will take any manufacturer's outlets, switches, or other electrical hardware. The number of wires entering a box is limited, as shown in Table 5—2.

In new work the boxes are usually mounted between studs on hangers or fastened to the studs themselves. Ceiling junction boxes for fixtures hang from headers nailed between ceiling joists or from specially designed metal hangers. These boxes are roomy enough to carry extra wires for distribution to other points. The square type is frequently used as a large outlet or switch box in unfinished areas, such as a basement. Gang boxes are outlet boxes with removable sides which allow two or more to be joined into a single large box. These are used whenever several switches and receptacles are to be grouped side by side. The gang is covered by a single combination plate.

For remodeling work in which boxes must be placed into existing walls, the so-called self-fastening boxes are good. These employ bent tabs at the sides or special screw clamps to hold them in sawed-out openings in the wall. For thin walls, where regular-size boxes are too deep, there are special boxes available which permit surface wiring.

Switches. A switch is a device used to connect and disconnect an electrical circuit from the source of power. The tumbler or toggle action switch is the one most often used in homes. Switches of this type may be one-pole or two-pole for ordinary lighting or receptacle circuits. If of the one-pole type, they must be connected to break the hot or ungrounded conductor of the circuit. If they are of the two-pole type, the hot and ground connection can be connected to either pole on the line side of the switch. The single-pole, single-throw type is the most commonly used. Switches are also available that can be operated in combinations of two, three, or more in one circuit. These are called three-way and four-way switches.

There are several variations of the toggle switch for special purposes. For instance, there are delayed-action switches that hold the circuit on for a few minutes after it has been turned off. These are most handy on exterior light circuits.

Receptacles or outlets. Portable appliances and devices are readily connected to an electrical supply circuit by means of an outlet called a receptacle. For interior wiring these outlets are installed as duplex receptacles and are now all of the three-wire type. The third wire on the three-wire receptacle is used to provide a ground lead to the equipment that receives power from the receptacle. The three-wire receptacle will take the regular two-prong plugs still found on many portable appliances. However, it is wise to ground a receptacle, and most local electrical codes require it.

On all three-wire receptacles, there is a green grounding terminal. When the metal outlet box is

located flush with the finished wall and is fastened so that the projecting metal tabs on the receptacle make firm contact with the metal outlet box, no wires have to be connected to this grounding terminal. Otherwise the terminal should be wired to a screw threaded into the back of the box. Modern boxes have prethreaded holes for this purpose, but with older ones you must drill a pilot hole in and drive in sheet metal screws to hold the grounding wires. When remodeling an electrical system where the present outlet boxes are not metal or are not grounded, the old-style two-prong, two-wire convenience outlets should be used.

WORKING WITH WIRE

In a two-wire cable, one wire will usually be covered with black insulation, the other with insulation that is partly or entirely white. In three-wire cable, the third wire will usually have red insulation on it. This enables the electrician to connect the various wires correctly, as explained below. Of the two main wires leading into a house from the outside, one is grounded or connected to the earth as a safety measure. An electrical ground is any conductor connected directly, or through other conductors, to the earth. The white (or neutral) wire of all alternating current systems must be grounded. This grounding assures that the conductor will always be at ground potential, thus reducing the effects of high voltage and lightning strokes. Such grounding also prevents shocks should exposed metal be accidentally touched. Thus, keep this important rule in mind:
Never connect the black (hot) wire to the white (neutral) wire.

Connect the black wire to the brass-colored terminal on switches, receptacles, sockets, and fuse boxes, and to the black wires on pull-chain fixtures. The white (neutral or ground wire, also called the continuous wire) is grounded at the electric service switch. Connect it to the silver or light-colored terminal of all receptacles, etc., and to the white wire on all lighting fixtures.

Three-wire cable is used between two three-way switches to provide two separate and independent control points for a light. An example of this type of installation is a garage light that can be turned on and off from inside the house or from the garage.

Working with armored cable. Armored cable may be fastened to wooden structural members with a one- or two-hole type mounting strap formed to fit the contour and size of the cable, or by staples made specifically for armored cable use. The cable is normally supported at the box entry by integral BX clamps built into the boxes, or by BX connectors. Whenever possible an armored cable installation should be run through holes centrally drilled in the

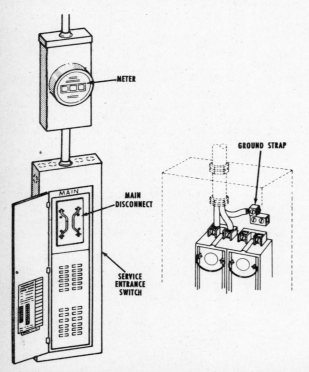

Figure 5–7. *(left)* Service entrance equipment; *(right)* detail of service entrance terminals.

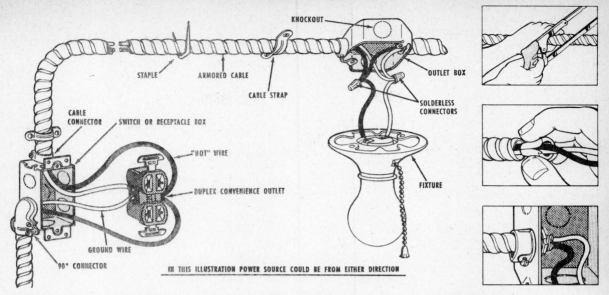

Figure 5—8. Armored cable installation. The procedure for preparing and attaching armored cable is given at the right.

building's structural members, and the holes should be at least 1/8 inch oversize to facilitate easy "pull through" of the BX. The flush-type mounting of BX accomplished by notching the joists and studs should be avoided whenever possible. This type of installation exposes the BX to possible short circuits by locating the cable in a position where it could be accidentally pierced by nails and materially weakens the structural member. When armored cable is run between joists and studs, it should be supported by staples or straps at least every 4 1/2 feet along the length of the cable run. These supports must also be installed within 12 inches of each box entry, unless the support interferes with installations that require extreme flexibility. This requirement assures the continuance of a satisfactory box connection by relieving the strain on the splices and connections within the outlet box. Cable runs installed across the bottom of ceiling joist and studding faces at least 7 feet above the floor must be supported on each joist or stud. They may also be installed on running boards.

When installing armored cable; take great care to avoid bending or shaping the cable in a manner that damages the protective armor. This type of installation damage may occur in drilled holes for BX; in corner runs; or when locating boxes on studs and joists. To prevent this, the radius of the inner edge of any bend must not be less than five times the cable diameter.

When a box connection is made, armored cable must be spliced or connected only to devices in standard boxes. All cable used, therefore, must be

cut long enough to run from box to box. To prevent cutting the cable too short, the BX should first be threaded through the mounting holes drilled in the joists or studs and attached to one box.

Though armored cable can be cut with a BX cutter specifically designed for the job, the majority of electricians generally use a hacksaw. When an outlet connection is being made, the cable should first be cut completely through about 8 inches longer on each end than required for the run. When you remove the armored cable from the wire, the armor should be cut approximately 8 inches from the cable end so that ample wire will be inserted in the box for connecting to the outlet device. These lead lengths may be increased when the wire run terminates in a fuse or circuit breaker panel box and a longer cable is required. The cutting of cable armor is a simple operation, but care must be taken to avoid damaging the wire insulation when making the cut. With the

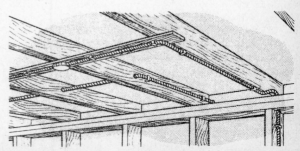

Figure 5—9. A typical armored cable wiring installation.

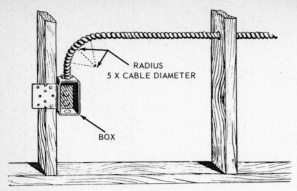

RADIUS
5 X CABLE DIAMETER

BOX

Figure 5–10. An armored cable bend.

hacksaw in one hand and the cable end held firmly in the other, make the cut with the blade of the hacksaw placed at right angles to the lay of the armor strip. The hacksaw and cable should form two legs of a 60-degree triangle. When the blade has cut almost through the armor strip, the cable end should be bent back and forth several times until it breaks. The loose armor can then be stripped from the wire leads by a twisting and pulling action. If one end of the cable has already been threaded and attached to a box, the cable should be pulled tight enough to assure a steady sawing surface. When cut from a coil, the armor is held firm by stepping on the coil cable end and pulling it tight. Rough or sharp ends of the cut are then smoothed with a file.

The fiber paper that is twisted around the conductors before the metallic armor is attached must be removed to allow free wire movement. Normally two or three turns of the paper are removed from under the armor by tearing the loose paper away from the wire at the armor end by a jerking action. The free space between the armor and the wires facilitates mounting the antishort bushing. When the ends of the cut armor are filed, only the outer burred edges are removed. The inner edges are always sharp and jagged at the cut end, and if not covered would tend to puncture the wire insulation and cause short circuits and grounds. To prevent this, a tough fiber bushing, commonly called an antishort, must be inserted between the armor and the wire to protect the wire against damage.

When the cable is used with a box having integral cable clamps, the knockout at the point of entry must first be pried out. Then the clamp-holding screw is loosened and the cable is inserted through the knockout opening and the leads threaded through the clamps. The armor is then forced snugly against the clamp end and the clamp screw is retightened, forcing the clamp into the ridges of the cable. When a BX connector is used in attaching the armored cable to a box, the cable is first inserted in the connector and the holding screw or screws are

tightened against the armor, securely connecting the cable and connectors. The BX connector is then inserted through a box knockout opening and is secured to the box by a locknut threaded on the connectors from inside the box.

Armored cable is preferred by many for exposed installations such as in unfinished basements, inside the garage, and near workbenches. The armor provides damage protection and adequate continuous ground to the metal outlet boxes. BX is also flexible enough so that it can be fed through small openings from attic or basement areas to boxes mounted on walls and ceilings. The cable is usually pulled into the concealed box with a fish wire or drop chain. The fish wire is used when the cable is to be fed from below the box location, whereas the drop chain is used when the installation is to be made from above. In these cases the junction box in which the power tap is to be made should be in a clear, readily accessible area since the fishing and catching of a fish wire and drop chain become a tedious and time-consuming operation if the junction box is concealed. If it is difficult because of building construction to feed the cable into the power tap box, the finished wall may have to be removed to allow entry. This will necessitate a replastering job after the addition has been installed.

Nonmetallic sheathed cable. NM cable (NM is the code designation for nonmetallic sheathed cable) is easier to work with than flexible armored cable and is preferred wherever it is concealed and not subject to mechanical damage.

When using NM cable, frequently called plastic cable, for exposed work, strap the cable every 3 feet on a supporting surface such as a stud, joist, wall, or ceiling. When run across the joists or through open spaces, the cable must be supported by a running board (see page 151) or drawn through holes drilled in the center of joists or studs. When bending the cable be careful not to damage the protective covering. Actually the minimum allowable radius of bend is five times the cable diameter. Though this bend limit is similar to the armored cable requirement, nonmetallic sheathed cable can be bent in a smaller arc. This is true because the cable diameters are smaller for the same wire gauge combinations.

In attics or roof spaces run the cable across the top of the floor beams, or across the face of the rafters at least 7 feet from the floor, and protect the cable by guard strips. If the attic is not reached by a stairway, guard strips will be required within 6 feet of the ladder hole.

For concealed work, strap the cable every 4½ feet (never use staples). Also be sure to strap within 12 inches of all outlets and switches. In new work, straps must be used for all runs whether concealed or exposed. In old work, straps must be used for exposed runs, but not for concealed runs.

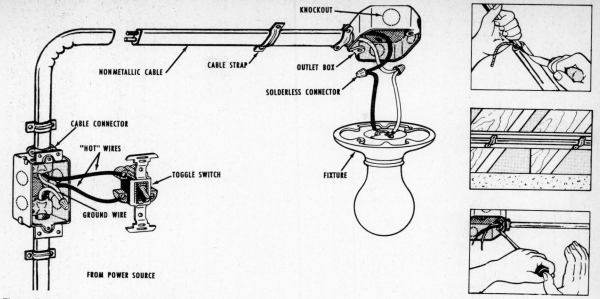

KNOCKOUT

NONMETALLIC CABLE

CABLE STRAP

OUTLET BOX

SOLDERLESS CONNECTOR

CABLE CONNECTOR

"HOT" WIRES

TOGGLE SWITCH

GROUND WIRE

FIXTURE

FROM POWER SOURCE

Figure 5–11. A nonmetallic cable installation.

Cable runs must be continuous from outlet to outlet because wire splices are permitted only inside a box. MN cable is prepared for box connection in the same manner as outlined for armored cable. In removing the protective sheathing from the conductors for connection, a pair of pliers or a knife rather than a hacksaw is used. In removing the covering a slit should be cut in the sheathing parallel to the wires without touching the individual wire insulation. A cut approximately 8 inches long for cable entry to ordinary boxes is satisfactory but can be increased to suit entry to panels. A knife is then used to remove the slitted sheathing. The moisture-preventive paper should also be removed from the wires. Frequently, a special tool called a cable stripper (Figure 5–12) is used instead of a

knife or pliers to remove the sheathing from NM cable, lead-covered cable, and portable cords. In operation, the stripper is inserted over the cable, squeezed together, and then pulled off the conductor. This action rips off the outer braid quickly and efficiently. The use of a stripper instead of a knife or pliers for outer braid removal is recommended since it cannot damage the wire insulation.

After the cable has been stripped, couplers, similar to those used for armored cable but made especially for NM cable, are used to fasten it into the knockout holes of existing boxes. This cable is also available with an extra ground wire, and it is recommended that you use this kind (Figure 5–13). Fishing and installing are otherwise the same as for armored cable.

Figure 5–12. A wire, or cable, stripper in use.

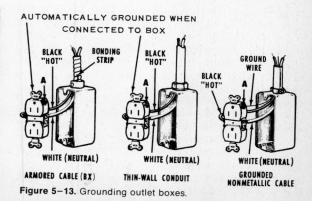

AUTOMATICALLY GROUNDED WHEN CONNECTED TO BOX

BLACK "HOT"   **BONDING STRIP**   **BLACK "HOT"**   **GROUND WIRE**   **BLACK "HOT"**

WHITE (NEUTRAL)   **WHITE (NEUTRAL)**   **WHITE (NEUTRAL)**

ARMORED CABLE (BX)   **THIN-WALL CONDUIT**   **GROUNDED NONMETALLIC CABLE**

Figure 5–13. Grounding outlet boxes.

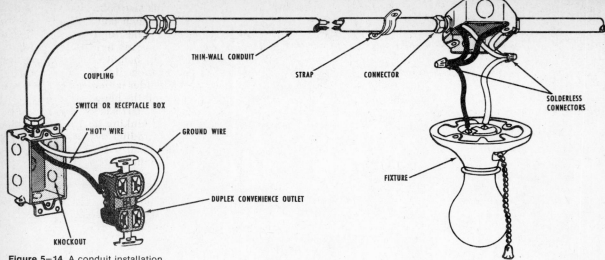

Figure 5–14. A conduit installation.

Conduit wiring. In many localities, particularly in cities and towns, regulations specify that all new work be done with conduit wiring. (New work is the wiring of additions in the process of construction.) The reason for using conduit wiring instead of armored cable or nonmetallic cable is that it is not so easily damaged. Also it is simpler, later on, to do minor rewiring because the wires can be pulled out of the conduit and larger ones installed if necessary.

As previously stated, electrical metallic tubing (EMT), commonly called thin-wall conduit, is more easily installed than rigid conduit by the average home handyman. For this reason, all references to conduit in this book are to the thin-wall type unless otherwise noted.

Thin-wall conduit and boxes are installed when the room addition is framed in, but before the paneling or gypsum board and finish floor are put in. However, the wires are not drawn through the conduit until the finished walls and flooring are installed. As a result, it is very difficult to wire an old house with conduit. As can be appreciated, conduit cannot be fed into a wall or ceiling through small holes. Entire sections of the wall, ceiling, or floor must be removed if conduit is used. For this reason, old houses are usually rewired with either nonmetallic sheathed or flexible armored cable.

When installing thin-wall conduit in a room addition, select the proper size conduit for the job: ½-inch conduit carries four No. 14 wires or three No. 12; ¾-inch carries four No. 10, five No. 12, or three No. 8; 1¼-inch carries four No. 6, three each No. 2, No. 3, or No. 4; 1½-inch carries three No. 1 wires; 2-inch conduit carries No. 1/0 or three No.

3/0 wires. Where the conduit runs along the side of a stud or joist it should be supported every 6 to 10 feet with a pipe strap or clamp. Where the conduit runs horizontally across the wall studs or joists, cut notches to provide a channel for it (Figure 5–15).

You can install conduit in new work without notching the upright studs. This type of installation is better because it will not weaken the supporting members of your ceiling and upstairs rooms, and it also eliminates considerable extra work. To install conduit, all the carpentry that is necessary is a

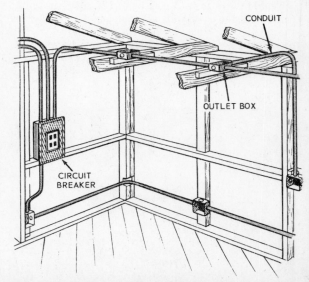

Figure 5–15. A typical conduit wiring installation.

small notch in the plate where you have a conduit bend. Conduit is then laid across the rough floor. Sleepers are then installed up to the conduit and then continued to the rough wall. After all the rooms are plastered or finished, the finished flooring (or the plywood or hardboard where resilient flooring is installed) is then nailed to the sleepers. It is also always advisable to cover the rough flooring with waterproof building paper.

While an electrician cuts conduit with a special tool that leaves no burrs, cutting can also be done with a hacksaw. But follow this with a good deburring job by reaming out the inside edges with a reamer, and using a file on the outside edges.

As implied by the name, thin-wall conduit has a thin wall that allows fairly tight bending without breaking. While this conduit can be bent in a vise, a better job is done with a special bending tool (Figure 5–16), which usually can be rented from your electrical supplier. In operating the bender, first place the conduit on a level surface and hook the end of the proper size tube bender under the conduit's stub end. Then, with the bending groove over the conduit, and using a steady and continuous force while firmly holding the conduit and bender with the body, push down on the handle and step on the foot step, bending the conduit to the desired angle. To make a 45-degree bend in this manner, move the bending tool until the handle is vertical. For accurately bending conduit stubs the bender must be placed at a predetermined distance from the end of the conduit. This distance is equal to the required stub dimension minus an amount commonly called a take-up height. This take-up height is based on a constant allowance determined by the

bending radii for various size conduits. The take-up height is 5 inches for ½-inch conduit, 6 inches for ¾-inch conduit, and 8 inches for 1-inch conduit. In the bending of an 11-inch stub in a ½-inch conduit, for example, the take-up height of 5 inches is first subtracted from the 11-inch dimension of the stub. The mark "B" on the bender is then set at the resultant value of 6 inches and the bends are made.

Extreme care must be used when bending metallic tubing to avoid kinking the pipe or reducing its inside area. The radius of the curve of the inner edge of any field bend must not be less than six times the internal diameter of the tubing when braid-covered conductors are used, and not less than ten times the interior diameter of the tubing when lead-covered conductors are used. Table 5–3 shows the minimum radii for field bends when braid-covered cable is used.

Table 5–3

Tubing size (inches, nominal inside diameter)	Minimum radius (inches)
³/₈	3
¹/₂	3³/₄
³/₄	5
1	6¹/₄
1¹/₄	8¹/₄
1¹/₂	9³/₄
2	12¹/₂

Remember that the National Electric Code permits only four 90-degree bends in any run of conduit between any two boxes.

The next task is putting the conduit in place, fastening it into knockout holes in the switch and outlet boxes, and supporting it along its length at intervals, every 6 feet on exposed runs; every 10 feet on concealed runs. Use only steel switch and outlet boxes in conduit installations. Be sure the edges of the boxes are far enough out from the studs so that they can be lined up level with the finished wall line. Also be sure that switch boxes are mounted so that there will be at least a 2-inch clearance from any doorframe. When connecting the conduit to boxes, fit the threadless end of the connector over the conduit and insert the connector through the box knockout; then tighten the locknut. Lengths of conduit can be spliced by using special double couplers.

After the conduit and boxes are installed, the wires are fished through the conduit. You can push the wires through short runs without difficulty. For long runs use a snake or fish tape (fish wire), available in various lengths (Figure 5-17). Push the wires through a short piece of conduit by twisting the ends together for the first few inches. Allow 6 to 8 inches of slack at each end of the conduit. On long conduit runs push the snake or fish tape

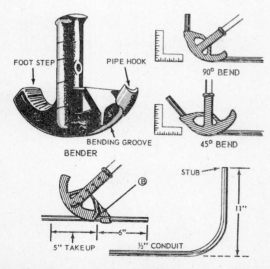

FOOT STEP   PIPE HOOK

90° BEND

BENDING GROOVE   45° BEND

BENDER

STUB

11"

5" TAKE UP   6"   ½" CONDUIT

BENDING 11-INCH STUB

Figure 5–16. Bending thin-wall conduit.

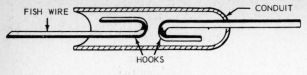

HOOKS BENT IN FISH-WIRE ENDS

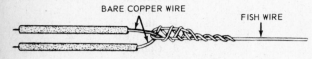

ATTACHMENT OF CONDUCTOR TO FISHING LINE

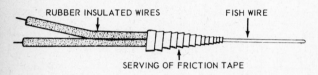

ATTACHMENT TAPED OVER

Figure 5–17. A fish-wire pulling arrangement.

through from one box to the other, tie the wires to it, and pull the wires back through the conduit.

Splicing and joining wires. Good electrical practice requires that conductors must be spliced or joined in a manner which insures that they will be mechanically and electrically secure without benefit of soldering. Soldering or splicing devices are used as added protection against insecure connections. The use of splicing devices is gradually supplanting soldering as the common method of conductor connection because of the ease of wiring and the high quality of the connections made by these devices.

Splices. A spliced wire must be as good a conductor as a continuous conductor. Figure 5–18 shows several variations of splicing used to obtain an electrically secure joint. Though splices are permitted in wiring systems, they should be avoided whenever possible. The best wiring practice (including open wiring systems) is to run continuous wires from the service box to the outlets. Under no conditions should splices be made in conductors encased in conduit.

Solderless connectors. There are several types of connectors used in place of splices because of

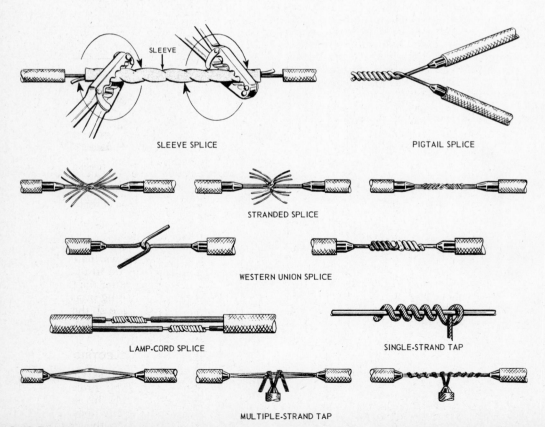

SLEEVE SPLICE

PIGTAIL SPLICE

STRANDED SPLICE

WESTERN UNION SPLICE

LAMP-CORD SPLICE

SINGLE-STRAND TAP

MULTIPLE-STRAND TAP

Figure 5–18. Typical wire splices and taps.

SPLIT-BOLT CONNECTOR

WIRE NUTS

Figure 5—19. Two types of solderless connectors.

their ease of installation. Since heavy wires are difficult to tape and solder properly, split-bolt connectors are commonly used for wire joining. Figure 5–19 illustrates two types of solderless connectors, popularly called wire nuts, which are used for connecting small-gauge and fixture wire. One design shown consists of a funnel-shaped metal-spring insert molded into a plastic shell, into which the wires to be joined are screwed. The other type shown has a removable insert which contains a setscrew to clamp the wires. The plastic shell is screwed onto the insert to cover the joint.

Soldering. All splices must be soldered before they are considered to be as good as the original conductor. The primary requirements for obtaining a good solder joint are a clean soldering iron, a clean joint, and nonacid flux. These requirements can be satisfied by using pure rosin on the joints, or by using a rosin-core solder.

To insure a good solder joint, the electric heated or copper soldering iron should be applied to the joints is still considered to be standard, the Scotch

Taping joints. Every soldered joint must be covered with a coating of rubber, or varnished cambric, and friction tape to replace the wire insulation of the conductor. In taping a spliced solder joint the rubber or cambric tape is started on the tapered end of the wire insulation and advanced toward the other end, with each succeeding wrap, by overlapping the windings. This procedure is repeated from one end of the splice to the other until the original insulation thickness has been restored. The joint is then covered with several layers of friction tape.

Though the method just described for taping joints is still considered to be standard, the Scotch electrical tape, which serves as an insulation and a protective covering, should be used whenever available. This tape materially reduces the time required

to tape a joint, and reduces the space needed by the joint because a satisfactory protective and insulation covering can be achieved with a single-layer taping.

Making wire connections. When attaching a wire to a switch or an electrical device or when splicing it to another wire, you must remove the wire insulation to bare the copper conductor. Figure 5–20 shows the right and wrong way to remove insulation. When the wire-stripping tool is applied at right angles to the wire, there is danger that the wire may be nicked and thus weakened. This may result in a short circuit. Consequently the cut is made at an angle to the conductor. After the protective insulation is removed, the conductor is scraped or sanded thoroughly to remove all traces of insulation and oxide on the wire.

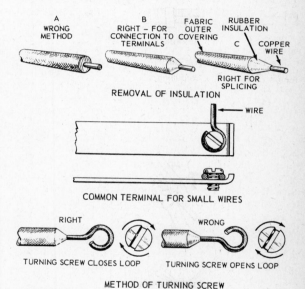

REMOVAL OF INSULATION

COMMON TERMINAL FOR SMALL WIRES

METHOD OF TURNING SCREW

Figure 5—20. The proper method of removing insulation and attaching wire to terminals.

Figure 5–20 also shows the correct method of attaching the trimmed wire to terminals. The wire loop is always inserted under the terminal screw, as shown, so that the tightening process tends to close the loop. The loop is made so that the wire insulation terminates close to the terminal.

INSTALLING AN ELECTRIC SERVICE

If a larger electric entrance service is required for your electrical remodeling project, its planning should be completed first. In some parts of our country, the power company does the complete installation from the pole to the electric meters. In other areas, you must supply everything from the top of the pole to the meter on the house, including three feet if extra wire is needed for the connection. In this latter case, you also must do all the wiring up to the pole, but you do nothing on the pole; it belongs to the power company. If any in-between poles are required, they are your responsibility, too. Among the items that must be furnished and installed are the lead-in wires, drip loops, entrance head, entrance wiring, meter socket, and service panel. Once the service installation has been completed, inspected, and approved by the utility company, they will complete the hookup by installing the electric meter and making the power connection at their pole.

As shown earlier in Figure 5–2, there are two basic types of entrance installation: underground and overhead. With the former, the entrance wiring usually comes from the top of the pole in nonmetallic conduit to a point about 6 to 8 feet above the ground, where the rigid steel conduit begins. This rigid conduit bends away from the pole and follows a dug trench (at least 18 inches deep) to or into the house. Then RHW-type wire of the proper size (see page 156) is snaked through the conduit. The meter may be installed inside the house or on an outside wall, but this must be checked with the power company.

On an overhead installation, the wires from the pole are fastened to insulators screwed to the house. These wires should clear the ground by at least 8 feet, driveways by 12 feet. The entrance head should be at least 10 feet above the ground. In fact, to connect wires from the entrance head to overhead wires the National Electric Code requires that the service entrance head should be installed above the top insulator of incoming power wires. Drip loops should be formed on individual conductors. This will prevent water from entering the electric service system. Rigid conduit is usually employed to bring the wiring to the meter. Use a metal strap every 4 feet to fasten the conduit to the house. Connect the conduit to the meter with conduit connectors. Use an entrance ell to turn the conduit into the house. The ell has two threaded openings corresponding to the conduit size. Use an adapter to fasten the conduit into the threaded opening at the top of the ell. Into the lower opening fasten a piece of conduit to run through the side of the house. Use a connector to attach the conduit to the electric service panel.

After the conduit is installed, push the wires through the top hub of the meter up through the conduit into and out of the entrance head. All three wires must extend at least 36 inches out of the service head to allow plenty of length for connecting them to the power lines. Then the wires are brought down from the meter to the entrance ell. Remove the ell cover and pull the wires through to the service panel inside the house.

Wires running from the meter socket to the service panel should be the same sizes as the entrance wires. Choose the service panel of a rating that meets your load requirements. The service panel that is equipped for circuit-breaker operation is better than the fuse type. It is available for either flush- or surface-mounting. Most panels will accept either aluminum or copper wires. As a general rule it is a good idea to locate the service panel as close as possible to the service entrance to keep the run of heavy wire short. Screw-type terminals on the service panel permit solderless connection of the heavy wiring.

Connect the two "hot" wires (red and black), for 240-volt service, to the power terminals of the panel. The neutral (white) wire should be hooked to the grounding terminal. (In a 120-volt service, the black wire is always the hot one.) Figure 5–21 shows the usual method of grounding a city-town system and a rural setup. With the city system, note the grounding conductor running from the neutral terminal of the electric service panel to the cold-water pipe of the water system. Attach wires securely to the pipe by a ground connector. It is considered best to make the water pipe connection on the street side of the meter. If impractical, connect to any point on the pipe, but install a jumper around the water meter as shown in the diagram.

The ground wire for rural systems does not go through the entrance panel, but is tapped off the neutral overhead wire, and brought down the side of the house and fastened to a ground rod or to an underground metallic water pipe system. Use a copper ground rod at least 1/2 inch in diameter, or a galvanized iron or steel pipe at least 3/4 inch in diameter. The rod must be at least 8 feet long, located at least 2 feet from the house, and driven at least 12 inches below the surface. Then attach the ground wire to the rod with noncorroding, pressure-type grounding clamps. The grounding wire should be No. 4 copper.

Service panels may be either series-wired or parallel-wired. With a series-wired arrangement, the main disconnect controls the power to all circuits. Your local power company will tell you what system you must use. Incidentally, as soon as the utility company wires the service to the pole and installs the meter, the entry at the top of the service is "hot." Be sure to keep away from it. In fact, whenever you work on the panel from the time your power is connected outside, stand on an insulated surface, a dry board if the floor is concrete. The main pull-out block should be removed or installed in the *off* position, of course, until all your circuits have been wired and until the service panel cover has been put on.

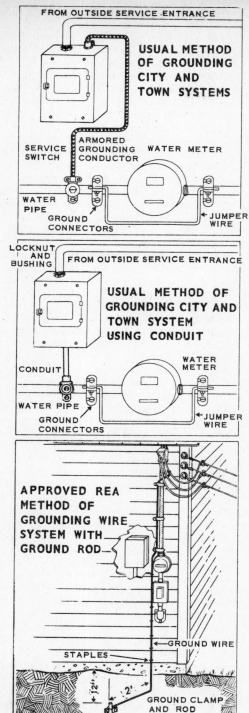

FROM OUTSIDE SERVICE ENTRANCE

USUAL METHOD OF GROUNDING CITY AND TOWN SYSTEMS

SERVICE SWITCH

ARMORED GROUNDING CONDUCTOR

WATER METER

WATER PIPE

GROUND CONNECTORS

JUMPER WIRE

LOCKNUT AND BUSHING

FROM OUTSIDE SERVICE ENTRANCE

USUAL METHOD OF GROUNDING CITY AND TOWN SYSTEM USING CONDUIT

CONDUIT

WATER METER

WATER PIPE

GROUND CONNECTORS

JUMPER WIRE

APPROVED REA METHOD OF GROUNDING WIRE SYSTEM WITH GROUND ROD

GROUND WIRE

STAPLES

2'

2'

GROUND CLAMP AND ROD

Figure 5–21. Methods of grounding city and rural electrical systems.

Adding a subpanel. Most service panels have at least two power takeoff lugs which may be used for adding new circuits. Circuit-breaker panel covers will probably have a couple of their knockouts still intact. You can install the new circuit breakers in these spaces. Fuse panels may have spare fuse sockets. You can get special half-thick circuit breakers that fit two to a knockout. This lets you add new circuits without adding a branch panel.

When a subpanel is used, it should be separately attached to the wall, or to the same board that holds the main panel. Use conduit in making the installation and keep the wire lengths as short as possible.

Wiring circuits. To connect a new circuit, turn off the main power and remove the screws that hold the panel cover on. Bring the circuit cable to the service panel and strip off enough outer covering to let the wires reach through a spare knockout and around inside the panel to the proper point of hookup. This can take a foot or more of wire. Mount the cable through the knockout with a cable connector. Wire the bare grounding wire to the entrance panel's back with a self-threading sheet metal screw. Scrape off the paint under the place where the wire will go.

Run the black wire to the spare fuse or breaker terminal and connect it. Run the white wire to a spare terminal on the neutral strip at the bottom of the box and connect it. Make the wire run inside the box as neatly as you can.

The other end of the cable should be wired into the first box in the circuit. Cables run between boxes, to connect them in a continuous circuit with the service panel. Connect the bare grounding wires to the back of the boxes at both ends with a screw. Or bend the wire back inside the cable connectors and wrap them around the connector screws before tightening. The box back connection is preferable. The black wires are connected to the brass terminals of every device. White wires are connected to the chrome terminals. Never connect the black and white wires together, except in certain switch runs. Then the white wire should be painted black.

Arrange your circuits so that one floor is not served by a single circuit. Then if a fuse blows or a circuit breaker is tripped, the entire floor will not be without power. In making wire runs remember that three-way switches need three wires in certain runs; four-way switches need some four-wire runs (see page 162).

Special circuit needed. A separate three-wire circuit must be installed for an electric range, electric water heater, electric dryer, and certain room air conditioners. A 100-ampere electric service is recommended to take care of a range, water heater, and regular dryer. However, when a high-speed dryer (about 8,500 watts) is connected along with a range,

Chapter 5

it is generally necessary to have an extra heavy-gauge wire and electric service to handle these appliances. Be certain that the electric service entrance and panel is heavy enough to handle the load. *Note:* check your local code to be certain that both the wiring and grounding methods conform.

Typical electric range or dryer hookup. An electric range operates on 240 volts at high heat and 120 volts at low heat. So it requires a separate three-wire No. 6 cable run from a 50-amp circuit in the main service panel to a heavy-duty wall receptacle. As shown in Figure 5–22, a flexible three-wire cord or "pigtail" is connected to the range or dryer terminals. The black wire to B, red to R, white or green to G or W. The other end of the cord has a three-prong plug to fit the range or dryer receptacle. Use of the cord and receptacle permits a range to be dis-

connected easily. Ground the metal frame of a range or dryer to the neutral terminal.

A regular electric dryer (about 4,200 watts) uses 240 volts and 120 volts for its motor and light. It also requires a heavy-duty wall receptacle (like the range) and a separate circuit from a 30-ampere pull-out fuse or circuit breaker in the main service panel or a connection to power takeoff lugs. Then to complete installation, connect a fuse or circuit-breaker safety switch and continue to dryer.

The installation of a high-speed dryer (about 8,500 watts) is the same as for a regular dryer except that it requires a 50-ampere circuit (also heavy-duty wall receptacle), the same as for the range. Be sure to check with your power company for the type of wire specified by local code. In many areas service entrance cable is used and the uninsulated wire is connected to the neutral terminal on a range or dryer.

Typical water heater installation. A double-element electric water heater is probably better for larger families because it permits a more constant supply of hot water. Double-element heaters have two thermostats. The single-element type has only one thermostat. The size of elements, type of thermostats, and method of wiring for heaters are usually specified by your power company. When the service panel has an unfused tap for a heater, use an indoor safety switch.

When making an electric water heater installation, follow the installation setup illustrated in Figure 5–22, with a fused safety switch and careful grounding. Power companies usually offer a very low rate for current used to heat water. This is known as an "off-peak-load" rate and is offered during hours when the demand for current is not great. The company will install a separate meter and time switch, which turns on or off at certain hours.

Split circuits. Most receptacles on the market today are designed to permit the connecting of each duplex outlet on a different circuit. To accomplish this a three-wire, 240-volt circuit is run from the entrance panel. The red wire is fused on the red-wired side of the box. The black wire is fused on the black-wired side. In each outlet box the black wires are connected to the brass terminal on the other side. The metal tab between the halves must be removed with pliers, so as to electrically separate the two halves of the receptacle. The white wires are hooked to one of the chrome terminals. Do not break off the connecting link on the chrome side since this will destroy ground continuity.

Another way of dividing the load among receptacles on a three-wire circuit is to carry the three wires only as far as the central junction box. From this junction box, you can then take off a pair of two-wire circuits, each one operating its own group of receptacles and lights. That is, at the junction

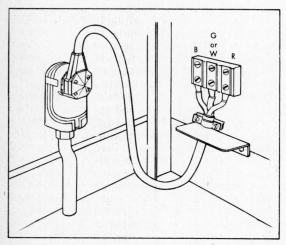

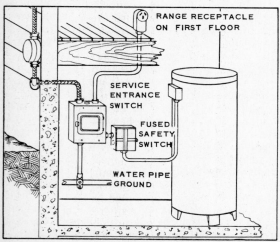

Figure 5–22. *(top)* A typical electric range or dryer hookup. *(bottom)* A typical water heater installation.

box, the black and white wires are spliced to form one two-wire circuit, while the red and white wires are the other two-wire circuit. This will mean that all the white wires are spliced together at the central junction box. In this splitting method none of the method tabs between the duplex receptacles should be removed.

Another splitting method in which the receptacle tabs are left intact is to alternate the use of the red and black wires at every other outlet box. For instance, the red wires are fastened to a brass terminal at the first outlet while the black wires are spliced together. At the second receptacle in the split circuit, the red wires are spliced together while the black wires are hooked to the brass terminal. To complete the wiring, the red and black wires are alternated at every other box. At every box, of course, the white wires are connected to the chrome terminals.

WIRING A NEW ADDITION

Working on a new addition is easier than doing work in an already constructed home. The installation of interior wiring in a new addition is generally divided into two major parts called *roughing-in* and *finishing*. Roughing-in is the installation of the outlet boxes, cable, wire, and conduit. Finishing is the installation of switches, receptacles, covers, and fixtures, and the completion of the service. The interval between these two work periods is used for inclosing walls, finishing floors, and trimming.

The roughing-in job sequence is as follows:

1. The first step in roughing-in a wiring job is to mount the outlet boxes. Mounting can be expedited if the locations of all boxes are first marked on the studs and joists of the building.

2. All boxes are mounted on the building members on their own brackets or with special brackets. For concealed installation, all boxes must be installed with the forward edge or the so-called plaster ring of the boxes flush with the finished walls.

3. The circuiting and installation of wire for open wiring, cable, or conduit should be the next step. This involves the drilling and cutting out of the building members to allow for the passage of the conductor or its protective covering. The production-line method of drilling the holes for all runs, as the installations between boxes are called, at one time, and then installing all of the wire, cable, or conduit, will expedite the job.

4. The final roughing-in step in the installation of conduit systems is the pulling in of wires between boxes. This can also be included as the first step in the finishing phase, and requires care in the handling of the wires to prevent the marring of finished wall or floor surfaces.

The finishing job sequence is as follows:

1. The splicing, soldering, and taping of joints or the proper employment of wire nuts in the outlet boxes is the initial step in the completion phase of a wiring job.

2. Upon completion of the first finishing step, the proper leads to the terminals of switches, ceiling and wall outlets, and fixtures are then installed.

3. The devices and their cover plates are then attached to the boxes. The fixtures are generally supported by the use of special mounting brackets called fixture studs or hickeys.

4. The service-entrance cable and fusing or circuit-breaker panels are then connected and the circuits fused.

5. The final step in the wiring of any addition requires the testing of all outlets by the insertion of a test prod or test lamp, the operation of all switches in the building, and the loading of all circuits to insure that proper circuiting has been installed.

Let us take a look at some techniques, not already described, that are necessary to complete a wiring of an addition. For instance, there are two different ways of wiring a ceiling light fixture and a switch box. The easier of the two is used when a main line cable can be brought up to the switch first. The main line cable is introduced into the box through a hole left by removal of a knockout plug. The two wire ends are then exposed by skinning off the insulation. The other cable to the light fixture is then brought into the box and its wires similarly treated. The two wires with white insulation are joined with a wire nut or a pigtail splice, soldered, and wrapped with rubber and friction tape. The two leads with black insulation are then connected to the two terminal screws of the switch. Only enough bare wire should be exposed to permit the wire to wrap around the screw once. It should be wrapped around the screw in the direction in which the screw is turned as it is tightened. Tightening the screw clamps the wire end firmly under the screwhead. After the leads are connected in the above manner, the cable ends are secured in the box by tightening the cable clamp screws. With this type of circuit closing the switch connects the two black leads through the switch contacts and permits current to flow to the light fixture. Also, with the switch off, only the grounded side of the circuit (white insulation) is connected to the light fixture.

The second method of connecting the switch and light fixture is used when the main cable can more conveniently be brought to the light fixture rather than to the switch box. A wire nut joint or pigtail splice (soldered and taped) is made in the light fixture box between the main line cable black wire and the other cable white wire. The black wire in the cable to the light switch box and the white wire in the main cable are then connected to the light fixture. The two wires in the cable to the light switch box (black and white insulation) are then connected to the switch. You will note that a con-

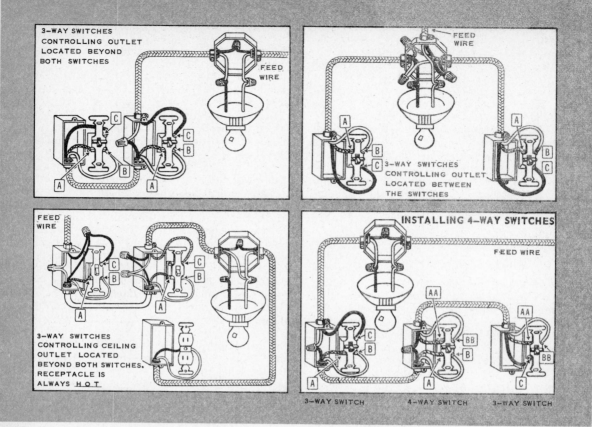

Figure 5—23. A method of connecting three- and four-way switches. In all cases the white wire from the switches must be painted black, both at the switches and at the light outlet.

siderably greater length of "hot" (black insulated) wire is used in this type of connection, but that the light fixture is still on the grounded side of the circuit (white insulated) when the switch is off.

Three-way switches are most frequently used to control one or more lights from two different points so that the light can be turned on or off by either switch; for example, in a long corridor or large room with entrances on opposite sides, or at the top and bottom of a stairway so that the light can be turned on as you start up the stairway and off when you reach the top. To connect three-way switches, follow the diagrams in Figure 5—23. Just be sure to connect the black, white, and red wires as shown. In all cases, the terminals marked A and B are the light-colored terminals to which red and white wires must be connected. Terminal C, in all cases, is the dark-colored terminal to which the black wire must always be connected. Check the diagrams carefully. Regardless of the location of the terminals, always connect the wires to brass terminals and dark terminals as noted.

You will notice that three-wire cable is required for some of the runs from box to box. In all cases the white wire from the switch must be painted black at the switch and at the light outlet. In the illustration (Terminal C) you can use two two-wire cables between switches, in case four-wire cable is not readily available.

A combination of three- and four-way switches is used wherever you wish to control one or more lights from three separate locations. If more than three control points are desired, just use an additional four-way switch for each. Connect each four-way switch as shown in Figure 5—23 for the center four-way switch here.

When mounting ceiling boxes in new work, use a type that is at least 1½ inches deep and anchor with an off-set bar hanger as shown here. The fixtures themselves are hung as described above. The installation of recessed fixtures is described on pages 61 and 64.

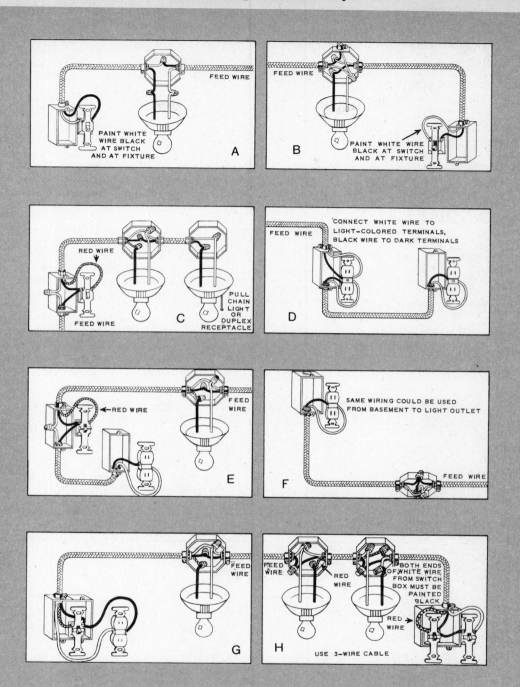

Figure 5–24. Other arrangements of switches: (A) To add a wall switch to control a ceiling light at the end of a run. (B) To add a wall switch to a control ceiling light in the middle of a run. (C) To install two ceiling lights on the same line, one being controlled by a switch. (D) To add a new convenience outlet beyond an old convenience outlet. (E) To add a switch and convenience outlet beyond an existing ceiling light. (F) To add a new convenience outlet from an existing junction box. (G) To add a switch and convenience outlet in one outlet box beyond an existing ceiling light. (H) To install one new ceiling outlet and two new switch outlets from an existing ceiling outlet.

OLD WORK REMODELING TECHNIQUES

By "old" work we mean, of course, the wiring or rewiring of a house where the finished ceilings, walls, and floors already exist. The big task in old work circuit wiring is getting the cable to the final location. That is easy enough when connecting an outlet in the basement laundry room for a washer-dryer, as the location is probably not far from the

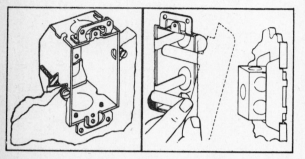

Figure 5—25. Special boxes are available for easy mounting. Push the box with the connected cable into the opening so that front brackets fit against the wall. Then tighten side screws to bring side brackets up snug against the wall. Metal box supports can ensure a strong job. Insert supports on each side of the box. Work the supports up and down until they fit firmly against the inside surface of the wall, and bend the projecting ears to fit around the box.

fuse box and there is no need for concealed wiring. Even appliance wiring for a kitchen is usually without complications because the cable is simply brought up through the basement ceiling behind the wall cabinet or sink. But it is a different matter when bringing wires to an upstairs bedroom for an air conditioner or to the living room or den, where there can be no breaking of walls.

When starting an electrical remodeling job, mark the outlines on the wall and ceiling. Remember that switch and outlet boxes must be located between the studs, preferably at a spot 4 to 5 inches from the stud. Switches should be located about 48 to 54 inches above the floor, convenience outlets about 12 to 18 inches above the floor, or slightly above table height in the kitchen and dining room. Wall light fixture outlets should be 66 to 70 inches above the floor. Always place switches at the opening side of the door, not on the hinged side. Use large-size (2½ inches deep) boxes if possible. Remember that boxes are available with built-in clamps for use with flexible armored cable, or with clamps for plastic-sheathed cable. A special outlet or switch box is made for fastening to plasterboard walls (walls of large plaster sheets nailed directly to studs, as opposed to lathed and plastered walls). There are boxes that clamp quickly and firmly in place on any kind of wall surface—tile, wood, wallboard, or plaster. Figure 5—25 shows how easy it is to anchor

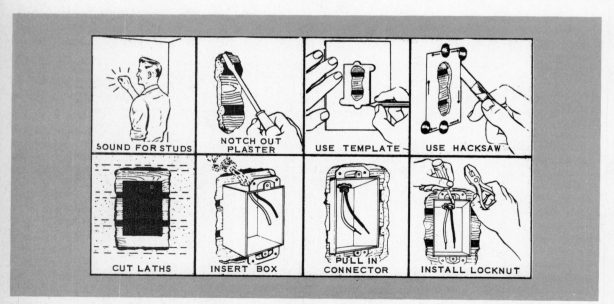

Figure 5—26. Installing an outlet box in an "old" plaster wall: If you fail to locate the studs by sounding, drill every 2 inches until the drill hits a stud. Make small holes just above the baseboard. Then determine the location for the box. Notch away the plaster, as shown, to expose one full lath but only part of the top and bottom laths. Use a template to outline the opening. Drill four ½-inch holes as indicated. Insert a hacksaw in the holes. Draw the saw toward you and hold your hand or a board against plaster to prevent cracking. Cut away the center lath completely and half sections from other two laths. Then draw the cable out of the wall, attach the connector (less the locknut), and pull lead wires through the knockout. Bring the connector into place in the box and tighten the locknut. The final step is to anchor the box securely to the lath with No. 5 wood screws.

a box securely both front and back. Adjustment screws eliminate all looseness. Knockouts can be used for either cable connectors or conduit. Place the box with the connected cable in the opening so that the front brackets fit flush against the wall and the side brackets are behind the wall. Then tighten both side adjustment screws until the box is solidly anchored.

After finding the desired location for the box, make sure that it is between framing members. Locate studs or joists with a stud locator or by sounding the walls by rapping with your hand. If you fail to locate the studs, drill to find the studs, using a 1/16-inch drill. Drill the holes every two inches until the drill strikes a stud. Drill just above the baseboard so the holes will not be noticed.

Once the studs are located, notch away plaster to expose one full lath but only part of the top and bottom lath. Then use a soft pencil and template to outline the position of the box. Drill four 1/2-inch holes as indicated in Figure 5–26. These holes provide space for a hacksaw blade. When the holes are drilled, cut the lath and plaster in the direction of the arrows in the illustration. When using a hacksaw blade, you should apply the cutting pressure as you draw the blade toward you to avoid the possibility of loosening plaster from the lath. Always hold your hand or a small board against the plaster as you saw, to prevent the plaster from cracking or chipping.

After the openings are cut for the outlet boxes, you must plan the manner in which the cable is to be run from the main line cable and between the switch and the fixture outlet boxes. In a one-story house, the problem is simplified by the fact that the work usually can be conducted from both the basement and the attic, except when either or both are finished rooms. In a two-story house, the job is more difficult and it will be necessary to make holes in the floor, wall, or ceiling in order to run the cable. Also, where fire stops have been nailed between the studs, the plaster must be broken out to

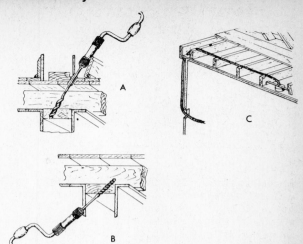

Figure 5–28. Method of running a cable from a ceiling fixture to a switch: (A) From a second floor remove a section of the baseboard and drill diagonally down through the floor and header. Replace the baseboard. (B) This diagram shows how to make the same hole in the header but from an opposite room. (C) If you have an open attic, this is the simplest way to run the cable.

permit the cable to pass around the fire stops. The holes can be patched after the job is completed. With papered walls, it is often possible to moisten a section of the paper where the hole is to made, slit it with a sharp knife, and peel it back. Then, after the plaster has been patched, the paper can be pasted back into place.

Let us assume that the ceiling light and switch are to be installed in a downstairs living room of a two-story house (Figure 5–28). From the basement, bore a hole up through the floor directly under the switch outlet box. This hole should come out inside the wall. Now, run a fish tape or wire up through this hole. (A fish tape, previously mentioned for use with conduit, is a tempered flat steel wire, 1/16 by 1/8 inch, comes in coils of 59-, 75-, and 100-foot lengths, and is sold at electrical supply stores. Ordinary steel baling wire can be used in some "fishing" jobs through enclosed areas, though it does not have the springy temper and stiffness that straightens out the tape after it hits an obstruction. Before using a fish tape, make a loop at the tip so the wire will not snag, and to form an eye for threading the electrical wires. Some tapes come with a knob at the end for use with a special "eye ball.") Manipulate it so that another person in the living room can catch it and pull it out through the hole cut in the wall for the switch outlet box. Attach the cable to the end of the fish wire and pull the cable through. It should be secured temporarily while the other cable is run from the switch outlet box to the fixture box in the ceiling (Figure 5–29).

The second cable will probably have to cross

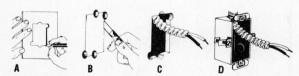

Figure 5–27. The installation of an outlet box in plasterboard or paneling is like that in Figure 5–26, except that the type of box used holds onto the plaster or similar flat material: (A) After finding the center between studs, outline the cutout on the wall with the template furnished with the box. (B) Cut out the plasterboard or wallboard with a hacksaw or compass saw. (C) Draw the cable through and fasten it into the box. (D) Place the box in position and draw up on the two screws on the sides. The side ears will draw up behind the wall, and the two ears at the top and bottom will hold from the front. (Before installing the box, adjust the top and bottom ears so that the front edge of the box is flush with the front of the wall.)

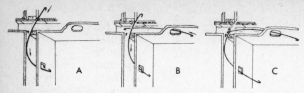

Figure 5–29. (A) "Snake" a short fish tape down through the floorboard hole and header hole from the second floor and bring the end out at a 4-by-5-inch plaster cutout. (B) Push a longer fish tape through the ceiling hole and hook the first tape. (C) Draw the short fish tape down and pull the long one through into the room.

some studs in the wall before it can be brought up to the ceiling between studs and then run to the fixture outlet box between the ceiling joists. This can be done by removing the baseboard so that the cable can be buried in the plaster or wallboard next to the floor. After the baseboards are removed, a hole is drilled in the wall close to the floor directly under the switch outlet box. The fish wire is then used to run the end of the cable through this hole and inside the wall up to the switch outlet box. A channel is then chiseled in the plaster or wallboard into which the cable can be laid and later covered when the baseboard is replaced. This channel will have to run around a corner if the ceiling joists are parallel to the wall where the new switch is to be. As the channel bypasses the wall studding, the wire can be run up between studs and then between the ceiling joists to the fixture outlet box.

At the proper place a second hole is made in the wall next to the floor. The cable is run into the wall through this hole. Then, from the next room, bore a hole through the plaster or wallboard and up through the plates or wood beam on top of the wall studs. This hole is for feeding the fish line down between the studs so that the cable can be drawn through the hole at the bottom of the wall and up between the studs. This hole is also used to feed the fish line to the fixture outlet box between the ceiling joists so that the cable can be drawn between the ceiling joists to the box.

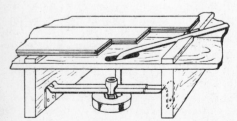

Figure 5–30. A ceiling box is supported by an adjustable bracket nailed to the rafters. The lower edge of the box must be flush with the surface of the finished wall. Note the long slot cut into the rough floor to accommodate the gradual bend of the conduit.

The selection of a ceiling box will depend on whether or not access is available to the ceiling from above (as through an attic) or whether it is a concealed ceiling (as between floors, or if the roof is flat). Where there is access, locate the spot for the box from above, and cut a hole down through the ceiling. The hole for the box should be slightly larger than the box. Keep in mind that the edge of the box must be flush with the room-side surface of the ceiling. Fasten the box in place with the same type of bracket described later in this chapter.

When the space is not accessible above the ceiling, the work must be done in the following manner:

1. Notch away the plaster or board to the size of a shallow box and carefully cut away the center lath.

2. Insert the hanger (remove the locknut and put the wire through the threaded stud). Holding the stud above the ceiling with one hand, pull the wire with the other hand and the hanger will center itself.

3. Connect the cable to the shallow box. Pull the wire (from the hanger) through the center knockout and install the locknut on the threaded stud. The fixture is hung as described previously.

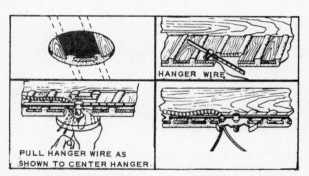

HANGER WIRE

PULL HANGER WIRE AS SHOWN TO CENTER HANGER.

Figure 5–31. Steps in mounting a ceiling box if the space above the ceiling is not accessible.

Raceways. If it is impossible to go into the wall, you can use raceways to get electric current to where it is desired. Attached to the outside (the room side), raceways are available in two basic types: (1) a covered metallic trough in which standard electrical cable or wires connect from the source to the outlets; and (2) heavy, plastic-enclosed cables to which special outlets are wired. The latter come in two general styles: one employs a standard plastic cable, the same type that is used for in-wall installation; the other is specially fabricated of plastic, in which the conductors are molded into the form so that they plug into special fittings to change direction, and the outlets snap into place along the molded strip. The metal-enclosed

REMODELING YOUR HOME'S LIGHTING

One sure way to give your home a lift in appearance is to modernize it with stylish lighting. The cost can be modest and you can improve one room at a time. If required, it is a perfect opportunity to improve your lighting. Create different effects not only with the attractive designs of fixtures themselves but with the ways illumination is applied—for accenting, highlighting, background lighting, or general illumination, from brilliant to subdued. Today there is an amazing variety of fixtures to match or complement your furnishings, everything from traditional and authentic period styling to striking contemporary. And you can even have built-in effects without major renovation.

There are three broad categories of lighting: (1) general area lighting; (2) local or functional lighting; and (3) mood or decorative lighting.

General area lighting. The amount of light needed for general illumination in any given room may be obtained from one source or from a combination of several. Factors to take into consideration are the size of the room and its use. The larger the room, the greater its requirements. For example, for a small bedroom of less than 125 square feet, you can create the necessary general lighting with three 40-watt bulbs or one 100-watt bulb. For an average-sized

Figure 5–32. A raceway fastened under kitchen wall cabinets.

raceway is generally recommended for areas where some mechanical abuse may be encountered.

Regardless of the type of surface wiring, installation is simple. Just follow the manufacturer's instructions on how to fasten the raceway to the wall and how to connect it to a duplex outlet.

Table 5–4. Recommended lighting for your home (watts)

Room	General area lighting		Local lighting		Remarks
	Bulb	Fluorescent	Bulb	Fluorescent	
Living, dining room	150	60–80	40–150	15–40	For small living rooms
Bedroom	200		40–100		Average size
Bath	100–150	80	Two 60s	Two 20s	Task lights on both sides of mirror
Kitchen	150–200	60–80	60	10 per foot of counter	Fixture over eating area or sink—150-watt bulb, 60-watt fluorescent
Halls, service	75	32			Plus low-wattage night lights
Stairway	75	32			Shielded fixtures at top and bottom controlled by three-way switch
Outdoor, entry and access	40				Wall brackets aimed down
Hall entrance	100	60			
Outdoor, yard	100–150 projector				Controlled from garage and house
Laundry	Two 150s	Two 80s			Placed over washing and ironing areas
Workshop	150	80	60	10 per foot of bench	Task lights aimed at machines
Garage	Two 100s				On ceiling, center of each side of car

bedroom of up to 225 square feet, you should have five 40-watt or four 50-watt bulbs. (Remember that this is for *general* lighting only; work areas must be considered and handled separately.)

Extending this generalization to larger rooms does not mean that a fixture accommodating more bulbs will do the job. Although this will increase the light level, the gain is not proportional to the number of bulbs added. The efficient way is to supplement the existing fixture with another one or more; in short, to disperse the light sources over a larger area.

A wall switch at the entrance to each room should control at least one light or fixture of general area light in the room. Then you will never have to walk into a dark room. The light can be a ceiling or wall fixture or a lamp that is plugged into a switch receptacle. Multiple switches are needed at all entrances more than 10 feet apart, as well as at the head and foot of stairways.

Local lighting. Sometimes called "task" or "work" lighting, this type of lighting is for visual jobs such as reading, sewing, playing the piano, etc. Generally it is provided by portable lamps placed close to the user, or by fixtures. When possible, local or functional lighting should contribute to the general area lighting.

Spotlighting is one of the more popular types of local lighting. Some spotlights are flush mounted and set into a ceiling. Others may be fastened on a ceiling or wall with screws. So-called pinup lamps may be hung on a wall with a picture hook. Many freestanding lamps, both floor and table models, are spotlights, and may or may not have flexible goosenecks or swivels to permit the direction in which their light is aimed to be changed at will. But while every house needs spotlighting, and has many places where this technique will be a big help, spotlights may hinder more than they help, unless used carefully. Because their light is so concentrated, any object placed in the beam will cast a very strong shadow. However, this may be avoided by observing any of these precautions:

1. Place the spotlight fixture so that its light reaches the work surface directly.

2. Use more than one spotlight for a given area. When multiple lamps are used in this way, the beam from each tends to reduce the shadows cast by the others.

Decorative lighting. This form of lighting is any light used for a decorative effect rather than a functional one. Of course, a source of decorative lighting can also contribute to either or both general area and local lighting.

Lighting fixtures. There are many different shapes, sizes, and types of light sources designed for a variety of uses. Both *incandescent* and *fluorescent lights* are used in homes. Incandescent bulbs have filaments of tungsten which give off light when heated by electric current. It is important to select a bulb of the wattage for which the fixture or lamp was designed. Too high a wattage can cause glare or present a safety hazard, while too low a wattage gives insufficient light. Some light bulbs can be switched to three different wattages to add flexibility. There are also a variety of shapes. Fluorescent lights come in many lengths, colors, and wattages. The color can be selected to enhance the interior decoration of the room in which the light will be used. Fluorescent tubes give more light per watt than do incandescent bulbs.

Selecting and installing lighting fixtures. Lighting fixtures furnish general and local lighting and, in addition, provide decorative accents. They may be installed in the ceiling or on a wall. Before a fixture is purchased, it should be seen lighted with the same wattage bulb that will be used at home. The appearance of the fixture both lighted and unlighted is important.

When purchasing a fixture, keep the following points in mind:

1. Top or side ventilation in a fixture is desirable since it will lower operating temperatures and will extend the lamp life. Never use a bulb larger than that recommended by the manufacturer.

2. The fixture should be designed to spread light uniformly and efficiently over the entire area that must be lighted. The best method of determining this is to see it in operation at your dealer.

3. The inside surface of shades or fixtures

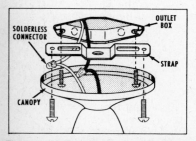
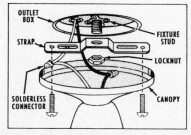
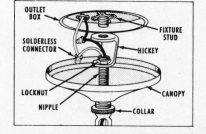

Figure 5—33. Three common methods of fastening a ceiling light fixture.

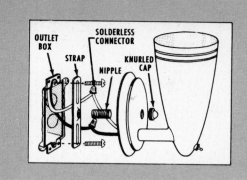 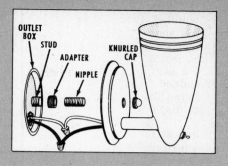

Figure 5–34. Wall fixtures are frequently mounted to smaller boxes of the outlet or switch type. If the fixture has a center nipple, obtain a bracket with a threaded hole in the center to take the nipple.

should be of a white-enameled or a polished material to reflect light.

4. Incandescent lamps should never be closer than ¼ inch to the enclosing globes or diffusion shields. Bare lamps should be visible from the normal viewing angle.

When you are replacing a ceiling light fixture or installing a new one, you can usually mount it by using either a threaded nipple in the center or screws near the edge. A nipple-mounted fixture is fastened to a stud in the outlet box. To splice to the wire coming through the center of the nipple, a "hickey" is usually added between the nipple on the new fixture and the old nipple on the outlet box. If the screw method of mounting is used, it is often necessary to employ an adapter strap because of the difficulty in lining up the screw holes of the junction box. The same adapter strap may be used to install a nipple-mounted fixture on screw mounting and vice-versa. Remember that a new fixture may be mounted by one or the other of these two methods; the one you are replacing may have been mounted the opposite way to that required by the new fixture.

To install a recessed fixture, first cut out an open space between the floor joists of the size recommended by the manufacturer. Some recessed fixtures have mounting straps, while others fasten with screws into the joints or wood strips which are placed above the opening across the lath. But before making any connections to your recessed fixtures, check the local electrical code since many codes require that a recessed fixture have a separate junction box attached to it.

Wall fixtures mount the same way as ceiling fixtures. Frequently, however, smaller adapter straps are used. Fixture wires are spliced to the junction box wires. Lighting fixtures do not use screw terminals like switches and receptacles. Solderless connectors or wire nuts (see page 157) are

used for this, and they eliminate the need for soldering joists. Since these are made of insulating material, the wires need not be taped and short circuits cannot occur. To use a wire nut, scrape the insulation off ½ inch of the ends of the junction box wires, and hold the two wires together. Slip the nut on and twist it clockwise. The nut has threads inside it that will thread onto the wires at the same time that it twists them together. Do not turn them up too tight or the wire may break; just turn the wire nut enough to hold firmly.

Structural lighting. Structural lighting is the term used by lighting designers to describe light sources built into the home as a part of its finished structure. Sometimes called "architectural" or "built-in" lighting, it denotes a custom installation, designed and assembled to fit a particular situation. Because structural lighting is built right into walls and ceilings, it can be designed to blend with any period decorative motif or color scheme. It can blend or contrast with its background. Since it has a very little styling, structural lighting does not become dated in appearance.

One of the major functions of structural lighting is to lighten and enhance walls and ceilings. This is important because walls and ceilings account for three-quarters, or more, of room surfaces in a home. The walls are the background of the home landscape. Light, well-lighted walls appear to recede. Hence, wall lighting extends the visual area, increasing the apparent space. With structural lighting, colors of wall coverings and draperies become more vivid and windows have daytime charm, even after dark. Because the major source of light in the room is the entire wall surface instead of a small fixture or lamp, the resulting room lighting is soft and relatively shadow-free. This "horizontal" lighting molds forms and features in a more flattering way than light from above or below.

There are three structural lighting techniques

Table 5—5. *Recommended types and sizes of structural lighting installations for residential interiors*

Location	Floor size of room (square feet)	Minimum length of installation when used in room with ceiling fixture (feet)	Minimum length of installation when used in place of ceiling fixture	Type (or combination) of structural lighting applicable
Living areas (includes living room, family room, recreation rooms)	Up to 185		12	Valance, cornice, wall bracket
	185– 250		16	Valance, cornice, wall bracket
	Over 250		1 foot of structural lighting for every 15 square feet of floor area	Valance, cornice, wall bracket
Dining room	Average	4		Valance, wall bracket
	Average	8		Cornice, cove
Dinette	Average	3		Valance, wall bracket
	Average	6		Cornice, cove
Bedroom	Up to 125	3	6	Valance, cornice, wall bracket
	125– 225	4	8	Valance, cornice, wall bracket
	Over 225		16	Valance, cornice, wall bracket
Vestibule	40–80		6	Wall bracket
Foyer	40–80		8	Cornice

for walls that are easy to install and have wide application throughout the home. The most popular is the lighted *valance.* This is always used with a window to provide "nighttime sunshine." The fluorescent *wall bracket* looks a lot like a valance, but is used mainly on inside walls away from windows. Easiest to install is the *cornice,* which is mounted at the junction of wall and ceiling and can be used with or without a window.

In many cases, the structural lighting technique is used instead of a lighting fixture for general lighting. In many rooms, added fixtures will be desired to provide specific task or decorative illumination. Walls can also be lighted by recessed louvered incandescent "hi-hat" fixtures. It is best to use 75-watt R-30 or 150-watt R-40 flood lamps. These should be centered 10 inches from a solid wall or 12 inches from a window wall. One fixture is used for every 32 inches of wall length.

Valance lighting. The lighted valance is always connected with the window. It usually directs light both upward over the ceiling and downward over the wall and drapery. Valance faceboards can be simple and unobtrusive, or they can be as decorative and stylish as the imagination will allow. A wide variety of faceboard materials are available that can be trimmed with moldings, scalloped, notched, perforated, papered, upholstered, or painted. Faceboards should have a minimum width of 6 inches and seldom should be wider than 10 inches. Nominal 8-inch lumber usually works quite well for valances 8 feet or longer.

The inside of the faceboard should always be painted flat white. The only exception to this would be the bottom 1½ to 2 inches on a very deep valance. It is possible that this bottom strip might be seen from outside the window and therefore can be painted to match the room decoration. If the back of the faceboard is not flat white, the valance will trap the light produced, and the resultant color of the light in the room may be distorted.

Wall brackets. The wall bracket is probably the single most useful structural lighting device in the home. It can be used in any room of the house. Basically, there are two kinds of wall brackets; the construction differs depending on whether the bracket is to be used high on the wall for general lighting, or lower on the wall for specific task lighting.

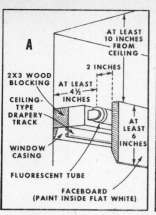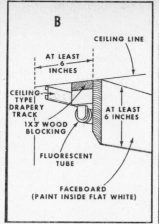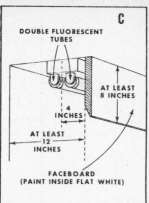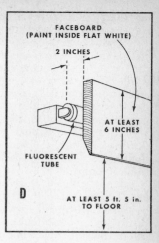

Figure 5–35. Common types of structural lighting: (A) valance; (B) cornice; (C) soffit; (D) bracket.

A high wall bracket is really a valance without a window. It is used as a source of general lighting for a room. Quite often it will be used to balance the illumination from a matching valance at an opposite window. Many of the same dimensions and construction techniques must be observed, as when installing a valance. The inside of the faceboard must be white. The fluorescent lamp and channel must be located as high up behind the shielding board as possible so the light will spread evenly and far out over the ceiling. The fluorescent tube should be at least 3 inches out from the wall to provide a smooth distribution of light over the wall. This reduces the chance of hot streaks of brightness above and below the shielding board. A minimum of 10 inches between the top of the shielding board and the ceiling is recommended, so no light is trapped above the bracket.

The low wall bracket is a "working light" commonly used where specific seeing tasks are performed close to a wall. They are used to highlight fireplaces and pictures; to provide functional lighting over desks, sofas, etc. For most of these low-on-the-wall uses, the bracket is mounted no higher than 5 feet 5 inches from the floor. Table 5–6 gives height locations for low wall brackets and the type of lamp that should be used.

Cornice lighting. The lighted cornice is positioned on the ceiling at the junction between the wall and ceiling. All of its light is directed downward to light the wall surface below. For this reason, the lighting effect produced is a dramatic one. It emphasizes wall textures and wall coverings, and lights pictures and other wall hangings. Also, because the wall is emphasized, the cornice gives an impression of greater ceiling height. Cornices

Table 5–6. Recommended mounting heights and lamps for structural lighting in specific task areas

Location	Mounting height	Recommended deluxe warm white fluorescent lamps
Single bed	52 inches from floor	30-watt lamp*
Double bed	52 inches from floor	40-watt lamp*
Extrawide bed or twin beds with single headboard	52 inches from floor	Two 30-watt lamps*
Lounge furniture	55 inches or more from floor	Choose lamp sizes to harmonize with length of furniture
Buffets	60 inches from floor†	30-watt* lamp
Desk	15–18 inches from desk top	30-watt or 40-watt lamp,* depending on length of desk
Mirror or picture grouping	Mount directly at top edge of mirror or above picture grouping	Choose lamp size to harmonize with length of furniture

*30-watt lamps are 36 inches long; 40-watt lamps are 48 inches long.
†Less if top wall bracket is closed.

are, therefore, ideally suited for low-ceilinged rooms such as basement recreation rooms.

Soffit lighting. The underside of an architectural member is known as a soffit. Often these spaces can provide a housing for light sources. Suitable soffits for lighting can be formed in furred-down areas over kitchen sinks and work areas, furred-down areas over bathroom mirrors, undersides of pass-throughs, niches, and beams. There are basically two uses for lighted soffits: (1) to direct light downward onto a horizontal plan; (2) to direct light outward to a vertical surface (such as a face in front of a mirror).

When a soffit is used to light a horizontal surface below it, the fluorescent channels should be equipped with polished aluminum reflectors. Reflectors will more than double the useful light output of the soffit if the bottom is closed with louvers or a material that does not diffuse the light to any extent. In living areas, the soffit has a more acceptable appearance if a lightly etched or configurated glass or plastic is used. To further reduce the brightness as viewed from seated positions in the room, the inside back vertical surface of the soffit can be painted in a matte black finish.

The soffit over the bath or dressing room mirror has the function of scattering light outward to light a person's face as he stands before the mirror. For this reason, the soffit is usually made shallower and a good deal wider to let more light escape. The bottom is covered with a highly diffusing glass or plastic. Reflectors are not needed. Incidentally, fluorescent channels should not be directly mounted on combustible materials. They should be mounted either with a surrounding air space or on fireproof materials.

Luminous ceiling panels. The comfortable lighting effects and the sensation of spaciousness created by luminous ceilings make them particularly suitable for applications in kitchens, bathrooms, entryways, recreation rooms, and even dining areas. Today, many manufacturers make packaged luminous ceiling assemblies which can be used for residential applications (see page 62).

The design of luminous ceilings varies with the room size, room proportion, and intended use. Usually these ceilings are applicable only in rooms with high ceilings where the plastic diffusers can be dropped 10 to 12 inches. For uniform lighting on the diffuser, lamps should be spaced in rows not more than one and one-half times their distance to the diffuser. Manufacturers of luminous ceilings can provide design and installation instructions for their particular products. An entire ceiling, however, need not be luminous to be effective and attractive. A simple method of luminous ceiling panel construction is to utilize the space between ceiling joists. This space is an ideal location for fluorescent lighting equipment if the ends are boxed in

and a plastic diffuser is suspended below.

Cove lighting. Coves are particularly suited to rooms with two ceiling levels. In these applications they should be placed right at the line where a flat, low-ceilinged area breaks away to a higher-ceilinged space. The upward light emphasizes this change of level and is very effective in rooms with slant or cathedral-type ceilings. But the lighting efficiency of coves is low in comparison with that of valances and wall brackets.

Coves (which are usually mounted high on the wall) direct all of their light upward to the ceiling where it is, in turn, reflected back into the room. The cove is known as a source of "indirect lighting." The illumination effect produced by cove lighting is soft, uniform, and comfortable. Since there is no light directed downward into the room from a cove, however, the resulting lighting effect is relatively flat and lifeless. For this reason, cove lighting should be supplemented by other lamps and lighting fixtures to give the room interest and provide lighting for seeing tasks.

For good cove lighting a few basic rules must be followed:

1. Cove lighting should be used only with white or near-white ceilings.

2. Keep the cove as far down from the ceiling as possible for wide distribution of light. There should be a minimum of 12 inches from the top of the shielding board to the ceiling.

3. Place the lamp at least 4 to 4½ inches out from the wall.

4. Paint the inside flat white. Butt the lamp sockets back-to-back.

Track lighting. Track lighting offers complete decorating freedom, providing endless opportunities to achieve function and accent lighting. Track lighting is a concept of accent light that can be as flexible as the imagination. It can be recessed, surface-mounted, or suspended by pendant stems. Most of these movable, adjustable track systems can be swiveled, angled, and pointed in any direction, or grouped for every functional design effect.

Installing dimmers. There are numerous occasions when the flexibility afforded by dimming is effective in adjusting the lighting to fit the mood. But dimmers are meant to control lights only. No motor-driven appliances—fans, for example—should be connected to an outlet controlled by the dimmer; neither should such electrical devices as radios or television sets. While dimmers range in size from 300 to 1,000 watts, the number of lamps or fixtures in the circuit does not matter, so long as their total wattage is less than the rated wattage of the unit. But, it is important to remember that no one dimmer is suitable for every possible lighting use in a home. Some dimmers are intended only for the control of permanent incandescent lighting fixtures, others are for floor and table lamps, and still different types are required for the control of fluorescent lights. With the last type, there are a few points to remember:

1. As a general rule, fluorescent dimmers require a three-wire cable connection from the dimmer to the fluorescent channels.

2. Special dimming ballasts are required for each channel and lamp.

3. Dimmer systems perform best when their circuits are grounded.

4. Dimming systems will operate the 30-watt or the 40-watt rapid start lamps, but will not operate them satisfactorily on the same circuit.

It is advisable to follow the manufacturer's instructions carefully for best results. The basic procedure of replacing an old on-off switch, however, can be outlined in only five steps:

1. Turn off the power by removing the fuse or by opening the circuit-breaker controlling line.

2. Remove the old switch unit and outlet box from the wall opening.

3. Enlarge the opening and fasten the outlet box in it.

4. Place the dimmer in the outlet box and attach the wires to its terminals.

5. Install the cover plate and turn the power on.

OUTDOOR ELECTRICAL WIRING

Outdoor wiring differs from indoor only in the fact that moisture and weather have to be taken into account. In fact, outdoor wiring, in many ways, is easier for the home handyman than interior wiring.

Electricity will do many things to make your patio, yard, or garden a great deal more fun. Therefore, plan enough outlets for all outbuildings such as garages, barns, and workshops. Also plan to enjoy outdoor living electrically by having plugs available for your grill, radio, rotisserie, percolator, or television. And use lights to glamorize your patio and grounds.

Installation of wiring. The style and construction of your home will determine how the circuits are run from the service panel to the outside. Most installations will be one of two types:

1. When the service is in the basement. In this situation, wiring is generally brought to the outside either through the masonry wall of the basement or through the sill on top of the foundation. Factors to be considered are whether the installation is to be underground or overhead. If underground, going directly through the basement wall and coming out below ground level on the outside is the least conspicuous method of installation. Where convenient shrubbery will hide the conduit, it may be easier to

Figure 5–36. Examples of outdoor lighting.

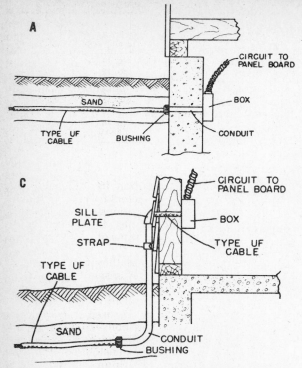

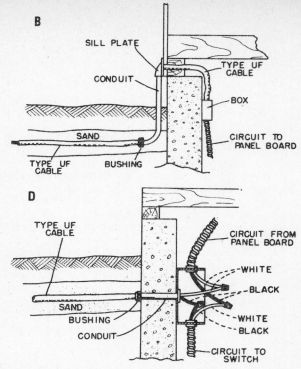

Figure 5-37. Exterior wiring suggestions: (A) running the circuit from a panel board through masonry; (B) running a circuit from a panel board through the sill; (C) running a circuit from a panel board through a garage wall; (D) a switch control for a group of outside lights.

come out through the sill. Either of these methods may be chosen when the wiring is to be overhead. In this case, since a length of conduit will have to run up the side of the house, it is best to come out of the basement at a point where shrubbery will partially conceal the installation. Occasionally, in frame construction, the circuit for overhead wiring can be fished up through the walls to a point of departure at the desired elevation of the house.

2. When the service panel is in the garage or house. In many newer homes, especially those without basements, the panel board is installed in the attached garage or in some other handy but inconspicuous part of the house. In such cases, the circuit is run from the panel board through the wall of the garage or house at the most convenient point. Thought should be given to the point selected so that installation is as unobtrusive as possible.

Circuits run underground offer a number of advantages to the homeowner. They are not subject to damage from storms or exposed to mechanical damage. Most important, such circuits are invisible and do not, therefore, mar the appearance of the grounds and gardens.

The most economical underground installation for both feeders and branch circuits is Type UF

(underground feeder) cable. This cable is approved by the National Electrical Code for direct burial in the ground without additional protection.

Underground cable is laid in a trench deep enough to prevent possible damage from normal spading. The bottom of the trench should be free from stones. This is easily accomplished by using a layer of sand or sifted dirt in the bottom of the trench. Cable is laid directly on top of this layer. When cable enters the building or leaves the ground, slack should be provided in the form of an "S" curve, to permit expansion with extreme changes in temperature. Where cable enters a building, after the cable has been installed, fill all openings through the foundation with sealing compound so that water from rain or melting snow cannot follow the cable into the building.

The National Electrical Code requires that underground feeder cables must be installed in continuous lengths from outlet to outlet and from fitting to fitting. Splices can be made only within a proper enclosure.

In some areas of the yard, where it is felt that digging might accidentally occur to the depth of the cable, a 1-by-2-inch running board can be laid over the cable before the trench is filled. Under driveways or roadways, or where heavy loading might occur, it is also desirable to use a board.

For outdoor wiring in sections of the country that are known to be termite infested or subject to attack by rodents, or wherever extra protection for the Type UF underground circuits is required, galvanized rigid steel conduit or lead-sheathed armor cable may be used for mechanical protection. When rigid conduit for the complete circuit run is used, feeders and branch circuits may be of any approved type of moisture-resistant wire such as Types TW, RW, or RHW.

Where the ground consists of a great deal of rock or ledge, it will be found a great deal easier and more economical to run outdoor wiring overhead. Overhead wiring can also be used effectively for certain lighting requirements such as floodlighting of tennis or badminton courts and for ornamental post lighting, provided, of course, that the overhead wire can be run high enough for proper clearance. Service drop, service entrance, or weatherproof wire of approved types may be used. Rigid conduit must be used for mechanical protection wherever the wire enters or leaves the ground. Drip loops (see page 146) at the point where the wire leaves the building and where it is attached to the pole are also required.

The height by which overhead wiring should clear the ground is generally controlled by local ordinance. In general, overhead wiring for outdoor lighting should follow the same rules laid down for services. Points to watch are clearances over driveways and walkways; possibility of damage caused

Table 5—7. Recommended wire size for outdoor circuits

Maximum length of circuit (feet)	Wire size	
	15-amp fusing	20-amp fusing
50	No. 14	No. 12
100	No. 12	No. 12
150	No. 12	No. 12
200	No. 12	No. 10
250	No. 10	No. 10
Size wire from junction box to outlet	No. 14	No. 12
Maximum load per circuit	1,800 watts	2,400 watts

by falling branches; isolation from window locations to prevent the conductors from being touched by persons at windows; locations such as flagpoles, TV masts, weather vanes, etc., that might foul the overhead wiring in windstorms or under conditions of ice loading.

Weatherproof outlets. Weatherproof outlets installed in the proper on-the-spot locations will allow you to plug in small garden lights, power equipment, appliances, and all of the many other kinds of equipment that are used to enhance the grounds or to provide more convenient outdoor living. With the outlets located where they are needed, the nuisance of dragging extension cords from the house and the hazard of tripping over cords are eliminated.

Weatherproof outlets are recommended for open porches even when they are roofed over. Weatherproof outlets should always be used in exposed areas such as on the side of the house or garage and on posts or masonry in the yard. Surface-mounted outlets on posts or masonry must also be enclosed in approved weatherproof outlet boxes. Flush-mounted outlets on porches or other locations that are roofed over are mounted in standard outlet boxes. All outlets, other than those intended solely for portable lighting equipment use, should be of the approved grounding type.

Outdoor lighting. There are four good reasons for installing outdoor lighting on the grounds around your home:

1. Beauty: flowers, shrubbery, and trees can be emphasized after dark.

2. Fun: outdoor lighting provides for sports, games, and barbecues after dark.

3. Convenience: outdoor lighting adds space for living and entertaining.

4. Safety: outdoor lighting prevents accidents and discourages trespassers.

Fixtures range in design from strictly functional types to those which are truly works of art. Between these two extremes are styles to satisfy most outdoor lighting needs. Functional fixtures, designed primarily to hold a light bulb, should be inconspicuous and often placed out of sight. Other

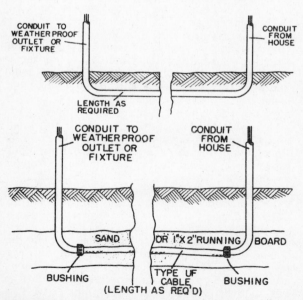

Figure 5—38. *(top)* Rigid conduit used for underground circuits; *(bottom)* type UF cable used for underground circuits.

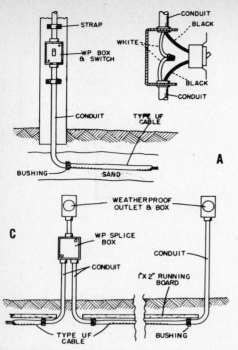

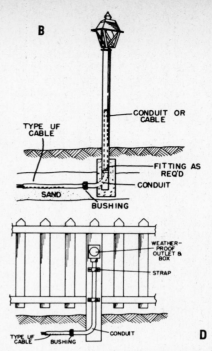

Figure 5–39. Outdoor wiring arrangements: (A) Outdoor weatherproof switch used to control a lighting fixture at a play area. (B) Ornamental post lighting fixture. (C) Weatherproof outlet enclosed in a weatherproof device box using a rigid conduit as both post and protection for wiring. The conduit is painted green to blend with the garden. (D) Weatherproof outlet enclosed in a weatherproof device box and surface-mounted on a fence post. The conduit is painted to match the fence.

fixture styles have a dual function: to be decorative and to produce useful light as well. Then, there are some fixtures one chooses simply because their beauty makes them look like jewels at nighttime. Generally, fixtures are made of aluminum, brass, steel, copper, or bronze. Select fixtures of sturdy construction and good finish to withstand all weather conditions.

No two gardens are alike, and no master plan can be adopted for a particular situation. A desirable outdoor lighting application will require experimenting to establish the best fixture placement, desired color effects, and the most enjoyable light usage.

COMMUNICATION SYSTEMS

Every home requires some form of signal from the outdoors to an inside room, so that the presence of visitors can be made known. While the electric bell and door chimes are the most common way to accomplish this, intercoms are becoming increasingly popular. There are also communication systems available which will announce two unwanted guests: burglars and fire.

Bell and door chimes. Signal equipment may occasionally be supplied for 120-volt operation, in which case it must be installed in the same manner as outlets and sockets operating on this voltage. Most bells and buzzers are rated to operate on 8, 12, 18, or 24 volts ac or dc. These operating voltages are known as low-voltage or low-energy circuits. They may be installed with minimum consideration for circuit insulation since there is no danger of shock to personnel or fire due to short circuits. The wire (called *bell wire*) is insulated with several layers of paraffin-impregnated cotton or with a thermoplastic covering. During installation, these wires are attached to building members with small insulating staples and are threaded through building construction members without insulators. They can even be placed behind baseboards and under moldings or floor boards.

In the majority of bell and chimes installations today, step-down transformers are employed in place of dry and wet cells for powering the signal system. The transformers are equipped to be mounted on outlet boxes and are constructed so that the 120-volt primary-winding leads normally extend from the side of the transformer adjacent to the box mounting. These leads are permanently attached to the 120-volt power circuits, and the low-voltage secondary-winding leads of the transformer are connected to the bell circuit in a manner similar to

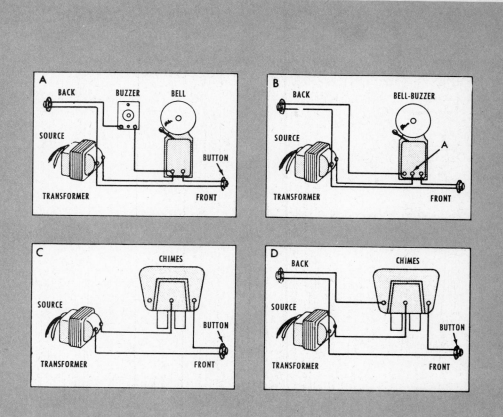

Figure 5–40. Arrangements of chimes, buzzers, and bells: (A) wiring for doorbell and buzzer; (B) combination bell-buzzer cir- cuit; (C) one- and two-note chimes at a front entrance; (D) one- and two- note chimes front and rear.

a switch-and-light combination. If more than one bell and push button is to be installed, they are paralleled with the first signal installation. A typical wiring schematic diagram for this type of installation is shown in Figure 5–40.

The installation of chimes is very similar to that of bells. For a set of two-door tubular chimes, three wires are needed, as with a pair of bells for two doors. One is a common wire and the other two run to the doors. It is a good idea to use wires with different-colored insulation to make identification easy.

Installing an intercom system. In addition to the normal functions of a home-intercom system, today's units feature hi-fi setups as well as radio. That is, a built-in AM/FM radio allows you to pipe music to every room at will; yet the intercom automatically overrides the radio.

Most intercom systems feature one master control with from three to six remotes. If you desire, additional masters and remotes may be added. As a rule, the master control is located near the telephone extension most frequently answered by members of the family. The individual remote units may be located where required or desired.

Wiring is simple. The master station, with its controls, is the only one needing a connection to a source of household current. A length of three- or four-conductor wire is strung from the master to the remote stations located in the various rooms. The wire is not bulky; hence it can easily be run along baseboards or around door and window framing. Often, the easiest way to run long leads is through the attic or along basement ceilings or beams. As for the actual hookup, follow the instructions furnished by the supplier.

Security sensor systems. Individual fire or burglar systems are available that may be installed by the average handyman. There are also sophisticated alarm systems in which one master unit can be used to detect fire, smoke, electrical power failure, freezing, flooding, and intruders. While there are many variations on the market, the wiring is simple, and actually hookup should be made as directed by the manufacturer.

Chapter 6

REMODELING YOUR HOME'S PLUMBING SYSTEM

Home plumbing is neither mysterious nor overly complicated. On the contrary, it is one of the easiest to do of all the various trades needed in home remodeling, especially when you become familiar with the tools and the wide assortment of products available. Today, with standardized fittings and tools available, almost anyone can acquaint himself with the general requirements and do a creditable job of plumbing.

But, before proceeding with any plumbing remodeling job, be sure to check your local plumbing or sanitary code. There are still a few cities in which all work on a residential plumbing job must be done by licensed plumbers. In some localities the code states that all soil and drain pipes must be installed by professionals, while a few communities permit anyone to do the work provided it is inspected and approved by licensed plumbers upon completion.

In any case, it is a good idea to obtain a copy of the local plumbing code and study it most carefully. The rules that appear in it usually follow the generally accepted practice of good plumbing. Remember that good plumbing does not depend as much on who does the job as it does on how the job is done. The comfort and health of your family depend on good workmanship and good sense when remodeling your home's plumbing system.

HOW A PLUMBING SYSTEM WORKS

The total plumbing system includes all pipes, fixtures, and fittings used to convey water into and out of the home. It can be divided into three basic areas: (1) the water-supply system; (2) the drainage system; and (3) the fixtures. The object of it all, of course, is to make water available where wanted in the home, and to get rid of the water, plus wastes, after it has served its purpose.

Water-supply system. In every plumbing system, there must be a source of water and the pipes to carry it to the fixtures. This water-supply system must be adequate to:

1. Assure you of pure water for drinking.

2. Supply a sufficient quantity of water at any outlet in the system, at correct operating pressure.

3. Furnish you with hot or cold water, as required.

In most incorporated areas the water source is a public or privately operated water "works" from which purified water is distributed through mains to which each user can be connected by arrangement with the proper authorities. However, if such a source is not available, you can install a private source of your own. In the latter case, the most efficient source in rural areas is the drilled well. In most cases, this is a job for a professional well digger. Wells are expensive and require special equipment for drilling. Local experts will be able to provide the answers to your questions concerning locating the well and its necessary equipment.

If you have a good well (ample water), all that you need to obtain "city-type" water service is the proper pumping equipment. You must have a pump that will deliver at all times the total maximum gallons per hour (gph) you will need. Water needs per day are based upon known average requirements (see Table 6–1), which are then converted by formula to arrive at the necessary pump capacity in gph.

Table 6–1. Water requirement calculations

Number of fixtures	
1	Bathtubs and/or showers
1	Lavatories
1	Toilets
2	Sinks and/or laundry tubs
1	Automatic clothes washer
0	Automatic dishwasher
2	Garden hose outlets
8	Total

FORMULA: 8 total × 60 min. = 480 gph pump capacity. (The minimum pump capacity recommended for a home is 540 gph.)

For all practical purposes a minimum discharge pressure of 30 pounds is sufficient to force water up to, and in good flow from, the highest faucet in a two-story home. (Many city water mains deliver water to basement mains at 30 pounds or a little more.) If, however, the pump will be situated many feet below the basement of your home (as with a pump and well in a valley or a house on a hill), a greater pressure will be required. The same applies if the pump will be at some distance from the house, or if it must deliver water to a distant outlet. In such cases a larger pump and/or motor will be required, or you may need a booster pump in your system.

Every automatic well pump requires a water-storage tank, which is kept filled by intermittent operation of the pump. As the tank fills, the water compresses the air locked in the tank, and this air pressure forces water from the tank up to and out an opened faucet. The pump must be equipped with an automatic pressure switch, which starts the pump when the tank (air) pressure drops below an established minimum and stops the pump when it reaches an established maximum. (The pump must, of course, be able to deliver this maximum pressure at the tank.) A well-designed, glass-lined tank is essential if you want pure water and no external condensate to dampen the tank area. An ample-size tank also will guarantee plenty of instantaneous water, even in excess of the pump's maximum gallons per minute capacity.

While there are several different types of water pumps on the market, the most popular for home use are the centrifugal jet and submersible types.

Remodeling Your Home's Plumbing System

The final selection should be made on the basis of advice from your well digger and your home requirements. Frequently, it is possible to use a booster pump rather than buying a new pump. That is, if the water pressure in the house, in a sprinkler system, or in a line to (for instance) a garage should be insufficient to produce the volume of water needed at the outlet(s), a booster pump will remedy the trouble. Connected to the main (or to the particular line to be boosted) the pump will increase pressure in relation to the amount of water passed through it, from 15 to 25 pounds. (For average home use the increase will be 20 pounds.) The pump has an integral motor and a flow switch that turns the motor on automatically when there is a demand for water.

Cold-water system. The main supply line coming into a house carries cold water. From this main supply, branches are taken off that lead to the various fixtures. The supply mains should be graded to one low point in the basement so that a drain cock will permit complete drainage of the entire supply system. Any portion of the piping which cannot be so drained must be equipped with a separate drain cock. As a rule, a pitch of 1/4 inch to each foot of pipe is sufficient to permit proper drainage. More information on the cold-water system in a home can be found on page 202.

Hot-water system. Hot water is obtained by routing cold water through a water heater. This heater may be part of the central heating plant or a separate unit. When part of a central system, a separate hot-water storage tank is generally provided to

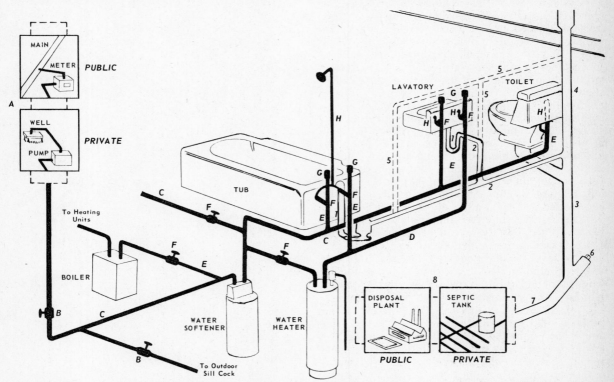

Figure 6–1. Major parts of the plumbing system. *Supply system parts:* (A) Water source, public or private. For our purpose it includes all piping up to the building. (B) Stop and waste valve. One is required at the low point of the system. (C) Cold-water main line (any line serving two or more fixtures). (D) Hot-water main line (any line serving two or more fixtures). (E) Branch line to fixture (any line, for cold or hot water, that serves one fixture only). (F) Shutoff valve, recommended for use in all branch lines and in main lines wherever a cutoff might be required. (G) Air chamber, recommended for any branch line terminating in a faucet. It helps eliminate chatter. (H) Fixture supply line. This is the portion of a branch line (above) that is installed when the fixture itself is installed and is adapted to its special requirements. *Drainage system parts:* (1) Fixture drain, the portion of a branch drain (below) adapted to the requirements of the particular fixture. Each drain must incorporate a trap (unless a trap is built into the fixture) that will hold water and seal the drain line against the escape of gases into house. (2) Branch drain, a line between a fixture and a soil stack. (3) Soil stack, a vertical pipe that collects from the branch drain or drains. Every installation must have one *main* stack, that is, a stack built of 3- or 4-inch pipe (depending on the building code), extending all the way through the roof. There may be a *secondary* stack or stacks, built of smaller (usually 2-inch) pipe, either throughout or in the vent portion only. (4) Vent, upper portion of a soil stack, through which gases escape to the outside and air enters the stack. (5) Revent, a by-pass for air between a branch drain and the vent portion of a stack. It is required by some codes. (6) Cleanout. One should be placed at every point where access may be needed to clear an obstruction (always at foot of each stack). (7) Building drain. It receives waste from the stack or stacks and carries it to the final disposal. (8) Final disposal, either the public sewer or a private septic tank.

hold the heated water. On the other hand, when a separate heater is used, the water is stored within the unit.

A separate heater unit may be electric, oil, or gas fired, but all are automatically controlled by a preset thermostat. Each style of heater comes in a wide variety of sizes. All automatic heaters have the necessary internal piping already installed, and the only connections required are the hot- and cold-water and fuel lines. Oil or gas-fired water heaters also require flues to vent the products of combustion.

A new hot-water heater might be necessary when you add new plumbing to your present system. Even if the present water heater is functioning properly (that is, it is not scaled up or rusted out), there may not be sufficient hot water available for your family. Actually the size of the hot-water storage tank needed in the house depends upon the number of persons in the family, the volume of hot water that may be needed during peak use periods (for instance, during laundering and bathing times), and the "recovery rate" of the heating unit. A good rule to follow when estimating the capacity of the tank required is 10 gallons per hour for each member of the family. For a family of four, for example, the hot-water demand will be 40 gallons of hot water per hour. This does not mean that the system will operate continuously at that capacity, but it must be capable of producing that amount of hot water to keep up with normal usage. If any unusual demands are anticipated, a larger capacity should be provided.

The recovery rate of water heaters varies with the type and capacity of the heating element. In standard conventional models, oil and gas heaters usually have higher recovery rates than electric heaters of similar size. For this reason, you would want a slightly larger capacity of electric heater than for either oil or gas.

Temperature and pressure (T&P) relief valves are on all hot-water heaters and hot-water storage tanks. Their function is to relieve pressure in the tank and water pipes should any other piece of control equipment in the system fail and the water temperature reach a point high enough to cause a dangerous pressure that would rupture the tank and pipes. Another important device on the heater is the drain cock or valve. Located at the bottom of the storage tank, it allows for the draining of the tank. A shutoff is also located on the cold-water intake pipe. *Note:* the hot-water valve or faucet is always placed on the left of a fixture as you face it.

Drainage system. Drainage (strictly controlled by code in most localities) is the complete and final disposal of the waste water, and of the sewage it contains. A drainage system, therefore, consists of: (1) the pipes that carry sewage away from the fixtures, and (2) the place where the sewage is deposit-

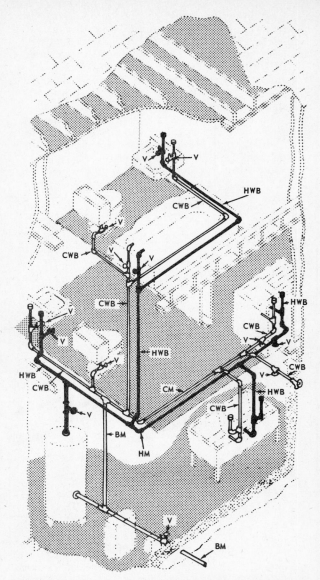

Figure 6–2. A typical water-supply system: BM = building main; CM = cold-water main; HM = hot-water main; CWB = cold-water branch; HWB = hot-water branch; V = valve.

ed. You may empty sewage into a city sewer, into a properly constructed septic tank, or (in a few cases) into a cesspool.

In the house, the waste lines are concealed in the walls and under floors. The vertical lines are called stacks, and the horizontal lines are called branches. The flow of waste water starts at the fix-

Because of the solid waste materials, soil lines are the largest in the system. Each time the soil lines are used, they are flushed. Also needed in a drainage system are the vents for the circulation of air.

To be safe, your drainage system has to meet five basic requirements:

1. All pipes in this system must be pitched (slanted) down toward the main disposal so that the weight of the waste will cause it to flow toward the main disposal system and away from the house. Because of gravity flow, the waste lines must be larger than the water-supply lines, in which there is pressure.

2. Pipes must be fitted and sealed so that sewer gases cannot leak out.

3. The system must contain vents to carry off the sewer gases to where they can do no harm. Vents also help to equalize the air pressure in the drainage system.

4. Each fixture that has a drain should be provided with a suitable water trap, so that water standing in the trap will seal the drain pipe and prevent the backflow of sewer gas into the house. The trap for the toilet (water closet) is built into it.

5. Re-vents should be provided wherever there is danger of siphoning the water from a fixture trap or where specified by local codes.

As we have seen, there is an important difference between the water-supply system and the drainage system. In the water-supply system, water flows under pressure; in the drainage system gravity causes the flow. Therefore, keep these points in mind: The supply system (hot and cold water) is continuous and closed; the drains are always pitched downward from the fixture to which they are attached and must always be vented. More details on the plumbing drainage system are given later in the chapter.

Fixtures. The fixtures provide the required means for using your water. In this sense, a faucet on the outside of your house (for attaching a hose) is a fixture. So is a laundry tub in the basement, or a shower, dishwasher, or toilet. Each has a purpose connected with your use of water; and each must have certain features to serve its purpose (for instance the hose faucet must be threaded so you can attach the hose; the shower must be designed to mix hot and cold water to give you water of the proper temperature, and so on). A great deal of thought should be given to fixtures: they are generally the most costly plumbing items, and should be exactly what you will need.

When selecting fixtures, the first step is to select those that are best suited to your purse and needs. Each fixture must be just right in size, color, styling, and accommodations. And the locations of fixtures in a room, such as in a bathroom, kitchen, or laundry, should be carefully planned for maximum accessibility and convenience. More on the

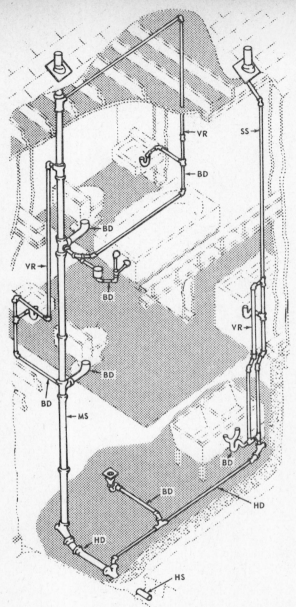

Figure 6-3. A typical drainage system: MS = main (soil) stack; SS = secondary (soil) stack; BD = branch drain; HD = house drain; HS = house sewer; VR = vent run.

ture trap, the device that stops sewer gases from entering the house. It flows through the fixture branches to the soil stack. It continues through the house drain and the house sewer and finally reaches the city sewer or, in a private system, a septic tank. Waste stacks carry only water waste. The lines taking the wastes from the toilet are called the soil lines.

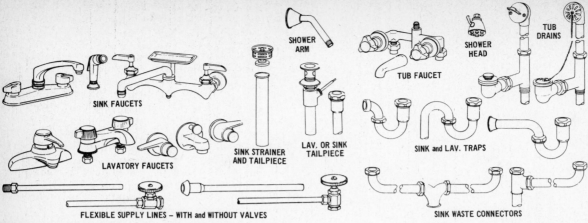

Figure 6—4. Typical fixture waste and supply fittings and trim.

selection of kitchen and bathroom fixtures can be found in Chapters 11 and 14. In addition to the usual bathroom and kitchen fixtures, these are some other popular accommodations to think about:

Extra bathroom	Electric clothes washer
Half bath	Electric dishwasher
Basement toilet	Electric garbage disposal
Basement or garage shower	Outdoor hose faucets
Sink for basement shop	Gardening sink
Laundry tub	Drain in garage

It is important to remember that the costliest single item in a plumbing remodeling job can be the main soil stack. If you cannot use the present main stack, you will have to have a secondary or optional vent. In planning fixture locations, keep the following in mind:

1. Every building must have a main soil stack built of 3- or 4-inch pipe (depending on the building code and kind of pipe) from the building drain up through the roof.

2. If there is one toilet, it must drain into the main stack. Extra toilets can drain into this same stack if not too far from it. The branch drain for a toilet must be the same diameter pipe as the main stack and must slope properly. If an additional toilet is too far from the main stack, you can provide a secondary (2-inch) stack that is increased to the proper (3- or 4-inch) size throughout the portion through which the toilet will drain. Or this additional toilet can drain into the main stack if you provide a 2-inch vent at the toilet.

3. Other fixtures (a tub, lavatory, sink) can drain into the main stack or a secondary stack. The branch drains must be 1½- to 2-inch pipe, depending on the fixture, and must slope downward.

4. Any secondary stack should be a minimum of 1½ inches in diameter and must either be vented

out through the roof or connect into the main stack at a point above any branch drain.

5. Any branch drain that enters a stack 8 feet or more below another branch drain should be re-vented to prevent siphoning off of the water in the lower fixture trap when the higher fixture is flushed. A re-vent should be the same size pipe as the branch drain.

6. All stacks must connect with the building drain, which must be of the same size pipe as the main stack, and must slope down all the way to the final disposal.

Planning an improvement. When adding a bathroom, your major plumbing problem will be how best to provide a soil stack for the new fixtures and how to connect this stack to your existing building drain. Of course, if your new room will butt against a wall in which there already is a suitable size soil stack, this problem is solved. More often, however, you will need to add a new soil stack. The easiest place to put this is inside one of your new walls, preferably the one closest to your building drain.

If you are creating a new bathroom within your present house walls by building three (or two) new partitions to enclose an area (like the space under a stairway, or in the corner of a large room, then you may be able to install a new soil stack inside one of the new partitions. In a one-story house this is easy to do as the stack can open right out through the roof for venting. If there is another floor above, however, you will have to run the stack up through a partition on the floor above, or plan to box it in. If this is impossible, you may be able to run the new stack up an outside wall, on the outside, and box it in to match the house exterior. In this case, the stack should be insulated against freezing.

When modernizing old homes, plan to locate plumbing facilities relating to the kitchen, bathroom(s), and the laundry as close together as possible since this makes the job much easier and less costly. Also try to keep the hot-water pipes and drains with their vent pipes as short as possible. This not only makes for more efficient plumbing but makes the installation and maintenance costs less.

SELECTING PIPE

Today, the home handyman plumber has a wide selection of pipe types from which to choose. But, regardless of the type, all pipe sizes for plumbing purposes are designated as the inside diameter or

Figure 6–5. Typical methods of concealing stack and horizontal pipes.

the actual size of the opening through which the water flows. Actually, the distance that water has to travel to the outlet is very important in determining the size of pipe. The inside walls of all pipes produce a surprising amount of frictional drag and, for this reason, the pipe should be as short as possible and have as few connections and bends as possible. In addition, piping for the distribution of water must be large enough to permit an equalized pressure and a sufficient supply to all outlet points. Branch pipes, for instance, can be somewhat smaller than the feeder lines coming up. The main risers can be smaller than the main supply line.

Types of water pipes and fittings. Water-supply piping is available in: (1) galvanized steel pipe; (2) rigid copper tubing; (3) flexible copper tubing; (4) rigid plastic pipe; and (5) flexible plastic pipe.

Galvanized steel pipe. This pipe is the same type as the pipe used for drainage, but ordinary (not sanitary) fittings are used with it for water-supply runs. Also, smaller sizes (seldom over 1-inch size) are used. The usual sizes required for water-supply runs are ½, ¾, and 1 inch, in 21-foot lengths (or shorter, threaded lengths, if specified). Fittings are similar in external appearance to the drainage fittings.

Table 6–2. Sizes for wrought iron and galvanized steel pipe

Nominal size (inches)	Outside diameter (inches)	Inside diameter (inches)	Number of threads per inch
¼	0.540	0.364	18
⅜	0.675	0.493	18
½	0.840	0.622	14
¾	1.050	0.824	14
1	1.315	1.049	11½
1¼	1.660	1.380	11½
1½	1.900	1.610	11½
2	2.375	2.067	11½
2½	2.875	2.469	8

Galvanized steel pipe is the most economical type available and will last for years. It also seems easiest for the amateur to assemble as the joints are simply screwed together. However, working in places too close to swing a wrench can become a problem, in which case copper or plastic may prove easier to handle. Also, galvanized steel pipe should never be buried underground.

Rigid copper tubing. Copper pipe is available in two types: hard (or rigid) and soft (or flexible) tubing. There are also five commercial grades of copper pipe: Type K, both hard and soft, is the heaviest and used generally in commercial work. Type L, both hard and soft, is lighter than K and is popular in residential water lines. Type M is made in hard tubing only and is used for light residential lines. (Your local plumbing code should be checked before installing Type M.)

Most rigid tubing in the home is in ⅜-, ½-, and

¾-inch sizes for in-house use (Type L) and in ¾-inch and larger sizes (Type K) for underground use; all are sold in lengths up to 20 feet. Solder-type fittings are always used and are very easy to assemble once you have learned how. By using the proper adapters, you may combine copper and threaded steel pipes in your installation.

Table 6—3. Sizes of types K, L, and M copper tubing

Nominal size (inches)	Outside diameter	Inside diameter		
	Types K, L, and M	Type K	Type L	Type M
⅜	0.500	0.402	0.430	0.450
½	0.625	0.527	0.545	0.569
¾	0.875	0.745	0.785	0.811
1	1.125	0.995	1.025	1.055
1¼	1.375	1.245	1.265	1.291
1½	1.625	1.481	1.505	1.527

Since copper tubing has a smooth bore, water flows through it with less resistance than through wrought iron. This feature permits replacement of a heavy iron pipe with a copper tube of smaller diameter. To determine possible replacement sizes involving this factor, check Table 6–4.

Table 6—4

Iron pipe size (inches)	Copper tube size (inches)
½	⅜
¾	½
1	¾
1¼	1
1½	1¼
2	1½

For distances over 20 feet, or for risers running up through the walls, it is safer to use a copper tube of the same diameter as the iron pipe it replaces.

Soft copper tubing. Soft or flexible copper tubing is the easiest metal pipe to install. Its walls are thinner than rigid copper and so the cost is less. It comes in 60-foot coils and is available in the same two types (L and K) and the same sizes as rigid copper tubing. Soft copper tubing has the advantage of turning corners without need of fittings. This means you can avoid complicated joints to round corners. Just bend the pipe around them. The only trick is to keep the tubing from sinking or flattening while you are bending it. If the diameter of the tubing is reduced, the flow of water through the pipe will also be reduced. Unless a special tube-bending tool is available, you should make the curves as gradual as possible. One method is to lay the tubing on a board, fastening down one end, then kneeling on the tube and raising the free end slowly. Move the knee toward the free end slightly, and raise again, repeating until the desired curve is obtained.

Another way of bending soft copper tubing requires a bending spring, an inexpensive device that is slipped down the pipe to the proper location. Grip the pipe firmly, placing your knee in the middle of the spring, and pull both ends until the desired bend is produced. The spring arrangement prevents kinking. Soft copper tubing can be bent by hand.

Soft copper tubing can be assembled with either solder-type fittings or flare-type fittings. The latter type hold simply by being tightened, and are very easy to assemble. However, flare-type fittings should never be used inside walls or anywhere they cannot easily be reached.

Rigid and flexible plastic pipe. Rigid plastic pipe in 10-foot lengths and flexible plastic pipe in 60-foot coils are similar in sizes and uses to copper tubing. The new CPVC (chlorinated polyvinyl chloride) pipes can be used in most water applications except that they are not made for hot-water systems (most can withstand pressures up to 100 pounds per square inch at temperatures of 180 degrees F) and, being nonconducting, they cannot be used in grounding. Plastic pipe hardware weighs only one-eighth as much as iron pipe, and one-third as much as copper tubing. The plastic surface prevents interior scale buildup and corrosion. Also, the natural insulation property of plastic reduces condensation on the outside of cold water lines. In addition, because of this natural insulation, the pipe can be installed just a few inches under the surface of the soil since freezing weather has no adverse effect on it. But, if the water is to be used for drinking, the pipe should bear the seal of the National Sanitation Foundation.

The plastic pipe can be connected to existing iron or copper piping with plastic-to-metal connectors and couplings. When joining plastic to an iron pipe system, try to use the lines where a connection is fairly close. This way you can disassemble the existing pipe from the connection and back to an existing elbow. A new iron tee replaces the elbow for the new connection. In copper lines, connections can be made almost anywhere. A CPVC take-off tee is used with copper tubing adapters. But before you start, check your local plumbing codes since some areas have not yet updated codes to permit use of plastic pipe. (Plumbing ordinances, as a rule, permit either galvanized steel or copper pipe for water-supply purposes.)

Valves and faucets. Valves are used in water-supply lines to shut off the flow of water when desired. A faucet is a valve used at the end of a water-supply line.

There are three general types of valves. First is the gate valve, which permits full flow of water when the "gate" in the valve is lifted out of the way. This type is used in water mains, but seldom in homes. The other two, the globe and the ground-key valves, do somewhat restrict water flow, even when open, but are more popular for home use. All valves are of either a threaded or a solder type. Stop-and-waste valves are of either a globe or a ground-key type fitted with a removable plug (or cap) for draining the shutoff side of the line (to prevent freezing of accumulated water). A check valve is one which permits water to flow in one direction only.

Fixture supply lines. Most exposed fixture supply lines are chrome plated for best appearance. Available in rigid and flexible types, they are equipped with proper fittings to join fixtures to their supply piping and are best ordered with the fixtures to guarantee correct fit.

Types of drainage pipes and fittings. There are three types of pipes used today for drainage systems: (1) cast-iron and threaded steel pipes; (2) plastic pipes; and (3) copper pipes.

Cast-iron and threaded steel pipes. Cast-iron pipe has long been used for stacks, building drains and sewers, and any drains buried underground. Pipes come in 2- and 4-inch sizes in 5-foot lengths, either with a hub at one end or with hubs at both ends (for making two shorter hub end pieces).

Table 6–5. *Pipe data at a glance*

TYPE OF PIPE	EASE OF WORKING	WATER FLOW EFFICIENCY FACTOR	TYPE OF FITTINGS NEEDED	MANNER USUALLY STOCKED	LIFE EXPECTANCY	PRINCIPAL USES	REMARKS
Brass, Threaded	No threading required. Cuts easily, but can't be bent. Measuring a job rather difficult	Highly efficient because of low friction	Screw on Connections	12 ft. rigid lengths. Cut to size wanted.	Lasts life of building	Generally for commercial construction	Required in some cities where water is extremely corrosive. Often smaller diameter will suffice because of low friction coefficient
Copper-Hard	Easier to work with than brass	Same as brass	Screw on or or Solder Connections	12 ft. rigid lengths. Cut to size wanted.	Same as brass	Same as brass	
Copper-Soft	Easier to work with than brass or hard copper because it bends readily by using a bending tool. Measuring a job not too difficult	Same as brass	Solder Connections	Coils - usually soft	Same as brass	Widely used in residential installations	
Copper Tubing, Flexible	Easier than soft copper because it can be bent without a tool. Measuring jobs is easy.	Highest of all metals since there are no nipples, unions, or elbows	Solder or Compression Connections	3 wall thicknesses: 'K'-Thickest 'L'-Medium 'M'-Thinnest 20 ft. lengths or 15 ft., 30 ft., or 60 ft. coils (Except 'M')	Same as brass	'K' is used in municipal and commercial construction. 'L' is used for residential water lines. 'M' is for light domestic lines only - check Code before using.	Probably the most popular pipe today. Often a smaller diameter will suffice because of low friction coefficient.
Wrought Iron (or galvanized)	Has to be threaded. More difficult to cut. Measurements for jobs must be exact.	Lower than copper because nipples unions reduce water flow.	Screw on Connections	Rigid lengths, up to 22 ft. Usually cut to size wanted.	Corrodes in alkaline water more than others. Produces rust stains.	Generally found in older homes	Recommended if lines are in a location subject to impact.
Plastic Pipe	Can be cut with saw or knife.	Same as copper tubing	Insert couplings, clamps; also by cement. Threaded & compression fittings can be used (Thread same as for metal pipe)	Rigid, semi-rigid & flexible. Coils of 100-400 ft.	Long life & it is rust & corrosion-proof.	For cold water installations. Used for well casings, septic tank lines, sprinkler systems. Check Codes before installing.	Lightest of all, weighs about 1/8 of metal pipe. Does not burst in below freezing weather.

Threaded, galvanized steel pipe, available in 1½- and 2-inch sizes in 21-foot lengths, is generally used with cast iron for branch drains and vent lines, and (sometimes) for secondary stacks. Steel pipe, however, must not be buried underground. So-called "sanitary" fittings must be used for assembling all drainage lines. These come in both hub-type cast iron and threaded iron. "Straight" (not sanitary) cast-iron and "ordinary" (not sanitary) threaded fittings are used in vent runs where gases only (no water) will pass through them.

Plastic pipe. Plastic pipe, called ABS-DWV pipe, is available in 1½- and 3-inch sizes in 10-foot lengths, for in-house use, and in 4-inch size for underground sewer-pipe installations. The ABS stands for the chemical composition of the pipe, i.e., Acrylonitrile-Butadiene-Styrene, and the DWV stands for Drain, Waste, and Vent. As the name implies, the pipe is not used for supply line, but solely for drains, waste lines, and vent stacks. For these purposes, it is very good. Boiling water, detergents, and various other solvents have no effect on the pipe. Being light in weight, it is easy to handle. The fittings are all uniform and exact in dimension, as is the pipe itself. Solvent cement is used to make all the joints. Incidentally, all ABS-DWV fittings are of the sanitary type and are used inverted wherever needed for vent-run connections.

Copper pipe. Lighter and easier to install than cast iron, copper pipe and fittings are available in 1½- and 3-inch sizes (pipe in 10-foot lengths) for all in-house drainage and vent runs. Drainage-type copper must not, however, be used underground. All fittings are the sanitary type and are used inverted where needed in vent runs.

Traps. The function of a trap, as previously mentioned, is to prevent air from entering the waste pipe while liquid is flowing, and thus it eliminates noise. It also stops unpleasant odors from entering the house from the sewer lines. Remember that many common sewer gases not only are obnoxious but can cause serious illness and even death.

The two most popular types of traps are "P" and "S" traps. When working in tight places, you can install "P" and "S" traps somewhat off the center line to avoid cutting into studs or joists. All fixture traps in the house must be constructed with a cleanout opening at the bottom of the curve so that waste collections can be removed when necessary.

Like exposed fixture supply lines, all exposed fixture drains and traps should be of chrome-plated brass.

Converting your plumbing ideas to an installation plan. To help order the necessary pipe and fittings, you must make an "installation plan." The plan illustrated in Figure 6–6 is for a typical cast-iron drainage system. The part labeled *Elevation* is a

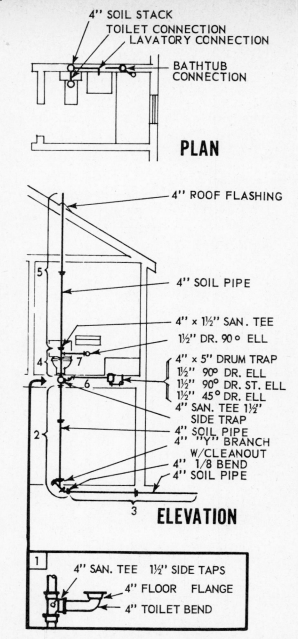

Figure 6–6. Converting a house plan to an installation plan.

side view to show the vertical "runs" of pipe, and the part labeled *Plan* is a top view (looking down) to show the horizontal runs. Wherever necessary, details should be shown in an enlarged boxed-in view arrowed to the point where the detail fits in (see number 1). The large numbers (such as 1 through 7) in the illustration give you the installation steps. All pipes and fittings should be labeled for ready identification. You should make similar plans for a water-supply system, too.

When making your plans, the following are some factors that should be taken into consideration: tion:

1. If a new main soil stack must be added, its location should be chosen first. This governs all other drainage piping requirements, and the water-supply piping can easily be adapted to any location made necessary by the soil stack. This stack must be straight, if possible, or have only gentle bends (if the building layout makes it necessary to have bends). It must be located directly behind the toilet or as close to it as possible. If there are two toilets, it should serve both, or a second stack is required. In this case, first consideration is given to the main stack, which will serve one toilet and most of the other fixtures. The second stack may be like the main stack or may use smaller (2-inch) pipe from the toilet upward. Any stack must have drainage fittings in the portion that carries drainage; but use ordinary fittings in the vent portion (that carries only air and gases). In very cold climates, outer walls should be avoided as pipes located in them may freeze. The bottom of any soil stack should be in a position where: (a) a cleanout can be conveniently located; and (b) the stack can easily be connected to the building drain.

2. Once the stack is located, the drainage lines should be placed. These lines must be sloped correctly, and each must emerge from the wall or floor where proper connections to the fixture can be made.

3. Re-vents should be located next (if used). These have the same requirements as drainage lines, except that ordinary fittings are used and they do not slope.

4. Any secondary soil stacks are now located. These have the same requirements as the main soil stack.

5. The building drain is the last part of the drainage system to be planned as its principal requirement is to collect from the soil stack(s) and drain to the final disposal. The sewer line must slope downward (all the way to final disposal) at the proper pitch. For construction of a building sewer see page 198.

6. Once the drainage system is planned, the water-supply system can be planned to keep all the pipes running (as nearly as possible) through the same wall openings (to save installation work). Your furnace (and chimney) location will probably determine the hot-water heater location (unless your heater is an electric one), and hot water pipes to various fixtures should parallel cold-water pipes to these fixtures (for convenience and the appearance of the installation). The point at which your water-source line enters the building will determine the meter (if any) location (as this must be at this point); and all pipes in the building should be planned to slope downward to a low point (as near as possible to the meter) so that you can locate a stop-and-waste valve at this low point.

Pipe sizes are usually determined as shown in Table 6—6.

ASSEMBLING PIPE AND FITTINGS

Standardized pipe fittings are available from any plumber's supply house and plumbing shop. These fittings are made for every type and size of job to be encountered in home plumbing. The term fittings includes all the connecting pieces that are necessary to join the lengths of pipe together to make up the plumbing system. Most of the fittings are threaded with standard pipe threads, except those used for soil pipes and drains, which have no threads.

One important requirement of good plumbing is to use as few of these fittings as is possible. In order to keep them at a minimum and the pipe lengths as short as possible, as previously stated, you should make a thorough study of the plumbing system to be used and carefully make a detailed drawing of it.

Cast-iron soil pipe. A cast-iron soil pipe is the most difficult for the home handyman to handle,

Table 6—6

Type of fixture	Lav-atory	Tub or shower	Toilet	Sink	Garbage disposal	Dish-washer	Clothes washer
Fixture drains Branch drains Revent Lines	1½-inch	1½-inch	3- to 4-inch	1½- to 2-inch	1½- to 2-inch	1½- to 2-inch	1½-inch
Fixture supply lines Branch lines	⅜-inch	½-inch	⅜-inch	½-inch		½-inch	½-inch

NOTE: *Main soil stack:* 3–4 inches. *Secondary soil stack:* Size of largest branch drain connected to it, in most cases. *Basement floor drain:* 2–4 inches. *Building drain:* At least the size of main soil stack. *Branch building drain:* At least the size of largest secondary soil stack emptying into it. *Cold-water main line* serving both the cold-water system and the hot-water heater: ¾-inch to 1-inch. *Cold-and hot-water main lines* serving two or more fixtures: Size of largest branch line served or, if fixtures will be used simultaneously, the next pipe size larger than that used for the largest branch line.

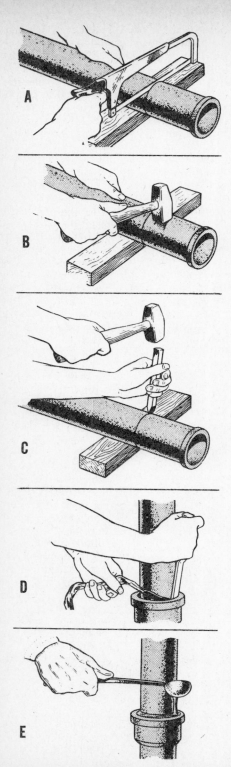

but it is the least expensive. The tools necessary for the assembly job can usually be rented from your plumbing suppliers.

Measuring. When pieces of pipe under 5 feet are needed, use double-hub pipe; then, when the pipe is cut, each end will have a hub. Carefully measure the length of pipe needed, making sure you allow the additional length necessary for engagement with the hub of the adjoining piece. Mark around the pipe with chalk where it is to be cut. Hub allowances are 2½ inches for 2-inch pipe; 3 inches for 4-inch pipe.

Cutting. To cut service-weight pipe, use a hacksaw and make a ⅟₁₆-inch cut all around the pipe (Figure 6–7A). Make sure your cut is square with the pipe to insure a clean, even break. Then tap the pipe with a hammer until it breaks at the cut (Figure 6–7B).

To cut extra-heavy pipe, first file around the pipe on the mark (using a triangle file) to scratch the surface and provide a guideline. Then lay a piece of 2 × 4 flat on the floor and place the pipe across it. Take a hammer and cold chisel, use your knee to turn the pipe, and make a light cut all around the pipe, once (Figure 6–7C). Continue cutting around the pipe, striking the chisel harder each time you go around, until the pipe breaks off.

Making connections. When the pipe is erected vertically, each piece is positioned with the hub end up. First make sure the ends of the pipes to be joined are clean and dry. Place the spigot (plain) end of the next-higher section into the hub to its full depth, and secure the upper pipe in position. Make absolutely certain the two lengths are perfectly straight up and down. Check with a level or taut cord. Then light a plumber's furnace and place the caulking lead in the melting pot. If your plumbing code requires a full inch of lead, use 1 pound of lead for each inch of pipe diameter. If it permits ¾ inch of lead, use 3 pounds for 4-inch pipe or 1½ pounds for 2-inch pipe.

Pack the joint with oakum while the lead is melting. Oakum comes in the form of a rope. About 1 ounce is required for each inch of pipe diameter. Wrap the oakum around the pipe at the joint, and drive it to the bottom of the hub space with the yarning iron (Figure 6–7D). Continue packing until the joint is filled to within about ¾ inch from the top of the hub. Make sure the oakum is packed tightly and evenly, as this makes the watertight seal. The joint is now ready for leading. *Warning:* Heat the ladle by placing it alongside the melting pot before dipping it into the molten lead. An explosion may result if a cold or wet ladle is dipped into molten lead.

When the lead is molten, dip it out and pour it into the hub (Figure 6–7E). Pour it evenly around the joint, and continue pouring until the lead is even with the top of the hub. Enough lead should be

Figure 6–7. Steps in the assembly of cast-iron soil pipe.

dipped to fill the joint in one pouring. When it cools, the lead must be packed down (caulked) to make the joint air- and watertight. Make sure the pipe is completely solid before starting. Other lengths of pipe may be positioned and packed with oakum while you are waiting. Then use a hammer and caulking iron to force the lead down. An inside caulking iron is used to pack the lead against the pipe, an outside caulking iron to pack it against the hub. Tamp the lead firmly all around several times in order to obtain a tight seal between hub and spigot.

The procedure for caulking a horizontal joint differs only in that an asbestos joint runner must be used to prevent the lead from running out of the hub as it is poured. Prepare the pipes and pack in the oakum, as before. Now place the asbestos joint runner around the pipe, fitting it just above the hub, and as tightly as possible. The clamp should be placed at the top of the pipe to form a funnel for pouring the lead. Tap the runner down against the top of the hub to prevent the lead from running out. Then take a full ladle of lead so that the joint may be made at one pouring, if possible. Pour the lead in at the top of the joint to overflowing. Remove the joint runner after the lead has cooled and solidified. A good horizontal joint will always have an excess of lead showing above the hub. Cut off the surplus lead with a hammer and cold chisel. Caulk the lead into the hub, following the same procedure given above.

Galvanized steel pipe.

All fittings for galvanized steel pipe are threaded. The pipe is cut to the length required, threaded on both ends, and screwed tightly into the fittings. In many cases, if your order calls for pipe precut to exact lengths needed, these pipes will all be threaded by the supplier.

Measuring. Pipe lengths to be cut should be measured very carefully, as allowance must be

Table 6–7

Pipe size (inches)	Distance pipe is screwed into fitting (inches)	
	Standard fitting	Drainage fitting
1/2	1/2	
3/4	1/2	
1	5/8	
1 1/4	5/8	5/8
1 1/2	5/8	5/8
2	3/4	5/8
3		7/8
4		1

made for the threads needed to engage the fittings. The best way to measure is to use the face-to-face method. First measure the exact distance from *face-to-face* of the fittings (see Figure 6–8). Next, refer to Table 6–7 to determine the extra length necessary for screwing into the fittings. Remember that double this length is necessary for two ends.

Example: The face-to-face measurement is 5 feet. If 3/4-inch pipe is being used, Table 6–7 shows that 1/2 inch is needed for engagement with the fitting at one end. If both ends are to be engaged with a fitting, then twice this, or 1 inch of extra length, is required. The total length of the pipe will be 5 feet 1 inch.

Cutting. Use either a hacksaw or a pipe cutter and cut squarely across the pipe. If the pipe is not cut squarely across and cleanly, threading will be difficult. For this reason, the pipe should be held in a pipe vise. Mount the vise solidly. Place it so there is ample room on each side for handling the longest pipe to be cut or threaded.

When using a pipe cutter, loosen its cutter wheel by turning the handle until the cutter will slide over the pipe (Figure 6–9A). Place the cutting wheel exactly on the cutting mark and tighten the handle until the cutting wheel is forced slightly into the pipe. Apply thread-cutting oil to the cutter wheel and the pipe. Rotate the cutter one complete turn around the pipe. Tighten the cutter wheel and go around the pipe again. Repeat until the pipe is cut off. Remove the burrs with a pipe reamer (Figure 6–9B) or file.

When using a hacksaw, mark the pipe where it is to be cut and tighten it in place in the vise. Hold the saw at a 90-degree angle to the pipe, and make your cut with smooth, even strokes. With the pipe still in the vise, remove the burrs with a pipe reamer or round file.

Threading. Care is required to insure clean-cut threads for engagement with the fittings. A stock and die are used. The stock contains a receptacle on one side in which the die sets, and an opening on the other side for inserting a guide. The guide makes it possible to start the die squarely. Each die is marked with its size. Select the same size die as the size of the pipe to be threaded. Loosen the

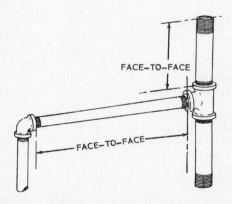

Figure 6–8. To get the correct length of pipe take the face-to-face measurements and add makeup distances.

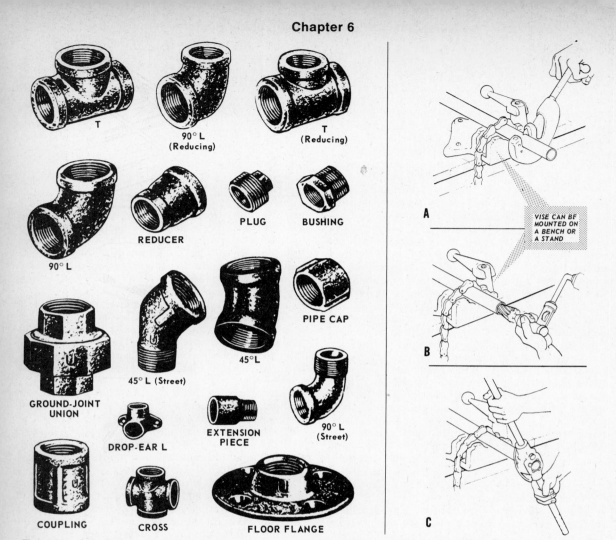

Figure 6—9. *(Left)* Typical galvanized malleable fittings; *(right)* steps in cutting and threading galvanized pipes.

thumb nut on the stock, slide the cover plate over, and insert the die. Make certain the printing on the die faces up toward the cover. Slide the cover plate back in place and tighten the thumb nut. Either an adjustable guide or individual guides can be used. Each individual guide is marked for the size of the pipe it fits. Select the correct guide, insert it in the opening in the stock, and tighten it in place with the lock bolt.

Place the pipe in the vise, and slide the stock over the end of the pipe with the guide on the inside. Push it onto the pipe until the die catches the pipe. Turn the stock slowly in a *clockwise* direction, keeping the die pressed firmly against the pipe. After cutting just enough thread so the die is firmly on the pipe, apply plenty of cutting oil to the

threads of the die and the pipe end. Continue to turn the stock, backing off about ¼ turn after each ½ turn forward, to clear away the chips. Continue threading, applying cutting oil often, until the pipe protrudes to the face of the die (Figure 6–9C). To remove the tool after threading, turn it *counterclockwise*. Wipe off the surplus oil, and all chips from the thread, before using the pipe.

Making connections. Pipe wrenches are used for connecting this pipe and fittings. Use a 10-inch wrench for pipes up to 1 inch; an 18-inch wrench for pipes up to 2 inches; and a 24-inch wrench for pipes up to 2½ inches. (Wrenches are sized according to the overall length of the wrench.) Use an open-end, adjustable-head, or monkey wrench on nuts, unions, and valves, and to hold fittings with flat surfaces to be gripped. Do not tighten the jaws of a pipe wrench too tightly or they will tend to crush the pipe (this wrench gets tighter when you turn it). Actually, pipe wrenches are intended for turning pipes and other round objects, and not nuts, bolts, or flanges that have flat gripping surfaces. The only exception is that a large pipe wrench may be used on a nut, bolt, or flange that is 1 inch or more across. Never use a pipe wrench on plated or polished surfaces as the finish will be marred. When using an adjustable wrench of any kind, always turn it so that the handle moves toward the open side of the jaws. This direction of turning tightens the wrench grip; opposite turning would loosen the grip and allow the wrench to slip. Never twist a wrench sideways. Use two wrenches when both fitting and pipe must be held. Position a left-hand wrench in front to loosen a joint; a right-hand wrench in front to tighten one.

Rigid copper tubing. Rigid copper tubing can be installed in much the same manner as wrought iron pipe, except that the ends are not usually threaded. This tubing is soldered to form a join. Where long lines are exposed, rigid copper has the best appearance. The cutter used can be a hacksaw or a pipe cutter. If a pipe cutter is used, then you should have a reamer also, to ream out the burr that is always left on the inside of the pipe after cutting. The burr will cause a turbulence in the water and cut down the rate of flow considerably, if left in the pipe.

Measuring. This tubing is measured face-to-face in the same manner as galvanized steel pipe; but add on the depths of the soldering hubs in the fittings to be used.

Cutting. If considerable tubing is to be cut, you will find it advantageous to build a jig for holding the tubing and guiding the hacksaw (Figure 6–10A). This will enable you to get an even, square cut. Use a fine-tooth hacksaw blade (preferably a No. 24). You can also use a tube cutter, without a jig. After the tubing is cut, remove all burrs by reaming.

Making connections. Since clean surfaces are essential, clean and brighten the end of the tube and the inside of the fittings to be soldered with steel wool or fine emery cloth. Do not use a file as it will score the surface. Also, the tube end must be perfectly round, not out-of-round or dented. Apply a thin coat of noncorrosive flux or soldering paste on the cleaned portions of both tube and fitting. Place the tube in the fitting and rotate it a few times to spread the flux coat evenly (Figure 6–10B). Remove the excess flux from the outside of the fitting.

Heat the connection evenly with a blowtorch by applying the flame directly to the fitting. Use two blowtorches simultaneously on the larger-size pipes, applying one to each side of the fitting to obtain uniform heating. When the flux bubbles out, remove the torch and touch the end of your solder

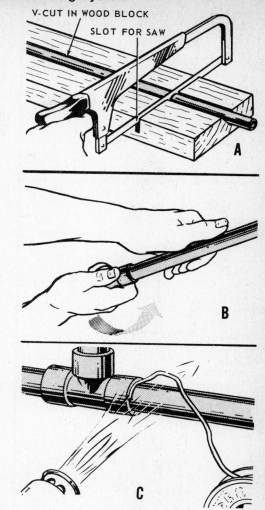

Figure 6–10. Working with rigid copper tubing.

stick to the edge of the fitting (Figure 6–10C). If the fitting and tube are hot enough, the solder will flow and fill the joint immediately. (The solder will be drawn into the space between the tube and fitting, even upward into a fitting, by capillary attraction.) When a line of solder shows completely around the joint, the connection is filled. Do not hold the flame on the connection after it is filled as further heating will only result in a loss of solder, which might make it necessary to start over again. When the joint is completed, remove all surplus solder. If you make other solder connections to the same fitting, wrap the finished joint with wet rags to prevent the solder from melting. But, in any case, make sure the pipe and fitting do not move while the solder is cooling. Movement may result in a weak joint.

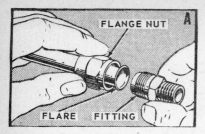
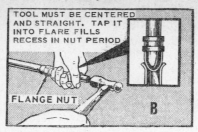
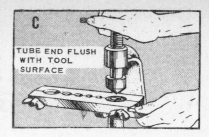

Figure 6–11. Methods of making connections with flexible copper tubing.

If you have not overheated the connection, the solder will be firm in less than a minute. If a soldered joint should leak, the entire run of pipe must be thoroughly drained, and the fitting must be removed and cleaned before the joint is re-soldered.

If you find it necessary to unsolder a connection, simply heat it until the solder runs, then pull the tube out. Use wet rags (as above) to keep from unsoldering other connections to the same fitting.

Flexible copper tubing. Like rigid pipe, flexible copper tubing can be installed with soldered joints, or the joints can be made with flare fittings. Flares are not recommended for inside wall construction, however, since it is possible for them to vibrate loose and drip. In open areas such as basements, garages, and utility rooms, however, flare fittings are fine. If used with solder-type fittings, flexible tubing is handled exactly like rigid tubing. The following describes the installation of flare-type fittings.

Measuring and cutting. Procedures for measuring and cutting flexible tubing are the same as those used for the rigid type. If the end becomes slightly out-of-round, flaring will reround it. After cutting, file off any burrs; the end must be perfectly smooth.

Making connections. Flare-type fittings have threaded flange nuts (Figure 6–11A) to hold the tubing in place. Remove the flange nut from the fitting and slide it onto the tube *before* flaring the tube. Flaring can be done either with a flaring tool (Figure 6–11B) or with a flanging tool (Figure 6–11C). Put a few drops of oil on the tube end when flaring it. Hold the tube in your hand; do not rest the opposite end on a solid object (as it might be damaged). Slide the nut back up to the end of the tube (it cannot come off now), and start it on the fitting threads. Finish making the connection by tightening the nut securely with wrenches (preferably open-end or adjustable-head wrenches), one on the nut, the other on the fitting. This forces the flare at the end of the tube up against the cupped end of the fitting to form a tight seal. Never use one wrench alone; if the fitting is not held stationary by a second wrench, it will turn and loosen the connection at the other end.

If a connection of this type must be broken, examine the flare to be sure it is still round and smooth. If damaged, the flare must be redone for reuse.

Plastic pipe. Most major cities now approve the use of plastic pipe for earth drainage systems and drain-waste-vent systems inside the home. This means that most plumbing, building and supply houses carry plastic pipe and the material is increasing in popularity.

Measuring. This pipe is measured face-to-face in the same manner, like galvanized steel pipe, but add on the depths the pipe will run into the fitting sockets.

Cutting. Use a hacksaw (Figure 6–12A) or other handsaw, or even your power saw, to cut this pipe, but never use a rotary pipe cutter. Whatever saw you use, the blade should be fine-toothed (9 to 14 teeth per inch), with little or no set. To be sure the cuts are square when using a handsaw, you can build a jig to hold the pipe and guide the blade (Figure 6–12B). If you use a vise or other holding device, wrap the pipe in cloth or other protective material to prevent damage to the pipe surface. Ream the pipe with a standard reamer or with a pocket knife.

Making connections. When making a plastic-to-plastic pipe connection, clean both the fitting socket surface and the surface of the pipe that will fit into the socket. With the proper solvent or cement for your type pipe (standard or drainage plastic piping) and a nonsynthetic bristle brush, apply

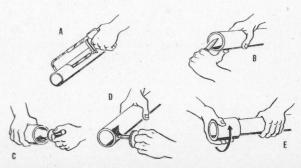

Figure 6–12. Assembling plastic pipe.

Figure 6–13. Arrows point to connections between plastic and galvanized piping.

the solvent or cement generously to the inside surface of the fitting socket (Figure 6–12C) and the outside surface of the pipe, over its circumference, covering an area at least equal to the socket depth (Figure 6–12D). Press the pipe and fitting firmly together, turning the pipe ¼ turn to evenly distribute the solvent (Figure 6–12E). Next, hold the pieces together for about 15 seconds, or until "curing" has begun, so that the pipe does not push out from the fitting. Clean off any excess solvent.

After making the assembly, check immediately for the correct positioning of the pipe and fitting and make sure they do not move until the solvent weld has "set." Proper alignment should be determined before the pieces are connected. If a solvent-welded joint has to be broken, the fitting must be sawed off and a new fitting used, unless you can salvage the fitting and a short length of pipe at each end by rejoining these assembled parts into a run with couplings.

To make a plastic-to-steel pipe connection, apply a special thread seal compound to both threads to join the plastic fitting to the steel. Afterwards, solvent-weld the fitting to the plastic pipe. Never use a pipe or chain wrench on plastic pipe or fittings. A strap wrench may be used or, on flat fitting surfaces, an appropriate toothless wrench. Where flange-type fittings or other types of bolted connections, such as expansion couplings, are used, a torque wrench should be used to tighten all bolts evenly. If the bolt tension is uneven, damage to the plastic components may result.

If you are able to break into your existing plumbing lines at a union, unthread the old piping back to the elbow you have chosen as a take-off point. Replace the elbow with a standard iron tee, which will then be threaded with a CPVC adapter. Be sure that the outlet of the tee points in the desired direction. Apply pipe dope to all threads and retighten the old iron piping into its former position.

If it is necessary to cut through a straight section of pipe, the procedure for installing a take-off differs. After cutting through the pipe in the area selected, remove the old pipe sections and thread in two CPVC male adapters with a coupling cemented to each. Make up a take-off assembly, consisting of two lengths of plastic pipe with a tee cemented between them. The total length of the assembly should be the distance between the coupling faces plus an allowance at each end to telescope into the coupling socket. Allow one diameter for each joint, that is, ½ inch for ½-inch pipes or ¾ inch for ¾-inch pipes. Check the take-off assembly by holding it in position before cutting; then cement the joints, making sure the tee is pointed in the desired direction.

Fixtures, drains, and supply lines. Connections different from any of those covered here are used for the "out-in-the-open" chrome-plated fixture pipes (see page 206).

INSTALLATION OF PIPES

There is, of course, no problem in installing pipes in an addition that is under construction; all pipes that are to be hidden in walls are positioned before the inner sides of the walls are finished. Then, again, if you are making your installation in an old building, but intend to assemble the piping in the open and box it in later, you will not have much breaking through of walls and floors to do. If, however, you plan to conceal all piping inside the existing walls and floors of an old house, you will have to remove some wall covering and flooring, and will probably have to cut through some joists (horizontal beams that support floors) and studs (vertical partition supports). "Breaking through" chiefly concerns drainage pipes because these are large and cumbersome. Water-supply pipes create no problems, as they are usually run in the same spaces with drainage pipes. Careful planning will eliminate unnecessary work.

Clearance needed for pipes. There must be sufficient space inside a partition, or a floor (if there is a ceiling below), for the pipes to be run through them. Measure the clear (air) space inside (see "X,"

Table 6–8

Pipe size (inches)	Cast iron (inches)		Plastic and copper (inches)	
	Pipe	Fittings	Pipe	Fittings
1½			1¾	2⅛
2	4	4		
3			3¾	3⅝
4	6¼	6¼		

in Figure 6–14 *top*). Space requirements for drainage pipes are shown in Table 6–8.

If you know the size of your studs (or joists) you can figure space as follows: A 2 × 4 stud partition has approximately a ¾-inch clearance inside it. It will not take even a 2-inch cast-iron pipe but will take a 3-inch copper or plastic pipe with fittings. A 2 × 6 stud (or joist) has approximately a 5¾-inch clearance. It will take a 2-inch cast-iron pipe. A 2 × 8 stud has approximately a 7¾-inch clearance. It will take up to a 4-inch cast-iron pipe. Because plastic and copper pipes are easily cut to any length desired, and fittings can therefore be located as desired, you can run 1½-inch pipe (without fittings) through a space as small as 1¾ inches,

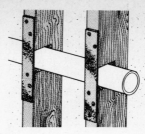

Figure 6–15. Reinforcing a notched stud.

or 3-inch pipe (without fittings) in a space of only 3¼ inches. Fittings are then planned to be where more space is available. Also, no turning space (for tightening) is required with plastic or copper, as it is with any threaded pipe.

Planning spaces for pipes. If a partition is too "thin," the easiest method of thickening it is to set 2 × 4 studs against the existing studs (Figure 6–14, *bottom*) after the walls have been opened and the plumbing installed. Then refinish your wall surface. (For examples of "thickened" partitions in rooms above or below a bathroom, which do not destroy the beauty of your home, see page 185). If an outer wall is being used, and you cannot break into it because the plaster is against the brick or other material used for the outer wall construction, you may have to add 2 × 6, or even 2 × 8, studs for sufficient thickening.

Since each stud in a partition shares its portion of the load, careless weakening of any stud is poor practice. Note in Figure 6–15 how the studs are notched and reinforced, and follow these rules:

1. Do not notch the lower half deeper than ⅓ without reinforcing it with a steel strap or furring.

2. Do not notch the lower half deeper than ⅔, even if it will be reinforced.

3. The upper half may be notched to ½ depth without reinforcing in a nonbearing partition if only two studs in a row are notched and there are at least two unnotched studs left.

Attic joists can be crossed over, and first-floor joists can be crossed under, without difficulty. However, joists between floors must be notched if pipes are to cross them. For this reason it is much

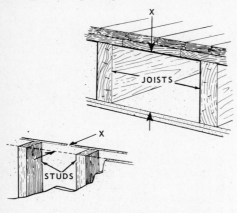

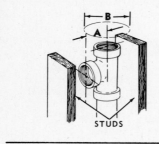

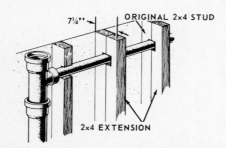

Figure 6–14. Rules for clearance of pipes: *(top)* necessary air. *(center)* Turning diameter. *B* space is needed with all threaded pipes for the assembly of fittings. *A* is the radius of the turn. *(bottom)* Method of building out wall to take the drainage pipe.

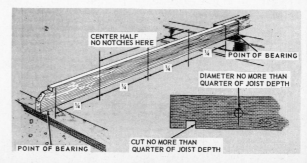

Figure 6– 16. Rules for notching a joist.

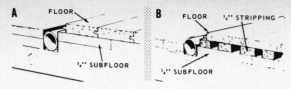

Figure 6–17. Other methods of running drain assemblies.

less difficult to run pipes between (rather than across) joists wherever possible. If necessary, notch the joists as shown in Figure 6–16, and follow these rules:

1. Never make any notch (at top or bottom) in the center half of a joist. Make the notching at the ends.

2. Never notch deeper than ¼ the height of the joist, and always reinforce it with a steel strap or 2 × 2 board across the cut.

3. A hole, instead of a notch, can be made anywhere in a joist providing: (a) it is centered between the top and bottom edge, and (b) its diameter does not exceed ¼ the height of the joist (Figure 6–17A and B).

Notching can sometimes be minimized by cutting through flooring, subflooring, and (if used) stripping, instead of the joists.

Toilet drains, which are a special problem, should be run between joists or below them whenever possible. However, if necessary, one (only) joist can be cut off at its end (nowhere else) provided the cut joist is then securely anchored by a header to joists at each side.

Planning bathroom wall alterations. Assuming you have sufficient wall thickness to conceal the pipes, typical wall alterations are as shown in Figure 6–18. All fixtures are placed against one wall, together with a medicine cabinet. This is the simplest and most economical arrangement. Only the one wall (as shown) has all the finish stripped off. Other fixture arrangements will necessitate stripping of other walls also. The dimensions *a*, *b*, and *c* will be given on your installation plan. If you should decide to determine these yourself, however, they—and all other dimensions indicated by the letters—can be determined from the roughing-in dimensions furnished with your fixtures.

Planning other wall alterations. The installation of a sink is similar to that of a lavatory, and the kitchen wall is prepared accordingly. Walls through which a soil stack passes may also have to be stripped. If cast-iron pipe is used, a 6- to 8-inch-wide opening is required from top to bottom of the stack. If plastic or copper is used, however, lengths can be joined and pushed up inside from the basement to minimize stripping required.

Service panels. Wherever a trap or valve must be installed inside a wall or floor, provide a removable panel so that it can be reached if necessary.

Bathtub pipes are always hidden in the wall behind the tub. Plan the tub installation to provide such a panel opening into a room or closet behind the tub.

INSTALLATION OF A DRAINAGE SYSTEM

When making any plumbing installation, begin with the drainage system. It is easier to install the water-supply piping afterwards. First check your shipment to be sure you have received all items and then study your plan to familiarize yourself with the arrangement of the pipes and fittings when installed. When installing any drainage system (plastic, copper, or cast-iron), you should follow the sequence of steps given below. However, each installation may vary in details from others, so the illustrations that follow should be considered to show only typical solutions.

Prepare and position toilet drain. Before installing any pipe you must make all necessary wall and floor openings for the stack and the bathroom plumbing. If your bathroom is above a room ceiling, cut away an 8-inch-wide strip of flooring from the center line of the toilet-bowl outlet to the wall (*d*,

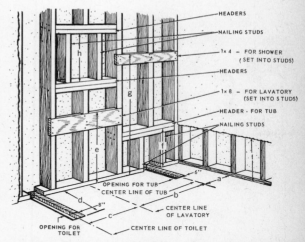

Figure 6–18. Dimensions necessary for bathroom wall alteration: *a* = half the width of the tub. *b* = distance from the middle of the tub to the middle of the lavatory. *c* = distance from the middle of the lavatory to the middle of the toilet. *d* = distance from the finished wall to the center of the toilet-bowl outlet (usually 12 inches) plus 4 inches. When measuring from the face of the stud (not the finished wall), allow for the thickness of the wall finish (¾ inch for lath and plaster, ½ inch for sheetrock or ½-inch plywood, 1 inch for rock lath and plaster). Example: rough-in is 12 inches, and wall finish will be ½ inch; then *d* = 12 + ½ + 4 = 16½ inches. If the partition or wall must be thickened for pipe clearance, allow for thickening when measuring. *e* = distance from the floor to the top of the lavatory plus 2 inches (usually 33 inches). *f* = distance from the floor to the top of the tub. *g* = height of the shower (usually 5 feet). *h* = area needed to frame the medicine cabinet.

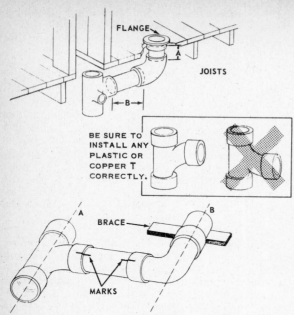

FLANGE

A

JOISTS

B

BE SURE TO
INSTALL ANY
PLASTIC OR
COPPER T
CORRECTLY.

A

B

BRACE

MARKS

Figure 6–19. Assembly of toilet drain.

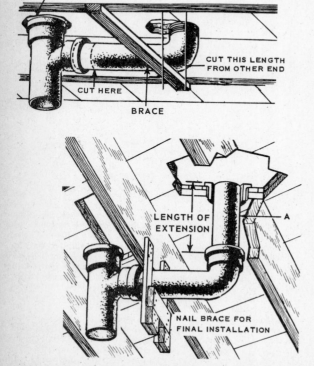

HOLE FOR TOILET
FLOOR FLANGE

CUT THIS LENGTH
FROM OTHER END

CUT HERE

BRACE

LENGTH OF
EXTENSION

A

NAIL BRACE FOR
FINAL INSTALLATION

Figure 6–20. Toilet drain hung in place.

Figure 6–18), then back through the wall finish and bottom partition header. This will provide space for installation of the stack T and closet-bend assembly from above. If there is no ceiling below, cut just two holes, one for the stack, the other for the closet-bend opening, and install the parts from below.

If you are using plastic drain pipe, the toilet-drain assembly will consist of a T, closet bend, two short lengths of pipe, and a floor flange. Copper pipe differs only in that there is no closet bend and a ¼ bend is used instead. To make either type of assembly, first calculate the vertical length of pipe (A, in Figure 6–19, top) needed between the flange (positioned to rest on finished floor) and the bend so that the latter will be at the depth required by your installation. Weld or solder the bend and vertical pipe lengths. Next, with the T and bend held in their places (any means will do for now), determine the length of horizontal pipe (B) required. Loosely assemble the T and horizontal pipe and bend them together. Do this with the parts lying on the floor and braced so the center lines (A and B, Figure 6–19, bottom) are parallel, and mark the pieces. Then weld or solder them together, being guided by the marks.

When cast-iron pipe is used, the fitting is much the same. If assembly will be between joists (Figure 6–20, top) only a T and closet bend are used, and the distances are adjusted (A and B, Figure 6–19, top) by breaking off parts of the toilet bend (along scored lines). If assembly will be below joists (Figure 6–20, bottom), a T, hub top with a ¼ bend, and vertical length of pipe are needed, and A and B are established as for plastic or copper. When all the pieces are ready, assemble and mark them as above, then brace them as required (Figure 6–21A), to caulk the joints. After completing the toilet-drain assembly, brace it in position (Figure 6–21B). Do not install the floor flange, however, until other work has been completed and you can finish the bathroom floor, so the flange will rest on it.

Installing building drains. There are two types of building drains: the underfloor drain and the suspended drain. For the former, if you have a plastic stack either plastic (4-inch sewer type) or 4-inch cast iron may be used for an underground building drain. With either a copper or a cast-iron stack, 4-inch cast iron generally is used for this drain. When converting from one kind of pipe, say plastic or copper, to another kind, for instance, cast iron, you must use an adapter. This adapter is generally located at the foot of the stack, just above ground (or basement floor).

Several types of suspended drains are shown in Figure 6–22. If you have a plastic stack, this drain also may be 3-inch plastic; with a copper stack it may be 3-inch copper—up to the Y assembly located in the basement wall or floor. With a cast-iron stack the drain will be 4-inch cast iron. In most cases, two cleanout assemblies using T-Ys, one at the foot of the stack, the other where the drain goes through wall or floor, generally are used, and the drain, from the second (in wall or floor) assembly outward, will be 4-inch plastic or 4-inch cast iron (the same as in an underfloor drain, discussed above). If only one cleanout assembly is used, all horizontal drains should be 4-inch pipe.

Locating the foot of the stack (underfloor drain). Use a string and plumb bob (or similar weight to hang string straight) and hang the string through the exact center of the toilet-drain T with the bob (or weight) ½ inch from the basement floor (or earth). When the string is straight and stationary, mark the floor (or earth) where the bob would touch.

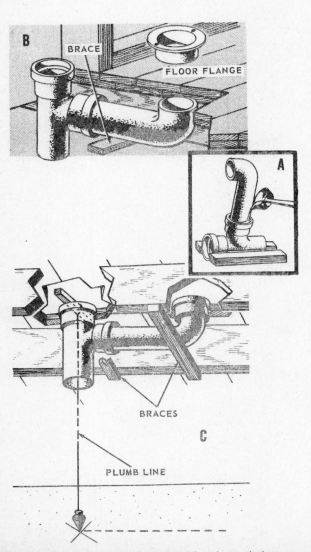

Figure 6-21. Drain arrangements for various house designs.

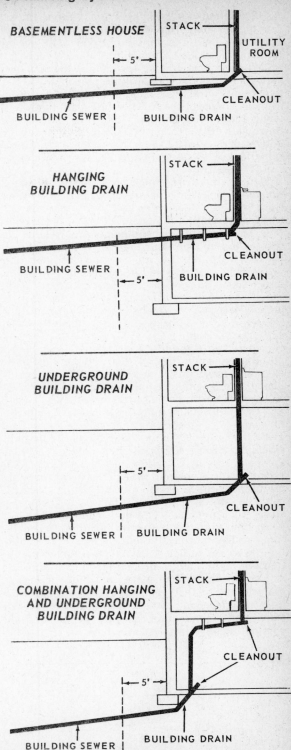

Figure 6-22. Installing an underfloor drain.

Preparing the building-drain trench. Draw a line on the floor from above the bob mark on the floor to where the building drain will go out through the house foundation. Dig a 2-foot-wide trench with this line at its center, digging deep enough so that the bottom of the trench at the start (where mark was) will be approximately 1 foot below the surface of the finished basement floor. Now grade the trench bottom, from this starting end downward to the other end, and firmly pack the bottom of this established grade. Proper grading is important. The grade should be 1¼ inches per 5 feet (Figure 6–23).

After completing the inside (above) trench, go outside and extend the trench at least 5 feet outward from the house. Connect the two trench portions by tunneling under (or through) the foundation. Make certain that the grade is correct all the way to the outside, and that the bottom is firmly packed. If you are installing a basement floor drain or other branch building drains (as from a secondary stack), prepare the trenches for these in the same way, each graded to slope down so that the branch can join the main building drain at a Y. However, refer to page 188 before planning such additional drains.

Installing the underfloor drains. Assemble the cleanout assembly first. If this is to be plastic, the assembly may consist of a cleanout T and two ⅛ bends, or a Y with cleanout adapter and plug and a ⅛ bend. If it is to be cast iron, there may be a test T and two ⅛ bends, or a Y with cleanout ferrule and plug and a ⅛ bend. In either case use the same method of aligning the parts as for the toilet-drain assembly (discussed above) and weld or caulk all the parts together. Position the above assembly in your trench, centered under the (still hanging) plumb bob. Brace it carefully so that it is exactly centered and aligned with the plumb bob and string; then pour concrete under and around it to permanently cradle it in this position. When the concrete has set, install the remainder of the building drain, out to 5 feet beyond the house foundation, setting in any Ys needed for branch drains. It is a good idea to also install all other underfloor drains now so that you can finish the basement floor and clean up before finishing the drainage installation. A floor drain assembly is prepared and cradled in concrete as described above.

Preparing and installing foot-of-stack cleanout assembly (suspended drain). Preassemble this assembly, in plastic, copper, or cast iron, in the same manner described for the cleanout assembly used with the underfloor drain. Weld, solder, or caulk all joints, installing, if necessary, a reducer or adapter at the top of the assembly to convert it for connection to the stack. When ready, join this assembly to the toilet-drain assembly, either directly (Figure 6–24, *top*) or with a length of pipe between (Figure 6–24, *bottom*). Length A may be needed if the drain must go through the wall at a certain height, and can be determined by using a chalk line. Brace the assembly firmly in place. *Note:* If length A extends up to a second-floor bathroom, build the stack up from the cleanout assembly, then fit and install the last piece.

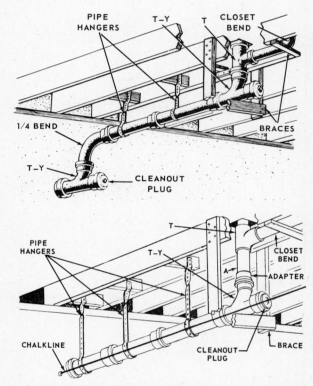

Figure 6–24. Preparing and installing a foot-of-stack cleanout assembly.

Installing a suspended drain. If you have not done so, use a chalk line to determine where the drain will go through the wall. Remember, it must pitch down at 1¼ inches per 5 feet. Make a hole through the wall at the place indicated and prepare the trench outside for at least 5 feet out from the wall. Install the drain from the foot of the stack out-

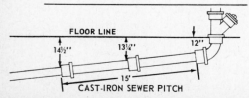

Figure 6–23. Proper pitch of the sewer line.

ward to 5 feet beyond the wall. If the drain includes a second cleanout assembly in the wall, preassemble the T-Y and ¼ bend (with any straight length of pipe needed between them) and brace these in position to help you fit the run to them. Permanently brace each section of pipe (every 5 feet) to joists above as you install it, and remember to keep the drain properly pitched.

Completing the main stack. If you have a suspended building drain (see above), the stack is now complete up to the toilet-drain assembly. If you have an underfloor drain, this portion is yet to be done. Build it straight up from the cleanout assembly, fitting the last piece as shown in Figure 6–25. To install the last piece, temporarily raise the toilet-drain assembly.

Build the stack on upward from the toilet-drain assembly and out through the roof. If there are any drainage or vent Ts needed, install each as you come to its place. Remember that each branch-drain T must be at the proper height so the drain will slope properly (1 inch per 4 feet). Refer to your plan on roughing-in measurements and plot each T position by using a stretched chalk-line to represent the drain that will be connected to it. Re-vent runs, on the other hand, slope slightly upward to the stack. With a cast-iron stack, special vent Ts are used; but with plastic or copper, sanitary Ts are used, and these must be inverted (upside down) in the stack when used for vent connections.

If there is a bathroom above the first one, preassemble and brace in position the second toilet-drain assembly (in same manner as the first), before building the stack up to it. This will make it easier to accurately fit the stack pipe to place it at the cor-

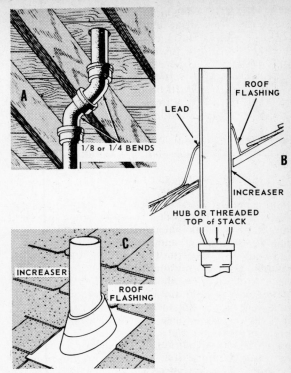

Figure 6–26. Roof work necessary for a main stack.

rect height. Should a roof rafter or other obstruction require turning the stack, make an offset as shown in Figure 6–26A. One-eighth bends are used if offset occurs in a drainage portion of the stack; ¼ bends, if in a vent portion. The topmost length of the stack should extend about 1 foot above the roof (if larger in diameter than the stack, it is made up by an increaser)—Figure 6–26B—and should be made watertight with a roof flashing (Figure 6–26C). The flashing is adjustable to roof pitch. Make sure the roof shingles (or other covering) overlap the flat part of the flashing at the top and sides. Seal the flashing to the stack pipe by peening in the sides against the pipe.

Installing branch drains and, if used, re-vent lines. Each branch drain is installed outward from the stack to end at the location required by your plan or roughing-in measurements (Figures 6–27 and 6–28). These drain runs may be plastic, copper, or steel, and generally come in 1½-inch sizes. The same is true of any re-vent lines required. With plastic or copper, sanitary Ts are used to join re-vent lines to the branch drains, and the re-vent lines are built upward from these Ts to join the inverted vent Ts already installed in the stack. With steel pipe, either a vertical vent T or a horizontal vent T (Figure 6–28) is required, and the vent run is built out and

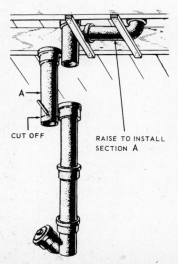

Figure 6–25. Completing a suspended main stack.

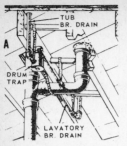
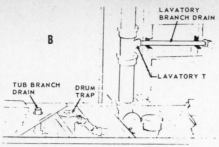
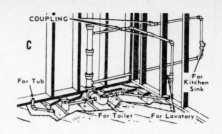

Figure 6-27. Technique of installing branch drains.

down from the stack T so that the final joint can be made by caulking the (unthreaded) steel-pipe end into the hub of the drainage-line vent T. Two (or more) vent runs may be joined by a T (or Ts) to run as a single line into the stack (Figure 6-27C).

Installing secondary stack, if used. If a secondary stack contains a toilet, it is installed just like the main stack, and its foot-of-stack cleanout assembly must also be positioned and joined to the building drain in the manner already described. If there is no toilet, however, the cleanout assembly location is not quite so critical. When installing the building drain (see above) and the branch drain to it from the secondary stack, simply hang a plumb bob approximately where the secondary stack will be, and position the cleanout assembly accordingly. Afterwards, build the secondary stack straight up from this cleanout assembly and install branch drains, etc., following the same general procedures given for a main stack.

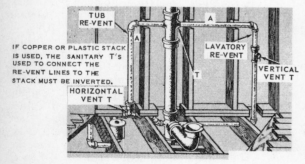

IF COPPER OR PLASTIC STACK IS USED, THE SANITARY T's USED TO CONNECT THE RE-VENT LINES TO THE STACK MUST BE INVERTED.

Figure 6-28. Installing re-vent lines.

INSTALLATION OF A WATER-SUPPLY SYSTEM

The water-supply system can be divided into two sections: the house-service line and the internal lines.

The house-service line. This line is the outside line, from source to house. It should be laid in as straight a line as possible from the water source to the most convenient point at which it can enter the building. Also, it should be buried below the frost-line and deep enough so traffic cannot disturb it.

If the source is a city or county water main, the water authorities will probably want to install (or at least approve) the house-service line. This line will end at a water meter (if one is used) installed by the water company. It should be of ample size to furnish all the water you will need at times of peak demand. This size may depend upon normal pressure in the water main, especially if it is usually low, or if your requirements are above average.

Should you have a private water source, the house-service line is considered to be all the piping up to your pressure tank, from which the internal main supply lines lead to the various branch supply lines and fixtures. Again, pipe size should be ample to provide for all the water flow that might be required at times of peak load.

Internal lines. All horizontal lines should have a slight slope back to the house-service line. A stop-and-waste valve should be installed at this low point so that the internal supply system can be drained when necessary. Pipe sizes should be chosen so that each line will have a sufficient capacity to serve all the fixtures to which it leads. Generally, use ¾- or 1-inch pipe for the portion of this line that serves both the cold- and hot-water system; use ¾-inch pipe for cold- or hot-water main supply lines; and use ½-inch pipe for branch lines to fixtures. Provide shut-off (gate) valves wherever convenient and on both lines at the water heater. Also, when using threaded pipe, install union couplings wherever the line may later have to be broken, such as in the lines to the hot-water heater (close to it).

Usually the main supply lines are installed under the first-floor joists, and are attached to these by hangers. The pipes can be run at right angles, or parallel to the floor joists. Union Ls and Ts can be used to advantage when connecting branch lines to mains; they eliminate the need for careful measuring and fitting. The hot- and cold-water lines run parallel, and should be spaced at least 6 inches apart (unless the hot-water pipes are insulated) to prevent the cold-water pipes from absorbing heat from the hot-water ones. Remember that the hot-water line is run into the left side of each fixture (as viewed by a user facing the fixture).

When laying out supply or feeder runs, try not to place any in outside walls, for no matter how well insulated, sooner or later they will cause trouble by freezing. All risers and feeder lines must be well blocked and securely fastened to support risers; use 2×4 braces with cleats nailed against a pipe on both sides with another nailed across the pipe to the cleats. When a riser runs from the basement to the first or second floor, a solid block of wood should be located under the elbow at the lower end, to support the weight of the vertical pipe. It will also keep the riser from hanging on the branch lines to the fixtures.

Pipe hangers and clamps should be employed to support overhead runs whenever possible. In the basement, where the run may be across the floor joists, the pipe can be clamped up against the joists with pipe straps or clamps, or can be supported just below the joists on pipe hangers or "plumber's tape," depending on the available headroom. (Plumber's tape is a long strip of galvanized steel about ¾ inch wide and perforated at intervals to receive ¼-inch bolts.) Secured by bolts to the structural members of the house, lengths of this tape form loops in which the pipes rest (Figure 6–29).

When it is absolutely necessary to run supply lines in or near outer walls, it is most important to insulate the pipe even though the wall itself is insulated. In fact, *all* cold-water pipes throughout the house should be covered with insulation. Such pipe insulation is not only a safeguard against freezing, but it will prevent summer condensation with its subsequent dripping and water-staining of walls and ceilings or the water-rotting of studs and wood around the pipe. Condensation in some areas of the country can become so great as to cause an actual flow of water down the outside of the pipe. Placing insulation around hot-water lines conserves hot water and achieves a saving on heating bills. Several types of wrap-on pipe insulation are available at plumbing supply shops and hardware stores. Install it as directed on the container or package.

Connections through the floor. Branch lines for the hot- and cold-water main supply lines are run below the floor joists to a first-floor bathroom. Fasten the pipes to the joists with pipe straps. If the pipes cannot be run below the joists (as with a bathroom on the second floor), run them just below the floor and across the tops of the joists, notching each joist to recess the pipes. Use plugs and caps to stopper the branch-line ends while patching walls and floors.

Connections through the wall. Figure 6–30 shows a typical installation in which the supply lines are run under the joists and the partition plate is notched for the vertical branch lines to the fixtures. If the bathroom is on the second floor, the supply lines are generally run up next to the stack and the branch lines are run horizontally through notches in the partition studs.

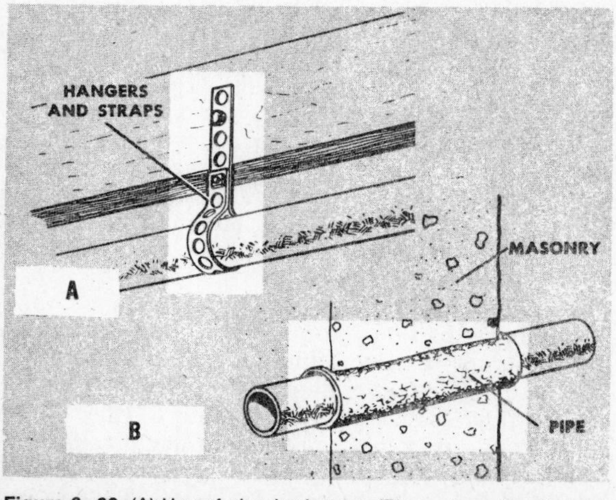

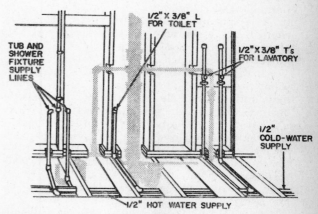

Figure 6–30. A typical installation in which the supply lines are run under the joists and the partition plate is notched for the vertical branch lines to the fixtures.

Use of air chambers. These chambers are short, "dead-end" lengths of pipe in which air is trapped and compressed by the water flow in the line. This trapped air absorbs the shock caused by sudden starting or stopping of the water flow in the line (as when faucets are turned on or off) and thus prevents "knocking" in the pipes. A serviceable chamber is shown in Figure 6–31. Use one in each branch line serving a hot or cold faucet.

Figure 6–29. (A) Use of plumber's tape; (B) passing a line through a masonry wall.

Chapter 6

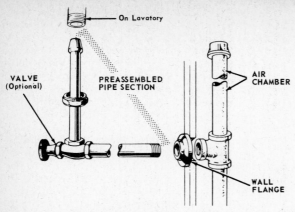

VALVE (Optional) — PREASSEMBLED PIPE SECTION — On Lavatory — AIR CHAMBER — WALL FLANGE

Figure 6–31. The use of a 12-inch air chamber for a lavatory.

To provide air chambers when the pipes are in the floor, run a horizontal line from each supply line to the nearest partition. Then make a 24-inch air chamber inside the partition to serve all the faucets on each supply line.

Provisions for a hot-water heater. Plan your supply lines to include the requirements for your hot-water heater. In most instances you will simply be replacing an older water heater in the same location. If you are considering relocation, the following should be kept in mind:

1. You can locate an electric model where convenient, but a gas- or oil-burning heater must be placed within 8 feet of a chimney large enough for proper venting through the flue.

2. National codes prohibit installation of gas water heaters in bathrooms or in any occupied room normally kept closed. Make sure there is adequate ventilation where such heaters are used. If a gas water heater is installed in an enclosed area (such as a utility closet), two ventilation openings for the replacement of air are necessary: one at the top and one at the bottom of the door or in the wall surrounding the utility closet. It is also necessary to have a way of replacing room air when exhaust fans are used.

3. Put the heater as close as possible to where you use the most hot water.

4. It is handy to have a floor drain, tub, or sink nearby. That will make it easy to drain water from your heater. It is also a good place to end the drain line of the temperature and pressure valve.

5. The tank or the pipes and your connections may leak in time. Put the heater in a place where a water leak will not damage anything. The manufacturer is not responsible for any water damage.

6. You must not put your heater in an area where it might freeze. You must turn off the electricity to the heater before you drain it, to protect the heating elements.

7. Make sure that you are able to reach the drain valve and all access panels when your heater is in place. This will make it easy to service your heater.

8. The heater must be level before you begin the piping.

In addition to water pipes, you must install gas piping for such heaters. If you are installing a water heater of the same size as the one replaced, all that is involved is reconnecting the gas line. If your replacement unit is larger, consult the installation guide packed with the unit for the proper pipe size. Indoors, this pipe can be black steel or flare, or compression-type copper (never soldered copper). Copper should not be used, however, inside of walls or in any inaccessible areas. Outdoors, gas pipe can be made of threaded steel (coated and wrapped), certain grades of copper, or plastic. Check your local codes for the proper material to use.

Planning connections. When installing fixtures during construction, place and connect the tub and/or the shower stall before finishing the walls and floor. Afterwards, finish your walls and floor, then install the toilet and lavatory.

If you are replacing old fixtures with new ones, you may have to open the walls for installation of the tub and lavatory. If so, check the roughing-in dimensions of the new fixtures against the branch-drain and supply-line openings (already there) to determine how the fixture drains and supply lines will connect with them. Also, refer to the instructions furnished with each fixture. Figure 6–32 shows typical branch-drain and water-supply openings (both in-wall and in-floor types) in relation to bathroom fixtures.

When handling fixtures, be very careful not to chip or scratch finished surfaces. Use pads to rest the fixtures on, when necessary, and use wooden blocks to brace them in position. Do not stand on or in a fixture with your shoes on.

Installing a toilet. There are two general types of toilets: those with the tank and bowl in one piece and those having a separate tank and bowl.

For setting the bowl (either type), most plumbing installations include a floor flange that rests upon the floor around the opening of the drain line (Figure 6–33A). This flange accommodates two upright bolts. To set any bowl that is held only by these bolts, simply place the bolts in the flange slots provided. If, however, your bowl requires four bolts, locate it on the floor properly over the flange, mark the spots for the two additional (front) bolts, then set these bolts into the floor at the positions marked. (If the floor is wood, use toilet-bowl bolts, which have wood threads at one end and machine threads at the other; if the floor is tile or concrete, set the heads of the machine bolts in prepared holes and fill the holes with cement to floor level.) Now turn

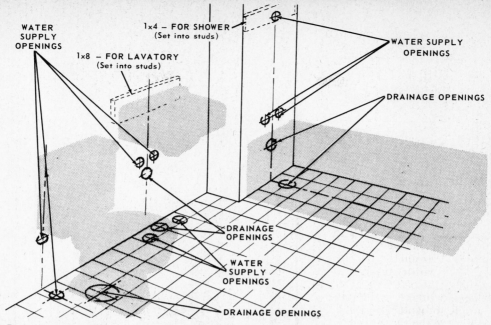

Figure 6–32. Basic information required to make proper connections of bathroom equipment.

the bowl upside-down (with papers under it to prevent scratching) and place one roll of putty completely around the rim, and a second roll completely around the discharge opening. Putty rings should be about 1 inch high. Arrange the one on the rim to squeeze inward (by rolling it toward the inner edge of the rim), but arrange the one on the discharge opening to squeeze outward, so that putty cannot get into, and clog, the opening. Either a rubber or a wax gasket (both are made for this purpose) is preferred to the putty on the discharge opening. If necessary, two rings or gaskets can be used if the floor level has been raised above the top of the floor flange.

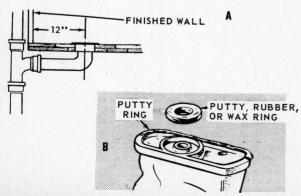

Figure 6–33. Preparing for toilet installation.

Now, lift the bowl up (it is heavy and may require two people to hold it) and set it gently down over the floor flange, letting it down as straight into the final position as possible, so as not to disturb the putty rings. Press down on the top center (not one end or the other) of the bowl with your full weight, and twist it slightly to settle it into the putty and firmly on the floor. It should be perfectly level when settled. Use a level, if in doubt, and wedge it up as necessary, but be sure that any wedging used does not lift it up to leave air gaps in either of the putty rings. When the bowl is squarely seated (with watertight seals at the putty rings), bolt it down to a snug fit, but do not forcibly tighten the nuts on the bolts.

With a separate tank toilet, the tank is set on the rear end of the bowl. It is usually held by two bolts (Figure 6–34B), and the water connection is sealed with a fitted gasket. Fixture supply lines (which should be purchased to fit the installation) are connected as shown in Figure 6–34C and D.

When a toilet is replaced, the old unit, of course, must be removed before the new one is installed. To accomplish this, turn off the water supply at the main source and open any cold-water faucet to relieve pressure in the pipes. Flush the toilet to drain the tank. Remove the remaining water with a sponge. Disconnect the water-supply pipe from the underside of the tank; also disconnect the pipe at wall or floor, using a pipe wrench. Then remove the old toilet. Temporarily stuff a rag into the sewer

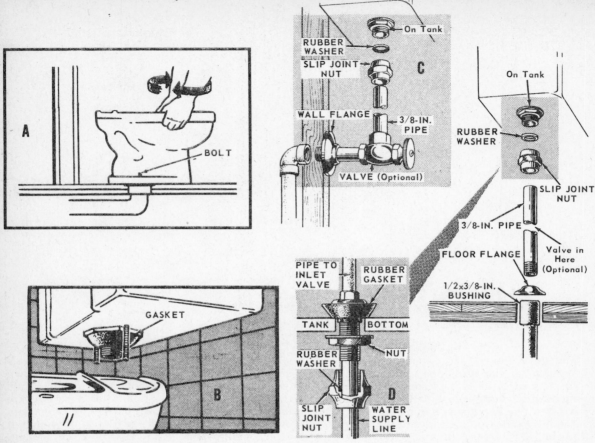

Figure 6–34. The installation of a toilet and tank.

outlet to prevent sewer gas from escaping. Clean the old sealing compound from the floor with a putty knife. Remove the old wax gasket or compound from the closet flange or from around the waste outlet opening in the floor. If the flooring is rotted, remove and replace it. If the old bowl was anchored by bolts screwed into the floor rather than with a closet flange, check the position of the bolt holes and waste outlet opening of the new bowl to assure a proper fit with the existing bolts. If not suitable, they will have to be removed and new bolts installed, or plumbing work will have to be done to install a closet flange.

A bidet (see page 394) is installed in the same manner as a toilet.

Installing a lavatory. Lavatories are wall-hung, pedestal, cabinet, or leg-stand types and are designed so that the top is approximately 31 to 35 inches above the floor level.

If yours is wall-hung, you will use one of the three types of wall brackets shown in Figure 6–35. To support the (single or double) bracket solidly, provide a horizontal 1-by-8-inch board firmly anchored to two studs and embedded flush with the wall behind where bracket will be. When the bracket is properly installed, the lavatory is simply hung on it (or them) against the wall. If there are legs at the front, these will be adjustable so that they can be made to rest squarely on the floor. If a pedestal is used, this can be mounted on bolts like the toilet bowl (see above). Cabinet types of lavatories do not require anchoring.

Typical floor and wall connections are shown in Figure 6–36. The fixture drain line must contain a trap, to stop sewer gases from entering your home. Use of a shut-off valve in each (hot- and cold-water) supply line is optional, but highly recommended as a great convenience when later servicing faucets.

To install a basic lavatory faucet, assemble the rubber washer on each shank, then insert the

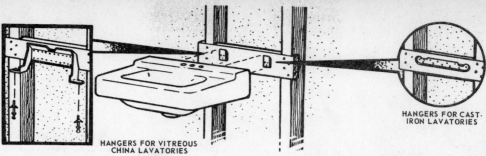

Figure 6—35. Three types of wall brackets.

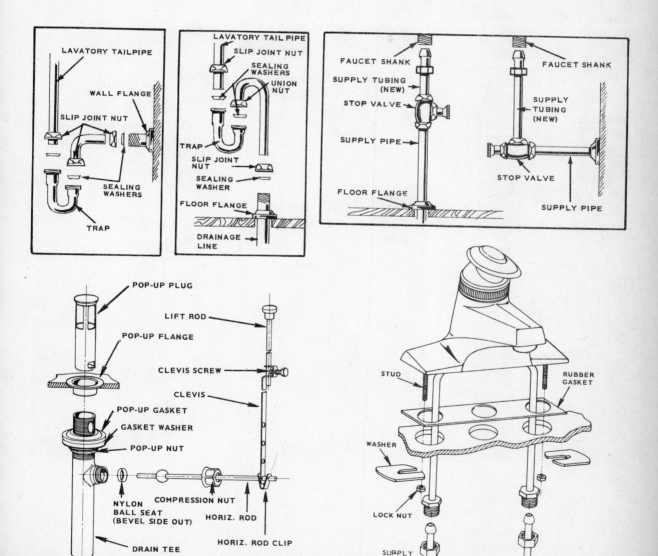

Figure 6—36. Necessary floor and wall connections.

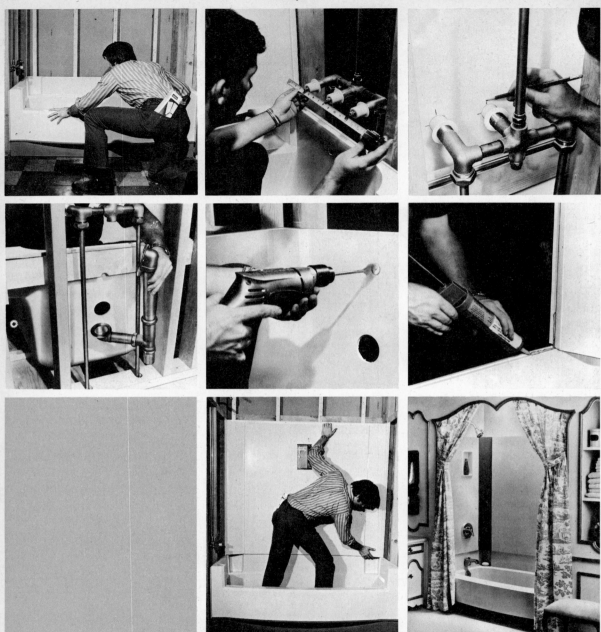

Figure 6—37. Steps in installing a fiberglass tub.

shanks through holes in the lavatory. Place the washer and locknut on each shank and tighten them with the faucet in position. Connect the water-supply pipes to the faucet and tighten the coupling nut securely.

When installing the standard type of lavatory drain, remove the stopper from the drain and assemble the rubber washer under the drain plug flange. Insert in lavatory, applying plumber's putty between the lavatory and washer. Attach other washers and install the locknut. Thread on and tighten the pop-up assembly, using a good pipe joint compound. Make sure the lift rod points to the rear of the lavatory. Tighten the locknut to secure the drain in position. Insert the stopper. Then loosely assemble the lift rod to the pop-up drain rod. Operate the pop-up drain and adjust it to position. Tighten the set screw to secure the linkage in the desired position. Tighten the sealing cap on the pop-up lever only enough to hold up the lift rod and knob.

To remove an old lavatory or vanity unit, turn off the water supply at the main source and open the lavatory or vanity faucets to relieve the pressure in the pipes. Drain the waste pipe trap (elbow) into a pail or pan by removing the plug from the bottom of the trap. Disconnect the waste pipe trap by unscrewing the large nut on each end of the trap with a parallel-jawed adjustable wrench. (If a drain plug is not provided, carefully disconnect the waste pipe trap and spill the water into a pail or pan.) Remove the waste pipe from the floor or wall nipple using the parallel-jawed adjustable wrench. Disconnect the water-supply pipes from the floor or wall nipples using the parellel-jawed adjustable wrench or an appropriately sized open-end wrench. The lavatory may now be lifted from its wall hanger. However, a vanity may require further disassembly. Inspect the underside of an enclosed lavatory or vanity top for attachments (screws or nuts) to the cabinet and remove them. Lift off the lavatory or vanity top. Inspect the back panel of the cabinet for attachments (screws or nuts) and remove these. Remove the cabinet. If a lavatory wall hanger is involved and found suitable for use with your new lavatory, both functionally and dimensionally, it may be left in place. If not, remove the attachments (screws or nuts) and hanger from the wall.

Installation of a tub. Modern steel and fiberglass tubs, designed to rest on the floor, completely fill the area (from wall to wall) in which they are located. When the space is just large enough for the tub, the wall covering (down to the studs) must be removed from the three adjoining walls. If the space is longer than the tub, with open walls at one end and the side only, then build the unopened end out to fill the extra space. After opening the walls, firmly nail 1-by-4-inch boards to the studs with their tops perfectly level and exactly at the height required to rest the tub flanges on them. Lower the tub into position with the flanges resting on the boards, and anchor each end of the tub to the end boards with screws through the flange holes provided. The walls can now be refinished to make a neat fit around the tub. (Note: No boards are required for cast-iron tubs.)

The drain fitting for your tub will be similar to the one shown on page 202, and should be accessible through a panel behind the tub. If your drainage system was properly installed, the tub branch drain (in the floor) will already contain a drum trap. All you need to do is connect the fixture drain to the branch-drain pipe in the floor below the tub. Connection is usually made with a slip-joint nut, the same as for the lavatory. Supply-line connections (also reached through the access panel) are also made in much the same manner as the lavatory connections.

The introduction of fiberglass units has greatly simplified the installation of tubs. In fact, the tub-shower unit shown in Figure 6–37 is ready for installation once the framing and rough plumbing are complete. Standard framing techniques, using wood studs, are all that is required to house the 60-by-32-by-74-inch tub-shower. Depending upon working conditions, there are two alternate assembly methods of installing this unit. If the back or either end panel of the unit is inaccessible once the unit is in place, the components are assembled and fitted together and then set into the stud pocket. However, when the three wall sections can be easily reached, the base may be installed first. Wall sections are then set in place and sealed before the unit is fastened to the studs. In either case, caulking is easily done with sealant that comes with each unit. To complete the installation, the assembled unit is then lined up in place and fastened to wood studs with large-head galvanized nails or to steel studs with dry-wall screws. The final step is setting and installing the standard waste and overflow fittings in premolded openings, and the shower head, mixing valve, and spout.

Installation of a shower stall. The prefabricated shower stall units of molded plastic and of metal are very popular with the home remodeler because they can be used in place of tubs to provide more floor area. Shower stalls can be quickly connected to the water outlets and drains without danger of leaking from the sides and bottom of the fixture. They are available in sizes ranging from 32 by 32, 36 by 32, 42 by 32, etc., to 60 by 32 inches. Square units 36 by 36, 42 by 42, etc., can also be obtained. But remember that only a 32-inch-wide, one-piece shower stall will pass through the rough framing of a 30-inch door.

Since the installation of each of these shower stalls varies with its manufacturer, no specific installation instructions are given here. The best advice that can be given is to follow the provided step-by-step directions to the letter. However, when a one-piece shower unit is installed, the pocket for the stall must be square and plumb, with the studs located as directed by the manufacturer. Since the one-piece unit combines the walls and base, no shower pan or hot mopping is required. The rough plumbing for the shower stall drain and water supply must be located in accordance with the dimensions given by the maker. Where access to valve connections is limited, consider using soft copper tubing from the risers to the valves from the supply

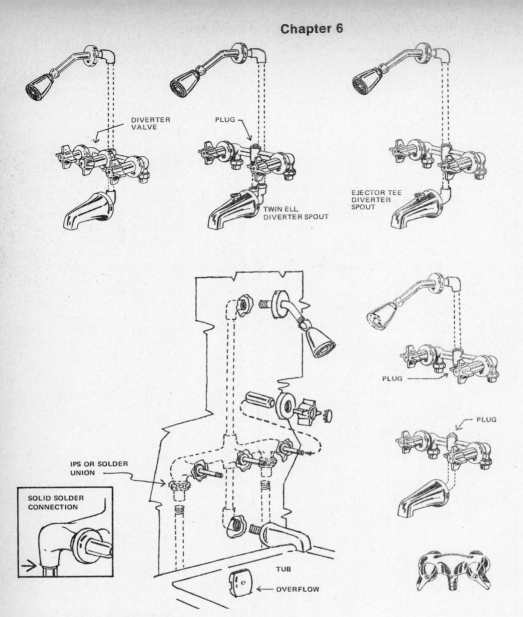

Figure 6—38. Shower-head and tub fixture arrangements.

lines. Connect the valves and risers before positioning the unit. The soft tubing will permit positioning of the valves and shower head after the unit is in place. For better floor support, apply a circle of cement or plaster about 18 inches in diameter on the floor around the drain pipe.

Once the shower stall is in place, level and plumb the unit. Then with No. 6 large-head galvanized nails, fasten the back wall of the unit to the studs, nailing through the nailing flange into the studs. Attach the side walls to the studs in the same way. If one end wall has been left loose, bring it up to the shower stall flanges and fasten it. The front vertical nailing flanges should be nailed to the studs on about 8-inch centers. Then the drain should be caulked and leaded. After the shower enclosure or shower curtain rod and other shower fittings are installed, the exterior of the shower stall pocket may be finished with the desired wall covering material.

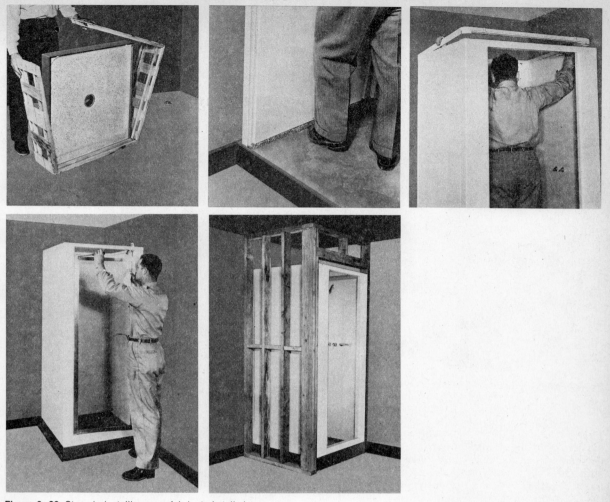

Figure 6—39. Steps in installing a prefabricated stall shower.

Installation of a prefabricated bathroom. The so-called instant bathroom contains almost everything required for a complete bathroom: floor, walls and ceiling, lighting, a built-in bathtub, lavatory, toilet, paper holders, medicine cabinet, and towel and grab bars. Available in several sizes, the entire bathroom is shipped in knocked-down form in three or four large but light, easy-to-assemble sections that can be handled by two men. Each section on most prefabricated units will go through a 30-inch doorway.

The manufacturer supplies complete drawings showing the rough plumbing details as well as instructions on how the unit goes together. As a rule, the bottom well or section goes in first and is carefully positioned over the toilet waste pipe. Then the preplumbed fixtures, tub, shower, and lavatory, are set in their proper locations. Then the two upper pieces are joined together with wing nuts. When the unit has been completely assembled, its integral plumbing is connected to the rough-ins. To complete the bathroom, install the light fixture and exhaust fan, hang the medicine cabinet, and fasten all other bathroom fittings in place.

In alteration work, a standard wall stud is built around the bathroom unit and is tied to the studs by metal straps. The stud wall may be covered with wallboard or paneling to complete the "instant bathroom."

Installation of a "pre-engineered" plumbing wall. Another great time-saver when installing an additional bathroom is the pre-engineered plumbing wall. The unit comes from the manufacturer completely assembled in a 2-by-6-inch wall frame.

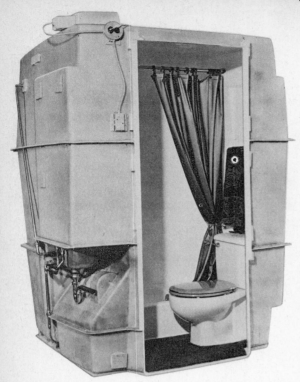

Figure 6–40. A typical prefabricated bathroom unit.

This unit can be recessed, frame and all, into an existing wall or against an existing wall. It can be used as a room divider. It can have a bathroom on both sides, or a bathroom on one side and a bedroom, lavatory, dressing room, or even kitchen on the other side. Since the plumbing wall is complete with a wall-hung toilet, and a lavatory and bathtub that drain into the wall inlets, installation necessitates drilling only four holes: one for a 3-inch waste line, one for a 3-inch vent line, and two for ½-inch water lines. While units vary slightly in size, most standard pre-engineered walls are about 90 inches long and 48 inches high.

Installation of sinks, laundry tubs, and other fixtures. Kitchen sinks are of many varied designs, and the method of mounting the sink depends entirely upon the kind of cabinet that holds it. Drain- and supply-line connections to a sink, however, are always the same in principle as those used for a lavatory. A trap must be provided and, if you will drain the sink waste into a septic tank, a grease trap in the drain line is also advisable (sometimes it is required by the local code). If used, a grease trap may be inserted anywhere in the branch drain from the sink. If a garbage disposal unit is used, it is connected in the drain line above the trap (which must

be exact in height, per the instructions contained with the unit) and the branch drain (clear to the stack) must be at least a 1½-inch pipe. When a dishwasher is used, this must also be provided with a trap.

Laundry tubs, washing machines, and other fixtures all have pipe connections similar to those already described. When these fixtures are in the basement, it is sometimes desirable, however, to use ordinary pipes and fittings (instead of chrome-plated ones) for the fixture connections. Always use traps of one kind or another.

Installation of a hot-water heater. Instructions for connecting a water heater to the plumbing system come with the unit. But, in general the following steps are involved in replacing a hot-water heater:

1. Turn off the gas supply at the meter or turn off the electricity at the fuse box.

2. Close the main water supply at the valve.

3. Release the water pressure by opening nearby hot- and cold-water faucets and allowing them to drain.

4. Disconnect and then drain the old heater and move the new unit into the correct position.

5. Purchase the necessary fittings to adapt existing plumbing to the new heater and to connect the cold- and hot-water supply pipes to the heater (identified by a marking on the top). Be sure the cold-water inlet connection contains the factory-furnished dip tube. The cold-water inlet line should contain a shut-off valve and union (Figure 6–41). The hot-water supply line should also contain a union.

Be sure to purchase a new temperature and pressure (T&P) relief valve that is approved by the local code and insert it through the opening provided. Tighten it with a wrench. Then run a pipe from the relief valve outlet (the pipe must be the same size as the outlet) to a suitable drainage point. Leave about a 6-inch air gap between the end of the pipe and drain. Do not install a shut-off valve in the relief drain line. Also do not thread, plug, or cap the end of the relief pipe.

For making the connection to the flue, if necessary, and to the power or fuel source, check the manufacturer's instructions. The basic power requirements for electric water heaters are covered in Chapter 5.

Replacing a lavatory or kitchen faucet. Often the replacing of a lavatory or kitchen faucet will remodernize the entire sink. To remove the old faucet, turn off the water supply at the main source. Open any cold-water faucet to relieve pressure in the pipes. Disconnect the trap and swing the trap in either direction for additional working space. If the new faucet has a mechanical drain, remove the existing tail pipe. Disconnect the water-supply pipes from the old faucet with a basin wrench. Discon-

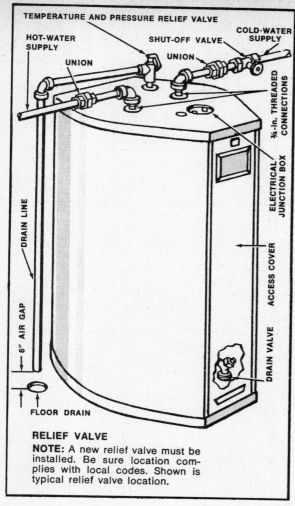

TEMPERATURE AND PRESSURE RELIEF VALVE

HOT-WATER SUPPLY

UNION

SHUT-OFF VALVE

UNION

COLD-WATER SUPPLY

¾-in. THREADED CONNECTIONS

ELECTRICAL JUNCTION BOX

ACCESS COVER

DRAIN VALVE

DRAIN LINE

6" AIR GAP

FLOOR DRAIN

RELIEF VALVE

NOTE: A new relief valve must be installed. Be sure location complies with local codes. Shown is typical relief valve location.

TEMPERATURE AND PRESSURE RELIEF VALVE

VENT PIPE

DRAFT DIVERTER

HOT-WATER SUPPLY PIPE

UNION

DRAIN LINE

GAS SUPPLY PIPE

GAS VALVE

UNION

6" AIR GAP

FLOOR DRAIN

TEE

DRIP LEG

PIPE CAP

½" GAS INLET

DRAIN VALVE

ELBOW

UNION

SHUT-OFF VALVE

¾" THREADED CONNECTIONS

COLD-WATER INLET LINE

RELIEF VALVE

NOTE: A new relief valve must be installed. Be sure location complies with local codes. Shown is typical relief valve location.

Figure 6–41. Typical hot-water heater installations: *(left)* electric; *(right)* gas unit.

nect the supply pipes at the wall or floor using a pipe wrench. Using a basin wrench, remove the old faucet locknuts and lift off the old faucet. Use a putty knife to remove the old putty from the sink.

When installing a new lavatory faucet, install nipples and valves on the existing water lines. Turn the handle on the valves clockwise to close a valve. At the main source, turn the water on so it is available to the rest of the house. Close the faucet that had been opened to relieve pressure. Refer to the instructions furnished with the new faucet before mounting it. Assemble the rubber washers on each shank; then insert the shanks through the holes in the lavatory. Place the washer and locknut on each shank and tighten, using a basin wrench. Install the mechanical drain (if included), following instructions given on page 207.

To reconnect the supply lines, measure from the faucet shank to the shut-off valve for length of pipe required. If it is necessary to shorten pipes, the straight sections may be cut to within 1½ inches of the flexible portion. (This does not apply to floor supplies.) Using a hacksaw or tubing cutter, make sure to keep the cuts squarely at 90 degrees with the pipe wall. Remove sharp edges and burrs with a file. Slip the coupling nut (supplied with the fau-

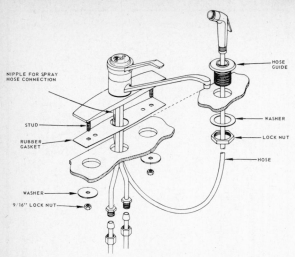

NIPPLE FOR SPRAY
HOSE CONNECTION

HOSE
GUIDE

STUD

RUBBER
GASKET

WASHER

LOCK NUT

HOSE

WASHER

9/16" LOCK NUT

Figure 6–42. A typical single-control faucet installation.

Figure 6–43. Simple steps necessary to install a personal shower.

cet), compression nut, and ring on the supply pipe as shown in Figure 6–42. Insert the straight section of pipe squarely into the valve until it seats firmly. Tighten the compression nut over the ring finger-tight. Insert the nosepiece into the faucet shank. Be sure it enters straight and square. Slip the coupling nut into position and tighten. Force the straight pipe in the valve as far as it will go and tighten the compression nut with an adjustable wrench. Be sure to connect the hot water to the left side of the faucet and the cold water to the right side.

When installing a single-control kitchen sink faucet, you should follow the same basic instructions given for the dual-control lavatory faucet. In both cases make certain to refer to the instruction sheet for detailed information on installing the faucet.

Installing a personal shower. One of the newer features of a modern bathroom is the so-called personal shower. This hand-held shower permits washing any part of the body without wetting others. It is particularly popular with women who want to shower without wetting their hair.

The personal shower consists of a flexible hose that can be fastened directly to an existing shower arm, or can be used with a diverter connection. The latter is the most popular since you do not have to do away with the standard showerhead. All you have to do is remove the present showerhead, insert the diverter, and replace the showerhead. The personal shower hose is then connected to the diverter outlet. To use a personal shower, pull the diverter control button "out"; to use the regular shower-head, push the diverter control button "in."

If your bath does not have a shower, you can install a diverter in the water-discharge nozzle of the tub and connect the personal shower hose to it. The operation of the diverter is the same as for the regular showerhead.

A PRIVATE FINAL DISPOSAL SYSTEM

In locations where a public sewer line is not available, a private final disposal system must be provided. The most common way of accomplishing this is to use either a cesspool or a septic tank.

A cesspool, the simplest private sewage disposal unit, is inexpensive to construct but requires periodic maintenance. It consists of an excavation from 5 to 7 feet in diameter and dug 7 to 10 feet deep. This is lined on the inside with bricks or concrete cesspool blocks set up without mortar. The sewage from the house flows into the tank, and the liquids pass through the openings in the bricks or blocks and are absorbed into the earth. The top of the cesspool must be provided with a tightly fitted concrete lid to keep out insects and vermin.

The major disadvantage of this type of system is that it can easily contaminate wells or nearby

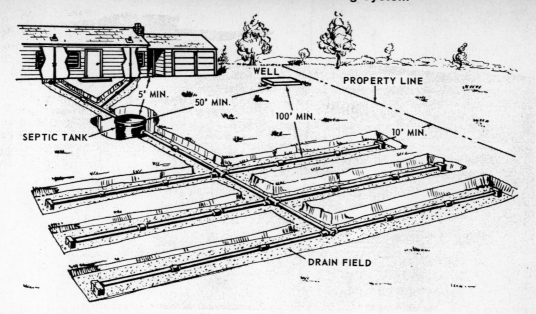

Figure 6—44. A well-planned and laid-out septic tank system.

water supplies. For this reason a great many communities have regulations prohibiting the installation of cesspools.

The septic tank, on the other hand, works on an entirely different principle. It is a safe and inoffensive method of disposing of sewage and helps to protect your water supply against pollution. Much of the solid matter entering the septic tank with the sewage is broken up into gases, liquids, and minerals through bacterial action.

In a well-built system the gases pass off readily without offense, liquids flow out of the septic tank into the tile lines, and the heavier solids, called sludge, settle to the bottom. A scum that forms over the top of the sewage in the tank aids in decomposition.

The five essential parts of a septic-tank system are: (1) the house drain; (2) the house sewer; (3) the septic tank; (4) the outlet sewer line; and (5) the disposal field. In most installations it is a good idea to install a grease trap in the septic-tank system. Kitchen sinks drain off a considerable amount of grease in the form of animal and vegetable fats. If grease is allowed to drain directly into a septic-tank line, it will tend to clog the pipes and prevent bacterial action in the tank. Actually, the best location for this trap is at the sink, or outside of the building and as close as possible to the kitchen sink stack. The closer it is to the stack, the less chance there is of grease accumulation in the waste pipe causing trouble. It will be necessary to remove the cover of the trap occasionally for disposal of the accumulated grease. It

would be well, when making the installation, to examine the strainer in your sink. If it is not good condition, replace it. A strainer is inexpensive and will do much to prevent trouble-making solids from being washed into and clogging your system. Incidentally, to facilitate inspection and repairs, it is good practice to keep a chart showing the exact location of the tank and other components. *Note:* It is best to have a septic tank installed by an expert.

IMPROVING YOUR WATER SUPPLY

Most water supplies, although drinkable and reasonably clear, are loaded with chemicals, minerals, gases, unpleasant tastes and smells, dirt, and decayed vegetable matter. When excessive quantities of minerals are present in the water supply, the life expectancy of the plumbing system can be cut to a serious degree. Certain minerals cause deposits to form in the pipes. Eventually, these deposits become large enough to interfere with the flow of water. In extreme cases, they have been known to stop it entirely. It is also likely that rust and corrosion may advance at a great rate owing to the presence of these minerals.

In another respect, minerals may not be as harmful as they are inconvenient. For example, a high iron content in water may impart a metallic taste and a dirty, brownish look to the liquid, but not be harmful to health. Probably the most common inconvenience that can be laid at the door of "hard water" (the high-mineral-content water we

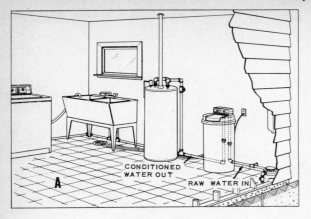

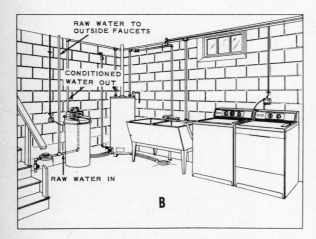

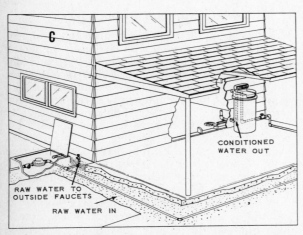

Figure 6—45. Installation of a water conditioner: (A) A typical first-floor installation for a utility room or breezeway where a floor drain exists. (B) A typical basement installation using overhead piping with a floor or washtub drain outlet. (C) A typical remote installation for a carport.

have been talking about) is the difficulty of washing with it. Soap will not lather and forms hard-to-dissolve curds, leaving an unsightly film on skin and clothes. To make hard water soft, the mineral content must be eliminated. This is easily done by piping the domestic water supply through a device called a water softener.

Most water softeners have few moving parts and consume little power. The water is treated as it flows through a special chemical that removes the objectionable minerals. Depending on the hardness of the water, the rate of consumption, and the unit's capacity, there comes a time when the chemical must be regenerated, or cleaned and renewed. Different types of chemicals and equipment may be required to treat your water problem. For this reason, an analysis of your water should be made. This may be performed by various local agencies, or you can obtain a kit from your plumbing supplier. After the water has been analyzed, you can determine the water softener best for you.

Location for your softener. To install a water softener, you will need to cut into the existing cold-water supply line ahead of your water heater and ahead of any cold-water outlet you want softened. Connections are made to the softener and then back to the water line. All of the lines downstream of your softener will then carry softened water. A grounded, plug-in connection to your household electrical system also is necessary. In addition, you will need an adequate drain for the softener. In order to minimize plumbing, it is generally recommended that you locate the softener as close as possible to the place where you interrupt the line. However, remember it is much easier to extend plumbing lines than it is to relocate a drain or move a major installation, such as a furnace or water heater. Consider these factors when choosing your softener location:

1. If you wish to conserve soft water, provide a separate hard-water line ahead of your softener to your outside faucets for lawn service.

2. An approved 115/120-volt, 60-hertz grounded receptacle should be within reach of the 6-foot power cord.

3. Allow sufficient space around the softener for easy access to add the salt and to make all connections.

4. Softeners should not be exposed to freezing temperatures and must be installed and operated in an upright position.

The actual assembly of the softener and its complete installation should be made as directed by the manufacturer. Should the water pressure in the house line run in excess of 75 pounds, it is recommended that a pressure regulator be installed in the supply side of the softener. This not only insures longer life, but it also cuts down water noise throughout your house.

CENTRAL VACUUM CLEANING SYSTEM

While not part of the house plumbing in the true sense of the word, a central vacuum cleaning system has a great deal in common with plumbing. It consists of a series of cemented-together 1¾-inch plastic tubes that run, like plumbing, through house walls or closets, terminating in wall or floor inlets where you plug in the hose. All the tubes tie into a central power head-dust collector located in the basement, utility room, or garage, depending on what is most convenient. The simple wiring necessary runs along and is taped to the tubing.

Planning an installation. In addition to the flexible hose and vacuum cleaner heads, there are three basic parts to the system: (1) the power unit; (2) the inlet valves; and (3) the plastic tubing that connects the two.

The power unit can be mounted in the basement, garage, utility room, or another remote area, preferably on a firm, outside wall away from heat-producing units, such as an incinerator, water heater, or dryer. Do not install a power unit in an attic. Closet installation can be considered where there is adequate ventilation such as louvered doors. It is important that you also plan the installation of the exhaust tube to the outdoors. It is usually best to exhaust out of the rear of the house, avoiding patios, windows, and entranceways.

Inlet valves are usually located centrally in the house in hallways, near the bottom of stairways. Inlet valves placed in halls and near doorways provide the maximum amount of cleaning coverage from the minimum number of valves, frequently making it possible to clean three or four rooms from one valve. Valves in these locations are seldom if ever obstructed by furniture placement. A valve located near the bottom of the stairway permits easy, convenient cleaning of the stairwell and surrounding areas. Start with the area farthest from the power unit and tentatively select a valve location that will provide maximum cleaning coverage. Using a 21-, 24-, or 28-foot-length cord, check to be sure all adjacent areas of the house can be cleaned from this location. Allow sufficient slack in the cord to provide for furniture placement and wall offsets. Be certain all areas can be cleaned including walls and ceilings.

Hoses are available in 21-, 24-, and 28-foot lengths, with 24 feet recommended because this length is more convenient to use and store. If a 24-foot hose will not adequately clean the area involved, try another valve site or use an additional valve, if possible, rather than the longer hose. The longer hose should be used when the installation of additional valves is not practical. Mark the location of the first valve and proceed toward the power

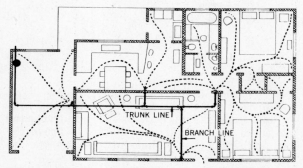

Figure 6—46. A typical installation layout for a central vacuum cleaning system.

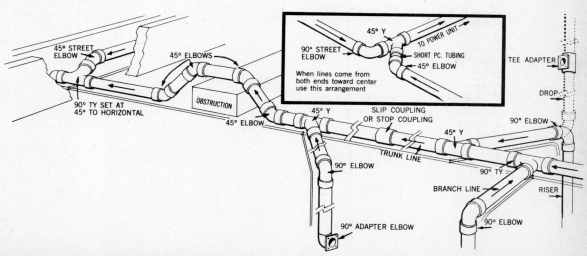

Figure 6—47. Method of installing tube lines.

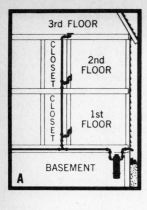

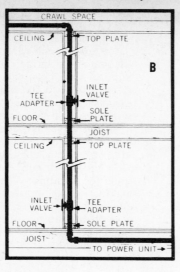

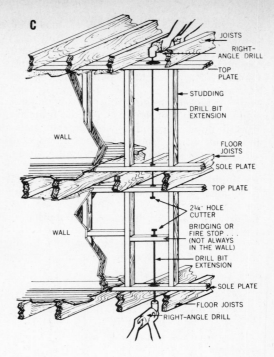

Figure 6—48. Solving installation problems.

unit, locating additional inlet valves until all parts of the house can be comfortably reached with the selected hose. It is preferable to plan on using wall valves; however, the same inlet valve can be placed in the floor if tubing cannot be installed in the wall.

Check the tubing path to each valve location to avoid possible obstructions, such as heating ducts, which may necessitate a slight relocation of the valve site. The best installation is accomplished by running a trunk line leading from the farthest inlet valve, in the easiest and shortest route, to the power unit, with branch lines running from the trunk line to the individual valves. Tube lines may be installed in partitions, in the attic, in crawl spaces, under or between floor joists, or on the face of walls or columns in the basement or open areas.

While the installation of a central vacuum cleaning system in single-story homes is comparatively simple, multi-story houses present special installation situations that require careful planning before the work is started. In a two-story house, it is sometimes preferable to run a trunk line directly into the attic or crawl space. From this point branch lines can be run across the attic to partitions and down within the partition walls to inlet valves on the floor below as needed. Tube lines carrying dirt upward should never exceed one story. There are several methods of gaining access for the tubing running up to the second floor or into the attic. The following are some possible methods:

1. Closet installation (Figure 6–48A). Frequently this is the easiest method of installing vertical tube lines, and it is particularly helpful when the closet on the second floor is directly above the one on the first floor. Tubing installed in a rear corner of the closet will be inconspicuous.

2. Installation in partition walls (Figure 6–48B). This installation is easier when one partition is directly above the other. When these are loadbearing partitions with the bottom blocked by a heavy beam in the basement, tubing can often be

Figure 6—49. Steps in installing a central vacuum cleaning system: (A) Use a 25-foot hose as the measurement in choosing the outlet site. (B) The wall opening is easily cut with a saber saw (the dimensions of the opening are furnished by the manufacturer). (C) The outlet pipes are linked to the attic feeder line by drilling a 1³/₄-inch opening into the top of the wall partition. The drilling point in this case was determined by using the heat duct (background) as the benchmark for aligning the wall outlet with the feeder line. (D) The outlet pipes, together with the doorbell wire secured by tape, are inserted in the wall through the attic access hole. (E) Prewired cover plate connects easily to the doorbell wire with tape or wire nuts. (F) The outlet pipes are connected to the feeder line by applying Pliobond adhesive; 90° or 45° ells are used to direct the feeder lines. (G) Taping the doorbell wire to the feeder lines results in a clean installation. (H) The central feeder line is connected to the power unit by a 90° ell. A utility valve left of the power unit permits a hose to be hooked up for convenient cleaning of the work area. (I) The exhaust from the unit is emitted outside through a feeder line.

fed down through a wall from the attic after holes have been cut in all cross members such as sole plates, top plates, and horizontal bridging or "fire stops" that may exist between studs. Be sure to select a section of the wall away from light switches, electrical outlets, wiring, and heating ducts.

3. Installation in a wall beside a soil pipe. Frequently the soil pipe in an existing house will run straight from the basement to the house roof in a wall often 6 inches or greater in thickness, rather than the conventional stud width, and seldom blocked off with cross bridging. In many existing homes, the holes that were cut in the top plate and sole plate of this wall to accommodate the soil pipe are much larger than necessary. When this situation exists, you have a ready-made avenue for vertical tubing all the way to the attic.

4. Installation in an outer wall (Figure 6–48C). Some houses are constructed in a manner known as "balloon framing." In this type of house, the studding in the outside walls will extend from the foundation to the top plate. In some houses there is no cross bridging between these studs, and it is possible to feed the tubing down inside the wall from the attic or crawl space all the way to the basement.

5. Cold air return installation. Sometimes the only practical way to install the tubing vertically to floors above is to run the tubing up inside the cold air return.

When a method of reaching the attic area is determined, plan the placement of branch lines to partition walls and plan the location of inlet valves on the floor below. Keep in mind it is possible to install an inlet valve into the vertical tube line by using a "tee" adapter in the line. For other details on the installation of a central vacuum cleaning system, check the manufacturer's instruction booklet most carefully.

Chapter 7

REMODELING THE CLIMATE IN YOUR HOME

Year-around climate control is not just for new homes, but can be installed in existing homes as well. New technological advances and methods are making it easier and more economical than ever for you to remodel the climate within your home.

In this chapter we are not going to suggest how you should go about adding a completely new heating system. A heating contractor should be called in to advise you on the changes necessary in your home to provide economical operation of a new heating system. Instead we will cover how to add heating to any remodeling project you have undertaken and how to remodel the climate in your home within your present heating system.

ADDING TO THE PRESENT HEATING SYSTEM

If you are adding living space or an extension onto your home that will require heating, or if any room in your home has not been getting sufficient heat, the installation of an additional radiator may be the answer. Since most home heating systems are slightly overdesigned to allow for extra heating capacity, the extra radiator will not reduce the heat in any of the existing ones.

Hot-water heating systems. Adding radiation units to an existing hot-water system is not difficult, but installation procedures differ somewhat depending upon which type of piping arrangement you have. Chances are that your present piped hot-water system is either a one-pipe or series-loop type. In the latter, there is no continuous separate main. Instead, the various radiation units are connected together, in series, to form a continuous loop and the two ends of the loop are connected to the boiler. Hot water then flows from unit to unit around the loop and back through the circulator to the boiler. Individual radiator valves are not used with the system since the flow through the entire series loop would be affected. If individual radiator control is necessary, a bypass, or a jumper, line must be installed (see page 228).

In a one-pipe system a single main pipe carries the hot water around (through one or more loops) and through the circulator back to the boiler. Individual radiation units are connected into this main, with a scoop (flow) tee, and flow is controlled by means of a radiator valve. This main is usually installed about 5 feet in from the outside walls and connected to the individual radiation units by branch piping.

Adding a new radiator. The first step in the installation of a new radiator is to determine where the radiator should be placed and to determine the best place to break into the hot-water line for the new extension. Choose a location that is easily accessible, so that you can do all the necessary cutting and fitting without being cramped for space. However, it is just as important to plan the shortest possible route for the new piping. The number of turns and the length of horizontal piping should be kept at a minimum. The best layout is one that is vertical, extending from the new radiator unit down to the hot-water line directly below. If a horizontal run of pipe is necessary, it must be pitched down toward the boiler so that hot water will return to the boiler. Of course, before you begin any work, be sure that the furnace has been shut down and all the water has been drained from the system.

There are three basic types of radiators used in hot-water heating systems: baseboard connector panels, cast-iron radiators, and connector cabinets. Let us see how each is installed.

Baseboard connector panels. These panels, better known as baseboard radiators, are designed to fit against the finished wall surface and above the finished floor. Several different designs of baseboard panels are available, and their sizes range from about 8 to 10 inches in height and from 2 to 2½ inches in thickness. The number of feet of baseboard radiation needed depends on the size of the room and on how much heat is lost in the area through doors and windows, whether there is a storm sash, the thickness and nature of the walls and insulation, and the location of the room in relation to the rest of the house. Given this information in the proper manner, your heating supply dealer will be able to give you the correct number of feet of radiation required for the room.

As a rule, the baseboard radiators are installed on the outside walls. If you have an addition under construction, make the panel installations after the wall covering and flooring are completed, but before the baseboards are installed. If remodeling an existing room, remove the baseboard along the walls in each room where your plan shows a panel. Try not to damage the baseboard, as short lengths will be needed to finish the walls between the panels. Do not attempt to recess the panels in the plaster.

Remove the assembled units from the cartons and lay them temporarily against the walls of the

Figure 7–1. Baseboard radiator units are designed to replace conventional wooden baseboards. In the hollow types, A and B, water or steam flows directly behind the baseboard face, from which heat is transmitted to the room. In the finned tube type, the water or steam flows through the tube and heats the tube and the fins. Air passing over the tube and fins is heated and delivered to the room through the slots.

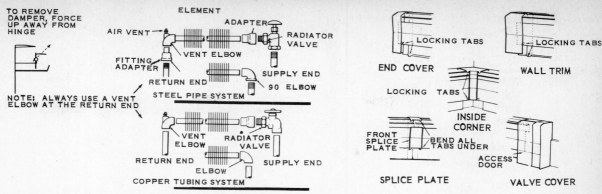

Figure 7–2. *(left)* Finned tube baseboard radiators connected with steel pipe and copper tube; *(right)* various covers and trim pieces used with baseboard radiators.

room in the locations shown on your plan. If radiation panels are to join at a corner of the room, always start there, and place each unit 3¼ inches from the corner. On straight runs, place the panels flush against the wall, butted together. If the room has wall-to-wall carpeting or if carpeting is anticipated, the panels should be installed higher on the wall to provide adequate bottom clearance. The rear panels may be set on a 1-inch board, which will serve as a gauging spacer. Another method is to measure up the wall a distance equal to the height of the rear panel plus the expected carpet thickness and snap a chalk line to serve as your guide. Now check the accessory pieces for the room (end enclosures, inside corners, etc.) and place them in their proper positions with the panels, as illustrated in Figure 7–2. Next, remove the front panels and the elements, and nail the rear panels with dampers against the walls at the studding. Start the nail holes through the panels with a center punch. If cutting of the panels is required, remove the dampers and slide the mounting brackets to new locations as needed. Be sure to install rear splice plates, inside covers, and all other accessories that fit behind the rear panels.

Place the elements on the mounting brackets with the cradles centered on the brackets. Slide into place all fittings (couplings, elbows, etc.) and check for the pipe riser holes. Mark and drill a small hole through the floor at the point where a riser should attach to the elbow, or valve, then go below and check under the floor to make sure there are no joists or other obstructions to interfere with the piping. If obstructions are encountered, continue checking with the drill until clear areas are found at each end. If necessary, you can shift a straight-row panel group several inches in either direction to get its piping in the clear, but you cannot shift panels in corners.

When you are certain each hole will be in the clear, mark the holes to be made and cut oval holes in the floor, with the long axis of each oval parallel to the wall (so riser pipes can move as panels expand or contract). For panels up to 25 feet overall length each oval is to be 1¼-by-1½-inch size. Increase the 1½-inch dimension by ⅛ inch for each additional 10 feet of panel length. It is easiest to bore a 1¼-inch-diameter hole, and lengthen it with a key hole saw, outward from the end of the panel. If it is necessary to shorten an element to fit the confines of the panels, use a fine-tooth hacksaw, and de-burr the cut inside and out. Twist off approximately six aluminum fins to allow for soldering to the fittings. Incidentally, either steel or copper piping may be used interchangeably. Cast-iron panels may be fitted with adapters for copper pipe, and conversely, finned copper tubing types may be fitted with adapters for steel pipe installation. Before permanently fastening, double-check the alignment of the loosely assembled core with the riser locations. If this proves to be correct, fasten the units with the piping.

Return the assembled elements to the rear panel, making sure that the cradles are properly centered over the brackets. The brackets may be moved to the left or right by springing them slightly from their channels. Finish all other piping, installing air vents and valves or supply elbows as per your plan. The system should now be filled with water, purged of air, and checked for leaks.

Then install front panels and front splice plates and lock all other hinged accessories, as required, under the bottom of the front panel. Finish the installation by using pieces of the wooden baseboard between the end covers and the nearest walls. If the walls are noticeably irregular, a quarter-round molding may be used to trim the top edge of the panels. Set all the dampers in the open position. Later you can adjust them to change the heat output if necessary.

FLEXIBLE TUBING IS EASILY RUN

BETWEEN JOIST AND STUD SPACES

DOORWAY

TREAD

PARTITION

TUBING CONCEALED BEHIND

MATCHING DUMMY ENCLOSURE

Figure 7–3. Many heating modernization problems can be simplified by using finger-thin hydronic piping. *(upper left)* Run tubing between joist and stud spaces. *(upper right)* At doorways tubing can be dropped below the joist level. *(lower left)* Between rooms run tubing through the partition. *(lower right)* A heating baseboard that does not run all the way across a wall is filled in with a dummy panel to conceal the tubing.

Cast-iron radiators. Because of their size and weight, cast-iron radiators are usually difficult to handle. You can more easily remove a radiator without marring the floor by resting the radiator legs on small boards and an old rug, and sliding it along, pushing the boards (or rug) ahead by foot, as required. If one of your radiators is too long to handle, it can be divided into two parts. Remove the tie rods, and place two wooden blocks under the center of the radiator. Carefully pry the radiator apart, alternately prying 1/16 inch at the top and bottom, with an iron bar. The wooden blocks will support the two sections when the radiator is finally divided. Take care not to damage or lose the short metal pieces, called push nipples, which join the sections at the top and bottom (Figure 7–4, *top*).

To reassemble the radiator in the desired location, lightly oil and install the two push nipples, then press the two sections squarely together. Install the tie rods and tighten the nuts one turn at a time, until the sections are firmly assembled. Afterwards, back each nut off 1/4 turn.

When the radiators are all properly positioned, check your present system and determine the direction of water flow through it. Install an air vent in the small threaded opening in the return end of each radiator (where the water leaves). When required, install a reducer bushing. Take the union elbow apart. Screw the spud (the piece with the large ring nut) into the return tapping of the radiator. Tighten the spuds securely by using a flat bar

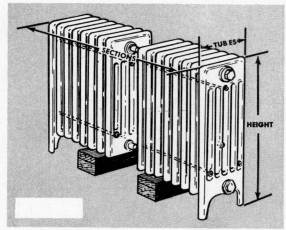

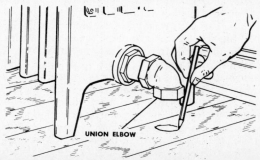

Figure 7–4. Working with cast-iron radiators.

and pipe wrench. Completely assemble the union elbow and install the radiator valve in the supply end of the radiator.

Mark the floor directly under the fittings at the two ends of the radiator (Figure 7–4, *bottom*), and drill small holes through the floor at the marks. Locate the holes on the underside of the floor and make sure joints or other obstructions will not interfere with the piping. Move the radiator slightly as required to avoid interference. Bore holes in the floor for the riser pipes (at right), when clear areas have been found. Place the radiator over the holes, install the riser pipes, and cover the holes with floor plates. Complete the piping as described in Chapter 6.

Convector cabinets. To install convector cabinets in a room, remove the baseboard from the wall behind it. Take the front panel off the unit and install an air vent in the small threaded hole in the return end of the heating element. Put a pipe plug in the similar hole at the supply end. A check of your system will quickly tell you which way the water flows through the cabinet.

Mark the floor for the riser pipe holes as shown in Figure 7–5. Drill small holes through the floor at each of the marks, then locate the holes on the underside of the floor, and check for obstructions that would interfere with the piping. If necessary, shift the unit slightly until clear areas for the riser pipes are found.

When ready, bore the riser pipe holes. Position the unit against the wall, and complete your piping. Afterwards, replace the front panel. Use short pieces of the baseboard to finish the wall between the cabinet and the nearest corners.

Zone control systems. When making an altera-

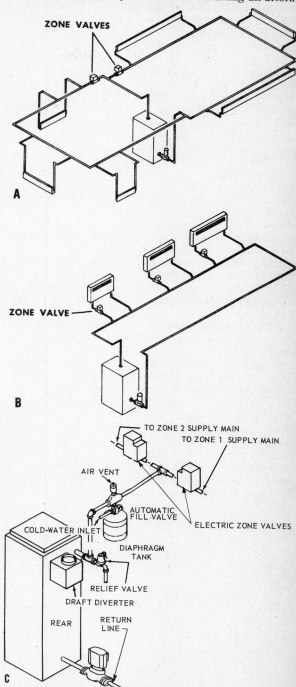

Figure 7–6. (A, B) Two methods of obtaining zone control; (C) typical piping with zone control valves.

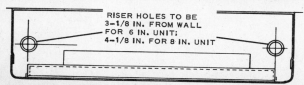

Figure 7–5. Working with convector cabinets.

tion or an addition to your home, it may be wise to have more than one piping system and to provide an independent control for each system. This arrangement of a zoned system is also used extensively when rooms are being added to the house because it is not necessary to disturb the existing piping to heat the new rooms. As previously stated, in most houses a single circulating pump can handle enough water to supply the complete heating system. If there are two or more loops in the system, separate electrical motorized valves can be used to provide multi-zone control. Each such loop contains its own zone valve and thermostat as in the two-zone system. The pump and burner (in the boiler) operate together on a call for heat from either thermostat, but hot water flows only to the zone requiring it.

Your installation may differ from the illustrations in Figure 7–6 since it is not always practical to install all the zone valves at the boiler. They may be placed in various locations throughout the system to simplify the piping arrangement. For example, the radiator in a room that overheats because of excessive sunlight can be thermostatically regulated without affecting the rest of the heating system. In areas where the zone valves will be concealed, provision should be made for easy access at a later date.

One-pipe (flow tee) system. If you plan to add a zone or a separate system for an addition, the entire main for a one-pipe arrangement is installed before any of the radiation units are connected to it. Start with the supply end of the main at the boiler and assemble the various pipe lengths and fittings. (To obtain the lengths of pipe you must measure between the necessary points as described on page 191.) Assemble the tees for the various loops, if used, and the tees for the radiation unit branches in their proper places, as the main is pieced together. Each branch-line tee must be located at least 1 foot from any elbow in the main. If you have to pass the main around beams, or other obstructions, use

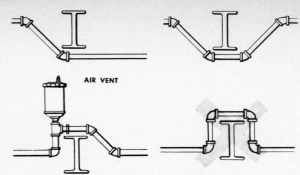

Figure 7–8. Recommended methods of passing obstructions.

one of the recommended methods shown in Figure 7–8.

As you assemble the main, make sure each connection is properly prepared and tight, before proceeding to the next one; it is almost impossible to repair a finished main without disassembling it all the way back to the faulty connection. Both ends of the main should be connected to the boiler with unions to facilitate the removal of accessories, and even the boiler itself, without disturbing the piping. Temporarily support the main every 8 or 10 feet as it progresses. Do not install the permanent hangers until all of the radiation units are connected.

When the main is finished, assemble the fittings to the two ends of each radiation unit. Connect the radiation units to it with two branch pipes, as shown in Figure 7–9. These parts will make a swing joint in each branch pipe that makes it easier to connect the piping. If the branch pipes are to be run between the joists, assemble the nipple and 45-degree elbow to the first branch-line tee in the main. Then measure and cut the length of pipe nec-

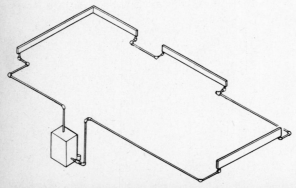

Figure 7–7. One-pipe hydronic (hot-water) system.

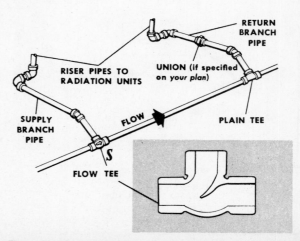

Figure 7–9. Connecting the branch pipe to the radiation units.

essary to connect the 45-degree elbow (above) with its swing joint. Wherever possible in a basement installation it is desirable to run the branches between the joists to save overhead space. The 45-degree elbow and nipple are not needed if the branch piping is to be run below the joists. In this type of installation, simply measure and cut the length of pipe necessary to connect the branch-line tee in the main with its swing joint. Repeat the steps given in the paragraph above to connect the second branch line to the first radiation unit. Then proceed to the next radiation unit, and so on, until all the units are connected to the main.

If your installation requires radiation units on the second floor or attic, they must be connected to the main by long riser pipes. Because there is usually less ceiling space in the basement than in the rooms above, installing these risers inside of partitions or walls (they can be put in outer walls if properly insulated) requires that, when steel pipe is used, each riser must consist of two shorter lengths coupled together as they are installed upward from below. Or you may substitute copper tubing and install it from above, uncoiling it as required.

In alteration work, you can install risers be-fore finishing the partitions, and the locations of all joists and studs will be obvious, so that they can easily be avoided.

When the room is already completed, however, you may be faced with two problems: (1) what to do about risers that must go through first-floor rooms, either from the basement up to the floor above, or from the attic down to the first-floor radiation units; and (2) how to locate wall studs and/or floor joists that might be in the way. You can, of course, plan the location for the risers, then strip off the necessary plaster or partition finish in order to install them. This often involves considerable work, and replastering the partition may prove to be difficult. Therefore, this solution is not recommended unless you are already planning major redecorations that would make the work necessary. It is easier, quicker, and more economical to run risers close against partitions, either in the open room or in a closet. If this is done in the open room, they can then be painted to match the walls, or can be decoratively boxed in.

Reread Chapters 3 and 4, and familiarize yourself with the usual arrangements of studs (in a partition) and joists (in a floor). Regardless of the type of

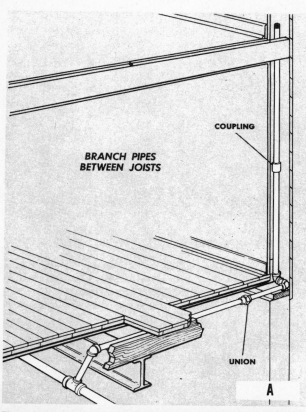
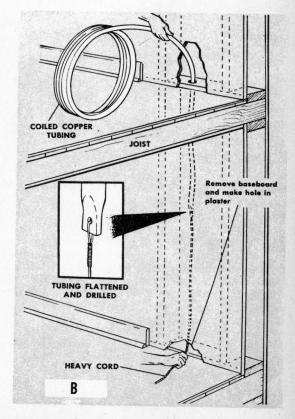

Figure 7–10. Methods of running steel pipe (A) and copper tubing (B).

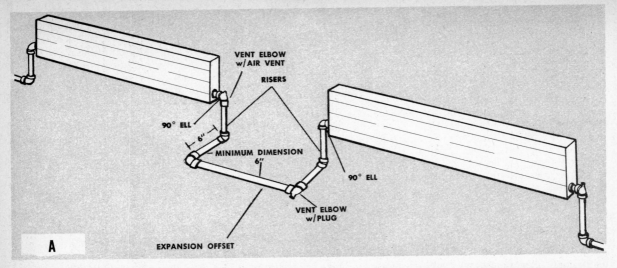

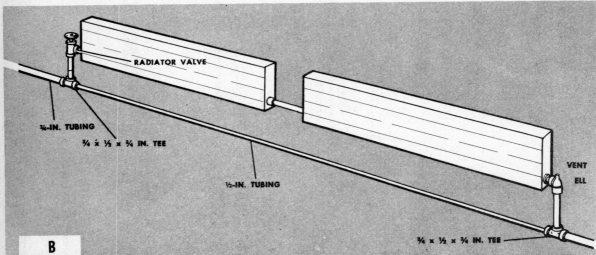

Figure 7–11. (A) Method of connecting units with jumpers; (B) method of controlling individual units.

wall finish used (plaster on wood or metal lath, plasterboard, etc.) or the type of floor covering used, studs and joists are generally spaced 16 inches apart, center-to-center. If you are running a riser through an old partition, you must only locate one stud and plan to set the pipes between this stud and the next one.

To run risers in a partition you will have to drill through the floor plate and, if your run goes to the floor above, through the ceiling plate. In rare cases you may also find a header in the way. Should you run into a header you will either have to open the partition to drill through it, or move over to the next stud space that is clear.

As mentioned several times earlier, there are several ways to find studs hidden in partitions. One

is to tap with a hammer and listen for the "solid" sound that indicates a stud. Another is to use a commercial stud locator. Perhaps the simplest method is to remove a section of the baseboard, then continually "explore" by driving a finishing nail into the plaster under the baseboard, until the nail strikes a stud.

Locating first-floor joists is not a problem, since these can be seen from the basement or crawl space. Second-floor joists present more of a problem. To find them, it is best to remove a section of the second-floor baseboard, and a small area of the plaster under the baseboard. Then drill a small hole through the floor where the baseboard will hide it. If the drill goes deeper than 2 inches and is still in wood, you are drilling into a joist. Otherwise, you have drilled through the floor and subfloor into a clear (joist-free) area.

If your riser runs from the basement up to a second-floor radiation unit, and is being installed inside an existing partition, it must (as already noted) pass through the floor and ceiling plates of the first-floor partition, and through the floor plate of the second-floor partition above. The two top holes can be drilled simultaneously from above by using a ratchet-type hand auger and a long (14-inch, or longer) bit. You will have to remove enough plaster to make room for the auger and bit, then drill straight down through the center of the second-floor floor plate and the ceiling plate below it. Drill a 1¼-inch hole. Afterwards, locate a spot directly below these holes (by taking careful measurements); then, from the basement or crawl space, drill the third hole through the first-floor floor plate. If your riser runs from a first-floor radiation unit up into the attic, you will have but one hole to drill through the ceiling plate of the partition. This is easily done from the attic.

When running risers in an open room, locate the studs and joists in the manner already described. Plot the locations for your holes carefully. If the riser passes through the first-floor ceiling into a floor (or attic) above, drill this hole before drilling any other holes required. Drill a 1¼-inch hole from above, being careful not to break through the first-floor ceiling plaster. Then drill a small hole through the ceiling plaster (to locate the hole). Go below and drill the larger hole upward through the plaster, so as not to chip or break it. If a hole through the first floor is also required, use a plumb bob and line to locate it; then drill down through the floor.

When the boiler is in a utility room and the main is in the attic, or when radiation units are to be in the basement, the pipe concealment problem is the same as in a second-floor installation. Connections between these riser pipes and the swing joints at the ends of each radiation unit are much the same as in a basement installation. The branch piping that connects the riser piping to the main must be pitched up toward the main for proper circulation when the radiator is below the main.

After all of the radiation units are connected to the main, check the piping to be sure it is properly pitched. Then support the main with hangers. For iron pipe the hangers should be spaced every 8 to 10 feet. Copper tubing less than 1½ inches in diameter should be supported every 6 feet.

Series-loop system. When installing a series-loop system, connect the vent ell and elbow to the radiation unit pointing downward. Install the risers below the joists. Fabricate the expansion joint with elbows, pipe, and fittings (Figure 7–11A). In like manner, complete the other jumpers to connect all of the radiation units in series.

When radiation units in adjoining rooms are close to the common partition wall, you may eliminate the jumper under the floor and simply run it through the wall from one unit to the next instead. You should buy a cover plate or dummy panel to match your radiation unit. Cut the cover plate or the dummy panel to fit between the radiator and the wall in order to conceal the piping above the floor. The radiation units joined in this manner will expand as one long unit. Therefore, when you make the riser pipe holes in the flooring, be sure to allow extra room for expansion.

The procedure just described is used only occasionally because of the extra cost of covers as well as the chance that a stud will complicate cutting through the wall.

The basic series-loop system does not permit individual control of the radiation units. You can easily see that cutting off the water to any one of the units would stop circulation through the entire loop. If you want to be able to regulate the temperature in a particular room, you can install a bypass (Figure 7–11B) around the radiation unit(s) for this room; then install a radiator valve at the supply end of the unit. When this valve is closed, the hot water will pass the unit and flow on through the rest of the system. Be sure to use ½-inch pipe for the bypass, instead of the ¾-inch pipe used in the rest of the loop. This smaller pipe is required so that, when the valve is open, the hot water will take the path of least resistance and flow through the larger pipe and the unit, instead of through the bypass. A bypass is not needed when baseboard convector panels are installed. Adjust the damper to regulate the heat.

A basement or second-floor radiation unit can be connected to the piping in a series-loop system as shown. A flow tee is installed in the supply

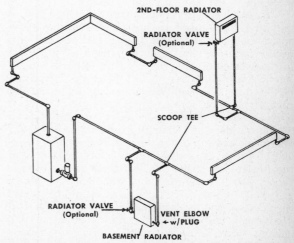

Figure 7–12. Method of connecting a basement or second-floor radiation unit in a series-loop system.

branch leading to the unit. Risers to the second floor should be installed as described on page 227 under one-pipe systems.

After all the radiation units are connected together, you are ready to install the supply and return lines. Measure and cut the lengths of pipe needed for these mains, and install each main beginning at the boiler.

Gravity hot-water system. Some older homes may still have a gravity hot-water system. When water is heated in the boiler, it expands and becomes less dense (lighter); then it rises through the supply piping and into the radiation units in the rooms above. After giving up its heat, the cooler (heavier) water flows down through the return piping to the boiler, to be reheated. Thus, circulation is effected entirely by the difference in weight between the hot water and the cooler water. As long as there is hot water in the boiler, the water will circulate and heat your home. A gravity system does not use a circulator pump.

When installing a radiator or branch line off a gravity system, follow the same procedure as described for a forced hot-water system.

Steam heating system. When the water in the steam heating boiler is heated, it boils and generates steam, which rises through the main and branch pipes to the radiators. After displacing the air in these units, which is released by the automatic air vents, the steam liberates its heat and condenses into water. Characteristic of the steam system is the single branch pipe to each radiator, through which the condensed water returns to the main against the inrushing steam. The main, which is pitched down from the supply end to the return end, carries this water around its single loop and back to the boiler for reheating, and also carries the steam upward to the branch pipes. The system operates as long as the boiler is hot enough to generate steam.

Steam heating systems use the same type of radiating units used in hot-water systems (baseboard convector panels, cast-iron radiators, and convector cabinets), and they are installed similarly. In older steam heat systems steel piping is usually found. Methods of assembling this type of pipe can be found in Chapter 6. When making any horizontal runs of pipe, be sure to pitch the pipe downward toward the supply line. The correct pitch for steam piping is a drop of 1 inch for every 10 feet of length.

Warm-air systems. Forced warm-air systems consist of a furnace, ducts, and registers. A blower in the furnace circulates the warm air to the various rooms through supply ducts and registers. Return grilles and ducts carry the cooled room air back to the furnace, where it is reheated and recirculated. If your home has a forced warm-air heating system, adding a room or improving the heating of an existing room offers few problems. In fact, all that is usually required are a few simple-to-install ducts

and registers. But, because each installation differs slightly from every other one, it is impossible to give specific, detailed instructions here for your particular plan. However, the following is the usual sequence of work:

1. Cut openings for registers and grilles.
2. Install supply-air registers.
3. Install return-air grilles.
4. Assemble pipes and ducts.
5. Install return-air runs.
6. Install supply-air runs.

Before starting the installation, you must, of course, figure out just where to run the pipes and ducts to supply heat to the room. Frequently this will dictate the type of registers and grilles that will be employed. As a rule, warm-air supply outlets are preferably located along outside walls. They should be low in the wall, in the baseboard, or in the floor where air cannot blow directly on room occupants. Floor registers tend to collect dust and trash, but may have to be used in installing a new system in an old house. High-wall or ceiling outlets are sometimes used when the system is designed primarily for cooling. However, satisfactory cooling as well as heating can be obtained with low-wall or baseboard registers by increasing the air volume and velocity and by directing the flow properly. Ceiling diffusers that discharge the air downward may cause drafts; those that discharge the air across the ceiling may cause smudging. Most installations have a cold-air return in each room. When the supply outlets are along the outside walls, the return grilles should be along the inside walls in the baseboard or in the floor. When the supply outlets are along the inside walls, the return grilles should be along the outside walls. In most room installations, the final layout choice will usually be a compromise between convenience and efficiency dictated by the design of your home. Once you figure out the system's configuration, how and where the ducts will run, it is a fairly easy task to determine the duct system parts needed. A heating supply dealer will also be able to assist in this matter.

Cutting openings for registers and grilles. Once your layout is completely planned and the materials are on hand, start the installation by cutting the openings for registers and grilles. A cardboard template (pattern) for each floor or wall opening required will greatly speed your work. If practical, simply place the unit to be measured on a piece of stiff cardboard and draw around the part for which the opening is to be made, using a sharp pencil that will closely follow the sides being outlined. Otherwise, take measurements and then transfer them to the cardboard. When cutting the cardboard, cut on the outer edges of your pencil lines. This way, the finished opening will be just enough larger than the unit so that the unit will fit in easily but snugly.

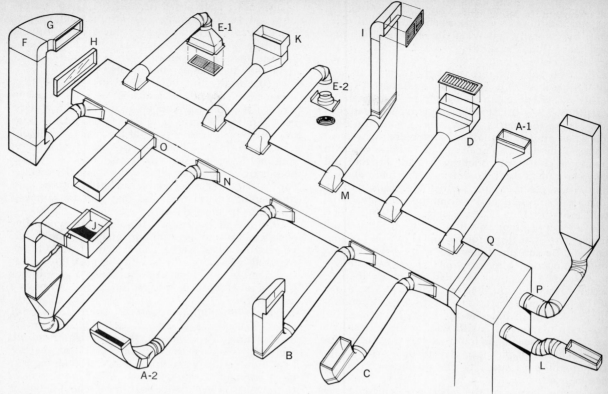

Figure 7–13. Parts used in a warm-air heating system: *A*-1 = 90-degree-angle boot; *A*-2 = straight boot with a 45-degree angle; *B* = center-end boot; *C* = center-end boot with a 45-degree angle; *D* = straight boot with a floor pan; *E*-1 = floor or ceiling outlet pan; *E*-2 = ceiling outlet; *F* = short-way 90-degree elbow; *G* = long-way 90-degree elbow; *H* = end cap; *I* = stack head; *J* = floor or ceiling outlet pan; *K* = stack reducer; *L* = flex elbow; *M* = top takeoff; *N* = side takeoff; *O* = flat takeoff; *P* = starting collar; *Q* = offset takeoff collar.

When joists are exposed on the opposite side, first find the approximate location in the room where the unit will go, as shown on your plan. Measure out from the wall the distance that the nearest edge of the unit is to be from the wall, and draw a short line on the floor. Move approximately 1 inch beyond this line and drive a thin, long nail through a floor crack so that the point is visible in the basement. Take the cardboard template down to the basement where the nail shows through. Get your directions straight, then hold the template up between the joists in a good position for the opening. Push the template straight up so that the nail point will puncture it, approximately 1 inch in from the edge nearest the wall. Take it down and write "Top" on the top side.

Return to your approximate location in the room, and place the template on the floor with the "Top" side showing, the punctured hole over the nailhead, and the nearest edge parallel to the wall. The edge of the template should line up with the

original line you drew on the floor. Draw a line completely around the template to outline your opening for cutting. For a ceiling opening, work in the attic and reverse the basement procedure.

When joists are not exposed on the opposite side, you will have to "search" for them. Find the approximate register location on your plan. Carefully remove the shoe molding and baseboard from the adjoining wall. Drill a 1-inch hole through the floor against the wall. When drilling the hole, if your bit goes deeper than 2 inches through the floor and is still in wood, you are drilling into a joist; if so, move about 2 inches to the left or right and drill a new hole. Prod through this hole with a wire to locate the joists at each side of it and mark their locations on the floor. Place your template and mark the register outline for cutting.

When a register is to be located in a wall, you will be using the space between the studs, and this opening must also be lined up with a floor opening between the joists. Therefore, both the studs and the joists must be located. Find the approximate register location in the wall, as shown on your plan. Start by carefully removing the shoe molding and baseboard from the selected wall. Using a hammer and cold chisel, remove enough plaster at the base of the wall below this location (in the area hidden by the baseboard) to find the studs nearest to the location. Stiff wire can be used to prod through the openings. Mark the stud locations on the wall surface where the marks show later. Locate the floor joists, as already explained, and mark their locations on the floor. You can now determine where to plan your continuous opening through the floor and between the studs. Take your register template and hold it in place, where neither the studs nor the joists will interfere, and outline the template on the wall for cutting.

To cut a floor opening with ordinary hand tools, start by drilling four 1-inch holes at the four corners. Be sure the holes are entirely within your outline, but touching the lines. Use a keyhole saw to cut along the lines between the holes, then remove the cutout portion of flooring and subfloor. If the opening is to be for a high-wall unit, enlarge one of the small holes at the base of the wall and reach up inside with a stiff wire or use a flashlight and mirror. Reach, or look, all the way up to the highest point of the desired wall opening to make certain the stud space is free of obstructions and can be used.

If you have a power saber saw, starting holes are not necessary. Start cutting through at about the center of each side line, then advance the saw to cut up to the corners.

To cut an opening in the floor under a wall, you will have to cut away a length of the 2×4 plate. Use a ratchet-type auger, or power drill, and drill 2-inch holes through the plate, one at each side line of the required opening. Use a wood chisel and hammer to complete the job, and then remove the plate. The floor opening can now, generally, be cut in the same manner used to cut an opening in an exposed floor, except that you will be working in a confined space. If you are on an upper floor and there is a wall below, the probability is that you will also have to cut through a ceiling plate in the lower partition. If so, you will find it easier to cut the sides of the opening by drilling 1-inch holes. Use a ratchet-type brace and bit or power drill; have the holes nearly touching, so that the ceiling plate is practically cut through at each side by the drilled holes. Finish the opening with a keyhole saw or chisel.

In a wall, always start cuts, when possible, in the area behind the baseboard where mistakes won't show; use a saber saw or keyhole saw with a drilled starting hole. First, saw horizontal lines in the wall following the template outline, then complete the cut.

To cut plasterboard or wallboard, use a fine-tooth saw and cut continuously around your outline. Since this material is heavy and brittle, support the piece being removed to keep it from breaking out and tearing the outline. When cutting through metal lath, use a metal-cutting blade.

To install horizontal ductwork in the joist space between a ceiling and floor, it is necessary to remove the flooring above the space that will be used. Find your joists, and draw lines on the floor to show their location. Start at the register wall and remove all flooring boards necessary to expose the subfloor between the two lines. Take out whole boards by prying them loose with a small wrecking bar or large screwdriver. Carefully remove and number the boards, so that they can be replaced exactly as they were.

On the subfloor, draw lines to show where the joists are. Cut out the subfloor flush with the inside edge of the joists. Nail a 1-inch strip of wood to the exposed joist sides, flush with the joist tops. After the duct is installed, you can relay the subfloor boards on the top of this nailing strip, and have a solid floor.

Installing supply registers. There are several types of supply registers, and each is installed in its own manner. For instance, the *rectangular ceiling register* has a face that fits into a ceiling register boot mounted between joists. Make an opening just large enough to hold the boot. Nail wood blocks to the joists at each side. Position the boot between the blocks, then attach it with nails. Install the face to the boot, and secure it with the screws provided.

To install a *round ceiling register*, cut a round opening in the ceiling just large enough for the round collar on the register boot; slip the boot in place from above. The flanges on the side of the square mounting plate may then be nailed to the joists to hold the boot securely. Center the ceiling register face over the collar on the boot; fasten it with the screws provided. These screws are long enough to pass through the ceiling and into the holes provided in the mounting plate.

The *wall register*, as a rule, consists of a face that attaches to a box called a "stack head." It requires a wall opening the length and height of the stack head. This opening may be at the baseboard, or higher in the wall. Fit wood blocks of the necessary width to fill the space between the sides of the stack head and the adjoining studs; nail the blocks to the studs. Slip the stack head into position and nail it to the blocks. When you are ready to install the register face, simply position it over the stack head and secure it with screws. In the case of a baseboard register, replace the baseboard and shoe molding.

A floor register generally consists of a face that fits into a pan. It requires a floor opening long enough and wide enough to hold the top opening of the pan snugly. Install the pan and nail through its sides into the opening edges to secure it. Place the register in the pan.

Installing return grilles. The opening for a floor grille should be the same size as the length and width of the shoulders on the underside of the grille. When the grille is in place, the flanges will rest on the floor. Be sure to install it, as noted on your plan, to be over a joist space or other clear spaces as specified.

Baseboard and wall-type grilles utilize stud space. Measure the height and length required for the wall opening; then make the wall opening a bit smaller so that the grille flange will cover the cut edges. Cut away the floor plate, making an unrestricted opening the full size of the stud space. Either a single or double stud space is used, depending on the width of the grille. Block off stud space above the wall opening if the run goes to the basement; below the opening, if the run goes to the attic. Nail wood blocks to the stud at each side or be sure there is other firm support for the screws, then attach the grille face to the wall. Reinstall baseboard and shoe molding. *Caution:* Before installing any grille of this type, be sure to check stud spaces for

obstructions and clear them all the way to the basement or attic. Cut every wall and floor opening as large as practicable. This will improve the air flow.

With the large wall grille used with a closet-type furnace, where the return duct goes straight through the wall, the center stud must be cut away and supported by a header. The duct leading into the furnace is installed first; the duct sides are nailed inside the opening, then the grille is installed.

Assembling pipes and ducts. Rectangular ducts vary in size, from the large sections used as main trunks in an extended plenum, down to the small size (usually 3¼ by 12 inches), which can be installed within the stud space of a wall. This small size is commonly referred to as "wall stack." Ductwork is shipped nested, with the seams open. Do not close the seams of a section that must be shortened until after it is cut to length.

When assembling ductwork, it is often necessary to shorten a section to fill out the last part of the run. Assemble all the sections except the last one, then hold it in place and mark it for cutting to length. Rectangular ductwork is cut in an open position with tin snips. After cutting, it is necessary to

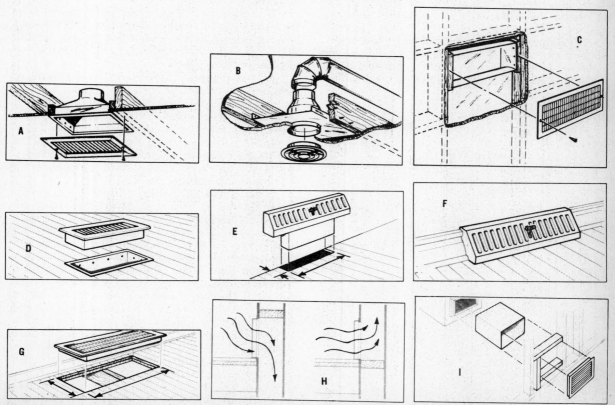

Figure 7–14. Installing return-air runs.

rework the cut end so that it may be properly joined to another section. Always cut off the plain end and make the shortened section approximately 1 inch longer than the space to be filled. Notch each corner of the cut end approximately 1 inch. Use a bending tool and form a new drive clip flange on the two short sides. Measure for the length required and mark the snap end for cutting. Plan to have the shortened section approximately three-quarters of an inch longer than the space to be filled. This will allow for engagement into the next piece. New snaps can then be formed to replace those cut off; use a small cold chisel. Locate them the way the original ones were located, using another stack section as a guide.

When large duct pieces are joined, the sections are assembled with connectors and drive clips. Most have "S" type connectors formed on the two long edges at one end of each section, though separate "S" connectors are sometimes used. Very wide sections use separate "L" type connectors. The two types are similar, except that the "L" connector has an outward projection to add support. The two short sides of each section are bent to receive the drive clips; if they are not bent, use the bending tool furnished to make a 180-degree bend on each short side; slide the tool all the way over the edge and bend the edge out and back until the tool touches the duct.

When joining two sections of equal width, and if the connectors are separate, place a connector over each long edge of one section at one end. Keep the connector ends flush with the duct sides. Join the next section to this one by inserting its long edges into the connector slots and pushing the two sections together. Keep the duct sides lined up. Close the two short sides of the joint with drive clips. The slots of a clip engage the turned-back duct edges. To install a clip, bend one end tab inward to a 90-degree angle to form a better working surface. Start the clip upward over the duct edges, then if necessary, tap the clip bottom lightly with a hammer to drive it in place; don't use the heel of your hand. Bend the top tab down over the duct, locking it into position. Support all main horizontal ducts with hangers spaced every 5 feet.

To join a narrower section to a wider one, use an increaser adapter. First, with tin snips, cut inward along the two corners of one side of the narrower section, exactly 6 inches. Cut off the end of the short side at a depth of approximately 5 inches, to leave a 1-inch tab. With your bending tool, bend this tab outward to about a 45-degree angle. Fit the increaser adapter over the opening, so that the S-cleat at its small end fits over the tab, and the S-cleats on the edges are engaged over the cut edges of the duct. If necessary, squeeze the S-cleats with pliers to make them tight. Now you can join the two duct sections in the same manner as described for sections of equal width.

Wall stack sections use snap-lock joints consisting of a snap end and a shaped end. Fit the snap end of one section between the flanges of the shaped end of the next section and push the two together until they lock.

All round pipes are shipped with seams open; they must be closed prior to use. There are two basic ways this is accomplished, as follows:

1. Snap-lock seams. With your two hands, shape the pipe round, overlapping the edges slightly. Press the tongue (which is on one edge) into the slot (on the other edge), and allow the seam to snap closed. Do not hammer this seam, as hammering will damage the locking edges.

2. Hammer-lock seams. Shape the pipe (as above) and hook the two edges together. Hang the shaped pipe over a length of 2×4, so that the seam lies flat along the narrow edge. Hammer the seam from end to end to close it tightly, but make certain the edges remain engaged while hammering.

When assembling a round pipe run, it is often necessary to shorten one pipe section to fill out the last part of the run. Assemble all the sections except the last one, then hold the last section in place and mark it for cutting. Always measure the last section while the pipe is still open; this will make it easier to cut to length. Always plan to cut off the plain (not crimped) end. Also plan to have the crimped end inserted up to the bead inside the piece into which it fits. If both ends are plain, plan to make the shortened section barely long enough to fill the space, with no overlap at either end. This joint can

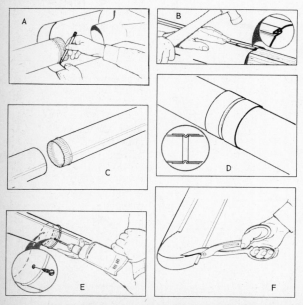

Figure 7—15. Technique of working with round pipe sections.

then be closed, using a pipe connector.

An open round pipe should be cut with tin snips while it is open. After cutting, use a screwdriver to pry open the seam edges where the seam has been squeezed closed by the snips; the pipe can then be closed.

When round pipe sections are joined, the crimped end of one pipe section or fitting slides inside the plain end of the adjoining section or elbow; the crimped ends should always face away from the furnace. For a tight joint, push the crimped end all the way in. For neatness, keep the seam edges in a straight line in the least noticeable position. Use two sheet metal screws to secure each joint. Drill holes for the sheet metal screws. Support the horizontal portions of assembled pipe with pipe hangers spaced every 10 feet.

When making openings in sheet metal, use the fitting, or a template the exact size of the desired opening, and mark the opening on the metal; remove the area of metal bounded by the mark. To start your cut, use a screwdriver and hammer to make a rip inside the area. Do this by holding the edge of the blade, not the end, against the metal and striking it. Complete the cut with tin snips, cutting out to the mark, and then around it. If more convenient, a saber saw with a metal-cutting blade may be used.

Installing return-air runs. Before beginning this work, study your plan and consider the best sequence for the various steps. Often, return-air runs will pass above supply runs, so return runs should usually be installed first. Determine from your plan where the return-air duct (or ducts) will enter the plenum chamber. Then hold an offset take-off collar up against the plenum side, one collar for each return-air duct. Hold the collar so that the outlet is at the desired position; the top of the fitting should be 1 inch below a floor joist or other combustible material. Outline the cutout on the plenum.

After marking all take-off collars, cut openings as outlined. You may wish to remove the plenum from the furnace for convenience in working. Push each collar into its opening, and secure it by flattening the metal tabs (formed by the cuts on the inner edge) against the inside of the plenum. Never install a grille directly in the side of a supply or return plenum since this is likely to interfere with the proper combustion of the furnace.

The joist space used to carry return air must be at least as large as called for on your plan. Measure the inside width and height; make certain the space is clear of braces or other large obstructions. Use double spaces where called for, or necessary, to obtain proper dimensions. Typical panned joist spaces are illustrated in Figure 7-16. Note the use of wood blocks and sheet metal to fully enclose the desired portions. Also note that the sheet metal bottom must be lowered below the joists, wherever it joins the return-air duct (so it will be same distance below the joists as the top of the duct). Use wood strips, as shown, to lower it. Cut the opening for the duct before nailing the sheet metal entirely in place. This opening must be made as large as possible. When planning your cut, allow enough material to provide a 1-inch tab turned down all around the opening. This will be set back against the return duct to secure the two sections together. Finish nailing the sides of the sheet metal to the joists. Do not install the end wood block until after the duct is installed and joined to the opening. This will allow access for working.

When stud space is used, remember to block off the space above the portion used for the return-air run, if the run goes down to the basement, or below it, if the run goes up to the attic. Provide full-size openings through the floor or ceiling, where they enter into the panned joist space or duct that carries the run toward the furnace. Remove all loose plaster, dust, and dirt insofar as possible; this will make for cleaner air circulation and more efficient operation. Be certain the stud spaces used are clear throughout. Cross members (fire stops) are frequently placed between studs when a house is built. These, or any other obstructions, must be removed.

When installing the ductwork, begin at the offset take-off collar and assemble the ductwork sections in position. Do not install the end cap on the last section to match the opening in the sheet metal panning. Install the duct section and, working through the open end, bend the tabs of the opening in the sheet metal panning back against the inner sides of the duct opening. Install the end blocks in the panned joist spaces, and nail the panning to the blocks. At the end of the return-air duct, install an end cap.

Installing supply-air runs. All warm-air runs within stud spaces must be ducted with wall stacks. Unlined stud spaces may be used only on the return system. All stack openings must be larger than the stack. Always refer to your plan for the proper size stack and fittings for each location. If the stacks can be installed from below, it is necessary only to make openings in the wall and floor for the stack. You must first make an opening under the baseboard, in order to cut through the floor from above. When the register is in an upper-floor wall directly above a first-floor wall, the requirements are the same as for a first-floor wall register except that an additional opening through the upper floor is required. Should the register be in a wall that is offset from, or at right angles to, the wall below, additional openings will be needed to lay the horizontal stack sections.

After all the openings are made, take a flashlight and look through the wall or floor space for such obstructions as fire stops or plaster.

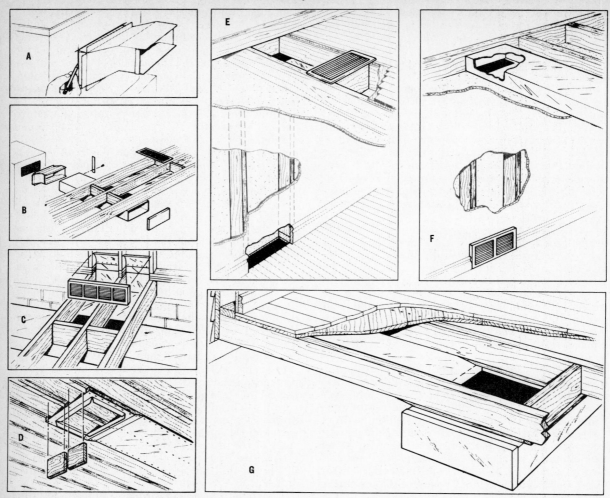

Figure 7–16. Installing supply-air and return-air runs.

When the stack is assembled in place, the snap end of any stack or fitting section must always be positioned toward the furnace. You should have a helper to hold the assembled stack while you attach new sections. Whenever possible, install the stack from below. Push one section up at a time, as high as convenient; attach the next section to it (secure both sections together with sheet metal screw) and continue until the top can be connected to its stack head or fitting. Cut any excess from the bottom section with your tin snips and install the proper boot, or other fitting. If you must work from above, use a long rope and wood block as shown in Figure 7–16K. Lower the stack while assembling it, section by section.

Assemble the pipes and/or ductwork and necessary fittings to complete the installation. Then install a volume damper in each branch run. You will have to balance your complete heating system

by using the dampers. This is accomplished by simply placing a thermometer in each room and then adjusting the dampers until the temperature suits you. There is a chance that the new branch will upset existing settings, but a few adjustments should work this out.

SUPPLEMENTARY HEATING

Frequently, when you are adding a room to your home, it is much easier and less costly to heat the area by supplementary means than to add to your present central heating system. Also supplementary heating may be the solution to those "hard-to-heat" rooms or where extra heat is needed in just one room alone (the bathroom, for example) for a short period of time.

Supplementary heating methods are many and varied. Some auxiliary heating units are portable,

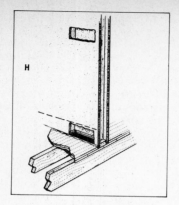

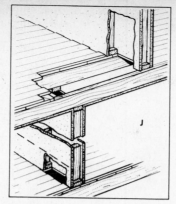

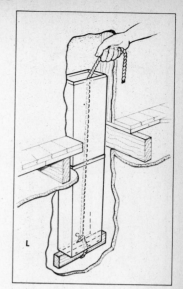

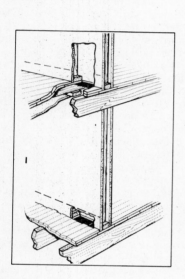

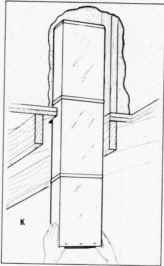

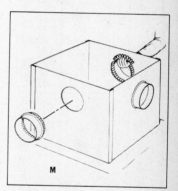

while others require permanent installation. Some units burn fuel gas and oil, and others use electricity. As a rule, convenience and availability are most important since the difference in operating costs is usually minimal because the area to be heated is relatively small.

Electric heat. Electric heat is very effective in new additions and hard-to-heat areas. In fact, it is the most popular way of furnishing supplementary heat to a room. It is easy to install. Units can be in the form of baseboard heaters, or wall or ceiling unit heaters. No matter what voltage your home has, the introduction of additional heating units will usually require new circuits. It is dangerous to connect a new heater to a circuit that may already be loaded to capacity (see page 144).

Baseboard heaters. Baseboard heaters can be used as the sole heating system or as auxiliary units where supplementary heat is required. They can be

installed to give highly efficient performance in new or old homes, additions, garages, or other locations where heat is desired, provided proper insulation has been installed. Most modern baseboard heaters are equipped with a thermal cutout that protects against overheating by automatically cutting out heating elements at a preset temperature. This safety device consists of a sensitive thermal element that runs the full length of the heater, sensing overheat conditions on any coverage of 6 inches or more segment. An automatic reset reenergizes the heaters when the condition causing the overheat is removed and the temperature falls below the preset control point.

As with steam or hot-water baseboard units, electric-type units should be centered on an outside wall or walls under window areas to counteract the downward flow of cool air caused by loss of heat through the glass. Drapes should be kept 6 inches

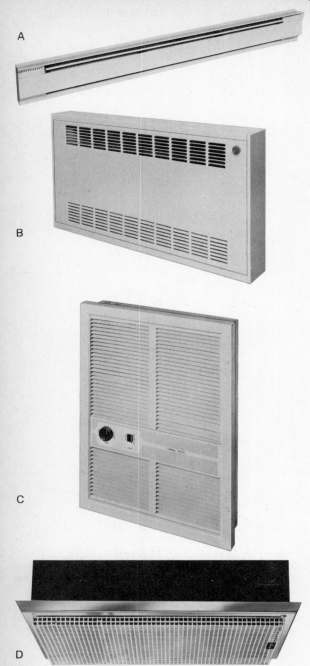

Figure 7–17. Electric heat units: (A) baseboard heater; (B) convector heater; (C) forced-air wall heater; (D) forced-air ceiling heater.

dealer will help you determine the length of the heating element needed.

The heaters and blank panels can be mounted against the plaster wall, semi-recessed by mounting directly to wall studs, or they can be mounted to insulation board used in solid masonry construction. That is, when heaters are to be mounted to solid masonry, the heaters should be mounted against the insulation board usually used in this type of construction. The usual mounting methods, such as screws with wood or lead plugs, are used to secure the heaters to the masonry wall.

Where a corner piece is to be used for continuing the installation of heaters on the adjoining wall, first install the corner unit, fastening it to wall or studs in a similar manner, then join the heater terminal boxes to the corner unit with Chase nipples or a comparable fastener.

Remove the front cover by pushing down on the top front cover support while lifting the front cover at the bottom. Remove the knockout or knockouts as required for wiring. For a semi-recessed method of mounting, place the heater in the proper location and fasten it to studs with screws through mounting holes. For surface mounting against a plaster wall, it is advisable to mark the stud positions on the wall before placing the heaters in the desired locations. This precaution is not necessary for solid masonry construction. Before fastening a heater, attach the connector for the electrical wiring and insert the wire through the connector into the junction box on the heater. Use round-head screws, drawing them up firmly first, then back off half a turn to allow for expansion from heat. It is possible to use 10d common nails in place of wood screws if desired.

Your supplier will tell you the wire size to use. Run a circuit of appropriate voltage to the outlet box for the thermostat and then down to the location of the junction box of the nearest heater unit. If a low-voltage thermostat and relay combination is to be used, run a high-voltage wire directly to the heater and the standard low-voltage thermostat wire from this to the heater. Electrical grounding of the metal housing must be provided as required by the National Electric Code. The maximum allowable connected load is 20 amps. If two or more heaters are to be connected, but separated, it is necessary to provide a connecting loop between the heaters.

Most heaters may be wired from either end. For a single heater, run the branch circuit wires to the wall thermostat and then to the junction box. Remove the wire nut joining the two conductors in the junction box and connect the branch circuit wires to these conductors. A ground screw is provided in each junction for the connection of the equipment-grounding conductor when nonmetallic-sheathed cable is used. Do not use a mounting screw for grounding.

above the top of the baseboard. If baseboard is required to cover wall to wall, then select the number of blank panels (without heating elements) needed to fill in the balance of the wall length. Your heating

Perhaps the most important advantage obtained from the use of electric heat is that of room-by-room control. With a thermostat in every room, careful consideration must be given to the selection and placement of the thermostat to insure the proper operation of the electric heating system. Thermostats should be located 52 to 60 inches above the floor on inside walls in locations that are subject to normal temperatures. For example, they should not be mounted near doors or windows, or adjacent to cold walls, or in drafts. Nor should they be mounted near heat sources such as ranges, refrigerators, televisions, lamps, hot-water pipes, or where exposed to direct rays of the sun. Avoid mounting the thermostat on a wall that has a heat-producing source on the adjacent or reverse side. For example, the thermostat should not be mounted on a dining room wall that is backed up by a kitchen oven.

To provide optimum comfort-level control, a thermostat must be able to sense the average room temperature. For this reason a wall-mounted thermostat is recommended. Thermostats built in to the various baseboard or wall heater units are subjected to the heat from these units and can cause wide variances in room temperatures. But, where it is difficult to run a thermostat circuit in the existing wall or where an integral thermostat is desired, the thermostat may be added to the baseboard. It is installed on the right-hand junction box.

Wall heaters. Built-in electric wall heaters are available in a wide range of shapes and sizes, with and without fans, thermostats, timers, and various other refinements. When selecting a unit remember that UL approval indicates the unit meets the safety standards of the Underwriters' Laboratories; the NEMA insignia indicates the manufacturer is a member of the National Electric Manufacturers Association, pledged to conform to the industry standards.

In new work, the metal box required for mounting the heater and the necessary wiring are installed before the finished wall surface is applied. In old work, an opening of the proper size must be provided. It can be done as follows:

1. Find the studs closest to each side of the heater unit and draw their center lines in vertical markings.

2. Locate a point 4 inches higher and 4 inches lower than the heater's vertical dimension.

3. Mark the wall opening along all the outermost lines in steps 1 and 2.

4. Cut through the wall covering on the marked lines. Use a cold chisel for plaster; a keyhole or saber saw may be used on dry-wall construction materials.

In either new or old construction, frame the opening for the box with horizontal 2 × 4's cut to fit snugly between adjacent studs. Toe-nail the framing into the adjacent studs and spike through into the cutoff stud ends. If you find that the opening ends on the center line of a stud, make the cut there. When the time comes to cover the wall, these half-exposed studs are ready for the wall-covering materials. If no nailing surface should remain, create one by nailing 1-inch (or thicker) stock to these studs as required. In most cases, place the bottom supporting header approximately 10 to 18 inches from the floor for fan-driven heaters. Radiant heaters must be mounted 24 inches from the floor. All heaters must not be less than 6 inches from an adjacent side wall.

Mount the wall box as directed in the instruction sheet, making sure that the flange of the box sets flush with the finished wall line. Run the necessary wiring through the knockout on the bottom of the wall box. Be sure to leave approximately 8 to 12 inches of slack in the cable to allow sufficient freedom for wiring. This amount of slack should be allowed within the wall so that cable can be pushed or pulled back and secured when the wiring is completed.

After the wall finishing operations have been completed, proceed to the wiring of the heater unit. Fasten the heater to the wall box using the screws provided by the manufacturer. The front grille and switch and thermostat knobs are then installed, and the heater is ready to operate.

Ceiling heating panels. Electric radiant heating panels for total or supplemental heat are avail-

Figure 7–18. A typical ceiling heating panel.

able for ceiling mounting. There are two types. One is installed in the same manner as a light fixture (see page 168), while the other is mounted flush in a standard T-bar suspended ceiling (see page 61). Their operation can be controlled by a simple on-off switch, thermostat, or interval timer.

For handyman installation there are two sizes available: a 2-by-4-foot panel, rated at a 500-watt capacity, and a 3-by-4-foot model with a 750-watt capacity. A 750-watt panel produces heat over a 150-square-foot area. Used as the sole heat source, two of these panels will comfortably heat a 150-square-foot, properly insulated room. The heating surface can be painted to match nearly any room decor. Because the units have no glass or moving parts, they are practically unbreakable, provide draft-free heat, and require no maintenance. The flat, lightweight panels can be placed in nearly any location, furnishing total heat for the entire home or for any special area of the home, such as the bathroom, kitchen, family room, enclosed sun deck, entryway, or hallway.

The installation of bathroom ceiling electric heaters is fully described on page 402.

Gas- and oil-fired heaters. Space heaters, in some areas of the country, are the most popular form of low-cost supplementary heating. They are automatic and engineered to circulate as well as radiate heat. In oil-fired units, kerosene or No. 1 fuel oil can be piped from an outside storage tank or led from one at the back of the unit. Installation is rather easy. Fuel lines to the heating unit should run much like plumbing (see Chapter 6). Copper tubing with flare fittings is suitable for either gas or oil. Your supplier will aid in the selection of the proper size unit for your planned use and will be able to advise you about any local ordinances that may affect its installation.

When installing a space heater or any other auxiliary heating unit, be sure to follow the manufacturer's recommendations as to necessary venting. Certain venting rules must be followed to insure safety, as well as observance of the guarantee provisions. Ignoring the basic rules of venting may prove dangerous. Failure to remove all the products of combustion is hazardous to the occupants. For this reason, check your chimney carefully. There must be good draft, no down draft, and no obstructions. If a gas heater is used, a special flue lining is needed. Frequently, a prefab chimney arrangement such as that described on page 245 is the easier solution to this important venting consideration.

Recessed wall units. These are space heaters designed to fit into a wall of a room. Available in gas or oil models, recessed wall units fit standard 16-inch stud spacing without projecting too far into the room. But as is the case with space heaters, venting is most important. When installing these heaters be sure to follow the manufacturer's instruc-

tions. In the case of gas units, both recessed and space heaters, it is best to have professional help, at least for the gas-line connection, which calls for an experienced pipe fitter.

Floor furnaces. At one time floor furnaces were considered a primary source of heat; most are now employed as a means of supplementary heat. They are easy to install, requiring an opening in the floor and proper framing to support the unit. Their use, however, is limited to rooms over basements or crawl spaces because of the unit's depth. Available with automatic temperature controls, floor furnaces must be installed as directed by the manufacturer.

Heat fins. If your home has either a hot-water or steam-heat system, it is often possible to heat the basement with so-called heat fins. In fact, these fins, made of sheet aluminum, when installed on steel pipe or copper tubing as shown in Figure 7–19, will take the chill off an average-size basement room with an 8- to 10-foot section.

The heat fins should be covered with protective shields if they are at reachable heights. These shields can be made of perforated sheet aluminum or similar screening.

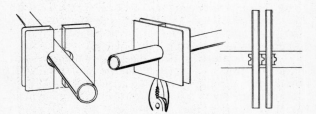

Figure 7–19. A stock heat fin can be installed on either steel pipe or copper tubing.

FIREPLACES

Traditionally, the open fireplace serves the home as a symbol of stability and unity. It is true that in these days of efficient central heating, fireplaces have little practical value, but they add a charm to everyday living that makes a good fireplace a must for many families. Where supplementary heating is desirable, the fireplace offers an effective as well as an attractive solution. While the traditional role of the fireplace has not changed, styles and needs have.

Remodeling a fireplace. If your old fireplace burns well, but looks old-fashioned, you can update it by remodeling. There are literally hundreds of possibilities for changing the appearance of your fireplace. You may want a medieval-turned-modern hood over the opening. You may merely want to replace the aged mantel with a new type, which can be purchased as a unit and nailed up the way the old one was. Or you may wish to create your own flush-faced fireplace from any one of, or a combination of, hundreds of new materials available.

The first step in most fireplace remodeling projects requires the removal of the old-fashioned mantle. To do this, pry the mantle out from the wall, using a small pry bar. When you are prying it carefully away, you will be able to see the nails that are holding the mantle to the wall, and pressure should be exerted at these points. Once all the nails holding the mantle are loosened, pull and lift it away from the wall.

If your remodeling plans call for a flush-faced fireplace, you must remove the brick or fieldstone veneer from the old fireplace, piece by piece, without disturbing either the firebrick or chimney. To do this most effectively use a cold chisel and a pry bar. You can cut away the old mortar with the chisel and pry the bricks or stones free from their mortar bond with the pry bar. If you encounter any metal ties that hold the masonry facing to the chimney or fireplace proper, cut them in half with the chisel to leave the chimney or fireplace intact. When removing the old masonry units, be certain to protect the floors with a paper or cloth covering.

Once the veneer has been removed, a frame is built (as described on page 243) to hold the flush wall material. This may be made of almost any of the wall finishing materials — plywood or hardboard paneling, solid wood boards, wall tiles, mirrors, and simulated stone brick — that are described in Chapter 3. They are installed on the flush fireplace frame as detailed in that chapter.

Raising the hearth. The raised hearth is the "in" design of modern fireplaces. While it is not a difficult job to make one, your present one must be changed proportionally or else it can become a smoking monster. Table 7–1 gives the proper proportions for a fire opening.

Table 7–1

A width at front (inches)	B width at back (inches)	C hearth-to-lintel height (inches)
28–33	21–25	28–30
34–38	26–30	28–30
39–44	31–35	30–33
46–52	36–43	33–39
52–56	44–48	39–44

Firebricks should be used throughout except for the final row, across the front, which may be a firebrick to match your present bricks. When setting the firebricks across the fire chamber, cement them down in a bed of mortar, but fill the joints between the bricks with fireclay. Most fireplace foundations can stand the additional weight of the raised hearth without any trouble.

When raising a hearth, check on whether or not the fireplace has some type of warm-air circulating device. As a rule this includes a metal jacket around the entire fireplace with a warm-air chamber fitted with cold-air intake ducts near the floor and warm-air ducts above the opening. To incorporate the circulating arrangement in the new fireplace opening, add the necessary lengths of duct as required, to bring the open ends flush with the new structure. The same face grille plates may be used, or you may wish to devise your own to match the mood of the new fireplace.

Glass screens. It is possible to give your fireplace a new look and, in addition, help to regulate the fire, even if the fireplace damper is faulty or if there is no damper at all. The special "heat-tempered" glass doors of the screen radiate heat from the fire in the same manner as an infrared heat lamp. Generally, the section of the frame below the doors is perforated and includes two sliding draft doors that allow you to control air intake. This ventilation system permits fingertip regulation of the fire, prevents any smoking of the fireplace, and eliminates the cold draft on the floor of the room.

The first step in the installation of a screen is to measure your fireplace according to the manufacturer's instructions, to make sure you order the correct size screen. When the screen is delivered, you simply drill four holes inside the fireplace opening (at the top and bottom of each side) with a carbide-tipped masonry drill. Lead plugs are then inserted in these holes to take the screws that attach the frame to the fireplace. Dismount the draft diverter from the frame temporarily so you can reach the lower mounting brackets and set the screen into the fireplace opening. Replace the draft diverter after the screen has been fastened in place with four screws driven into the lead plugs. Due to the natural irregularity of the brick or stone of the fireplace, there may be cracks between the frame and the fireplace. These do not impair the appearance of the screen since the frame overlaps the fireplace opening. These invisible gaps are filled by stuffing fiberglass insulation behind the frame. This completes the installation.

Cleaning a fireplace. Sometimes it is possible to give a fireplace a "new" look by just cleaning it. To clean off smoke stains from the masonry, mix 1½ pounds of caustic soda (from a hardware store) in 1 gallon of hot water. Apply this mix to the stained areas with a fiber scrubbing brush to clean off the stains, then rinse with two flushings of clear water. Be careful not to splash the caustic on any painted surfaces. If this mix does not take off the stains, try a muriatic acid solution (10 parts water to 1 part acid, available at most paint or hardware stores). Mix the acid solution in a container made of any material but metal, apply it with a natural fiber brush, and wear rubber gloves. Rinse off the acid solution at once with plenty of clear water.

Adding a new fireplace. At one time, building your own fireplace was a very ambitious project, but today, thanks to prefabricated fireplace units and chimney kits, it is a relatively simple one. Before starting any fireplace project, consult the local building code, especially the requirements for installation of factory-built fireplaces and chimneys.

Today, there are two basic types of prefabricated fireplaces: the built-in style and the freestanding style.

Built-in fireplaces. There are several ways the built-in fireplace can be installed, as shown in Figure 7–20. Consider the traffic pattern in your room and check the construction of your home above and below the fireplace before making a choice. A corner location may be best where space is limited.

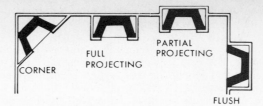

Figure 7–20. Various locations for a fireplace.

The fireplace may be installed directly on the floor, or an elevated wood or masonry platform may be used. When placed on a combustible floor, a fireproof hearth extension is usually required. (This may be purchased with the fireplace unit.) The ex-

Figure 7–21. Prefabricated fireplace units in various settings.

Figure 7—22. Framing details for a built-in prefabricated corner fireplace.

tension may be on the same level as the fireplace, or it can be recessed into the floor. Both the fireplace and the extension should be on a flat, level surface. A projecting fireplace will accent large natural finishing materials such as fieldstone.

The total height of the fireplace and chimney, in most cases, should not be over 45 feet. The installation will be easier and cost less if joists or rafters are not cut as the chimney is assembled. A 15-degree elbow is available with most units, and it can be used to offset the chimney to miss a rafter or joist.

The fireplace may be positioned and then the framing built around it, or the framing may be constructed and the fireplace then pushed into the opening. The fireplace may touch combustible materials at the bottom, sides, and back. Chimney sections must have at least a 1-inch clearance to combustible material. Firestop spacers must be installed at every ceiling level. They will provide the necessary clearance. Install the fireplace no closer than 36 inches to any unprotected combustible wall,

perpendicular to the fireplace openings. This does not apply to corner installations or walls with insulated shields. A floor that supports a fireplace does not have to be reinforced unless the material used for facing is very heavy, i.e., large areas of brick, fieldstone, etc.

As you install your fireplace, you may want to include space for a face finishing material. You can use plasterboard, plywood or wood paneling, ceramic tile, or any of the materials mentioned in Chapter 3. The material or facing may be installed even with the wall, or it may project in front of the wall. If you want the facing and wall to be even, you must recess the fireplace unit back the thickness of the facing.

The hearth or the area in front of the fireplace should be of fireproof material. If the floor is wood, you can cover it with bricks, ceramic tiles, sheet asbestos, or metal. Typically a hearth should be 12 to 20 inches deep, and extend about 8 to 10 inches on either side of the opening. If you prefer the fireplace and hearth raised above the floor, you can get a

Figure 7—23. Method of installing a fireplace with a prefabricated chimney.

raised base or you can build your own platform out of wood. If the fireplace is on a platform, you may bring the facing around the bottom of the opening. Do not block off the air opening at the bottom of the fireplace.

Freestanding fireplaces. Freestanding prefabricated fireplaces are the easiest to install. Most building codes specify that the back and sides of the freestanding fireplace be kept a certain distance from combustible materials, unless it has a high-temperature insulation barrier built into it, as is the case in models designed for wall installation. Most models must be set at least 18 inches away from the wall. The unit should stand on a base made of a

Figure 7—24. Three designs and applications of freestanding fireplace units.

fireproof material such as brick, metal, or tile.

Once the fireplace has been assembled according to the manufacturer's instructions, locate it where you plan to make the complete installation. To obtain the most efficient of any fireplace, built-in or freestanding, it should be located as close to the chimney as is practical. Keep the smokepipe connection to the chimney flue short and direct, using as few elbows as possible. Select a spot close to a window, or a location where the chimney can run through the interior of the house or an outside wall. If the fireplace flue is to run through the interior of the house, consider positioning it where it is possible to box in the chimney or run it through an

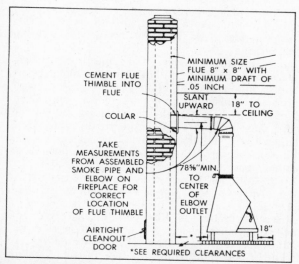
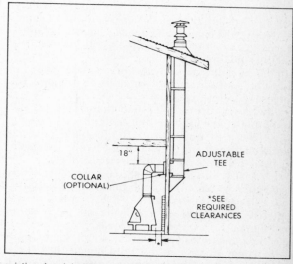

Figure 7—25. *(left)* Proper venting into an existing chimney; *(right)* using a prefabricated chimney. Required clearances vary with

existing local building codes. These codes should always be followed to the letter.

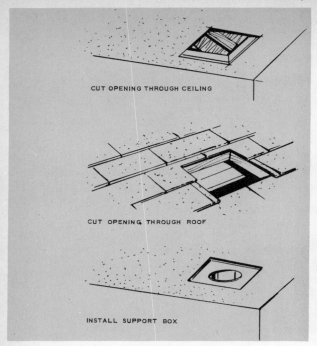

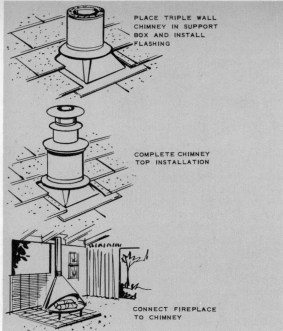

Figure 7—26. Steps in installing a prefabricated chimney.

interior closet. A space approximately 19 inches square is required to do this. In fact, fireplaces on two floors, one directly above the other, are becoming increasing popular. It is only a little more work to put in two fireplaces instead of one, and both can share the same chimney housing. But, if you plan to use an existing chimney flue, be certain that it is not serving any other major appliance. Most flues are not capable of handling the products of combustion of two appliances. If the flue is overloaded, there is a good chance that one appliance may interfere with the draft for the other, and the result is usually smoking difficulties.

The installation of a prefabricated chimney for either a freestanding unit or built-in fireplace involves the following steps:

1. Cut an opening through the ceiling for the support box. Try to locate the center of the opening so a joist will not be cut. Cut out the opening as directed by the manufacturer. Then install headers between the joists for extra support.

2. Install the chimney support box. Place the metal support box up through the opening until the bottom is against the ceiling. Excess metal above the joists may be cut off. With the box of collar in position, nail it securely to the joists. If the chimney goes through an upstairs room in a corner or along a wall, it should be covered with a partition. This will help avoid personal injury as well as protect the chimney. Be sure to keep at least a 1-inch space

between the chimney and the partition.

3. Cut an opening through the roof. Locate the center of the opening to avoid cutting a rafter or beam. If this cannot be avoided, even by using an elbow, headers must be placed between remaining rafters or beams to help support the roof members. Make the cut to the size recommended by the manufacturer. Remember that roof openings should be at least 1 inch larger, to keep the 1-inch minimum clearance from the chimney pipe to combustibles. When making a cut, save the shingles for covering the flashing.

4. Run the chimney smokepipe from the fireplace to the roof support box. After the roof support box is in place, the chimney smokepipe or wall pipe can be installed up to the roof. Smokepipe can be cut and shaped as described on page 234. The pipe must be kept 1 inch from combustibles. The support box and the roof flashing act as spacers. Firestop spacers must be used any time you go through another floor.

5. Complete the chimney top installation. Once the chimney or wall pipe has been brought through the roof, the chimney top should be installed as directed by the maker. Keep in mind that the chimney outlet must be at least 3 feet above the roof cutout. It also must be at least 2 feet above the highest point of the roof within 10 feet in a horizontal plane. Flash the chimney unit as directed and then renail the shingles on the top and sides with roofing

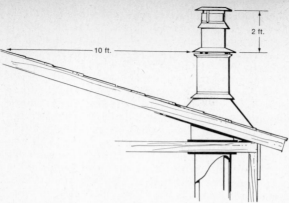

Figure 7–27. The top of the chimney should be at least 3 feet above the roof and at least 2 feet higher than any point of the roof within 10 feet. It is always best to extend the chimney above the peak.

nails. Do not nail through the lower portion of the flashing above the shingles. Chimney hoods are made of aluminum painted a neutral gray or with a simulated-brick finish.

6. Connect the fireplace to the chimney. Align the flue collar of the fireplace with the chimney pipe. The last section of the chimney pipe is installed by using an adapter between it and the fireplace flue pipe.

When a chimney flue is installed through a wall or window to an outside chimney installation, a special tee is used. For best operation, the chimney smokepipe should not run horizontally for a distance exceeding ½ the vertical height of the chimney serving the fireplace. When the pipe goes through an outside wall, the horizontal flue should be pitched at least ¼ inch for every foot of pipe used between the fireplace and the tee. This way you can be assured that the smoke will flow upward and not become trapped in the outlet and cause a smoke problem. Details of the outside installation of a chimney are shown in Figure 7–27. Your heating supplier will help you determine the amount of piping and other items you need for the chimney installation.

Other fireplace items such as fireplace hoods are available in prefabricated form. If you follow the manufacturer's directions for assembling them, they are usually quite easy to install.

AIR CONDITIONING

The precise definition of air conditioning recognized by the American Society of Heating, Refrigerating, and Air Conditioning Engineers is: "The process of treating air so as to control simultaneously its temperature, humidity, cleanliness, and distribution to meet the requirements of the conditioned space."

Many people think of air conditioning as cooling only. Actually, the dehumidification function performed by an air conditioner is equally important, particularly in those areas where summer weather is not only hot but "muggy" and extremely humid, and there are quite a few of these areas in the United States. Air conditioning also filters the air that is circulated through the house, reducing dust, dirt, pollen, smoke, and other air pollutants that might otherwise be present. This air-cleaning function cuts down on the amount of cleaning of the home itself, its draperies and rugs, and even the family's clothing. At the same time, filtration of the air before circulation may be beneficial from the standpoint of health, since people who are subject to asthma, hay fever, and other pulmonary disorders traceable to airborne allergens may obtain relief in an air-conditioned home.

There are two general types of air conditioning systems: (1) central, which accomplishes the four functions of air conditioning throughout the entire house; and (2) room conditioning, which performs its tasks only in the room in which it is placed.

Central air conditioning. Central air conditioning is available in two types of units: "single package" and "split system." A single package unit is one in which all components—compressor, condenser, cooling coil, and all the rest—are contained within one enclosure; a split system, as might be expected, has the cooling coil and sometimes some of the other components separated from the condensing unit (compressor and condenser); the latter is

Figure 7–28. An electric fireplace unit.

247

placed outside the house on a slab so as to exhaust the heat extracted from inside the house. A single-package central system is sometimes installed inside the conditioned space with a duct or other provision for exhausting the heat to the outside.

Many variations of these basic types have been developed within the past fifteen years, so that you have a wide variety of models from which to choose the one combination that is "tailor-made" for your particular home. For instance, if you have a forced warm-air heating system, you may have an air conditioning installation that will utilize the same fan and ductwork used to distribute heat from the furnace in winter. This type of installation may be either a split system or a single package. If the former, only the cooling coils need be installed in the plenum of your furnace (the plenum is the big heat

Figure 7–29. The map shows minimum air changes recommended for an air-cooling system in various regions of the United States: in shaded areas, one change every one and one-half minutes; in other areas, one change every minute.

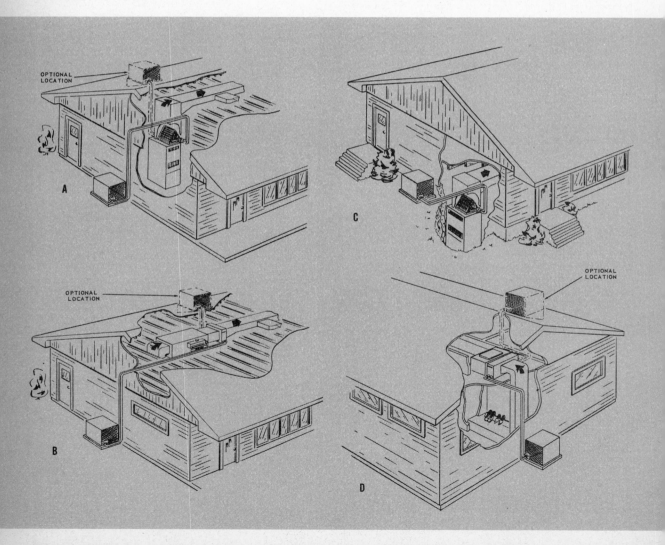

chamber out of which the ducts run to various parts of the house), and the compressor, condensing unit, and other operating parts may be outside. If a single package is used, it may be placed in the basement beside or adjacent to the furnace and "tied in" with the ductwork or plenum through a separate connection duct.

On the other hand, if the home is heated by hydronic or electric heat, or some other form of heat not using ductwork, either a split system or a single package may again be used. Such an installation will require the installation of ductwork, and may be somewhat more expensive than using the heating ducts, but it is feasible. An example of an installation in a home having other-than-warm-air heating is the attic-type installation, in which the cooling coils and blower fan are mounted in the attic

floor to distribute cooled air downward into the rooms through grilles.

Figure 7–30 illustrates several other possible central air conditioning installations. Since each installation is really a "custom" job, it is important

Figure 7–30. Air conditioner applications: (A) Upflow furnace on the ground floor with coil above the furnace. (B) Horizontal furnace in the attic with horizontal coil. (C) Upflow furnace in the basement with coil on top of the furnace. (D) Blower and coil in a closet. The central hall is used for ductwork. (E) Residence with a basement in which the unit passes through the wall. (F) Installation in a house on a slab. The unit passes through the wall, and the central hall is used for ductwork. (G) Distribution system in the attic. (H) Standard system using the present furnace. (1) Independent cooling system, in which the first floor is treated like a one-story house. To cool the second floor, install in the attic a separate blower coil with its own condensing units, distribution system, and ceiling outlets and inlets.

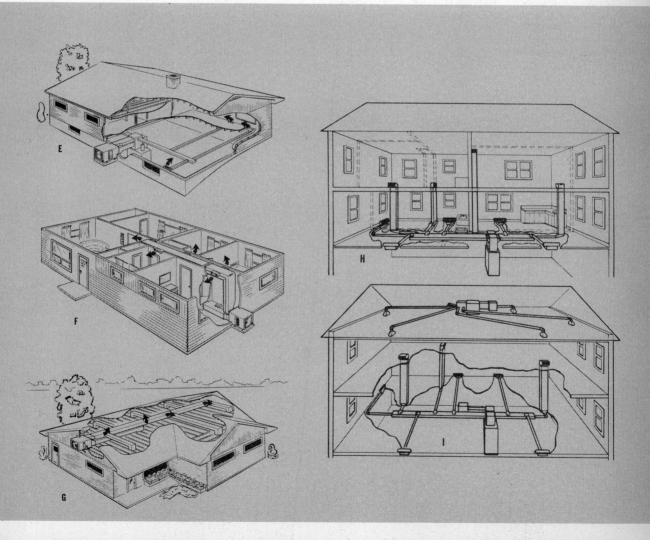

that you consult with an "expert" such as the supplier when planning the system best suited to your needs and purposes even though installing a complete central air conditioning system is no longer the complicated job it used to be, and a few of the new systems include detailed instructions for the home craftsman. Ready-made pipes and ducts just snap together with special fittings and are installed in much the same manner as described on page 230. Also, the once difficult job of charging the system with refrigerant has been eliminated. Precharged flexible tubing is available in the lengths needed to couple the cooling and condensing units, with no need to handle the gas directly. While an air conditioning installation is not too difficult a task, many equipment suppliers insist on professional installations in order for their warranties to be valid.

Local building codes should also be checked. Many stipulate that heating and air conditioning installations must be checked by an inspector before the system can be put into operation, and some require that part or all of the work be done by a licensed contractor. Also, in some localities you may need to apply for a building permit. But, even if the building codes and supplier let you install it, you should seek expert help in planning an air conditioning system. Here are some factors that must be considered in determining the proper layout of your system.

What capacity? In making his survey of your home, the expert will determine how much "heat gain" can be expected in the house under hot weather conditions. This heat gain comes from the sun, from hot and humid outside air, which "seeps" in around windows, doors, and other openings, from the electric lights and other heat-generating appliances in the house, and from the body heat given off by the occupants of the home. He will also check on the thickness and composition of the insulation in the roof and walls, because this has a great bearing on the amount of heat gain.

In arriving at the capacity required, the expert needs to know the area of your home, the type and color of the roof, the number of windows, and the direction in which they face, what sort of landscaping, the size of the family normally expected to occupy the house, and the volume of "traffic" through outside doors during a normal day. When these facts are established, the expert determines, by use of a load estimating form developed by the Air-Conditioning and Refrigeration Institute, or another accepted basis for calculation, that the equipment to be installed should have sufficient "capacity" to remove the heat built up by all the "heat gain" factors. In other words, "capacity" is the ability of a system to remove the heat in the house.

In air conditioning terms, capacity is expressed in British thermal units per hour. That is, the capacity of an air conditioner is said to be the number of these units, abbreviated as Btu's, that it can remove from the conditioned space in one hour.

Electrical requirements. Any air conditioner rated at 8,500 Btu's or more will require 240 volts, a separate fused circuit, and enough amperage for its motors. Your house's wiring may need to be modified to accommodate the electrical requirements of the cooling and condensing units.

Duct and register placement. If your present ductwork is planned for both heating and summer air conditioning, no duct changes are needed. However, most installations that were designed for heating alone do require some modification before they can be used for air conditioning. There are two reasons for this.

1. Satisfactory summer air conditioning requires the movement of a larger volume of air than is needed for heating. Often, the supply- and/or return-air ducts are not large enough to carry this greater volume of air.

2. Warm air rises above cool air. For this reason, a forced-air heating system draws its return air from the colder floor area. An air conditioning system should draw its return air from the warmer ceiling area. In many homes, it would be difficult and costly to install new return ducts at ceiling level. However, satisfactory results can often be obtained with existing furnace ducts by using diffusing-type supply registers that will keep the room air well mixed. This reduces the likelihood of a layer of hot air forming at the ceiling.

Because warm air tends to accumulate on the upper floor of a multi-story home, a distribution system designed only for forced, warm-air heating generally proves to be unsatisfactory for cooling a multi-story house with open stairwells. There are two ways of solving the problem.

1. Single system. This method utilizes the existing system to cool both floors, by adding a new large-capacity return duct from a high wall or ceiling inlet grille on the second floor. This return should be large enough to draw off at least 60 percent of the return air from the second floor. Preferably, this new return should be centrally located, in a hallway or stairwell. In some cases, it can be run up through first- and second-floor closets; otherwise, it can be secured to the wall. The return can then be boxed in, to improve appearance. If such a centrally located return is used, all the second-floor doors must be left open, or you can cut an opening through to the hall above each door. Make such openings 1 inch below the ceiling. Block off the upper part of the stud space in which the opening is located to prevent hot attic air from entering. Use a plain 12-by-6-inch wall grille to cover each side of the opening in the hall and room walls.

2. Independent cooling system. This method treats the first floor like a one-story house. Then, to

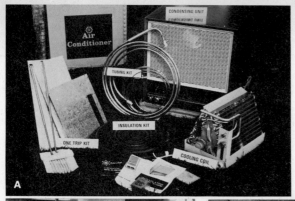

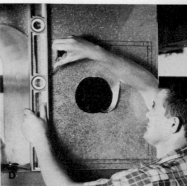

Figure 7–31. Installation steps for a central air conditioning unit: (A) Items needed for the installation. (B) A typical existing forced-air furnace. (C) The plenum hole is cut with tin snips. (D) The location measurements for the cover are marked, and the cover holes are drilled. (E) The plenum hole is finished, and the coil support rods are installed over the duct flanges. (F) A sealing compound is placed around the perimeter of the plenum hole and on the baffles where the coil is to rest. (G) The cooling coil is installed in the furnace plenum. (H) The cover is screwed into place, and refrigerant tubing is run from the condensing unit outside to the cooling coil. (I) The condensate drain trap is connected to the floor drain. (J) The refrigerant tube lines are connected to the condensing unit.

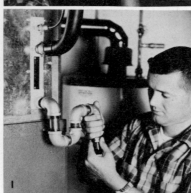

cool the second floor, a separate blower coil is installed in the attic, with its own condensing units, distribution system, and ceiling outlets and inlets.

In homes with hydronic heat or those without a central heating system of any kind, an independent air conditioning system, based on a blower coil, may be installed. Figure 7–30I shows a typical installation. The blower coil, which is in the attic, must have the same sort of auxiliary drain pan described for use with the coil for a horizontal furnace application. Installation of ducts, registers, and grilles is the same as for a conventional furnace system (see page 230). Note that a blower coil system is a "split system," in that it is connected by refrigerant lines to an outside condenser (a coil in a furnace works in much the same way). Vapor-barrier duct insulation is very important here, since all ductwork is exposed to attic air.

Installation of a remote condenser unit must conform to the local code. The maximum distance between the condensing unit and evaporator is governed by the maximum tubing length permitted, which is given in the manufacturer's instruction manual. As a rule, it is a good idea to have the condenser close to the house. If the air stream through the condenser will be parallel to the side of the house, the unit can be located as close as 12 inches; otherwise, a minimum distance of 2 feet between the wall and the air inlet, or 4 feet from the discharge side, should be kept. When planning your air conditioning arrangement, try to position the condenser in a shady spot on the east or north side of the house. Always try to locate the unit away from bedroom windows, both yours and your neighbors', so its noise will not be offensive.

Most central cooling systems come with all necessary controls, and they are made operative according to the installation manual. When locating the thermostat, place it in the most important room in your house, usually the living room, on an inside wall, away from any direct sunlight or sources of indoor heat like television sets and radios. In addition, keep it away from furniture that might reduce air circulation around it.

Room air conditioners. Room air conditioners produce and circulate conditioned air within the room in which they are located. They can be placed on a window sill or in a wall. The latter type fits into a through-wall sleeve that is built into the wall. Most window models are made for the double-hung window up to 40 inches wide, although accessory kits are available for windows up to 60 inches wide. Other models are made for casement windows, and a few for awning-type windows.

The cooling capacity of room air conditioners ranges from about 4,000 to more than 30,000 Btu's. If you give your dealer adequate information, he will be able to calculate the capacity needed to obtain the proper size. The National Better Business

Bureau, in a pamphlet on room air conditioners prepared in cooperation with the National Electrical Manufacturers Association, suggests taking the following steps before contacting the dealer:

1. Draw a simple rough floor plan of your house or apartment. Indicate which direction is north. Measure the length and width of the rooms and indicate these on the plan. In heavier pencil show the living zone or sleeping zone (or if it is just a room) that you wish to air-condition. Show where doors or archways are located. Also show the size and locations of windows. Glancing at this plan, the dealer can see the relationship of the conditioned zone to the rest of the house. He can also advise you where the air conditioner should be placed in order to deliver the best patterns of air circulation.

2. Also, be prepared to answer the following questions: (a) is the roof or is the ceiling above the conditioned area insulated? (b) What is the approximate height of the ceilings? (c) How many people are in the family? (d) Are there any doors continuously open, or archways between the areas?

When you select a room air conditioner, the following are a few features to look for: (a) a thermostat, which limits wide fluctuations in temperature; (b) a built-in overload device that shuts off the compressor to avoid overheating of the motor windings; (c) a condensation disposal arrangement to get rid of the water removed from the air; and (d) a fresh air outlet, which provides for ventilation with or without cooling and exhausting of odors and stuffiness. There are three basic types of filters used

Figure 7–32. A room air conditioner may be installed in a window *(left)* or an outside wall *(right)*.

in air conditioners: metal mesh and plastic filters (which can be cleaned and reused) and fiberglass filters (which must be replaced from time to time). Always remember, a clogged filter greatly reduces cooling capacity, an unnecessary loss of comfort control when you consider the ease with which it can be maintained or replaced.

Installation of a room air conditioner.

In locating a room air conditioner, try to place it as far from the door as possible to prevent drafts and cross-ventilation from interfering with its cool air. Make sure there are no obstructions in front of the air conditioner, such as drapes or furniture pieces. Position the vents to point upward so that the cool air drifts back to the floor. Doors and windows should be weather-stripped to prevent cool-air loss. When too much outside air enters through cracks and openings, the unit will have to work harder to remove the excess heat and humidity from the room.

The actual installation of a window-type unit will depend on how it is to be held in the window. The manufacturer's instructions are usually explicit on how this should be accomplished. While manufacturers' instructions vary slightly, they all follow a basic procedure.

The first step is to take the metal outer case apart and slide out the cooling unit. Fit the metal case into the window opening and fasten it to the sill with screws. Then lower the sash so as to lock the top of the case in place. Remember to do this, because if you are not careful, you might drop the whole unit on the ground below. To seal the air conditioner into place, measure, then cut and fit the side panels that close off the space between the unit and the sides of the window. It is also a good idea to add weather stripping. Now you are ready to lift the cooling unit into its case. You might need help for this, since the cooling unit is heavy. Then fit the grille and filter trim in place, and you have completed the installation. All you have to do is plug it in or install it into your electrical system.

When an in-the-wall installation is used, the best location is under a window. If a radiator is in the way, you may be able to relocate it away from the window. If that is not possible, locate the conditioner as close to the window as you can. Have the unit low in the wall so it will be less noticeable and the controls more accessible.

The opening in the wall of the house must be wider than the unit's casing to permit framing the opening. Allow at least 2 inches in width for this framing. In a brick or block wall a steel lintel is placed over the opening and its ¼-inch thickness is all the allowance necessary. That is, to set a lintel in an 8-inch brick wall, the outer half of the course of bricks over the opening is removed, as is a half brick to each side. The angled lintel is then set in a mortar bed of 4-inch width at each end, with

the lintel's vertical leg against the other half of this course of brick. The removed brick is then replaced on a mortar bed on the lintel.

In a frame wall, the one stud cut through is cut 4 inches above the opening, and a double 2 × 4, spiked together, is inserted as a lintel across the opening. It extends to adjoining studs at each end and is toenailed to them. The cut stud rests on top of the lintel and is toenailed into it. For a brick veneer wall, insert the doubled 2 × 4 lintel in the frame portion. Additional brick need not be removed. The brick mortar above the opening is removed from both sides to a depth of 4 inches, and the angled lintel is inserted from the inside, the lower leg being pushed into this recess, with the vertical leg pressed against the brick above it. Mortar seals the joint between the brick and lintel.

The actual installation of a unit will vary slightly according to the make. In most cases, slide the inner workings out of the metal box and fit the box into the prepared space. Again, be certain that you bolt down the unit so that it does not drop out. Now rebuild your wall around the unit, and follow the rest of the steps given above for the window unit. Put in the cooling unit, fit the grille, filter, and trim, and the unit is ready for operation once it is plugged in.

Cooling with water. In dry climates, you will find that the most common and effective method of cooling with water is the water-evaporation method, which is satisfactory only when the humidity is low. It is used extensively in hot, dry climates. Figure 7–33 shows the areas of the United States where water-evaporation cooling is satisfactory.

In water-evaporation cooling, water is sprayed on excelsior (or some other good water-absorptive material). A fan then draws air through the excelsior. The water in the excelsior evaporates and cools the air; the cooled air, in turn, cools your home. An air velocity of 150 feet per minute through the excelsior provides maximum cooling. Slightly higher velocities keep the circulated air from becoming saturated.

Figure 7–33. Shaded areas on the map indicate regions where evaporation cooling is effective.

Twenty to 40 house-air changes per hour are necessary. Water-evaporation cooling requires 5 to 10 gallons of water per hour to cool an average-size house.

Installation and operation costs for a water-evaporation cooling unit that is large enough to cool an average-size house will depend on your locality. The installation of a water-evaporation cooling system should be made according to the manufacturer's instructions.

HUMIDITY CONTROL

"It is not the heat, it is the humidity" is a popular way of acknowledging humidity as an important factor in human comfort. Practically everyone knows that excessive humidity makes for discomfort in summer, but relatively few realize that the situation is reversed in winter. During hot weather we are interested in taking moisture out of the air. We almost forget about the need for adding more moisture to the air in our homes during cold weather. As a matter of fact, very few homes have adequate humidity in winter unless they are extremely tight in construction and have an unusually steady source of evaporating moisture. The dryness of most homes is due to the basic physical principle that cold air holds very little moisture, yet the same air when heated can drink up large amounts of moisture.

If there is too little moisture in the air of your home, you may suffer from itchy skin or dry, irritated nasal and throat passages. Many medical authorities relate low humidity to increased susceptibility to colds and respiratory infections. Low humidity can also cause woodwork to dry and shrink, furniture joints to loosen, and leather goods and furnishings to become brittle. At humidities under 30 percent, static electricity may cause irritating shocks and room dust may increase. In addition, when the air is too dry, you feel colder because of excess moisture evaporation from your body. As a result, you need a higher room temperature to feel comfortable. Studies show that for a drop of 30 percent in humidity, the room temperature must be raised five degrees to maintain the same body comfort balance as before. Such an increase in your home's indoor temperature could result in a 10 to 15 percent increase in your fuel bill. Heating costs usually increase 2 to 3 percent for each degree the room temperature is raised above seventy degrees. In addition, a dry house often shrinks. This tends to open cracks around the doors and windows of your home, allowing even more heat loss.

Over the years many types of simple evaporative humidifiers have been developed. Most are helpful in relieving air dryness but do not have the capacity for complete control. One common type of air circulating system uses an evaporating pan inside the furnace unit. Another type uses a series of absorbent plates. The lower surfaces of the plates are immersed in a water pan. The upper surfaces are exposed to the circulating air stream inside the furnace. The pan is kept filled with water through the operation of an automatic valve. For improved accuracy of control the valve can be operated by a humidity control.

For hydronic systems, water pans are hung on the sides of the radiators, or evaporating plate humidifiers can be concealed within hot-water convectors. The heat from the radiator or convector and the circulating air causes the water to evaporate. Another way of adding humidity is through use of power humidifiers.

Power humidifiers. Power humidifiers provide a new opportunity for accuracy in home humidity control, both for hydronic heating and for warm-air systems. Whereas most other humidifiers tend to be only partially effective in meeting extreme conditions, today's power humidifiers can offer the full capacity to add moisture to the air as needed. In addition, power humidifiers have the advantage of quick response to control. However, because of their large capacity, power humidifiers must be accurately controlled to meet changing needs without over-humidifying.

While there are many types of power humidifiers available, they all work on one of the following three basic principles: (1) evaporator types rely on the fact that warm air moving over water can pick up moisture by simple evaporation; (2) atomizer types mechanically break up water into fine particles that surrounding air can readily absorb; and (3) vaporizer types heat water to the temperature at which it changes to vapor. For home applications, the first two types are the most popular.

The most efficient evaporative type employs a revolving drum that is covered with a spongy plastic pod. As the drum is driven by a small electric motor, it revolves through a small water reservoir. This reservoir is fed by a 1/4-inch copper tube, which is connected to a float valve. The moisture picked up by the slowly turning drum evaporates from its spongy pad in the moving air that passes through the humidifier.

With the atomizer type of humidifier, a fine water spray is forced into a tiny nozzle or onto a metal disk into the warm-air plenum, and this moisture is then distributed throughout the house. But with this type of unit, water hardness is frequently a problem because the spray or nozzle often becomes clogged with lime scale and requires cleaning.

The installation of either type of humidifier is not a difficult job, just as long as you follow the manufacturer's instructions most carefully.

While both the evaporative and atomizer types are primarily designed for use with forced warm

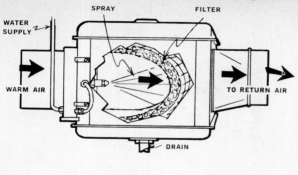

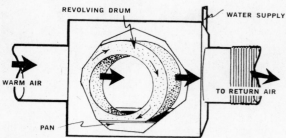

Figure 7–34. Two popular types of power humidifiers.

damage sills, draperies, or furniture. Sometimes the moisture may form inside the walls and freeze as it collects, and later drip out to blister or stain the outside paint. Such damage can be very costly to you over the years.

There are many types and sizes of power dehumidifiers available. Most are simply small refrigeration units that remove the moisture by chilling the air temporarily as it passes through the unit. Most models allow you a choice of a pan (which requires emptying) to catch the water, or a drain connection to carry the condensed water away.

Most dehumidifiers include a built-in automatic control. Those that do not can be provided with a plug-in control. Automatic control gives you the advantage of starting your unit automatically before humidity conditions get out of control. In addition, it automatically shuts down the unit to save power costs and wear when operation is no longer required.

Another cure for too much moisture is ventilation, insulation, heat control, or any combination of these—all of which are discussed in detail later in this chapter. The best solution to both the problem of too little and too much moisture is a year-round air conditioning system.

air, power humidifiers of these types are available that operate independent of any heating source. Many of these are placed in wood cabinets and can be used in your living or dining room without being conspicuous. They have reservoirs that are filled every day or can be connected to a water supply. Some are even controlled by an automatic humidistat, a device that senses the relative humidity the way a thermostat senses temperature.

Humidifiers are rated according to their water output. A house with about 16,000 cubic feet of space, an average of 7 to 8 rooms, needs a unit that provides approximately a half-gallon per hour to maintain a relative humidity of about 40 percent at 72 degrees, a desirable level. (Relative humidity is the percentage of moisture in the air at a certain temperature compared to the total amount the air can absorb at the same temperature.) A larger house with a 30,000 cubic-foot area, 10 to 14 rooms, would require a unit with an output of 1 gallon per hour. When you buy a humidifier, the dealer should be told the cubic footage or number of rooms.

Power dehumidifier. If there is too much moisture in the air, as often occurs in summer, it reduces the evaporation rate of your body so you feel hot and sticky, clothing gets damp and wrinkled, woodwork swells and drawers stick, and mold and mildew may form. In cold weather, if the indoor humidity is too high, moisture collects on windows and walls, and it may drip down and stain and

THERMAL INSULATION

The secret of a comfortable home is, of course, insulation. Most materials used in home construction have some insulating value. Even air spaces between studs resist the passage of heat. However, when these stud spaces are filled or partially filled with a material high in resistance to heat transmission, namely thermal insulation, the stud space has many times the insulating value of the air alone.

The inflow of heat through outside walls and roofs in hot weather or its outflow during cold weather have important effects upon (a) the comfort of the occupants of your home and (b) the cost of providing either heating or cooling to maintain temperatures at acceptable limits for occupancy. During cold weather, high resistance to heat flow also means a saving in fuel. While the wood in the walls provides good insulation, commercial insulating materials are usually incorporated into exposed walls, ceilings, and floors to increase the resistance to heat passage. The use of insulation in warmer climates is justified with air conditioning, not only because of reduced operating costs, but also because units of smaller capacity are required. Thus, whether from the standpoint of thermal insulation alone in cold climates or whether for the benefit of reducing your cooling costs, the use of 2 inches or more of insulation in the walls can certainly be justified.

Insulating materials. Commercial insulation is manufactured in a variety of forms and types, each

Figure 7—35. *(left)* Roll blanket insulation can be stapled in place. *(right)* Loose-fill or vermiculite insulation can be poured directly from the bag.

with advantages for specific uses. Materials commonly used for insulation may be grouped in the following general classes: (1) flexible insulation (blanket and batt); (2) loose-fill insulation; (3) reflective insulation; (4) rigid insulation (structural and nonstructural); and (5) miscellaneous types.

Flexible insulation. Flexible insulation is manufactured in two types, *blanket* and *batt*. Blanket insulation is furnished in rolls from 40 to 100 feet in length and in widths suited to 16- and 24-inch stud and joist spacing. Usual thicknesses range from 1 to 7 inches. The body of the blanket is made of felted mats of mineral or vegetable fibers, such as rock or glass wool, wood fiber, and cotton. Organic insulations are treated to make them resistant to fire, decay, insects, and vermin. Most blanket insulation is covered with paper or other sheet material with tabs on the sides for fastening to studs or joists. One covering sheet serves as a vapor barrier to resist movement of water vapor and should always face the warm side of the wall. Aluminum foil or asphalt or plastic-laminated paper are commonly used as barrier materials.

Batt insulation is also made of fibrous material preformed to thicknesses of 2 to 6 inches for 16- and 24-inch joist spacing. It is supplied with or without a vapor barrier. One friction type of fibrous glass batt is supplied without a covering and is designed to remain in place without the normal fastening methods.

Loose-fill insulation. This type of insulation is usually composed of materials used in bulk form, supplied in bags or bales, and placed by pouring, blowing, or packing by hand. This includes rock or glass wool, wood fibers, shredded redwood bark, cork, wood pulp products, vermiculite, sawdust,

and shavings. A 3-cubic-foot bag (the average size) will fill these volumes:

Thickness (inches)	2	3	3⅝	4	5	5⅝
Square feet	20	13	11½	10	8	6½

Fill insulation is suited for use between first-floor ceiling joists in unheated attics. It is also used in sidewalls of existing houses that were not insulated during construction. Where no vapor barrier was installed during construction, suitable paint coatings, as described later in this chapter, should be used for vapor barriers when blown insulation is added to an existing house.

Reflective insulation. Most materials reflect some radiant heat, and some materials have this property to a very high degree. Materials high in reflective properties include aluminum foil, sheet metal with tin coating, and paper products coated with a reflective oxide composition. Such materials can be used in enclosed stud places, in attics, and in similar locations to retard heat transfer by radiation. These reflective insulations are effective only when used where the reflective surface faces an air space at least ¾ inch or more deep. Where a reflective surface contacts another material, the reflective properties are lost and the material has little or no insulating value. That is, reflective insulation without filler material must always be placed so there is a dead air space on both sides.

Reflective insulations are equally effective regardless of whether the reflective surface faces the warm or cold side. However, there is a decided difference in the equivalent conductance and the resistance to heat flow. The difference depends on (a) the orientation of the reflecting material and the dead air space, (b) the direction of heat flow (horizontal, up, or down), and (c) the mean summer or winter temperatures. Each possibility requires separate consideration. However, reflective insulation is perhaps more effective in preventing summer heat flow through ceilings and walls. It should likely be considered more for use in the southern portion of the United States than in the northern portion.

Reflective insulation of the foil type is sometimes applied to blankets and to the stud-surface side of gypsum lath. Metal foil suitably mounted on some supporting base makes an excellent vapor barrier.

Rigid insulation. Rigid insulation is usually a fiberboard material manufactured in sheet and other forms. However, rigid insulations are also made from such materials as inorganic fiber and glass fiber, though not commonly used in a house in this form. The most common types are made from processed wood, sugarcane, or other vegetable products. Structural insulating boards, in densities ranging from 15 to 31 pounds per cubic foot, are fabricated in such forms as building boards, roof decking, sheathing, and wallboard. While they have moderately good insulating properties, their primary purpose is structural.

Roof insulation is nonstructural and serves mainly to provide thermal resistance to heat flow in roofs. It is called "slab" or "block" insulation and is manufactured in rigid units ½ inch to 3 inches thick and usually 2 by 4 feet in size.

In home remodeling, perhaps the most common forms of rigid insulation are sheathing and decorative coverings in sheets, planks, panels, or in tile squares. Sheathing board is made in thicknesses of ½ and ²⁵/₃₂ inch. It is coated or impregnated with an asphalt compound to provide water resistance. Sheets are made in 2-by-8-foot size for horizontal application and 4-by-8-foot or longer for vertical application. The surface may be smooth or textured, and even prefinished.

Miscellaneous insulation. Some insulations do not fit in the classifications previously described, such as insulation blankets made up of multiple layers of corrugated paper. Other types, such as lightweight vermiculite and perlite aggregates, are sometimes used in plaster as a means of reducing heat transmission. Other materials are foamed-in-place insulations, which include sprayed and plastic foam types. Sprayed insulation is usually inorganic fibrous material blown against a clean surface that has been primed with an adhesive coating. It is often left exposed for acoustical as well as insulating properties.

Expanded *polystyrene* and *urethane* plastic foams may be molded or foamed in place. This usually must be done with spray equipment by a professional. The big advantage of foamed-in-place plastic is that it goes in over piping, wiring, and similar items. While doing this, it not only hides these features but also solidifies into a mass that seals and reinforces them, in addition to serving its prime purpose. For electric heating, standard urethane foam thicknesses have been set at 2 inches in floors, 1¼ inches in walls, and 2½ inches in ceilings.

Plastic foam insulation is also available in board foam, in ½ inch to 2 inches in thicknesses. The foamed boards of both polystyrene and urethane can be sawed to shape and generally worked like plywood. Although foamed boards cost more than either batts or blankets for the same insulating value, they are most effective in use on some areas such as masonry walls when making a basement livable or in converting a concrete block garage to living quarters.

The data given in Table 7–2 will provide some comparison of the insulating value of the various materials. These are expressed as *k* values or heat conductivity, and are defined as the amount of heat, in British thermal units, that will pass in 1 hour through 1 square foot of material 1 inch thick per 1 degree F temperature difference between faces of the material. Simply expressed, *k* represents heat loss; the lower this numerical value, the better the insulating qualities.

Table 7–2. *Thermal conductivity values of some insulating materials*

Insulation group		*k* range (conductivity)
General	Specific type	
Flexible		0.25–0.27
Fill	Standard materials	.28– .30
	Vermiculite	.45– .48
Reflective (two sides)		(a)
Rigid	Insulating fiberboard	.35– .36
	Sheathing fiberboard	.42– .55
Foam	Polystyrene	.25– .29
	Urethane	.15– .17
Wood	Low density	.60– .65

ªInsulating value = slightly more than 1 inch of flexible insulation (resistance, $R = 4.3$).

Insulation is also rated on its resistance or *R* value, which is merely another expression of its insulating value. The *R* value is usually expressed as the total resistance of the wall or of a thick insulating blanket or batt, whereas *k* is the rating per inch of thickness. For example, a *k* value of 1 inch of insulation is 0.25. Then the resistance *R* is ¹/₀.₂₅, or 4.0. If there are 3 inches of this insulation, the total *R* is three times 4.0, or 12.0. By the way, the *R* value or number, by federal law, is now printed on the vapor barrier, bag, or carton of all insulation material. That is, the *R* numbers you see printed on insulation boards, batts, and blankets are for that thickness of insulation. The *R* numbers on bags of loose-fill insulation are per inch of installed thick-

Figure 7–36. Locations that should be insulated.

ness. The higher the *R* number, the more the insulation value. Two different types of insulation with the same *R* number have equal insulating value. Sometimes the *R* number depends on whether the insulation is used in a wall, floor, or ceiling. Then several *R* numbers will appear on the material. For example, a 4-inch flexible insulation may read: ceilings, R-12; walls R-14; and floors R-16. Incidentally the insulation values recommended for *full* insulation in cold climates are: ceiling R-19, walls R-11, and floors R-13. In terms of fiberglass flexible insulation in cold climates are: ceiling R-19, walls ings, 3 inches in walls, and 4 inches between floor joists in unheated spaces.

The *U* value is the overall heat-loss value of all materials in the wall. The lower this value, the better the insulating value. Specific insulating values for various materials are also available. For comparison with the table of thermal conductivity values given earlier, the *U* value of window glass is as follows:

Glass	U value
Single	1.13
Double	
Insulated, with ¼-inch air space	.61
Storm sash over single glazed window	.53

Where to insulate. To reduce heat loss from the house during cold weather in most climates, all walls, ceilings, roofs, and floors that separate heated from unheated spaces should be insulated. Insulation should be placed on all outside walls and in the ceiling. In houses involving unheated crawl spaces, it should be placed between the floor joists or around the wall perimeter. If a flexible type of insulation (blanket or batt) is used, it should be well supported between joists by slats and a galvanized wire mesh, or by a rigid board with the vapor barrier installed toward the subflooring. Press-fit or friction insulations fit tightly between joists and require only a small amount of support to hold

them in place. Reflective insulation is often used for crawl spaces, but only one dead-air space should be assumed in calculating heat loss when the crawl space is ventilated. A ground cover of roll roofing or plastic film such as polyethylene should be placed on the soil of crawl spaces to decrease the moisture content of the space as well as of the wood members.

In 1½-story houses, insulation should be placed along all walls, floors, and ceilings that are adjacent to unheated areas. These include stairways, dwarf (knee) walls, and dormers. Provisions should be made for ventilation of the unheated areas.

Where attic space is unheated and a stairway is included, insulation should be used around the stairway as well as in the first-floor ceiling. The door leading to the attic should be weather-stripped to prevent heat loss. Walls adjoining an unheated garage or porch should also be insulated.

In houses with flat or low-pitched roofs insulation should be used in the ceiling area with sufficient space allowed above for clear unobstructed ventilation between the joists. Insulation should be used along the perimeter of houses built on slabs. A vapor barrier should be included under the slab.

In the summer, outside surfaces exposed to the direct rays of the sun may attain high temperatures and, of course, tend to transfer this heat toward the inside of the house. Insulation in the walls and in attic areas retards the flow of heat and, consequently, less heat is transferred through such areas, resulting in improved summer comfort conditions.

Where air conditioning systems are used, insulation should be placed in all exposed ceilings and walls, as when you are insulating against cold-weather heat loss. The shading of glass against the direct rays of the sun and the use of insulated glass will aid in reducing the air conditioning load.

The best way to insulate the exterior walls in an existing home is to have insulation blown in.

This work should be done by a professional. It takes skilled mechanics to remove sections of siding, drill through sheathing into each stud space, probe walls for any obstacles and know how to overcome them, control the amount of insulation to achieve complete coverage, and replace the siding and seal up the wall so that no signs of the job are visible. In addition, special expensive pneumatic equipment is required to blow in the fibrous or granular fill properly.

While a blown type of installation job is not for the home handyman, there are other ways to insulate the outer walls of a house. For instance, if you are planning a major interior remodeling job, the insulation installation can be combined with the other work. If new paneling is to be installed, fur out the walls using 2 × 2 strips nailed to each of the studs through the existing finishing material. Staple the insulation batts or blankets to the furring and then apply the new wall surface. The 2 inches of insulation, while not as good as the blown job or complete installation, will add comfort to the room and save heating dollars.

The foamed plastic insulation boards mentioned on page 257 may be installed over a sound wall without the use of furring. The foam is glued to the wall with wall paneling adhesive, and then the finish wall is glued to the insulation boards. The foam material requires no added vapor barrier; it is a good one in its own right. The same method of installation may be used on masonry walls, too.

Ventilation of attic and roof spaces is an important adjunct to insulation. Without ventilation, an attic space may become very hot and hold the heat for many hours (see page 267). Obviously, more heat will be transmitted through the ceiling when the attic temperature is 150 degrees F than if it is 100 to 120 degrees F. Ventilation methods suggested for protection against cold-weather condensation apply equally well to protection against excessive hot-weather roof temperatures.

The use of storm windows or insulated glass will greatly reduce heat loss in your home. Almost twice as much heat loss occurs through a single glass as through a window glazed with insulated glass or protected by a storm sash. Furthermore, double glass will normally prevent surface condensation and frost forming on inner glass surfaces in winter. When excessive condensation persists, paint failures or even decay of the sash rail or other parts can occur.

How to install insulation. Blanket insulation or batt insulation with a vapor barrier should be placed between framing members so that the tabs of the barrier lap the edge of the studs as well as the top and bottom plates. This method is not often popular with the contractor because it is more difficult to apply the dry wall or rock lath (plaster base). However, it assures a minimum amount of vapor loss

compared to the loss when tabs are stapled to the sides of the studs. To protect the head and soleplate as well as the headers over openings, it is a good practice to use narrow strips of vapor-barrier material along the top and bottom of the wall. Ordinarily, these areas are not covered too well by the barrier on the blanket or batt. A hand stapler is commonly used to fasten the insulation and the barriers in place.

For insulation without a barrier (press-fit or friction type), a plastic film vapor barrier such as 4-mil polyethylene is commonly used to envelop the entire exposed wall and ceiling. It covers the openings as well as window and door headers and edge studs. This system is one of the best from the standpoint of resistance to vapor movement. Furthermore, it does not have the installation inconveniences encountered when tabs of the insulation are stapled over the edges of the studs. After the dry wall is installed, the film is trimmed around the window and door openings.

Reflective insulation, in a single-sheet form with two reflective surfaces, should be placed to divide the space formed by the framing members into two approximately equal spaces. Some reflective insulations include air spaces and are furnished with nailing tabs. This type is fastened to the studs to provide at least a ¾-inch space on each side of the reflective surfaces.

Fill insulation is commonly used in ceiling areas and is poured or blown into place. A vapor barrier should be used on the warm side (the bottom, in the case of ceiling joists) before the insulation is placed. A leveling board will give a constant insulation thickness. Thick batt insulation is also used in ceiling areas. Batt and fill insulation might also be combined to obtain the desired thickness with the vapor barrier against the back face of the ceiling finish. Ceiling insulation 6 or more inches thick greatly reduces heat loss in the winter and also provides summertime protection.

When adding a slab-type alteration foundation to your home, there are special insulation needs. There should be perimeter insulation all around the outside of the slab. In cold climates this insulation should be carried in for a distance underneath the floor. This keeps the edges of the house slab from being much cooler than the rest of the floor. Of course, if your slab foundation has no perimeter insulation, you can add it by digging down below the frost line around the perimeter of the house and installing 2-inch-thick foam plastic panels. Backfilling holds them in place. Plastic foam is especially good for perimeter insulation because it is unaffected by moisture.

Precautions in insulating. Areas over door and window frames and along side and head jambs also require insulation. Because these areas are filled with small sections of insulation, a vapor barrier must be used around the opening as well as over the header above the openings. Enveloping the entire wall eliminates the need for this type of vapor-barrier installation.

In 1½- and 2-story houses and in basements, the area at the joist header at the outside walls should be insulated and protected with a vapor barrier. Insulation should be placed behind electrical outlet boxes and other utility connections in exposed walls to minimize condensation on cold surfaces.

Floors above unheated crawl spaces are best insulated with batts, blankets, or insulation board. Batts and blankets should be stapled between floor joists with their vapor-barrier side up. To support the insulation, use wooden battens or chicken wire. The easiest way to install insulation board is to cut it slightly wider than the space between the joists and then press it in by hand. It also can be put in by resting the insulation on ledger strips nailed to the sides of the floor joists. But unless closed-cell foam plastic insulation board is employed, a continuous vapor barrier should be placed on top of the board by laying down a sheet of plastic under the floor boards.

Vapor barriers. Most building materials are permeable to water vapor. This presents problems because considerable water vapor is generated in a house from cooking, dishwashing, laundering, bathing, humidifiers, and other sources. In cold climates during cold weather, this vapor may pass through wall and ceiling materials and condense in the wall or attic space; subsequently, in severe cases, it may damage the exterior paint and interior finish, or even result in decay in structural members. For protection, a material highly resistive to vapor transmission, called a *vapor barrier,* should be used on the warm side of a wall or below the insulation in an attic space.

Among the effective vapor-barrier materials are asphalt-laminated papers, aluminum foil, and plastic films. Most blanket and batt insulations are provided with a vapor barrier on one side, some of them with paper-backed aluminum foil. Foil-backed gypsum lath or gypsum boards are also available and serve as excellent vapor barriers. Some types of flexible blanket and batt insulations have a barrier material on one side. Such flexible insulations should be attached with the tabs at their sides fastened on the inside (narrow) edges of the studs, and the blanket should be cut long enough so that the cover sheet can lap over the face of the sole-plate at the bottom and over the plate at the top of the stud space. However, such a method of attachment is not the common practice of most installers. When a positive seal is desired, wall-height rolls of plastic-film vapor barriers should be applied over studs, plates, and window and door headers. This system, called "enveloping," is used over insula-tion having no vapor barrier or to insure excellent protection when used over any type of insulation. The barrier should be fitted tightly around the outlet boxes and sealed if necessary. A ribbon of sealing compound around an outlet or switch box will minimize vapor loss at this area. Cold-air returns in outside walls should consist of metal ducts to prevent vapor loss and subsequent paint problems.

Paint coatings on plaster may be very effective as vapor barriers if materials are properly chosen and applied. They do not, however, offer protection during the period of construction, and moisture may cause paint blisters on exterior paint before the interior paint can be applied. This is most likely to happen in buildings that are constructed during periods when outdoor temperatures are 25 degrees F or more below inside temperatures. Paint coatings cannot be considered a substitute for the membrane types of vapor barriers, but they do provide some protection for houses where other types of vapor barriers were not installed during construction.

Of the various types of paint, one coat of aluminum primer followed by two decorative coats of flat wall or lead and oil paint is quite effective. For rough plaster or for buildings in very cold climates, two coats of the aluminum primer may be necessary. A primer and sealer of the pigmented type, followed by decorative finish coats or two coats of rubber-base paint, are also effective in retarding vapor transmission.

Because no type of vapor barrier can be considered 100 percent resistive, and some vapor leakage into the wall may be expected, the flow of vapor to the outside should not be impeded by materials of relatively high vapor resistance on the cold side of the vapor barrier. For example, sheathing paper should be of a type that is waterproof but not highly vapor resistant. This also applies to "permanent" outer coverings or siding. In such cases, the vapor barrier should have an equally low perm value. This will reduce the danger of condensation on cold surfaces within the wall.

SOUND INSULATION

Development of the quiet home or the need for incorporating sound insulation in a remodeled home is becoming more and more important. In the past, the reduction of sound transfer between rooms was more important in apartments, motels, and hotels than in private homes. However, home designs now often incorporate a family room or "active" living room as well as a "quiet" living room. It is usually desirable in such designs to isolate these rooms from the remainder of your home. Sound insulation between the bedroom area and the living area is usually desirable, as is isolation of the bathrooms and lavatories. Isolation from outdoor sounds is also often advisable. Thus, sound control has become a vital part of home design, construction, and remodeling, and will be even more important in the coming years.

In older homes, the two best ways to sound-insulate a room are to apply acoustic tiles to the walls and ceiling and to fill the spaces between studs in the walls and the joists in the ceiling or floor with insulation. Acoustic tile is a porous substance (see page 56) that absorbs much of the sound striking it instead of allowing it to pass on through the wall or ceiling. The insulation in the walls, ceiling, or floor also helps to prevent the passage of sound from one room to another. These two treatments choke off most of the airborne sound.

Part of the sound, however, travels through the structure itself and not through the air. It is carried through the wood studs from one wall surface to another, or through the joists from a floor to a ceiling. For efficient soundproofing of new rooms in your home, additional barriers can be installed at every joist or stud. This is a somewhat more expensive construction, but is essential for maximum efficiency.

One sound-insulating method is to stagger the wall studs (and then weave insulating blanket between them). A second method is shown in Figure 7–37. As you can see, the insulating blanket is nailed into place on the studs with furring strips and the lath is nailed to these strips. For floors, similar methods can be employed. The method shown at the upper left of the figure makes use of furring strips that hold the insulating blanket to the underside of the joists and also serves as a nailing base for the ceiling lath of the room below. At the lower right, a staggered joist construction is shown.

The best way to reduce the noise coming up from a room below is to install a suspended ceiling in the room below (see Chapter 3). Another way, as just described, is to install an insulating pad in the floor cavity. Carpeting on the floor will also reduce sound transfer, but it is not as effective as the other two methods. Heavy draperies and upholstered furniture will absorb sound, too.

Ordinary doors represent a fairly good sound barrier, but sound does pass through the wood panels and around the door edges. The door edges can be sealed by installing regular insulating strips around them. Covering the door with plywood sheets will greatly reduce sound travel through it. Insulating board, cut to fit into the panel recesses, will also serve effectively. There are special soundproof doors available, which are made of several layers of insulating material held between the door panels. Outside noises can be kept to a minimum by keeping storm windows closed and making sure that any gaps around them are tightly sealed and caulked.

Kitchen appliances such as dishwashers, com-

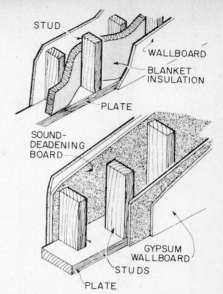

Figure 7–37. How to sound-insulate a wall.

pactors, and garbage disposals, or other vibrating appliances, should be installed with flexible connectors. For instance, V-shaped loops should be employed to connect appliances like clothes washers and dishwashers to the wall. This will greatly reduce the transmission of vibrations from the appliance to the wall, which can in turn transmit the vibrations throughout the house. Setting the appliances on a rubber mat will also absorb vibrations and noise.

When installing any new plumbing work, remember to keep the number of bends to a minimum and use the proper size pipes (see page 185). This will reduce high-pressure water noise and will increase the water pressure.

VENTILATION

Condensation of moisture vapor may occur in attic spaces and under flat roofs during cold weather. Even where vapor barriers are used, some vapor will probably work into these spaces around pipes and other inadequately protected areas, and some through the vapor barrier itself. Although the amount might be unimportant if equally distributed, it may be sufficiently concentrated in some cold spot to cause damage. While wood shingle and wood shake roofs do not resist vapor movement, asphalt shingle roofs and built-up roofs, for example, are highly resistant. The most practical method of removing the moisture is by adequately ventilating the roof spaces.

A warm attic that is inadequately ventilated

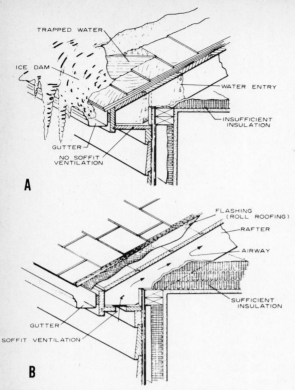

Figure 7–38. Snow and ice dams: (A) Ice dams often build up on the overhangs of roofs and in gutters, causing melting snow water to back up under shingles and under the fascia boards of closed cornices. As a result ceilings inside and paint outside are damaged. (B) Eave protection for snow and ice dams: Lay smooth-surface 45-pound roll roofing on roof sheathing over the eaves extending upward well above the inside line of the wall.

and insulated may cause formation of *ice dams* at the cornice. During cold weather after a heavy snowfall, heat causes the snow next to the roof to melt. Water running down the roof freezes on the colder surface of the cornice, often forming an ice dam at the gutter which may cause water to back up at the eaves and into the wall and ceiling. Similar dams often form in roof valleys. Ventilation thus provides part of the answer to the problems. With a well-insulated ceiling and adequate ventilation, attic temperatures are low and melting of snow over the attic space will be greatly reduced.

In hot weather, ventilation of attic and roof spaces offers an effective means of removing hot air and thereby materially lowering the temperature in these spaces. Insulation should be used between ceiling joists below the attic or roof space to further retard heat flow into the rooms below and improve comfort conditions.

It is common practice to install louvered openings in the end walls of gable roofs for ventilation.

Air movement through such openings depends primarily on wind direction and velocity, and no appreciable movement can be expected when there is no wind or unless one or more openings face the wind. More positive air movement can be obtained by providing openings in the soffit areas of the roof overhang in addition to openings at the gable ends or ridge. Hip-roof houses are best ventilated by inlet ventilators in the soffit area and by outlet ventilators along the ridge. The differences in temperature between the attic and the outside will then create an air movement independent of the wind, and also a more positive movement when there is wind.

Where there is a crawl space under the house or porch, ventilation is necessary to remove moisture vapor rising from the soil. Such vapor may otherwise condense on the wood below the floor and facilitate decay. A permanent vapor barrier on the soil of the crawl space greatly reduces the amount of ventilating area required.

Tight construction (including storm windows and storm doors) and the use of humidifiers have created potential moisture problems that must be resolved through planning of adequate ventilation as well as the proper use of vapor barriers. Blocking of ventilating areas, for example, must be avoided, as such practices will prevent ventilation of attic spaces. Inadequate ventilation will often lead to moisture problems that can result in unnecessary costs to correct.

Area of ventilators. Types of ventilators and minimum recommended sizes have been generally established for various types of roofs. The minimum net area for attic or roof-space ventilators is based on the projected ceiling area of the rooms below. The ratio of ventilator openings are net areas, and the actual area must be increased to allow for any restrictions such as louvers and wire cloth or screen. The screen area should be double the specified net area shown in Figure 7–39 of the various roof types.

To obtain an extra area of screen without adding to the area of the vent, use a frame of the required size to hold the screen away from the ventilator opening. Use as coarse a screen as conditions permit, not smaller than No. 16, for lint and dirt tend to clog fine-mesh screens. Screens should be installed in such a way that paint brushes will not easily contact the screen and close the mesh with paint.

Gable roofs. Louvered openings are generally provided in the end walls of gable roofs and should be as close to the ridge as possible. The net area for the openings should be 1/300 of the ceiling area. For example, where the ceiling area equals 1,200 square feet, the minimum total net area of the ventilators should be 4 square feet.

As previously explained, more positive air movement can be obtained if additional openings

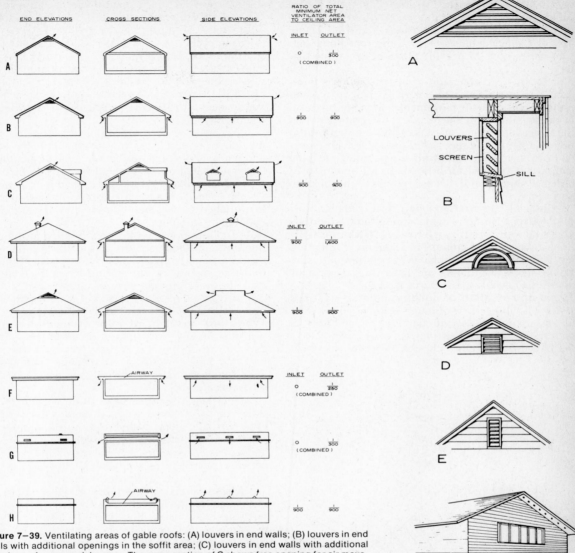

Figure 7–39. Ventilating areas of gable roofs: (A) louvers in end walls; (B) louvers in end walls with additional openings in the soffit area; (C) louvers in end walls with additional openings of eaves and dormers. The cross section of C shows free opening for air movement between the roof boards and the ceiling insulation of the attic room. Ventilating areas of hip roofs: (D) inlet openings beneath the eaves and outlet vent near the peaks; (E) inlet openings beneath the eaves and ridge outlets. Ventilating area of flat roofs: (F) ventilator openings under overhanging eaves where the ceiling and roof joists are combined; (G) openings for a roof with a parapet where roof and ceilings are separate; (H) openings for a roof with a parapet where roof and ceiling joists are combined.

Figure 7–40. Outlet ventilators: (A) triangular; (B) typical cross section; (C) half circle; (D) square; (E) vertical; (F) soffit.

are provided in the soffit area. The minimum ventilation areas for this method are shown in Figure 7–39A, B, and C. Where there are rooms in the attic with sloping ceilings under the roof, the insulation should follow the roof slope and be so placed that there is a free opening of at least 1½ inches between the roof boards and insulation for air movement.

Hip roofs. Hip roofs should have air-inlet openings in the soffit area of the eaves and outlet openings at or near the peak. For the minimum net areas of openings, see Figure 7–39D and E. The most efficient type of inlet opening is the continuous slot, which should provide a free opening of not less than ¾-inch. The air-outlet opening near the peak can be a globe-type metal ventilator or several smaller roof ventilators located near the ridge. They can be located below the peak on the rear slope of the roof so that they will not be visible from the front of the house. Gabled extensions of a hip-roof house are sometimes used to provide efficient outlet ventilators.

Flat roofs. A greater ratio of ventilating area is required in some types of flat roofs than in pitched roofs because the air movement is less positive and is dependent upon the wind. It is important that there be a clear open space above the ceiling insulation and below the roof sheathing for free air movement from inlet to outlet openings. Solid blocking should not be used for bridging or for bracing over bearing partitions if its use prevents the circulation of air.

Perhaps the most common type of flat or low-pitched roof is one in which the rafters extend beyond the wall, forming an overhang. When soffits are used, this area can contain the combined inlet-outlet ventilators, preferably in a continuous slot. When single ventilators are used, they should be distributed evenly along the overhang.

Types and location of outlet ventilators. Various styles of gable-end ventilators are available ready for installation. Many are made with metal louvers and frames, while others may be made of wood to fit the house design more closely. However, the most important factors are to have sufficient net ventilating area and to locate ventilators as close to the ridge as possible without affecting the appearance of the house.

One of the types of ventilators commonly used fits the slope of the roof and is located near the ridge. It can be made of wood or metal; in metal it is often adjustable to conform to the roof slope. A wood ventilator of this type is enclosed in a frame and placed in the rough opening much as a window frame.

A system of attic ventilation that can be used on houses with a wide roof overhang at the gable end consists of a series of small vents or a continuous slot located on the underside of the soffit areas. Several large openings located near the ridge might also be used. This system is especially desirable on low-pitched roofs where standard wall ventilators may not be suitable.

It is important that the roof framing at the wall line does not block off ventilation areas to the attic area. This can be avoided by the use of a "ladder" frame extension. A flat nailing block used at the wall line will provide airways into the attic. This can also be adapted to narrower rake sections by providing ventilating areas to the attic.

Types and location of inlet ventilators. Small, well-distributed ventilators or a continuous slot in the soffit can provide inlet ventilation. These small louvered and screened vents can be obtained in most lumberyards or hardware stores and are simple to install.

Only small sections need to be cut out of the soffit; these can be sawed out before the soffit is applied. It is more desirable to use a number of smaller well-distributed ventilators than several large ones. Any blocking that might be required between rafters at the wall line should be installed so as to provide an airway into the attic area.

A continuous screened slot, which is often desirable, should be located near the outer edge of the soffit near the fascia. Locating the slot in this area will minimize the chance of snow entering. This type may also be used on the extensions of flat roofs.

Crawl-space ventilation and soil. The crawl space below the floor of a basementless home or room addition and under porches should be ventilated and protected from ground moisture by the use of a soil cover. This includes such barrier materials as plastic films, roll roofing, and asphalt-laminated paper. Such protection will minimize the effect of ground moisture on the wood framing members. High moisture content and humidity encourage staining and decay of untreated members.

Where there is a partial basement open to a crawl-space area, no wall vents are required if there is some type of operable window. The use of a soil cover in the crawl space is still important, however. For crawl spaces with no basement area, provide at

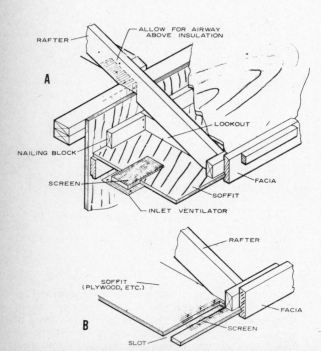

Figure 7–41. Inlet ventilators: (A) small inlet ventilator; (B) slot ventilator.

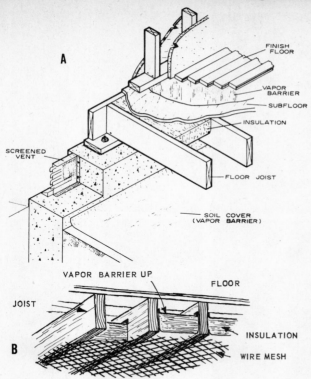

Figure 7–42. (A) Crawl-space ventilator and soil cover; (B) method of holding insulation under floorboards.

least four foundation-wall vents near the corners of the building. The total free (net) area of the ventilators should be equal to $1/160$ of the ground area when no soil cover is used. Thus, for a ground area of 1,200 square feet, a total net ventilating area of about 8 square feet is required, or 2 square feet for each of four ventilators. The use of a larger number of smaller ventilators having the same net ratio is also satisfactory.

When a vapor-barrier ground cover is used, the required ventilating area is greatly reduced. The net ventilating area required with a ground cover is $1/1600$ of the ground area or, for the 1,200-square-foot house, an area of 0.75 square foot. This should be divided between two small ventilators located on opposite sides of the crawl space. Vents should be covered with a corrosion-resistant screen of No. 8 mesh.

The use of a ground cover is normally recommended under all conditions. It not only protects wood framing members from ground moisture, but also allows the use of small, inconspicuous ventilators.

Exhaust fans. One of the best ways to remove air contaminators such as odors, moisture, smoke, and excess heat is with an exhaust fan. This is especially true in kitchens, bathrooms, basements, utility rooms, and recreation rooms.

An exhaust fan, to be efficient, should be placed in relation to the work it has to do. For example, if you want to remove cooking odors and smoke, a hood-fan directly over your range is most efficient. To take heat and moisture out of your laundry room, place the exhaust fan as near as possible to the washer and dryer. "Make up" air should come from other rooms in the house and sweep through the entire room. In locating your fan, also consider the ductwork that carries contaminated air outside. Actually, because ductwork is concealed in the walls, it is often neglected. Unnecessary elbows should be eliminated during the early planning stage as they drastically reduce the flow of air from the fan. Remember that all ductwork

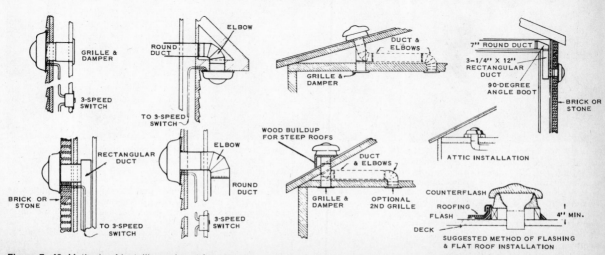

Figure 7–43. Methods of installing exhaust fans.

Figure 7—44. Installation of an exhaust fan: (A) Hood and vent packages, plus accessories, are combined with stock sheet-metal ducts and electrical devices for the job. (B) Holes to accommodate ductwork are made in the cabinet and ceiling. The first length of ductwork is inserted, and the hood is put in place over the range. (C) The ductwork layout determines the vent location. Cut a hole in the roof between rafters for the outside roof cap, then slide accessory roof flashing under the shingles so that it fits over the hole. (D) The duct is assembled in the attic, and a length is pushed up through the roof. This is a two-way duct, venting both the bath and the kitchen. Keep the runs short and insulate the duct in the open attic. (E) Remove the motor cover and push RX cable through the fitting and tube into the open motor compartment. Tighten the two screws on the fitting to keep the cable in place, then position the unit. (F) Strip the cable for a length of 6 inches and connect with wire nuts to motor leads. Arrange the wires under the clip so that they will not tangle with the revolving cooling blades on the end of the motor. (G) After the motor housing has been screwed on, caulk around the upper edge of the installation where it meets the roof. The exposed flashing on the lower side serves as a drip ridge. (H) The last step is to secure the cover in place. On roofs with a pitch of more than 15 degrees, build a platform under the unit to level it. After a switch has been installed in the kitchen, the job is done.

should be as short and direct as possible. More on the exhaust fan ductwork can be found in Chapter 10.

Proper fan performance also depends on choosing a fan of the correct power. The various rooms needing exhaust fans have different requirements of air movement, and the Home Ventilating Institute has determined the following appropriate standards: The *kitchen* demands a complete change every four minutes or fifteen times per hour; the *bath* needs eight air changes per hour to remove humidity; and the *laundry* or *utility room* should have an air change every ten minutes, or six changes per hour.

To calculate the correct amount of CFM (cubic feet per minute) required for each room, measure the square feet of floor area, and then use the following formula for each room:

Kitchen   Square feet × 2.00 = CFM for fifteen air changes per hour
Bath   Square feet × 1.07 = CFM for eight air changes per hour
Laundry   Square feet × 0.80 = CFM for six air changes per hour

All the above figures are based on an average 8-foot ceiling. If your ceilings are in excess of this, increase the CFM rating as compensation. Thus, a bathroom with floor dimensions of 9 by 5 feet would require 48 CFM. Since the nearest standard rating is 50 CFM, this would be your most effective choice.

Attic exhaust fans. Next to air conditioning, the best method of cooling a home is with an attic exhaust fan. When properly installed, this blower fan system removes all the hot air from the home in a few minutes and brings in cooler air from outdoors. The attic exhaust fan does not reduce air temperature, but the air movement it creates helps cool your body by evaporating perspiration, causing what is more than just an illusion of comfort. Furthermore, the fan does reduce the room temperature because it replaces hot, indoor air with cooler night air drawn from outside. By adjusting windows and doors according to the needs and conditions of your rooms, you can send fresh, moving air through the entire house.

Fan size. In the average home, the attic is the warmest area of the house in the summer. Hot air rises, and in the attic it is trapped and further heated by the sun on the roof. A thermometer placed in the attic at noon may register as high as 140 degrees, yet not drop below 115 degrees even when the outside temperature falls considerably as evening unfolds. It is a fan's task to blow the hot air out of the house. Therefore, the capacity needed should be determined by the number of cubic feet inside the house that the fan must move. In hot southern areas, the fan should be capable of changing all the

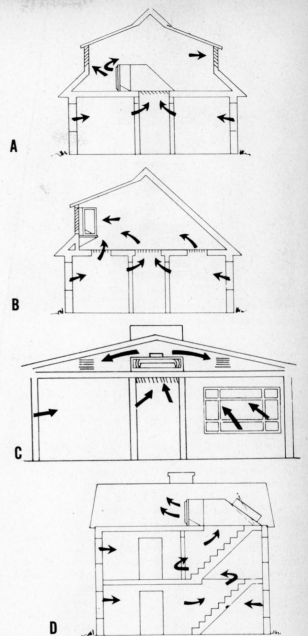

Figure 7—45. Locations of attic exhaust fans: (A) Centering an attic fan under the roof is the best arrangement in single-story ranch-style houses. The fan is directly above the automatic shutters, and the exhaust vents are in the gables. (B) in houses having a stairway to the attic, the suction fan may be installed over the stairway opening. A tight-fitting door provides easy access to the attic from below. (C) This location is suitable for both one- and two-story houses. It affords an opportunity to direct the fan discharge toward unobstructed attic areas for ready exhaust. (D) When the fan is mounted on a wall, the entire attic should be airtight, because all of it is used as a suction chamber. Louvers should be adjustable so that they may be shut in cold weather.

Figure 7—46. A fan mounted in front of a louver.

For this purpose, an opening or openings must be provided. Actually, this air-discharge space must have a total surface area in direct proportion to the size of the fan. The opening should provide 1 square foot of free space for about each 700 cubic feet of air moved per minute. In our Georgia house example, 10,232 cubic feet, at least 14⅓ square feet of free space are necessary.

Where louver openings are covered by screen wire to exclude insects, increase the free-space figure by 50 percent. Where the louver opening is covered with ½-inch mesh wire, such as is used to exclude birds and rodents, increase the figure by 20 percent. If the louver itself is adequate, but these wire covers make it too small, a wire-covered framework can be built to increase the screen area to compensate for the loss of free air space. This will make enlarging the louver unnecessary in some cases.

The task of installing a vent in the gable ends involves the following four steps:

1. Mark off the opening.
2. Cut through the siding, sheathing, and studs (if necessary).
3. Frame in the opening to support the louver.
4. Nail the louver in place and install flashing to overlap the top edge of the louver. Caulk around all joints and edges, to seal out leaks.

Locating an attic fan. If you are installing a fan in an attic that is unused and has gable ends, the fan can be mounted in either of two ways. It can be mounted directly in front of a louver on the wall so that as it discharges air through this opening, a vacuum is caused in the attic, which in turn draws air up from below; or it can be mounted in the ceiling of the floor below and directly over the air passage from below, where it will force air into the attic under pressure to find its way out through louvers.

Hipped roofs (without gable ends) usually require the building of a small dormer to accommo-

air in the house in one minute. In cooler northern climates, the speed of exchange can be reduced to 1½ minutes.

To determine the size of the attic fan you will need, find the volume of the air that must be moved. To do this multiply the house length by the house width by the room height by the number of floors of living space. (All dimensions should be in feet.) The basement is not considered as a floor. Once the total volume is figured, deduct 10 percent for areas such as closets that the fan will not be required to ventilate. Then if you live in the shaded area of the map shown in Figure 7–29, divide the volume by 1.5. This will give you a minimum CFM requirement. If you live in the unshaded area, your minimum CFM requirement will be the same as the volume that should be moved. For instance, for an average two-story house in Georgia measuring 32 feet long and 22 feet wide, and has 8-foot ceilings, multiply $32 \times 22 \times 8 \times 2$ (stories). The answer will be 11,364 cubic feet. Deducting 10 percent reduces this figure to 10,232. This house would need an attic fan with a capacity of at least 10,232 cubic feet per minute. If the house was in North Dakota instead, the fan would have to move only two-thirds as much, or about 6,822 cubic feet per minute.

Once the house's volume in cubic feet has been determined, refer to the fan manufacturer's catalog for the required fan size.

Air discharge. Air that the fan pulls into the attic from below must pass freely to the outdoors.

Figure 7–47. *(opposite)* Installing an exhaust fan directly over a ceiling grille: (A) After the ceiling opening has been cut according to the manufacturer's instructions, the ceiling joists that cross the opening are exposed. (B) If the joist ends will need support after they have been cut, add support by anchoring threaded rods to the ends and rafters with steel braces. (C) Next, cut away the interfering joists flush with the edge of the opening. The work may be done with a hand or a power saw. (D) The cut ends of the joists are notched so that the framing remains flush with the opening. The framing stock should match the joists. (E) The opening here is framed in with 2 × 6's, which are nailed to the joists at every point of contact. Nail 1 × 4 plates on top to complete the framing. (F) The fan assembly is lifted or hoisted into the attic through the opening and set down on the framing, covering the opening. (G) A view from below shows the notched joists, the box frame, and the edge of the 1 × 4 plate and the fan in position, resting on the framing members. (H) A shutter, which is held by screws into the framing, fits the opening from below. When the fan is turned on, the louvers open automatically.

date the fan. Sometimes it is possible to create openings at the eaves by installing several small louvers. Flat-roofed homes, on the other hand, generally require a "penthouse" type of installation which includes a separate structure built into the roof to house the blower unit.

Before the fan is mounted, the air passage route from the lower floors to the attic should be determined. The fan should be located so that the air will be drawn from all parts of the house at once, if at all possible. In one-floor houses, the ideal location is in the ceiling of a central hallway; in two-story houses the best location is in an upper hallway or over a stairwell. This opening is cut between ceiling joists, framed with 1-by-8-inch lumber, and a seat is prepared for the grille. On the attic side of the opening, a platform is constructed to accommodate the type of fan selected if it is to be mounted directly over the grille.

When a ceiling mounting is employed, the attic itself need not be airtight, since the air will be forced out through the louvers and any other openings. But where a wall-mounted installation is used, the attic should be reasonably airtight or the efficiency of the system declines. Frequently, it is a good idea to build a suction box from the ceiling grille to the fan, thus bypassing the attic completely. This will permit the air from the rooms below to pass directly to the fan and to the outside.

The grilles of wood, metal, or composition materials are usually purchased with the attic fan. Most open and shut automatically as the fan is turned on or off. Some louvered grilles are even equipped with fusible links, which will automatically close the louvers in case of a fire. When locating the grille, try to position it so that a minimum number of ceiling joists will be cut.

Once the location of the ceiling opening has been decided on, the grille opening is started by cutting from the room side. The actual size of the cutout will be determined by size of the grille used. After the rough cutout from below has been made, go into the attic and cut away the joists over the grille opening. Then frame out the opening by using headers the same size as the joists. (The framing details are handled in the same manner as for attic stairs; see page 137). Before nailing headers in place, it is usually necessary to bring the fan into the attic since it may not fit through the opening with the headers installed. After the headers have been nailed in place, mount the grille.

Mounting an attic fan. With the grille in place, the final step is to mount the fan. Here again, the mounting system employed determines the construction details. For instance when the fan is mounted directly in front of the louver on the wall, it is usually best to suspend it on springs to absorb vibration and sound. On the other hand, where the fan is mounted directly over the ceiling grille, the unit is usually set on vibration (shock) absorbers to avoid noise and vibrations from being heard throughout the house.

Since most fans in the system are of relatively high power (from $1/3$ to $3/4$ hp), wiring should be done with No. 12 or heavier wire. All wiring must be done in accordance with local codes. Switches should be located at convenient places for the operation of the fan.

Some attic fan models are equipped with two-speed motors that control the volume of air that is moved in the house. The low-speed feature is most desirable in the winter when the exhaust fan can be used for short periods to help maintain a low relative humidity in the home. This is accomplished by exhausting the moist inside air and allowing the drier outside air to infiltrate and replace it.

Chapter 8

EXTERIOR HOME REMODELING

Chapter 8

Home remodeling does not involve just the interior of the home. There is a great deal that can be done to modernize a home's exterior. By adding new windows, doors, walls, and roof you can give your home a new look. Frequently it is even possible to give the exterior of your home a new appearance by removing trim or adding new trim. For example, the simple straight-line trim around the front of your house can be replaced with different trim to add beauty to your entrance. Paint is, of course, the easiest way to give the exterior of a home a new look. Let us take a look at some of the real face-lifting projects.

WINDOWS

Modern windows come prebuilt, preglazed, and frequently prefinished and ready for installation. There are even some that are completely encased in rigid vinyl for weather protection and to eliminate painting. Since windows are available in a wide range of sizes, there is little difficulty in finding a replacement for any old one. But if you decide to change the windows in your home or if you are making an addition, it is a good idea to consider improvement rather than just replacement. With a little extra work, it is usually possible to increase the size of the opening and install a larger window or set of windows to update both the inside and outside of your house.

Types of windows. Windows are available in many types, each having advantages. The principal types are double-hung, casement, stationary, awning, and horizontal sliding. They may be made of wood or metal. Heat loss through metal frames and sashes is much greater than through similar wood units. Glass blocks are sometimes used for admitting light in places where transparency or ventilation is not required (see page 91).

Insulated glass, used both for stationary and movable sashes, consists of two or more sheets of spaced glass with hermetically sealed edges. This type has more resistance to heat loss than a single thickness and is often used without a storm sash. Tables showing glass size, sash size, and rough opening size are available at lumber dealers, so that the wall openings can be framed accordingly. Typical rough openings for windows are shown on page 275.

Double-hung windows. The double-hung window (Figure 8–2) is perhaps the most familiar window type. It consists of an upper and lower sash that slide vertically in separate grooves in the side jambs or in full-width metal weatherstripping. This type of window provides a maximum face opening for ventilation of one-half the total window area. Each sash is provided with springs, balances, or compression weatherstripping to hold it in place in any location. Compression weatherstripping, for example, pre-

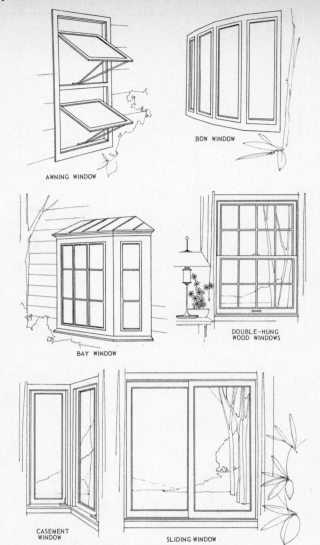

AWNING WINDOW

BOW WINDOW

BAY WINDOW

DOUBLE-HUNG WOOD WINDOWS

CASEMENT WINDOW

SLIDING WINDOW

Figure 8–1. Types of windows.

vents air infiltration, provides tension, and acts as a counterbalance; several types allow the sash to be removed for easy painting or repair. The jambs (sides and top of the frames) are made of nominal 1-inch lumber; the width provides for use with drywall or plastered interior finish. Sills are made from 2-inch lumber and sloped for good drainage. Sashes are normally $1\frac{3}{8}$ inches thick, and wood combination storm and screen windows are usually $1\frac{1}{8}$ inches thick.

Sashes may be divided into a number of lights by small wood members called _muntins._ A ranch-type house may look best with windows whose top and bottom sashes are divided into two horizontal

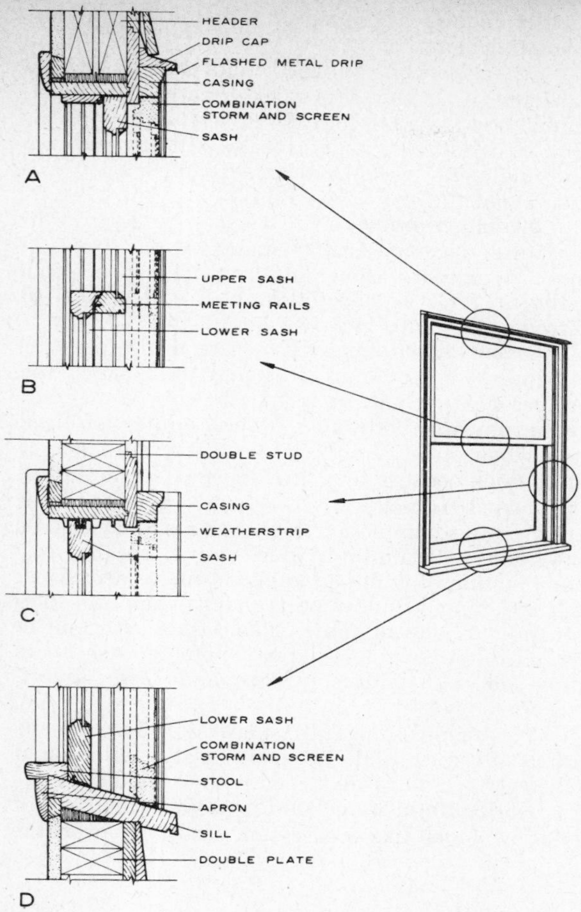

Figure 8-2. Double-hung windows. Cross section: (A) head jamb; (B) meeting rails; (C) side jambs; (D) sill.

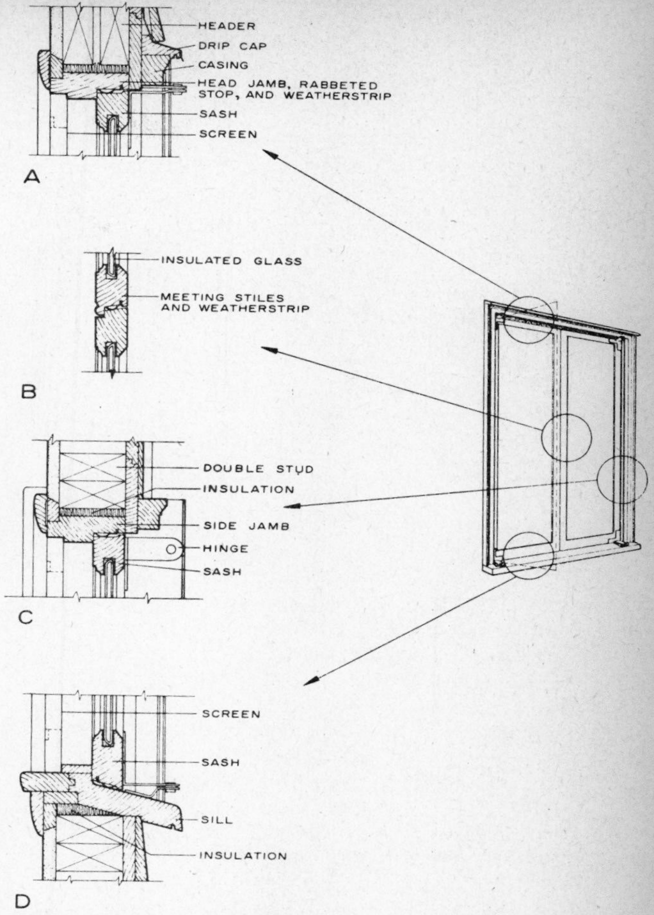

Figure 8-3. Out-swinging casement sash. Cross section: (A) head jamb; (B) meeting stiles; (C) side jambs; (D) sill.

lights. A colonial or Cape Cod house usually has each sash divided into six or eight lights. Some manufacturers provide preassembled dividers that snap in place over a single light, dividing it into six or eight lights. This simplifies painting and other maintenance.

Assembled frames are placed in the rough opening over strips of building paper put around the perimeter to minimize air infiltration. The frame is plumbed and nailed to the side studs and header through the casings or the blind stops at the sides. Where nails are exposed, such as on the casing, use the corrosion-resistant type.

Hardware for double-hung windows includes the sash lifts that are fastened to the bottom rail (although they are sometimes replaced by a finger groove inserted in the rail) and sash locks or fasteners located at the meeting rail. They not only lock the window, but draw the sash together to provide a "windtight" fit.

Double-hung windows can be arranged in a number of ways, as a single unit, doubled (or mullion) type, or in groups of three or more. One or two double-hung windows on each side of a large stationary insulated window are often used to affect a window wall. Such large openings must be framed with headers large enough to carry roof loads.

Casement windows. This type of window (Figure 8-3) is characterized by a side-hinged sash, usually designed to swing outward because it can be made more weathertight than the in-swinging style. Screens are located inside these out-swinging windows, and winter protection is obtained with a storm sash or by using insulated glass in the sash. One advantage of the casement window over the double-hung type is that the entire window area can be opened for ventilation. Weatherstripping is also provided for this type of window, and units are usually received from the factory entirely assembled with hardware in place. Closing hardware con-

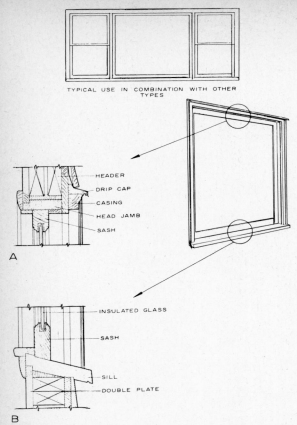

Figure 8–4. Stationary window. Cross section: (A) head jamb; (B) sill.

usually required because of the thickness of the insulating glass.

Other types of stationary windows may be used without a sash. The glass is set directly into rabbeted frame members and held in place with stops. As with all window-sash units, back puttying and face puttying of the glass (with or without a stop) will assure moisture resistance.

Awning windows. An awning window unit (Figure 8–5) consists of a frame in which one or more operative sashes are installed. It is often made up for a large window wall and consist of three or more units in width and height.

Sashes of the awning type are made to swing outward at the bottom. A similar unit, called the hopper type, is one in which the top of the sash swings inward. Both types provide protection from rain when open. Jambs are usually $1\frac{1}{16}$ inches or more thick because they are rabbeted, while the sill is at least $1\frac{5}{16}$ inches thick when two or more sashes are used in a complete frame. Each sash may also be provided with an individual frame, so that any combination of width and height can be used. Awning or hopper window units may consist of a combination of one or more fixed sashes and one or more of the operable type. Operable sashes are provided with hinges, pivots, and sash-supporting arms.

Weatherstripping and storm sash and screens are usually provided. The storm sash is eliminated when the windows are glazed with insulated glass.

Horizontal-sliding window units. This type of window looks like a casement sash. However, the

sists of a rotary operator and sash lock. As in the double-hung units, casement sash can be used in a number of ways, as a pair or in combinations of two or more pairs. Style variations are achieved by divided lights. Snap-in muntins provide a small, multiple-pane appearance for traditional styling.

Metal sashes are sometimes used, but, because of low insulating value, should be installed carefully to prevent condensation and frosting on the interior surfaces during cold weather. A full storm-window unit is sometimes necessary to eliminate this problem in cold climates.

Stationary windows. Stationary or picture windows (Figure 8–4) used alone or in combination with double-hung or casement windows usually consist of a wood sash with a large single light of insulated glass. They are designed to provide light, as well as for attractive appearance, and are fastened permanently into the frame. Because of their size (sometimes 6 to 8 feet wide) $1\frac{3}{4}$-inch-thick sash is used to provide strength. The thickness is

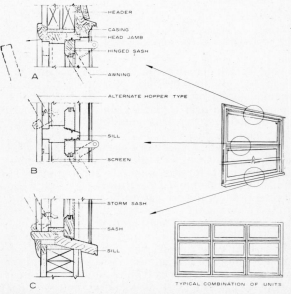

Figure 8–5. Awning window. Cross section: (A) head jamb; (B) horizontal mullion; (C) sill.

sashes (in pairs) slide horizontally in separate tracks or guides located on the sill and head jamb. Multiple window openings consist of two or more single units and may be used when a window-wall effect is desired. As in most modern window units of all types, weatherstripping, water-repellent preservative treatments, and sometimes hardware are included in these fully factory-assembled units.

Installing a picture window. One of the easy ways to update your home, both inside and out, is to add a picture window. As stated earlier, most such windows are manufactured as a complete unit, ready to be installed into the wall. A number of types are sold by various makers. The technique of installation varies but little for the various kinds.

The job can be done from inside or outside the house, depending on the type of exterior wall and how quickly the window will be installed. If there is extensive remodeling being done on the interior at the same time and dust in the room is not a problem, it is easier to remove the gypsum wallboard or plaster and frame the new opening from the inside. If it is desirable not to make dirt inside the house and the job can be done in a day or a weekend, remove the siding or shingles along with the sheathing to expose the framing. Do not try to cut into the wall with a power saw; you might hit wiring, and insulation will fly around. Remove the insulation and any wiring that might be in the area to be enlarged for the new window. Relocate the wiring.

Since the opening for a picture window is more than three studs wide, it is necessary to shore up the ceiling just inside the opening so that the second floor or attic joists will not sag. The shoring can be simply a length of 2 × 4 held flat against the ceiling by two or three vertical 2 × 4s wedged tightly against the main floor. Once the shoring is in place, the studs can be removed to create the new opening.

As shown in Figure 8–6, frame the new opening to the required rough opening size specified for the window selected. Note that the trimmer studs on each side of the opening support the header, which is needed to bridge the opening and support the structural load above it. The header is made by doubling two 2 × 6s or 2 × 8s, depending on the

width of the opening. Double 2 × 4s are the sufficient header size for openings up to 3 feet; 2 × 6s should be used for openings up to 6 feet; and 2 × 8s for headers over openings from 6 to 12 feet. Install short cripple studs beneath the sill framing and between the lintel and the top plate of the wall framing, spacing them 16 inches on centers, the same as the framing studs. Staple the insulation back into position around the new opening.

Once the opening is framed on the side of the wall that was removed, an accurate opening to match can be cut in the untouched wall simply by sawing along the edge of the header, the trimmer studs, and the rough sill.

If the outside of the wall was removed, cut the sheathing to fit around the opening and nail it in place. Then set the window in place and level it, using shims if necessary to hold it in position. Fasten the window by driving nails through the outside casing into the trimmer studs on each side. For additional support, drive nails or screws up through the window head into the overhead beam (the header or lintel). Knee brackets, available from the window manufacturer, are recommended under a unit that is cantilevered out beyond the wall. Knee brackets are not needed beneath a full-height unit set on an extension of the flooring. The drip cap, usually made of vinyl or aluminum and supplied by the manufacturer, is nailed along the top edge of the window frame.

Bow and bay windows installed beneath a wide second floor or roof overhang require nothing more than caulking to seal joints against the weather, but a decorative roof is required above the window when it is installed in a flat wall. This roof, often supplied knocked down by the manufacturer, is installed against the wall sheathing and sealed by nailing flashing over the joints, later to be covered with roofing and further protected by fitting the siding or shingles around it.

Complete the job by re-installing the shingles or siding around the new window and caulk the meeting joints on all sides of the window for a tight seal. Install the stool, apron, and casing around the interior of the window and paint or stain these members as desired.

When any other type of new window is installed, the same basic procedure is followed as for a picture window. That is, cut a hole in the wall for the new window, removing the studs, sheathing, and siding from the new opening. Install a new 2-by-6-inch header and two 2 × 4s from the header to the horizontal 2 × 4 that rests on the floor. Make a new sill of double 2 × 4s. Install the new window as directed by the manufacturer, and complete the repair of the finish surfaces, inside and out, as described for picture windows.

To enlarge an existing window opening, it is first necessary to remove the old sash. To do this,

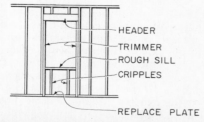

Figure 8–6. Rough framing for a window.

HEADER

TRIMMER

ROUGH SILL

CRIPPLES

REPLACE PLATE

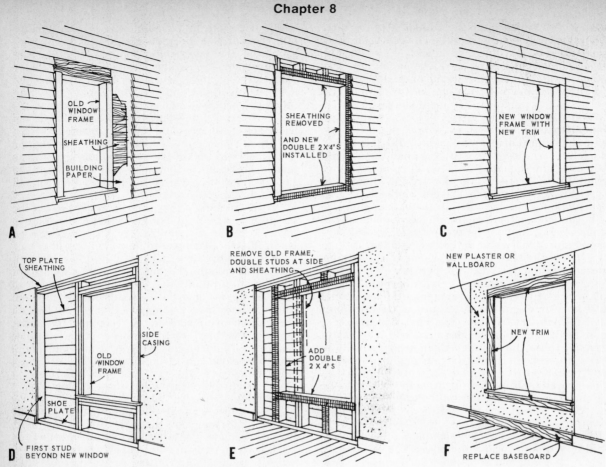

Figure 8—7. Steps in the replacement of an old window.

remove the inside trim and outside casing. With a crowbar gently force the window away from the studs, removing the nails until the window is free. Then mark the size of the new window and cut out the necessary opening. Add the necessary new framing, double 2 × 6 headers at the top and twin 2 × 4s at each side. A double 2 × 4 sill completes the framing. The new window can be secured in position, and the wall refinished around it.

Replacing a window. If you just wish to replace an old window with a new one, remove the old unit as previously described. Then replace the window with a new one of the same size. It may be necessary to shim the new window at the top and sides to make it level.

Odd-shaped openings such as those originally fitted with tall, narrow windows, can be reduced in height by blocking the opening to the required size. Usually, these tall windows were set low in the wall, with the head at door height and the sill close to the floor, so just nailing new sill framing across

the opening at a height appropriate for the new window often will bring the rough opening to size. If the opening is still a bit wide, nailing trimmer studs at one or both sides will reduce the width.

Replacement windows set in framed walls and some brick veneer and masonry walls do not always require jamb extenders; recessing the window so that the inside of the jamb is flush with the interior wall may be sufficient. Jamb extenders of various widths are available to adapt windows readily to a wide range of standard wall thicknesses. Where wall thicknesses are not standard, jambs can be fitted by ripping off enough material from the edges of an oversize set of jamb extenders to bring them flush with the existing interior wall surface. Alignment of these jamb extenders is easy and fast; the tongued edge of the extender fits snugly into a groove in the jamb and is secured by nailing.

Unless the existing exterior wall covering is to be replaced with new material, any gaps around the new window and the existing siding or shingles should be filled in with matching material and the joints caulked where the siding material meets the exterior casing. A plywood panel or any low-maintenance material, trimmed with molding for a decorative effect, can be nailed beneath the new window if necessary to fill the space formerly occupied by a tall window, or a veneer of used brick can be laid up to the sill to retain the continuity of a masonry wall.

The interior wall should be refinished. The installation of a stool and apron at the sill and interior casing around the jamb completes the replacement window on the inside.

Closing up a window. The procedure for closing up a window is much like that used for a doorway (see page 101). That is, first remove the interior and exterior trim and casings. Take out the two sashes and the frame. Add new 2-by-4-inch studs, as necessary, to the space occupied by the old windows. The new studs should be 16 inches or closer on centers. Then add insulation to the formerly open area of the windows. Nail ¾-inch plywood sheathing to the studs on the outside wall. Staple building paper to the sheathing and nail matching siding on the paper-covered sheathing. If it is not practical to match your present siding, nail a piece of ½-inch exterior plywood to the sheathing and paint it a complementary or contrasting color. On the interior, the space formerly occupied by the window can be finished with plaster, plywood, or gypsum board, and in the various other methods described in Chapter 3.

SLIDING DOORS

FOLDING DOORS

COLONIAL

COMBINATION DOORS

MODERN

DUTCH DOORS

PATIO DOORS

TRADITIONAL

Figure 8—8. Types of exterior doors.

EXTERIOR DOORS

Exterior doors are usually 1¾ inches thick and not less than 6 feet 8 inches high. The main entrance door, as a rule, is 3 feet wide, and the side or rear service door 2 feet 8 inches wide. The frames for these doors are made of 1⅛-inch or thicker material, so that rabbeting of the side and head jambs provides stops for the main door. The wood sill is often oak for wear resistance, but when softer species are used, a metal nosing and wear strips are included. As in many of the window units, the outside casings provide space for the 1⅛-inch combination or screen door.

The frame is, of course, nailed to studs and headers of the rough opening through the outside casing. The sill must rest firmly on the header or stringer joist of the floor framing, which commonly must be trimmed with a saw and hand ax or other means. After finish flooring is in place, a hardwood or metal threshold with a plastic weatherstop covers the joints between the floor and sill. The exterior trim around the main entrance door can vary from a simple casing to a molded or plain pilaster with a decorative head casing. Decorative designs should always be in keeping with the architecture of the house. Many combinations of door and entry designs are used with contemporary houses, and manufacturers have millwork that is adaptable to this and similar styles. If there is an entry hall, it is usually desirable to have glass included in the main door when no other light is provided in the hall.

Types of exterior doors. Exterior doors and outside combination and storm doors can be obtained in a number of designs to fit the style of almost any house. Doors in the traditional pattern are usually the panel type. They consist of stiles (solid vertical members), rails (solid cross members), and filler panels in a number of designs. Glazed upper panels are combined with raised wood or plywood lower panels. For methods of hanging doors and installing hardware, see Chapter 3. Incidentally, most exterior doors employ three hinges rather than the two used in the interior type.

Exterior flush doors should be of the solid-core type rather than hollow-core to minimize warping during the heating season. (Warping is caused by a difference in moisture content on the exposed and unexposed faces.)

Flush doors consist of thin plywood faces over a framework of wood with a wood-block or particle board core. Many combinations of designs can be obtained, ranging from plain flush doors to others with a variety of panels and glazed openings. Bold designs can be achieved with wide molding, painting in colors that contrast strongly with wide molding, and painting in colors that contrast strongly with the door face. Various degrees of prominence

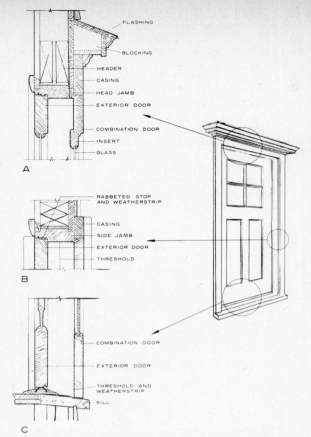

Figure 8—9. Exterior door and frame. Exterior door and combination door (screen and storm) cross sections: (A) head jamb; (B) side jamb; (C) sill.

can be assigned to the design by choosing brighter or more subdued shades, or even using the same color as the rest of the door, letting the 3-D effect come through subtly.

Wood combination doors (storm and screen) are available in several styles. Panels that include screen and storm inserts are normally located in the upper portion of the door. Some types can be obtained with self-storing features, similar to those in window combination units. Heat loss through metal combination doors is greater than through wood doors of similar size and construction.

Exterior door locks. New locks and escutcheon plates can give new beauty to most entrance doors. The first step in replacing an old lock is to remove it completely from the door. Generally it is a good idea to fill all the holes created by the removal of the lock. An exception to this procedure occurs with some of the modern locks, which have large escutcheons that will cover the old holes. To fill the old mortise, make a plug of soft pine. When

Figure 8–10. How a flush door *(left)* can be changed by the addition of stock molding.

Figure 8–11. Upgrading an old lock: (A) Remove the worn-out, broken lock. (B) Remove the latch. (C) Use the template packed with the new lock to mark the area to be enlarged. (D) If a jig is available (usually on loan from a hardware dealer), use a hole saw to enlarge the area so that it will accept the new lock mechanism. However, if the hole requires only minor enlargement, use a wood rasp or a similar tool. (E) Cut away excess wood in the edge of the door, if necessary, to accommodate a new latch plate. (F) Install the latch. (G) Insert the lock mechanism from the outside of the door. (H) Attach the mounting plate on the inside of the door and snap on the trim and knob. (I) The completed installation.

driving in the plug, make sure that the grain follows the grain of the stile. Fill all the screw holes with wood putty or plastic; let it dry and then sand it smooth.

When installing the new lock, use the cardboard template, or pattern, which comes with the lock, to locate all holes. To drill the large holes necessary with some locks, use an expansion bit, or start with a smaller hole and enlarge this with a keyhole saw. The cut for the face plate can be made with a chisel and hammer. Using the plate as a pattern, mark off the area that must be removed and carefully cut a shallow mortise just inside the mark.

After all the cuts are on the door, the new lock can be installed. Since each lock has its own special features, it is most important to follow the manufacturer's instructions to the letter. Figure 8–11 shows a typical installation of a front door lockset. You will note that the deadbolt is mounted first. Then the latch, grid-handle, and inside mechanism are installed, and the mounting screws are tightened.

The last item to install is the striker plate against which the door latch hits as the door closes. Rub some chalk on the tip of the latch and close the door. Repeat this for the deadbolt. Cut a couple of notches in the frame where these marks indicate a depression is needed. (The plate also requires a shallow mortise so it will fit flush with the frame.) Hold the striker plate in position, mark off the two mortises, and then cut them out inside the marks. To complete the job, attach the striker plate with the screws provided.

New thresholds. Most exteriors require a piece of trim called a threshold to seal the space between the bottom of the door and the door sill. In older homes, the thresholds were made of oak or some other hardwood that was worked to a special shape for this purpose. But, since probably no other spot in the entire house is subject to as much wear and tear as the thresholds, they become worn and splintered after long years of service. This can be both unsightly and dangerous.

To remove the old wood saddle or threshold, pry it out carefully with a pinch bar. Rather than installing another piece, most homeowners seem to prefer those made from an aluminum extrusion. Available in a clear anodized finish or gold color, these modern units have special vinyl strips inserted into the threshold or to matching pieces attached to the door. Thresholds of this style are most effective in giving a good under-the-door seal. If you still wish to have wood, there are hardwood thresholds available with vinyl sealing strips. In either case, the manufacturer's instructions should be followed when making the installation.

While it is not necessary to use thresholds on interior doors, you may wish to install one of the various sealing strips on the market to reduce sound transmission and prevent air movement. Many door sealers operate in an automatic fashion. That is, the sealing strip lifts upward when the door is opened and drops to the floor when the door is closed.

Installing sliding glass doors. Sliding glass doors are one remodeling project that will produce a magical transformation almost anywhere in the home. Off the bedroom, den, kitchen on the ground level, or on a deck, they permit all the beautiful scenery of the outdoors to become a part of the room. The changing seasons offer a panoramic view to highlight the seasonal accessories inside and delight all who enter the room. In effect, there is a living fourth wall that requires no decorating yet looks constantly fresh as the outdoors. A sliding door, for example, can quickly change a small, dark room into a bright, spacious-appearing area. It also provides quick access to the patio or garden of your home. Fortunately, the installation of sliding glass doors is not usually too difficult a task.

Sliding glass door frames come either preassembled, ready to set into an opening, or knocked-down, requiring assembling on the job. While the latter requires an extra step in the installation, the pieces are cut to size and the corners are fitted and mitered so that the framework can be easily assembled inside its opening in the exterior wall. Regardless of how the frame is shipped, sliding glass door units usually have at least one fixed and one operating panel. Some may contain as many as three or four panels. Be sure that the sliding glass door unit that you select has insulating glass and quality weatherstripping, so as to reduce heat loss and prevent condensation.

The installation of sliding door frames is similar to the procedure described for picture windows and exterior doors. The framing details as to size of lumber and installation technique are the same as those for putting in a picture window, except that the opening is continued to the floor, as with an exterior door (Figure 8–12).

Though sliding door units may be installed in any outside wall, it is simpler and quicker if you select a location where there are already existing doors and windows. If possible, pick a location where the combined widths of the doors and/or windows will be the same as the width of the new glass sliding door unit you plan to install. As with picture window installation, the work may be started inside or out. If any heat ducts, plumbing lines, electrical wiring, or other utilities are involved, be sure that they are relocated before cutting the outside wall. If possible, try to plan the job so that you can cut the complete opening and install the unit on the same day. If some unexpected delay should be encountered, a heavy canvas or sheets of plywood can be nailed temporarily over the opening to

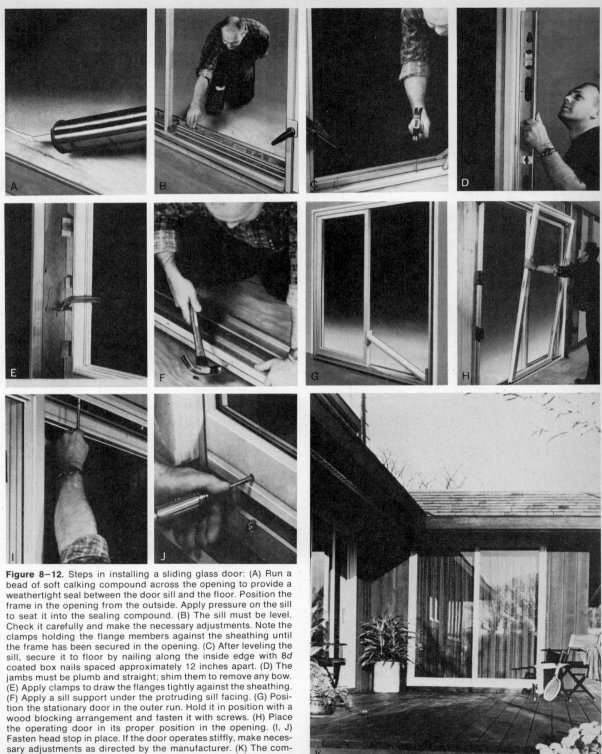

Figure 8–12. Steps in installing a sliding glass door: (A) Run a bead of soft calking compound across the opening to provide a weathertight seal between the door sill and the floor. Position the frame in the opening from the outside. Apply pressure on the sill to seat it into the sealing compound. (B) The sill must be level. Check it carefully and make the necessary adjustments. Note the clamps holding the flange members against the sheathing until the frame has been secured in the opening. (C) After leveling the sill, secure it to floor by nailing along the inside edge with 8*d* coated box nails spaced approximately 12 inches apart. (D) The jambs must be plumb and straight; shim them to remove any bow. (E) Apply clamps to draw the flanges tightly against the sheathing. (F) Apply a sill support under the protruding sill facing. (G) Position the stationary door in the outer run. Hold it in position with a wood blocking arrangement and fasten it with screws. (H) Place the operating door in its proper position in the opening. (I, J) Fasten head stop in place. If the door operates stiffly, make necessary adjustments as directed by the manufacturer. (K) The completed job.

protect the inside of your home. Because of the size of the opening, be sure to shore up the wall as described on page 275.

To start the installation, mark the area for the rough opening on both the inside and outside walls, using the exact measurements from the actual assembled framework, rather than trusting the dimensions given in the catalog or other descriptive literature. When marking the opening, remember to allow for the thickness of the doubled 2 × 4 studs that will be required at each side, and for the header at the top. In most cases, double 2 × 6s placed on edge and nailed flat against each other, are needed for openings under 6 feet in width. Double 2 × 8s are required for openings from 6 to 8 feet in width, while double 2 × 10s should be used as headers for larger openings. Remove the interior and exterior wall coverings as described on page 276.

Once the wall coverings have been removed, cut off the studs at the desired height, leaving stubs at the top to rest on top of the new header. Nail in place the new floor-to-ceiling studs at each side of the opening, then nail the shorter studs (on which the header will rest) flat against these full length studs. After lifting the header into place, toenail the side studs and those above the opening into it. Then cut the soleplate off flush to the side framing to complete the opening.

Before the frame is set in place, a bead of sealing compound should be laid across the opening to provide a weathertight joint. Then position the frame in the opening from the outside, applying pressure to seal it into the sealing compound. Remember that the jamb must be plumb and straight if the door is to slide properly. Shim the side jambs with wedges, as you would for regular door frames. Secure the frame in place as directed in the instructions; this is usually done with screws or with coated box nails.

Before seating the threshold of the frame directly on the subfloor or slab floor, run a bead of sealing compound across the opening to insure a weathertight seal between it and the floor. Check to be sure the threshold is level and make any necessary adjustments. Fasten it to the floor and recheck the frame for plumb.

Position the stationary door in the outer run, being sure the bottom rail is straight with the threshold. Force the door into the run of the side jamb with a 2 × 4 wedge. Check the alignment of the fixed panel and then fasten it into position.

The operating door is now placed in the opening. Position the rollers of the door on the rib of the threshold, tip the door in at the top, and apply the head stop. Check the door operation. If the door operates stiffly or is not parallel with the side jamb, adjustment of the shims is necessary. To complete the job replace the siding and outside trim; then replace the wall covering and trim inside.

Weatherstripping. Before leaving the subject of exterior doors and windows, it would be wise to mention weatherstripping, since this is one remodeling improvement that will increase comfort in your home and will help to reduce fuel consumption.

While there are many kinds and grades available, weatherstripping may be divided into three basic classifications: metal, fabric, or a combination of the two. Rigid metal varieties usually require some extensive cutting and shaping of the door and frame and windows, to interlock properly when set in place. (Since both the work and the tools are specialized, most homeowners have the work done by professionals. Also, much of the needed materials are available to professional workers only and not obtainable at all in many communities.) Once installed, rigid metal weatherstripping is practically invisible and will last the life of the door or window. Incidentally, most modern windows come with metal weatherstripping already installed.

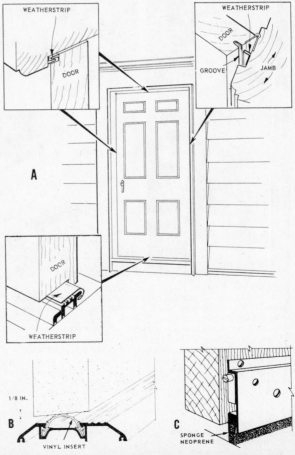

Figure 8-13. (A) A typical door weatherstripping; (B, C) two types of thresholds.

There are other types of weatherstripping on the market that can be applied by the average home handyman, although they are not as long-lasting and invisible as the rigid metal type. Complete instructions are furnished by the manufacturers and, for the best results, they should be most carefully followed.

EXTERIOR WALL COVER

Over the years, the exterior walls of your home take a terrific beating from the elements, and sooner or later, in spite of proper maintenance, you may have to concede defeat and give the walls a new covering. When the time comes for the remodeling of the exterior walls, you have a wide choice of materials to use and a number of ways to apply them.

Types of siding. There are six basic exterior siding materials available to the remodeling homeowner: (1) wood, (2) asbestos, (3) composition, (4) alumi-

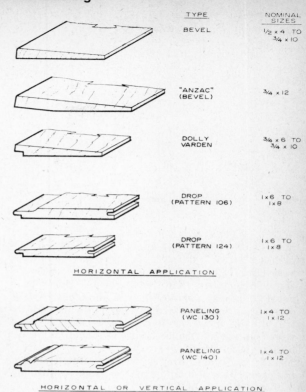

Figure 8–15. Wood siding types.

Figure 8–14. Siding can make a big change in the appearance of a house.

num, (5) steel, and (6) vinyl.

1. **Wood siding.** One of the materials most characteristic of the exteriors of American houses is wood siding. The essential properties required for siding are good painting characteristics, easy working qualities, and freedom from warp. Such properties are present to a *high* degree in the cedars, Eastern white pine, sugar pine, Western white pine, cypress, and redwood; to a *good* degree in Western hemlock, ponderosa pine, the spruces, and yellow poplar; and to a *fair* degree in Douglas-fir, Western larch, and Southern pine.

Material used for exterior siding that is to be painted should preferably be of a high grade and free from knots, pitch pockets, and waney edges. Vertical grain and mixed grain (both vertical and flat) are available in some species such as redwood and Western red cedar.

Some wood siding patterns (Figure 8–15) are used only horizontally and others only vertically. Some may be used in either manner if adequate nailing areas are provided. Descriptions of each of the general types follow.

Plain bevel siding can be obtained in sizes from ½ inch by 4 inches to ½ inch by 8 inches, and also

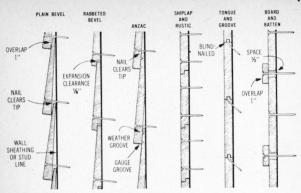

Figure 8–16. Installation of various sidings.

in sizes of ¾ inch by 8 inches and ¾ inch by 10 inches. "Anzac" siding is ¾ inch by 12 inches in size. Usually the finished width of bevel siding is about ½ inch less than the size listed. One side of bevel siding has a smooth planed surface, while the other has a rough resawn surface. For a stained finish, the rough or sawn side is exposed because wood stain is most successful and longer lasting on rough wood surfaces.

Dolly Varden siding is similar to true bevel siding except that shiplap edges are used, resulting in a constant exposure distance. Because it lies flat against the studs, it is sometimes used for garages and similar buildings without sheathing. Diagonal bracing is then needed to provide racking resistance to the wall.

Regular drop sidings can be obtained in several patterns, two of which are shown in Figure 8–16. This siding, with matched or shiplap edges, can be obtained in 1-by-6-inch and 1-by-8-inch sizes. This type is commonly used for lower-cost dwellings and for garages, usually without benefit of sheathing. Tests conducted at the Forest Products Laboratory have shown that the tongued-and-grooved (matched) patterns have greater resistance to the penetration of wind-driven rain than the shiplap patterns, when both are treated with a water-repellent preservative.

Fiberboard and *hardboard sidings* are also available in various forms. Some have a backing to provide rigidity and strength while others are used directly over sheathing. Plywood horizontal lap siding, with a medium-density overlaid surface, is also available as an exterior covering material. It is usually ⅜ inch thick and 12 and 16 inches wide. It is applied in much the same manner as wood siding, except that shingle wedges are used behind each vertical joint.

A number of siding or paneling patterns can be used horizontally or vertically. These are manufactured in nominal 1-inch thicknesses and in widths

Figure 8–17. Hardboard sidings.

from 4 to 12 inches. Both dressed and matched and shiplapped edges are available. The narrow- and medium-width patterns will likely be more satisfactory when there are moderate moisture content changes. Wide patterns are more successful if they are vertical grain, to keep shrinkage to a minimum. The correct moisture content is also important when tongued-and-grooved siding is wide, to prevent shrinkage to a point where the tongue is exposed.

Treating the edges of both drop and matched and shiplapped sidings with water-repellent preservative usually prevents wind-driven rain from penetrating the joints if they are exposed to weather. In areas under wide overhangs, or in porches or other protected sections, this treatment is not as important. Some siding has received preservative treatment at the factory.

Wood siding for vertical application. A method of siding application, popular for some architectural styles, utilizes rough-sawn boards and battens applied vertically. These boards can be arranged in several ways: (a) board and batten, (b) batten and board, and (c) board and board (Figure 8–18). As in the vertical application of most siding materials, nominal 1-inch sheathing boards or plywood sheathing $5/8$ or $3/4$ inch thick should be used for nailing surfaces. When other types of sheathing materials or thinner plywoods are used, nailing blocks between studs commonly provide the nailing areas. Nailers of 1 by 4 inches, laid horizontally and spaced from 16 to 24 inches apart vertically, can be used over nonwood sheathing. However, special or thicker casing is sometimes required around doors and window frames when this system is used. It is good practice to use a building paper over the sheathing before applying the vertical siding.

Sidings with sheet materials. A number of sheet materials are now available for use as siding. These include plywood in a variety of face treatments and species, paper-overlaid plywood, and hardboard. Plywood or paper-overlaid plywood is sometimes used without sheathing and is known as panel siding, with $3/8$ inch often considered the minimum thickness for such use for 16-inch stud spacing. However, from the standpoint of stiffness and strength, better performance is usually obtained by using $1/2$- or $5/8$-inch thickness. These 4-by-8-foot and longer sheets must be applied vertically with intermediate and perimeter nailing to provide the desired rigidity. Most other methods of applying sheet materials require some type of sheathing beneath. When horizontal joints are necessary, they should be protected by a simple flashing.

An exterior-grade plywood should always be used for siding, and can be obtained in such surfaces as grooved, brushed, and saw-textured. These surfaces are usually finished with some type of stain. If shiplap or matched edges are not provided,

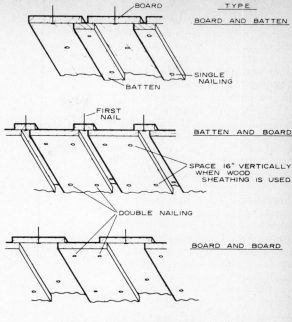

Figure 8–18. Vertical board siding.

some method of providing a waterproof joint should be used. This often consists of caulking and using a batten at each joint and a batten at each stud if closer spacing is desired for appearance. An edge treatment of water-repellent preservative will also aid in reducing moisture penetration. Allow $1/16$-inch edge and end spacing when installing plywood in sheet form.

Exterior-grade particleboard might also be considered for panel siding. Normally $5/8$-inch thickness is required for 16-inch stud spacing and $3/4$-inch for 24-inch stud spacing. The finish must be with an approved paint, and the stud wall behind must have corner bracing.

Paper-overlaid plywood has many of the advantages of plywood and, in addition, provides a very satisfactory base for paint. A medium-density overlaid plywood is most commonly used.

Hardboard sheets used for siding are applied the same way as plywood, that is, by using battens at vertical points and at intermediate studs. Medium-density fiberboards might also be used in some areas as exterior coverings over certain types of sheathing.

Many of these sheet materials resist the passage of water vapor. Hence, when they are used, it is important that a good vapor barrier, well installed, be employed on the warm side of the insulated walls. These factors are described in Chapter 7.

Wood shingles and shakes. Wood shingles and shakes are desirable for sidewalls in many styles of houses. In Cape Cod or colonial houses, shingles may be painted or stained. For ranch or contemporary designs, wide exposures of shingles or shakes often add a desired effect. They are easily stained, and thus a long-lasting finish can be obtained on those species commonly used for shingles.

Western red cedar is perhaps the most available species, although Northern white cedar, bald cypress, and redwood are also satisfactory. The heartwood of those species has a natural decay resistance, which is desirable if shingles are to remain unpainted or unstained.

Western red cedar shingles can be obtained in three grades. The first-grade shingle (No. 1) is all heartwood, edge grain, and knot-free; it is primarily intended for roofs, but is desirable in double-course sidewall application where much of the face is exposed. Second-grade shingles (No. 2) are most often used in single-course application for sidewalls, since only three-fourths of the shingle length is blemish-free. A 1-inch width of sapwood and mixed vertical and flat grain are permissible. The third-grade shingle (No. 3) is clear for 6 inches from the butt. Flat grain is acceptable, as are greater widths of sapwood. Third-grade shingles are likely to be somewhat thinner than the first and second grades; they are used for secondary buildings and sometimes as the undercourse in double-course application. A lower grade than the third grade, known as under-coursing shingle, is used only as the under and completely covered course in double-course sidewall application.

Wood shingles are available in three standard lengths, 16, 18, and 24 inches. The 16-inch length is perhaps the most popular, having five butt thicknesses per 2 inches when green (designated as 5/2). These shingles are packed in bundles with 20 courses on each side. Four bundles will cover 100 square feet of wall or roof with an exposure of 5 inches. The 18- and 24-inch-length shingles have thicker butts, five in 2¼ inches for the 18-inch shingles and four in 2 inches for the 24-inch lengths.

Shakes are usually available in several types, the most popular being the split-and-resawn. The sawed face is used as the back face. The butt thickness of each shake ranges between ¾ inch and 1½ inches. The shakes are usually packed in bundles (20 square feet), five bundles to the square.

2. ***Mineral fiber shingles and siding.*** Introduced as siding material shortly after World War I, mineral fiber or asbestos-cement composition was the first siding that offered an alternative to wood, and its natural resistance to fire and termites earned it immediate popularity. Today, most mineral fiber shingles and siding have been combined with long-wear additives, including a protective coat of acrylic resins. Most brands now carry twenty-year guarantees.

Mineral fiber siding products are generally made to look like conventional wood shingles or clapboard. Several of them are convincing imitations of hand-split shakes. Mineral fiber siding is one of the lowest priced of all exterior coverings.

3. ***Composition siding.*** There are two basic types of composition or insulated siding, and, except for slight differences in the manufacturing process, asphalt and mineral-impregnated siding are essentially the same. Saturating a heavy felt-like material with formulated asphalt, and then evenly coating the surface with a thick asphalt compound containing crushed mineral granules, produces a shatterproof and weather-resistant siding material. Similar in appearance to asphalt roofing shingles and sheeting, insulated siding comes in panels of standard lengths.

Composition or insulated siding had a big boom during the 1940s and early 1950s when there was extensive mass building of low-cost development homes. It was widely used as an inexpensive replacement and re-siding material. Since then, however, the use of asphalt and mineral-impregnated insulated siding has declined in the same way as has the use of wood and asbestos, because superior, modern re-siding materials have replaced them. Today, they are generally considered to be old-fashioned and unattractive. Not only do they "date" a house by some twenty years, but their use tends to cheapen its basic value.

Mineral fiber shingles and similar nonwood exterior materials are installed in almost the same manner as wood shingles (page 287), but make certain that they are applied in accordance with the manufacturer's directions.

4. ***Aluminum siding.*** In the early 1950s, aluminum siding was something new, but it quickly caught on as a re-siding material because it was easy to handle and could, in fact, be installed directly over old siding materials such as wood, stucco, concrete block, and other surfaces that are structurally sound. It is available in a variety of vertical and horizontal panel styles, in both smooth and textured designs. Aluminum siding is frequently installed with a backer or insulation board behind each piece of siding.

Aluminum siding may be purchased in its natural silver-white or a wide selection of colors ranging from several whites through bright and soft pastels to charcoal grays. Manufacturers stress that aluminum siding requires minimal maintenance and note that the chemically applied plastic finish will last for a number of years before painting is necessary. Actually, many companies guarantee their finishes up to 20 years and will allow you to pass on these guarantees when the house is sold.

5. ***Steel siding.*** Steel siding is a fairly recent

innovation; steel companies hoped to duplicate the wide acceptance of aluminum as a siding material. Ironically, the steel producers had to turn to aluminum in order to make steel suitable for siding. To lessen the natural corrosion of steel, cold-rolled sheets must first be hot-dip coated with aluminum and, like aluminum siding, then chemically coated with plastics such as acrylic and vinyl. Galvanized steel, electronically coated with zinc, is also used, but, here again, before the steel sheets are made into siding, they too must be coated with various plastics, including vinyl, for ease of maintenance. Steel siding, therefore, is actually aluminum siding with a steel core and, as a result, is more rigid and resistant to dents. It shares all of the characteristics of aluminum siding but one. Steel siding is almost twice the weight of aluminum and, not surprisingly, is more difficult to handle.

Steel siding is available in both vertical and horizontal types, smooth or textured, and six or seven colors. It carries a twenty-year guarantee against repainting.

6. *Vinyl. siding.* The expanding technology of plastics has created vinyl siding, but vinyl is not new to siding, having been used for more than two decades either as a paint or as a bonded coating on aluminum or steel siding, imparting to these siding products both a variety of colors and increased ease of maintenance. In the mid-1960s, vinyl came into its own as a siding material when the plastic compound, now containing colorants and reinforced with heat stabilizers and other processing aids, was developed into extruded, rigid panels. Vinyl's adaptability allows it to be manufactured and tailored to provide an infinite variety of colors, shapes, sizes, and even textures to suit your tastes and preferences. In remodeling, the use of an insulation backer board is optional.

Vinyl siding's great appeal lies in the fact that it requires little, if any, maintenance, and regular repainting is unnecessary because the colors added during the production process totally permeate the material. Vinyl siding, therefore, will not chip, peel, or flake. Nor will it scratch, rot, or dent. Manufacturers guarantee vinyl siding for twenty years, and claim thirty-five years or longer without painting or upkeep other than washings.

Installing shakes or shingles. Wood shingles and shakes are applied in a single- or double-course pattern. They may be used over wood or plywood sheathing. If sheathing is 3/8-inch plywood, use threaded nails. For nonwood sheathing, 1- by 3- or 1- by 4-inch wood nailing strips are used as a base. In the single-course method (Figure 8–19), one course is simply laid over the other. The shingles can be second-grade because only one-half or less of the butt portion is exposed. Shingles should not be soaked before application but should usually be laid up with about 1/8- to 1/4-inch space between adjacent shingles to allow for expansion during rainy weather. When a "siding effect" is desired, shingles should be laid up so that they are only lightly in contact. Prestained or treated shingles provide the best results for this system.

In a double-course system (Figure 8–20), the undercourse is applied over the wall, and the top course nailed directly over a 1/4- to 1/2-inch projection of the butt. The first course should be nailed only

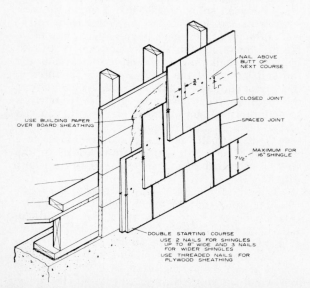

Figure 8–19. Single-coursing of sidewalls (wood shingles or shakes).

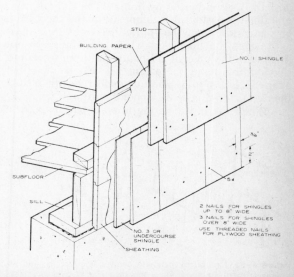

Figure 8–20. Double-coursing of sidewalls (wood shingles or shakes).

enough to hold it in place while the outer course is being applied. The first shingles can be a lower quality, such as third grade or the undercourse grade. The top course, because much of the shingle length is exposed, should be of first-grade shingles.

Exposure distances for shingles and shakes of various lengths can be estimated by the recommendations in Table 8–1.

Table 8–1

Material	Length (inches)	Single coursing (inches)	Double coursing (inches)	
			No. 1 grade	No. 2 grade
Shingles	16	7½	12	10
	18	8½	14	11
	24	11½	16	14
Shakes (hand-split and resawn)	18	8½	14	
	24	11½	20	
	32	15		

In estimating the quantity of shingles (or any other siding) needed for sidewalls, you should calculate the actual areas to be covered in terms of square feet. Door and window areas should be deducted. Take this square-foot figure to your local building supply dealer, and he will give you the proper quantity to do the job.

While wood shingles or shakes can be applied over old siding or other wall coverings that are sound and will hold nailing strips, it is usually a good idea to remove the old wall cover since the added thickness could cause considerable problems around door and window frames. The thinner mineral fiber (asbestos) and composition and sheet shingles and siding may be applied over old siding just as long as the door and window casings are not flush with the present siding. Aluminum, steel, and vinyl siding, being quite thin, are usually installed over the old siding, without backer board, unless the old material is in very poor condition.

When the old covering is employed as a base for new siding, make the following wall preparation:

1. Renail all loose boards or shingles. Repair any split boards.

2. Check flashing around doors and windows. If it is defective, repair it, or remove and replace it. Use sheet copper or aluminum.

3. Make the surface level by nailing a beveled wood strip or wood lath below each course of siding material. Strips of insulating board may also be used to level the surface.

If you decide to remove the old siding, be sure to check the condition of the flashing. If it is defective, remove and replace it. Also, if the old sheathing is not covered with asphalt-saturated felt or building paper, apply either material as follows: After cutting the paper into 12-inch strips, start along the bottom edge of the wall, nailing the paper with large-head galvanized nails. Continue nailing, spacing the nails 10 inches apart. Be sure to allow horizontal lengths of paper to lap 3 to 5 inches. Continue the paper up the wall, allowing each succeeding course to lap 6 inches. Never apply more felt or paper than you can cover with shingles during that day. Incidentally, some manufacturers recommend that you apply a layer of felt or paper over old siding when it is used as a base for new siding.

As previously stated, shingling should begin at the lowest point on the house wall. To be certain of a leakproof joint between the foundation and the wall at the sill, shingles should be carried down over the foundation at least 2 inches and preferably 4 inches. At this point a double layer of shingles is applied, one directly over the other, with vertical joints between shingles staggered 2 inches in each row, or course. Run a chalk guideline from end to end of the wall face, check it with a level, and place the first row along this line. In fact, it is best to establish the chalk line in relation to the eaves or the top and bottom of the windows after determining the lowest corner of the house. Snap a chalk line at the required height. Of course, if there are obvious irregularities in the levelness of the sill, you can make a compromise by adjusting this course off-level and gradually bring succeeding courses to a level line. The double course laid directly over the first is extended downward ¼ inch to provide a drip edge.

Closed or open joints may be used in the application of wood shingles to sidewalls at your discretion. Spacing of ¼ to ⅜ inch produces an individual effect, while close spacing produces a shadow line similar to that of bevel siding.

Shingles and shakes should be applied with rust-resistant nails long enough to penetrate into the wood backing strips or sheathing. In single-coursing, a threepenny or fourpenny zinc-coated "shingle" nail is commonly used. In double-cours-

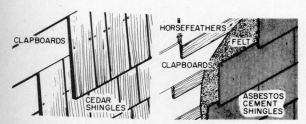

Figure 8–21. Method of installing cedar shingles (*left*) and asbestos cement (mineral fiber) shingles (*right*) over old clapboards. Horsefeathers are thin strips of tapered wood available in bundles at your lumberyard.

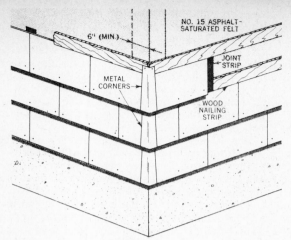

Figure 8–22. *(top)* An asbestos cement (mineral fiber) shingle application with metal corners. *(bottom)* The same shingle with a butt corner joint.

ing, where nails are exposed, a fivepenny zinc-coated nail with a small flat head is used for the top course, and threepenny or fourpenny size for the undercourse. Nails should be placed in from the edge of the wood shingle a distance of ¾ inch. Use two nails for each shingle up to 8 inches wide and three nails for shingles over 8 inches. In single-course applications, nails should be placed 1 inch above the butt line of the next-higher course. In double-coursing, the use of a piece of shiplap sheathing as a guide allows the outer course to extend ½ inch below the undercourse, producing a shadow line. Nails should be placed 2 inches above the bottom of the shingle or shake. Rived or fluted processed shakes, usually factory-stained, are available and have a distinct effect when laid with closely fitted edges in a double-course pattern. Wood shingles and shakes may be joined to form corners, using an interlacing pattern, or simply butted together at meeting edges.

Installation of siding.

One important factor in the successful performance of various siding materials is the type of fasteners used. Nails are the most common of these, and it is poor economy indeed to use them sparingly. Corrosion-resistant nails, galvanized or made of aluminum, stainless steel, or similar metals, may cost more, but their use will insure spot-free siding under adverse conditions.

Two types of nails are commonly used with siding, the finishing nail having a small head and the siding nail having a moderate-size flat head. The small-head finishing nail is set (driven with a nail set) about 1/16 inch below the face of the siding, and the hole is filled with putty after the prime coat of paint is applied. The flathead siding nail, most commonly used, is driven flush with the face of the siding, and the head later covered with paint. Ordinary steel-wire nails tend to rust in a short time and cause a disfiguring stain on the face of the siding. In some cases, the small-head nails will show rust spots through the putty and paint. Noncorrosive nails that will not cause rust are readily available.

Siding to be "natural finished" with a water-repellent preservative or stain should be fastened with stainless steel or aluminum nails. In some types of prefinished sidings, nails with color-matched heads are supplied. In recent years, nails with modified shanks have become quite popular. These include the annularly threaded shank nail and the helically threaded shank nail. Both have greater withdrawal resistance than the smooth shank nail and, for this reason, a shorter nail is often used. Exposed nails in siding should be driven just flush with the surface of the wood. Overdriving may not only leave a hammer mark, but may also cause objectionable splitting and crushing of the wood. In sidings with prefinished surfaces or overlays, the nails should be driven so as not to damage the finished surface. As with wood shingles and shakes, it is best to remove the old siding before applying new material.

Bevel siding.

Siding may be installed starting with the bottom course. It is normally blocked out with a starting strip the same thickness as the top of the siding board. Each succeeding course overlaps the upper edge of the lower course. Siding should be nailed to each stud or on 16-inch centers. When plywood or wood sheathing or spaced wood nailing strips are used over nonwood sheathing, sevenpenny or eightpenny nails (2¼ and 2½ inches long) may be used for ¾-inch-thick siding. However, if gypsum or fiberboard sheathing is used, the tenpenny nail is recommended to penetrate into the stud. For ½-inch-thick siding, nails may be ¼ inch shorter than those used for ¾-inch siding.

The nails should be located far enough up from the butt to miss the top of the lower siding course. This clearance distance is usually ⅛ inch. This allows for slight movement of the siding due to mois-

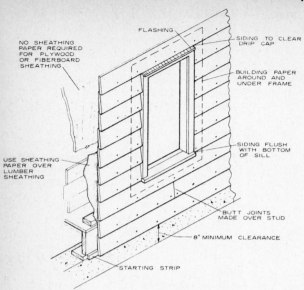

Figure 8—23. Installation of bevel siding.

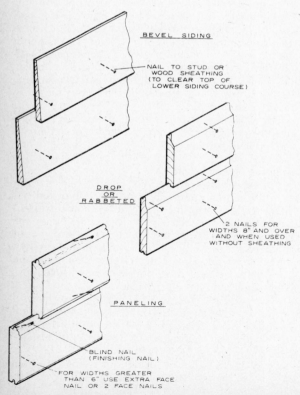

Figure 8—24. Nailing of siding.

ture changes without causing splitting. Such an allowance is especially required for the wider sidings of 8- to 12-inch widths.

It is good practice to avoid butt joints whenever possible. Use the longer sections of siding under windows and other long stretches and utilize the shorter lengths for areas between windows and doors. If necessary, butt joints should be made over a stud and staggered between courses as much as practical (Figure 8 – 23).

Siding should be square-cut to provide a good joint at window and door casings and at butt joints. Open joints permit moisture to enter, often leading to paint deterioration. It is good practice to brush or dip the fresh-cut ends of the siding in a water-repellent preservative before the boards are nailed in place. Using a small finger-actuated oil can to apply the water-repellent preservative at end and butt joints after the siding is in place is also helpful.

Drop and similar sidings. Drop siding is installed in much the same way as lap siding except for spacing and nailing. Drop, Dolly Varden, and similar sidings have a constant exposure distance. This face width is normally $5\frac{1}{4}$ inches for 1-by-6-inch siding and $7\frac{1}{4}$ inches for 1-by-8-inch siding. Normally, one or two eightpenny or ninepenny nails should be used at each stud crossing, depending on the width. The length of the nail depends on the type of sheathing used, but penetration into the stud or through the wood backing should be at least $1\frac{1}{2}$ inches.

Horizontally applied matched paneling in narrow widths should be blind-nailed at the tongue with a corrosion-resistant finishing nail. For widths greater than 6 inches, an additional nail should be used, as shown in Figure 8 – 24.

Other materials such as plywood, hardboard, or medium-density fiberboard, which are used horizontally in widths up to 12 inches, should be applied in the same manner as lap or drop siding, depending on the pattern. Prepackaged siding should be applied according to manufacturers' directions.

Vertical sidings. Vertically applied matched and similar sidings having interlapping joints are nailed in the same manner as when applied horizontally. However, they should be nailed to blocking used between studs or to wood or plywood sheathing. Blocking is spaced from 16 to 24 inches apart. With plywood or nominal 1-inch board sheathing, nails should be spaced on 16-inch centers.

When the various combinations of boards and battens are used, they should also be nailed to blocking spaced from 16 to 24 inches apart between studs, or closer for wood sheathing. The first boards or battens should be fastened with one eightpenny or ninepenny nail at each blocking, to provide at least $1\frac{1}{2}$-inch penetration. For wide underboards,

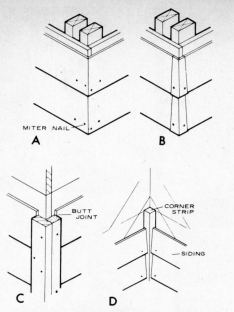

Figure 8-25. Siding details: (A) miter corner; (B) metal corners; (C) corner boards; (D) interior corner.

two nails spaced about 2 inches apart may be used rather than the single row along the center. The second or top boards or battens should be nailed with twelvepenny nails. Nails of the top board or batten should always miss the underboards and not be nailed through them. In such applications, double nails should be spaced closely to prevent splitting if the board shrinks. It is also good practice to use a sheathing paper, such as 15-pound asphalt felt, under vertical siding.

Plywood and other sheet siding. Exterior-grade plywood, paper-overlaid plywood, and similar sheet materials used for siding are usually applied vertically. When used over sheathing, plywood should be at least ¼ inch thick, although ⁵⁄₁₆ and ³⁄₈ inch will normally provide a more even surface. Hardboard should be ¼ inch thick, and materials such as medium-density fiberboard should be ½ inch.

All nailing should be over studs, and total effective penetration into wood should be at least 1½ inches. For example, ³⁄₈-inch plywood siding over ¾-inch wood sheathing would require about a sevenpenny nail, which is 2¼ inches long. This would result in a 1⅛-inch penetration into the stud, but a total effective penetration of 1⅞ inches into wood.

Plywood should be nailed at 6-inch intervals around the perimeter and 12 inches at intermediate members. Hardboard siding should be nailed at 4- and 8-inch intervals. Joints of all types of sheet material should be caulked with mastic unless the joints are of the interlapping or matched type or

battens are installed. A strip of 15-pound asphalt felt placed under uncaulked joints is good practice.

Installing vinyl siding. Vinyl siding is available in:

1. Horizontal. The most common types of horizontal siding in use are the double 4-inch exposure, and the single 6- and 8-inch exposures. They simulate the wood clapboard siding in appearance.

2. Vertical. The V-groove and the board and batten are the most popular vertical siding. They can be used in combination with the horizontal siding, particularly on gable ends. They are available in various exposures.

A complete line of accessories is available including inside corner posts, outside corner posts, starter strip, V-channel, F-channel, drip cap, inserts, and trim. They are designed to give every installation a professional, finished appearance, and make all joints weather-resistant. In addition, there are three types of backer board (see page 49) available, fiberboard, polystyrene foam, and honeycomb, which are used with vinyl paneling under certain circumstances. The backer board comes in lengths and widths to match fit the different types of siding. It need only be dropped in place behind the siding. In some cases trim accessories with wider channel openings may be required to accommodate the increased thickness of the insulated siding.

The inside and outside corner posts are installed first as directed by the manufacturer. As a rule, position the first nail at the top of the upper slot; the rest of the nailing should be in the center of the slots, 8 to 12 inches on centers. This allows for expansion and contraction to occur at the bottom. When the siding is installed, a ¼-inch space should be maintained in the channel section of the corner post. Vinyl can be cut with a power saw, tinsnips, and utility knife. A snaplock punch can be used to punch ears or lugs in the cut of the siding to be used for the top or finishing course.

Use only aluminum or other corrosion-resistant nails when installing vinyl siding. Nail in the center of the slot, approximately 16 inches on center. Some siding and accessories have parallel hammer-stop rails to prevent tight nailing. Do not nail tight. The panels should float on the nails to provide for expansion and contraction. Nail into studs where possible. Be sure nails hold securely, and that the nailing base is sound.

On uneven walls or masonry surfaces furring or strapping may be used to provide an even and nailable base. Shim out the furring at the high and low spots to get a final even surface. Furring may be vertical or horizontal, and strapping should be placed alongside all door and window frames and building corners. Accessories must be attached over strapping. Do not furr out farther than necessary; the alignment of the siding at doors and windows may be difficult if excessive furring is used.

Using a chalk line or cord as a guide, install a

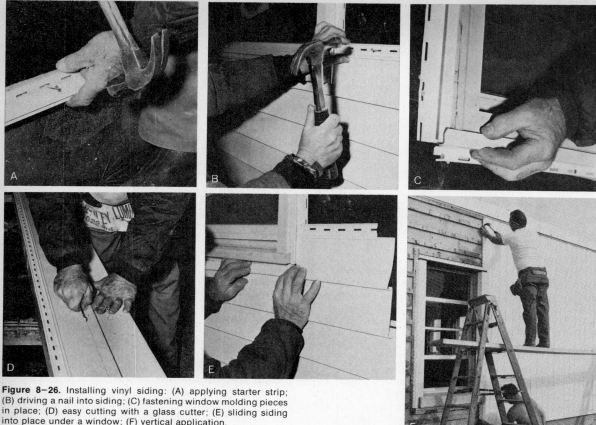

Figure 8–26. Installing vinyl siding: (A) applying starter strip; (B) driving a nail into siding; (C) fastening window molding pieces in place; (D) easy cutting with a glass cutter; (E) sliding siding into place under a window; (F) vertical application.

starter strip along the bottom of the building. Allow space for corner posts, J-channels, etc. Keep ends of the starter strips at least ¼ inch apart to allow for expansion. Nail in the center of the nailing slots. Align with the windows and eaves.

The first panel is placed in the starter strip and securely locked. If backer board is used, it is dropped in place, behind the siding panel, bevel edge down (if beveled) and towards the wall. Panels are fastened with nails that are centered in the nailing slots. Check the course to insure proper alignment with windows and eaves. Allowances should be made for expansion and contraction by leaving approximately ¼ inch at all corner posts and channels. If individual corner caps are used, cut back the panels ¼ inch from the corner. Vinyl panel ends should be lapped approximately one-half of the factory-prenotched end. Succeeding courses are similarly installed. Stagger the end laps so that one is not directly above the other, unless separated by three courses. Check every fifth or sixth course for alignment. Do not force the panels up or down when nailing in position. A panel should not be

under vertical tension or compression when it is nailed. Always overlap the joints away from entrances and from the point of greatest traffic. This will improve the overall appearance of the installation.

When fitting around openings, nail the J-channel on the sides of the doors and windows. A vinyl undersill trim or finish trim should be used under windowsills to receive the cut edges of the siding. Vinyl window head flashing should be installed above all doors and windows unless they have been previously flashed. Then either J-channel or undersill trim may be used at the window or door heads. It may be necessary to furr out under the windowsills so as to align the surface of the panels.

When the top is being finished, the appropriate accessory is installed along the bottom of the rake board. Furring may be needed to allow the last panel to be set at the proper angle.

Aluminum and steel siding are installed in much the same manner as vinyl. Always be sure to follow the instructions of the manufacturer to the letter.

Masonry veneer. Brick or stone veneer is used for all or part of the exterior wall finish for some styles of architecture. It may also be used as an exterior wall for an addition.

You do not have to remove the old siding when using a masonry veneer. But you must consider how many inches the present roof extends beyond the sides of the house. Where there is a large overhang, the new veneer can be brought right up to the roof without any difficulty. Extending the roof is a hard job, and probably is not necessary. There are other ways when the overhang is short. For instance, a veneer may be brought up to first-floor height, and the gable refinished in wide siding or prefinished panels. If your house does not have gables at the front side, the veneer can be carried up to the eaves easily. Sometimes the relocation of the gutters might have to be considered. It is a good idea to decide these points in advance.

The next consideration is the material to be used. There are bricks, fieldstone, cut stone, irregularly shaped slate, and simulated stone. These heavy materials cannot be supported by a frame wall and therefore must rest on a firm footing tied to the foundation. The veneer itself is tied into the framework of the house by metal strips.

As with nearly all masonry projects, this one begins with digging. Follow the present foundation down to the flooring. If it extends out 6 inches or more, you have no problem, as your new foundation may rest on that. If the footing is less, it must be built out to that distance by adding more concrete. Actually the main consideration is the footing in steps, as illustrated in Figure 8–27. To save materials that cost more, you can use concrete block or poured concrete, up to within a few inches of ground level, and start the veneer at that point. The new foundation should be tied to the old with mortar. To make it stick, wash all earth from the old wall first, then coat the wall with grout, a loose mixture of coarse sand and cement.

Once the foundation is ready, you can lay up the brick veneer wall as described in Chapter 2. When you reach a window opening, follow the line of the trim, bring the brick up under the sill, and

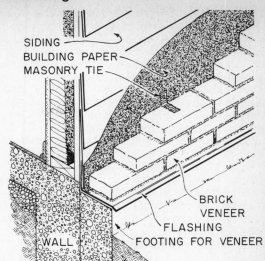

Figure 8–28. A typical brick veneer construction used when remodeling over old siding.

cement all joints between wood and brick. When this veneering system is used, the window frame and sill will be set in rather than protruding from the house. Across the tops of doors and windows, if the brickwork is to extend higher, it is necessary to use an L-shaped steel lintel long enough to have a bearing surface of at least 6 inches at each side of the opening. This is set back ½ inch from the outside, and the next course is laid along the lower flange of the lintel. Building supply dealers will furnish you with the right-size lintel for your project.

You will find it necessary to include metal ties, which are nailed to the frame wall in studs if possible, and extended out into the mortar joints of every other course. These ties are corrugated metal and serve to hold the veneer wall tightly to the house wall (Figure 8–28).

One word of caution in laying brick: if you find one brick out of line, do not try to reset it if the mortar has begun to set. Moving it will admit air into the mortar, which will quickly crumble. Instead, remove the brick and mortar, and reset the brick with fresh mortar.

Fieldstone walls are usually built 4 inches thick, and the stones are cut to assorted sizes. A scaled layout pattern, sometimes furnished by the stone supplier, is needed for laying these. Its purpose is to guide you in placing each stone in the proper place. When irregularly shaped stones are used, the artistry of the individual is necessary for an attractive result, and care must be taken to "come out even" at the openings.

Sandstone and slate may also be used for veneer. The technique is different here, however. A

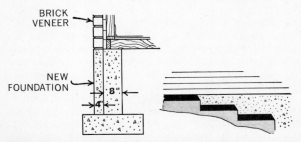

Figure 8–27. *(left)* The brick veneer must rest on a firm footing bonded to the house foundation. *(right)* If a house is built on a slope, use step-type footing beneath the veneer.

wire mesh (heavy duty) is spread over the siding and nailed there securely. A thin coat of mortar is spread over the mesh, and the surface is scratched sharply and then left to dry. Ties are nailed to the house at intervals. Then the stones, 1½ to 2 inches thick, are cemented to the wall, and each stone tied in. Care must be taken that every joint be filled flush to provide a binder to individual stones. Mortar for this job should be richer, 1:¹⁄₁₀:1½, or 1 part cement, ¹⁄₁₀ part lime, 1½ parts sand.

Real stone, thinly cut, such as that described on page 88 is suitable for exterior work, too. To install it, either remove the old siding and cover the sheathing with 15-pound felt or fasten exterior plywood sheathing over the old siding. The stone itself is then fastened to the sheathing with clips, as illustrated on page 88. Be sure to use waterproof mortar. No foundation is necessary when putting up this type of stone veneer.

ROOF COVERINGS

The average homeowner pays little attention to his roof, until it leaks. When it is time to replace a roof, you should be familiar with the choice of materials available and have an understanding of their proper application. Properly selected and applied, a roof covering provides a house with year-round protection and dramatic eye appeal. Two points are worth emphasis: (1) a leaking roof must be repaired or replaced immediately; and (2) a worn roof detracts from the appearance of a house and probably should be replaced before it actually starts leaking.

Materials. Materials used for pitched roofs are wood, asphalt, and asbestos shingles, and also tile and slate. Sheet materials such as roll roofing, galvanized iron, aluminum, copper, and tin are also used. Perhaps the most common covering for flat or low-pitched roofs is the built-up roof with a gravel topping or cap sheet. Plastic films, often backed with an asbestos sheet, are also being applied on low-slope roofs. While these materials are relatively new, it is likely that their use will increase, especially for roofs with unusual shapes. However, the choice of roofing materials is usually influenced by cost, local code requirements, house design, or preferences based on past experience.

In shingle application, the exposure distance is important, and the amount of exposure generally depends on the roof slope and the type of material used. This may vary from a 5-inch exposure for standard-size asphalt and wood shingles on a moderately steep slope to about 3½ inches for flatter slopes. However, even flatter slopes can be used for asphalt shingles with double underlay and triple-shingle coverage. Built-up construction is used mainly for flat or low-pitched roofs, but can be adapted to steeper slopes by the use of special materials and methods.

Roof underlay material usually consists of 15- or 30-pound asphalt-saturated felt and should be used in moderate- and lower-slope roofs covered with asphalt, asbestos, or slate shingles, or tile roofing. It is not commonly used for wood shingles or shakes. In areas where moderate to severe snowfalls occur, cornices without proper protection will often be plagued with ice dams. These are formed when snow melts, runs down the roof, and freezes at the colder cornice area. Gradually, the ice forms a dam that backs up water under the shingles. Under these conditions, it is good practice to use an undercourse (36 inches wide) of 45-pound or heavier smooth-surface roll roofing along the eave line as a flashing. This will minimize the chance of water backing up and entering the wall. However, good attic ventilation and sufficient ceiling insulation are of primary importance in eliminating this harmful nuisance. These details are described in Chapter 7.

Metal roofs (tin, copper, galvanized iron, or aluminum) are sometimes used on flat decks of dormers, porches, or entryways. Joints should be watertight and the deck properly flashed at the juncture with the house. Nails should be of the same metal as that used on the roof, except that steel nails may be used with tin roofs. All exposed nailheads in tin roofs should be soldered with a rosin-core solder.

Reroofing operation. Reroofing is a dangerous job unless you are familiar with roof work. Many homeowners have suffered serious injuries in falls from roofs and ladders. It is not for a home handyman, even with experience, to try to install anything but the asphalt strip-type shingle. Leave the other types of roofing material and surfaces to the professional roofer.

The usual minimum recommended weight for asphalt shingles is 235 pounds for square-butt strip shingles. This may change in later years, as 210 pounds (weight per square) was considered a minimum several years ago. Strip shingles with a 300-pound weight per square are available, as are lock-type and other shingles weighing 250 pounds and more. The heavier shingles last much longer, require less maintenance, and have greater fire and/or wind resistance. Naturally these shingles cost more, but they do eliminate roof worries for twenty to twenty-five years or even longer. Asphalt shingles are also available with seal-type tabs for wind resistance. Many contractors apply a small spot of asphalt roof cement under each tab after installation of regular asphalt shingles to provide similar protection. The square-butt strip shingle is 12 by 36 inches, has three tabs, and is usually laid with 5 inches exposed to the weather. There are 27 strips in a bundle, and three bundles will cover 100 square feet. Incidentally, roofing is estimated and sold in squares. A square of roofing is the amount required to cover 100 square feet of roof area. In

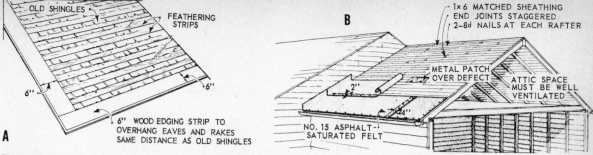

Figure 8–29. (A) Treatment at rakes and eaves when reroofing in a windy location. (B) Essential features of a satisfactory wooden roof deck.

order to estimate the amount required for any given roof, compute in square feet the total area to be covered, divide this amount by 100, and then add a certain percentage for waste and cutting. The percentage to add must be determined by individual experience. A good general average is 10 percent. Simple roofs, uncomplicated by dormers or other irregularities, will require less material, while complicated roofs will require more.

Reroofing procedures vary with the type of roofing material. Asphalt shingles, for example, can be applied directly over most existing roofs without the necessity of tear-offs. But asphalt shingles cannot be applied over hard or brittle materials such as tile and some slates that do not permit the driving of nails. A roof of wood shakes in need of reroofing requires a tear-off because the shakes do not offer a smooth surface for nailing. Application of asphalt shingles over asphalt or wood shingles can be done successfully, and the extra layer of shingles provides additional insulation and also eliminates the cost of tear-off.

Before reroofing, the condition of the old roof and its supports should be inspected for damage. If the roof deck or its supports is found to be warped, rotted, or otherwise unsound, old roofing should be removed so that the deteriorated roof structure can be repaired or replaced. If necessary, the chimney should be pointed, and damaged gutters relined, cleaned, rebuilt, or replaced. Flashing should be installed in valleys wherever needed and under-roof ventilation checked for adequacy. Metal drip edges should be applied along the eaves and rakes, and a flashing strip applied along the eaves.

Roofing nails used in applying asphalt shingles over old roofing must be long enough to penetrate through the old roofing and ¾ inch into the roof decking below. They are longer than nails used in new construction or where the old roofing has been removed.

Reroofing over old wood shingles. If an inspection of the old roof indicates that old wood shingles may remain, carefully prepare the surface

of the roof to receive the new roofing as follows:

1. Remove all loose or protruding nails, and renail the shingles in a new location.
2. Nail down all loose shingles.
3. Split all badly curled or warped old shingles and nail down the segments.
4. Replace missing shingles with new ones.
5. Where the roof is in a location subject to the impact of unusually high winds, cut back the shingles at eaves and rakes far enough to allow the application at these points of 1-inch-thick wood strips 4 inches to 6 inches wide. Nail the strips firmly in place, allowing their outside edges to project beyond the edge of the deck the same distance as did the wood shingles. To provide a smooth deck to receive asphalt roofing apply a "backer board" over the wood shingles or use beveled wood "feathering strips" along the butts of each course of old shingles.

If old asphalt shingles are to remain in place, nail down or cut away all loose, curled, or lifted shingles; remove all loose and protruding nails; remove all badly worn edging strips and replace them with new ones; and just before applying the new roofing, sweep the surface clear of all loose debris.

Reroofing over asphalt shingles. When new asphalt roofing is to be laid over old roll roofings or old asphalt, proceed as follows to prepare the deck:

1. Slit all buckles and nail segments down smoothly.
2. Remove all loose and protruding nails.
3. If some of the old roofing has been torn away, leaving sections of the deck exposed, examine such areas to note any loose or pitchy knots and excessively resinous areas.

When the framing supporting the existing deck is not strong enough to support the additional weight of roofing, or when the decking material is so far gone that it will not furnish adequate anchorage for the new roofing nails, the old roofing, regardless of type, must be removed before you apply the new roofing. Then prepare the deck as follows:

1. Make repairs to the existing roof framing where required to level and true it to provide adequate strength.

2. Remove all rotted or warped old sheathing (delaminated units in the case of plywood) and replace with new sheathing.

3. Fill in all the spaces between the boards with securely nailed wood strips of the same thickness as the old deck; or move existing sheathing together and sheath the remainder of the deck.

4. Pull out all protruding nails and renail the sheathing firmly at the new nail locations.

5. Cover all large cracks, slivers, knotholes, loose knots, pitchy knots, and excessively resinous areas with sheet metal securely nailed to the sheathing. Just before applying the new roofing, sweep the deck thoroughly clean of all loose debris.

For working on sloping roofs, some means of maintaining a foothold is desirable. A long straight ladder with hooks at the end may be laid on the roof ridge. Another device, called a "roof jack," is made of two metal straps to which a board is attached. The upper ends of the metal straps have holes or notches through which nails can be driven into the roof to hold the jack in place. When the jack is moved, the nails are driven on down into the roof.

Laying the shingles. When the shingles arrive, the bundles should be piled flat for storage so that strips will not curl when the bundles are opened for use. To start the reroofing job itself, it is recommended that horizontal and vertical chalk lines be used to insure good shingle alignment. Since minor variations in the dimensions of asphalt shingles are unavoidable, it is essential that closely spaced chalk lines be used to control the placement of shingles so that cutouts will be accurately aligned horizontally, vertically, and diagonally on the roof. Where a roof surface is broken, start laying shingles

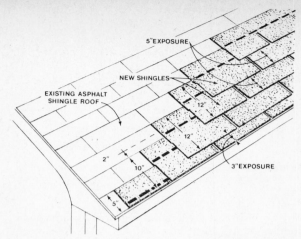

Figure 8–31. Proper exposure when reroofing under normal conditions.

Figure 8–32. Random spacing of three-tab square butt strips.

from a rake toward a dormer or into a valley. Where unbroken, begin at the rake that is most visible. If both rakes are equally visible, start at the center and work both ways.

The actual laying of asphalt strip shingles begins with the application of a starter course whose function with both square butt and hexagonal patterns is to back up the first regular course of shingles and fill in the spaces between tabs. The starter course is laid with tabs facing up, over the eave edges. With square butt shingles, cut about 3 inches off the first starter course shingle to insure that all cutouts will be covered. With hex strips the first shingle is not cut. The starter course for the self-sealing type of shingle should have the exposed (tab) portion removed and the sealant adjacent to the eaves.

The number of nails per strip and the placing of the nails are both vital factors in good roof application. With three-tab, square butt strip shingles use a minimum of 4 nails per strip. Align each shingle carefully. Start nailing from the end nearest the

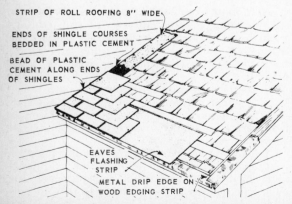

Figure 8–30. The use of flashing against a vertical wall when reroofing over old material.

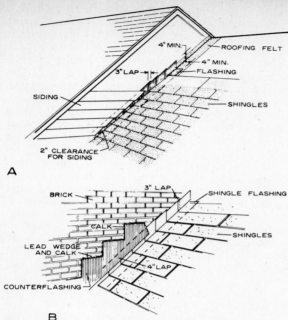

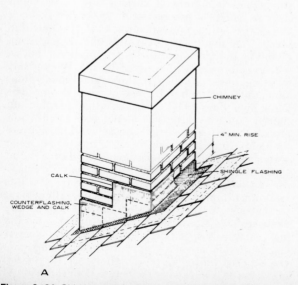

Figure 8-33. Roof and wall intersection: (A) wood siding wall; (B) brick wall.

shingle just laid, and proceed across. This will prevent buckling. Drive the nails straight so that the edge of the nailhead will not cut into the shingle. Nailheads should be driven flush, not sunk into the surface. Proper nailing increases roof strength and resistance to high winds.

Flashing and reroofing. Serviceable old chimney metal flashing should be left in place and reused, but if badly deteriorated it should be removed and replaced. To do this, apply a strip of roll roofing approximately 8 inches wide on the reconditioned roof surface at the front and sides of the chimney. It should be laid so that it abuts the chimney on all sides and should be secured to the old roof with a row of nails along each edge. At the junction where it meets the chimney, apply a heavy coating of plastic asphalt cement to each course of shingles, holding the lower edge slightly back of the exposed edge of the covering shingle, and bending it up against the masonry to which it is secured with a suitable asphalt cement. Nails are driven through the lower edge of the flashing into the roof deck. These nails are covered with the plastic cement, which is used to secure the end shingle to the horizontal portion of the flashing, and also by the shingle itself. The operation is repeated for each course. The flashing units are wide enough to lap each other at least 3 inches, the upper one overlaying the lower one each time. The masonry should then be cleaned with a wire brush for a distance of 6 or 8 inches above the deck, and a suitable asphalt primer should be applied to the masonry surface.

After the primer is applied, plastic asphalt cement should be troweled over the shingles for a distance of approximately 2 inches and up the chimney against the masonry surface for 4 to 6 inches. A strip of mineral-surfaced roll roofing wide enough to cover the cement should then be pressed into the cement, the side pieces being returned around and over the ends of the front piece, and around the back of the chimney for a distance of about 6

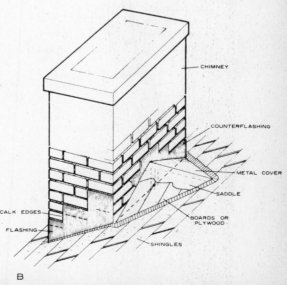

Figure 8-34. Chimney flashing: (A) flashing without a saddle; (B) flashing with a chimney saddle.

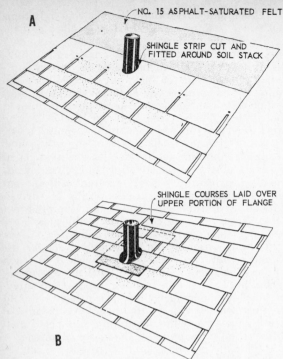

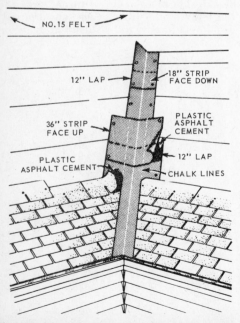

Figure 8–35. Vent pipe fitting on a roof: (A) Roofing is applied up to the pipe and fitted around it. (B) Shingling is completed past and above the pipe.

Figure 8–36. The use of roll roofing for typical open-valley flashing.

inches. If the original construction did not provide a cricket behind the chimney, the base flashing at this point should consist of a 36-inch-wide strip of mineral-surfaced roll roofing, applied to lie 24 inches up the roof over the old roofing and 12 inches up the rear face of the chimney. It should be bedded in plastic asphalt cement applied over the old roofing and against the primed masonry surface. The cement should be well troweled into all irregularities between the roof deck and the masonry, and the upper edge should be secured by nailing into a mortar joint.

Almost all roofs have vent pipes protruding from the deck. Such pipes always have flashing around them. Old metal flashing around the protrusion should be examined carefully. If it has deteriorated, remove it and apply new flashing. If the metal flashing is in good condition, proceed as follows:

1. Lift the lower part of the flange and apply the shingles underneath it up to the pipe.

2. Replace the flange, bedding it in asphalt roof cement.

3. Protect the junction of the metal sleeve and the flange with an application of roof cement.

4. Proceed to apply shingles around the pipe and up the roof.

Among flashing jobs, one of the most vital is the construction of good valleys where two sloping roofs meet at an angle. The recommended flashing material for valleys is 90-pound, mineral-surfaced asphalt roll roofing of a matching or neutral color. Because valleys often must take care of a heavy flow and a considerable backing up of water, the flashing must be laid to extend well beyond the anticipated shingle line. A first flashing strip, preferably 18 inches wide, is centered lengthwise in the valley and laid mineral surface down. After this strip is nailed, a second strip, 36 inches wide, is laid over the first, mineral surface up, and nailed in place. The sealing of the valley flashing is completed as the asphalt shingles are applied. That is, when you are ready, roofing is applied. When ready to shingle over a valley flashing, snap chalk lines along the full length of the valley, on each side. The chalk lines should be 6 inches apart at the ridge and should spread apart $1/8$ inch per foot as they approach the eaves. Lay each course of shingles up to the chalk lines and trim to fit. Clip off the upper corner of each shingle diagonally, from a point about 1 inch in to a point about 1 inch down, to direct water into valley. Secure each shingle, as it is laid and trimmed, to the valley lining with cement so that a tight seal is formed. Do not permit any exposed nails along the valley flashing. Follow the manufacturer's specifications for exposure. Normal exposure of square butt strip shingles is 5 inches. Lay the exposed butt edge of the tab even with the top of the cutouts in the course below. The exposure of hex strip shingles is normally $4^{2}/3$ inches. Because

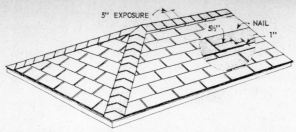

Figure 8–37. The application of hip and ridge shingles.

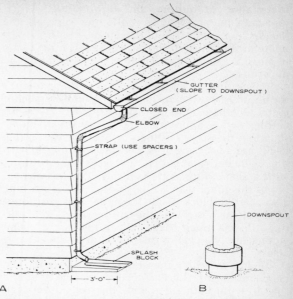

Figure 8–38. Downspout installation: (A) downspout with splash block; (B) drain to a storm sewer or dry well.

the top edge of the cutouts is the same length as the exposed lower edge of the tabs, the shingles are self-aligning and will produce the proper hex pattern when carefully laid.

Hips and ridges. Special shingles for finishing hips and ridges are supplied by manufacturers, and their application is covered by the manufacturers' direction sheets. Hip and ridge capping also can be made from the shingles used to cover the roof (Figure 8–37). Never use metal ridging with asphalt roofing. Corrosion may discolor the roof.

The following gives the steps to follow in applying special shingles:

1. Bend each ridge shingle lengthwise down the center so that it extends an equal distance on each side of the ridge. In cold weather the shingle should be pliable before bending.

2. Beginning at the bottom of the hip, or at one end of a ridge, apply the shingles over the hip or ridge, exposing them 5 inches. Secure each ridge shingle with one nail on each side, 5½ inches back from the exposed butt end, and 1 inch up from the side edges.

GUTTERS

Gutters play an important part in both the protection and beauty of your home. They keep water from sloshing down the side of the house and beating a path along the ground into your basement. That is, if they leak, you will have not only water dripping into unwanted places, but perhaps ugly rust stains on the house as well.

Selecting gutters. Modern gutters are made of wood, metal, or plastic. While wood was one of our first gutter materials, its popularity has decreased rapidly in the last few years because of its weight, cumbersomeness, and cost, plus the fact that it needs frequent applications of wood preservative to prevent rot. As a result, metal and plastic are the most frequently used types of gutters in home remodeling today.

Metal gutters are available in four varieties: galvanized steel, enameled galvanized, aluminum, and enameled aluminum. The least expensive, galvanized steel gutters must be primed with a rust-

inhibitor and then painted. Care must be taken to paint all exposed areas, or corrosion will occur.

Aluminum gutters do not rust when left unfinished since they have their own natural protective coating against the elements. But, because they are lighter than steel, they are subject to denting by a ladder or similar objects. The long-life, baked-on enamel finish permits color-matching without the problems of painting. However, keep in mind that steel gutters will rust if their enameled surface is scratched and the metal exposed. Also remember never to mix aluminum and steel gutters, since contact between the two metals starts electrolytic action and corrosion.

Plastic gutters made of polyvinyl chloride (PVC) will not corrode and never need painting. The major problem with plastic gutters is their high coefficient of thermal expansion, which means that if not properly installed they may buckle in hot weather. They also do not have the stiffness of the steel gutters.

To determine the amount of material necessary, measure the length of the gutters around the house. Most gutters are available in 10-foot lengths; figure how many multiples of 10 feet are required. Some manufacturers produce longer lengths of gutters, but these are more difficult to handle. Once you have figured out the length of gutters and downspouts needed, plus the various accessories such as elbows, corners, and hangers, take the list to your local building supply dealer.

Installation of gutters and downspouts. When replacing gutters remove only one run, all the lengths along one side of the house, at a time. Try not to break or distort the old gutter when removing it, since it makes a fine guide when assembling the new runs.

Once the old gutter is on the ground, line up the appropriate fixtures and the required number of gutter lengths parallel to it. Mark the new pieces for cutting to the appropriate size. Use a carpenter's square to mark the cutting lines. As for the cutting itself, use a hacksaw or power saw with a metal cutting blade for metal gutter; the plastic one can be cut with a sharp, fine-tooth handsaw. To prevent flexing of the gutter wall while sawing the gutter, slide a wood filler-block inside the gutter and position it as closely as possible to the cutting point. After cutting, file the rough edges and, in the case of metal gutters, apply a coat of rust-inhibitor to the cut surfaces.

Before installing the new gutters, check the fascia board for rot. If it is defective, replace it, but be sure to paint both sides and edges of the replacement piece.

The downspout end of the gutter must be located at the lowest point on the fascia board. To achieve this, snap a chalk line on the fascia board to

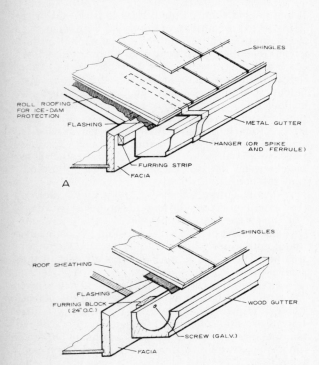

Figure 8–39. Gutter installation: (A) formed metal gutter; (B) wooden gutter.

the desired slope of the gutter. Whenever possible, the degree of slope should be $1/8$ inch per foot in order to insure proper water drainage.

Installing plastic gutters. To install the gutter hangers, line them up with the chalk line and nail them to 18-inch centers. (Up to 24-inch spacing may be used in areas where there is no danger of ice build-up in the gutters.) Be sure the section of each hanger in contact with the fascia is perpendicular to the chalk line. Use only noncorrosive screws or nails. Hangers must be located so that when the gutter is snapped in place it will properly receive the water that runs off the roof. In installations where no fascia board exists, special gutter hanger rods are required. These rods are nailed to the roof edge and bent to the desired angle.

Collector boxes or expansion joints should be used on long runs in order to avoid problems with expansion and contraction. Allowance for movement is made by properly aligning hangers and by not placing hangers closer than 18 inches on corners adjacent to long runs. In gutter installations where the ends are not confined so as to prevent excess lateral shifting, it is advisable to secure the gutter to prevent any possibility of creeping. This may be accomplished by drilling a nail hole as high as possible in the mid-point of the back wall of the gutter section. Then nail the gutter to the fascia using shims, if necessary, to maintain the proper alignment. Where the ends of the gutter are confined between walls or rake boards, a $1/2$-inch space should be maintained on each end.

On buildings with inside and/or outside corners, always start a gutter system installation at a corner. Attach the corner securely to one gutter end prior to placing the section into the hangers. Once the section is clamped firmly into the hangers, attach the other gutter end. On a small hip roof building, by using hangers only and properly spacing them, the required allowance for expansion-contraction can be planned for. This is done by placing on successive corners one hanger 6 inches from a corner, and the next hanger around the corner, 18 inches from the corner. If this practice is followed on each corner, allowance will be made for the expansion-contraction that is required.

For assembling details follow the manufacturer's directions most carefully. As a rule "pop" rivets and PVC cement are used to fasten sections together. Elbows usually connect outlet tubes and collector outlets to the downspout. Select the proper elbow and insert its fluted end into the adjoining elbow, making certain the fluted end is pointed downstream. Connect the elbows with a section of downspout cut to the proper length, when the soffit is so wide that elbows cannot be joined directly to each other. Short lengths of downspout may be used for this purpose by cutting $1\frac{1}{2}$-inch slits on diagonally opposite corners of the short length of the down-

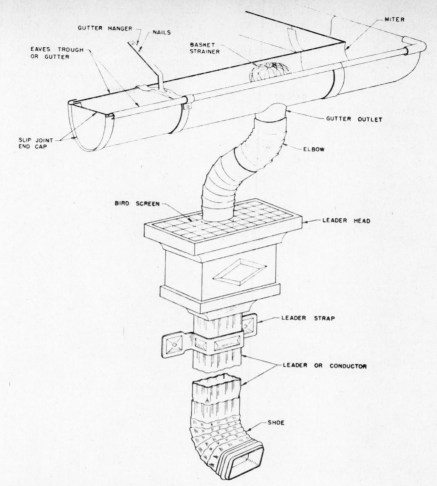

Figure 8—40. Factory-made roof drainage products.

spout, then squeezing this end of the downspout and inserting it into the large end of the elbow. Downspouts are fastened to the wall with downspout straps. Use only aluminum screws or nails; other kinds will corrode and weather-stain the vinyl. Be sure they are long enough to anchor the downspout securely to the wall. If the gap between wall and downspout is too wide, shim the downspout strap away from the wall with 1-inch wood stock. Coat each screw or nailhead with PVC cement to make it match the gutter system. Use two straps on each 10-foot length of downspout and three straps on two joined 10-foot sections.

Installing metal gutters. Most metal gutters are installed with large spikes that pass through the sides into the fascia board. A metal tube, called a ferrule, mounts around the spike and maintains the

spacing of the gutter sides. These spikes should be located 24 to 30 inches apart depending on snow conditions.

Two other methods of hanging metal gutters can be employed. The first uses sickle-shaped hangers, which are fastened to the fascia boards about every 30 inches, then the gutters are laid on top of the hanger. This method eliminates the need for drilling holes in the gutter and thus is easier than spiking the gutters in place. However, the sickle-shaped hangers are more expensive than the spikes.

The second method of hanging metal gutters is to use strap hangers, which have flanges that are nailed in place under the roofing material. This type of hanger is best used on new work, since there is always a chance of damaging the existing roofing when prying it up to install the hanger.

Installation procedures for elbows and downspouts are very similar to those used for plastic sections. To perform their maximum service, downspouts should be installed so as to carry water as far away from the foundation line as practicable. While there are several ways of achieving this, the three most popular are: (1) a concrete splash block, directly under the downspout; (2) a dry well, located at least 10 feet from the foundation; and (3) a storm sewer, which is connected directly to the main sewerage system. More information on drain water runoff from the gutter system is given in Chapter 12.

Chapter 9

IMPROVING THE HOME BY PAINTING AND WALLCOVERINGS

Paint can transform your home far more quickly and inexpensively than any other material available. A new coat of paint on your walls can bring with it a sparkle and beauty that will affect every member of your household and make your furnishings seem twice as attractive. But paint is more than beauty; it is protection too. Paint will add years to the life of your home, or your walls, or your furniture. Applied correctly, it may have to be renewed only at long intervals, depending on your own requirements and tastes.

In the last few years, enormous advances have been made in paint technology, and it is true that anyone can do a superb paint job today, if only reasonable care is taken. The proper preparation of surfaces is a vital factor in successful painting. Paints must be matched to surfaces or to requirements just as carefully. But, before taking a look at these two important points of improving your home with paint, let us consider the methods of applying it.

METHODS OF APPLYING PAINT

In order to do a good job with a minimum of trouble, choose the right tools and learn how to handle them properly. When painting your home, outside or inside, you have a choice among three tools: a brush, a roller, and a sprayer. Which one to use for the painting job you plan depends upon the surface to be painted.

Using a brush. The use of a brush assures good contact of paint with pores, cracks, and crevices. Brushing is particularly recommended for applying primer coats and exterior paints. It is also the most effective way of painting windows, doors, and intricate trim work. For spray work, window glass must be masked, a tedious affair for the most part.

Selecting a brush. Brush prices vary considerably; the greatest difference between one brush and another lies in the bristle stock, which may be made from either natural or synthetic sources. Natural bristle brushes are made with hog hair. This type of brush was originally recommended for applying oil-base paints, varnishes, lacquers, and other finishes, because natural fibers resist strong solvents.

Synthetic bristle brushes are made from a synthetic fiber, usually nylon. Today's nylon brushes are recommended for both latex (water-soluble) and oil-base paints, because this tough synthetic fiber absorbs less water than natural bristles do, while also resisting most strong paint and lacquer solvents. In addition, nylon bristles are easier to clean than natural bristles.

Brush quality determines painting ease, plus the quality of the finished job. A good brush holds more paint, controls dripping and spattering, and applies paint more smoothly to minimize brush marks. To assure that you are buying a quality

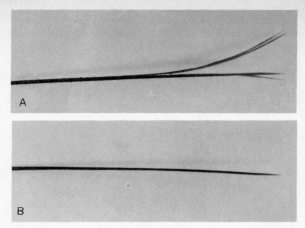

Figure 9–1. (A) A flagged bristle has split ends, which help to load the brush with more paint while assisting the paint to flow smoothly on the surface. Cheap brushes have less flagging or none at all. (B) A tapered bristle also helps the paint to flow and releases it smoothly. Check to see that the base of each bristle is thicker than the tip. The tip thus has a fine painting edge for even and accurate work.

brush, check the following factors:

1. Flagged bristles (Figure 9–1A) have split ends that help load the brush with more paint, while permitting the paint to flow on more smoothly. Cheaper brushes will have less flagging, or none at all.

2. Tapered bristles (Figure 9–1B) also help paint flow and provide smooth paint release. Check to see that the base of each bristle is thicker than the tip. This helps give the brush tip a fine painting edge for more even and accurate work.

3. The fullness of a brush is important too. As you press the bristles against your hand, they should feel full and springy. If the divider in the brush setting is too large, the bristles will feel skimpy, and there will be a large hollow space in the center of the brush.

4. Bristle length should vary. As you run your hand over the bristles, some shorter ones should pop up first, indicating a variety of bristle lengths for better paint loading and smoother release.

Size (inches)	Application
1–1½	Touch-up and little jobs, such as toys, tools, furniture legs, and hard-to-reach corners.
2–3	Trim work, such as sashes, frames, molding, or other flat surfaces. An angular-cut brush helps do clean, neat sash or narrow trim work and makes edge cutting easier.
3½ or 4	Larger flat surfaces, such as floors, walls, or ceilings.
4½–6	Large flat areas, particularly masonry surfaces, barns, or board fences.

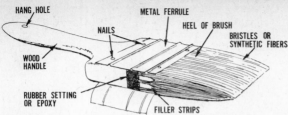

Figure 9–2. Anatomy of a good paintbrush: The handle should be perfectly balanced and shaped comfortably to the hand. A metal ferrule secures the bristles to the handle. A good rubber-base or epoxy setting prevents the bristles from coming loose. Filler strips of wood, metal, or plastic help to shape the bristles into a natural taper and to form a reservoir in the center of the brush that provides a good paint flow.

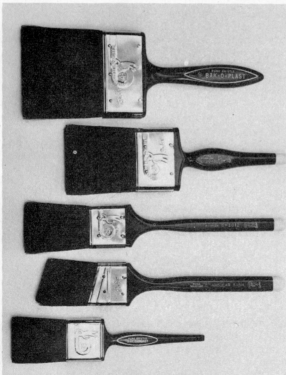

Figure 9–3. Five brushes to meet all home painting needs: *(top to bottom)* 4-inch wall brush; 3-inch enameling brush; 2-inch trim brush; 2-inch sash brush; 2-inch varnish brush.

5. A strong setting is important for bristle retention and maximum brush life. Bristles should be firmly bonded into the setting with epoxy glue, and nails should be used only to hold the ferrule to the handle. Brush size and shape are also important. The choice of a brush width is determined by the amount of open or flat area to be painted. The table on the bottom of page 304 may be used as a guide, but should not be considered a limiting factor when selecting a brush.

Brushing technique. Hold the brush by gripping the wide part of the handle between your fingertips near the metal ferrule. The rest of the handle should be held between your thumb and forefinger, as you would grip a pencil. This is the best way to hold the brush except when working overhead. In this case wrap your hand around the handle with the thumb resting against the handle's inside curve. Use long, steady strokes and moderate, even pressure; excessive pressure or "stuffing" the brush into corners and cracks may damage the bristles.

Always work toward the "wet edge," the previously painted area, making sure not to try to cover too large a surface with each brushload. When loading the brush with paint, do not dip more than half the bristle length into the paint. Tap the bristle tips lightly against the inside rim of the can to remove excess. Never wipe the brush edgewise across the rim. This removes more paint than necessary, causes the brush to separate or finger, and causes tiny bubbles that make it hard to get a smooth job.

Brush care. A good brush is an expensive tool, and it pays to invest the necessary time and effort to take care of it properly. Clean brushes immediately after use with a thinner or special brush cleaner recommended by your paint or hardware store. Use turpentine or mineral spirits to remove oil-base paints, enamels, and varnish; alcohol to remove shellac; and special solvents to remove lacquer. Remove latex paints promptly from brushes with soap and water. If any type of paint is allowed to dry on a brush, a paint remover or brush-cleaning solvent will be needed. Use the following procedure to clean paint brushes:

1. After removing excess paint with a scraper, soak the brush in the proper thinner, working it against the bottom of the container.

2. To loosen paint in the center of the brush, squeeze the bristles between thumb and forefinger, then rinse the brush again in thinner. If necessary, work the brush in mild soap suds, and rinse in clear water.

3. Press out the water with a stick.

4. Twirl the brush in a container so you will not get splashed.

5. Comb the bristles carefully, including those below the surface. Allow the brush to dry by suspending it from the handle or by laying it flat on a clean surface. Then wrap the dry brush in the origi-

Figure 9—4. Method of cleaning brushes: *(left)* Soak the brush in a proper thinner, working it against the bottom of the container. To loosen paint in the center of the brush, squeeze the bristles between the thumb and forefinger, then rinse again in the thinner. *(left center)* If necessary, work the brush in mild soap suds; rinse in clear water. Press out the water with a stick. *(right center)* Twirl the brush in a container so that you will not be splashed. *(right)* Comb bristles, including those below the surface, carefully. Allow the brush to dry either by suspending it from the handle or by laying it flat on a clean surface.

nal wrapper or in heavy paper to keep the bristles straight. Store the brush suspended by its handle or lying flat.

Using a roller. Paint rollers are faster than brushes when working on large, flat surfaces. It has been estimated that this comparatively new painting tool is today being used to apply over 75 percent of all interior wall and ceiling paint, and it is being used in an impressive share of outdoor painting tasks as well.

Selecting a roller. It is important to choose the proper type of roller for the particular job to be done. Modern paint rollers are available in various sizes and with handles of different lengths. Many are built so that extensions can be screwed into their handles. This makes it possible to paint ceilings or stairwells as high as 12 feet while standing on the floor, or to paint the floor without stooping. You can enamel a baseboard much faster with a roller than a brush and thus will have to spend less time in an uncomfortable position. Be sure to protect the wall and floor when you paint the baseboard.

Roller covers are available in a variety of widths suitable for use on different-size areas (Figure 9–5). For walls and ceilings, the best size roller for the amateur is the 7- or 9-inch model. For finished woodwork, doors, and trim, the best choice is the 3-inch model. There are smaller sizes available to cut in corners and for use on window frames and moldings. There are even doughnut-shaped rollers that will coat both sides of a corner at the same time. To help you paint a wall without getting the paint on the ceiling, there are special edging rollers, too. Flat painting "pads" (some with guide wheels) are available for use on fencing, siding, shakes, and other hard-to-get-at surfaces. Most paint trays are designed for use with a roller up to 9 inches wide. Roller frames can have a compression type cage, or the roller cover can be held on with an end cap held by a wing nut. Compression frames permit easier and faster roller cover mounting or removal. If you apply floor or ceiling paint with your roller, be sure the frame handle has a threaded end that will permit an extension pole to be added.

The fabric on the roller cover should conform to the type of paint to be applied. Lambswool rollers are excellent with oil-based paints, but they should not be used with water-thinned latex paints. Water softens and swells rayon and lambswool. These roller fabrics lose their resilience, and the fibers mat together, when used in latex paints. Oil or alkyd paints and varnishes are usually thinned with mineral spirits or turpentine. Roller fabrics of all types are not affected by these thinners. Toluol and Xylol are sometimes used, however, and these thinners may swell polyurethane foam covers. Lacquers and two-component epoxy enamels are generally thinned with solvent mixtures that contain ketones. Ketone solvents will degrade Dynel, acetate, and polyurethane foam roller covers. Mohair rollers can be used with any type of interior flat paint, but are recommended especially for applying enamel and wherever a smooth finish is desired. Rollers made from synthetic fibers can be used with all types of flat paint, inside and out.

In buying a roller, be sure the roll can easily be removed and changed. If both oil and water paints are to be applied, get a roll for each. Make sure that neither water nor oil will soften the tube (frequently

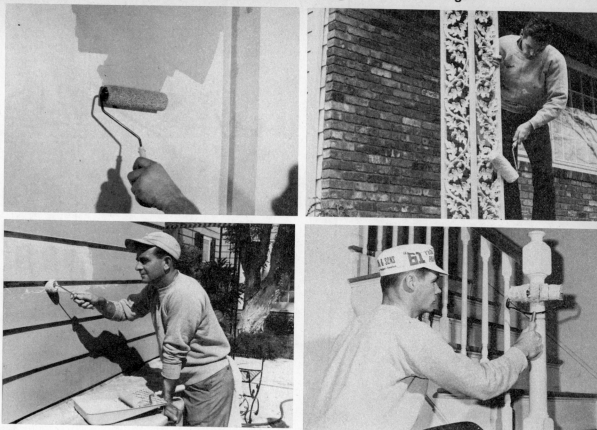

Figure 9–5. Suitable rollers are available for every type of job.

treated cardboard) that supports the pile. It may be better to get a roll with the material stretched over a plastic tube.

Walls can be made uniquely attractive by using a special roller to stipple a contrasting color over another one. Stippling rollers come in a wide assortment of design-producing sleeves. With these rollers, however, a different rolling technique must be used. The roll should be started at the left-hand side of the wall at the ceiling line, and the roller drawn evenly in a straight line to the floor. The second stroke should not overlap, but simply fit against the edge of the first.

Another factor to consider when choosing a roller is the length of the nap or pile. This can range from $\frac{1}{16}$ to $1\frac{1}{2}$ inches. A handy rule to remember is the smoother the surface, the shorter the nap; the rougher the surface, the longer the nap. Use short-napped rollers for most walls, ceilings, and woodwork and smooth concrete. The longer naps are for rough masonry, brick, stucco, wire fences, and other

irregular surfaces. Your paint dealer can help you with this choice or you can use the following chart:

Pile	Application
Standard: $\frac{1}{4}$- or $\frac{3}{8}$-inch	Most ceiling, wall, or floor work.
High: $\frac{3}{4}$- or $1\frac{1}{2}$-inch	Exceptionally rough surfaces, such as stucco, masonry, brick, and wire fences.
Stipple (carpet weave)	For a stipple-textured finish or rolling on mastic materials.

Roller technique. Before applying the paint with a roller, first cut in the edges of the wall and hard-to-reach areas with a brush or with an edging roller, taking care not to get paint on the ceiling or the adjacent wall.

Some roller models have a roll that may be filled with paint, which soaks through a perforated backing into the pile cover. However, most rollers used by amateurs are manually loaded from a tilted tray, which usually has a corrugated bottom. Before

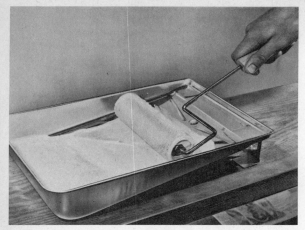

Figure 9–6. To save time when painting with a roller, line the tray with foil or heavy paper. Color changes are thus easy to make, and tray cleaning is eliminated.

ways start in a dry area and roll toward one just painted, blending in the laps.

Roller care. Rollers should be thoroughly cleaned after each use. You should use the same cleaning liquids as those recommended for brushes for the various types of coatings. Pour the liquid into a shallow pan and roll the tool back and forth in it. Then roll out the paint and thinner on newspaper. The roller cover can also be cleaned by putting it into a large-mouth jar filled with thinner (or water, if you are using a water-thinned paint), and then shaking the jar.

The paint tray should also be cleaned after each use. If you line it with newspaper held in place with masking tape, before use, your cleaning will be much easier. Tin or aluminum foil serves better with water-base paints, since newspapers may disintegrate when wet with water. After the roller has been washed, wipe with a clean dry cloth and wrap in aluminum foil. This will keep it soft until the next time it is used.

Using a paint sprayer. Paint sprayers are particularly useful for large areas. Spraying is much faster than brushing or rolling and, although some paint will likely be wasted through over-spraying, the savings in time and effort may more than compensate for any additional paint cost. Once you have perfected your spraying technique, you can produce a coating with excellent uniformity in thickness and appearance. In many localities, paint sprayers may be rented on a daily or weekly basis from paint dealers or tool rental shops.

Surface areas accessible only with difficulty to the brush or roller can readily be covered by the sprayer. All coats can be applied satisfactorily by the spray technique *except for the primer coats.* Spraying should be done only on a clean surface

paint is poured into the roller tray, it should be thoroughly mixed in the can to assure even pigment distribution. The tray should be propped so that about two-thirds of the bottom is covered with paint.

Next, dip the roller into the tray. Dip it into the edge of the paint, rolling the tool back and forth over the slanting corrugated section of the tray to distribute the paint evenly over the entire surface of the roller and to remove excess paint. If the roller drips when lifted from the tray, it is overloaded. The excess should be wiped off on the dry side of the tilted tray before you begin your stroke.

Apply even pressure when rolling paint on a surface. Even if the general direction of the painting may be downward, make your first stroke upward to avoid dripping. Work up and down first, doing about three strips, then work the roller horizontally to assure even coverage. As you progress, al-

Figure 9–7. Using a spray gun is the quickest way to paint.

since the paint may not adhere well if a dust film is present. Pre-preparation of the paint is of critical importance, however, when a sprayer is to be used. Stir or strain the paint to remove any lumps, and thin it carefully. If the paint is lumpy or too thick it may clog the spray valve; if it is too thin the paint may sag or run after it is applied. Follow the manufacturer's instructions on the paint label for the type and amount of thinner to be used.

Sprayer technique. Before you begin, ask your paint dealer to show you exactly how the sprayer works, and to give you pointers on how to use it to best advantage. For best results:

1. Adjust the width of the spray fan to the size of the surface to be coated. A narrow fan is best for spraying small or narrow surfaces; a wider fan should be used to spray table tops or walls.

2. Before spraying any surface, test the thickness of the paint, the size of the fan, and the motion of the spray gun. Excessive thickness can cause rippling of the wet film or lead to blistering later.

3. Hold the nozzle about 8 inches from the surface to be painted.

4. Start the stroke or motion of the hand holding the sprayer while the spray is pointed slightly beyond the surface to be painted. This assures a smooth, even flow when you reach the surface to be coated.

5. Move the sprayer parallel to the surface, moving back and forth across the area with an even stroke. Spray corners and edges first.

6. Use a respirator to avoid inhaling vapors.

7. Cover everything close to the work area with drop cloths, tarps, or newspapers. The "bounce-back" from a sprayer may extend several feet from the work surface.

Paint sprayer care. Clean the sprayer promptly before the paint dries. After using oil-based or alkyd paints, clean the sprayer with the same solvent used to thin the paint. After using latex paint, clean the sprayer with detergent and water. Fill the sprayer tank with the cleaning liquid and spray it clean. If the fluid tip becomes clogged, it can be cleaned with a broom straw. Never use wire or a nail to clear clogged air holes in the sprayer tip.

EXTERIOR PAINTING

As stated earlier in this chapter, one of the easiest and certainly one of the most effective ways to improve or alter the appearance of your home is by the application of a coat of paint, and this is especially true in the case of your home's exterior. You do not have to be an expert on color to select the right paint for your exterior decorating; your good taste and judgment and a few guidelines should be enough to assure the choice of a proper color scheme for your home.

First, decide specifically what you want to accomplish through painting; which features of your home deserve to be pointed up and which should be played down. If, for example, your two-story home appears too tall and narrow, emphasize the horizontal look by using a light body color to bring out the shadow lines of the siding, accent the fasciae, and the like. If the house has no wings or attached garage to balance the height, use the same body color for both stories, or a darker color above a lighter one. If you have a small house, the same emphasis on the horizontal should be employed. A small house surrounded by plentiful foliage benefits greatly from a light color. Where a large door on an attached garage diverts attention from the house proper, disguise it by painting it the same color as the body of the house. A house with a confusing profusion of projections or one with a number of odd-sized windows is also helped by the single-color treatment.

After you have determined what you want your paint job to do, consider the limitations imposed by the house itself and by its location. The roof is an important factor, for its color is not easily changed. Your home's surroundings, too, are important. The neighbors' color schemes must also partially determine your own choice. If your home is in a natural setting, you have greater freedom of choice; nature is very accommodating, and there are not many colors that actually clash with foliage or flowers, no matter how bright.

Finally, decide how you can best take advantage of the patterns presented by the design and materials of the house. All trim boards should be painted the same color to provide unity throughout, even if body colors vary on different areas. Accenting a well-designed doorway or properly proportioned shutters can be very effective. Table 9–1 gives a few suggested color schemes.

Selection of exterior paint. Even though there are a number of different types of paint, selection need not be too much of a problem. First consider the type of surface. Are you painting wood, metal, or masonry? Some paints can be used on all three; others on two. The condition of the surface may also be important. Old chalky surfaces, for example, are not generally a sound base for latex or water-base paints.

Next consider any special requirements. For example, nonchalking paint may be advisable where chalk rundown would discolor adjacent brick or stone surfaces. Or if mildew is a problem in your area, you may use mildew-resistant paint. Lead-free paints may be used in areas where sulfur fumes cause staining of paints containing lead pigments.

Color is a third consideration, but it is mostly a matter of personal preference. Some colors are more durable than others, and some color combinations are more attractive than others. Your paint dealer can help you with decisions on color durability and combinations.

"House paint" is the commercial term for exterior paints mixed with many different formulations. It is the most widely used type of paint. Formulations are available for use on all surfaces and for all special requirements such as chalk or mildew resistance. White is the most popular color.

Exterior paint comes in both oil-base and latex (water-base) types. The vehicle of oil-base paint consists usually of linseed oil plus turpentine or mineral spirits as the thinner. Latex paint contains water as the vehicle thinner; its vehicle consists of fine particles of resin emulsified or held in suspension in water.

Another type of water-base paint has a vehicle consisting of a soluble linseed oil dissolved in water. This paint has the properties of both oil-base and water-base paints.

The advantages of latex paints include easier application, faster drying, usually better color retention, and resistance to alkali and blistering. Also, they can be applied in humid weather and to damp surfaces. Brush and tool cleanup is simpler because it can be done with water.

Use the chart on page 311 as a guide in selecting paint. Your paint dealer can also help you. The following are some specific suggestions:

Wood surfaces. Wooden clapboard siding, one of the most commonly used exterior building materials, lends itself to almost any house paint formulated for wood surfaces.

Shingles of various decorative woods, on the other hand, may have a natural grain, which is pleasing to the eye and can be coated with a clear water-repellent preservative. However, color can be added by applying two coats of a quality pigmented stain, which will enhance beauty of the shingles, seal the surface, and provide protection against the weather.

Wooden trim, such as window sashes, shutters, and doors, should be attractively coated with a colorful exterior enamel. These coatings, which dry with a relatively glossy surface, are available in ei-

Table 9–1

If the roof of your house is	You can paint the body	and the trim or shutters and doors															
		Pink	Bright red	Red-orange	Tile red	Cream	Bright yellow	Light green	Dark green	Gray-green	Blue-green	Light blue	Dark blue	Blue-gray	Violet	Brown	White
Gray	White	x	x	x	x	x	x	x	x	x	x	x	x	x	x		
	Gray	x	x	x			x	x	x	x	x	x	x	x	x		x
	Cream-yellow			x	x		x		x	x							x
	Pale green				x		x		x	x							x
	Dark green	x				x	x	x									x
	Putty		x		x	x					x			x	x		x
	Dull red	x				x			x					x			x
Green	White	x	x	x	x	x	x	x	x	x	x	x	x	x	x	x	
	Gray		x			x	x	x	x								x
	Cream-yellow			x	x			x	x	x						x	x
	Pale green			x	x		x		x								x
	Dark green	x		x		x	x	x									x
	Beige				x					x	x	x		x	x		
	Brown	x				x	x	x			x						x
	Dull red					x		x		x							x
Red	White		x		x				x		x			x			
	Light gray		x		x				x								x
	Cream-yellow		x		x							x	x	x			
	Pale green		x		x												x
	Dull red					x		x		x	x						x
Brown	White			x	x		x	x	x	x	x		x	x	x	x	
	Buff				x				x	x	x					x	
	Pink-beige			x					x	x						x	x
	Cream-yellow			x					x	x	x					x	
	Pale green								x	x						x	
	Brown				x	x	x										x
Blue	White			x	x		x					x	x				
	Gray			x		x						x	x				x
	Cream-yellow			x	x									x	x		
	Blue			x	x	x							x				x

ther water- or oil-based mixtures, and in a variety of sheens. Those which have the smoothest surface are called "high-gloss" enamels, while others are classified as "semi-gloss" coatings.

Masonry surfaces. Masonry surfaces—brick, cement, stucco, cinder block, or asbestos cement—can be revamped with a variety of paint products. One of the newest ideas in painting brick is a clear coating that withstands weather and yet allows the natural appearance of the surface to show through.

Cement-based paints are also used on masonry surfaces. Colorful rubber-based coatings, vinyl, and alkyd emulsion paints, are also used on masonry. Almost all exterior house paints may be applied to masonry, however, when surface preparations are made properly.

Asphalt shingle siding, on the other hand, requires a rather special treatment calling for exterior emulsions formulated for these surfaces.

Metal surfaces. Galvanized iron, tin, or steel building materials are available in various types, all of which may rust if not protected against moisture. Copper building materials, although they will not rust, will give off a corrosive wash that will discolor surrounding areas. Aluminum, like copper, will not rust, but will corrode if not protected.

Conventional house paints or exterior enamels can be applied to these surfaces. But there are some rust-inhibiting coatings that would be best suited for the job. Ask your paint dealer which paint is formulated for application to the metal used on the exterior of your home.

Porches, decks, and steps. Porch floors and steps are usually constructed of wood or concrete, factors that should be kept in mind when choosing paint. The most important point to remember, however, is that foot traffic on these areas is extremely heavy, so the paint used must be durable. Most paint stores stock special porch and deck paints that can wear well under this hard use, but the selection of a primer coat will vary according to the building material used. Wooden porches and steps, for instance, can be primed with a thinned version of the top coat, while cement areas may need to be primed with an alkali-resistant primer.

Best results in painting concrete porches and steps can be obtained with a rubber-based coating or similar product. Roughening the surface slightly with muriatic acid is recommended before painting concrete that is hard and glossy, but in any case all instructions on the label should be closely followed.

Table 9–2

	House paint (oil or oil-alkyd)	Cement powder paint	Exterior clear finish	Aluminum paint	Wood stain	Roof coating	Trim paint	Porch and deck paint	Primer or under-coater	Metal primer	House paint (latex)	Water-repellent preservative
Masonry												
Asbestos cement	X·								X		X	
Brick	X·	X		X					X		X	X
Cement and cinder block	X·	X		X					X		X	
Concrete/Masonry porches and floors								X			X	
Coal-tar-felt roof						X						
Stucco	X·	X		X					X		X	
Metal												
Aluminum windows	X·			X			X·			X	X·	
Steel windows	X·			X·			X·			X	X·	
Metal roof	X·									X	X·	
Metal siding	X·			X·			X·			X	X·	
Copper surfaces			X									
Galvanized surfaces	X·			X·			X·			X	X·	
Iron surfaces	X·			X·			X·			X	X·	
Wood												
Clapboard	X·			X					X		X·	
Natural wood siding and trim			X		X							
Shutters and other trim	X·						X·		X		X·	
Wood frame windows	X·			X			X·		X		X·	
Wood porch floor								X				
Wood shingle roof					X							X

NOTE: The dot in X· indicates that a primer sealer, or fill coat, may be necessary before the finishing coat (unless the surface has been previously finished).

Estimating the paint quantity. For a rough estimate, you can figure the amount of paint you need for flat surfaces by simply multiplying the height (or length) times the width of the surface and dividing the result into the coverage estimate on the paint can label. That is, figure the siding area below the roof line by adding the length of your house to the width, multiplying by the height, and multiplying that number by two. For example, the square footage of a house 40 feet long and 20 feet wide would be $(20 + 40) \times 12 \times 2 = 1,400$ square feet. For pitched roofs and gables, multiply the height of the peak from the roof base by half the width of the area, doing this for each peaked area; then add the area of each gable to the below-roof-line siding area. In our example, this is $6 \times 10 \times 3$ gables $= 180$ square feet; the total area to be painted thus is $1,440 + 180 = 1,620$ square feet.

If the label states that paint coverage is approximately 420 square feet per gallon, four gallons will be adequate for one coat. Second coats generally require less paint. But remember that these are *average* estimates of coverage. Some surfaces are more absorbent than others, and your paint dealer can give you the benefit of his experience in tailoring an estimate to the particular surfaces you are going to be covering. Be ready to provide him with exact measurements of the areas to be covered.

Your dealer will also be able to advise you about the number of coats that will be required for different surfaces and different types of paints. Do not make any purchases until you and the dealer have reached agreement on the approximate amount of paint, thinner, primer, and other supplies you may need. If a particular dealer is lacking in patience in reaching this agreement, find another dealer.

As has been stressed many times in this book, it pays to buy quality products, and this is especially true with paint. The actual cost of paint, to cover the average house, is very small when considering the total cost of labor and time. Quality pays be-

cause of the lasting characteristics of good paint. There is more time between repaintings, with the result that labor costs are reduced.

Surface preparations. The finest paint, applied with the greatest skill, will not produce a satisfactory finish unless the surface has been properly prepared. The basic principles are simple. They vary somewhat with different surfaces and, to some extent, with different paints, but the goal is the same, to provide a surface with which the paint can make a strong, permanent bond. In general, these principles include the following:

1. The surface must be clean, smooth, and free from loose particles such as dust or old paint. Use sandpaper, a wire brush, or a scraper to clean the surface.

2. Oil and grease should be removed by wiping the surface to be painted with mineral spirits. If a detergent is used, it should be followed by a thorough rinse with clean water.

3. Chipped or blistered paint should be removed with sandpaper, a wire brush, steel wool, or a scraper.

4. Chalked or powdered paint should be removed with a stiff bristle brush, or by scrubbing with water mixed with household washing soda or TSP (trisodium phosphate, sold in hardware stores). If the old surface is only moderately chalked and the surface is relatively firm, an oil primer can be applied without the prior use of a stiff brush. The primer rebinds the loose particles and provides a solid base for the paint.

5. Loose, cracked or shrunken putty or caulk should be removed by scraping.

6. If new putty, glazing compound, caulking compounds, and sealants are used, they should be applied to a clean surface and allowed to harden before the paint is applied. If the caulk is a latex type, latex paint can be applied over it immediately without waiting for the caulk to harden.

7. Damp surfaces must be dry before paint is applied, unless you are using a latex paint.

Wood surfaces. Wood siding and other exterior wood surfaces preferably should not contain knots or sappy streaks. But if new siding or wood does contain them, clean the knots and streaks with turpentine and seal them with a good knot sealer, such as shellac. The knot sealer will seal in the oily extractives and prevent the staining and cracking of the paint in the knot area. Smooth any rough spots in the wood with sandpaper or other abrasive. Fill cracks, joints, crevices, and nail holes with glazing compound, putty, or plastic wood and sand them lightly until flush with the wood. Always sand in the direction of the grain, never across it. Dust the surface just before you paint it.

New wood surfaces to be stain-finished should first be sanded smooth. Open-grain (porous) wood should be given a coat of paste filler before the stain

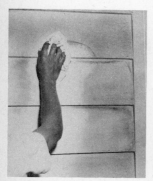

Figure 9–8. *(left)* Remove dust and dirt with a sturdy cloth or a stiff brush. *(right)* Use a nail set and a hammer to sink nailheads below the surface of the wood. Seal any knots or pitch spots with shellac to avoid subsequent brown discoloration.

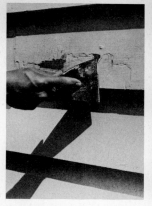

Figure 9–9. *(left)* If the old paint is damaged, scrape to the original surface with a broad knife and a wire brush. Smooth all rough areas and remove rust marks with sandpaper or steel wool. *(right)* There may be areas, especially under eaves or on trim, where the old paint is "shiny." Since paint does not adhere well to slick surfaces, roughen these areas with sandpaper or a wire brush.

Figure 9–10. Clean and prime gutters and downspouts. Remove rust and peeling paint by scraping or wire-brushing. Wash protected areas under eaves with water: a strong stream from a garden hose does the best job. Apply primer when surface is dry.

is applied. (Paste fillers come in various matching wood colors.) The surface should then be resanded. Read the manufacturer's instructions carefully before applying paste fillers.

Old surfaces in good condition, just slightly faded, dirty, or chalky, may need only dusting before being repainted. Very dirty surfaces should be washed with a mild synthetic detergent or TSP and rinsed thoroughly with water. Grease or other oily matter may be removed by cleaning the surface with mineral spirits.

Remove all nail rust marks. Set the nailheads below the surface, prime them, and putty the hole. Fasten loose siding with nonrusting-type nails. Fill all the cracks. Compounds for this purpose are available from paint and hardware stores. Sand the area smooth after the compound dries. Remove all rough, loose, flaking, and blistering paint. Spot-prime the bare spots before repainting. Where the cracking or blistering of the old paint extends over a large area, remove all the old paint down to bare wood. Prime and repaint the old surface as you would a new wood surface. Sand or "feather" the edges of the sound paint before you repaint.

Old paint may be removed by sanding, scraping, or burning, or with chemical paint remover. Scraping is the simplest but hardest method. Sanding is most effective on smooth surfaces. Chemical paint remover can be expensive for large areas. Only experienced persons should attempt burning. Remember that it is of utmost importance to correct the condition that caused the blistering, cracking, or peeling of the old paint, before you repaint. Otherwise, you may run into the same trouble again.

Metal surfaces. Clean new metal surfaces such as aluminum or tin with a solvent such as mineral spirits to remove the oil and grease applied to the

metal as a preservative by the manufacturers. Apply a special primer before painting (see page 315.)

It is usually a good idea to allow galvanized steel, such as that used for roof gutters, to weather for about six months before painting. If earlier painting is necessary, wash the surface with mineral spirits or VM&P (Varnish Makers & Painters) naphtha; then apply a primer recommended specifically for galvanized surfaces.

Rust and loose paint can usually be removed from old surfaces with sandpaper or with a stiff wire brush. Chipping may be necessary in severe cases. Chemical rust removers are available from paint and hardware stores.

Oil and grease may be removed with a solvent such as mineral spirits. Then rinse the surface thoroughly.

Masonry surfaces. New concrete should weather for several months before being painted. If earlier painting is necessary, first wash the surface with a solvent such as mineral spirits to remove oil or grease used for hardening the concrete during the "curing" process. Fresh concrete may contain considerable moisture and alkali, so it is probably best to paint it with latex paints.

Patch any cracks or other defects in masonry surfaces. Pay particular attention to mortar joints. Follow the procedure described earlier on page 29.

Clean both new and old surfaces thoroughly before painting. Remove dirt, loose particles, and efflorescence (the crystalline deposit that appears on the mortar between the bricks in a brick wall) with a wire brush. Oil and grease may be removed by washing the surface with a commercial cleaner or with a detergent and water. Loose, peeling, or heavily chalked paint may be removed with sandblasting.

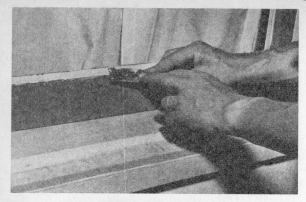

Figure 9–11. *(top)* Loose or dry putty removed during the preparatory stage should be replaced with fresh putty. Cracks and nail holes in siding can also be filled with putty to obtain a smooth surface. *(bottom)* Calk around windows and doors if necessary. Tightly calked joints help to weatherproof a house and prevent seepage that may damage paint film.

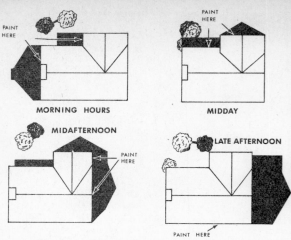

Figure 9–12. In warm or hot weather follow the sun around the house so that you are always painting in the shade.

If the old paint is just moderately chalked but is otherwise "tight" and nonflaking, coat it with a recommended sealer or conditioner before you repaint with a water-base paint. Some latex paints are modified to allow painting over slightly chalked surfaces. Follow the manufacturer's directions. After cleaning the surface, wash or hose it, unless efflorescence was present.

When to paint. You can easily ruin your paint job if you forget to consider the weather. Excessive humidity or extremely cold weather can cause paint troubles. Latex or water-base paints allow more freedom in application than do oil-base paints; the former can be applied in humid weather.

1. Paint when the weather is clear and dry and the temperature is between 50 and 90 degrees F. Never paint when the temperature is below 40 degrees F.

2. Do not paint in windy or dusty weather or when insects may get caught in the paint. Insects are usually the biggest problem during fall eve-nings. Do not try to remove insects from wet paint; brush them off after the paint dries.

3. Start painting after the morning dew or frost has evaporated. Stop painting in the late afternoon or early evening on cool fall days. If the siding has been thoroughly soaked wet by rain, let it dry several days before applying paint. However, when latex paint is used, as previously stated, some moisture can be left on the surface.

4. In hot weather, paint surfaces after they have been exposed to the sun and are in the shade. That is, follow the sun around your home; never precede the sun. Too much heat will result in an improperly cured finish, meaning shorter life or later paint trouble.

Application of exterior paint. Before starting any paint job, be sure that all the tools and materials are at hand. Along with the proper paint, you will need extra cans for mixing the paint and paddles for stirring it. You will need strainers for removing lumps that might mar the smooth finish and rags for cleaning up spatters. You also need drop cloths for protecting porch roofs, floors and steps, and shrubbery and plants.

For most exterior work, some type of ladder is required. This could be a stepladder (good for heights up to 10 feet), a single ladder (available in sizes up to 20 feet), or an extension ladder (for heights above 20 feet). On large houses, scaffolding may be needed. This, of course, should be erected by someone with experience. In many cities, incidentally, it is now possible to engage skilled painting contractors to paint all the hard-to-reach high places, while the homeowner prepares and paints the lower, easy-to-reach areas. In such cases, the painting contractor usually demonstrates methods

Figure 9–13. Even though your paint dealer has mixed your paint mechanically, mix it again just before and during painting. *(left)* Stir the contents of the can from the bottom up; *(right)* "box" the paint by pouring it from one can to another.

of application and advises the homeowner on painting procedures.

Exterior paint may be applied by brush, roller, or spray. While a roller is faster than a brush, the latter gives better penetration on wood surfaces. With a roller, you still need a brush for "cutting in." This means extra tools to clean. However, rollers work well on masonry and metal surfaces as well as large, flat wood surfaces such as floors and decks. Proper depth on the roller cover is important and varies from one surface to another (see page 307).

Spraying, as previously stated, is the fastest method of applying paint. But you may not get proper penetration on wood surfaces. On masonry surfaces, holes that are difficult to fill with a brush or roller can be coated adequately by spraying. Surrounding surfaces must be well protected when spray painting.

Read the paint can label carefully before you start to paint. It will contain specific directions for applying the paint. As a rule new paints are generally ready for use when purchased and require no thinning, except when they are to be applied with a sprayer. Get the advice of the paint salesman when you buy the paint, and check the label before you mix or stir. Some manufacturers do not recommend mixing, as it may introduce air bubbles.

If mixing is required, it can be done at the paint store by placing the can in a mechanical agitator, or you can do it at home with a paddle or spatula (Figure 9–13). If you open the can and find that the pigment has settled, use a clean paddle or spatula and gradually work the pigment up from the bottom of the can, using a circular stirring motion. Continue until the pigment is thoroughly and evenly dis-

tributed, with no signs of color separation. If the settled layer should prove to be hard or rubbery, and resists stirring, the paint is probably too old and should be discarded.

Between jobs, even if it is only overnight, cover the paint container tightly to prevent evaporation and thickening, and to protect it from dust. Oil-base and alkyd paints may develop a skin from exposure to the air. When you finish painting, clean the rim of the paint can thoroughly and put the lid on tight. To ensure that the lid is airtight, cover the rim with a cloth or piece of plastic film (to prevent spattering) and then tap the lid firmly into place with a hammer.

If you are using a gallon of paint, transfer it to a larger container or pour about half into another container. It will be easier to handle and there will be room for the brush.

Number of coats. Three coats of paint are recommended for new wood surfaces, one primer and two finish coats. (Two-coat systems are sometimes used and give long service when properly designed and properly applied.) On old surfaces in good condition, one top coat may be sufficient.

On bare surfaces or surfaces with little paint left on them, it is best to apply a primer and at least one top coat. A primer does two things: it penetrates a porous surface and grips tightly, and it makes a firm base for the second or finish coat, which may not be able to penetrate as well as the prime coat. The paint you buy bears a label on which recommendations for a primer coat are made. Apply the primer coat after you clean and repair the surface, but before you putty cracks or other defects.

Allow the primer coat to dry according to the manufacturer's label instructions. Allow longer drying time in humid weather. Apply the finish coats as soon as the primer has dried sufficiently. (If you must wait a month or more, wash the surface thoroughly before applying the top coats.) Allow about 48 hours' drying time between oil-base finish coats. Two coats of latex paint may be applied in one day.

On metal surfaces, prime both new metal and old metal from which the paint has been removed. Copper should be cleaned with a phosphoric acid cleaner, buffed and polished until bright, and then coated before it discolors. Copper gutters and downspouts do not, however, require painting. The protective oxide that forms on the copper surface darkens it or turns it green, but does not shorten the life of the metal. Copper is often painted to prevent staining of adjacent painted surfaces. Zinc chromate types of primers are effective on copper, aluminum, and steel surfaces, but other types are also available for use on metal.

Galvanized steel surfaces, such as gutters and

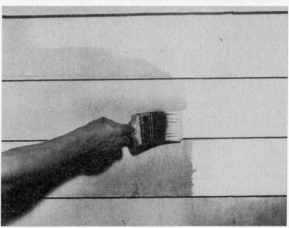

Figure 9—14. *(top)* Dip the brush about 2 inches or approximately halfway into the paint, and tap the excess off against the inside of the can. Repeat this procedure several times. *(bottom)* Apply paint generously along the joint of the siding, distributing it evenly as you brush.

Figure 9—15. *(top)* Brush the paint out well, taking care to coat the under edge of the clapboard. *(bottom)* Feather the ends of your brushstrokes to assure smoothness where one painted area joins another. Do not bear down too hard on the brush.

downspouts, should be primed with recommended special primers, since conventional primers usually do not adhere well to this type of metal. A zinc-dust zinc-oxide type of primer works well on galvanized steel. Exterior latex paints are sometimes used directly over new galvanized surfaces, but do not use oil paints. Unpainted iron and steel surfaces rust when exposed to the weather. Rust, dirt, oils, and old loose paint should be removed from these surfaces by wire brushing or power tool cleaning. The surface should then be treated with an anti-corrosive primer. After the primer has dried sufficiently on any metal surface, apply one or two finish coats of paint.

New masonry surfaces should be primed, preferably with a primer specifically made for masonry. Common brick is sometimes sealed with a penetrating type of clear exterior varnish to control efflo-

rescence and spalling (flaking or chipping of the brick). This varnish withstands weather, yet allows the natural appearance of the surface to show through. Coarse, rough, and porous surfaces should be covered with a fill coat (block filler), applied by brush to thoroughly penetrate and fill the pores.

How to paint. Every paint job will go faster if you follow the right sequence. Paint the windows, trim, doors, gutters, and downspouts before you paint the body of the house. The reason for this is that you avoid placing the ladder against freshly painted siding. Porches, storm windows, screens, and shutters should be left for last.

As was described earlier in this chapter, dip the brush half the length of the bristles into the paint (Figure 9–14). Tap the brush gently against the side of the can, but do not wipe it across the lip. Hold the brush comfortably near the handle base, applying light pressure with your fingertips. The bristles should flex slightly toward the tip as you begin the stroke, but you should not bear down on the brush. Use long sweeping arm strokes, keeping an even pressure on the brush. Apply both sides of each brushful. End each stroke with a light, lifting motion. Always apply the paint to an unpainted area and work it into the wet edge of the previously painted portion. When you finish an area, go over it with light, quick strokes to smooth brush marks and to recoat any thin spots.

When cutting in around windows, protect the glass from paint smears by using masking tape or a metal shield. Use an angular sash brush that is at least 1½ inches wide. To start each stroke, touch the tip to the surface a slight distance from the edge, holding the brush edgewise or sideways. Press the brush lightly with a slight twisting motion so that the bristles will fan out to form a sharp, knife-like edge. Move the brush along slowly, gradually working the tip outward to the edge until it just barely touches the glass. When working on a window, paint the parts in the following sequence:

1. Mullions (strips on the grass).
2. Horizontals of the sash.
3. Verticals of the sash.
4. Verticals of the frame.
5. Horizontals of the frame and sill.

When finishing a window be sure to paint the edges of the casings and do the underside of the sills. Leave the windows slightly ajar at the top and bottom to keep them free; open and close them several times a day until the paint is thoroughly dry.

When painting casement windows, open them and paint the top, side, and bottom edges first. Finish with the rails, frames, casing, and sills.

The painting of exterior doors should also follow a sequence. Start by painting the top panels.

Paint the molding edges first. Then do the remaining panel area by brushing first across, then up and down. After doing all the panels, paint the remaining area and finish with the door edges. If the door swings out, paint the lock-side edge with exterior paint. If it swings in, paint the hinged edge with exterior paint. Paint flush doors the same way you would a wall or other flat surface, painting the edges first and then filling in the large area. Complete the job by painting the door frame and jambs.

When painting siding, start at a high point of the house, at a corner or under the eave. Paint from the top to the bottom and then begin again at the top. Complete one sidewall before starting another. In fact, finish a complete side, or at least up to a door or window, before stopping for the day. It is most important that you do not start a new can of paint in the middle of a board or large wall area. If the remaining paint in a can will not finish an area, mix some of the new paint with the partially filled can before starting the area. This will help blend the color.

When painting siding, paint the underside first, then the vertical flat area. Begin at a corner board and brush the paint out well after laying a brushful in two or three spots. Finish with sweeping strokes, using the tips of the bristles and lifting the brush gradually to a thin feather edge. Paint a strip as wide as you can reach safely and comfortably from your ladder.

Because shingles and shakes have many exposed edges they are susceptible to the absorption of moisture. Moisture may also enter the wood from the back of the shingle. For this reason, the best results are usually obtained by coating the shingles with specially formulated shingle stains (see page 318), which allow moisture to escape without causing blistering and cracking of the coating film.

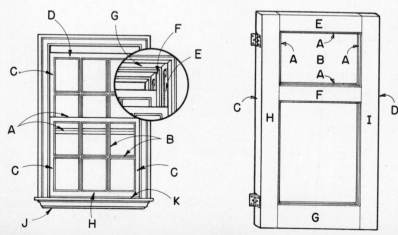

Figure 9—16. The proper sequence for painting windows and doors.

Figure 9—17. When using a roller, pour a small amount of paint into the well of the roller tray. Work the paint into the roller by rolling it in paint in the tray. Be sure the entire surface is covered. Remove excess paint by rolling the roller over the ribbed portion of tray. Apply the paint in even strokes with a light pressure, rolling first in one direction and then overrolling in the other.

Sometimes a thicker coating is desired than can be obtained with a stain. This can best be accomplished with the use of exterior latex paint. These paints deposit films that are more porous than high-gloss oil-type paints and are more likely to allow the escape of moisture without blistering, cracking, or peeling. The application of high-gloss coatings to rough surfaces such as shingles and shakes is not generally desirable from an appearance standpoint, in addition to the reasons given above. Wood staining can usually be avoided by sealing the surface with a properly formulated solvent primer or a latex primer especially designed for resistance to staining. It is strongly suggested that the manufacturer's recommendations be followed carefully in selecting and applying a coating system for wood shingles and shakes.

Natural finishes and stains. All natural wood finish preparations are either: (1) the penetrating type, water-repellent sealers that produce little or no surface film, or (2) varnish-type finishes that form a built-up surface film.

Penetrating finishes. A penetrating type of sealer is designed to soak into the wood. Since there is little or no surface film, these materials offer little protection against change in color of the wood, and do not protect the wood against wear and abrasion where protection is needed. But because of the lack of a surface film, the finish cannot crack or peel (and requires less scraping and sanding when your house is ready for another coat). Penetrating sealers, also called water-repellent preservatives, can be applied only over bare, unfinished wood or over previous coats of the same type of sealer.

Penetrating sealers are available both clear and lightly pigmented in a variety of colors. The pigmented types react like a stain, coloring the wood but also allowing the natural grain to show through. In addition, the pigmented types will generally protect your siding better than a clear type because pigmentation shields the surface against damaging sun rays. This results in more resistance to fading and weathering. Penetrating sealers have no luster, but a top coat of varnish can be applied where a gloss finish is desired.

Many penetrating sealers also contain a wood preservative such as pentachlorophenol, phenyl-mercury-oleate, creosote, and various metallic salts like copper naphthenate. These materials, combined with water-repellent oils, help to resist dry rot and fungus.

Because of its lower cost, linseed oil is sometimes used in place of prepared penetrating sealers. Unfortunately, however, linseed oil does not give much protection against moisture and, since it dries rather slowly, it picks up a great deal of dirt and dust while tacky. Linseed oil is also highly vulnerable to fungus and mildew, and repeated applications darken Western red cedar and redwood excessively.

Varnishes. While spar varnish was used for years to give exterior woodwork a clear, glossy finish, the polyurethane type is most widely used today. Polyurethane varnishes withstand hard use, are long-lasting, and are particularly suited to window, door, and trim surfaces. But they are not too well suited for large wood expanses because their hard surface has a tendency to crack with weathering, which will necessitate a good deal of sanding and scraping before a new coat can be applied. In addition, polyurethane varnishes do not work very well over oil stains.

In recent years, the introduction of the so-called "resin-free, processed-oil varnishes" has solved this problem for large areas such as siding. These varnishes, as the name implies, are made of processed oils formulated to produce a surface coating that appears and acts like a varnish, but the film is neither as hard nor as brittle as a polyurethane varnish. When applied, it is not as likely to crack, and it will withstand the expansion and contraction of the wood. Because these processed oils form a comparatively soft film, they should not be used on windows, doors, trim, and other hard-use surfaces.

Oil-base varnishes are available in both gloss and flat finishes, and may be had clear or with pigmented added.

Stains for shingles. Quality stains are formulated with penetrating types of oils and, whether semi-transparent or solid color, usually provide a flat finish. Where the retention of the natural wood grain and texture is desired, shingle stains are unexcelled. They are available in several wood tones, and it is possible with stain to maintain the beautiful natural look of cedar better than with clear treatments. It is important to use stains in accordance with the directions of the manufacturer; proper mixing and application are essential because of the thin consistency of the product.

One coat may be enough if you are re-staining in the same tint, but two or three coats may be needed for an extreme color change. If you plan to apply a light-colored stain over a dark wood (or over wood that has been previously stained a dark color), then choose one of the heavily pigmented stains. Estimate at least a two-coat job. All of these stains dry to a dull finish.

Bleaches. Frequently a natural silvery gray appearance is sought, similar to that seen on old shingled buildings that have been exposed to salt air along the seacoasts. There are a number of weathering and bleaching compounds on the market that speed the natural weathering process. Their final effect will depend upon the character of the product used. Bleaching oils are applied with a brush or spray.

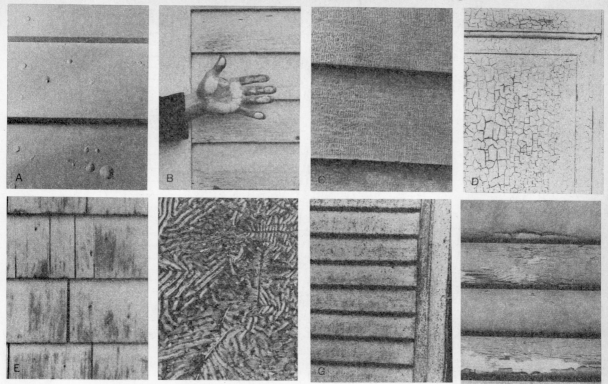

Figure 9–18. Common paint problems: (A) blistering; (B) chalking; (C) alligatoring; (D) checking; (E) bleeding; (F) wrinkling; (G) mildew; (H) peeling.

Application. As in all paint work, follow the manufacturer's directions to the letter, particularly in respect to the number of coats required and the sequence to follow in building up the finish. When employing a varnish-type finish, avoid excessive thinning. Do not thin penetrating sealers. On new work, if the wood finish does not contain a wood preservative, it is usually wise to apply a first coat of penetrating preservative. This treatment provides maximum protection against termites, mildew, and rotting.

When a natural wood finish is applied, the usual precautions associated with any exterior paint job apply. That is, the wood surface must be free of loose matter such as dirt, dust, and flaked and cracked old film. Nail all the loose boards, countersink the nailheads, and fill the holes with tinted putty to match. Fill all cracks and open joints with caulking compound or tinted putty. If mildew is present, proceed as suggested on page 313.

Never apply natural wood finish in foggy or damp weather, and wait at least 24 hours after a rain. The temperature should be above 45 degrees F, though it is unwise to apply such wood finishes when directly exposed to a hot sun. Any of the standard methods of applying paint are satisfactory for shingles and shakes—brush, roller, or spray. The "airless" spray may be preferred to the standard type because it makes it possible to lay down a thicker film.

Ladder safety. The most dangerous phase of house painting involves the use of a ladder. For safety's sake observe the following precautions:

1. Make sure that the ladder is not defective. Check the rungs and rails carefully. Any cracked wood or loosened metal should be repaired before the ladder is used. Check any ropes and pulleys also to make sure that they are securely fastened and work properly. Check the locking mechanism to be certain that it works freely. It is a good idea to keep this well oiled at all times.

2. To raise a straight or extension ladder, brace one end against the house foundation, a step, or a curb. Raise the other end and walk in, working the hands alternately rung after rung. Be sure that the ladder is positioned firmly both on the ground and on the top, never against a window or screen or a weak gutter. If the ground is soft or the surface is

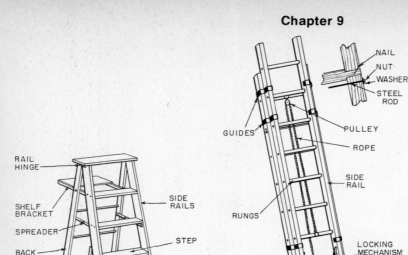

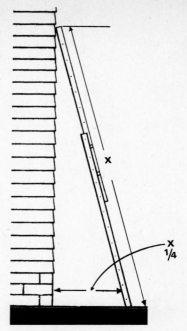

Figure 9—19. Basic parts of two types of ladders used for most house painting: *(left)* stepladder; *(right)* extension ladder.

Figure 9—20. Set the ladder at a safe angle when you paint.

macadam, install metal cleats at the base. You can avoid ladder pitching by placing a plank under the base or legs, or by driving a stake into the ground, set firmly against the bottom rung. Keep in mind that a stepladder is firmly footed only when the spreader is fully opened and press-locked. Do not try to climb a stepladder in any other position; it will probably topple or slip.

3. Check the angle of a straight or extension ladder against the wall. It should be set so that its foot is away from the wall one-fourth of the distance to the point of support (Figure 9–20). Remember that if the base is too far away from the wall, the rungs might not be able to support the weight; if the base is too close to the wall, then the ladder might topple backwards. If you use scaffolding, make sure that it is secure.

4. Always face the ladder when climbing up or down. Hold on with both hands. Carry tools and supplies in your pocket or haul them up with a line. Also keep your shoes clean when climbing. It is always wise to scrape off any dirt or mud; corrugated or square rungs add to safety, but not with dirty shoes.

5. Be sure that the paint bucket, tools, and other objects are secure when you are on a ladder or scaffolding. Falling objects can injure persons walking below.

6. Do not overreach when painting. Move the ladder frequently rather than risk a fall. A good rule is to keep your belt buckle between the rails.

7. Lean toward the ladder when working. If you must have both hands free to do a job, then "lock" yourself to the ladder. Slip one leg over a rung and hold the rung below with the heel of your shoe. But, keep one hand free, ready to grab the ladder just in case. Never "push off" when painting a spot directly under the ladder. That is, do not shove the ladder away from the wall and let it momentarily "float." It is during this time that a gust of wind could carry the ladder away.

8. Never stand with both feet on the top level. On a stepladder, it is wise not to go higher than the second step from the top; while on a straight ladder, the third step from the top is the highest you should go. If you must go higher, get a longer ladder.

9. Watch out for and avoid any electrical wiring within the area of work. This is especially important if you are using a metal ladder.

10. When painting second roofs, do not rest or place the ladder on the tar or shingles of the first roof. Tar melts and shingles are prone to sliding. Nail a 1 × 2 brace into the roof; this will prevent the ladder's legs from sliding. Always wear rubber-soled shoes when on rooftops.

11. No matter where the job, avoid setting a ladder up in front of a door. For if someone opens the door, down you go. If you must work in front of a door, then have a helper stand in front of the locked door.

Figure 9–21. *(left)* When working from a ladder, work from the top down, doing the gutters and eaves first if they are to match the siding color. *(right)* It makes no difference whether you work from the left or the right, but before you move or shorten the ladder, finish an entire area (about 4 or 5 feet square).

12. If it is necessary to move the ladder a short distance, place your foot against the base and pull on the rungs until the ladder is vertical. Slip your arm through the space between the rungs at about shoulder height and hold the ladder against your side. Use your other hand to brace the ladder. Walk slowly, watching the top (now and then, for you also must watch your step on the ground) to make sure that the ladder remains vertical. To carry a ladder horizontally, lift it at its center of gravity, and put it over one shoulder. Keep the front end raised so that it is at least 5 to 6 feet off the ground.

INTERIOR PAINTING

Exterior painting and interior painting are similar in some ways but different in others. Because of the differences, the two types of painting are treated under two separate headings. Some repetition is, of course, unavoidable, but it will be kept to a minimum.

Color and remodeling with paint. Two major problems that face the home decorator when he is planning a painting job are the selection of color and deciding which type of paint is best for the purpose. Since there are so many sources of information on color, only a few facts that are related to paint and are especially important will be given here.

In selecting colors from paint chips, remember that the color will be intensified and appear much darker on the wall than it does in the small sample. Colors intensify when used in large amounts.

Some colors are predominantly warm and others are cool. Warm colors are stimulating and exciting; they include such colors as the reds, pinks, yellows, oranges, and yellow-green. Because they seem to advance, warm colors will make a room appear a little smaller than it actually is. If your room is located on the east, north, or northeast side of the house, you may wish to use a warm color for the walls.

Cool colors, blue, violet, green, and blue-green, remind us of the cool things in nature. These colors will give a room an appearance of coolness and are good to use on walls in rooms with the exposure from the west, south, or southwest. Since cool colors are receding, they make a room appear somewhat larger and more subdued than the warm colors, and they give a feeling of restfulness to a room. Unless a room has good natural and artificial lighting, dark colors on the walls may make the room appear dark and gloomy. Light colors are more likely to give a cheerful background. Whether the finish is dull or shiny is almost as important as the color. A dull finish gives walls soft tones for background, while a shiny high gloss reflects light and may cause a glare.

In redecorating walls, you must consider the

ceiling as part of the project. For best light reflection in a room, the ceiling should be very light in color. A white or off-white is best. For a bedroom that is used only for sleeping and dressing, it is not necessary to be so careful about light reflection. If the room is used for studying, reading, sewing, or other close work, light is very important. You may use the same color on the ceiling as on the walls or add white to the wall color for a lighter ceiling. A little of the wall color may be added to white for the ceiling to make the two surfaces blend more closely. If the ceiling is extra high and you wish to make it appear lower, paint it a little darker than the wall. This will also make your room seem a little darker, especially at night. Another solution to the extra-high ceiling is to bring the ceiling color down on the upper wall to form a border. This might be 6 to 18 inches depending on the height of the ceiling. If the ceiling is extra low, painting it white will add apparent height.

Woodwork is a part of the background. The trend today is to make it as inconspicuous as possible. In many new houses woodwork around doors and windows is completely eliminated. It is usually more pleasing to keep the color of the woodwork as near that of the walls as possible, since door and window shapes often cut into the walls and do not always form pleasing divisions. If the walls are painted, use the same color of paint on the woodwork. This will help to unify the background and make a small room appear larger. Contrasting color in the woodwork calls attention to it and breaks the area into sections.

If woodwork has good proportions, and door and window frames create a pleasing design, you can give them a natural finish. In some old houses, the woodwork is unusual and could be made a center of interest by using contrasting colors for walls and woodwork. When walls have a patterned paper with a number of different colors and values, it is better to use the predominant value for the woodwork.

Selection of interior paints. Interior paints can be roughly categorized into one of three broad families: (1) flat paints that dry with no gloss and are most frequently used on walls and ceilings; (2) gloss finishes (usually used in kitchens, bathrooms, and on woodwork generally) that are available in various lusters from a low satin finish to a very high gloss; and (3) the primers, sealers, and undercoats that are used as bases. All of these paints are available in different grades or qualities, and many in both solvent-thinned (mineral spirits, turpentine, or benzine) or latex (water-thinned) forms.

Latex interior paints are generally used for areas where there is little need for periodic washing and scrubbing; for example, living rooms, dining rooms, bedrooms, and closets. Interior flat latex paints are used for interior walls and ceilings since they cover well, are easy to apply, dry quickly, are almost odorless, and can be quickly and easily removed from applicators. Latex paints may be applied directly over semi-gloss and gloss enamel if the surface is first roughened with sandpaper or liquid sandpaper. If latex is used, follow the instructions on the container label carefully.

Flat alkyd paints are often preferred for wood, wallboard, and metal surfaces since they are more resistant to damage. In addition, they can be applied in thicker films to produce a more uniform appearance. They wash better than interior latex paints and are nearly odorless.

Enamels, including latex enamels, are usually preferred for kitchen, bathroom, laundry room, and similar work areas because they withstand intensive cleaning and wear. They form especially hard films, ranging from a flat to a full gloss finish. Fast-drying polyurethane enamels and clear varnishes provide excellent hard, flexible finishes for wood floors. Other enamels and clear finishes can also be used, but unless specifically recommended for floors they may be too soft and slow-drying, or too hard and brittle. Polyurethane and epoxy enamels are also excellent for concrete floors. For a smooth finish, rough concrete should be properly primed with an alkali-resistant primer to fill the pores. When these enamels are used, adequate ventilation is essential for protection from flammable vapors.

For walls that are rough and have patched plaster, or to hide uneven seams in wallboard, a textured finish may be used. A special paint, thicker than ordinary paint, is used for a textured finish. A heavy coat of paint is applied to the wall surface and the desired texture added while the paint is still wet. Interesting textures may be achieved by the use of a brush, sponge, or a paint roller; however, some skill is needed to obtain a regular effect.

Varnishes form durable and attractive finishes for interior wood surfaces such as wood paneling, trim, floors, and unpainted furniture. They seal the wood, forming tough, transparent films that will withstand frequent scrubbing and hard use, and are available in flat, semi-gloss or satin, and gloss finishes. Most varnishes are easily scratched, and the marks are difficult to conceal without redoing the entire surface. A good paste wax applied over the finished varnish, especially on wood furniture, will provide some protection against scratches. Polyurethane and epoxy varnishes are notable for durability and high resistance to stains, abrasions, acids and alkalies, solvents, strong cleaners, fuels, alcohol, and chemicals. Adequate ventilation should be provided as protection from flammable vapors when these varnishes are being applied.

Shellac and lacquer finishes are similar to those of most varnishes, and are easy to repair or recoat. They apply easily, dry fast, and are also useful as sealers and clear finishes under varnish for wood surfaces. The first coat should be thinned as recommended on the container. After it is applied the surface should be sanded very lightly, and then finished with one or more undiluted coats. Two coats will give a fair sheen, and three a high gloss.

Liquid and paste waxes are used on interior surfaces. They provide a soft, lustrous finish to wood and are particularly effective on furniture and floors. Waxes containing solvents should not be used on asphalt tile; wax emulsions are recommended for this purpose. Waxes should be applied to smooth surfaces with a soft cloth and rubbed with the grain. Brushes should be used to apply liquid waxes to raw-textured wood. Wax finishes can be washed with a mild household detergent, followed by rinsing with a clean, damp cloth. A wax finish is not desirable if a different type of finish may be used later, for wax is difficult to remove.

Unless you are an experienced painter, shop for a salesman or a paint store owner before you shop for paint. Find one who is willing and able to help you match the paint to the job. Read labels and company leaflets carefully. They are usually well written, accurate, and helpful. Table 9–3 provides some additional paint information.

Estimating paint quantity. To determine the amount of paint needed, measure the square feet of wall area to be covered, then take these measurements to your paint dealer. He should have a chart that shows the amount of paint required for the area.

To get the square feet of the wall area, measure the distance around the room. Then multiply this figure by the distance from the floor to the ceiling. For example:

Your room is 12 by 15 feet and 8 feet high.

$12 + 12 + 15 + 15 = 54$ feet, the distance around the room. Multiply this by the height of the wall. $54 \times 8 = 432$ square feet of wall area.

There are windows and sometimes doors that do not require paint, so you will deduct this space. For example, in your room there are one door, 7 feet by 4 feet, and two windows, each one 5 feet by 3 feet. Multiply height by width to get the square feet in each.

$7 \times 4 \times 1 = 28$ square feet of door space.

$5 \times 3 \times 2 = 30$ square feet of window space.

Add these to get the total amount of space to be deducted from the room size. $28 + 30 = 58$ square feet. Subtract this from the total.

432 square feet $- 58$ square feet $= 374$ square feet of wall area to be painted. If the door is to be painted the same color as the walls, do not deduct the door area.

Table 9–3. *Paints for interior surfaces (what to use and where)*

	Flat enamel	Semi-gloss enamel	Gloss enamel	Interior varnish	Shellac-lacquer	Wax (liquid or paste)	Wax (emulsion)	Stain	Wood sealer	Floor varnish	Floor paint or enamel	Aluminum paint	Sealer or undercoater	Metal primer	Latex (wall) flat	Latex gloss on sealer
Masonry																
Asphalt tile							X									
Concrete floors						X·	X·	X			X				X	
Kitchen and bathroom walls		X·	X·										X			X·
Linoleum							X									
New masonry	X·	X·											X		X	X·
Old masonry	X	X										X	X		X	X·
Plaster walls and ceiling	X·	X·											X		X	X·
Vinyl and rubber tile floors						X	X									
Wallboard	X·	X·											X		X	X·
Metal																
Aluminum paint	X·	X·										X		X	X·	X·
Heating ducts	X·	X·										X		X	X·	X·
Radiators and heating pipes	X·	X·										X		X	X·	X·
Steel cabinets	X·	X·												X		X·
Steel windows	X·	X·										X		X		X·
Wood																
Floors				X	X	X·	X·	X·	X	X·	X·					
Paneling	X·	X·		X	X	X·		X	X						X·	X·
Stair risers	X·	X·		X	X			X	X							X·
Stair treads					X			X	X	X	X					
Trim	X·	X·		X	X	X		X					X		X·	X·
Window sills					X											

NOTE: The dot in X· indicates that a primer sealer, or fill coat, may be necessary before the finishing coat (unless the surface has been previously finished).

Be sure to buy enough paint to complete the job, especially if you are having colors mixed. The second mixing may not match exactly. If the paint you choose is not available in the exact tint you want, will you mix it yourself or have the dealer do it for you? It may be advisable to have the dealer do the mixing even though it may add to the cost. Careful mixing is essential to the finished product, for a paint that is not well mixed may leave an uneven, spotty appearance. Whether you use more than one coat will depend on the type and color of paint you are using, the condition of the walls, and the color you are covering.

Besides paint and the applicator (brushes, roller, or spray gun), other materials you might need include: extra pans or cans for stirring the paint, old cloths to wipe up spills and drops of paint, masking tape to cover window glass and other surfaces to prevent smearing them with paint, a stepladder or sturdy table to stand on for reaching high areas, newspapers or drop cloths to cover the floor, and cleaning materials for brushes.

Surface preparation. As with exterior painting, preparation for interior work depends on the surface and its condition. For example, the amount of wall preparation needed will depend on whether you are

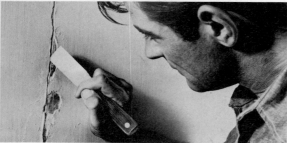

Figure 9–22. *(top)* Fine cracks in walls and holes in wood trim can be filled with spackling compound. Mix with water to a firm paste, and press the paste into the cracks with a spatula or a putty knife. When dry, the patched areas can be sandpapered smooth. *(bottom)* Use your finger to force material into tiny cracks or corners. Large cracks will need patching plaster. On cracks 1/16 inch wide or wider, undercut to an inverted-V shape for anchorage. Wet the edges of the old plaster so that the new plaster will bond. Mix patching plaster according to directions and fill cracks. Remove the excess and smooth the surface with a putty knife.

working with new walls or old ones that have had a previous treatment. If it is an old surface, the preparation needed will depend on whether the surface is plaster, wallboard, or wood, and on the type of finish used previously.

Walls previously papered. You can paint papered walls if the wallpaper is well-bonded to the wall and contains no ink that will smear or stain. Test the paper by painting a small section and allowing it to dry.

Wallpaper that is covered with a latex-base paint is very hard to remove from the wall. Although the latex-base paint gives a satisfactory finish over wallpaper, you must consider the amount of work that will be needed when the paper has to be removed in later years.

Removing old wallpaper. If wallpaper is torn, loose from the wall in spots, or has colors that will smear, take it off and clean the walls before painting. To remove paper, soak it thoroughly with warm water, using a large sponge or a long-handled mop to apply the water. (Steam paper-removing equipment is frequently available at tool-rental stores and is easy to use.) After the paper is softened, you can pull or tear it from the wall. If several layers of paper are on the wall, you may need to take it off layer by layer. You may need to remove stubborn areas with a blunt-edged tool, such as a spatula or broad-edged putty knife. Be careful not to damage the wall.

After all the paper is off, wash the walls with a solution of paint cleaner and warm water to remove all the paste. Rinse with warm water, and allow the walls to dry thoroughly before painting.

Walls previously painted. Walls that have been painted with a casein or calcimine paint cannot be painted again without first removing the old paint, unless you use the same type of paint. You can remove calcimine or a casein paint by washing the walls with a solution of paint cleaner and warm water. With a large sponge, begin with the ceiling and wash down the walls. When the calcimine is removed, rinse the walls with clear warm water and allow them to dry thoroughly before applying new paint. If the walls have been papered, then painted, they cannot be washed.

If the previous paint, other than calcimine or casein, is in good condition, check to see that it is free from dust, grease, or other foreign matter. A primer or seal coat is usually not needed when the painted surface is in good condition. If the old paint has a glossy finish, you may need to sandpaper the surface lightly so that new paint will adhere. You can also remove the old gloss with a special commercial liquid.

Patching cracks. Patch all cracks and nail holes in plaster walls before you apply paint. You can fill small hairline cracks with a spackling compound or crack filler, using a putty knife to put the

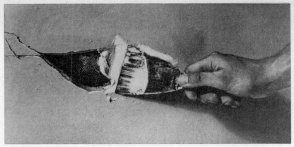

Figure 9—24. Plaster that can be scratched with a fingernail is not thoroughly dry. When the patched areas are dry and smooth, they should be spot-primed either with the paint selected as a finishing coat or with an appropriate primer. Directions on the paint label will tell you which of the two is preferable.

Figure 9—23. *(top)* For large broken areas, clean out the old plaster and tack a piece of wire screen or hardware cloth to the lath to anchor the plaster. Fill the hole and smooth the plaster level with surface. If shrinkage occurs in drying, a second filling may be necessary. *(bottom)* Large cracks or holes in plaster should be repaired a day or two before painting to provide adequate drying time. For wallboard and plasterboard, be sure to cover seams with joint cement. Apply a uniform coating 5 inches wide over the entire length of the seam. Place perforated joint tape on top of the cement. Draw a broad knife firmly over the tape to squeeze out any excess cement. Apply another thin coat of cement on top of the tape, feathering the edges as you work. When the cement is dry, sand it lightly until it is smooth.

filler in the cracks. For larger cracks and breaks, cut out the holes and remove the loose plaster. Cut an inverted "V" with the smallest part of the opening at the outside of the plaster surface and the largest part near the wall lath. Fill the crack with patching plaster. Dampen the edges to prevent cracking while drying. Sand the patches smooth after they are dry. For most types of paint, especially the alkyd type, plaster patches must have a primer or seal coat before the final coat of paint is applied.

New walls. The wall surface should be smooth, completely dry, and free from dust, grease spots, and any other foreign matter. Some paints cannot be applied on fresh plaster. Be sure to read the directions on your paint container to see if it can be used on fresh plaster.

Certain types of paint require the use of a primer or seal coat before you can apply them. This is especially true on plaster and wallboard because certain spots are more porous than others and will not absorb the same amount of paint. This will give a spotty final finish, or there may be areas that are glossy while others have a flat finish. A primer or seal coat will seal the pores of the wall surface and give an even absorption of paint.

Select a primer that best suits your needs for the type of paint you have chosen. If the primer you are using comes in white only, you may wish to add a little of your paint to give a better base for the final coat of paint.

Woodwork. Woodwork requires about the same preparation for painting as the walls. Whether a primer is needed will depend on the type of paint you use on new woodwork.

On previously painted woodwork, if the paint is chipped, peeling, or in bad condition, completely remove the paint. You can do this with a varnish or paint remover or by sanding. If the paint is in good condition and still has a glossy surface, sand off the gloss so that a new coat of paint can adhere to the surface.

To give a smooth surface, fill nail holes and cracks with a commercial crack filler. After the filler is dry, sand it smooth before applying the final coat of paint.

Unpainted or new woodwork to be finished with enamel or oil-base paint should be primed with an enamel undercoat to seal the wood and provide a better surface. If the unpainted wood is not primed, the enamel coat may be uneven. Unpainted wood to be finished with topcoat latex should first be undercoated. Water-thinned paint could raise the grain of the bare wood and leave a rough surface.

If the woodwork is to have a clear finish, the following should be kept in mind:

1. Soft woods such as pine, poplar, and gum usually require a sealer to control the penetration of the finish coats. When a stain is used, a sealer is sometimes applied first in order to obtain a lighter, more uniform color.

2. Open-grain hardwoods such as oak, walnut, and mahogany require a paste wood filler, followed by a clear wood sealer.

3. Close-grain hardwoods such as maple and birch do not require a filler. The first coat applied

may be a thinned version of the finishing varnish, shellac, or lacquer. More information on clear wood finish can be found on page 330.

Masonry surfaces. Smooth, unpainted masonry surfaces such as plaster, plasterboard, and various dry-wall surfaces can be primed with latex paint or latex primer-sealer. The color of the first coat should be similar to that of the finish coat. But coarse, rough, or porous masonry surfaces such as cement blocks, cinder blocks, and concrete blocks cannot be filled and covered satisfactorily with regular paints. Block filler should be used as a first coat to obtain a smooth sealed surface over which almost any type of paint can be used. Unpainted brick, while porous, is not as rough as cinder block and similar surfaces and can be primed with latex primer-sealer or with an exterior-type latex paint.

An enamel undercoat should be applied over the primer where the finish coat is to be a gloss or semi-gloss enamel. Follow carefully the manufacturer's label instructions for painting masonry surfaces.

Metal surfaces. Unpainted metal surfaces should be primed for protection against corrosion and to provide a base for the finish paint. Interior paints do not usually adhere well to bare metal surfaces, and provide little corrosion resistance by themselves. Primer paints for bare metal surfaces must be selected according to the type of metal to be painted. As explained on page 315, some primers are made especially for iron or steel, others for galvanized steel, aluminum, or copper.

An enamel undercoat should be used as a second primer if the metal surface is to be finished with enamel; that is, apply the primer first, then the undercoat, and finally the enamel finish. Most enamel undercoats need a light sanding before the topcoat is applied.

Application of interior paint. Before you brush, roll, or spray a drop of paint, there are certain preparations you should make to ensure a good job with a minimum of effort, errors, and spattering. The precautions may seem obvious, but they are often overlooked. For instance, read the instructions on the label of the paint container. Then move as much furniture as possible out of the room. Cover pieces you cannot move with drop cloths. Remove any hardware, such as plates over light switches, that is not to be painted over. Cover the floor with papers or drop cloths to prevent spotting. Be sure the wall and ceiling are completely free from dust and grease before you apply either the sealer or the paint.

When you have assembled all the equipment and the wall is in condition for painting, read again the instructions on the label of the paint container. Follow these carefully. You can expect much better results when you do. If you are using a paint that requires a primer, apply the prime coat and allow it to dry.

Stir the paint thoroughly as directed on the container. Do not thin paint unless absolutely necessary, then use only the thinning agent the paint manufacturer recommends. Pour some of the paint into another container to work from, unless you are using the self-feeder type of roller or spray gun. Keep the paint can tightly closed when not in use.

When you buy new paint of good quality from a reputable store, it is usually in excellent condition. However, after stirring the paint thoroughly (if it is a type that should be stirred), you should examine it for lumps, curdling, or color separation. Do not use the paint if there are still any signs of these conditions. Old paints that, upon removal of the container lid, release a foul odor (especially latex paints) or show signs of lumps or curdling, are probably spoiled and should be discarded. If there is a "skin" on the surface of the paint when you open the container, remove as much of the hardened film as possible with a spatula or knife and strain the paint through a cheesecloth or fine wire mesh such as window screening. If you fail to do this, bits of the skin will show up with exasperating frequency to spoil the appearance of your paint job.

Remember to clean up paint as you go along. Wet paint is easy to remove; dry paint is hard to remove. Use turpentine or another thinner to remove oil paint, and water to remove latex. *Caution:* If paint is dropped on an asphalt tile floor, do not attempt to remove it with mineral spirits or turpentine since this may permanently damage the tile. If the paint will not come off with a dry cloth, let it dry and then scrape it off.

To keep yourself clean, rub special paint protective cream onto your hands and arms. A film of this cream will make it easier to remove paint from your skin when the job is done. Old gloves or throwaway plastic gloves and aprons are also useful.

Painting sequence. When painting rooms, do the ceilings first, walls second, then woodwork (doors, windows, and other trim). The place floors occupy in the sequence depends upon what is being done to them. If floors are simply being painted, they are done last, but if they are to be completely refinished, including sanding or scraping, do them first, then cover them with paper or drop cloths while painting the room.

The basic application techniques, brushing, rolling, or spraying, described earlier in this chapter hold for most interior painting jobs.

Ceilings. When using a roller for ceiling work, brush on a strip of paint around the entire perimeter of the ceiling. Roll the first stroke away from you. Do not roll too fast or you will spatter the paint. Slow down as you reach the wall. Ease into the junction of wall and ceiling so as to get as little paint as possible on the wall.

Figure 9–25. If you plan to paint both the walls and the ceiling, start with the ceiling. A single ladder will do, but two stepladders holding a long plank will allow you to cover a large area quickly, comfortably, and safely. Use a strong plank and be sure that the ladder legs are firmly placed on the floor.

If you are using a latex paint that does not show lap marks, paint a narrow strip around the entire perimeter of the ceiling. You will fill in the center area later with your roller. If you are using an alkyd paint, it is best to work across the narrow dimension of the ceiling. Start in a corner and paint a narrow strip 2 or 3 feet wide against the wall (Figure 9–25). After loading your roller, roll on a strip of the same width, working from the unpainted area into a still-wet wall-side strip. When you get to the far side of the room, paint the area near the wall with a brush or roller and a paint guard. As you roll along, work backward into the wet edge of the previous strip. Criss-cross your strokes to cover the area completely. Light strokes help to eliminate lap marks. It is a good idea to attach a tightly fitting cardboard disk around the handle of the roller to guard against any paint that may drip or run down the side of the roller.

When using a brush, also begin at a corner and paint a strip 2 to 3 feet wide across the ceiling. You may find it easier to brush on the paint and then

Figure 9–26. Painting a ceiling with a roller.

cross-brush in the opposite direction, but always do the final brushing in the same direction. After you have completed the first strip, do another section about the same width. Continue in this manner until the ceiling is completed. Always work toward a wet edge of the last section to avoid lap marks.

You will find it easier to paint the ceiling if you place a 1½-inch plank at the proper height securely on the treads of two solidly footed, completely opened stepladders. This eliminates climbing up and down again and again. Of course, an even easier method is to use a long-handled roller, which permits you to paint the ceiling while standing on the floor. You may have to use a ladder only to cut in the edges.

Walls. Use the same basic procedure for painting the sidewalls as you did for the ceilings. When using a brush, start painting in a corner and complete a strip 2 to 3 feet wide from ceiling to baseboard, brushing from the unpainted into the painted area. Flat paint can be applied in wide overlapping arcs. When a few square feet have been covered, "lay off" with parallel upward strokes. That is, make all final brush-off strokes until one wall is completed. Leave the trim and woodwork until all walls are painted.

Figure 9—28. Before using a roller, paint the corner and the area next to the ceiling and baseboard with a brush *(left)* or a paint pad *(right)*.

You cannot do a smooth paint job in the corners with a standard 7- or 9-inch roller. Therefore, unless you plan to use a special corner roller, paint the corner, top of the wall next to the ceiling, and the bottom wall next to the baseboard with a wide brush before using the roller. When using any paint other than latex, remember to do this only as you are ready to paint each strip. If the corners are allowed to dry before the inner area is painted, lap marks will show.

To use the roller, start about 3 feet from the ceiling and roll up, then down. Roll across if necessary to fill in spots that you missed with the up and down motions. Always begin a strip by working from the dry area to the wet one.

Figure 9—27. When using a brush, dip the bristles to only one-third of their length into the paint and tap the brush gently against the inside edge of the can to release dripping paint. Starting at the ceiling line, paint down in 3-foot strips, brushing from the unpainted area into the painted area. Flat paint should be applied in wide overlapping arcs. When a few square feet have been covered, "lay off" with parallel upward strokes.

Figure 9—29. When using a roller, pour a little paint into the deep end of the tray. Work the paint into the roller by moving the roller back and forth in the tray until paint is evenly distributed around it. Move the roller across the wall in slow, smooth strokes, working first in one direction and then in another. Quick strokes and heavy, uneven pressure may cause bubbles or spatters. Apply the paint from top to bottom as recommended for brushing.

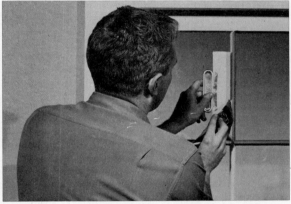

Figure 9-30. When painting windows, you can keep paint off the glass by using masking tape *(top)* or a paint guard *(bottom)*.

Trim and baseboards. When painting a window, adjust it so you can paint the lower part of the upper sash. Then raise the upper sash almost to the top to finish painting it. The lower sash comes next. With the window open slightly at the top and bottom, it can be finished easily. Paint the recessed part of the window frame next, then the frame, and the window sill last. Spatters on the glass can be wiped off when wet, or removed with a razor blade when dry.

When painting a door, do the frame first. Then paint the top, back, and front edges of the door itself. If the door is paneled, paint the panels and panel molding first, starting at the top. Keep a clean cloth handy to wipe off any paint that gets on the area surrounding the panels. Paint the rest of the door last, starting at the top.

The baseboards are painted last. A cardboard or plastic guard held flush against the bottom edge of the baseboard will protect the floor and prevent dirt from being picked up in the brush. Do not let paper or drop cloth touch the baseboard while the paint is wet.

Trim work is often painted with enamels and semi-gloss or gloss paints. These materials flow on more generously and with much less pressure than flat paints. Completing a small area at a time, brush on the paint with horizontal strokes, then level off with even, vertical strokes. Work quickly and never try to go back and touch up a spot that has started to set.

Natural finished walls. Although some wood panel products mentioned in Chapter 4 are available prefinished, many are not. Table 9-4 lists some of the more common finishes for hardwoods and knotty pine, cedar, cypress, and other woods.

Figure 9-31. A cardboard guard prevents you from smearing paint on the ceiling or the floor.

Figure 9-32. After the nailheads have been coated with properly colored plastic wood *(left)*, wood sealer can be applied with either a cloth *(center)* or a brush *(right)*.

Table 9—4

Type of finish	Finishing materials used	Method of finishing
Light natural	1. Two coats satin-finish lacquer or varnish 2. Good-quality paste wax	Apply coat of satin finish; steel-wool when dry. Apply second coat of lacquer or varnish; steel-wool the second coat and then wax.
"Pickled" effect	1. White plywood sealer, or undercoater 2. Two coats satin-finish lacquer or varnish 3. Good-quality paste wax	The white plywood sealer should be thinned 10 to 20 percent with mineral spirits or turpentine. Allow to set three to five minutes. Rub into the pores and wipe clean, not leaving a "painty" effect. Allow to dry twenty-four hours. Lightly sand with fine sandpaper. Apply one coat lacquer or varnish; when dry, steel-wool. Apply second coat. Steel-wool when dry; then wax.
Slightly "pickled" effect	1. Natural paste wood filler 1. White plywood sealer 3. Two coats satin-finish lacquer or varnish 4. Good-quality paste wax	Apply a coat of natural paste wood filler mixed with about 10 percent of white plywood sealer. Rub well into the pores and wipe off thoroughly. Let dry for twenty-four hours. Apply first coat of lacquer or varnish. When dry, steel-wool and dust off. Apply second coat, steel-wool, and dust off when dry; then wax.
Blond effect	1. White plywood sealer 2. Two coats satin-finish lacquer or varnish 3. Good-quality paste wax	The white plywood sealer should be thinned 10 to 20 percent with mineral spirits or turpentine. Allow to set three to five minutes. Rub into the pores and wipe clean, not leaving a "painty" effect. Allow to dry twenty-four hours. Lightly sand with fine sandpaper. Apply one coat lacquer or varnish; when dry, steel-wool. Apply second coat. Steel-wool when dry; then wax.
Full flush finish	1. Wood filler (shade desired) 2. Two coats satin-finish lacquer or varnish 3. Good-quality paste wax	Apply paste wood filler of desired shade, rub well into wood, and clean off. Let dry twenty-four hours, and apply first coat of lacquer or varnish. When dry, steel-wool and dust off; then apply second coat. Steel-wool and dust off when dry; then wax.
Oil-stained effect	1. Clear or white plywood sealer (tinted) 2. Two coats satin-finish lacquer or varnish 3. Good-quality paste wax	Apply oil stain made of white or clear plywood sealer thinned about 20 percent with turpentine or mineral spirits and tinted with colors-in-oil to the desired tone. (Use white sealer as base for gray and pastel and clear sealer for oak, maple, and darker shades.) Let this coat set a few minutes; then rub well into pores and wipe off thoroughly. Let dry for twenty-four hours. Apply first coat of lacquer or varnish. Steel-wool when dry, dust off, and apply second coat; steel-wool, dust off when dry, and wax.
Colonial or Cape Cod effect	1. Clear plywood sealer (tinted) 2. Pure white shellac 3. Good-quality paste wax	Thin the clear plywood sealer 10 to 20 percent with mineral spirits or turpentine. Thoroughly mix in approximately $1/2$ ounce (by weight) burnt umber in oil and approximately $3^1/2$ ounces (by weight) raw umber in oil to the gallon. Brush on and wipe off in three to five minutes, depending upon the intensity of color desired. Let dry overnight and apply a thin coat of pure white shellac. Sandpaper dry and wax thoroughly.
Modern gray effect	1. White plywood sealer or undercoater tinted 2. Two coats satin-finish lacquer or varnish 3. Good-quality paste wax	First tint the white plywood sealer with a little lamp-black ground in pure linseed oil and a touch of light Chrome yellow to equal the shade on the panel. The tinted white plywood sealer should be thinned 10 to 20 percent with turpentine or mineral spirits. Allow to set three to five minutes. Rub into pores and wipe clean, not leaving a "painty" effect. Allow to dry twenty-four hours. Sand lightly with fine sandpaper. Apply a coat of lacquer or varnish; steel-wool when dry. Apply a second coat of lacquer or varnish; steel-wool the second coat; then wax.
Sheraton mahogany effect	1. "Acid" stain, medium mahogany color 2. Light mahogany paste filler 3. Pure white shellac 4. Two or three coats good-quality varnish	Apply medium mahogany-color "acid" stain evenly. When dry, sand sand lightly with fine sandpaper. Apply light mahogany paste filler following manufacturer's directions. Sand lightly. Apply thin coat of pure white shellac. Apply coat of good-quality varnish and sandpaper lightly when dry. Apply second coat of varnish. Sand with very fine sandpaper. Rub with rubbing compound.
Light Sheraton effect	1. Extralight mahogany filler 2. Two coats satin-finish lacquer or varnish 3. Good-quality paste wax	Apply extralight mahogany paste filler, following manufacturer's directions on the can. Let dry overnight. Lightly sandpaper with fine sandpaper. Apply coat of satin lacquer or varnish; steel-wool when dry. Apply second coat of lacquer or varnish; steel-wool when dry; then wax.

NOTE: It is a good idea to use a filler on open-pored woods. On walnut use standard walnut wood filler; on mahogany, use standard light or dark mahogany wood filler; for antique oak effect on oak, korina, elm, ash, etc., use antique oak wood filler; for natural finish use natural wood filler or tint it to the desired shade with colors in oil. For flush finish with white pores use special white wood filler.

Figure 9–33. In new work it is often best to prepare the wood before installing it. (A) The secret of fine wood finishing is a smooth surface. Sanding may be done in any direction with a vibrating power sander. (B) The best results can often be obtained by staining the wood before nailing it into place. (C) For a warm and glowing tone, rub the stain off the wood while it is still wet. (D) Once the boards have been installed, apply a coat of lacquer to the paneling. Rub the boards down with steel wool when the lacquer is dry. (E) To bring out the natural sheen of the wood, apply a good paste wax, then buff. (F) The completed room.

Floor finishing or refining. While many good floor seals, varnishes, or shellacs are readily available, the problem of having good floors goes much deeper than the final finish. As with all finishing jobs, preparatory work, sanding, and buffing go a long way in their effect on the final appearance of the floor. Motor-driven sanding machines, usually equipped with a vacuum cleaner that removes the dust produced by sanding, may generally be rented at low cost from your local hardware store.

Three sanding cuts or traverses are recommended for the average floor, although acceptable results sometimes are achieved with only two. The first cut may be made crosswise of the grain or at a 45-degree angle. Succeeding cuts should be in the direction of the grain. It generally is best to use No. 2 or 3 sandpaper for the first traverse, No. 1 or 0 for the second, and No. 00 or 000 for the third. With parquet floors, it is impossible to sand with the grain of the wood, hence a finer grit must be used

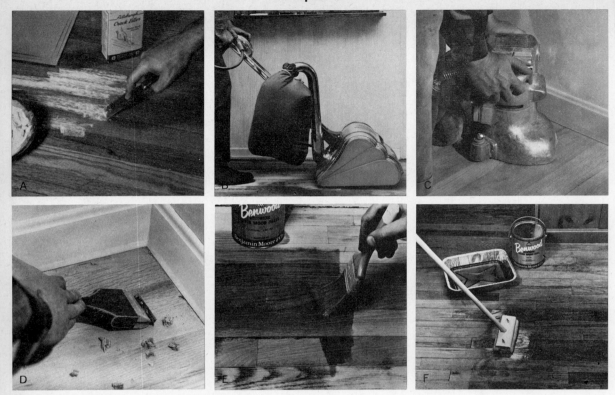

Figure 9–34. Refinishing a floor: (A) Before sanding a floor prior to refinishing, go over it carefully, countersinking all nailheads and filling all cracks. (B) Run a rented power sander from end to end of wood flooring, never across the boards. Never stop the sander in one spot with the sandpaper in contact with the floor. (C) An edger (also a rental tool) gets up close to the baseboard. (D) A hand scraper may be used in corners and under fixed objects. (E) Wood filler should be applied with a brush, then wiped. (F) Apply the final coat with a mop.

on the sanding machine and special care must be observed.

Start sanding by moving the machine slowly forward and gently lowering the sanding drum into contact with the floor. Keep the machine moving by walking slowly forward. Take short steps and keep your feet close to the machine. At the end of the forward cut, the sanding drum must be raised clear of the floor before the machine comes to a standstill. To start the backward cut, the machine must again be in motion as the drum is lowered in contact with the floor. Sanding must be done with the grain and enough taken off to get down to the clear wood.

After each of the three sandings with the drum sander the disc sander is used (changing the sandpaper each time to correspond with what was used in the drum sander) to finish up in areas inaccessible to the drum sander, such as along baseboards and stair treads. To remove the old finish from corners, behind radiator pipes, or in other areas inaccessible to the disc edge sander, use a hand scraper and sandpaper. If any spots remain, they may be

bleached out by using a solution of one teaspoonful of oxalic acid in a cupful of hot water. This acid is a poison and should be handled with care. Cracks may be filled with white dry lead worked into a putty, or by adding fine sawdust to glue melted in a double boiler.

When a dark-colored floor is desired, one coat of stain should be applied before any filler or other finish. A flat varnish brush 3 to 4 inches wide may be used for application. Prepare samples of the required color on pieces of scrap flooring or on the closet floor, where variations in shade will not be noticed. When the desired shade has been achieved, begin in the corner of the room furthest from the door. Care must be taken that the stain is applied evenly. Excess stain is wiped off with a soft cloth before it has had time to set.

One coat of good-quality paste wood filler should be applied after the stain has dried thoroughly. The purpose of wood filler is to fill the minute surface crevices in the wood. By making the surface perfectly smooth, it prevents the top coating of the finish from sinking into the pores, a condition that would cause a comparatively rough finish. For a natural or light-colored floor, use colorless wood filler; for a dark floor, use the colored type. It is generally applied with a short-bristled 4-inch brush and is first brushed across the grain, then with the grain. Care should be taken to avoid covering too large an area at once. Before the filler in each new area becomes hard, the excess must be wiped off with burlap or excelsior so that the coat of filler is uniformly even with the surface of the wood. The filler then is allowed to dry for 24 hours. Since the filler raises the grain somewhat, the floor should be sanded lightly, with No. 0 sandpaper, before another finishing material is applied.

Most of the varnishes used on floors today are of the new synthetic resin formulations, principally the epoxies and polyurethanes. They may be applied by brush or roller. In the case of the latter, use a short-napped roller with a long handle. Most of the plastic varnishes are self-leveling and fast-drying. You may find it desirable to apply another coat in a few hours. If you use a urethane product, you should lightly hand sand the floor with fine sandpaper to ensure a really smooth finish, before the second coat is applied. Two coats of finish are usually sufficient, although a third coat will produce a higher gloss and provide additional wear. The final coat should dry overnight.

Shellac at one time was a popular floor finish. Today, it has been replaced by the new lacquer-type coatings. These products are designed for application with brush or roller and produce an attractive lustrous finish with good durability. They are faster-drying (as little as 10 minutes) than shellac.

Floor sealers are also very popular floor finishing materials. They differ from other finishes in that they not only are a surface coating but also penetrate the wood fibers and seal them together. In effect they become a part of the wood itself. They wear only as the wood wears, do not chip or scratch, and are practically immune to ordinary stains and spots.

Floor sealer may be put on with a brush, a squeegee, or a paint roller. It is applied first across the grain, then with the grain. After a period of 15 minutes to 2 hours, depending upon the specific instructions of the manufacturer, the excess should be wiped off with a clean cloth or a rubber squeegee. For best results the floor should then be buffed with steel wool. A second coat is frequently recommended for new floors or floors that have just been sanded.

A painted finish is by no means new. It has been in common use for softwood floors since before the days when all floors were carpeted. However, in the last few years the trend for painted floors from a decorative standpoint has grown in popularity, because of the possibilities they afford for harmonizing with the walls and furnishings. The floor surface must be clean, dry, and perfectly smooth. Ordinarily, two coats of paint will be sufficient, but where floors are subjected to a great deal of foot traffic, three coats should be used. All coats should be thinned according to manufacturers' directions.

HOW TO HANG WALLCOVERING

Wallcoverings (of which wallpaper is still number one) are one of the most versatile of all home improvement devices. They can make a room appear cozy or formal, restful or active, gay or dignified. By careful selection of colors and patterns in a wallcover, a room can be made to appear smaller or more spacious than it actually is. The ceiling can be made to appear higher or lower according to the needs of the room, and wallpaper can turn a dark gloomy room into a pleasant gay one. Certain types of wallcover seem to give more character and atmosphere to a room than painted walls do.

Before selecting a wallcover, visit stores that have a wallcover department and look through every book. As you look, try to visualize the paper on your own walls. Tilt the samples in a perpendicular line so that you will see the paper as it will appear on the walls. If possible, hold two rolls side by side to get the full effect of matching the patterns.

Types of wallcovering. Wallpapers, or wallcoverings as they are now called, are available in almost any design you can think of. Floral patterns, scenics, plaids, stripes, vines, fruits, pastoral scenes, animals, birds, or fowl, feather designs, geometrics, and modern abstracts are among the designs you will find. But not all wallcoverings have a pictorial pattern. Some have a textured appearance which looks like a fabric weave. Others are embossed. You will also find a selection of good solid-color papers. Special papers are made for the ceilings, and some of these harmonize in color with the sidewall patterns.

Companion papers, to be used in adjoining rooms, are also available. These coverings have different designs, but the background color is the same. Companion coverings may also be used in one room. A patterned covering may be used on one wall and a plain matching color cover on the other three walls. This is a good treatment for a long narrow room. The narrow end wall may be made to appear wider or to seemingly advance toward the center of the room.

Special features to look for in wallcovers are washability, resistance to stains, and colorfastness. Some wallcovers are more washable than others. Coverings for the kitchen or bathroom must be washable and resistant to steam vapor and grease stains. Some wallcoverings have the margins already trimmed off. This saves time and effort, but the covering will usually be a little more expensive than untrimmed paper. Other factors affecting cost are the weight and grade of the material, the number of colors, the detail of the design, and the size of the roll.

There is a wide variation in the weight and grade of different wallcoverings. Thin, low grades of paper tear easily and often stretch and wrinkle badly when wet with paste, making them hard to work with. Good grades of paper are firm and easy to handle even when wet. Extra thick, stiff paper may be a problem for the beginning paperhanger.

Some companies make prepasted papers that are ready to hang without using paste. This makes paperhanging easier for the beginner. Instructions for hanging come with the paper.

Wallcovers are available in many patterns, colors, and surface types. Because of these wide variations, you must observe certain precautions in decorating with wallcoverings. Look at your room with a critical eye, and decide what character you want it to have. You must consider the personality of the person or persons who will use the room. Should your paper have a pattern or be a solid color? If there are other areas of design in the room, walls probably should be plain. Too much design gives a feeling of activity and confusion.

Measure the walls carefully to see if they are perfectly straight with floor and ceiling. If the walls are not perfectly straight, do not select a covering with a definite stripe or plaid pattern. An embossed covering or one with a small all-over design may be most suitable for walls with many imperfections. If you wish to give rooms in an old house a modern appearance, a distinctive weave pattern will provide a good background. A room crowded with furniture will appear more cluttered with patterned walls. Large designs and deep dark colors usually make a room appear smaller. Light solid colors and small designs make small rooms seem larger. Small delicate patterns may seem lost in large rooms.

Wall hangings, such as pictures and textiles, show up to a greater advantage on plain walls. Extremely high ceilings can be made to appear lower by stopping the side wallcovering a foot or so below the ceiling and treating the rest of the wall the same as the ceiling. A horizontal stripe pattern can give the same effect, while vertical stripes give the opposite effect. Select striped patterns with care. A covering with great contrast in color or value of the stripe and the background may become tiresome.

When selecting a wallcovering, consider the activities taking place in a room. Quiet delicate designs and colors are more appropriate in rooms intended for sleeping, resting, reading, and conversation. The living room and bedrooms usually fall in this category. For more active rooms, such as the den and family room, more bold, vivid designs and colors may be used. Because the hallway and the dining room usually are not occupied for long periods of time, they may have more outstanding patterns and colors. Kitchen walls should be cheerful and restful. Avoid a spotty scattered pattern and the too realistic designs that copy nature in every detail. A conventionalized or stylized design is more satisfactory over a long period of time.

As stated earlier in the chapter, warm colors, such as tints of red, pink, yellow, orange, and yellow-green, give a feeling of warmth to a room. They have a stimulating effect and make a room appear smaller than it really is. The cool colors, green, blue, cool gray, lavender, and blue-green, are receding and make a room appear a little larger. These colors are restful and good to use on walls of rooms that get too much sunlight.

Consider woodwork as a part of the background and avoid great contrasts between the color and value of the woodwork and walls. Contrasting colors emphasize the woodwork and tend to break the room into different areas of walls, windows, and doors. Painting woodwork the same color as the background or the predominant color in the wallcovering helps to tie the woodwork and walls together and make a unified background for the room furnishings.

Well-designed wallcovering may be the source of a color scheme for a room, and it can tie together all the colors used in a room. Wallcovering for a room should be harmonious in color and design with that of other rooms or hallways that open into it. In selecting paper for the ceiling, remember that a light-colored ceiling reflects more light than a dark one. A glossy-surface paper will produce more glare than will a soft, nonglossy paper.

Estimating the amount of wallcovering needed. To estimate the amount of wallcovering required for a job, keep in mind that the roll is a standard unit of measurement in the wallcovering industry. The material may come in double A or triple A roll bolts, but the roll is still the standard unit of measurement, and each roll contains approximately 36 square feet. However, when hanging the material you will always have a certain amount of waste while trimming and cutting the strips to size, so you will actually obtain approximately 30 square feet of usable material out of each roll.

To figure how many rolls you will need for a given room, first measure the distance around the room. Then multiply this figure by the distance from the baseboard to the ceiling. This will give the number of square feet of wall area. For example:

Your room is 15 by 20 feet and 8 feet high.

$15 + 15 + 20 + 20 = 70$ feet, the distance around the room. Multiply this by the height of the wall. $70 \times 8 = 560$ square feet of wall area. But there are doors and windows that require no paper, and you must deduct this space. For example, in your room, there are one door, 7 feet by 4 feet, and two windows, each one 5 feet by 3 feet. Multiply height by width to get the square feet in each.

$7 \times 4 \times 1 = 28$ square feet of door space

$5 \times 3 \times 2 = 30$ square feet of window space

Add these to get the total amount of space you will deduct from the room size.

$28 + 30 = 58$ square feet

Subtract this from the total. 560 square feet − 58 square feet = 502 square feet of wall area to be papered.

Now, divide this figure by 30; this room would require approximately 17 rolls of wallcovering. Estimate the number of rolls of ceiling covering needed in the same way, multiplying the length of the ceiling by the width to get the square feet.

For a quick reference aid in estimating the amount of coverage needed, use Table 9–5.

Table 9–5. *Wallcovering estimating chart*

Distance around room (feet)	Single rolls for wall areas Height of ceiling			Number of yards for borders	Single rolls for ceilings
	8 feet	9 feet	10 feet		
28	8	8	10	11	2
30	8	8	10	11	2
32	8	10	10	12	2
34	10	10	12	13	4
36	10	10	12	13	4
38	10	12	12	14	4
40	10	12	12	15	4
42	12	12	14	15	4
44	12	12	14	16	4
46	12	14	14	17	6
48	14	14	16	17	6
50	14	14	16	18	6
52	14	14	16	19	6
54	14	16	18	19	6
56	14	16	18	20	8
58	16	16	18	21	8
60	16	18	20	21	8
62	16	18	20	22	8
64	16	18	20	23	8
66	18	20	20	23	10
68	18	20	22	24	10
70	18	20	22	25	10
72	18	20	22	25	12
74	20	22	22	26	12
76	20	22	24	27	12
78	20	22	24	27	14
80	20	22	26	28	14
82	22	24	26	29	14
84	22	24	26	30	16
86	22	24	26	30	16
88	24	26	28	31	16
90	24	26	28	32	18

NOTE: This quick reference chart is based on a single roll covering 30 square feet; deduct one single roll for every two ordinary-size doors or windows or every 30 square feet of opening. It is wise to buy one or two extra rolls in case you ruin some of the covering in hanging. Most dealers will take back uncut rolls. You may wish to keep some covering for patching.

In addition to wallcovering material, you will need the following materials and equipment for doing a good job of paperhanging: a ladder to reach the ceiling; a large flat surface or table; a large pail for paste; a brush or paint roller for applying paste; a smoothing brush to smooth the paper on the wall (a fiber brush about 10 inches wide or a clean clothesbrush will do); a rotary beater or similar device to mix the paste; a pair of large sharp shears; a trimming knife or razor blade to trim the wallpaper; newspapers to cover the table while applying paste; wallpaper paste, unless you are using prepasted wallpaper; a yardstick or T-square for measuring straight edges; a plumb line (long string with weight tied to one end). If the walls need repairing, you may need patching plaster to fill the holes and cracks, a putty knife, paperhanger's size, a scraper, and sandpaper.

Kits containing tools needed for hanging wallcoverings are available at wallcovering stores, often on a rental basis.

Preparing the wall. No wallcovering job will be better than the surface on which the covering is hung. The walls must be properly prepared for the wallcovering to hang smoothly and look good for a long period of time. The preparation needed depends on the type of finish the walls have had previously, the material of the wall, and whether the wall is new or old.

Before doing any work on the walls, turn off the electricity and remove switch and wall outlet plates as well as light fixtures.

Papered walls and ceilings. If the old paper is in good condition, well bonded to the wall, and in not too many layers, you do not need to remove it. You can put new paper over the old without resizing the wall.

If the paper is loose in just a few places, remove it, and sand the edges of the hole smooth with sandpaper. When bare plaster is exposed, size it and allow the sizing to dry before applying a new covering.

Completely remove old paper that is in poor condition. You can do this as described on page 324. After all the paper is off, wash the walls with a solution of paint cleaner and warm water to remove all the paste. Rinse with warm water and allow the walls to dry thoroughly.

Fill cracks or holes with patching plaster, then apply a coat of size to the entire wall. You can buy size at a paint store, complete with instructions for use. But, be sure to check the wallcovering manufacturer's directions as to the type of sizing to use. The easy way to apply size is by using a paint roller.

Painted walls. Walls that have been painted with a gloss or semi-gloss enamel are too slick to provide a grip for the wallcovering paste or adhesive. You can remove this gloss by sanding the wall lightly with medium-grade sandpaper or by using a commercial gloss-removing liquid. Then wash the surface using a strong washing compound, rinse it with clean water, and allow it to dry before applying a coat of size.

Walls painted with flat paints should be washed down completely with a good washing

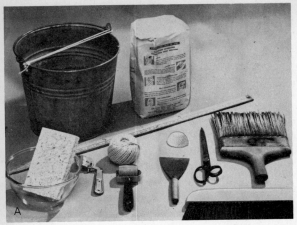

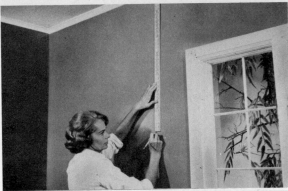

Figure 9-35. Hanging wallpaper: (A) The material list comprises wallpaper paste, a bucket and brush for applying the paste, a plumb line and chalk, a razor knife, a yardstick, a metal straight-edge (a flat scraper will do), a sponge and bowl, shears, a seam roller, and long smoothing brush. (B) Measure the height of the wall from ceiling to baseboard, the distance around the room at the baseboard, and the height and width of each door, window, or other area that will not be covered to determine the quantity of wallcovering that is needed. (C) When hanging the paper, do not count on your eye to give you a completely straight first strip on the wall. Use a plumb line. Tack it near the ceiling where you want to start with the wallcovering. Hold the weight tight at the end of the line and snap the string. This leaves a vertical chalk mark on the wall. (D) Long strips of wallcovering covered with wet paste are easy to handle when you use the professional's folding trick called booking. After pasting the bottom section, fold it paste to paste toward the center without creasing. Do the same with the top section. Get the edges even and press gently so that the material will separate easily. (E) To hang, unfold the top section and place it on the wall so that it overlaps the ceiling joint by about 2 inches. Tap the upper section of the strip with the smoothing brush to hold it to the wall. Now open the lower folded section, slide it into position, and brush. (F) Use a smoothing brush, not your hands. Employing downward strokes with the brush in the center of the strip improves the appearance of the seams. (G) Using a wall scraper as a guide, trim the excess material at door casings, baseboard, and ceiling moldings with a sharp single-edge razor blade. (H) Use clean water and a sponge to rinse all baseboards, casing, and ceiling moldings before the paste dries. (I) Wallcovering is hung around windows and doors just as it is on walls. Check for matching, then paste. Position the strip along the edge of the last strip hung. Make a diagonal snip at the corners, fit the wallcovering into place, and trim.

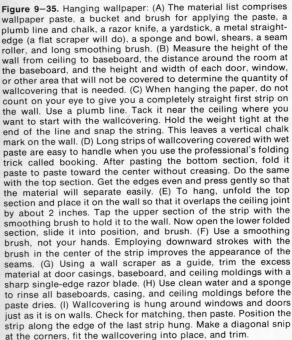

compound. This removes grease, grime, and dirt. Wash from the bottom up, and do the ceiling last.

Composition walls or dry-wall construction. Be sure all seams have been taped and spackled so that joinings will not show through the wallcovering. Set nails with a hammer, leaving a dent in the dry-wall surface. Cover the dent with spackle and level it to the surface. Allow the spackle to dry, apply a second coat, and when it is dry, cover the unpainted dry walls with a flat primer-sealer before hanging the wallcovering. This prevents damage to the wall when the wallcovering is removed.

Hanging the wallcovering. The hanging of wallcovering can be divided into three steps: (1) preparing

the paste and measuring; (2) cutting and matching the wallpaper; and (3) pasting and hanging.

Preparing paste and measuring. Mix the wallpaper paste or adhesive according to instructions on the package. Mix in a large pail, but do not mix too much paste at one time. The paste should be mixed until it is free of lumps and adheres to the hand like a smooth glove. You can tie a string across the top of the paste bucket to hold the brush out of the paste when you are not using it.

To cover the four walls of a room, the hanging operation should be started at a window or door. If you are hanging a large pattern in a room with a fireplace, center the first strip over the fireplace and work away from the fireplace in both directions. Whether the starting point is a window or door casing, or the fireplace, measure along the wall to a distance that is 1 inch *less* than the width of the wallcovering. If, for example, the width of the paper is 24 inches, measure in 23 inches from the corner or door casing. The extra inch is to provide an overlap of the corner or casing to compensate for one that is not perfectly straight, which is usually the case.

Drop a plumb line from the ceiling to the baseboard along the mark and snap a chalk line down along the wall. To make a plumb line, hang a weight (large washer, or even your scissors) at the end of a string. Tack the string at the top of the wall so that it is closer to the starting door or window than the width of your wallcovering roll. The weight should hang just above the floor. Rub colored chalk into the string, hold the string near the weight, and snap the taut string against the wall. This will make a perfectly vertical colored chalk mark on the wall. Another plumb line should be made as each new wall is begun.

Cutting and matching. Make all strips of the wallcovering a little longer than the ceiling to baseboard measurement to allow for matching and trimming at the ceiling and baseboard. If the covering does not require matching, cut the first strip about 6 inches longer than the measurement, then cut all the other strips the same length. Be sure a complete design is at the top of each strip. Check to see that the join marks match on each strip.

If the design must be matched, cut the first strip 8 to 12 inches longer than the ceiling to baseboard measurement, depending on the size of the design. To allow for trimming, be sure the point of the design that you want to meet the ceiling is 3 or 4 inches below the top of the strip. This assures an even line all around the ceiling. Unroll a second strip on top of and the same length as the first one, then place it alongside the first strip to see that the design and join marks match. Cut the second strip even with the top of the first strip. Cut all the strips the same way, placing each one on top of the pile with the pattern side up.

When all the strips are cut, turn the pile over with the pattern side down. Trim if necessary. That is, some wallcovering has a selvage on both sides. Sometimes the dealer will trim this off for you. If he does not give this service, you can easily do the trimming. Usually one side is all that needs trimming because the next strip will lap over to cover the selvage on the other side. You may trim the selvage before applying paste to the strip or after you have folded the pasted strips together. You can trim two thicknesses of pasted paper at one time if you have the edges of the strips exactly together.

If your paper does not have a firm line to follow for trimming the selvage, draw a line with a pencil and yardstick. You can cut the selvage with sharp shears or a trimming knife and a straightedge, such as a carpenter's square or yardstick.

Pasting and hanging. Place the first strip, pattern side down, on a large smooth table. Apply paste to the wallcovering beginning at the top and brushing toward the bottom. When you have covered about half to two-thirds of the strip with paste, fold the top down to the center with the pasted sides together. Be sure the outside edges are exactly even. Do not crease the paper where it is folded. Next apply paste to the rest of the strip and fold the bottom up as you did the top, with the pasted sides together. This makes it easier to handle the pasted strip without danger of smearing paste on other strips. The outside edges of the strips must be even. Use enough paste. Blisters may appear later if you miss a spot.

Repeat the pasting process with each strip as you get ready to use it. Do not apply paste until you are ready to hang the strip.

Place the smoothing brush on top of the ladder so it will be handy when you need it. Now unfold the top fold of your covering. Place the strip in position where the design meets the ceiling line at the desired point, with the covering overlapping onto the ceiling. Press the covering firmly to the wall. Let the bottom fold out, and as it drops down, press it to the wall, making sure it is even with the plumb line. Place your hand flat on the paper and press it with the palm, not the fingertips. Smooth down the center first, then the edges.

When you are sure the first strip is straight, take the smoothing brush and go over the whole strip with long sweeping strokes both vertically and horizontally. If wrinkles appear, lift the bottom to where they are and brush them out. It is important that the first strip be straight.

If the left edge overlaps the frame, trim the paper with a trimming knife or make a scored line with the sharp point of the shears, then trim along the line. Trim the excess covering at the ceiling and baseboard in the same way. Push the covering firmly down around the door or window frame and baseboard.

Hang each succeeding strip in the same way, working the covering into place so that the pattern matches. Let each strip overlap the previous one about $1/16$ inch. Roll the seams flat, using a seam roller.

After hanging each strip, see if you have smeared paste on it. If the wallcovering is waterproof, use a dry cloth. Do not allow paste to dry on the pattern.

Hang the wallcovering over electric outlets, then take a knife or shears and cut out the area around the switches. Replace the plates. You may wish to mark the spots as you cover over them so they will be easy to find when you are ready to trim out the area.

If you started by hanging your covering at a door or window, there will be other doors and windows in the room that will present a different problem. To solve this problem, simply match the strip of covering to the last strip you have hung. Let the wallcovering overlap the door or window frame. Press it in place along the ceiling line and down the side that is not overlapping the frame. For a square corner, make a diagonal cut from the overlapping edge to the top corner of the frame. Crease the covering against the edge of the frame at the top and along the side. You can do this easily with the blunt edge of your shears. Then lift the paper lightly and cut off the excess paper. Press the edges firmly around the frame. Treat the bottom of the window in the same way as the top. Use a separate strip to match the center panels at the top and bottom of the windows and over the doors.

Wallcovering in the corners often buckles or splits. To prevent this, make a seam at every corner, cutting the paper to make it overlap the next wall about 1 inch. Smooth the strip in place and press it firmly into the corner, extending it about 1 inch on the adjoining wall. The next strip will overlap this extra inch.

One of the major problems when doing walls occurs in a dormer bedroom or a refurbished attic. Here, at least one wall will slant, probably two, and they can be broken up into any number of odd shapes by the roof and the windows. But such walls are less difficult to cover than they seem. The same principle of extending the material beyond the edges and at all corners applies, as does the necessity for cutting sections that will match that we encountered around doors, and windows set flush with the walls. What distinguishes the dormer situation is that, since some of the walls slant, not all the areas to be covered are rectangular. The choice of pattern becomes extremely important. Stripes will work out well, if you want a stimulating zig-zag effect, but an informal scattering of flowers or branches might be better; many mis-matches are inevitable where vertical and slanting walls meet. It is a good plan to first cut on the bias those strips that do not require trimming either at the top or bottom, just as if you were going to hang them on an ordinary straight wall. The fact that they may be placed on a slanting ceiling has nothing to do with preparing the strips. Vertical guidelines here and there will be useful, and, depending on whether or not you have a helper, you could hang these "straight" coverings beginning at the top or working up from the bottom. Or, if the room is a high one, you could hang the strips in sections. As for all the triangles that may occur in a dormer room: measure, cut, and number the strips for each position before you apply paste.

In a room completely hung with wallcovering, the ceiling will be covered first, the walls next, and borders—wide or narrow—last. The merit of borders, in addition to the finishing touch they give a room, lies in their ability to conceal (or distract from) poor joining and trimming. If you know you are going to use a border at the ceiling line, you do not have to add that extra inch or two and then trim it off quite so meticulously. Borders are not as easy to find as they should be, but sometimes you can cut your own border trims from the pattern you are using, or take a narrow border from a deeper one. Wide or narrow, borders are measured and pasted like any other wallcoverings, and are usually started in the most obscure corner, working from there continuously around the room. As the repeats on narrow widths are small, a mis-match at the corner where they began will not be noticeable. Small border papers used as trimming throughout a "tailored" room would be mitered like a picture frame at the corners of the doors and windows they outline.

Covering a ceiling. As was just stated, a ceiling should be hung before the walls are. The strips should always be hung across the room, rather than length-wise, as shorter strips are easier to handle. These strips will be cut and pasted as were those you prepared for the wall, with the same allowance of about 1½ inches at each end, that amount to be used at the top to fill in the corner where ceiling and wall join. Here the surplus covering will be cut off according to what is planned: either a pattern continuing all or part way down the wall, or the use of some sort of molding. If the same pattern is used on both walls and ceiling, it is an advantage when the main entrance to the room is opposite its narrow side, not its length. Then the wall pattern can be hung so that it seems to continue up and across the ceiling, adding apparent height to the room and counteracting its shallowness. Should a guideline for the first ceiling strip be advisable, you should determine it by measuring along the short wall to a distance just less than the width of a strip of the wallcovering (so that it can overlap the edge where it starts), and employing a T-square to begin drawing the line at right angles,

continuing it with a yardstick. You should plan to end the ceiling job on the less critical side of the room, perhaps just above the main entrance. The last strip will almost certainly be a partial strip, and there will be no possibility of controlling a match, if you are using a pattern.

Ceiling paper is much easier to hang when two people work together, for one person can place and smooth, while the other holds up the rest of the strip. If necessary, though, you can support the strip with a second ladder, or make yourself a little scaffolding with a plank stretched between two ladders. Be sure to follow the same procedures of smoothing out wrinkles, sponging off excess paste, and trimming while the paper is wet, as you did when hanging the wallcovering.

Prepasted wallcoverings. When using prepasted wallcoverings, read the manufacturer's instructions before starting. Prepasted strips are cut and matched as are all other types of wallcoverings. Reroll the strip from the bottom to the top with the pattern inside (Figure 9–36). Roll it loosely so the water can easily reach the entire prepasted surface. Most companies furnish plastic-coated cardboard water trays that you can place on the floor next to the wall. They are just the right width for the strips of wallpaper.

Check the manufacturer's instructions as to the length of time that the rolled strip should remain in the water tray. Be sure to leave each strip in the water for the same length of time so that each strip will dry and fit uniformly. Use tepid water in the water tray. Check the manufacturer's instructions as to the length of time that wallcoverings should "relax" after wetting. Place the water tray at the end of the cutting table or at the baseboard. Hang prepasted strips in the same way you would hang other wallcoverings.

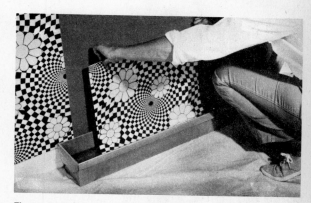

Figure 9–36. Use a water tray when you hang prepasted wallcoverings. The water should be tepid. Check the manufacturer's instructions for the length of time that the rolled strip should (a) remain in the water tray and (b) relax after wetting. Place the tray at the end of the cutting table or at the baseboard. Hanging is the same as for other wallcoverings.

Figure 9–37. Uses for wallcoverings.

Murals and panels. Murals and panels present no difficulty in hanging; the planning of where and at what height they are to be hung is the biggest part of the job. In many museums and art galleries today, the paintings are hung lower than they formerly were. Presumably this gives a more contempo-rary and intimate look, as well as adding height to the room. But the furniture you use in conjunction with panels or a mural will determine at what level you want the interest centered. Just remember to relate any murals or panels to your furnishings as if they were pictures, and do not "sky" them. Since

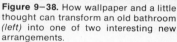

Figure 9—38. How wallpaper and a little thought can transform an old bathroom *(left)* into one of two interesting new arrangements.

mural subjects are printed on plain-colored or textured precut strips that are much longer than the average height of a wall, it is simple, once you are sure, to cut the strips to your own requirements. In placing them, be certain to use a plumb line.

Special wallcoverings. There are several other types of wallcoverings that can be used to beautify your home.

Vinyl wallcoverings are hung much like the ordinary "paper"-type wallcovering just described except that special adhesives are employed and the "strippability" must be considered. The latter may involve the use of a lining paper for both a neater job and quicker removal. Properly hung, vinyls can be stripped off in one sheet if a corner is loosened.

When working with vinyls, you will have to be a little more careful smoothing out air bubbles and blisters behind the material since the fabric is stiffer and more airtight than ordinary paper. Many professionals use a window squeegee or broad putty knife to smooth the vinyl against the wall, rather than the smoothing brush or sponge normally used on wallpapers. Pay particular attention to the edges of each strip and roll them several times after you have completed each section to make certain they do not curl back or lift up where strips meet edge to edge. Butt joints neatly; do not overlap them at all.

Flocked patterns are among the oldest and newest in existence. In recent years flocking has been added to almost any surface to which it will stick, but it still appears most widely in damask-type patterns that simulate cut velvet. Flocks need a little more preparation than the average wallcovering. In the first place, it is best to use a lining paper with flocks, as the raised flocking reflects extra light and betrays any unevenness of the wall. Second, they require the use of special, noncellulose paste, and this must be prevented from getting on the flocked surface, as much as possible. For this reason the selvage on a flocked paper is retained until after a strip has been pasted. If paste does get on the surface, it must be sponged off and dried with a soft cloth immediately. Prolonged soaking of the paste on the back and over-brushing of the surface should also be avoided. This and other pertinent information and complete hanging instructions come with every purchase of flocked wallcovering.

Foil patterns are a comparatively new development. Very thin sheets of gold, silver, and aluminum leaf, long used in the decoration of interiors and objects, led to the making of metallic papers from powder. These could be "polished" to a high shine, but foil coverings are gradually superseding most metallic-powder papers because of their superior brightness. Foils are actually a thin sheet of metal on a paper or cloth backing. In spite of their toughness they need to be hung (as do flocks) over a thoroughly dried-out lining paper, and each sheet of foil, after being pasted with a special adhesive, should be allowed from five to seven minutes' "rest," for absorption and softening.

There are two methods of applying foil: by pasting the back of each strip, one at a time, or by applying the adhesive directly to the wall, preferably lined with paper, which a single strip will cover. Foil does not expand or shrink, so air pockets must be punctured, and the material pressed against the wall to set it. If flocking is added to foil (currently a popular practice), the characteristics of each material must be taken into account when hanging the product. Whereas a seam roller of hard rubber could be used on foil (which is frequently mottled with color and encrusted with vinyl-impregnated substances), only a brush of soft natural bristles should be used to smooth any surface that is flocked.

Chapter 10

GIVE YOUR KITCHEN A NEW LOOK

The kitchen in your home should be custom planned to provide for the needs and personal preferences of your individual family. Of course, what psychologists call "living patterns" affects planning of the entire home, but how you live is most important in designing the kitchen. This is the center of family living. In fact, in most homes, the kitchen is not just a place of preparing meals; it is also the family gathering place, an informal setting for entertaining, and an inviting area for relaxation. Of course, your family may view it differently. Perhaps the lady of the house would just like a cheerful, efficient kitchen where she can enjoy cooking convenience.

It is a good idea to make a list of your family's likes and dislikes about the kitchen. If you ask any homemaker who has lived with her kitchen for a period of time, chances are that she will have some pretty strong opinions on what can be done to improve it, whether it is a vintage type dating back to the turn of the century or a modern version of a room she designed herself.

WHAT MAKES A GOOD KITCHEN?

Good kitchens do not just happen. They start with careful planning to blend the ideal in attractiveness with practical working principles. Size of family, ages, activities, working and eating habits, availability of help, even the physical characteristics of the principal users of the room, all have a bearing on planning a kitchen that is right for the individual family. If you can, enlist the help of a kitchen designer, architect, interior designer, utility home ser-

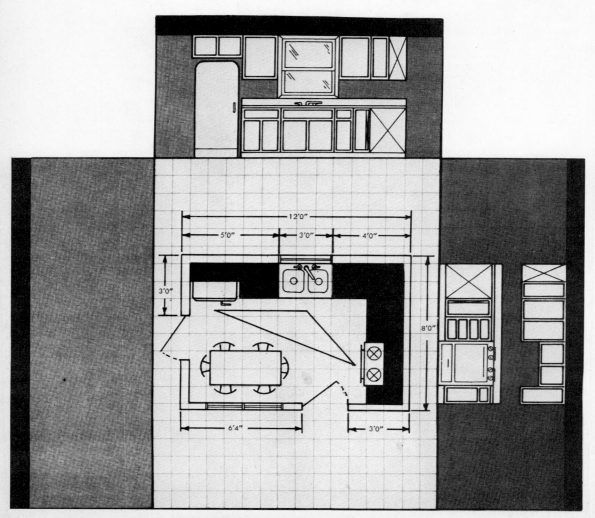

Figure 10—1. Example of how to make a kitchen layout.

vice representative, or other professional. Gather ideas from books, magazines, kitchen displays, advertisements, and the homes you visit. Make notes and clip pictures of appliances, cabinets, floor coverings, color schemes, wall coverings, layouts, construction details, and accessories that appeal to you. List the things that must be in the kitchen and the things it would be nice to have if the budget permits.

Study the local building codes; they affect the installation of ranges, food waste disposers, dishwashers, lavatories, and venting systems among other things. It is a good idea to submit plans for approval before the work is done. It may be expensive to change things if the finished job does not pass inspection.

In planning your remodeling project, measure the kitchen at counter height, 36 inches from the floor. Draw an outline of it to scale (¼ inch to a foot is easy to work with) on graph paper. Show windows and doors, including casings, door swings, columns, radiators, and other details that will affect the layout of the kitchen. Cut out pieces of paper drawn to the same scale to represent appliances you know you will use. If you are undecided about the size and style of some you will be buying, cut out models for all those you would consider. Then work out as many arrangements as possible, drawing copies of those that look workable. It is helpful to include floor plans of adjacent rooms; a dining room closet may be converted to a pantry opening into the kitchen, or a door may be eliminated from the kitchen if an adjoining bedroom can open to a different part of the house. Note which walls must stay and which can be removed. When the floor plan pleases you, do elevation drawings to scale to show what each wall will look like. These plans can be the springboard for your work with an expert or, after much critical examination, can be your plans for a do-it-yourself job.

Traffic patterns and floor plans. "Form follows function," our great designers tell us. And certainly nothing could be more true in planning to remodel a kitchen. You want it to be beautiful, but it also must be efficient. No matter how beautiful it is, if it is not functional, it is not good. A few steps saved every day can be many miles saved over the life of the kitchen. Therefore the first thing to do is to consider the homemaker's working habits. Since most women spend about 50 percent of their time in the kitchen, it must be planned for that time to be used as fruitfully as possible. That means tailoring the kitchen to the homemaker's needs—making it fit her patterns of work, her particular preferences, her individual ways of getting things done. For example, if she is left-handed her kitchen had better be left-handed. If she likes to do a lot of baking, her oven had better be able to handle it, or maybe she will need two ovens. If she uses her freezer a lot, it

had better be close at hand. If she has small children, she will want to be able to keep an eye on them when she has to be in the kitchen.

Many people make the mistake of assuming that more space is the solution to any problem of kitchen design. Sometimes it is. Other times, it may simply mean that the homemaker has farther to walk before she gets to her other problems. Usually, inefficiency is the fault of poor planning (often in older homes) rather than of size.

Efficient use of space is considerably more important than sheer space itself. The minimum floor space needed for a modern efficient kitchen is about 100 square feet. If you have more space, fine, up to about 150 or 160 square feet. Beyond that the homemaker will probably have to walk too much. Around 160 square feet should handle just about everything a homemaker wants, except when the family room or a large breakfast room is combined with the kitchen. In fact, what is involved in kitchen traffic flow is nothing more or less than whether you end up with a good design, and the traffic moves smoothly most of the time. If it is a bad design, people get in each other's way. Actually the key to a good design is an efficient "work triangle" (Figure 10–3).

The work triangle. Every kitchen should have three distinct areas of equipment, and ideally they should be arranged in a triangular pattern with work flowing continuously from right to left. That sounds a lot more complicated than it really is. All it means is that, preferably, the kitchen design should arrange the work areas something like this:

1. Storage center, which consists of the refrigerator and/or freezer, and plenty of cabinets.

2. Clean-up center, which consists of the sink, disposer, compactor, and automatic dishwasher.

3. Food preparation center, which consists of the range or built-in cooking top and oven, counter space, and space for storage of cooking utensils. This is the kitchen's "work triangle."

The clean-up center (the sink) should be considered the mid-point of the triangle. The total of the three sides of the triangle should not be more than 22 feet nor less than 13 feet, according to the generally accepted standards of kitchen efficiency. The most trafficked leg of the triangle is that between the sink and the range. Therefore, this would ideally be the shortest leg of the triangle. The next most heavily traveled route is between refrigerator and sink; this leg of the triangle might be from 5 to 8 feet. In planning your kitchen around the triangle, try to prevent the normal traffic lanes of the home from crossing the triangle, thus reducing the kitchen layout's efficiency.

As far as the rest of the kitchen traffic flow considerations are concerned, common sense is most important. Obviously, you do not want doorways funneling traffic right into the middle of the work

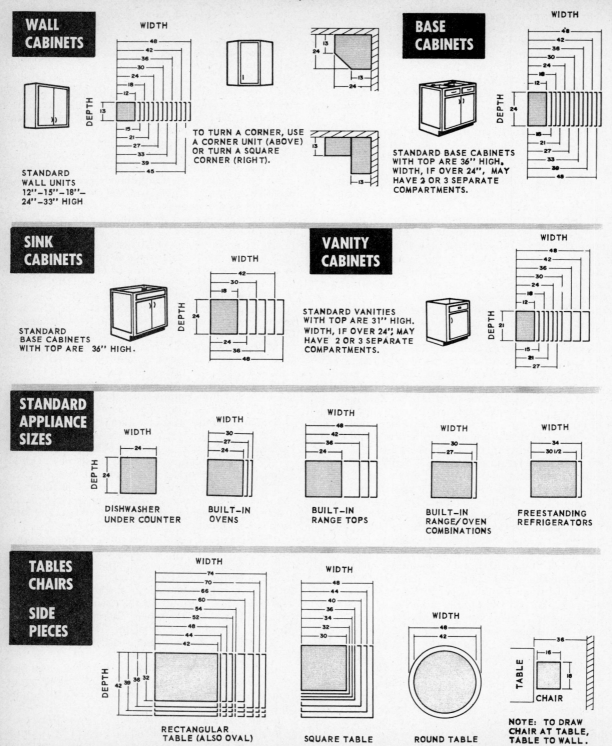

WALL CABINETS

WIDTH

STANDARD WALL UNITS 12"–15"–18"– 24"–33" HIGH

TO TURN A CORNER, USE A CORNER UNIT (ABOVE) OR TURN A SQUARE CORNER (RIGHT).

BASE CABINETS

WIDTH

STANDARD BASE CABINETS WITH TOP ARE 36" HIGH. WIDTH, IF OVER 24", MAY HAVE 2 OR 3 SEPARATE COMPARTMENTS.

SINK CABINETS

WIDTH

STANDARD BASE CABINETS WITH TOP ARE 36" HIGH.

VANITY CABINETS

STANDARD VANITIES WITH TOP ARE 31" HIGH. WIDTH, IF OVER 24", MAY HAVE 2 OR 3 SEPARATE COMPARTMENTS.

WIDTH

STANDARD APPLIANCE SIZES

WIDTH — DISHWASHER UNDER COUNTER

WIDTH — BUILT–IN OVENS

WIDTH — BUILT–IN RANGE TOPS

WIDTH — BUILT–IN RANGE/OVEN COMBINATIONS

WIDTH — FREESTANDING REFRIGERATORS

TABLES CHAIRS SIDE PIECES

WIDTH — RECTANGULAR TABLE (ALSO OVAL)

WIDTH — SQUARE TABLE

WIDTH — ROUND TABLE

TABLE / CHAIR

NOTE: TO DRAW CHAIR AT TABLE, TABLE TO WALL.

Figure 10–2. Dimensions of typical kitchen equipment and other items.

Give Your Kitchen a New Look

TO END A ROW OF BASE CABINETRY YOU MAY LIKE A SHELF UNIT OR

TO TURN A CORNER, USE A LAZY SUSAN FOR BEST USE OF SPACE. OR, LIKE THE WALL CABINETS, TURN A SQUARE CORNER.

AN END UNIT WITH DOORS.

UTILITY (TALL) STORAGE

UTILITY CABINETS ARE 24" DEEP FOR PANTRY & UTILITY STORAGE.

WIDTH
DEPTH

PANTRY STORAGE

PANTRY CABINETS ARE 13" DEEP FOR PANTRY, BROOM, OR SHELF STORAGE.

WIDTH
DEPTH

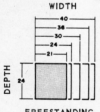

WIDTH
DEPTH

FREESTANDING RANGE/OVEN COMBINATIONS

WIDTH
BUILT-IN REFRIGERATOR

WIDTH
WARMING OVEN SEPARATE FROM OVEN

WIDTH
ICEMAKERS UNDER COUNTER

WIDTH
BUILT-IN FREEZERS

WIDTH
FREESTANDING FREEZER

AVERAGE DINING & SMALL SIDE CHAIR

SIDE CHAIR

LARGE SIDE CHAIR (WING)

BARREL CHAIR

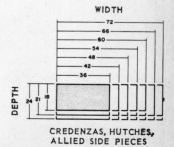

WIDTH
DEPTH

CREDENZAS, HUTCHES, ALLIED SIDE PIECES

COMFORTABLE SEATING ALLOWS 24" PER PERSON.

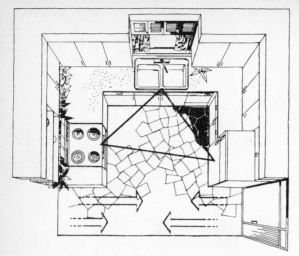

Figure 10—3. The work triangle.

triangle. Or you would not want the kids traipsing through the entire kitchen just to hang up their coats after school. The number of doorways, their location, and the direction of door swing affect the efficiency of the kitchen arrangement. Generally, doorways in corners should be avoided. It is also desirable to avoid door swings that conflict with the use of appliances or cabinets, or with other doors. Rehang the door on the other side of the jamb or hinge it to swing out rather than in. In the latter case, make certain that the door does not swing into the traffic path in halls or other activity areas. A sliding or folding door avoids the problem. But aside from such general thoughts on good traffic movement, there are no hard and fast rules of traffic flow.

Eating area. Most American families eat more meals in the kitchen or space adjacent to it than in a formal dining room. It is great to have a table and chairs for this purpose, but only if the available space is at least 8 to 9 feet wide. To conserve

Figure 10—4. Ways of including an eating area in a kitchen design.

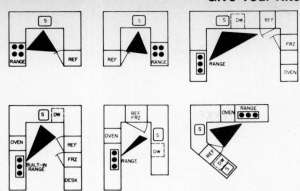

Figure 10—5. Six arrangements for a U-shaped kitchen.

First, of course, is a location convenient for serving. The homemaker does not want to have to walk across the room a half-dozen times every time she is serving a snack or lunch. Also the amount of space available is important when planning the family's dining area. A too-small or cramped eating area is a major annoyance that will pop up to haunt you every time food is served. For comfortable dining, allow at least 24 inches of table or counter elbowroom for each person, if possible.

Be sure to leave plenty of room for moving chairs, serving, and general traffic around the table. That usually requires at least 30 inches of clearance on each edge of the table that will be in use. When a counter is planned, a minimum depth of 15 inches is adequate for family breakfasts or for quick snacks. But, it is better to allow a 24-inch depth or more if the counter is extended for serving dinner or for a line-up of buffet foods. This depth provides space for the casseroles, large platters, and accessories that are employed for dinners and special parties.

When planning built-in seating and a table in the kitchen, be sure to set aside a space no less than 4 by 5½ feet. This space is designed to serve four people in comfort.

The four basic kitchen floor plans. Once you have reached at least tentative conclusions about the work centers and family eating area, it is time to

space a table may be used with a bench built against a wall, or a breakfast bar may be built in. If there is a peninsula dividing the kitchen work area from the dining area, a snack bar built onto it solves the quick meal problem. A dining bar should be about 29 inches high if chairs are used, about 40 inches with high stools. Allow 2 feet of counter or table space for each place setting. A counter should be at least 15 inches deep for meal service. But, whether you end up with a counter or a table arrangement, you will want to keep several thoughts in mind.

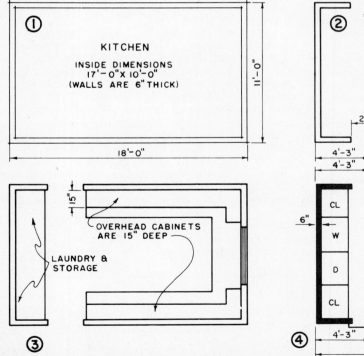

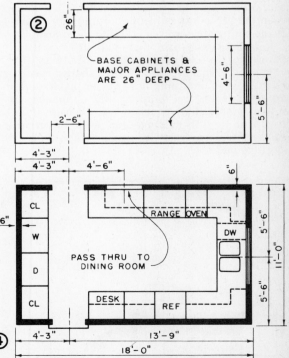

Figure 10—6. Follow these four steps in laying out a U-shaped kitchen.

begin thinking about your basic floor plan. There are four basic kitchen floor plans, each with infinite variations, for you to choose from.

The U-shaped kitchen (Figure 10–5). In spite of the fact that experts seldom agree on anything, most kitchen design experts agree that this arrangement is the most desirable kitchen plan from the standpoint of efficiency. The short distance between the work centers cuts down on wasted steps, and the overall plan adapts beautifully to both large and small kitchens.

The center of the "U" provides a natural space for either an eating area or an island sink and work counter. In many large kitchens, the "U" is found at one end of a kitchen-family room area, with one leg of the "U" being an island or peninsula that divides the two areas. If you use this plan, try to have the kitchen at least 10 or more feet wide at the base of the "U." If you try to make it narrower, you will probably end up with a cramped work area at the sink and inefficient storage areas tucked into the corners.

The L-shaped kitchen (Figure 10–7). Next in popularity to the U-shaped kitchen as a favorite design is the L-shaped kitchen. In fact, many people prefer it because it gives them greater freedom in the location of appliances and work centers. The design is adaptable to almost any space, large or small, and lends itself to a very efficient work triangle. In larger areas, it is often used with an island location for a sink or a built-in cooktop. The open area of the "L" offers a great opportunity for a comfortable eating area or even a family-room area. Extra storage space can be included easily, and the flexibility of the total design is almost limitless.

If you are leaning toward an L-shaped design, be sure to keep one thing in mind: in planning the work triangle, be sure to arrange the appliances so the food preparation sequence runs logically from refrigerator to sink to range and oven to serving area. You will save the homemaker thousands of steps if you do.

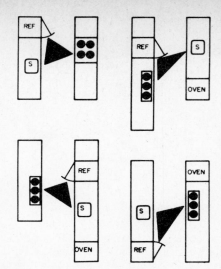

Figure 10–8. Four arrangements for a corridor kitchen.

The corridor kitchen (Figure 10–8). This floor plan uses a minimum of space for a maximum of counter space and appliances. Translation? It is probably the most efficient design in terms of sheer square-foot utilization. However, the traffic pattern tends to get pretty cluttered unless there is an alternate door for traffic flow. Normally, there is not enough floor space for more than one person to be in motion at a time.

The corridor kitchen is particularly good for long, narrow rooms. An eating area can be added at the open end, if space permits, and there is usually plenty of storage space in this design. Always make sure it is at least 8 feet wide, though, or the homemaker will be stepping on herself.

The single-wall kitchen (Figure 10–9). Normally this floor plan is used only when the available space is too narrow for any other arrangement. Although it will fit into many small homes, it makes it difficult for you to get either a short work pattern or enough counter space. If necessity makes this the only logical choice, supplement it by converting a nearby closet into extra kitchen storage

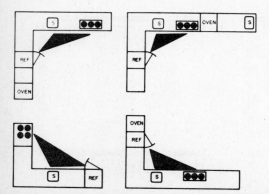

Figure 10–7. Four arrangements for an L-shaped kitchen.

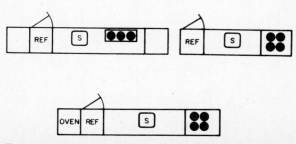

Figure 10–9. Three arrangements for a single-wall kitchen.

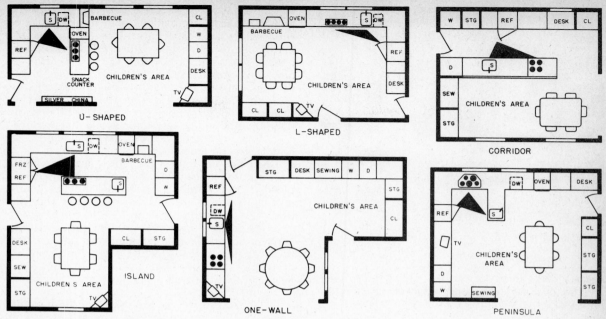

Figure 10—10. Six family kitchen plans.

space, with a large pantry cabinet, for example, or by adding a mobile cart or two to give extra counter work space. As far as an eating area is concerned, that will probably have to fit into an adjoining room where space is available, either in the dining room or a family room.

Occasionally the single-wall or line-a-wall plan will work out nicely in a large open-plan kitchen-family room, but even then one of the other plans would probably give you more efficiency and usable space.

Family kitchen. The so-called family kitchen is just an open version of any of the four basic plans (Figure 10–10). Its function is to provide a gathering place for the entire family in addition to providing space for the everyday kitchen functions. Because of the dual function, a family kitchen is normally divided into two sections. One section includes the three work centers, while the other contains the dining area and family-room facilities.

Kitchen laundry. If you can find space for a clothes washer and dryer in another convenient location, it is better not to put them in the kitchen; clothes and food just do not mix well together. It is convenient, though, to have the laundry center near the kitchen to help in dovetailing your tasks (page 377). But, if the laundry appliances must be in the kitchen, try to place them out of the refrigerator-sink-range area. Allow at least 4½ feet of wall space for a standard-size washer and dryer; be sure to check the measurements of the models you will use. When space is very limited or a standard washer

cannot be installed, a compact spinner washer 24 inches wide by 30 inches high by 15 inches deep can be stored out of the way and rolled to the sink for use. A matching compact dryer of the same size may be operated on 120 volt electricity; it can be hung on a wall, placed on a base cabinet, or stood on the floor. If there is room for a washer, but not enough

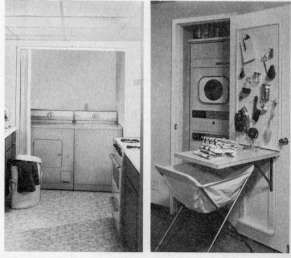

Figure 10—11. Two kitchen laundry arrangements. The arrangement at the right features an over-under washer-dryer unit.

Figure 10—12. Frequently a family-play area can be designed as part of a kitchen.

space or the required utility connections for a standard-size dryer, a compact dryer can be mounted on top of some washers with the use of a special kit.

WORK CENTERS AND APPLIANCES

At the heart of each work center is one or more appliances, and no matter which basic floor plan you use, U-shaped, L-shaped, corridor, or single-wall, the placement of your appliances will determine the centers of activity.

The storage center. This area is where each meal usually begins. As previously mentioned, the storage center includes the refrigerator and freezer, as well as lots of cabinet space. If the homemaker likes pantries, this is where the pantry belongs. If she prefers cabinet food storage, this is where the appropriate cabinets belong. Tailor everything to the homemaker's habits and preferences, but be sure to group it all efficiently so she does not have to keep walking from one side of the kitchen to the other. Try to include at least 1½ feet of counter space next to the refrigerator, with the refrigerator door opening toward it. If you have a side-by-side refrigerator-freezer, remember it is easier to reach across the closed freezer door to load and unload the fresh food section than to reach around an open door to a counter on the wrong side. Of course, if you have a side-by-side refrigerator-freezer, it is a good idea, when possible, to have an equal amount of space beside the freezer.

While the remodeling of a kitchen does not automatically call for new appliances, it is a good time to take a long look at the ones you have, and at the ones you could have. For the extra money, they can save a lot of extra steps, and there is never a better chance to put a whole dream kitchen together than right now.

In recent years, advances in design and insulation have made it possible to put a refrigerator of surprisingly large capacity into the floor space formerly required for a unit with a much smaller capacity. This is primarily due to the discovery of new urethane insulation materials, which permit the walls of the refrigerator to be thinner, thus increasing the interior capacity. Be sure to decide whether you want a left- or right-hand opening door, though, and be sure that the opening is convenient to the counter space you have planned to use for loading and unloading.

As far as the style of the unit is concerned, you have a wide choice. First of all, you can have completely separate units, a refrigerator and a matching up-right freezer, sitting side-by-side. Or you can have a two-door refrigerator-freezer combination, with the freezer at the top, or along one side. The latter space arrangement is found with the new vertical two-door designs. While some units come as narrow as 30 inches wide, it is best to count on at least 36 inches of wall space for most refrigerators on the market. Check the specifications of the model you intend to use for the height of the box and recommended clearance for air circulation as well as for width. Avoid putting a refrigerator in a corner, beside a wall, or next to a line of cabinets; it is usually necessary to open the door more than 90 degrees to remove crispers and shelves.

An automatic icemaker requires a cold water line. If you are building an addition to or remodeling the kitchen, put in the line. Many refrigerator-freezers are designed so that icemakers can be installed either at the time of purchase or later on; chances are you will be using the line in the future if not now.

A separate freezer is not used as many times a day as the refrigerator; it may be located out of the main kitchen work area, perhaps in a line of tall cabinets on another wall if it is an upright model, or in a garage or utility room.

There are also a variety of built-in combination units, as well as separate individual refrigerator and freezer units. Whatever style you choose, make sure you are getting the features you want.

The clean-up center. As every homemaker knows, she uses the clean-up center before, during, and after meals, so it is a good idea to get it located as centrally as possible. The center consists of the sink, garbage disposer, trash compactor, and automatic dishwasher, as well as adequate counter space on both sides.

The sink. Whether or not the sink is actually an appliance is something we will worry about later; suffice it to say that it is probably the most important single piece of equipment in the kitchen. It is used more often, for more things, and in more ways than any other item in the kitchen. Thus, locating it in the best possible spot is vital to the whole kitchen plan. For instance, if there is a window at least 40 inches above the floor (enough to allow for a backsplash), you may want to place the sink under it. If there is a peninsula dividing the work area of the kitchen from the dining area, this makes an excellent site for a sink. Gourmet cooks often favor putting the sink in an island work counter in the middle of a kitchen.

Sinks come in three basic types:

1. Enameled cast-iron sinks are manufactured with a heavy wall thickness of iron; a fused-in enamel is applied to all exposed surfaces. The enamel on cast-iron sinks is four times thicker than on other types of sinks. This provides much greater resistance to cracking, chipping, and marring. Cast-iron sinks are available in colors or in white. The solid, heavy construction makes them less subject to vibration and, therefore, extremely quiet when installed with a disposer.

2. Procelain-on-steel sinks are formed of sheet steel, in one piece, and are sprayed and fired to produce a glass-like finish much like the surface found on cast-iron sinks. But, because of the unique physical characteristics of the material used, the finish on porcelain-on-steel sinks is only one-fourth as heavy as that on cast-iron sinks. These porcelain sinks are available in colors and in white.

3. Stainless steel sinks are the lightest of the three and will provide a lifetime of service. The surfaces are easy to keep clean and are stain resistant. Since stainless steel is the finish, this type of sink is not available in colors. But the natural finish blends well with most color schemes.

In these three materials, there are single bowls, double bowls, deep bowls, shallow bowls, big bowls, little bowls. There are sinks with twin compartments set at an angle for use in corners; or you can simply place a conventional sink diagonally across a corner if that location is indicated.

The final selection of style and color is up to you. Most people prefer the double bowl, but it is wise to remember that one large sink (21 to 24 inches) takes less space than a double one (33 inches, for example) and is quite satisfactory if there is a dishwasher. Most sinks are 21 or 22 inches from front to back, and the bowl itself usually is 16 inches from front to back, but these dimensions vary slightly according to manufacturer and style.

While the usual depth of a standard bowl is about 7½ inches, this can vary to some degree, too. For instance, a triple-bowl sink may have a small vegetable sink between two standard bowls, and this may be only 3½ inches deep. In kitchens where space is at a premium, there are sinks at a depth of 5½ inches which permit one bowl to fit over a built-in dishwasher.

Frequently, if space permits, it is a good idea to have two separate sinks in the kitchen for two work centers, or an extra small sink for father's bartending, mother's plant watering, or the kids' finger-painting. Also consider installing a sit-down sink. This is a sink that puts the homemaker close to the work and takes her off her feet at the same time. It makes no difference if she is short or tall; the sink can be installed at the height most convenient to her.

Sinks may come with faucets and other attachments, or simply with punched holes so faucets can be purchased separately. One of the more popular sink attachments is an undersink heater, which serves at a tap instant near-boiling water for coffee, dehydrated soups, gelatin desserts, and the like.

Allow 24 inches on one side of the sink for a dishwasher. Be sure to avoid placing the dishwasher at immediate right angles to the sink; if it must be around the corner from the sink, place it 24 inches from the corner so you can stand at the sink and pivot to load the open dishwasher. You will need at least 24 inches of counter space on each side of the sink. There should be storage space nearby for hand towels, dish towels, dish cloths, and aprons; vegetables such as onions and potatoes; a chopping board; vegetable peeler; pots and pans used for foods cooked with water; and other items used first at the sink.

The garbage disposer. A food waste disposer installed under one sink will eliminate messy food waste and simplify clean-up after meals, since you can peel fruits and vegetables, scrape plates, dump coffee grounds, and empty cereal bowls directly into the sink. The quality disposer can handle bones, fruit pits, egg shells, shrimp shells, in fact, almost any food waste. Some of the more efficient models have cutter blades that can handle fibrous waste such as corn husks, celery stalks, and artichoke leaves. Disposers are so efficient in handling food waste that today approximately 100 cities require their installation in all new housing starts or major improvements. Research by the United States Public Health Service has pointed out that septic tank–soil absorption systems that meet the FHA minimum property standards can handle the additional loads from food waste disposers. The addition of ground food waste may reduce the time between tank cleanings by approximately one-third.

There are two basic types of disposers: the batch-feed and the continuous-feed. The former is controlled by a built-in switch. Waste is placed in the chamber, the cold water is turned on, and the lid is put in place. In some cases the lid must be turned or positioned a certain way to start the motor; in others a sealed-in magnet activates a hermetically sealed switch so that the disposer starts as soon as the lid is dropped into place. A continuous-feed disposer is controlled by a separate electrical switch installed nearby. It is a little less expensive than a batch model, but the cost of installing the switch almost equalizes the price. With a continuous-feed model you can feed waste into the disposer as it is operating.

Most garbage disposers are designed to fit any single or double sink with a 3½-inch to 4-inch opening, and require a 120-volt ac outlet. You should check local plumbing codes and requirements to determine the amount of fall necessary and the method of connection. Detailed instructions for installation are provided with each model and, of course, they should be followed to the letter.

Trash compactor. There should be provision near the sink for a container for waste bottles, cans, and papers. Or you may wish to install an appliance that will compress cans, bottles, paper, cartons, and food waste into a compact package for disposal. A typical model fits into the space of a 15-inch-wide base cabinet. It requires no plumbing or special wiring, and can be used wherever it can be plugged into an ordinary 120-volt outlet.

Automatic dishwasher. The installation of a built-in dishwasher is not difficult, and some manufacturers are supplying simple instructions for do-it-yourself installation where the local code permits.

A typical space requirement for a built-in dishwasher is 34 inches high, at least 24 inches wide, and 24 inches deep. The dishwasher fits into the space of a standard 24-inch base cabinet. In an existing set-up, if there is a 24-inch base cabinet that can be removed, well and good. If not, it is possible to take out a wider cabinet or two cabinets that total at least 24 inches and use fillers on each side to fill the remaining space. Fillers are usually available from cabinet suppliers and some lumber yards. When existing cabinets were built on the job, some carpentry or cabinetmaking may be needed to open the space and finish the adjacent cabinets. Do not place the dishwasher at an immediate right angle to the sink. If the dishwasher must be around the corner from the sink, allow an intervening space of at least 18, and preferably 24, inches from the corner. Also, because the refrigerator generates cold and a dishwasher produces heat and steam, these two appliances will last longer and work better if they are separated by a 3-inch insulated filler strip.

A dishwasher takes a 120-volt, 60-hertz a.c. individual circuit, fused for 20 amperes. Three-wire electrical service to the dishwasher is recommended for connection to the terminal block and for grounding. To avoid the hazard of electrical shock, the dishwasher must be installed before it is used.

The water supply needed is 140 to 150 degrees F hot water at 15 to 120 pounds per square inch pressure. The water pipe should be ½-inch outside-diameter copper, with a ⅜-inch female pipe thread connection at the valve. A ½-inch by ⅜-inch male

compression elbow is provided as an accessory. An 8-foot flexible drain hose with a ½-inch inside diameter is furnished. It is not recommended that the drain line be extended beyond the length of the hose provided, but should this be necessary, attach the hose to a line of larger inside diameter.

The most desirable drain system for a built-in dishwasher is through a drain air gap mounted at the sink or at countertop level. This accessory protects against a siphoning of the wash or rinse water and also prevents the possibility of food waste entering the dishwasher in the event of a plugged drain line.

Portable dishwashers vary somewhat. One model, for example, is 33⅛ inches from top to the bottom including the caster, 23⅖ inches wide, and 27¾ inches deep. The handle projects another 2 inches. This portable dishwasher has a hose 34 inches long from the cabinet to the end of the faucet connector, and an electric cord 6 feet long. It requires a 120-volt, 60-hertz, 20-ampere circuit, and it has a three-prong plug that must be connected to a properly grounded electrical outlet. The inlet and drain hoses are handled through a single connector to the faucet.

The food preparation center. Primarily, the food preparation center includes the range, or built-in cooktop, and oven. It also includes ventilating equipment, counter space next to the range, and a serving area located for the convenient transferring of food to the table. Also make sure to include adequate storage for cooking utensils nearby and do not have the dishes stored too far away.

Range-oven. Recent tests show that the average homemaker makes more trips between the range and the sink than between any other two points in the kitchen. To cut down on the daily mileage, locate the range 4 to 6 feet from the sink without a traffic lane between them. Ideally, the range should be handy to the dining area you use most often. But do not place it next to a door that opens onto a constant parade of children; a cabinet at least 15 inches wide between the door and the range will prevent accident possibilities with hot food. Do not forget to allow space on each side of the range for elbowroom and for pan handles, with at least 21 inches of counter on one side for serving. Your local building codes may also have something to say about range placement. Check their requirements first.

While a built-in range top and separate oven(s) are generally considered the most convenient of all range styles, they use up the most wall space. They also cost more to install, and replacement of the oven is difficult if the new model does not fit the cabinet for the old one. A separate oven should not be located directly next to the range; counter space is needed next to each. If necessary, you may locate the oven out of the busiest kitchen area. A wall

Figure 10–13. *(left)* A tabletop range is a feature of this kitchen. *(right)* A tabletop range and a built-in oven are installed in a brick-wall room divider.

oven should be installed so the inside top surface of the fully opened door is between 1 and 7 inches below your elbow height. If a double-oven unit is used, the bottom of the upper oven at counter height (36 inches) is about right for most women. Never install a built-in oven too high. High mounting can result in burns and makes it difficult to remove pans. Allow 21 to 24 inches of counter on at least one side of the oven; a heat-resistant surface here is a joy to busy bakers. Avoid having the wall oven at the end of a line of cabinets where the door will open into a traffic lane. Also avoid installation in a corner. Easier loading, unloading, and cleaning are possible with space all around the open oven door.

Make certain that your new unit has either self-cleaning or continuous-cleaning features. With a pyrolytic self-cleaning type of oven, the walls of the oven can get as soiled as those of a conventional oven. When the oven is cleaned, controls are set that lock the door shut for safety, and the oven is heated to about 1,000 degrees F. The process takes from 2 to 3½ hours for the complete cleaning of the oven. In a catalytic continuous-cleaning oven, there is a catalyst in the porcelain enamel of the interior oven panels that helps to oxidize spatter as it hits the surface. The oven never gets terribly soiled, unless there is a spill-over, but it may not look entirely clean. Grease that is deposited on oven surfaces from meat cookery tends to disappear as the oven is used for baking. The catalytic system does not require extraordinary temperatures so no door latch is needed, and the oven is not taken out of use for

cleaning. Range dealers have information about the two types of ovens.

Either one of these ovens will serve well, so make sure the new range has one of them. As to the range itself, you can get one of several kinds; the familiar freestanding unit of counter height, a freestanding unit of the "over and under" design (with an oven on the top, an oven on the bottom, and the cooktop in between), a drop-in or slide-in unit, a separate built-in cooktop and wall oven, or an eye-level oven and cooktop stacked on a base cabinet. The most cooking facility for the least space is a 30-inch-wide range with an eye-level oven above the range top and another oven below it. However, a very short woman often finds it difficult to handle a hot roasting pan in the high oven; a very tall woman may find her view of the back burners on the range blocked by the upper oven. Have the homemaker stand in front of the model being considered and have her go through the motions of cooking to see if she can work with it safely and comfortably.

Conventional freestanding ranges and slide-in models that appear to be built in are available in widths from 20 to 42 inches. These ranges, and drop-in ranges that are set on a base cabinet support, are gaining in popularity. All styles of ranges and ovens are available with either gas or electricity as the fuel, and if both types of fuel are available in your area, you should consider their individual advantages carefully before making a choice. Both gas and electric models offer a wide variety of special features such as automatic timers, rotisseries, special broiling devices, and special colors. You may want to consider the new electronic ranges, too. They cut down cooking time fantastically.

Ventilating equipment. As was stated in Chapter 7, every kitchen should have a good ventilating system. Walls, draperies, cabinets, and everything else will stay clean and new-looking much longer if grease and smoke are whisked out of the kitchen before they get a chance to settle.

There are two basic types of ventilating fans available: ducted and non-ducted. You may also want to consider built-in cooking equipment that comes with its own ventilating system.

There are three basic ways in which fans are combined with range hoods:

1. The fan is built right into the hood itself and does not take any of the cabinet space above it.

2. The fan is not in the hood but is instead installed in the cabinet space directly above the hood.

3. An exhaust fan is simply mounted in the wall above the cooking surface of the range and is vented directly to the outside.

Wall-mounted hoods should extend at least to the front of the cooktop and 3 inches to 6 inches out on each side. On peninsula or island installations, the hood should overhang the cooktop 3 to 6 inches

Figure 10—14. This modern barbecue unit, which may be installed in a standard wood or metal kitchen cabinet, brings barbecue cooking conveniently indoors for year-round enjoyment. Units of this type are available for use with charcoal, gas, or electricity as fuel. One style of unit drops in a countertop with the front concealed.

on all four sides. The more overhang the better in these wide open spaces because of air turbulence, which tends to make cooking vapors spread. The factors affecting the depth of a hood are its length, width, and distance from the cooking surface and placement of the exhaust inlet. Cooking vapors should be picked up from the top of the hood where they have concentrated, and the larger the hood the more depth is necessary to hold these vapors. A 5- or 6-inch depth has practically no holding power and allows cross-drafts to spread the vapors. A 9-inch depth holds vapors in a wall-mounted hood that is fairly well closed in on the sides with cabinets. A 14-inch depth is needed where the hood is placed as high as a person's head, and on large island and peninsula installations an 18- or 20-inch depth is desirable. The arrangement of the kitchen sometimes limits hood depth, but it is often possible to change kitchen arrangements when you are aware of the importance of "vapor holding capacity."

When a hood is installed, the bottom of the hood should be placed at least 24 inches from the burners. If you get the hood any closer to the heat source, the cook cannot see into her pots and pans, especially if the hood is wide enough to cover the front burners, as it should be. Twenty-seven to 30 inches is the safe distance for the placement of the hood and generally makes the most attractive installation. Thirty-four inches is the maximum distance and should be used only for wall-mounted hoods, which are better protected from cross-drafts.

For a regular four-burner cooktop, 300 CFM (cubic feet per minute) is enough blower capacity. This is the capacity of one single blower. If you have a regular kitchen range with four burners and an oven, you need 600 CFM available (one dual blower). In a case like this, you will have separate switches for the two blowers so you can use one by itself for light cooking. Miscellaneous cooking equipment like an electric fry pan will do fine with one 300-CFM blower. An indoor barbecue unit needs 600 CFM all the time. If you have more than one piece of cooking equipment under a hood, vent each as if the other were not there. Do not expect a dual blower placed over a barbecue to take care of a cooktop beside it. The blower should be directly over the equipment it is to handle. On an island or peninsula a 600-CFM blower is always necessary because air must be picked up from all directions. For this reason, a single switch operates a dual blower.

Non-ducted ventilating systems can be hung on the wall above a freestanding range or cooktop, or can be suspended beneath the wall cabinets over the cooking surface. They are ideal for any location where ducting to the outside is either difficult or not desirable (such as over an island installation), and are very easy to install. However, they are not quite as efficient as the ducted systems. They draw air through a filtering system and then return it to the room, filtering out the smoke, grease, and odors with special charcoal filters.

Barbecue grilles. Outdoor cookery has become so popular that the barbecue grille has inevitably moved indoors, allowing the devotee of charcoal-broiled steak to enjoy this succulent treat the year-round. Drop-in models are available; they use charcoal, gas, or electricity for fuel. Whichever type is used, adequate venting is a necessity. This is usually provided by an exhaust fan inside a hood directly over and slightly larger than the grille unit. For top performance of any indoor barbecue, as previously noted, the Home Ventilating Institute suggests hood fans that move 600 cubic feet or more of air per minute.

In some grille arrangements, the vent is right on the cooking surface, eliminating the need for a hood (Figure 10–15). Instead, the surface vent pulls heat, odors, smoke, and grease downward, then ducts them outdoors. If the cooking top is on an outside wall, installation of a vent is simple. If not, ducts can be run under the floor to an outside wall.

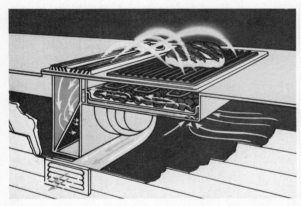

Figure 10–15. A popular ventilation system that moves odors, smoke, and grease downward and outward.

CABINETS, COUNTERTOPS, AND STORAGE

If there is one thing a good kitchen has to have, it is plenty of places to put things. Places to put things *in*, places to put things *on*, places to put things *beside* and *between* and *above* and *below*. In short, you need storage space, and lots of it.

How to choose kitchen cabinets. While the kitchen cabinets are by no means the whole storage story in a remodeled kitchen, they are the most important single part of it. Therefore, consider your storage needs carefully, and then choose the cabinets that meet those needs.

You will find that cabinet sizes are standardized. The standard base and wall cabinets you buy are made in widths varying in 3-inch modules from 9

to 48 inches. Manufactured and finished in a factory, they have sides and backs and usually have adjustable shelves. They come in a variety of materials: solid lumber, plywood with fine wood veneer facings over an inner core, prefinished hardboard over a wood frame, and steel. They come in a variety of period styles, from Early American to French Provincial and Spanish, and in a variety of colors and finishes to suit any decorative scheme. Some boast reversible door panels that permit covering with wallpaper or other material for a completely personalized scheme. The price differences in stock cabinets are not as great from one quality to another as they can be with the options offered by one manufacturer. (Fancy moldings, special decorative finishes, and special interior fittings can run the price up.) Drawer cabinets are typically more expensive than comparable door units with an interior shelf. If your budget is tight, consider using simple cabinets of good quality and installing your own plastic turntables and other custom fittings.

If you have the equipment, time, and skill, you can make the cabinets right on the job. But, in most cases, the manufactured kitchen cabinets on the market today are far superior to what any cabinetmaker can custom-produce for your kitchen. This is true because the home carpenter, no matter how skilled, usually does not have access to completely kiln-dried lumber and cannot produce the baked-on finish that makes the best manufactured cabinets so easy to keep clean and helps to maintain dimensional stability. But, if your kitchen cabinets are to be built on the job or in a local cabinet shop to your specifications, see if the shelves can be made adjustable. If that is not feasible, it would be helpful if spacing between the shelves is not exactly the same all around the kitchen; there will be some tall items and some shallow ones to store as well as many in-betweens.

Wall cabinets, whether bought or custom-built, and including those above the range and refrigerator or in corners, should extend at least 10 linear feet. Most wall cabinets are 12 to 13 inches deep. They are usually hung with the top line 84 inches above the floor; utility cabinets are 84 inches above the floor. The height of the basic wall cabinet may be 30 to 33 inches, depending on style. This gives ample clearance (15 to 18 inches) between the counter (36 inches from the floor) and the bottom of the wall cabinet.

If a cabinet is to be placed over a sink, allow 24 inches above the sink rim for standard-depth wall cabinets. This space can be cut to 16 inches if the wall cabinets are custom-made only 6 inches deep. For safety as well as convenience there should be 27 to 36 inches between a range top and wall cabinets; consult the local code. Allow for the depth of the range hood. Cabinets less than 15 inches wide have limited use except for trays, so try

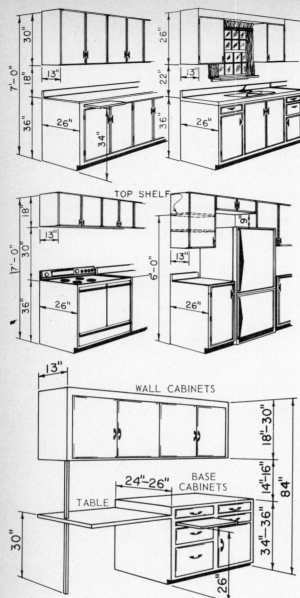

work surface is at 36 inches. Dishwashers and most ranges are designed for the 36-inch counter height, although some range tops may be positioned 2 or 3 inches lower than the side rim. Since it is less tiring to work at a counter a few inches below one's elbow height (measured with the upper arm straight down, the forearm parallel to the floor), many women find it desirable to have one section lower, possibly at 33 inches. This lower counter could be at the end of a peninsula, or may be provided by a sturdy pull-out chopping board. A sit-down counter should be 26 to 30 inches from the floor. A manufacturer's specification sheet will give exact sizes of base and wall cabinets, so that you can work out a cabinet plan to fit your chosen appliances and your wall space. You can order filler strips for those gaps where you do not come out exactly even in your measurements.

Worthwhile cabinet features include magnetic door closures and good rollers on the drawers. Trays that roll out easily are excellent for storing heavy pots and pans. Depending on the decorative look desired, you may choose handsome handles, knobs, and hinges; or you may prefer concealed hinges and finger grips. Avoid hardware with open ends that can catch on pockets and other parts of the clothing.

Installing cabinets. Manufactured kitchen cabinets are available already assembled and in a knocked-down form. The latter are less costly and come finished and unfinished. Most pre-assembled cabinets are finished at the factory. To assemble the knocked-down cabinets, follow the manufacturer's instructions to the letter.

Cabinets are fastened to the walls either by the hanger method or directly to studs. With the former, the cabinet manufacturer supplies steel hanger

Figure 10–16. *(top and center)* Typical heights of kitchen cabinets; *(bottom)* dimensions of cabinets and working surfaces.

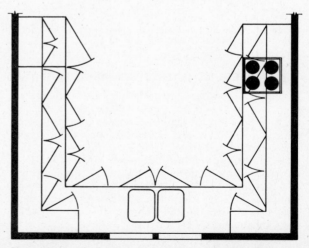

Figure 10–17. Cabinet doors should open away from the work area.

to plan the layout without too many narrow units. For good appearance, it is more important to line up wall and base cabinets for vertical symmetry than to worry about horizontal symmetry.

Prefabricated base cabinets are about 24 inches deep; the counter about 25 inches. The standard height of base cabinets including toe space is 34½ inches; so that with a 1½-inch-thick counter the

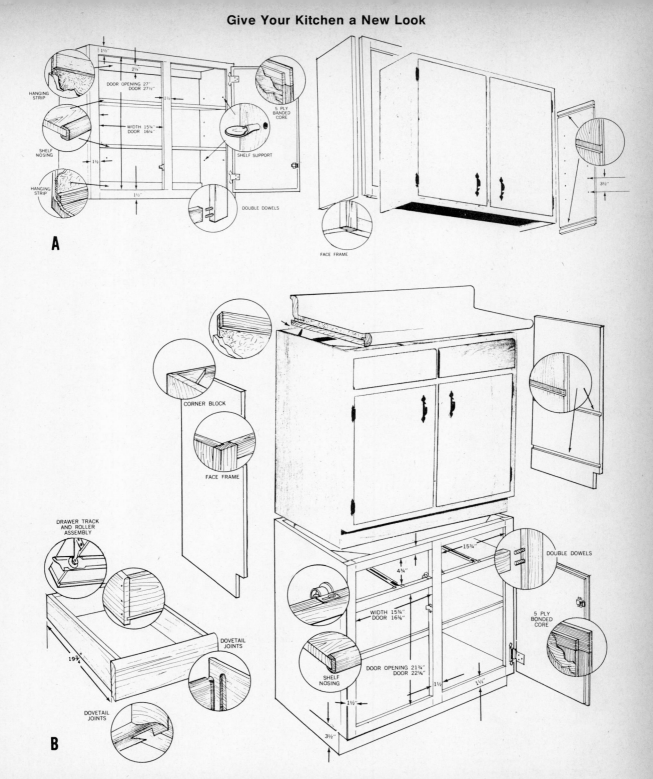

Figure 10–18. Construction details of a typical factory-built wall cabinet (A) and of a typical factory-built base cabinet (B).

1

Cabinets must be attached to studs for full support. Studs are usually located 16" on center. Locate studs with stud finder, tapping with hammer or nail driven through plaster at height that will be hidden by cabinets. Cabinets must always be attached to walls with screws. **Never use nails!**

2

Cabinets must be installed perfectly level — from a standpoint of function as well as appearance. Find the highest point of floor with the use of a level.

3

Using a level or straightedge, find the high spots on the wall on which cabinets are to be hung. Some high spots can be removed by sanding. Otherwise, it will be necessary to "shim" to provide a level and plumb installation.

4

Using the highest point on the floor, measure up the wall to a height of 84". This height, 84", is the top height of wall cabinets, oven and broom cabinets. 84" cabinets can be cut down to 81".

5

On the walls where cabinets are to be installed, **remove baseboard and chair rail. This is required for a flush fit.**

6

Start your installation in one corner. First assemble the base corner unit, then add one unit on each side of the corner unit.   This — as a unit — can be installed in position. Additional cabinets are then added to each side as required.

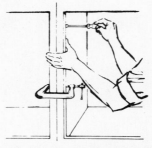

7

"C" clamps should be used in connecting cabinets together to obtain proper alignment. Drill 2 or 3 holes through ½" end panels. Holes should be drilled through to adjoining cabinet. Secure T-nut and secure with 1½" bolt. Draw up snugly. If you prefer you may drill through side of front frame as well as "lead hole" into abutting cabinet, insert screws, and draw up snugly.

Figure 10–19. Typical instruction sheets accompanying factory-built cabinets.

8 Each cabinet — as it is installed to the wall — should be checked front to back and also across the front edge with a level. Be certain that the front frame is plumb. If necessary, use shims to level the cabinets. Base cabinets should be attached with screws into wall studs. For additional support and to prevent back rail from "bowing," insert block between cabinet back and wall. After bases are installed cover toe-kick area with material that is provided.

9 Attach counter top on base cabinets. After installation, cover counter tops with cartons to prevent damage while completing installation.

10 Wall cabinets should then be installed, beginning with a corner unit as described in step #6. Screw through hanging strips built into backs of cabinets at both top and bottom. Place them ¾" below top and ¾" above bottom shelf from inside of cabinet. Adjust only loosely at first so that final adjustments can be made.

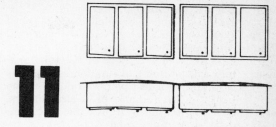

11 Wall cabinets should be checked with level on cabinet front, sides, and bottom to insure that cabinets are plumb and level. It might be necessary to shim at wall and between cabinets to correct for uneven walls or floors. After cabinets and doors are perfectly aligned, tighten all screws.

Problem Doors:

There are very few "perfect" conditions where floors and walls are exactly level and plumb. Therefore, it is necessary to correct this by proper shimming so that the cabinet is not racked or twisted and so that cabinet doors are properly aligned.

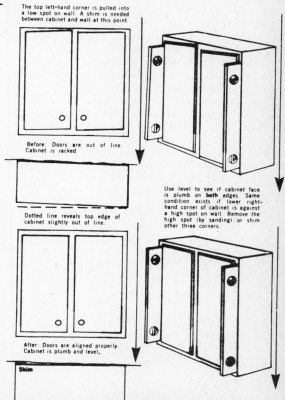

The top left-hand corner is pulled into a low spot on wall. A shim is needed between cabinet and wall at this point

Before: Doors are out of line. Cabinet is racked

Dotted line reveals top edge of cabinet slightly out of line.

Use level to see if cabinet face is plumb on **both** edges. Same condition exists if lower right-hand corner of cabinet is against a high spot on wall. Remove the high spot (by sanding) or shim other three corners.

After: Doors are aligned properly. Cabinet is plumb and level.

Shim

brackets that are fastened to wall studs by means of wood screws. The cabinets are then hung on the hangers. A somewhat less complicated method consists of screwing the cabinets directly to the wall studs. The screws should be long enough to go through the wall material and penetrate well into the studs. But, regardless of how the cabinets are fastened to the walls, they must be installed perfectly level, from a standpoint of function as well as appearance. Find the highest point of floor with the use of a level. Also, using a level or straightedge, find the high spots on the wall on which the cabinets are to be hung. Some high spots can be removed by sanding. Otherwise, it will be necessary to "shim" the low spots to provide a level and plumb installation. Using the highest point on the floor, measure up the wall to a height of 84 inches. This height, 84 inches, is the top height of the wall cabinets and oven and broom cabinets. On the walls where cabinets are to be installed, remove the baseboard and chair rail. This is required for a flush fit.

Start your installation in one corner. First assemble the base corner unit, then add a unit on each side of the corner unit. This, as a unit, can be installed in position. Additional cabinets are then added to each side as required. C-clamps should be used in connecting cabinets together to obtain proper alignment. Drill two or three holes through the end panels. Holes should be drilled through to the adjoining cabinet. Secure a T-nut and draw up the two cabinets snugly with a bolt. If you prefer, you may drill through the side of the front frame and drill a "lead hole" into the abutting cabinet, insert the screws, and draw them up snugly.

Each cabinet, as it is installed on the wall, should be checked front to back and also across the front edge with a level. Be certain that the front frame is plumb. If necessary, use shims to level the cabinets. The base cabinets should be attached with screws into the wall studs. For additional support and to prevent the back rail from "bowing," insert a block between the cabinet back and the wall. After the bases are installed, cover the toe kick area with the material that is provided by the cabinetmaker.

Once the base units are fastened in place, attach the countertop to the cabinets. This countertop may be purchased with the kitchen cabinets, or it may be built on the job, as described later in this chapter.

The wall cabinets should then be installed, beginning with a corner unit, in the same way the base units were. Screw through the hanging strips built into the backs of the cabinets at both the top and bottom. Place them about ³/₄ inch below the top and ³/₄ inch above the bottom shelf from inside of the cabinet. Adjust the screws only loosely at first so that the final adjustments can be made after the cabinets have been checked with a level. The wall cabinets should be checked with a level on the cabinet front, sides, and bottom to insure that the cabinets are plumb and level. It might be necessary to shim at the wall and between the cabinets to correct for uneven walls or floors. After the cabinets and doors are perfectly aligned, tighten all screws.

To close the gap between the tops of the wall cabinets at the ceiling, soffits are frequently employed. They are framed from 2 × 3s in the manner shown in Figure 10–20. A ceiling plate is spiked to the joists above, and the wall cleat is spiked to the studs. The short 2 × 3s between the main members are toenailed in place. Afterward, the face of the soffit is covered with wallboard or any convenient sheet material. When the cabinets are hung, gaps remaining between the bottom of the soffit and the tops of the cabinets will be hidden by a cove molding that is the last item to be affixed.

Countertops. The selection of the proper countertop is most important. That is, space to put things *on* is just as important as space to put things *in.*

Let us first consider the decorative aspect. The countertop should blend with the cabinets, yet add its own note of beauty, texture, and pattern to the kitchen. At the same time, it must harmonize with the floor and wall colors.

Now for the functional aspects of the countertop. Remember one important fact: the countertop will take almost as much wear and abuse as the floor, so above all it has to be rugged and easy to clean. There are several materials you want to consider.

Laminated plastic. This material is still the most popular countertop. It is easy to care for, it wears well, and it comes in the widest variety of colors and patterns. Some have a matte finish that will not show scratches, but it is a little harder to clean than the shinier finishes. New methods of texturing even make it possible to get laminated plastics with the feel of leather, wood, or slate. The standard countertop grade is ¹/₁₆ inch thick, wears extremely well, and is not injured by grease spatters. However, it should not be used as a cutting

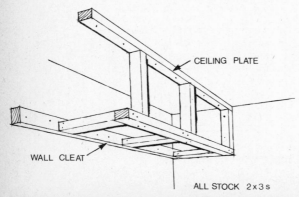

CEILING PLATE

WALL CLEAT

ALL STOCK 2 x 3s

Figure 10–20. Installation of a typical kitchen soffit.

Figure 10–21. Steps in applying a laminated plastic countertop: (top left) After the parts have been cut to size, apply contact cement to both surfaces. (top right) Position the parts, keeping the surfaces separated by wrapping paper until they have been aligned. (bottom left) After the parts have "contacted," apply pressure by hand or with a rolling pin. (bottom right) The edges may be beveled with a hand plane or an electric router.

surface, and hot utensils or small appliances should not be set directly upon it. The following paragraphs give information on installing laminated plastic.

The core stock of most kitchen countertops is either ³/₄-inch exterior plywood or particleboard (also known as flakeboard). Laminated plastics usually are available in sheets a few inches larger than standard 4- by 8-foot (or 4 × 10 or 4 × 12, etc.) panels, to allow for the edge trimming that is necessary. When figuring the amount of material needed, remember to avoid joints as much as possible by using the longest lengths available. For example, if you are going to build a 9½-foot-long top, buy a 10-foot length of base core and laminate rather than joining an 8-foot piece with a 1½ footer. If the countertop has to turn a corner, you will probably have to join pieces.

To start the laminating job, cut the plastic to size, allowing ⅛ to ¼ inch waste on the edges. To cut the laminated plastic with a hand saw use a fine-tooth saw with a low-angle stroke to avoid chipping the edge, and saw with the decorative side up. With a circular electric saw, saw with the decorative side down. Hold the saw firmly against the

sheet. With a radial arm power saw, use a fine-tooth blade and saw with the decorative side up.

The laminate is bonded to the core stock with contact cement. There are many good brands available. Before applying the cement to the base, make sure the surface is clean, dry, and smooth, with no holes or voids. When replacing an old top, first remove the old material from the counter, using a putty knife or scraper to get rid of adhesive and fragments of material. Then scrape or sand the surface to leave it clean and dry. Any core material that has rotted or become delaminated should be replaced with new plywood or particleboard.

With a clean paint brush, apply an even coat of contact cement to the back of the laminated plastic sheet. Also apply an even coat to the wood surface to which it is to be glued. Take care to get complete coverage on both surfaces. Allow the cement to dry, following the instructions on the can. Bare wood surfaces are often porous enough to absorb some of the cement. In such cases, apply a first coat of contact cement to the wood, allow it to dry, and then apply a second coat. Apply the cement to the back of the laminate sheet as soon as you have placed the second coat on the wood. Read the label on the contact cement can carefully for specific instructions on application, drying time, and room temperature.

Once the two cemented surfaces touch, the contact cement bonds immediately and no further adjustment of position is possible. Therefore, it is extremely important to position the sheet properly before the glued surfaces touch. This is best done by the following method: Cut a heavy sheet of brown wrapping paper into several pieces. Place these on the wood surface so they overlap each other and completely cover the glued area. Place the laminate sheet on the paper and position it for perfect fit. Move the first piece of paper out a few inches at a time, gently pressing the laminate to the wood surface as you go. Then remove the remaining paper sections.

After the sheet is in place, apply heavy pressure to the surface. Start in the center and roll toward the edges. Be sure to cover every square inch of the surface. A 3-inch hand roller will provide the heaviest concentration of pressure. For hard-to-reach areas, hold a smooth block of wood on the surface and apply pressure by tapping it with a hammer. Remove excess cement from the surface by rubbing it with your fingers. It will "ball up" and come off quite easily.

Edges are most commonly finished by using one of the following two methods:

1. Laminated plastic edges are the most used way of finishing countertops. For best appearance, "build up" the core thickness by gluing and screwing 1½- or 2-inch-wide strips of the ¾-inch particleboard or plywood to the underside of the exposed edges. Sand the surface, if necessary, to make sure the strip and the original edge form a flat, smooth surface. Cut a strip of the laminate sheet a minimum of ¼ inch wider than the edge to be covered. (Always apply the edge band first, before applying the sheet to the top surface.) Coat the wood edge twice and the back of the laminate strip once with adhesive, as described previously. Apply the strip and roll with firm pressure. Use a router with a flush trimming bit, or a block plane and a hand file, to trim the excess laminate flush with the top and bottom of the wood surface. Then apply the laminated plastic sheet to the top as already explained. Trim off excess material. Use a router with a 22½-degree bevel trimming bit, or a hand file, to bevel the edge joint.

2. When finishing with a metal edge molding, apply the laminate sheet to the top surface and trim it flush with the edge. When purchasing the metal molding strip, make sure that the drilled holes are of the proper width to cover the entire thickness of the exposed edge, including the laminate. Apply the molding strip to the entire edge with screws of a

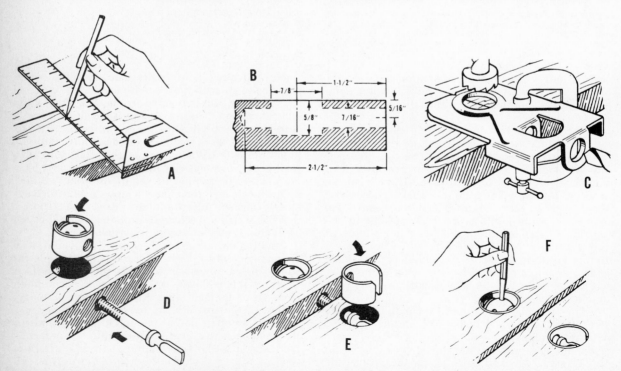

Figure 10–22. A tight-joint fastener is an easy means of fastening countertop sections. Follow the installation steps from A through F.

type to fit the molding you have purchased.

To build a backsplash, follow the same procedure as for the top. Actually, the backsplash is only a double thickness of core stock, 2 to 4 inches high and the same length as the top. Use the straight cutter for all edges that will butt up against another piece of laminate, and bevel the rest. When all of the surfaces have been laminated, clamp the backsplash to the top and fasten it with long wood screws, driven up through the underside of the top, and go through the top into the backsplash. If you have two sections to join, you can use a special-purpose fastener called a tight joint. As shown in Figure 10–22, all it involves is butting the two sections to be joined, drilling holes in core strips on the edge of each section, then slipping in and tightening up the fasteners to join the sections. Complete instructions come with the fastener. Frequently, a metal core is used to close the joint between the backsplash and countertop.

For a so-called "continuous top," post-formed plastic laminates are used. This is a method of forming a backsplash and rounded front and consists of heating a special type of $1/16$-inch laminate and then bending it in a special mold. Post-formed laminates are usually made by firms that make completed sink cabinets and bathroom vanities. Post-formed laminates must still be mounted on plywood just as flat sheets are.

If you are going to mount a sink in the countertop, the cutout for it should be made at this point, before attaching the top to the cabinet. Locate the position of the sink and use the rim as a template to insure accurate measurement of the sink cut-out. The cutout should be $1/16$ inch oversize to permit freedom for the "leg" of the sink rim. Your sink rim kit will come complete with fastening clips and corner brackets to support the sink until the clips are installed. Nail or screw these brackets in place, caulk the inside of the rim, fit the rim to the sink, and set the assembly in place. Finally, install the clips around the edge of the sink according to the rim manufacturer's instructions.

Ceramic glass. This is a new space age material that is ideal as a heatproof working surface near your range. You can cut, knead dough, roll pastry, or cool candy on it. It is extremely smooth, easy to clean, and does not stain. Glass ceramic comes in a range of sizes; it cannot be cut on the job.

Marble. An insert of marble can be used in the same way as ceramic glass, but it is more likely to break, needs more care, and has a greater tendency to stain. A new solid plastic that looks like marble is becoming popular as countertop material. This so-called "man-made" marble has the stain and heat resistance you want plus the characteristics of wood (you can saw it, shape it, sand it) for maximum adaptability.

Stainless steel. Stainless steel also makes a

Figure 10–23. A ceramic tile countertop is easy to install. After adhesive has been applied to the countertop surface, mosaic tile sheets can be placed in position. Once the tiles have set, grout can be applied as described for Figure 3–42. The completed job provides a serviceable countertop.

good heatproof insert, but will show cuts and scratches more quickly. It wears very well, is heatproof and moistureproof, and will not crack, chip, or break. Stainless-steel countertops or inserts should be installed by a skilled workman.

Laminated hardwood. The good old chopping block is still the gourmet cook's favorite for slicing or chopping. Hot pans should not be set directly upon it, and prolonged moisture should be avoided. However, if the wood is oiled occasionally, it will serve faithfully for years, and the surface can always be sanded down if it gets too chopped up.

Laminated hardwood countertops are available in a wide range of standard sizes from 12 to 120 inches. They are usually a full $1\frac{1}{2}$ inches thick and 25 inches deep, and come with or without a 1-inch-thick backsplash. They come ready for installation on top of the base cabinets. Follow the manufacturer's instructions carefully for best results. Hardwood block inserts are available that come with a standard stainless-steel sink frame (see page 353) or that are the drop-in type that can fit in a hole cut into the countertop.

Other storage space. There is the time, while still in the planning stage, to make sure you are finally going to get all the storage space that is needed. Every family's storage needs are a little different; they stem directly from the activities and interests of each member of the family, and knowledge of those activities will help anticipate ways to solve

Figure 10–24. Two examples of an attractive planning center in a kitchen.

the line of cabinets and brings all the stored items within easy reach. Pantry units can also be cleverly designed with hinged shelf sections on both sides, opening like leaves of a book to make everything accessible. Some manufacturers offer ready-made ones. Slanting shelves, supermarket style, can also be used for canned goods storage, with cans lying on their sides so that a replacement rolls into position as one is removed.

Figure 10–25. Four storage arrangements that you may use in remodeling your kitchen.

the storage problems they create. I could not begin to cover all the storage possibilities in one chapter (homemaker magazines are full of new suggestions for storage in every issue), but I would like to list a few of the more important areas you should consider as you start planning your own personal storage utopia.

How about a planning center? A planning center will give you a great storage place for your recipes, bills, grocery lists, correspondence, and anything else you refer to frequently. If it is built around a telephone desk, it is possible to create a little "business office" right in the newly remodeled kitchen.

In a U-shaped or in an L-shaped kitchen, the planning desk can be placed at either end of the principal work areas; or place the desk along the free wall that is opposite the cabinet-appliance line-up. In the one-wall and the corridor kitchens, try to fit your desk along the end of the kitchen, just outside of the traffic path. That is, locate the desk, which should be about 29 inches high, out of a traffic lane, both so that the homemaker can work at it without interruption and so that passersby will not be dropping off baseball mitts and other clutter. Be sure it is not near the spatter of a sink or range. It may be wise to provide space above the desk for recipe books. A file drawer will help keep children's medical and school records, appliance instruction books, and the family's business and social records organized. A typewriter can be located on a spring-up platform that lifts out and up to the correct working height.

How about a pantry? There is much to be said for the old-style walk-in pantry or a wall of floor-to-ceiling cabinets for storage of canned and packaged foods, small appliances, dishes, and glassware. When wall space is limited, plot the pantry with a pull-out unit that uses the full height and depth of

How about kitchen linen and broom closets? With all the linens that are used in the kitchen, everything from napkins and tablecloths to dish towels and cleaning and dusting utility rags, the life of the homemaker can be made easier if the linens are all concentrated in one convenient space.

Brooms and mops keep getting in everyone's way, until you provide them with their own little closet or storage space. Overhead, you will have room for several shelves to hold cleaning items. Also, chances are the kids are in and out of the kitchen a dozen times a day on their way to and from school and play. You will save everyone time and steps if you have a closet near the kitchen door.

How about a place for small appliances? The

portable appliance problem, where to store them and where to plug them in, grows with each new invention. Many a gift appliance is tucked away in a hall closet when it could be at work in the kitchen. Therefore, plan a "small appliance center" that includes counter space or storage space and enough circuits and outlets for the proper operation of the appliances. When there is ample counter space, it is a great labor-saver to keep the frequently used portable appliances out and ready. If you wish to screen them from view, you could create cupboards from countertop corners by building doors diagonally under the wall cabinets. A stand mixer can be mounted on a typewriter-style shelf that swings up from a base cabinet, and many portable appliances and appliance heads can be mounted on the wall.

It is desirable to have two circuits for the use of portable appliances, with outlets to serve each section of the counter. You may want to use an electric fry pan, toaster, and coffeemaker at the same time. Heating appliances draw more current than motor appliances; check wattages and avoid overloading the circuits. Put in enough outlets to serve appliances that will stay plugged in, such as a can opener or rechargeable battery for a knife, and leave some free for other uses.

In a large kitchen it may be better to store appliances according to use: a coffeemaker near the sink because it takes water as the first step in use, a toaster near the breakfast table, a mixer at the baking center, and an automatic fry pan near the range or barbecue hood.

How about a drink cabinet? Entertaining is fun, and much more convenient when your drinks, glasses, and the rest of your supplies are all right at hand in one single storage unit. This would also be a nice place to put your wine rack.

Most households have a few serving trays, and they are white elephants to store, unless you remember to include a few tall, narrow slots in one of your base cabinets.

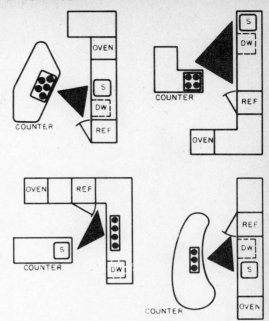

Figure 10—27. Four island kitchen arrangements.

How about the problem of blind corner cabinets? To capitalize on corners, try laying out the kitchen in a parallel-wall plan rather than in a U-shaped (two corners) or L-shaped corner plan. Or take advantage of the corner cabinets with turntables offered by cabinet manufacturers. Some have front panels at right angles with a pie-shaped segment cut out of the circle; others have diagonal front panels to get more usable space on the turntable. There are also ready-made cabinets with swing-out panels that bring the contents of the blind corner to the front of the adjacent cabinet.

You may find it less expensive and reasonably satisfactory for storage of seldom-used items to put in a separate plastic turntable and gain access to the corner through the adjacent cabinet door. (The side of the cabinet would have to be cut out and a plywood base laid in the corner if stock cabinets are used.) Avoid placing a range and a dishwasher at right angles in a corner as this cuts off all access from the kitchen to the corner storage space.

When the corner is part of a peninsula dividing the kitchen from a dining area, it is possible to open the cabinet toward the dining side, using it for dish or placemat storage. A drawer for silver can be included. When the corner is on an outside wall, it may be possible to open the storage space through the outside wall and use it for garden tools.

How about an "island" or a "peninsula"? Many women with big kitchens have learned the delights of a center "island" that brings work areas

Figure 10—26. Two ways of solving bottle problems.

Figure 10—28. Island kitchen arrangements in use.

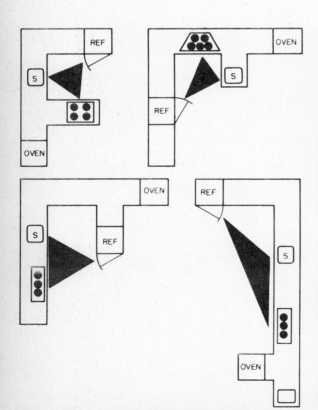

Figure 10—29. Four arrangements for a peninsula kitchen.

Figure 10—30. A peninsula kitchen arrangement in use.

closer together and adds valuable work and storage space. You may want to set a range or dishwasher and sinks in your island (Figure 10–27). Just remember to leave at least 3 feet of space between the island and nearby work centers if the range and sink are on opposite walls; do not place the island between them unless the lady of the house is out to break a hiking record.

If the island is to be a real "cook's table," by all means design a rack above it with hooks to hold pans and large cooking tools. Add storage facilities for other basic utensils and supplies and perhaps a wooden, marble, or glass ceramic top section.

A peninsula can bring the three kitchen work centers closer together and reduce the size of the work triangle (Figure 10–29). Often, the center floor space in a kitchen is not put to good use. A large, old, square kitchen or an open, new kitchen can benefit from the addition of a peninsula. Even a short line-up of cabinets extending into the center of the room can divide the working and eating areas and give additional storage and work tops. A peninsula is often designed so cabinets open from both sides. This feature is particularly good if the table-setting supplies are housed in the peninsula. Wall cabinets can be hung over the top of the peninsula, or you can leave the view open.

How about some open shelves and hanging storage? Doors and hardware are the expensive parts of kitchen cabinets, so a few open shelves for auxiliary storage will be both convenient and economical. Remember though, dust will collect on open shelves.

Every well-planned kitchen offers several great possibilities for hanging storage, spice racks, cup hooks, small shelf units, hanging trees, knife racks, and the like.

Figure 10–31. Pantry storage arrangements.

There are as many interesting storage solutions as there are perplexing storage problems. If you cannot solve a particular problem yourself, take it to your kitchen cabinet dealer for his suggestions.

KITCHEN LIGHTING

In the field of kitchen design, it is amazing how often the subject of lighting is treated lightly. After all, lighting is a part of decorating, and decorating is a part of lighting.

In a purely technical sense, whenever you look at an object, you do not see the object itself but rather the light reflected from it. So every surface in your kitchen becomes a part of your lighting design. Reflected light is always tinted with the color of the reflecting surface. That is why the paint on the wall may look far more intense in color than the paint chip from which you selected it. Colors live in light; man actually becomes color blind in the dark. Colors literally become gray and lifeless in poor illumination. That is why you need to ask yourself some questions. Is the lighting level adequate over the range? Is a fixture located to eliminate shadows and glares? Does the window over the sink allow a blinding afternoon sun to make the clean-up center an unbearable place to work?

The following are some of the things you will want to think about and plan for in your kitchen design.

Kinds of lighting. In any room, and especially in a kitchen, there are several kinds of lighting, each with its special purpose, level, and limitations. For the kitchen, you will want to know more about three basic kinds:

1. General lighting to illuminate the whole room.

2. Local or task lighting to provide adequate illumination for the special tasks of food preparation, cooking, clean-up, and dining.

3. Decorative lighting to emphasize the warmth and charm of a dining nook.

Let us study the types of lighting in a little more detail so you will know how to make the lighting in your new kitchen work more effectively for you.

General lighting. As was detailed in Chapter 5, this is the "fill-in" lighting that provides the soft glow throughout any room, enhancing its decoration and making it more livable. It also provides the lighting you might need for general housekeeping, scrubbing or vacuuming floors, cleaning walls, and such tasks.

General lighting can come from hanging fixtures, fixtures mounted on the ceiling, or recessed fixtures mounted in the ceiling. It also can come from a "light ceiling" where light floods through an entire translucent suspended ceiling.

How much light do you need? It is difficult to tell in terms of light bulb wattages, because wattages are not accurate measures of light intensity. However, the following system will give you a rough guide. Measure your kitchen to find how many square feet of floor space you have. Then simply apply the following minimums. If you are more comfortable with more light, do not hesitate to move up from the minimums.

For ceiling-mounted or suspended fixtures in the kitchen, you should have: *incandescent*—2 watts per square foot; *fluorescent*—1 watt per square foot. For valance, cornice, or wall-bracket types of indirect lighting, you will need 5 to 6 watts of fluorescent lighting per square foot of floor space.

For non-directional recessed lighting (fixtures mounted in the ceiling), the minimums are: *incandescent*—3 watts per square foot; *fluorescent*—1½ watts per square foot.

General lighting reduces the contrast in brightness between task lighting and lighting on other surfaces in the room. It also adds some flexibility in changing lighting effects and creates a more pleasant working environment.

Task lighting. With plenty of general illumination, you will want to start planning local lighting for the special tasks of your kitchen. Among the things you will want to plan are lighting level, lighting color (most people find warm colors more acceptable), and location.

If the sink or range has wall cabinets on either side of it, you can mount lights in or on the soffit. However, a faceboard should be located on the bottom edge of the soffit to keep the light from shining in the eyes of the person working there. If the sink or range is not located under a soffit, you may want to recess your lighting fixtures in the ceiling.

Another approach is to mount either fluorescent or incandescent fixtures on the ceiling. In addition, you might want to drop a heat lamp from the ceiling over your cutting board. This provides both illumination and warmth to keep foods piping hot while they are being readied for serving.

If you use a ventilating hood over the range, you will find that many come equipped with a light fixture built in.

The general food preparation is often done on the countertop and under wall cabinets. The wall cabinets themselves often provide a good mounting surface for lighting fixtures. Make sure, though, that the bare bulbs are not in the line of vision.

For task lighting, use a 20-watt fluorescent or a two-socket (60 watts each) incandescent for every 30 inches of counter. Above the sink, use two 30-watt fluorescents. At the range, use a 30-watt tube or two 60-watt incandescents in a hood. Occasionally, there might be a countertop without any cabinets overhead (such as a peninsula, island, or snack bar design). You can use surface-mounted or recessed ceiling fixtures. If the countertop is used for informal dining, you might prefer a pull-down fix-

ture to bring the light closer at those times.

Light for informal dining. While the kitchen is seldom used for the "candlelight and wine" romance of more formal dining, many people like to eat snacks, brunches, and lunches there. These occasions are often filled with the warmth of gay laughter and friendliness, and the lighting for this area should reflect these attitudes. Usually, it is best to provide some kind of fixture over the center of the table (or snack bar) to provide downlight that is shadowless, yet relatively low in intensity. The fixture can be hung from the ceiling or on a swinging bracket mounted on the wall.

A pulley lamp can be utilized to allow you to adjust the light level over the table. Be careful, though, in locating the fixture on the ceiling. Your furniture arrangement of such things as hutches or buffets can force you to place your table off center, but you want to make sure your light is centered over the table. The softness and warmth of incandescent lighting are usually thought to be more comfortable for dining than the brighter illumination of fluorescent lighting.

Windows. Windows furnish the natural light to brighten working areas and supplement the artificial light. Minimum property standards of the FHA specify a window area totaling, in square feet, 10 percent of the floor area. (Good kitchens should have at least 15 percent.) Skylights or glass panels in outside doors count as part of the total window area.

Windows also form an important part of the decorating plan. A paned window fits into many traditional kitchens, but would be an unusual choice for some contemporary rooms. Decide on the type of window, then on the window treatment that you would like. Start your window plans by thinking about the exposure of the kitchen to sunlight; consider the view from the window, the need for privacy, possible glare from uncovered windows at night, and the proximity of the window to spatter from the sink or range. A good north window usually provides a nice view while it keeps the sun from shining directly into your eyes while you work. East windows are not too bad because the morning sun does not seem to have quite the intensity of the hot afternoon sun. South and west windows begin to allow the glare of the sun into the kitchen about 1 P.M. and continue to do so for as long as seven hours. This may be more sunshine than you desire.

A variety of curtains, shades, and special screens can help solve the problem for you and still give you as much sun as you like. Cafe curtains, casement cloth curtains, window shades laminated to match wallpaper, Roman shades (fabric curtains that are pulled up venetian-blind style into horizontal folds), beaded curtains, and shutters are among the decorator possibilities. Many materials are treated to make them easier to clean. A coordinated look can be achieved by matching the dishwasher front panel to the curtain or shade.

Some women like to have glass shelves across the window to hold plants. Others like to frame the window with fabric or a decorative wood valance across the top and down the sides. If you leave the window bare, remember that garden lighting (see page 175) will help reduce reflection at night.

Lighting is very important to any remodeled kitchen. It not only enhances the beauty of the room but makes it comfortable to work in. Therefore plan it carefully.

Kitchen wiring. A most important part of lighting is providing adequate wiring and current for the fixtures. Part of your lighting considerations are wall switches and other outlets. You might want to put in three-way switches so you can turn the general lighting on as you enter from the dining room and turn it off as you exit into the utility room or basement.

For the light over the dining area of your kitchen, you might want a dimmer switch so you can regulate the light intensity to fit your mood and meal. You should also plan other conveniences such as the appropriate number of wall outlets for your small appliances. You will probably need a separate outlet each for your toaster, mixer, blender, coffeemaker, can opener, radio, knife sharpener, waffle grille, and a few extras. Each outlet should be located where you can use the appliance most conveniently.

When planning kitchen wiring, bear in mind the following data:

1. An electric range requires a 240-volt circuit all its own.

2. An electric dryer also requires a 240-volt circuit of its own.

3. Almost every gas range needs a convenient 120-volt wall outlet for its clocks, lights, and rotisserie.

4. For food protection, a freezer should have its own 120-volt circuit (so the circuit breaker cannot be tripped accidentally by overloading the circuit at another outlet).

5. A refrigerator should also have its own 120-volt circuit for the same reason.

6. A dishwasher must have its own 120-volt circuit.

7. Several 20-ampere, 120-volt circuits should be available to provide wall outlets for different small appliances. (Most home circuits are rated at only 15 amps, barely adequate for just one heating-type small appliance.) Keep in mind that a 20-amp circuit requires heavier wiring throughout. Do not try to get away with putting a 20-amp fuse in a 15-amp circuit.

8. Your outlets should have grounded three-prong receptacles because most new small appliances will have grounded three-prong plugs. This helps eliminate shock hazards from a faulty appliance.

When planning the lighting of your kitchen remodeling, plan to add more wiring and electrical capacity than is needed. You will be surprised at how quickly all the extra capacity and wiring are used.

FLOOR, WALLS, AND CEILING OF YOUR KITCHEN

In Chapters 3, 4, and 10, we discussed materials and how to install them on floors, walls, and ceilings. Now let us see which are best for your kitchen.

Floors. What kinds of flooring should be used in the kitchen? There are many factors that should be considered before making any selection. For example, the durability desired, amount of moisture present, amount of resistance to alkali and grease wanted, traffic expected, and degree of quietness wanted should all be determined when selecting the type of flooring material for a kitchen. Another important consideration is the fact that the kitchen floor coordinates the color scheme. This is usually one of the most important design features in tying the kitchen design together. It correlates the rich warmth of the cabinets to the colors of the walls, appliances, countertops, and drapes.

With these thoughts in mind, let us look at what you probably want the floor to do for you. First, the floor should provide a measure of safety. That means it should be smooth (nothing to trip over) without being slippery, and it should be level.

A second consideration, because the homemaker spends a lot of time in the kitchen, is that the floor should provide some comfort. This means the floor should have resiliency. It should absorb the shock of your footsteps, and it should be easy to stand on.

People who work on solid floors (concrete, for example) find them extremely tiring to stand on hour after hour. On the other hand, a floor that is too soft can also be tiring. The luxury of deep pile carpeting and extra thick sponge padding might enhance your living room, but it can be a deterrent to comfort in the kitchen.

Cleanability is something else that should be considered in selecting a kitchen floor. The easier to clean, the better. That is the reason why many people prefer firm-surfaced floor coverings.

Beauty is also something that is wanted in a kitchen floor, in the form of design, color, pattern, texture, or a combination of these. The floor selected should be carefully coordinated with the basic design of your kitchen.

These are the factors you will be balancing in the selection of your kitchen floor material. Balance them carefully as you mull over the following selections. There is, of course, an almost infinite variety of materials, colors, textures, and patterns. But they can be sorted into three major classifications and some minor ones before you have to choose the exact flooring material you think would be best for your kitchen.

First, we classify floor coverings by hardness, then by their basic material. After deciding on hardness and basic material desired, you choose your brand name, texture, pattern, and color. Keep in mind that this is merely a brief overview of the floor coverings available.

Hard surfaces. The really hard surfaces do have certain advantages and features you might like. For instance, *flagstone* gives a very permanent flooring with beautiful texture and a random pattern that is intriguing. The disadvantages: flagstone is heavy and the floor must have adequate support (see page 128); and, while flagstone is hard and close-grained, it can still be stained. Also, long hours of standing on a flagstone floor can be uncomfortable.

With *brick*, again you have a weight problem. But you also have a striking floor that will wear longer than any other in your home, plus the advantage of being able to work out some truly unusual original patterns. Staining can definitely be a problem with brick. The discomfort of standing can also be a drawback.

Ceramic tile is a hard surface that overcomes the major disadvantages of the previous two. It is scratch resistant, fireproof, waterproof, and never needs waxing. The weight is no problem, and cleaning is easy. It can last the life of the home and has amazing variety in the sizes, shapes, patterns, and finishes.

Resilient surfaces. These surfaces are ones that most people think of when they think of kitchen floor coverings. They have been designed to include the advantages you like in a kitchen floor.

Linoleum comes in sheets and tiles, and it can heal itself of minor cuts and scratches. It is light in weight and has resiliency. A good coat of wax does help it stay clean between washings. The selection of linoleum patterns and colors is extremely wide. Remember waxing and removing wax occasionally will be necessary, except in the case of so-called "permanently" waxed types.

Vinyl has moved into the top spot in the popularity poll for kitchen floor coverings. It is available in sheets and tiles or as a poured floor covering. It has excellent wearing properties, and certain glossy-finish vinyls need no waxing. Also, many vinyls now have a sandwich construction with foam in the middle for extra softness and resiliency. Again, the choice of patterns, textures, and colors is extremely large.

For years, *wood* was the number one flooring, even for a kitchen floor. But wood is sensitive to water, so it went out of style. Now, new finishes have encouraged some people to bring back the warmth and beauty of real wood to kitchen floors. There really is no substitute for its appearance.

Soft surfaces. These floor coverings can provide the maximum comfort underfoot. They absorb shocks of walking and cushion footsteps like no other covering can. They reduce noise, and also absorb spilled liquids and often hold them against the underflooring. (If the underflooring is not water resistant, this could be a problem.)

The sophisticated development of synthetic fibers has lead to the use of kitchen *carpeting*. The fibers themselves are often highly resistant to staining. But the weave of the carpeting can lock in the stains so they are fairly hard to remove.

Carpet tiles are a "do-it-yourself" alternative to carpeting. These tiles can be laid quickly. Usually they have a foam backing that holds the woven fabric in place and provides built-in padding. If you have a permanent burn or stain, you can replace one tile instead of a whole floor.

Area rugs can offer accents of color to certain spots and provide a measure of standing comfort in some areas. These rugs really serve more as decorative elements than as floor coverings. They should be non-slip and of a type you will not be tripping over.

Wall coverings. An almost infinite variety of materials exists for use on walls, and more are being developed every day.

Paint. Paint offers you an infinite variety of colors and hues. You can have it mixed to the precise shade and color you choose. It will have a fair lifespan. Keep in mind that paint for a kitchen should be either semi-gloss or gloss. This improves its cleanability.

There are, of course, some disadvantages to paint. In areas where there is high wear, such as around light switches, paint can wear off in a year. In addition, paint does not have much variety in textures or patterns.

Wallpaper. Here, as in Chapter 9, the word wallpaper is being used in a general sense. Wallpaper can be paper, plastic-coated paper, foil, coated paper, cloth, or plastic-coated cloth. Each kind has its advantages and disadvantages.

For kitchen use, a plain paper style of wallpaper is not recommended. Dirt builds up on it fast. Grease is absorbed into the paper. Plastic-coated papers and cloths tend to overcome this drawback. The plastic is cleanable with a damp rag. Also, the plastic-coated covering seem to have a higher resistance to sun fading.

There are many variations in the quality of the paper and the coating. The better ones naturally cost more money. But they are usually worth the difference in their resistance to dirt and their easy cleanability. Then, there are the straight cloths. These are often specialty wall coverings used for their unique texture. Among them you will find burlap and Japanese grasscloth. Both provide a handsome texture and highlight to any wall. But both have serious drawbacks for kitchen use. They are perhaps more susceptible to grease and dirt than paper. Cleaning them is not easy either.

Ceramic tile. Some people tend to forget about tile as a wall covering, yet it has some truly outstanding features for use in a kitchen. Ceramic tile is highly resistant to food acids, impervious to grease, and almost completely scratch-proof. It is also fireproof and waterproof. It never needs waxing or painting. Cleaning can be done with a damp cloth, and most cleaning agents can be used on it. An extensive selection of colors and shapes of tiles offers infinite possibilities in pattern design on the wall.

Plastic or metal tiles do not have quite as broad a selection of shapes and sizes. They also do not have as great a resistance to scratching and dirt.

Paneling. The various types of paneling suitable for kitchens use include wood (prefinished and unfinished), hardboard (with baked-on finishes, plastic laminates, and lacquer finishes), particleboard (with all kinds of surface finishes), and other types of wallboard (with all kinds of finishes). What is the best? It depends on what you want. Most paneling never needs painting, is easy to clean, and has a good resistance to dirt. The smoother the surface of the paneling, the higher the resistance.

Wood paneling, where it fits your decor, is hard to beat for warmth, beauty, and texture, plus its easy cleanability. However, you might want the effect of travertine stone, leather, linen, decorator tile, tapestry, or rough-sawn barnwood. You can get them all in paneling, as well as complete murals and a host of other panel designs.

Most paneling is printed and textured so artfully you will have a difficult time telling it from the real thing. Paneling is usually much easier to take care of.

Brick and stone. These materials can provide a wonderful feeling of warmth and create an outstanding highlight wall in a kitchen. Real brick and stone have a permanence matched only by ceramic tile. But real bricks and stones do have certain disadvantages. They are porous and grease will sink right in, as will dirt of any kind. In addition, bricks and stones add enormous weight to a wall, so the wall may have to have extra support.

These disadvantages have led manufacturers to develop imitations. Many of these come in sheets or squares. Most are made of some kind of plastic. They are easier to clean and far lighter in weight than the real material. Most of them are less than $1/2$ inch thick.

Ceilings. Almost everything that has been mentioned for use on walls can be applied to your kitchen's ceiling—paint, wallpaper, tile, or panel-ing—to give you the broadest possible spectrum of colors, textures, and patterns. But it is important to remember that most experts agree that ceilings should be relatively light in color, especially in a kitchen. This maximizes the reflection of light to provide more even lighting in the kitchen.

In addition to using wall coverings on ceilings, you will want to think about several other options.

Suspended ceiling. Is your present kitchen ceiling too high? Too cracked and ugly? Then you might want to use a new suspended ceiling. This is one of the most economical ways to cover an old ceiling, as well as a nice way to lower it. When you put in a suspended ceiling, you can add recessed light units that fit right into the proper squares.

Light ceiling. Above this type of suspended ceiling, you have a large number of fluorescent fixtures. The ceiling itself is made up of translucent plastic diffusers that soften and spread the light uniformly and shadowlessly through the kitchen.

Acoustical tile. For kitchen use ordinary acoustical tile is not usually recommended. While it might reduce the noise level in the kitchen and stop sounds from going to other parts of the house, it also absorbs dirt and grease very readily. There seems to be no satisfactory way of cleaning it. It can be painted, but painting sharply reduces its sound-deadening ability. Therefore, other ceiling finishes are better. Keep in mind, though, that new developments in acoustical tiles occur from time to time. Some manufacturers now have vinyl-coated ceiling tiles that have sound-deadening properties along with better cleaning properties.

Beams, arches, and cornices. These are not a part of the ceiling, but they often add to the beauty of it. (What would a colonial kitchen be without a beamed ceiling?) As described on page 65, light-weight foamed plastic is now being fabricated into very realistic looking beams and arches and even the artistically scrolled cornices of other eras. These can be finished or painted to match any color scheme.

COMMON PROBLEMS AND SOLUTIONS

Whenever you plan to remodel a kitchen, some problems commonly arise. Even if the home is only a few years old, it seems that the windows are where you do not want them. Or the chimney flue forms a jutting corner right where you want a cabinet. The following are some of the more common problems and ways of solving them. Most of these require a fair skill in carpentry and a good knowledge of basic home construction. Some call for abilities in plumbing and wiring.

Problems with things that stick out. One of the most common problems is that something juts out just where you do not want it. Depending on what is out of place for you, there usually is a solution.

Radiators. While radiators provide a good form of heating and are often found in older homes, they are a real problem when one of them sits right where you want new cabinets. What can you do? Here are three basic solutions to solving the problem of a radiator in the kitchen.

1. Cover it. Build a cover that matches or complements the rest of your new kitchen design. But make sure this cover allows proper circulation to heat your kitchen adequately.

2. Move it. Is there another location in the kitchen for your radiator? Perhaps moving it to another wall might improve your kitchen design and your heating, although this can be costly. If you move a radiator, you probably will still want to cover it (see No. 1 above).

3. Replace it. The old-style radiator can often be replaced with a new baseboard unit that gives you more versatility in decorating the walls. But you may want to think a long time about whether you can locate this baseboard unit under the front edge of your kitchen cabinets. Not only will you lose some space in the cabinets, you also will be putting a fair amount of heat into the cabinets. This could have an effect on the items you store there.

The other solutions might include changing the form of heating and/or cooling you use. A solution of this type will involve you in some expenses in changing (or supplementing) your heating and cooling system (see Chapter 7).

Pipes. Do you have unsightly pipes running up the wall of your kitchen? An amazing number of older homes do have this problem. There are two relatively simple solutions.

1. Enclose the pipes in the wall. This means that you must cut the pipe and install elbows to move the pipe into the wall itself. And that means cutting a slot in the wall for the pipe, then patching the wall afterward. This is a lot of work, but the most satisfactory solution.

2. Box in the pipes. This is an easier solution. Simply build the wall out around the pipes using a simple wooden box construction. Then paint or paper the addition to match the rest of the wall. This is more of a compromise solution, and it does leave a jutting corner in the room.

Flues. Sometimes the chimney flue seems to run right through the kitchen. If you are lucky, it is already in the wall. If you are not, you have a problem. A chimney flue cannot be readily moved and enclosed in the wall (but a heating duct can). A chimney flue, however, can be boxed in in the same manner as pipes.

Another solution is to accept the limitations of the flue location and design around it. You can wallboard it and hide it. Or you can dramatize it and highlight it. Try adding brick (imitation or otherwise) to it to make it more dramatic. Or put cookbook shelves up the wall.

Problems inside the wall. Just about as common as things that jut out are problems that are already in the wall. That is, doors, wiring, and plumbing lines never seem to be where they should be. Wiring and plumbing are not *usually* too serious a problem. The more obvious problems are discussed below.

Doors. Your problem with a door might be that: (a) it is not where it is supposed to be; (b) it should not be there at all; or (c) it will bang into the cabinets or appliances every time it swings open. Recognize the type of problem, and you can find a solution.

1. Move the door. If it is in the wrong location, the door, doorway, and moldings can be removed and the hole can be filled in. Then a new opening can be cut in another wall and the door can be placed where it belongs.

2. Remove the door. If it swings into furniture, cabinets, or appliances, simply take the door out of the doorway. The doorway can then be changed into an archway if you like, or a curtain of beads can be hung in its place.

3. Replace the door. You can solve a swinging door problem with a new type of door, swinging cafe doors, bifold doors, or pocket doors. (A pocket door is a sliding door; the pocket is the part of the wall it slides into.) A pocket door may require major structural changes in the wall (see page 97).

Windows. Redesign a kitchen, and the windows will pop up in the wrong places with amazing frequency. The following are some ideas you can use to overcome the problems.

1. Move the window. Remove the window and fill in the wall. Then cut in a new window where your design shows it should be. This calls for a good knowledge of the framing necessary to provide good support (see page 276).

2. Replace the window. Maybe a smaller one would fit your plan and still let enough light in. Or maybe glass bricks might work better where the window was.

3. Make the window into a light box. If you are building a new room up against the window, you do not have to take out the window. Instead, add a picturesque scene and some interesting lighting, so you can still look out your "window" to a synthetic outdoors. This approach would help keep a small kitchen from appearing even smaller.

Walls. Frequently, there is the problem of a wall not being where it should be in your new plan. Perhaps you need to remove it. But, before doing so, check the wall most carefully; it may be a load-bearing one (see Chapter 2).

Sometimes you might need to add a wall. This is simpler and can be accomplished as described in Chapter 3.

Partial kitchen remodeling. Up to this point, we have been discussing only a complete kitchen remodeling job. But if you cannot afford to do the

Figure 10–32. A laundry center in a bedroom *(left)* and in a family room *(right)*.

whole job, consider a partial remodeling. Wooden cabinets can be sanded and repainted and be perfectly satisfactory if they are structurally sound, countertops can be replaced with new plastic laminates, floors can be resurfaced, and so on.

LAUNDRY CENTER

One of the most frequently used areas of the home, but often the most neglected from the standpoint of planning, is the laundry. Most households probably wash at least three times a week, perhaps every day if they have a family with small children.

Location of laundry. When you are remodeling and plan to include an efficient laundry, first decide on a good location for it. Modern-day home planners are avoiding locating in the basement if at all possible, and with good reason. A study conducted at Kansas State University showed that the upstairs location of a laundry can reduce footsteps by as much as one-half. With laundry appliances available in pleasing designs and so many attractive colors, there is no need to hide them away.

Generally, the laundry location will be determined either in terms of the most efficient location for the laundry function, or in terms of the location most convenient to other homemaking tasks. The first approach would call for putting the laundry center in the bedroom-bathroom area, where the bulk of laundry is collected and clean laundry is stored. This would cut down greatly on transportation of laundry to and from the center. The other

approach might involve the inconvenience of carrying laundry across the length of the house, or up and down stairs, but would be handy to the kitchen or other work areas, enabling a homemaker to supervise several tasks at the same time.

Bedroom-bath area. Most items in your family wash are used and stored in this location. Arranging to have the laundry center here can save many steps and eliminate the need for carrying the laundry back and forth. The center can be in a large bathroom, where plumbing facilities already are available, provided adequate storage space can be found. The work of collecting soiled clothing and distributing clean laundry is virtually eliminated. While bathrooms large enough for an adequate laundry center are rare in existing homes, the bathroom laundry is something to consider if you are remodeling. In some cases where a washer and standard-size dryer will not fit, a washer and a wall-hung portable dryer might be the answer. No additional sink is needed because the lavatory is handy.

Frequently a spare bedroom can be used as a laundry as well as sewing center. A corner of your master bedroom is a possibility, especially if the wall is common with the bathroom so that plumbing is not a problem.

A wide hallway or extra-large closet, though usually found more often in older homes, should not be overlooked as a laundry center possibility in new home plans. The hallway offers good possibilities for pass-through storage and a plumbing tie-in with the bathroom. It would also be close to bedrooms and linen storage. In all these examples, doors can be used to close off the laundry center when it is not in use.

Near the kitchen. The kitchen area, where the homemaker spends most of her working day, may be a desirable location for a laundry. Plumbing costs can be minimized with a kitchen location. However, a partition or counter peninsula should be used to separate the laundry area from the food-preparation area. This is, plan to keep laundry and food preparation areas separated. A pantry, off the kitchen, has the advantage of being near that busy work center without actually being in it. In some cases it may be possible to combine the homemaker's "office" with the laundry equipment.

For a family-room laundry center, folding or sliding doors are desirable to close off the area when the work is completed. This can be combined with a general storage area or perhaps the home entertainment equipment. Though it may not be convenient to the bedroom-bath area, the family room makes a pleasant area in which to do the laundry.

The utility room is a common location for laundry equipment. If the rear entrance to the house is in the utility room, it becomes a natural place to wash up after outside work or play or to store work clothes.

Where the climate is warm, the breezeway, patio, carport, and garage become possibilities for laundry, although these locations work best when they are near clothes collection points.

If the basement is the only place in your home where space is available for the laundry, it can be made quite pleasant at nominal expense. A clothes chute is desirable, and the work will be easier if provision is made for a sit-down work area, good ventilation, light, and other conveniences.

Space requirements. The space required for your laundry center will vary with the type of appliances selected, and the other activities planned for the area. A washer and dryer require a space of from 4 feet 6 inches up to 5 feet 3 inches wide, and 30 inches deep, depending upon the widths of the appliances chosen. The amount of space needed for a washer and a portable dryer depends on whether the dryer is wall-hung, set on a counter, or equipped with casters and rolled out of storage only when needed. If the dryer is wall-hung, over a narrow sorting counter next to the washer, for example, only 3 feet 6 inches would be required. But adequate work space should either be provided or be accessible nearby.

A University of Illinois study of home laundry operations shows that the amount of work space needed for most women is relatively constant. The following recommendations are the minimum to permit freedom of action. These measurements are in addition to space for the appliances.

Washer and dryer: 5 feet 6 inches wide by 3 feet 6 inches deep in front of the appliances.

Washer or dryer alone: 3 feet 8 inches wide by 3 feet 6 inches deep in front of the appliance.

If the appliances are located in a traffic area, or if the washer and dryer are opposite each other, the work space should be increased to at least 4 feet deep.

Ironing: A space at least 5 feet 10 inches wide by 4 feet 3 inches deep will be required for an ironing board, a chair, and a laundry cart or basket. If a clothes rack is used, 2 feet 4 inches of working space should be allowed in addition to the rack measurements.

Non-automatic laundry equipment: Two rinse tubs are necessary when a wringer washer is used; thus a larger laundry area is required. The minimum space requirements, including equipment and working space, are 8 feet 6 inches wide by 7 feet deep. If clotheslines are used, 20 feet of clothesline for each member of the family is recommended. Lines should not be placed less than 20 inches apart.

Secondary uses of the laundry center. To help justify the space needed for an adequate laundry center, consider additional uses for the space. Many of the facilities required for the laundry can be used for other purposes, depending on the location in your home and the amount of space available. Ironing is a part of sewing, as well as of laundering. Thus, the laundry center may be combined with a sewing room. The laundry sink can also be used for arranging flowers or as a place to wash up. Using the space as a family hobby center is another possibility.

Other considerations. Proximity to plumbing is vital in locating your laundry center. Hot and cold water and a drain are needed for the washer. Installation costs will be lower if existing plumbing can also serve the laundry appliances. Ideally, the laundry center should share a wall with the kitchen or bath.

Electricity and gas connections must be considered. A 120-volt electric connection is required for a washer, and others are needed for an iron, a sewing machine, and other uses. The washer should be on a circuit by itself. With the exception of the portable model, a 240-volt connection is necessary for an electric dryer. Some standard-size dryers can operate on 120 volts, but if so, the drying time is nearly doubled. A gas supply line of rigid pipe and flexible copper tubing is standard for gas appliances. A gas dryer also needs a 120-volt connection for the motor. All laundry appliances should be connected to an electrical ground. A local serviceman or the electric utility is the best source of advice on the most effective grounding method for the area.

If the laundry center is not in your bedroom-

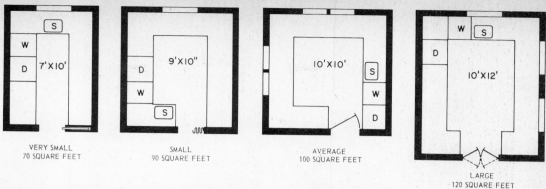

Figure 10–33. The size of a utility room varies with the budget and needs of the homemaker.

bath area, some method of transporting soiled laundry should be provided. In a two-story house, this may be a chute from upstairs directly to the laundry center. In a one-story house, if the center is near the bedroom-bath area, consider pass-through sorting bins. If your home is one story and the center is not convenient to the bedroom-bath area, a rolling cart will ease the job.

The farther the water heater is from the washer, the more loss there is in the water temperature. It is wise, therefore, to consider installing the water heater in the laundry center, if it is practical.

A mechanical water softener may also be desirable if the water has a high mineral content (see page 215).

Laundry layout. Where the laundry center is located, the amount of space allowed for it, and other activities planned for the area will influence what goes into it. While it may not be possible to install an ideal laundry center, certain requirements must be met if it is to be efficient. Even if space for your laundry center is extremely limited, there are certain basics necessary for even a minimum installation. They are: the appliances (washer and dryer); storage for soiled clothes (preferably at least three bins); counter space for sorting, pre-treating (nearby water supply necessary), and folding; and storage for laundry aids.

An optimum laundry center would include the following:

1. Laundry equipment. This consists of an automatic washer and dryer. You may choose, because of floor space or preference, a combination washer-dryer. Remember to inquire about load capacities of the appliance you select. If you have a big family, a large-capacity washer and dryer will save you time and money.

2. Space to pre-sort and store soiled clothes. Changing laundering habits and the variety of washable fabrics now being used have intensified the need for pre-sorted storage. Providing storage for each of the categories into which the laundry is sorted makes it easy to know when a washer load of each has accumulated. A minimum of three storage units is required for adequate pre-sorting by laundry procedure. Five or six are desirable, particularly if the family laundry includes large amounts of delicate items or washable woolens. Types of storage containers can vary. Tilt bins or large rollout drawers built in under a counter are convenient. The bins or drawers can be labeled, and your family can put laundry in the proper bin as it is soiled.

3. Storage for laundry aids and stain removal supplies. Adequate space must be provided near the washer for all detergents, bleaches, and other laundry aids used. To eliminate stooping, and to keep these items out of reach of small children, overhead storage is best. However, it may be necessary to set aside some under-the-counter storage for extra-large boxes of detergent and heavy bleach bottles. The most frequently used items should be easiest to reach. Stain-removal supplies can be stored in a drawer, or on the shelf with other laundry aids.

4. Sink for pre-treating and other laundering needs. This sink should be located between the sorting bins and the washer. However, if the kitchen or bathroom sink is located nearby, it can be used instead.

5. Space to fold clothes and store those that require ironing. It is most practical to remove items from the dryer one at a time, hang or fold them immediately, and sort them according to where the clean clothes are to go. A counter is most desirable for folding, but if the space is inadequate, the tops of the appliances can be used. A shelf over the appliances is useful for the temporary storage of folded items. However, if the washer is the top-loading type, the shelf should be high enough to allow the top to open without interference.

6. Place to hang permanent press items. A full-length hanging closet next to the dryer is especially desirable for hanging permanent press items as they

377

Figure 10—34. A complete laundry-sewing center.

are removed from the dryer. A clothes rack can also be used for this purpose or, if no room is available, a wall hook can be installed.

7. Provision for sewing supplies. Mending should be done before clothes are washed, so tears do not get larger. Mending supplies — needles, thread, and scissors may be all that are needed — can be stored in a small drawer or in one of the cupboards. However, if much garment construction is done, a full sewing center will be desirable. A shelf that pulls up and out from under the counter (similar to a typewriter shelf in a desk) is especially handy for a portable sewing machine, because it eliminates the need to lift the machine. Perforated board on the inside of a cupboard door is convenient for hanging scissors, thread, and other sewing accessories.

Planning the center. When planning the laundry center arrangement, consider the homemaker's height and build. Working surfaces should be at a comfortable level. A counter is at the correct work height when the homemaker can stand and rest her hands on the counter with her arms comfortably relaxed from the shoulder. She should not have to raise her hands above the level of her elbows while folding clothes. Women of average height maintain good posture and avoid fatigue when working at a counter 36 inches above the floor. The depth of the counters depends on the length of the homemaker's arms, her body build, and her physical agility.

Wall cabinets should be low enough so she can reach the top shelf easily. For the average woman this is about 72 inches from the floor. Shelves

Figure 10–35. Three methods of venting a dryer.

should be adjustable.

Placing the dryer on a riser to prevent stooping is often convenient, especially for the older home-maker. The riser can be a solid base, or it can contain a drawer.

Because one of the purposes of a laundry center is to ease the homemaker's workload, it should also be easy to keep clean. Wall cabinets built to the ceiling or soffit, and flush drawers and doors without paneling prevent dust from accumulating. Wall coverings or paint should be washable. Durable, stain-resistant countertops make cleaning simpler.

A pleasant decor can do a great deal to make work more pleasant. Therefore, choose cheerful colors and patterns and have good lighting. This is especially important if the laundry center must be located in an otherwise drab basement. Follow the suggestions given earlier in this chapter for kitchen countertops, floors, walls, and ceilings, since the problems these surfaces pose are about the same for both areas. The laundry area also needs good general lighting, plus specific illumination for the pre-treating, mending, and ironing centers.

Cabinets, cupboards, counters, and closets can be purchased ready-made, or they can be custom-made by a cabinetmaker. Or you can make them right on the job, just as you do the kitchen units. The installation of the cabinets and counters is also achieved by following the same procedures as those used for their kitchen counterparts.

Standard airflow-type automatic clothes dryers, gas or electric, should be vented to the outside air (Figure 10–35). The vent may extend from the back

or either side of the dryer. Some models may also be vented straight down through the floor, then outside, making it possible to install the dryer flush to the wall. Complete vent kits, suitable for all dryers, are readily available. They contain all the necessary parts and instructions for making the installation. Whether the vent must go through a masonry wall, a window, or a frame wall, there is a kit specifically designed to meet the situation.

When making your installation, the following are a few guidelines to a good venting installation:

1. Select an inconspicuous place to locate the exhaust vent. Fine lint can accumulate outside the exhaust, resulting in an unsightly appearance on shrubs or flowers.

2. The best vent duct system is that which is shortest, straightest, and concealed where possible.

3. Best results are obtained when the venting length complies with the manufacturer's recommendations. A long vent run tends to reduce the efficiency of the dryer's airflow system. It is generally unwise for the vent system to include more than two elbows or to vent more than a total length of 30 feet, with 4 feet subtracted for each elbow used.

4. The vent hood, installed at the end of the system on the exterior of the house, has a flap door that opens only when the dryer is in use, to exhaust the moisture-laden air.

5. To avoid lint accumulation within the tubing, all joints should be made so the exhaust end of one length of pipe is inside the intake end of the next pipe.

6. For the same reason, moderate angles (90 degrees or greater) should be used when making elbow connections. A severe angle can mean a potential lint buildup.

7. The vent outlet should not terminate under the house or porch, or in a chimney, since the resultant accumulation of lint could create a fire hazard.

8. To permit sufficient air circulation, the vent exhaust hood should be 12 inches or more above ground level.

Chapter 11

REMODELING OR ADDING A BATHROOM

Figure 11−1. A simple remodeling job can transform a bathroom.

Bathroom remodeling can be as simple as replacing an old-style sink with a new vanity unit or as complex as adding a garden bath or a full health center with sauna, whirlpool, and exercise gear. Regardless of how ambitious your project, remember not to let your current bath inhibit your planning; bathrooms are no longer the minimal, utilitarian, limited spaces they once were. True, a bathroom's function is much the same today as it was more than half a century ago, and the basic equipment has not changed a great deal. What has happened is that glamour has stepped in and turned the bathroom into a fashionable unit as well as a functional one.

PLANNING BATHROOMS

A house is a good house insofar as it fills the needs and desires of the people who live in it. That goes

for bathrooms, too. The bathroom arrangement must be "right" for the house, which, in turn, must be "right" for the family that lives there. Thus, begin your overall remodeling planning by considering all the ways a bath area will be used. The family bathroom, in particular, deserves careful study.

The answers you give to the following questions will help to determine the size, location, and arrangement of the family bathroom. You may decide you need a second bathroom or a separate wash-up area.

1. Will the family bathroom be used as a wash-up area? In the small house the family bathroom also serves as a wash-up area for men coming in from outdoor chores or sports and by children coming in from play. Locate it so it can be reached from the rear entrance without going through other rooms of the house.

Figure 11−2. Decorating can make a big difference in a bathroom. All three of these bathrooms have the same equipment; only the decorations differ.

Remodeling or Adding a Bathroom

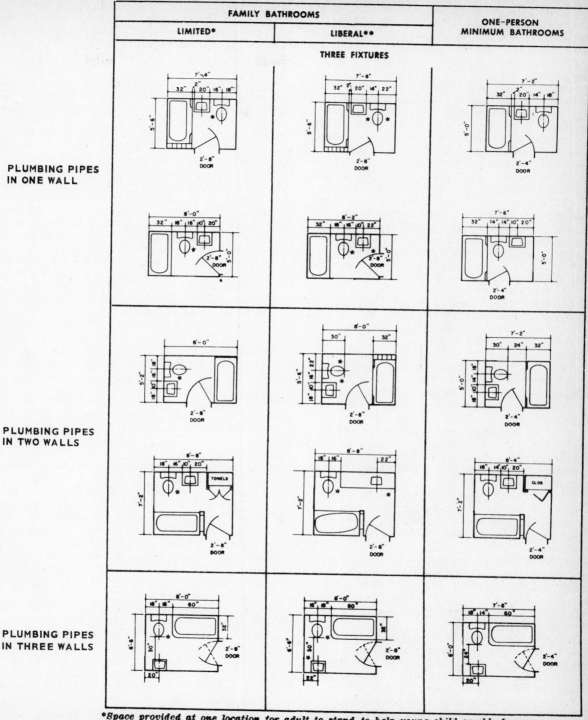

Figure 11–3. Suggested bathroom arrangements.

*Space provided at one location for adult to stand to help young child or elderly person.
**Space provided at two locations for adult to stand to help young child or elderly person.

Chapter 11

2. Will the bathroom be used for the care of infants and small children? If the bathroom is to be used for the care of infants and small children, make it spacious enough for the extra equipment needed. If you use a folding bath table to bathe and dress a baby, keep in mind that such a table is approximately 3 feet long and 20 inches wide. A large lavatory with swing-away faucets or a small kitchen sink set in a counter will be more convenient for bathing a baby than a regular-sized lavatory. An adjoining counter can be used for dressing the baby. A storage cabinet for baby clothes and supplies is an added convenience. Use sliding doors or eliminate the doors on the cabinets above the lavatory and counter for safety and convenience.

3. Will the bathroom be used by several persons getting ready for school or work at the same time? The large family with a number of individuals getting ready for school or work at the same time may want to consider the convenience of additional fixtures, an extra, separate lavatory or toilet, and a stall shower in addition to the tub.

4. Will the bathroom be used for the care of family members who are ill or feeble and need assistance? If your household includes elderly or ill persons who need assistance in the bathroom, plan sufficient space for the person who is to be helped. If a family member is confined to a wheelchair, see that the door to the bathroom is wide enough so the wheelchair can be pushed through. The bathroom should be large enough to accommodate the wheelchair and to permit someone to help the invalid from the chair.

5. Will the bathroom also be used as a dressing room? Counter areas, generous mirrors, good lighting, and ample storage space are desirable appointments in the bathroom that is also used as a dressing center.

6. Will the bathroom be used for hand or machine laundering? In the small home without a basement or separate workroom the most convenient location for laundry equipment may be in the bathroom.

Suggested bath arrangements. Young families are usually relatively small families who, because of a small budget, live in a relatively small home: a ranch, split-level, or small two-story house. A striking bath is one of the best ways to dress up a simple house when remodeling.

When considering bath arrangements, keep in mind that most one-bathroom houses have a tub, because of children and older people. After that, the shower is usually the preferred way of bathing. The lavatory should not be placed next to the tub, because this creates several inches of dirt-catching area. It is far better to place the toilet near the tub and the lavatory on the other end of the room, because it usually can be tucked into a corner. A lavatory bowl hanging on the wall with the naked pipes exposed will not do, even in minimum baths. If there is not a complete built-in vanity, there should at least be a good-size shelf. In addition to generous cabinet storage, there must be some place to set the razor down, not to mention the toothpaste, hair spray, combs, and brushes.

These are only a few things to remember when planning a bath. Of course, a new home affords full opportunity for planning the selection and arrangement of plumbing fixtures to meet individual requirements. Usually it is just a question of placing the fixtures in the most convenient arrangement in the space available. The remodeling of a bathroom, however, brings up the question of how to first utilize existing plumbing without many costly changes. A floor plan should be selected that will make use of the present vent stack and water supply line if possible. Sometimes a new bathroom is created in an existing home by building two or three partitions to enclose a hall, bedroom, or storage room. In this case, especially in one-story homes, a new stack and drain can be installed without excessive cost. In any case, the planning of a bathroom should take into consideration the availability of the plumbing connections and the requirements of local building codes. See Chapter 6 for full details on plumbing system considerations when remodeling.

As with kitchens, there are four basic fixture layout plans for bathrooms. They are as follows:

1. The one-wall bathroom. A one-wall plan is ideally suited to a room that is long and as narrow as $4\frac{1}{2}$ feet. It has the advantage of having all plumbing connections, drains, and vents in one wall.

2. The U-shaped bathroom. This is the most practical plan to best utilize space in a square-shaped room. Plumbing, however, is more complicated since it is not confined to one wall.

3. The corridor bathroom. This is a practical arrangement for a small bathroom between two bedrooms with access from each (especially suitable for a small home or apartment with space for just one bath). The corridor space should be at least 30 inches in width. This arrangement requires two plumbing walls.

4. The L-shaped bathroom. This is the most common arrangement for small bathrooms. It provides the maximum amount of clear floor space. This plan can be achieved with one plumbing wall, when the bathtub is installed across the end of the room.

There are, of course, many variations of these four basic fixture arrangements. For help in planning a family bathroom or any bath area, study the arrangements on pages 283 and 285. The space allowances around fixtures in these plans are based on research in which both the use and the cleaning of the bathroom were considered.

Remodeling or Adding a Bathroom

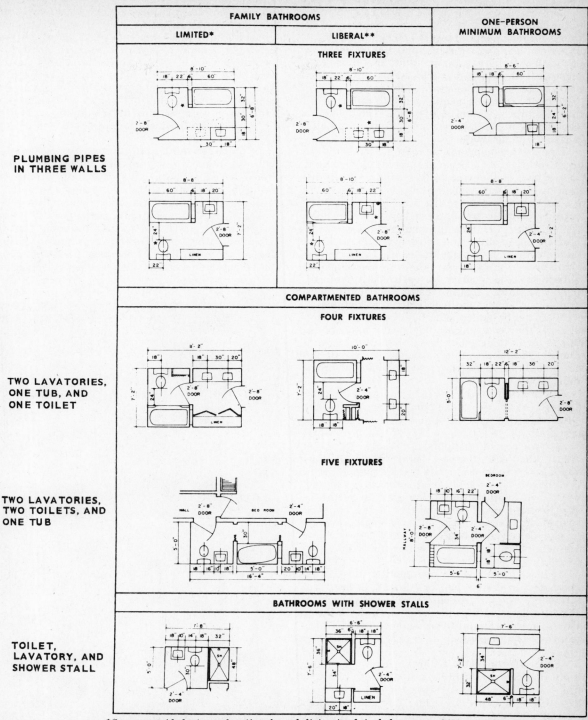

Space provided at one location for adult to stand to help young child or elderly person.
**Space provided at two locations for adult to stand to help young child or elderly person.*

Figure 11–4. Suggested bathroom arrangements.

Dimensioned plans for each arrangement of a family bathroom give a choice of two sizes. The limited arrangements show one location where a mother can stand comfortably and help a child, or one adult can help another adult; the liberal arrangements show two such locations. In the one-person baths, clearance between, to the side of, and in front of fixtures is held to a minimum. In all family bathroom plans, doors are 2 feet 8 inches wide. Doors in the one-person or minimum baths are 2 feet 4 inches wide.

Five arrangements for compartmented baths are shown on page 285. Three of these areas have four fixtures; two of them have five fixtures. Three different arrangements of bathrooms with toilet, lavatory, and shower stall are also shown on page 285.

Location of bath areas. Most families wish they had two things: *more* bathrooms and *bigger* ones. There are space-stretching tricks for both purposes. Therefore, once you decide on the kind and number of bath areas you need, the next step is to consider the best possible location for each. Oddly enough, the new bathroom can be located almost anywhere in the house, subject to the following restrictions:

1. In the basement. The bathroom can be anywhere in the basement as long as the main house drain is lower than the basement floor, or the headroom of the basement is sufficient to permit the bathroom floor to be at a level above the house drain.

2. First floor level. The bathroom may be located anywhere on the first floor, just as long as the bathroom drains can be sloped downward to the main drain.

3. Upper or attic floors. The only restriction here is that the planned bathroom's soil pipe should not run across joists to reach the main drain.

When the location of a new bathroom is planned, as stated in Chapter 6, it is important to keep it as close to other plumbing facilities in the home as possible. In this way, a great deal of pipe and labor can be saved. Thus, when locating the new bathroom, keep in mind the following money saving tips:

1. Place the new bathroom next to the existing one or next to the kitchen or laundry. In fact, if at all possible, the fixtures should be located back-to-back with those on the other side of the wall. Doing this will mean that only very short lengths of pipe are necessary to connect into the old drain and supply lines.

2. Arrange the new bathroom over (or under) an old one or over (or under) the laundry or kitchen. In cases where the new fixtures cannot be located so that they connect directly into simple extensions of old pipes, any over or under setup will reduce piping costs and work.

3. Do not rule out the possibility of using an inside bathroom. Most building codes, as well as the FHA, no longer require a window as long as the bathroom has a ventilating fan. Therefore, if carpentry and piping costs are reduced substantially by locating the new bathroom in the center of the home, it may be a wise choice to do so. It is never a wise decision to install the bathroom in an area where extensive remodeling is required. The expense of tearing out and putting up walls, changing windows and doors, plus other alterations, is usually higher than the cost of running pipes to an area not presently piped.

Compartmented bathrooms. Compartmented baths are popular with families with growing children. The addition of one or two fixtures, and the multiple use of others, adds convenience and flexibility. In remodeling, a compartmented bath often makes the best use of space, particularly if a large area is being converted into a bathroom. That is, compartmenting can go a long way toward easing the bathroom bottleneck. The basic idea is to separate functional areas so that one person does not

Figure 11–5. Two practical compartmented bathrooms.

enter the bathroom, close the door, and tie up everything.

A compartmented bathroom allows others to use the facilities not being used by the person who got there first. It is the best way yet to get the children off to school in the morning. Minimal compartmenting, almost a must in the one-bathroom house, amounts to separating toilet from bath and vanity area. There are all kinds of practical and attractive dividers, from opaque glass to louvered doors, that can be used for this purpose. And the doors really must be sliding or folding to make the most of a little space. Enclosing the tub area with a sliding glass door, for example, can double the function of a bathroom without taking up an inch of extra space. In fact, you can get the effect of two full baths in a relatively limited area by using two toilets, two lavatories, and one tub, the tub being the most expensive item.

To counteract the feeling of a small, enclosed space, about the best trick of all is to give the bathroom mirrors, mirrors, and more mirrors. You will want mirrored cabinets, of course, but what about a mirrored shower door also? Mirrors create a sense of space; they add glamour.

Another small-bathroom trick involves tiling. A patterned ceramic tile floor makes the bathroom look smaller. Solid-colored tile has the same effect in the bathroom that wall-to-wall carpeting has in any other room of the house: it gives you an unbroken expanse of color, which makes the bathroom appear larger. As a matter of fact, wall-to-wall carpeting is no longer a rarity for the bathroom itself. It is practical as well as rich-looking, and it can make a fairly minimal bath seem almost luxurious, as well as larger.

Two more tips on space: To make a small wash basin look bigger, and certainly more glamorous, surround it with a counter top. And remember that a luminous ceiling stretches space overhead just as a solid-colored floor does underfoot.

Double entry. The double entry bath is another possibility. Although this device seems to be losing its former popularity, it cannot be overlooked in a discussion of bathroom treatment in small, inexpensive homes.

This is the bathroom with two doors, one going into each bedroom, which give the occupants of both bedrooms a sense that the bath "belongs to me." Generally speaking, however, this is the least private of all bathrooms, because one is never quite sure whether anyone is already in the bath. There is always the chance that the last person opened his door, closed yours, and forgot about opening both doors afterwards.

The half-bath. Many relatively small homes call for half-baths or powder rooms. The question is, where do you put them? In a ranch home, 80 percent of the owners prefer the half-bath adjacent to the owners' suite. In two-story houses, most prefer a downstairs powder room. A word of caution should be mentioned on both scores. In the first place, turning the half-bath of the owners' suite into a full one by installing a shower makes the house far more pleasant to live in and more valuable when it comes time to sell, and the cost of doing this is not that much more. There is also the alternative, chosen by many families, of having one family bath until they can afford a second bath exclusively for the owners' suite. The space for the second bath already is there, being used in the meantime for storage.

The main question in adding a half-bath in a two-story house is one of location. Should the half-bath be placed to the rear of the home, off the family room, where it is often combined with a laundry or mud room or both? This is a great arrangement for families with small children, but kind of grim for their guests. The children can come in the back door after a morning spent digging to China, kick off their dirty shoes in the mud room, wash up in the adjacent lavatory, and enter the main living area

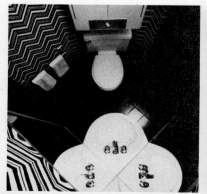  

Figure 11–6. Powder rooms can be made attractive and interesting.

Figure 11—7. If time is spent in design, bathrooms can be interesting rooms.

in almost spotless condition. However, this does not make a very successful powder room for guests, unless a lot of attention has been devoted to the laundry room decor. It would be possible, of course, to match the vanity with handsome cabinets above the washer and dryer, where clothes and laundry supplies can be stored out of sight, or to cover the washer and dryer completely with floor-to-ceiling louvered doors.

Many people, however, prefer a high-style powder room that is intended primarily for guests. In this case, it becomes one of the glamour centers of the home and should be discreetly placed to the front of the house. Actually, the powder room is a place to try decorating ideas you have always wanted to use before, but never dared to try. Since no one stays in the room very long, you can be much more dashing here than in any other room in the house. This room is usually small, so you can follow either of two courses in selecting your wall covering: you can use a see-through type of pattern, such as a caning or trellis design, or you can have fun, using a bold, zippy pattern that takes over the whole room. Mirrored walls, as previously stated, are a great visual spacemaker, and overcome the claustrophobic effect of a small room.

A three-bathroom family usually is a family with lots of children of all ages. Having a combination laundry room and bath on the second floor of a two-story home appeals to a number of mothers, because it means saving steps; the washing is done right where most of it is accumulated. A disadvantage of a laundry-bath combination, however, is the danger of overflow, which would damage carpeting and plaster below. As mentioned earlier, decor is very important when one combines laundry with bath facilities. So is storage space. Nothing is more appreciated, not only in laundry-bath combinations, but in more conventional bathrooms, than triple hamper storage that allows the housewife to pre-sort clothes for the washer.

Another welcome item in the laundry-bath, especially if there is a small baby in the family, is a kitchen-size sink. You can pop baby right in and forget the bathinette merry-go-round of setting up, taking down, and storing. The addition of a kitchen spray attachment not only is wonderful for rinsing off baby but is also useful in any bathroom in the house for shampooing.

One word of caution about second-story bathrooms: the family bath should not be located directly at the head of the stairs on the second floor. All too often, it is easily visible from the lower front entrance hall or a corner of the living room. Greater privacy can sometimes be achieved by moving the door 2 feet.

When planning and locating a bathroom you should determine the mood or feeling you are ultimately going to create in your bathroom. Do you

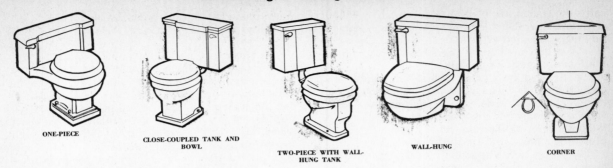

ONE-PIECE CLOSE-COUPLED TANK AND BOWL TWO-PIECE WITH WALL-HUNG TANK WALL-HUNG CORNER

Figure 11—16. Common toilet (water closet) designs.

ance and easily cleaned, but much more expensive than two-piece models); (2) close-coupled tank and bowl (the tank, a separate unit, is attached to the bowl; (3) two-piece with wall-hung tank; (4) wall-hung (completely wall-hung toilets make it possible to clean the floor under and around the toilet); and (5) corner toilet (a great space saver). Some manufacturers also offer a one-piece, freestanding toilet with a low tank that is just slightly higher than the seat of the toilet.

Table 11-2. *Approximate dimensions for toilets*

	Tank		Extension of fixture into room (inches)
	Height (inches)	Width (inches)	
One-piece toilet	$18^1/_2 - 25$	$26^3/_4 - 29^1/_4$	$26^3/_4 - 29^1/_4$
Close-coupled tank and bowl	$28^1/_2 - 30^7/_8$	$20^5/_8 - 22^1/_4$	$27^1/_4 - 31^3/_8$
Wall-hung toilet	$27 - 29^1/_2$	$21 - 22^1/_4$	$26 - 27^1/_2$ (concealed tank, 22)
Wall-hung tank	$32 - 38$	$17^3/_4 - 22$	$26^1/_2 - 29^1/_2$
Corner toilet	$28^3/_4$	$19^1/_4$	31

The toilet is the only one of the plumbing fixtures currently available that must automatically perform a full cycle of functions:

1. Flush quietly, completely, and efficiently.
2. Shut off the water flow to the bowl at the end of the flushing action.
3. Refill the flush tank to the proper depth and then shut off the water from the supply line.

Part of the cycle is performed by the mechanism in the tank, but proper flushing action is also dependent upon a properly designed toilet bowl. There are three different flushing actions commonly used for residential construction. These different actions result from bowl design, and although they have been available for years, few individuals are familiar with their differences or the advantages of one over the other. Consequently, price has frequently been the determining factor in bowl selection, resulting in later dissatisfaction with the functioning of the toilet. The three flushing actions are illustrated in Figure 11−17 and described here:

1. Washdown. The washdown toilet bowl discharges into a trapway at the front, and it is most easily recognized by a characteristic bulge on the front exterior. It has a much smaller exposed water surface inside the bowl, with a large flat exposed china surface at the front of the bowl interior. Since this area is not protected by water, it is subject to fouling, contamination, and staining. The trapway in the washdown bowl is not round, and its interior is frequently irregular in shape due to the exterior design and method of manufacturer. Characteristi-

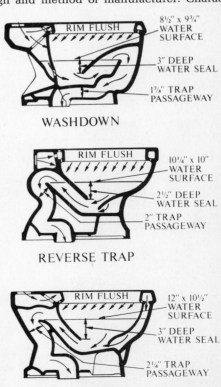

WASHDOWN

RIM FLUSH
$8^1/_2$" x $9^3/_4$" WATER SURFACE
3" DEEP WATER SEAL
$1^7/_8$" TRAP PASSAGEWAY

REVERSE TRAP

RIM FLUSH
$10^1/_4$" x 10" WATER SURFACE
$2^1/_2$" DEEP WATER SEAL
2" TRAP PASSAGEWAY

SIPHON JET

RIM FLUSH
12" x $10^1/_2$" WATER SURFACE
3" DEEP WATER SEAL
$2^1/_4$" TRAP PASSAGEWAY

Figure 11−17. The three major flushing actions employed in toilets.

cally, the washdown bowl does not flush as well or as quietly as other bowls. The washdown bowl is no longer accepted by many municipal code authorities, and several manufacturers have deleted it from their manufacturing schedule.

2. Reverse trap. The reverse trap bowl discharges into a trapway at the rear of the bowl. Most manufacturers' models have a larger exposed water surface, thereby reducing fouling and staining of the bowl interior. The trapway is generally round, providing a more efficient flushing action.

3. Siphon jet. The siphon jet is similar to the reverse trap in that the trapway also discharges to the rear of the bowl. All models must have a larger exposed water surface, leaving less interior china surface exposed to fouling or contamination. The trapway must be larger, and it is engineered to be as round as possible for the most efficient flushing action.

In addition to the standard toilets, custom models are available that give the appearance of furniture like the *chaise percée* of old. There are also toilets that have built-in features such as a planter or ventilator mechanism (a jet-aspirator) for removing odors before they reach the room. The non-overflow toilet and the water-saving toilet are other innovations in this area. Modern toilet seats offer a decorative effect in both color and design.

The bidet. Bidets provide the ultimate in personal hygiene. Widely used for decades in Europe and South America, they are now gaining popularity in the United States. A companion to the toilet, a bidet is a fixture that is used for cleaning the perineal area of the body after using the toilet. Many doctors believe that this washing practice prevents skin infections and irritations in the genitourinary area. The thermal effect and soothing action created by water under pressure striking the body are also advantageous in the care of post-operative patients or elderly people.

The user sits astride the bowl of the bidet facing the controls, which regulate water volume and temperature. Water enters the bidet either via the douche-type rinse-spray or through the flushing rim that helps maintain bowl cleanliness. A mechanical stopper permits water to accumulate in the bowl when desired. The bidet unit usually requires a space approximately 15 by 30 inches and is available in the same colors as other bathroom fixtures. The optimum location for a bidet is alongside the toilet. When planning a compartmented bathroom, do not place the bidet in one compartment and the toilet in another.

The bidet is not the only European amenity that has become increasingly popular in the American market. Belatedly, but rapidly, the sauna, a Scandinavian innovation, is finding its way into many American homes, with lots of American improvements, of course. A steam room, or a dry-heat sauna, provides a kind of stimulation and relaxation no ordinary bathing facilities can offer. These thermal baths cleanse the body from the inside out, and offer a variety of both cosmetic and physical effects. Many bathtubs and stall showers can have steam facilities added; some saunas can be installed in areas no larger than a closet.

The condensation factor, however, cannot be ignored. The volume of water vapor produced in a steam room is tremendous. Moisture entering the walls of your house as invisible vapor, and condensing there, can weaken plaster, rot wood and even attract termites. The sauna, which is a dry-heat bath, produces a comparatively small amount of vapor. In both cases, however, the solution is sim-

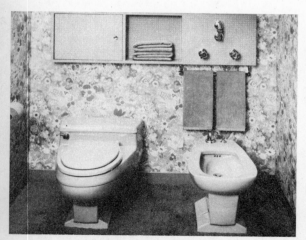

Figure 11–18. A toilet and bidet arrangement is becoming popular in American homes.

Figure 11–19. A sauna closet is often made a part of the bathroom.

ple: every wall enclosing a steam room or sauna should include a vapor barrier. More information on saunas can be found in Chapter 12.

The sauna or other kinds of steam bath gear are frequently used in conjunction with various types of spa equipment to form a health center bathroom (see page 417). Built-in whirlpool attachments, exercise equipment, ultraviolet sunlamps, and gymnasium units are some of the things that can go into such a bathroom.

Another plumbing arrangement popular in European homes is to supplement a full family bath with a wash bowl vanity in one or more of the bedrooms, depending upon the size of the home and family. The purpose, of course, is to provide privacy and to eliminate one person's tying up all the facilities. This arrangement is especially nice in a guest room and very practical in a nursery.

The European bathtub (there is usually only one, even in large homes) is invariably big and usually equipped with a personal shower spray attachment (see page 214) conveniently placed over the soap dish. It is a wonderful way to rinse off after bathing in either a sitting or a standing position, marvelous for shampooing, or for bathing the baby.

Finally, would England really be England without those heated towel-warming racks? Many well-traveled Americans have so enjoyed stepping out of the bath and into a warm toga-size towel that they are installing towel-warmers in their own homes.

Fixture fittings and hardware. There is a wide array of fixture fittings and hardware available to help give your bathroom a custom-made look. For instance, ornate fittings and decorated lavatory bowls, reflecting the styles of earlier eras, are returning in use to give new elegance to the bath and dressing room. Elaborately decorated bowls, former-ly made only to order, are now available as stock items. A recent survey by a national magazine showed that one of the most popular innovations in bathroom fixtures has been the introduction of the single-control faucet for lavatory and tub-shower, with a push-pull dial control mechanism or a lever. The advantages of these devices include space saving, simplicity of one-hand or, with the lever, even elbow operation, and the safety factor implicit in being able to set a dial or lever to a predetermined, known temperature that is comfortable. Maintenance is also reduced to a minimum since there is only one moving part. For shower safety, there is also available a thermostatic device that prevents scalding.

In the category of bathroom fittings are such items as grab bars, soap dishes, clothes hooks, and paper holders. These fittings are available in many finishes including polished or muted brushed chrome, brass, bronze, and gold and silver plate. Decorated ceramic fittings are also available.

WALLS AND FLOORS

The variety of materials for bathroom walls and floors on the market today is so diverse that almost anything within the realm of reason is easily within the reach of your pocketbook.

Wall materials. The varied materials used to finish bathroom walls today are pleasing to the eye, remarkably practical, and easily cleaned. Some of these decorative wall materials will last many years; others will need to be renewed from time to time. You have a choice of paint, ceramic or plastic tile, plastic-coated hardboards, plastic laminates, wallpapers, or fabric-backed wall coverings. The kind of wall finish you select will depend on how much money you want to spend, your personal taste, and the way the bath area is used. Be careful, when selecting materials in color, to choose those that you and your family will not tire of quickly.

If you decide to *paint* the walls, choose a paint that is recommended for bathroom use, that is, one that withstands moisture, is resistant to mildew, and is easy to clean. A gloss or semi-gloss enamel is usually recommended. Follow the application directions carefully (see Chapter 9 for more information). Painted surfaces are not recommended for the interior of shower stalls because they do not withstand the constant wetting (for long periods) and are subject to wrinkling, blistering, and discoloration.

You may want to consider rigid wall coverings, such as *plastic-coated hardboards*. These are available in a nice assortment of colors and may have a plain finish or be scored to resemble tile. They are also available in marble effects and wood grains. Rigid *plastic laminates*, familiar as counter coverings, are increasingly popular as bathroom wall

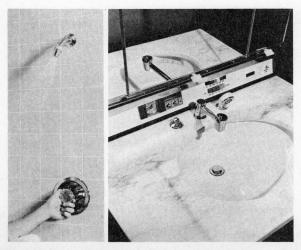

Figure 11–20. Modern types of bathroom water fixtures.

covering. Some laminated panels have a polystyrene core that will adapt to the irregularities of the wall surface to which it is applied. The panels can be installed over existing tile walls, masonry walls, plaster walls, or any other sound, reasonably smooth wall surface. A new one-coat adhesive system instead of contact cement reduces installation time. That is, the panels come in five sizes and are factory coated with adhesive in a non-active state to assure proper adhesion and coverage. After the panels are cut and fitted, an adhesive activator is applied with a roller, and then the panels are put into place by applying pressure all over with a J-roller or wood block and hammer. *Sheet vinyl* with a moisture-resistant backing can also be used for bathroom walls and counters. See Chapter 3 for instructions on how to install this.

Washable wallpaper is practical for the bathroom and, if applied with a moisture-resistant or waterproof adhesive as recommended by the manufacturer, can be used successfully even on the wall around the tub. However, it is wise to test a sample of the paper to make certain that the colors are fast and that it can be cleaned satisfactorily.

Coated fabric wall coverings are well suited to bathrooms, and they are colorful and easy to apply. One type is made of paper stock bonded to rugged woven cloth, coated with a vinyl resin, and printed in various patterns and colors. Still others are fabrics to which pure vinyl has been applied by heat and pressure, or several coats of enamel have been baked on.

Ceramic tile and *plastic tile* are in wide demand as bathroom wall coverings. Ceramic tile is made from clay that has been fired; it comes glazed and unglazed. Glazed tile, the type commonly used for walls, has a white body with a vitreous glaze of the desired color on the face. Unglazed tile has a dense vitreous body and is the same color throughout.

As was stated in Chapter 3, ceramic wall tiles come in a wide variety of colors and a number of sizes; a commonly used size for bathroom walls is approximately $4\frac{1}{4}$ by $4\frac{1}{4}$ inches. These tiles can be ordered from the factory assembled in blocks on mesh or paper sheets. Tiles assembled in blocks can be installed in less time than it takes to install individual tiles.

Plastic wall tile is inexpensive and comparatively easy to install, but as stated in Chapter 3, it has never been too popular with the home remodeler. However, like ceramic tile, plastic tile is available in numerous colors that can be coordinated nicely with any decorating scheme.

The performance of any wall finish depends on the care with which it is installed and maintained. Always follow the manufacturer's recommendations exactly for the type of adhesive and backing material, and for the method of installation. Backing material around tubs and showers should be thoroughly sealed with waterproofing materials prior to the application of the wall finish. For recommended construction of base joints around showers and tubs, see Figure 11−21.

Floor materials. The four main floor materials are resilient coverings such as vinyl and linoleum, ceramic tiles, plastic seamless materials, and carpeting. Ceramic tile is the older and, to some, the only way to cover a bathroom floor. Unglazed mosaic tiles also make a most durable floor. Another choice might be quarry tile. Floor tiles, of course, come in various shapes — hexagons, octagons, rectangles, small squares, larger squares, and Spanish and Moorish shapes. Most tile companies manufacture floor tiles whose colors harmonize with those of their wall tiles. Details on how to install ceramic and quarry tiles can be found on page 126.

Seamless floors are also good-looking. These floors, as described fully on page 132, actually formed on the job, are built up in layers, with polyurethane chips embedded in a polyurethane glaze. They are sometimes referred to as seamless floors

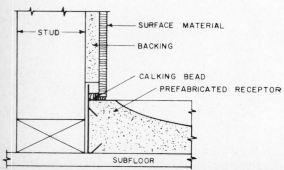

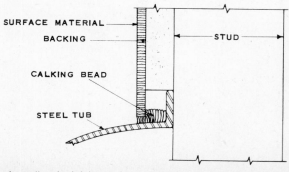

Figure 11−21. *(left)* Recommended construction of a shower stall joint using a precast receptor; *(right)* recommended construction of a wall and tub joint.

When shopping for accessories, do not limit yourself to the bath shop. Pottery canisters from a kitchen shop can be used to store bath salts, a dish from an antique shop can hold soaps, or an old hatstand rescued from the attic and spray-painted a brilliant color can be used to hold towels.

Do not forget pictures as bathroom accessories—flower prints in gold frames for a powder room, military prints for a boy's bathroom. Sculpture, a collection of seashells, framed butterflies, posters, a collection of small mirrors, unusual containers for soap or guest towels can all add to the charm of a bathroom. If you have a green thumb, the bathroom, with its high humidity, is a wonderful place to grow plants, either in a planter top for the toilet (several manufacturers produce these), in containers, or in built-in planter boxes. Plants that might be considered for bathrooms include philodendron, grape ivy, fittonia, orchids, and Chinese evergreen. If container plantings are used, provide a tray or other arrangement to prevent unsightly water drainage marks on the floor.

Windows. The treatment of your window is also a definite part of your bathroom decorating. Try to avoid having your tub beneath a window. It makes it difficult to open and close the window, and if water from the shower strikes the window, there is danger that the water will penetrate from the window into the wall below and destroy the plaster and other construction materials. Normally, beaded or frosted glass is used for bathroom windows to preserve privacy. Louvered shutters, Roman shades, woven blinds, decorative window shades, or shutters with inserts of filigree, caning, or fabric can be used, adding to the decorating scheme while reinforcing a feeling of privacy. If you prefer draperies or curtains, remember that ruffly, delicate materials suffer from the humidity. Duck, sailcloth, denim, and other tightly woven materials are better choices.

One thing that is sometimes overlooked is the relation of the bathroom color scheme to other rooms nearby. Decorate the powder room in the same colors you are using in the adjacent foyer or entrance hall. Tie the master bathroom scheme in with that of the master bedroom.

Remember color is your greatest ally in achieving a beautiful bathroom. The fixture's pastel colors can form the background for a brilliant, colorful scheme, with high-intensity colors in the accents. Or they can harmonize quietly with subtle, elegant low-key schemes.

VENTILATION, LIGHTING, AND HEATING

Looking at the bathrooms in many new homes, you would think that indoor plumbing was the latest triumph of American ingenuity. Motels, even the unpretentious ones, have bathrooms that are better equipped for modern living than those in many expensive new homes. Take the matter of electrical outlets, for example. Travelers find outlets conveniently placed for electric razors and toothbrushes.

Maintaining the desired physical atmosphere in the bathroom, of course, is a most important consideration. And the three factors in creating this proper physical atmosphere are ventilation, lighting, and heating.

Ventilation. Every bathroom or wash-up area should be ventilated either by a window or an exhaust fan. Natural or forced ventilation is necessary, in most areas, to comply with local building codes and to meet requirements of lending agencies.

If your bathroom is ventilated by a window, avoid locating the tub under the window, if possible. If there is no other location for the tub, a window that opens with a crank is easier to operate than a double-hung window.

To help prevent excessive humidity in the house, exhaust fans vented to the outside can be installed in all bathrooms whether or not they have windows. Fans are particularly necessary in humid climates. In fact, no new bathroom should be built without an exhaust fan certified by the Home Ventilating Institute. In three minutes' time, an exhaust fan can do what an open window cannot: completely change the air in the bathroom, eliminating objectionable odors as well as after-shower steam. Fans even come with timers, which shut themselves off automatically. Exhaust fans in combination with lights and heater are good choices for small bathrooms. Lights and exhaust fans can be installed with one wall switch, but separate switches are preferred if such an installation is permitted by codes and ordinances.

Lighting. Most people expect to flip a switch for light in the bathroom, twenty-four hours a day. If there is a window, the curtains or blinds required for privacy rarely admit enough light even at high noon. And in recent years, with the development of efficient ventilating systems, it has become practical to group bathrooms, stairs, and hallways in the center of the house, giving the windows to activity areas that need them more.

Bathroom lighting, as with other home lighting, falls into two basic categories: general illumination of the room as a whole, and lighting for specific areas.

General lighting can range from a ceiling fixture to a luminous ceiling. In fact, many homeowners favor the soft, diffused light from luminous ceiling panels. Just recently, another solution has come to the fore: natural overhead illumination from a skylight.

Skylights, as described on page 427, come in all shapes and sizes: round, square, rectangular, and even angled to fit the degree of roof slope. Some are ventilated; others have double layers of plastic or glass for insulation. They may be either clear or opaque.

Wherever the lights are placed, you do not want them too bright. Instead of improving vision, high-intensity light impairs it. The answer is low-intensity light from several sources, rather than a few dazzling pinpoints. If you start with good general illumination, you will need less light shining directly on you to see really well. Specialized lighting is needed for some areas, however. A bracket lamp near the toilet is convenient for bathroom reading; stall showers and enclosed tubs need an overhead fixture set flush with the ceiling; and so on. Waterproof lights are available for use in the tub or shower area, but do not place light switches where they can be reached by someone in the tub or shower. If the toilet is in a separate compartment, it should have its own light fixture. The vanity area is the section of the bathroom that needs the most light. A single fluorescent fixture over a mirrored medicine cabinet is the budget solution, but has definite disadvantages. It creates badly placed shadows on the face of a man who is trying to shave and is not flattering to the woman who is applying make-up. A better choice would be a pair of lights on each side of the medicine cabinet, either wall brackets or hanging lights. Each fixture should be capable of utilizing a 100-watt bulb. Theatrical lighting (exposed bulbs mounted around the cabinet) or soffit lighting (lights mounted in the ceiling or bulkhead concealed by a translucent panel) are also possibilities for lighting the vanity area. Actually, one thing that *all* bathrooms need is close-up light for personal grooming. Some people prefer the warmth of incandescent bulbs; others like the shadowless illumination of fluorescent fixtures. There are differences of opinion on placement of the lights, too. Light cannot light the whole face evenly. Light from both sides of the mirror fills in features that would otherwise be left in shadow, but side lights have the disadvantage of intruding on the field of vision, especially if they are closer together than 25 inches.

Women are divided about 50–50 when it comes to choosing between lights placed above a mirror or at its sides. Men almost unanimously choose side lighting because it provides under-chin visibility for shaving. Bathroom cabinets are now available with a wide assortment of matching light fixtures: fluorescent or incandescent, top or sides.

There are several special-purpose lamps, such as heat lamps, sun lamps, ozone lamps, and night lights, which you may wish to consider for the bathroom. Heat lamps are good ideas for instant heat when you step out of a tub or shower, while sun lamps can help you keep a tan year-round.

Ozone lamps are used to eliminate odors and keep the air in the bathroom fresh. They should be mounted above eye level since ozone lamps should not be viewed directly. Night lights are helpful to prevent any stumbling around in the dark. When planning to employ any of these special-purpose lamps be sure to follow the manufacturer's recommendations for their installation and use.

Because it is easy to touch water and metal while switching on lights in the bathroom, as mentioned earlier, make certain that lights are controlled by wall switches out of reach of anyone in the bathtub or shower, or anyone using a water faucet. Defective wiring and frayed cords on electrical equipment can result in severe electrical shock. Locate a grounded convenience outlet near the lavatory at a comfortable height for electrical appliances used in the bathroom. Full details on how to install electrical fixtures can be found in Chapter 5.

Electrical outlets. While you are planning your lighting, be sure to consider all the electrical appliances you might want to use in your bathroom. There are electric shavers, electric toothbrushes, water pics, hair dryers, curlers, and setters, facial saunas, electric manicure implements, and exercisers. Think about storing these appliances at the same time you are planning the electric outlets where you will attach them. Will you store them in the vanity, in the medicine cabinet, or in a linen closet?

Heating. Almost every bathroom needs auxiliary heat, to raise the temperature quickly when you step from the bath. A wall heater can also fill in on chilly days during the late spring or early fall, when the main heating plant is not running.

As was stated in Chapter 7, the two most popular auxiliary heaters are electric or gas space type. (The former is easiest to install.) Plan the location of the heater most carefully in a bathroom. That is, place the wall heater where there is no possibility of a person being burned on it or of towels or curtains catching fire from it.

Make certain that an electric heater is properly grounded (see page 238) and is equipped with a thermostatic control so that it will shut off at a given temperature. If a gas heater is employed, make sure that it is vented and has safety pilot shut-off fixtures.

Portable heaters are not recommended as a source of heat for a bathroom. In bathrooms where space is at a premium, a ceiling heater may be the answer. This handy unit combines a circulating air heater with a ventilating fan and two overhead lights. It works with lights alone, lights and fan, or heater and fan.

Chapter 12

MAKING THE MOST OF YOUR BASEMENT

Chapter 12

Your basement offers the opportunity for you to put many additional conveniences into your home without adding to the area your house covers. Here your skill and imagination have free play, for almost anything can be built into a basement. You may wish to devote most of the space to an adult recreation or rumpus room, an arts and crafts center for the whole family, a home gymnasium for the youngsters, or a workshop. At the same time you can provide for a gardener's corner, a built-in playpen with a raised floor for the baby, and a great deal of general storage space.

Figure 12–1. An unfinished basement *(top right)* becomes a quaint ski retreat in the following pictures. Approached with creative verve, even an ugly Lally column (steel pole) succumbs to clever remodelers, who have painted it red and adorned it with decals from ski resorts.

PLANNING YOUR BASEMENT

When you plan a basement room, first consider its use. Then try to visualize the best materials for carrying out the plan. In order to enjoy the result of your efforts, plan carefully and wisely to make sure that these two important problems are solved.

If the new room is to be a workshop, for instance, some of the important considerations will be accessibility from the outside for bringing in materials; light and air; adequate space for the location of power tools and benches; accessibility to electrical outlets, water, and so on. Think also of the location in relation to the floor above and the transmission of noise to the living and sleeping areas. All of these considerations are not likely to be satisfied by any one location, so you must decide which are the most important and plan to satisfy those.

An enclosed space for a laundry, for a vegetable-storage room, or for general storage must also be planned to satisfy definite requirements. It usually helps to visualize the setup if you mark off the arrangement of fixtures accurately to size on the floor.

It is always a good idea when planning the basement to put down on paper a scaled layout of your complete plans, even if your present intention

is to finish only a portion of the total area. Your plans might, for example, call for the basement to be divided into four areas, a family playroom, a workshop, a laundry room, and a section for the heating or other utility units. The family room could be completed first, the others at a later date. With an overall plan, you would not have to make any alterations in your first room when you get around to completing the rest of the project.

A basement room or rooms, of course, presents other problems to the planner. In the first place, considerable open floor space is required, so the location should be relatively free from objectionable pipes, low girders, and inconveniently located posts. Although many of the illustrations in this chapter show rectangular rooms, a playroom may assume any shape that seems convenient for use and practical in construction. If winter heating is a necessity, the location may be planned to take advantage of existing heating arrangements.

After planning your layout, carefully inspect the existing basement before proceeding with construction. Here are a few preliminaries to take care of:

1. Remedy leaks and dampness.
2. Insulate water and heating pipes.
3. Repair and relocate electric wiring for new

Figure 12—2. Basement layouts for different purposes.

fixtures and outlets.

4. Check for sufficient light and proper ventilation.

Overcoming dampness. Perhaps the most basic requirement for a pleasant basement is that it be completely dry and dampproof. Architects and builders distinguish between dampproofing and waterproofing by defining dampproofing as action to reduce the passage of water through the wall by capillary action (that is, carried through the wall as it would be carried upward in a wick). Waterproofing is designed to prevent a flow of running water through the wall, as may happen when water from the eaves or melting snow pours onto the soil outside the house.

Actually, the latter is the most frequent cause of dampness in the basement; that is, surface water collects near the outside foundation walls, penetrates them, and comes inside the basement. The

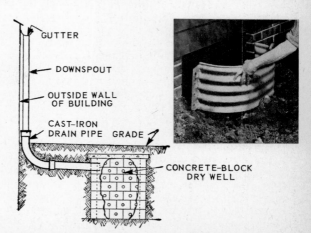

Figure 12—3. Typical dry-well arrangement *(left)* and areaway *(right)*.

Chapter 12

Figure 12—4. Methods of sealing the joint between the basement floor and the wall.

water from roofs should be carried away by adequate gutters, conductors, and downspouts (see Chapter 8). The downspouts should be connected to a drain emptying into a storm sewer, dry well, open water course, or other suitable outlet. Many communities prohibit the draining of surface water into sanitary sewers. Where downspouts are not connected to an outlet, it is advisable to place a spatter board or splash block of good size at the outlet to divert the roof water away from the wall.

Quick shedding of water is essential, and in many cases this may be accomplished by proper grading. The usual method is to place additional filling against the basement wall and grade it down to a sharp, smooth slope that extends at least 8 or 10 feet from the wall. The slope should be sown with good grass seed or sodded, and then rolled firmly and evenly. If it is necessary to grade above basement window sills, an areaway should be built around them. You can use asbestos sheets or masonry for the sides of the areaways. Ready-made metal areaways are available at most building supply houses. Be sure to line the bottom with cinders, gravel, or crushed stone to provide drainage. The soil around the foundation should be planted generously to help resist erosion.

Another method sometimes used to turn surface water away from basement walls is to lay a concrete pavement, walk, or gutter, 2 or 3 feet in width, around the house with a gradual slope away from the walls. Where the sidewalk joins the wall, the wall surface should be roughened, cleaned, and moistened, and the concrete rounded up to meet the face of the wall. This method will make a good bond and turn water away from the joint between the wall and sidewalk. Of course, always make sure that the gutters and leaders are not clogged and that water runs through them freely.

Interior treatments. If your basement is still damp, after these precautions, you can *probably* effect a permanent cure by working from the inside with special waterproof coatings and waterproof cement that are currently on the market. Available at paint and hardware stores, and through many building material suppliers, these powdered waterproofing compounds are most effective in stopping seepage, as well as in checking leaks in masonry

walls. Among the most popular varieties are the so-called heavy-duty cement compounds, which are mixed with water before applying. While mixed and applied like ordinary powdered cement paint (see page 313), they are much heavier in consistency and have sealers added to prevent seepage. They can be applied only over an unpainted masonry wall, or over walls that have been previously painted with ordinary powdered cement paint. But before applying, be sure to clean the walls with a stiff wire brush to remove dirt and any loose particles of concrete.

While cleaning down the walls, check for any holes or cracks in the basement wall. If there are any, they must, of course, be filled before the waterproofing is applied. To do this, cut out the crack with a cold chisel to form a wedge with the inside wider than the outside. This will prevent the patch from falling out after it dries. Use a stiff wire brush to remove any dirt or loose concrete from inside the crack. Wet down the sides of the crack and mix a mortar using a quick-setting hydraulic cement. (Follow the manufacturer's instructions for the proper mixture.) Force the mortar in, making certain that it completely fills the opening, and smooth off the outside surface. Keep the patch moist until it sets.

Once the walls have been cleaned and all cracks filled, the waterproofing material should be applied as directed by the manufacturer. As a rule, powdered waterproof compounds require the wetting down of the wall before they are brushed on. While one coat is usually sufficient to do the job, two coats should be used where seepage is severe.

Other popular waterproofers that work well on porous masonry are the so-called "blockfillers." Some have an alkyd or a modified oil base, while others use special latex or plastic binders. Like the powdered types, these materials should be applied only over a sound surface in which all cracks or holes have been filled with waterproof cement. While blockfillers are suitable for mild seepage problems or occasional leaks, they should not be used for sealing basement walls where there is a definite hydrostatic pressure on the outside areas.

About the only waterproofing compound that may be applied on the inside wall to stop hydrostatic pressure is the epoxy-type coating. During application, two separate liquids, a resin and a reactor, are mixed together and then applied on just about any sound masonry surface, painted or unpainted. But since epoxy-type waterproofers are fairly expensive, it may be necessary to use the material only in a specific area. For instance, since most hydrostatic leaks appear along the joint where the floor and walls meet, it may be necessary to apply epoxy sealer only along this area. Brush on two coats, extending up about 1 foot from the bottom and about 3 inches onto the floor. At the same time, also apply the epoxy to any porous sections that are notice-

406

able, and over any cracks or holes that may be visible, particularly around pipes or wires that pass through the walls.

If the basement floor presents a dampness problem, the waterproof procedure will depend upon its condition and its eventual use. For example, if the floor leaks periodically and through hair-line cracks, it can be treated with blockfillers (if the floor is unpainted) or with an epoxy sealer (if the floor is painted or if the problem is hydrostatic in nature) in the same way as are the walls. If the basement floor is to be covered with a wood floor (see page 110), the wet floor can be given the asphalt and felt treatment. That is, a coat of either asphalt or coal-tar pitch is applied to the floor as a base, and a layer of 15-pound roofing felt or polyethylene plastic sheeting is put over it. Before the bituminous coating is brushed or trowled on, the floor should be primed, using an asphalt primer with asphalt coatings and a coal-tar or creosote primer with coal-tar coatings. When laying the felt, make certain that all bubbles and bulges are ironed out.

On the other hand, a floor that is badly cracked and leaking periodically should be replaced. When headroom is available, you will be reducing basement height by 2 inches; this may be done by topping the existing floor with a 2-inch layer of 1:2:3 mix concrete. This should be reinforced by lightweight steel-wire mesh, not lighter than No. 14 gauge, placed in the middle of the new layer. To prevent cracking, the floor should be kept moist for a period of not less than three days.

Immediately before the new concrete is poured, a dry floor should be roughened, cleaned, and welted and a cement-sand grout (1 part cement to 2 parts sand volume) scrubbed in to form a bond. If the old floor has been penetrated by seepage, a bituminous coating should be applied to the surface of the old floor before the new concrete topping is set in place.

Exterior treatment. Should interior basement repairs fail to stop dampness, the only recourse is outside waterproofing. Begin by digging a trench around the complete foundation as deep as the footings. A line of 4-inch-diameter plastic or clay drain tile should be laid at the bottom of the trench at a pitch of 1 inch in 4 feet (Figure 12–5). The tile should be connected with a sewer, dry well, or other outlet at a lower level. The cracks between the joints should be covered on top with strips of roofing paper or tarpaper to prevent sediment from running into the pipe. The pipe should be carefully laid and protected against settling or leakage by surrounding it with fine screened gravel or broken stone tamped firmly around it. Following this, coarser gravel up to 1 inch in size should cover over the pipe to a depth of 1 or 2 feet. Before backfilling with earth to grade level, it is well to spread burlap or bagging or to place sod, grass side down, on top

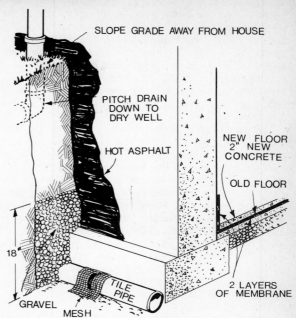

Figure 12–5. Methods of waterproofing a basement.

of the stone to prevent fine material from falling or washing down into the stone.

While the foundation wall is exposed, it is wise to apply a layer of bituminous coating, even if this was done as part of the original construction. Before applying the coating, scrub the concrete surface clean to remove all caked-on dirt. Then brush or trowel on a heavy layer of bituminous coating, covering this with sheets of roofing felt overlapped at least 10 inches where they meet. To complete the waterproof membrane covering, apply another coat of asphalt or coal-tar pitch. Allow this to harden for a day or so before replacing the soil, and shovel the earth in carefully to avoid damaging or breaking the membrane.

Condensation. Even with a watertight floor and walls, condensation can cause dampness problems in your basement. Just as a pitcher of ice water will "sweat" on a hot summer day, so too will a cold basement wall cause drops of moisture to condense on the surface when warm humid air accumulates on the inside. When this moisture has a chance to build up, it will create damp spots that are often mistaken for seepage.

To differentiate between the problems of condensation and seepage, make the following simple test: Cut two sections of heavy cardboard about 2 feet square (an old carton will do), and lay one on the floor, holding it down with weights around the edges and in the center. Tape the second to a foundation wall about 1 foot up from the floor. Wedge a board across the center to press this part tight to the wall. After 48 hours, remove the cardboards. If the area covered is now damp, the moisture represents seepage into the basement. The drier air had been absorbing it as fast as it penetrated, and the basement was apparently, though not actually, dry. Conversely, if the covered areas are dry, and the remaining walls are damp, then condensation is responsible for the dampness.

Fortunately, condensation problems in the basement are usually fairly easy to cure. For example, since the major cause of condensation is humid air in the basement, the first step is to provide for adequate ventilation for its escape to the outside. Keep basement windows closed during humid periods, and keep them open when the air outside is relatively dry. (More on basement ventilation is covered later in this chapter.) Make sure that all moisture-producing appliances such as clothes dryers are vented directly to the outside. Electric dehumidifiers and chemical dehumidifying appliances will also help to reduce condensation, but these are effective only if the basement windows are kept closed.

Uninsulated cold-water pipes are a source of annoyance because of the condensation formed on them during the summer months. Play safe and insulate them before undertaking new construction; then you can be sure that no damaging water spots will appear on the ceiling. There are several easily applied products that will take care of this trouble. A wrapping of hair felt is a standard remedy for sweating pipes. Builders' supply companies and hardware stores also feature mastic preparations that may be painted on, or tapelike materials that are easily wrapped about pipes.

Pipes and heating ducts. One of the problems in starting to finish your basement is what to do with various pipes and heating ducts. In most cases, you probably will want to conceal these pipes by either: (1) leaving the pipes alone and building around them, or (2) relocating the pipes behind proposed walls and ceiling.

Pipe concealment. Pipes, as described in Chapter 6, are usually supported by metal straps. When the pipes are held snugly against the wall or against wall joists, furring strips will usually set the ceiling far enough below to avoid contact with, and yet conceal, the pipes. This is also true of walls. Use 1×2 furring along walls and joists with $\frac{1}{2}$-inch pipes, 2×2 furring for 1-inch pipes.

When the piping is suspended below the joists, either it must be raised or the ceiling lowered. If the basement is sufficiently high, install a suspended ceiling (see page 61). This conceals not only the piping but heating ducts and wiring as well. Everyone is not fortunate enough to have the headroom; therefore you may have to relocate the pipes.

While a drain pipe can pose special problems,

Figure 12–6. A simple method of concealing ugly drain pipes.

as a rule, where it travels across the basement wall in an almost horizontal position, it can easily be enclosed behind the newly finished wall. Where the drain runs directly into the basement floor from above, it can simply be boxed in (Figure 12–6). But before *any* pipes are enclosed by a wall or ceiling, note the position of all shut-off valves and clean-out plugs. If they are widely scattered, try to relocate them in one location. A trap door arrangement in the ceiling or wall will permit access to them should an emergency arise. Remember that it is far better for a few of these mechanical necessities to be exposed than to find them sealed off when a problem presents itself.

Relocating. In basements where headroom is at a premium, relocating the pipes may be the only solution. Frequently, it is possible to do this by raising the main cold-water line (which usually enters the basement at a low point) and cutting a length off each riser that transports water to the floor above. The feed from the main water line may run vertically and then across the joists, at an angle to fit the branch between joists, along a joist, or the pipes can be passed through the joists. Details on how this can be done are given in Chapter 6. When relocating pipes, remember that copper tubing and plastic pipe are the easiest types to handle.

Because of the difficulty and hard work involved, it is not wise to plan on moving the main house drain line. However, if the outside sewer line is lower than the basement footings, it is possible to run the vertical portion of the drain directly from the upper floors to the basement floor, then under it, and to the sewer or septic tank line. When this is done, a section of the floor must be broken open, and the drain pipe run from the sewer line to the basement and under the floor to the point of vertical rise, maintaining the proper upward slope all the way (see page 198). Then the vertical length is supported while the drain pipe sections in the basement are removed, and the connection made between vertical and horizontal lengths. By using Y-section, in the new lengths, you can install a toilet or drain in the basement.

Heating ducts or pipes. While the heating unit itself can be set off from the remainder of the basement in a "utility" area (see page 414), its ducts or pipes can cause problems. For instance, if you have a warm-air system, about the only thing that can be done is to box in the ducts, since relocation is impractical. This is also true in the case of steam heating systems; it is not a good idea to try to relocate steam pipes.

With a forced-feed hot-water system, it is frequently possible to draw the pipes more closely to joists and nearer to walls. It is also possible to relocate these heating pipes in much the same manner used in moving water pipes.

If it is not possible to conceal heating pipes or ducts, they sometimes can be painted or decorated to blend with the decor of the room.

Wiring. Take care to protect all electric wiring during construction. It should be unnecessary to warn against the consequences of short circuits caused by damaged wiring, or improperly installed outlets. But, it is best to decide where to place any electrical outlets and lighting fixtures before the walls, ceiling, and floor are finished. For complete information on how to install electrical wiring and fixtures as well as how to estimate your line load, see Chapter 5.

Light and ventilation. Natural light and air are as necessary in the basement as elsewhere in the house. This is especially true if you expect to spend much time in the room, and wish to have it usable the year around. Many basements could be made lighter by enlarging window openings or by putting in additional ones; if this is done, proper lintels should be placed over the openings and precautions taken to insure stability of the wall. Keeping the spaces in front of basement windows clear, especially by removal of shrubbery, grass, and weeds, allows a maximum amount of light and air to enter.

To improve the basement's air supply, a window ventilator of the kitchen-fan type (see Chapter 10) may be used. As moist air is heavy, it has a tendency to remain near the floor so that it is sometimes difficult to remove it by simply exhausting the air at window height. A window air conditioner (see page 253) is a good investment for any basement room.

Enlarging basement windows by cutting out the

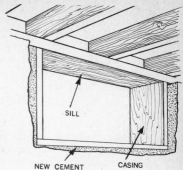

Figure 12–7. Details of adding a new window to a basement room.

SILL

NEW CEMENT   CASING

masonry with a cold chisel and substituting larger frames is not too difficult in many cases (Figure 12–7). If the bottom of the window frame remains above the level of the grade, either casement or pivoted swing-out windows can be installed in the new framing. Windows that are close to or below the grade require an areaway, as described earlier under "Overcoming dampness." Such windows may be of the swing-in casement type or the steel-framed, tilting type. To reflect additional light the inside of the areaway should be painted light yellow or cream.

If your home is built on a slope, it is often possible, even though the major portion of the basement is below grade, to open up an entire basement wall to provide a door and big glass expanse. This is a particularly fortunate arrangement if the wall that can be opened up to the sun and a view faces south. Such a design makes the room warmer in the winter, cooler in the summer, and cheery the year around. There are also modern houses that have the living room raised to make possible an unexcavated basement. Since opening one wall of the basement can make a world of difference in the atmosphere of your recreation room, you may want to make a major alteration and excavate the ground from the outside, making a sunken terrace outside the basement room where you can have a big window and door. Not only will this plan allow extra light and freedom of movement in and out, but it will form an ideal spot for a built-in fireplace with a storage cabinet for fuel and utensils. It is suggested that you leave the excavation work, and the installation of doors and windows, to a professional as you may be dealing with a wall that serves as a structural support for your house. The enclosing wall can be of concrete, cement block, or brick, or you can cover it with a bamboo paling fence or trellis so that when you look out of the basement wall you see greenery.

WALL TREATMENT

As detailed in Chapter 3, there is a wide choice of suitable materials available for basement finished walls: gypsum board in plain and varied effects, insulation wallboard and hardboard in sheets, tile, and planks, genuine wood paneling, and plywood in many finishes. But before any of these products can be installed, the basement walls must be waterproofed. This can be done by applying one of the many available waterproof coatings to the inner surface of the masonry, as described earlier in this chapter.

Furring for exterior walls. After the walls have been waterproofed, furring strips (1 × 3s or 2 × 3s) are commonly used to prepare the exterior walls (those built to cover the masonry foundation walls) for interior finish. As described in Chapter 2, there are several methods of fastening furring strips to masonry walls. One of the most popular ways of securing the furring strips is to use concrete nails or steel cut nails, which can be driven directly into the masonry. Another method is to use metal anchors, which consist of flat perforated plates with a spe-

Figure 12—8. *(top)* Furring is applied horizontally to a masonry wall. Nails set on metal, with the points out, are attached to the wall with adhesive, furring is tapped onto the nails, and the nails are clenched. *(bottom)* Vertical boards are applied to furring with 2½-inch finishing nails set through the tongue into the furring. The succeeding board hides the nails.

cial adhesive. The furring strips are then hammered onto the nails, and the nail points are bent over into the wood. Still another method is to drill holes into the masonry, insert expansion shields or fiber plugs, and fasten the furring strips with wood screws driven into the shields or plugs.

The quickest and easiest way of fastening strips into masonry, of course, is to use a powered stud gun. While these guns are expensive to purchase for one-time use, they can frequently be rented from some hardware dealers and building suppliers. When using a gun, you do not have to drill any holes; you just shoot the metal fastener right in the wood into the masonry. Cartridges are sized so that they will penetrate properly. When using a powered gun, do not fire the fasteners into any wall that you are not sure is solid masonry. Also, never fire into a wood wall.

The direction in which furring strips are anchored to the wall depends basically upon the type and size of wall finishing material used:

1. When using 4 × 8-foot sheets or narrow solid wood paneling boards, nail the 1 × 3-inch furring strips horizontally, placing one at floor level, another at ceiling level, and two others in between at about 28 to 32 inches, center-to-center.

2. When using 16-inch panels, nail the 1 × 3-inch furring strips vertically, spaced 16 inches, center-to-center.

When installing, make certain that each furring strip is level and employ shims where necessary to assure a plumb wall. This plumbness can be checked by holding a long straightedge across the faces of several strips. Space the steel cut nails, adhesive-type anchors, or concrete nails approximately 16 inches apart along the furring strips. The spacing for the other types of wall anchors varies: hammer-driven anchors are placed about 24 inches apart while lead shields and fiber plugs are placed approximately 36 inches apart.

When applying the furring strip to frame out around basement windows, make sure that there is sufficient clearance at the sides so that the window may still be opened. You can frame the inside of the window recess and extend your wall covering into this space. Also, before applying the finishing wall material to exterior basement walls, it is a good idea to staple a layer of polyethylene plastic sheeting over the furring strips. This gives an added protection against dampness.

Insulated foundation basement walls. There has been a trend in recent years to insulate the foundation walls with either blanket-type insulation or foamed plastic insulation. When blanket insulation is used, either 2- by 2- or 2- by 3-inch furring strips are employed. That is, a 2- by 2- or 2- by 3-inch plate is anchored to the floor at the junction of the wall and floor. A 2- by 2-inch or larger top plate is fastened to the bottom of the joists or to joist

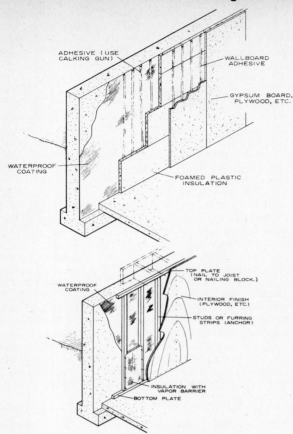

Figure 12–9. Two methods of insulating basement walls.

lation should be followed. Most foam-plastic insulations have some vapor resistance in themselves, so the need for a separate vapor barrier is not as great as when a blanket type of insulation is used.

Partition wall framing. Your floor plan for the finished basement is your guide for positioning the partition walls (those built to divide the area into rooms or sections) to close one part of the basement off from another. First, plan every measurement on paper, allowing space between the partitions for equipment that must remain accessible. The plan will also make it easier to compute your lumber needs. Next, mark the basement floor with chalked guide lines, using the measurements based on your plan. Since none of the basement partition walls will be load-bearing, 2 × 3 lumber can be used for the framing in most cases. The only possible exception to this is when a partition is located directly beneath a steel I-beam. In such cases 2 × 4s are preferred to accommodate the width of the columns and beam and maintain an unbroken wall line on both sides of the partition. Of course, if this partition is to be finished off only on one side, the narrower lumber could be employed, with the framing kept flush with the beam and columns on that side. Wall studs are spaced 16 inches apart, center-to-center, for 16-inch wall material; otherwise, they may be placed 24 inches on centers.

The standard wall, which has a wall covering material on either side of the frame, is constructed by anchoring 2 × 3s to the floor (sole plates) and ceiling (top plates) and 2 × 3s as studs between these boards. The actual partition wall construction is basically the same as that described in Chapter 2. However, there are a couple of points to keep in mind: When the partition runs at right angles to the ceiling joists, nail the top plate at the joist with 12d

blocks, or anchored to the wall. Studs or furring strips, 2 by 2 inches or larger in size, are then placed between the top and bottom plates, anchored at the center, when necessary, with concrete nails or similar fasteners. Electrical outlets and conduit should be installed, and insulation with vapor barrier placed between the furring strips. The interior finish of gypsum board, fiberboard, plywood, or other material is then installed. Furring strips are commonly spaced 16 inches on center, but this, of course, depends on the type and thickness of the interior finish.

Foamed plastic insulation is sometimes used on masonry walls without furring. It is important that the inner face of the wall be smooth and level without protrusions when this method is used. After the wall has been waterproofed, ribbons of adhesive are applied to the wall and sheets of foam insulation installed. Dry-wall adhesive (see page 72) is then applied, and the gypsum board, plywood, or other finish is pressed in place. Manufacturers' recommendations on adhesives and methods of instal-

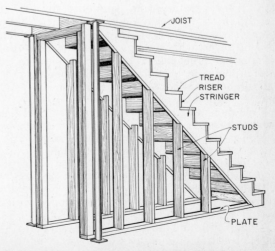

Figure 12–10. Framing around basement stairs.

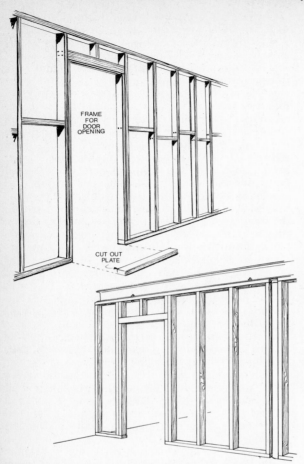

Figure 12—11. *(top)* Simple framing used in basement improvement; *(bottom)* fastening framing to a metal I-beam with bolts.

on all four sides to both plates. The one exception to this is the studs that flank the door openings. These should be nailed only on the edges and away from the opening; do not nail in the direction where the plate is to be cut.

Once all full-length studs are nailed in place, cut two studs the height of the door plus 1 inch for the top frame plus ¼ inch for door clearance. Nail these studs to the full-length studs and to the bottom plate. Set the header in place and nail through the studs. A short jack or cripply stud is then fastened between the header and the top plate. To complete the door opening, cut away the bottom plate.

For openings that do not reach the floor, such as a pass-through, construct a double frame of studs all around the opening. The double framing at the bottom and top are connected to the sole and top plates with short jack studs.

To conceal obstructions such as meter boxes (Figure 12–12), soil drain lines, heating ducts, and low-hanging pipes, build a box frame around them, attached to the walls and joists. While the exact shape of the structure will vary depending on the nature of the obstruction, the important thing to remember is to provide for a solid nailing surface for material that will cover the boxed-in frame, usually the same paneling that is used in the rest of the basement room. Valves, clean-outs, and meters, as previously stated, must be provided with access doors.

When you install a non-standard wall, use a material that is finished on both sides, for example,

nails. If the partition runs parallel to the joist, it may fall directly beneath a joist, in which case it is simply nailed to the joist. There will be a problem here, however, with nailing surfaces for the ceiling material, so either nail 1- or 2-inch lumber to the sides of the plate, or use a larger-size framing material, like a 2 × 6 or a 2 × 4, for the top plate, so that it extends beyond the studs.

Where a wall is parallel to the joists, but falls between them, nail headers every few feet between the joists, 1½ inches above the lower edges. Then nail a 2 × 4 or 2 × 6 all along the top length of the plate to provide sufficient nailing surfaces for ceiling material. Fasten the top plate to the 2 × 4 or 2 × 6. While doing this, make certain that both plates are parallel by using either a straightedge with a level or a plumb bob.

When both top and bottom plates are nailed in place, measure and cut studs to fit tightly between them. Use 8*d* (eightpenny) nails to toenail the studs

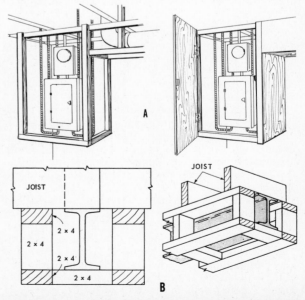

Figure 12—12. (A) Details of framing in a metal box; (B) one method of framing a metal I-beam.

perforated hardboard or translucent plastic sheets. Then all you have to do at this time is anchor a 2 × 3 to the floor and another to the ceiling. Use finished lumber in this instance as this wood will be exposed when the wall is finished. Use a flat-head screw in place of a lag bolt to anchor the 2 × 3 to the floor. Countersink the head so that it is flush with the top of the 2 × 3.

CEILING TREATMENTS

The installation of a ceiling in a portion or all of the basement not only will improve the looks and value of this part of the house, but will prevent dust and drafts from infiltrating into the upper floors.

Figure 12—13. Two ways of adding interest to basement stairs.

Ceilings of insulation board, plasterboard, asbestos cement board, hardboard, plywood, and wood can be installed the way walls are installed. However, insulating and acoustical tile are now more popular. Methods of installation are outlined under "Ceilings" in Chapter 3.

It is a good policy (and required by many building codes) to make the ceiling over the furnace or heater fire-resistant. Some of the more economical materials that will serve this purpose are galvanized sheet metal, plasterboard, asbestos cement board, and plasterboard lath or metal lath covered with cement plaster. This protecting panel is usually 8 to 10 feet square (consult your local code). The remainder of the ceiling may be finished with any material desired.

If you have overhead pipes with sufficient headroom beneath, it may be desirable to conceal them completely with a false ceiling. A framing of 2- by 2- or 2- by 4-inch furring is dropped from the ceiling rafters far enough to clear the overhead piping. A dropped or suspended ceiling may be constructed as described in Chapter 3.

Pipes can also be boxed in and made to look like beams. Dummy beams may be installed to give the effect of beams spaced at regular intervals. Before the exposed pipes are enclosed, however, they should be thoroughly checked for any signs of leakage or condensation.

If you do not finish the ceiling, you can give the room an appearance of height by painting the beams a light color, and painting the pipes, underflooring, and bridging a darker shade or a contrasting color.

FLOOR TREATMENTS

As described in Chapter 4, there are several floor surfacing materials suitable for below-ground use. In addition to these, paint can be used. Painting, if correctly done with proper materials and preparation, is a very satisfactory and inexpensive way of finishing the floor. Unfortunately, however, many painted floors turn out badly, owing to dampness and alkali in the cement, which softens and discolors the paint. Grease from soapy water around the washing machine and laundry tubs is also a frequent cause of paint failure. The floor must be cleaned thoroughly before painting. Flushing it off with water alone is not sufficient. The surface must be scrubbed thoroughly with a grease-dissolving compound, until all grease and soap are removed. To make such a solution, dissolve 1 pound of trisodium phosphate in a gallon of warm water. Follow the scrubbing with a final rinse of hot water.

To remove small spots of grease, oil, and soap, place sawdust or fine shavings on such spots and soak them overnight with a solution of 1 pound of lye to a gallon of water. Brush away sawdust a day

  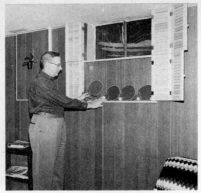

Figure 12–14. Adding storage facilities to a basement: *(left)* A flush-mounted metal pull is used to detach a removable wall panel; when in place, as shown, wood-grained scoring hides the joints between the fixed and removable panels. *(center)* With the panel removed, you can see the magnetic catches at each end of the 1 × 2s used to hold it in place. To replace the panel, slip the top up into the ceiling molding. Then the panel drops into a 5/32-inch groove in the platform, where the magnetic catches are prepositioned. The 2 × 4 rail locks table halves in place on the platform built above the cove base. *(right)* This innovation provides storage for paddles and balls while decorating a high, small basement window. When the lower set of shutters is closed, the 3½-inch-deep ledge where paddles are kept resembles a windowsill. The framed panel to the left of the window is hinged to swing open for access to the circuit breaker box.

later and scrape the spot clean. Then wash the spots down with a trisodium phosphate solution.

There are two types of paint that are used on basement floors, rubber-base and oil-base paint (see Chapter 9). Paints made with a chlorinated-rubber base are quite new and are more reliable on concrete than oil-base paints are. However, oil-base paints made for use on concrete are easier to use, are considerably less expensive, and wear well if there is no moisture in the concrete. Cleaning is a necessary preliminary step with either paint unless the concrete is new. Both paints are applied with a brush, and the manufacturer's directions should be followed to the letter.

Instructions for installing resilient flooring and wood are given in Chapter 4.

OTHER CONSIDERATIONS

When you work on the completion of your basement, there are several areas that require special considerations. The problem of camouflaging unsightly household necessities, for example, can also be solved with a little thought. For instance, a movable cabinet for old-fashioned laundry tubs not only hides their ugliness but also serves a useful purpose as a table; unobtrusive casters permit its easy removal on wash days, and it can be utilized from the rear as a stand for the ironing board.

Your basement stairs can be converted from a potential hazard to an inviting and safe stairway. The addition of risers and a good-looking balustrade will add to the appearance of the steps and strengthen the structure. It is a good idea, from the standpoint of safety alone, to box in the basement stairs. The generally neglected space under the steps can be converted to a useful storage locker.

Heating. If your heating plant keeps the basement comfortably warm in the coldest weather, a lattice grille built in a partition may be adequate. If the heating plant is within the room, it may be practically concealed by means of a lattice structure. However, modern heating plants usually give off very little heat in the basement, except from uncovered pipes and ducts, so it may be necessary to provide other means of heating.

In the case of a hot-air plant, a separate pipe should be run from the furnace to the room. With a hot-water or steam system an overhead radiator serves the purpose. (A floor radiator is impractical because it would be below the level of the water in the boiler, which would not circulate properly.) If none of these methods solves your problem, or if your heating plant is already taxed to the limit to heat the upper floors, the installation of a gas or electric radiator is recommended. This is a self-contained unit requiring only a gas or electric connection. Other auxiliary heating system ideas suitable for a basement or for a basement room are given in Chapter 7.

Heater enclosures. It is not uncommon these days to see the main heating plant located at one end of the finished basement. The modern basement heater is usually a good-looking piece of equipment, and all except the hand-fired coal-burning units are clean, unobjectionable mechanical devices. However, the furnace can be enclosed by using decorative shades, tall window shutters, porch blinds, or a screen. A permanent enclosure can be constructed of fixed Venetian blinds and

Figure 12—15. Three suggestions for a basement recreation center.

will not only successfully conceal the most unsightly of furnaces, but also permit a free circulation of air.

When one side of the heater section can be left open to an unfinished part of your basement, the problem of air circulation is simplified; the other two sides can then be enclosed in knotty pine or wallboard, with a door at the front, or a fairly tight latticework enclosure can be erected on the studding, with latticework doors.

Outside basement entrance. At one time, almost all houses with basements had outside entrances. These were fitted with sloping wooden doors that lifted up, and the youngsters used them with gusto for sliding down. About a decade or so ago this building practice was abandoned, and homeowners without such entrances lost these advantages:

1. Convenience in reaching basement storage areas from outside;

2. Avoidance of tracking through the house all those outdoor items destined for winter storage downstairs;

3. Adequate cross-ventilation in the basement;

4. A separate outside entrance to a finished basement.

Typical basement entrances are of two types: those that are at right angles to the foundation, and those that parallel the foundation. Each has two or more retaining walls or bulkheads holding back the

Figure 12—16. Steps required to replace wooden basement doors with metal ones.

earth and a sloping base section for steps. In many cases, the old-time basement entrances are in need of rejuvenation. While the entranceway walls are usually in good shape, the wooden super-structure usually falls victim to the elements. Fortunately, steel basement replacement doors are available, and their installation, as shown in Figure 12–16, is a job that can be undertaken by most homeowners.

If your home is without an outside basement entrance, this home improvement project involves the following steps:

1. Making an excavation to expose a portion of the house foundation;

2. Erecting a retaining wall or bulkhead to hold back the soil;

3. Breaking through the foundation;

4. Installing steps and a door.

Hired labor can give you a fast start on the excavation and breaking through the foundation if you decide not to do it all yourself. The digging is not difficult since the bottom of the excavation slopes to meet the stair incline, and the width need be little more than maximum door width (3 feet) plus 8 inches at each side for a concrete block wall. Once the foundation is exposed, it is broken through with a large cold chisel and hammer or a rented pneumatic hammer, either of which goes quickly through concrete block or brick foundations, but somewhat more slowly through poured concrete. The opening is smoothed off and faced with 2 × 6 lumber set in new mortar. The house sill over the opening serves as the necessary lintel. The bulkhead should be carried approximately 6 inches above grade to prevent water from flowing down the new stairs, and the new entrance door is installed on the bulkhead top as indicated in Figure 12–17.

Stairs may be built on wood stringers (see page 137) or constructed of concrete blocks or poured concrete, or, to save time and labor, prebuilt stringers can be used (Figure 12–18).

Figure 12–17. Steps required to add an outside entrance to a basement.

Figure 12–18. Adding metal-wood steps to a basement areaway.

Figure 12—19. Two bar ideas for a recreation center.

Lighting for seeing and decoration. Lighting your basement, utilizing new lamps and lighting ideas, can dispel much of the underground atmosphere, besides creating any kind of atmosphere you desire. To begin with, you will want highly functional lighting, overall room lighting that, if you so wish, casts away all shadows and almost takes the place of daylight. You can use built-in fluorescent or incandescent ceiling lights and add to this supplementary light from lamps placed at the "task" centers. A shop, for instance, depends on good lighting, adjustable to minute work, as well as high-level overhead lighting. A standard industrial heavy-duty fixture that you can buy or even make yourself serves this purpose. For detail work there are flexible lamps that operate on swivels and arms so complex they can follow your work closely.

For reading, for television, or for card playing, you will want the best light for your eyes and for enjoyment. A ceiling-mounted fixture on a reel principle is suggested for games at the card or dining table. When the table is pushed aside for dancing or games, this light can be sent up to the ceiling, out of the way.

Valance and cove lighting (see page 170) from the edge of the room will enlarge the horizons of your room. For cove lighting, place two continuous rows of 40-watt single fluorescent lamps approximately 6 inches from the edge of the cove, staggered to give an unbroken line of light with no dead spots between the fixtures.

Basement sauna. Although saunas are frequently installed in a bathroom (see page 394), and even closets, the basement is the most popular spot for this healthful addition to any home. A sauna, of course, is a small, wooden room heated with a powerful stove, usually electric, to around 200 degrees. The heat is comfortable, because the humidity is kept very low, under 6 percent. The dry heat bath is some 80 degrees hotter than an average steam room, with none of the discomfort sometimes associated with bathing of this type.

There are two ways to build a sauna room. One is to get the complete package that includes the room, heater, and controls. The other is to buy only the heater and controls and build a custom-made room. The costs of either method are comparable.

The typical complete-package sauna is 6 feet 8 inches high, and is built in 4- by 6-, 6- by 6-, 6- by 9-, or 6- by 12-foot units as well as in a few special sizes. But, whatever the size, the precut kit includes walls, ceiling, benches, and floor of California redwood or cedar, the heating unit and electrical controls, sauna rocks, and a carpet. There is no plumbing to install, and most package units are put together with the aid of a wrench. That is, the walls of prebuilt redwood or cedar lock together, as do the floor and ceiling. Both woods, cedar and redwood, are fine for sauna use because of their high insulating factors. They make the sauna easier to heat and they remain cooler to the touch.

When a custom-built arrangement is constructed, the room is framed with 2- by 4-inch studs, in much the same manner as the walls of the home are constructed (see Chapter 2). The walls are then usually insulated with 3-inch-thick insulation batts, and the inside wall and ceiling covered with ½-inch gypsum board.

The heart of the sauna room is the heater. While there are sauna gas heaters and even coal- and wood-burning units available, the electric type is by far the most popular as it is compact and requires no flue, and the heat control is very accurate. There are two types of electric sauna heaters presently used. One is equipped with a fan, while the

Figure 12—20. A typical closet-type sauna.

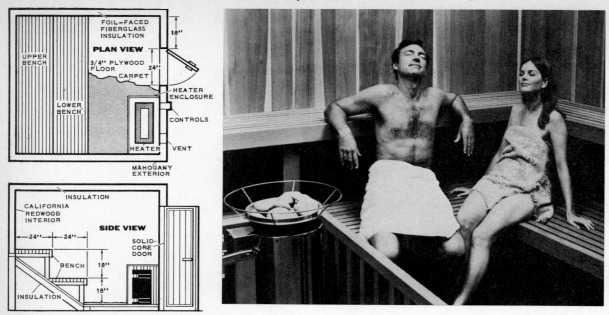

Figure 12—21. A family-type sauna suitable for a basement.

other is not. The advantage of the former is that it takes only about 15 minutes to warm up the room. The advantage of the fanless heater, which depends on convection for air circulation, is that it is almost completely silent. It may take far longer to heat the sauna (1 hour), but it heats walls, floor, and benches, as well as the air, in that time.

Most heaters are located in the room, and a heater guard is installed around the unit for the protection of sauna users. Most larger electric heaters require a 240-volt line. If you do not have the extra circuits available, you may have to switch to a larger service to accommodate a sauna heater. Electric heaters for one-man saunas operate on 120 volts, but they use 1,500 watts and require a circuit all to themselves. They demand all the power a 15-ampere circuit can provide.

There are a number of luxuries that can be add-ed to your room that will aid in making sauna bathing one of the most relaxing experiences in the world. One is a hygrometer which shows how quickly the relatively humidity drops as the sauna temperature increases. Another is an "old country" wooden bucket and ladle, which are used for sprinkling water on the sauna rocks for those who enjoy the "steam shock." There is even an audio transducer that attaches to the sauna exterior, producing a stereo sound effect inside.

Certain aspects of remodeling will be the same for every basement room, such as the roughing-in, ceiling installation, wall paneling, floor tiling, etc. But beyond that, your individuality takes over. While many ideas are shown in this chapter, the limits on what you can do are imposed only by your own good taste and, to a lesser extent, by your budget.

Chapter 13

MAKING THE MOST OF YOUR ATTIC

If you are crowded for living space in your home, how about using the attic? In many houses the attic can be converted into two large rooms that can be used as extra bedrooms with bath, or into one large recreation room. It can also be converted into a playroom, sewing room, office, or even a den. The ceiling of course will pose a problem. The walking area of an attic is limited because of the slanting roof, but you can utilize the available space by careful planning. The low areas can be used for beds, desks, built-ins, etc.

PLANNING THE ATTIC

Each attic, of course, presents a different situation, depending on the usable area and the pitch of the roof. In general, if the rise of the roof is less than 8 feet, there will be insufficient headroom for a usable room. The minimum standing headroom is considered to be 6 feet 6 inches, and the average person requires 4 feet of headroom when seated. Therefore, the points at which walls 4 feet high will intersect the sloping rafters determine the width of the prospective room. Unless the house is unusually large, a rise less than $\frac{1}{3}$ of the span leaves attic space with too little headroom. The length of the room will be dependent upon the length of the house, the placement of the stairs, the location of any interior chimneys, or any other obstruction.

If the attic is small, or only one room is to be finished off, the problem is relatively easy; the plan generally depends upon the location of the stairway. Where space exists for two or more rooms,

preliminary measurements of the available area should be made into a rough floor plan so that you can visualize just how the location of the stairway will influence the arrangement of the rooms. In many houses the attic stairs are centrally located, providing an ideal layout with rooms opening from a small central hall. Where the stairway enters the attic at one end, generally there is not sufficient headroom available for a lateral hallway, and the floor plan must permit entry into a living or general-purpose room first, with the bedroom at the opposite end.

Your procedure depends first on the attic, whether it is long and rectangular under a low-pitched gable roof or whether it is more nearly square with a high-pitched roof. Because of the limited height available in relation to the overall size in the smaller home, it may be necessary to include the entire attic space along the length and slant a portion of the walls along one or both sides. The alternative is the installation of dormers such as are described later in this chapter.

Before going any further, it is wise, especially in older homes, to check the strength of the existing joists and their ability to carry the new or added weight of materials and furnishings. Some houses have not been designed for upstairs living quarters. The best guide for determining this is to use the FHA Minimum Property Standards chart reproduced in Table 13–1.

The data in Table 13–1 refer to acceptable spans for joists under "habitable" rooms in the attic; for baths and hard-use rooms such as a recreation

Figure 13–1. A typical attic area before and after remodeling.

Table 13-1

If joist is (inches)	And spacing is (inches)	Safe span is
2 × 6	16 o.c.	10 feet 4 inches
2 × 6	24 o.c.	9 feet
2 × 8	16 o.c.	14 feet
2 × 8	24 o.c.	12 feet 4 inches
2 × 10	16 o.c.	17 feet
2 × 10	24 o.c.	15 feet 6 inches
2 × 12	16 o.c.	19 feet 8 inches
2 × 12	24 o.c.	17 feet 10 inches

NOTE: o.c. means "on center."

room, deduct at least 12 inches from the spans shown in the third column of the table. Also subtract another 12 inches from the span if the joists used are any wood other than Southern yellow pine or Douglas fir. If the joists need strengthening, nail a member of equivalent size, 2 × 6, 2 × 8, etc., next to each existing ceiling joist so that it bears on the same members that the in-place joist does. Use 16d nails spaced 6 inches apart, and if the ceiling below is plaster, scrape away any plaster-keys so that the joists will lie flush. Double the joists under any partition that will run parallel to them. If the joists are less than 2 × 6s, you will have to strengthen or replace them with stronger members.

FRAMING

The general rules of framing an attic area follow those outlined in Chapter 2, with a few variations. That is, the basic framing of an attic includes the following four steps:

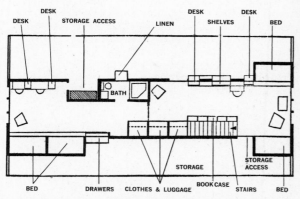

Figure 13—2. Many old houses that were built close to or in town are as long and narrow as this house. They would lend themselves perfectly to a similar remodeling, but even if the space is divided in half, room for two beds and a study area can be provided. Though not visible in any of the photographs, a folding door has been installed between the bathroom and wardrobe closets. This permits one person to study without being disturbed by talk in other parts of the attic. The bath is narrow but functional. The square tub fits into the tight space available. Moreover, costs were lowered because the bath was planned directly over existing plumbing.

1. Laying a sub-floor if the joists are exposed.

2. Joining the sloping portion of the roof with the floor by installing knee-walls.

3. Locating and erecting collar beams to form the frame for the ceiling.

4. Laying out and constructing partition walls to divide the attic into rooms.

Installing the sub-floor. Your attic may have a rough sub-floor already laid, or, as is the case with many expansion attic homes, it may have only a partial sub-floor. In the latter case, the sub-floor will have to be completed first. The easiest material to install is sub-floor grade plywood. It makes a quickly installed, tight, strong, and even sub-floor. Three-quarter-inch plywood should be laid over the joists, and 8d nails should be placed every 6 inches on bearing at the edges of the panels and one every foot on bearing away from the edge.

You can also use 1- by 4- or 1- by 6-inch boards, either square-edge, or tongue-and-groove, for sub-flooring. As a rule, the less expensive grades of lumber may be used for the sub-floor. Knots, or even knot holes, are not objectionable. The sub-floor is laid across the joist at right angles. The diagonal method provides bracing across the joists, and permits the finish floor to be laid in any direction. It is wise not to spare the nails in laying a sub-floor. At least two 8d nails should be used where each sub-floor board crosses a joist; for example, two nails for 4-inch boards, and three nails if 6-inch boards are used. The nails should be driven flush so that the floor is smooth, with no heads protruding.

Before applying the sub-flooring, make the necessary provisions for lighting, heating, and plumbing if cables, ducts, or pipes are to run under the floor. During the laying of the sub-flooring, care should be taken not to hammer too hard since the vibrations in the floor joists might loosen or crack the ceiling below.

Constructing the knee-walls. Most attic rooms will have sloping ceilings following the roof line. When a partition is constructed along this line, it is gener-

ally best to secure the base sole plate, then fasten the short knee-wall studs alongside each rafter (Figure 13–3). These will usually be on 16-inch centers, except in very old houses. In most cases, the minimum height advisable for knee-walls is at least 4 feet. Make certain that you provide for this height when locating the position for the floor sole plates. The knee-wall studs to form the attic side walls are attached to a floor sole plate and the rafters. The sole plate lumber and knee-wall studs should be the same dimensions, usually 2 × 4s.

To line up the knee-wall studding, nail a temporary knee-wall stud at each end of the wall at the proper height. Use a level to insure that they are plumb. Then snap a chalk line between these studs along the floor and across all the rafters. This allows you to properly line up each knee-wall stud. The temporary studs should be removed after the chalk line has been snapped.

Place the base sole plate on the floor just outside the chalk lines and nail it down with 16d nails through the sub-floor and into each joist. Alternate nails on one side of the sole plate, then the other.

Measure and cut a knee-wall stud that will reach from the sole plate up to the roof rafters. The bottom of the stud is cut square, while the top may be cut at an angle to match the roof angle, or cut straight across. In the latter case, be sure you have sufficient nailing area. After cutting a sample stud, try it at various points along the knee-wall to see that roof sag does not make shorter studs necessary. Once you get the stud so that it fits everywhere, use it for a pattern to cut all the remaining studs. Toenail each stud to the sole plate with a pair of 8d nails and nail its top into the roof rafter above with two 12d nails. The location of roof rafters will determine the location of knee studs. But remember that knee-wall and end-wall studs should be doubled and blocked apart 1 5/8 inches with 2 × 4 scraps where the partitions meet the wall to provide a nailing face for wall covering materials on each side of the partition.

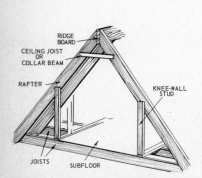

Figure 13–3. Basic parts of attic construction.

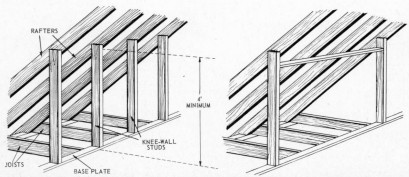

Figure 13–4. (left) Knee-wall studs in place. (right) Method of supporting rafters if there is to be a knee-wall opening.

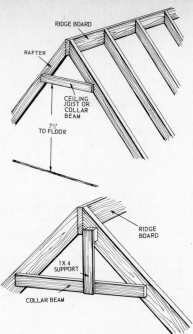

Figure 13–5. The ridge board and collar beam setup typical of most attics.

When installing the knee-walls you may wish to use some of the under-eaves space for storage; in this case don't attach the studs in the storage access areas. Frame this area by attaching a plate, the same size lumber as the studs, between the two studs forming the outside of the storage area. It is wise to double the studs at both sides of the opening. The doors for the access area can be installed after the wall finishing material has been installed.

Installing the collar beams. Once both knee-walls have been erected, collar beams or ceiling joists should be installed. Many building codes specify that the bottom of the collar beam should be a minimum of 7 feet 6 inches from the floor. Most attics already have collar beams overhead; they hold the rafters together, and are usually spaced on every third set of rafters. If these are level and at the proper height, they can serve as a guide for the other collar beams. That is, simply install similar beams between the rafters where they are missing. Again, a line and straightedge will help to insure your keeping them level and maintaining a smooth ceiling line.

If the present collar beams are not level, which is often the case, or are not at the proper height, it is best to install new collar beams. Use 2 × 4s for collar beams on spans under 15 feet; 2 × 6s on longer spans. On these longer spans, nail a pair of continu-

ous 1 × 4s over the top of the collar beams as stiffeners.

To start installing the collar beams, locate one at the correct height at each end of the room. (Get the proper overall ceiling height by measuring up from the floor at the four corners of the room.) Then snap a chalk line across the rafters. The collar beams should be placed on each rafter at the chalk line height and nailed with three 16d nails on each side of the rafter.

Installing partitions. If you have included separate rooms with partitions to divide them in your planning, this is the next and last step of the attic framing. Usually this job is started by framing the end walls. As a rule, these wall studs can be located at either every 16 inches or every 24 inches. In addition nailing surfaces for wall materials must be provided all the way around, sides, top, and bottom. At a point about at floor level, install headers between the studs to provide a nailing surface there. A cleat nailed to the end rafter flush with its lower edge is an easy method of obtaining a nailing sur-

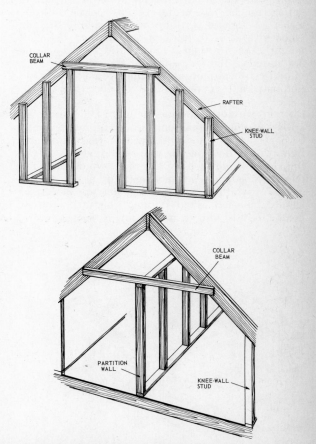

Figure 13–6. Partition wall arrangements used in most attic improvement projects.

face up toward the roof peak. Unless an end wall stud falls conveniently just inside the knee-wall corner, you will have to cut and install a stud there. To provide a nailing surface along the knee-wall–roof joint, cut and nail in two rows of headers there. One row fits between the knee studs; the other fits between the roof rafters.

The installation of interior partitions is very much like installing wall frames in any other part of the house (see page 46). They can be erected with studs on either 16- or 24-inch centers; either 2 × 3s or 2 × 4s can be used, but double studding should be employed around doors. If possible, any partition that will run parallel to the floor joists below should be centered over a joist.

The first step in erecting an interior partition is to cut the lower sole plate and the partition studs to length, and nail through the plate into the studs. This assembly is put into place on the floor and the lower sole plate is nailed down. Then the studs are toenailed into the collar beams. Interior corners, where a partition is butted up against a side wall, require an additional stud (or studs) as a nailing surface for the edge of the corner sheet of wall material. Full-length partition framing should include wood bridges or blocks between studs at chair-rail height to ensure rigidity. Extra bridges or blocking are added to the sides of door framing to prevent vibration when doors are slammed. Incidentally, do not install a floor sole plate in the door frame openings.

Dormer windows. Dormer windows not only increase available headroom in attic rooms, but may be necessary to provide the proper ventilation and light. Unless the house is so located that one side of the sloping roof faces to the rear, two dormers are usually needed to balance each other in appearance. For widths over 8 feet the shed type of dormer should be used. Shed dormers, because of their greater width, offer a maximum of headroom and

light. But, unless you are familiar with the type of carpentry required to frame a dormer, it is a good idea to have this part of the job done by an experienced carpenter. As soon as the dormer is enclosed you can take over and finish the job.

After deciding on the location and type of the dormer you want, mark off its area by driving two long nails through the roof from the inside. Place these nails at "ceiling" height on the inner side of the two rafters between which the dormer will be located. On the roof, remove all shingles from the markers down to the eaves, and to about 1 foot on the markers. Then saw out the roof boards in a straight line from the mark to the eaves. Pry the cut-out boards from the rafters, and the opening is begun. All that remains is to cut through rafters that are in the way. But, before removing the roofing be sure that a heavy tarpaulin is available in case of bad weather.

First put in double studs or corner posts under the two rafters that form the outside width dimensions of the dormer. Then, making cuts across the intervening rafters, remove them. Once the cut is made, the rafter can be easily pried up from the sole plate. Nail a timber or header across the cut ends of the rafters (using a timber of the same dimensions as the rafters), supported by the double studs. Your opening is now complete.

Framing of the dormer itself is fairly simple. Toenail the corner posts onto the sole plate, or sill. Next, nail a 2 × 4 across the lower edge of the header you nailed to the cut ends of the rafters, and on this seat fit the new dormer rafters, extending them outward to the new plate nailed across the corner posts. From this point on, the framing must fit the type of dormer you have chosen.

The *shed dormer* (Figure 13–7) requires only a series of new rafters from the double header to the sole plate, spaced 16 inches on center from the corner post to the inside double stud, all of these being

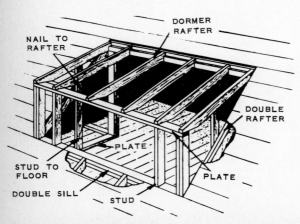

Figure 13–7. Details of a shed dormer.

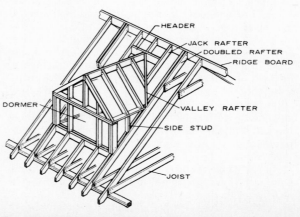

Figure 13–8. Details of a gable dormer.

angled to fit under the framing rafter. Try to locate a bearing wall as near to the center of the attic as possible to more surely guarantee support for the ridge pole or plate. If you have some spare pieces of 2- by 4-inch lumber, give the dormer roof added support by installing short lengths of studding between the dormer ceiling joists and the dormer rafters. The pitch of the dormer roof will naturally be shallower than that of the regular house roof, and this will be added support against the weight of snow if you are situated in a northern area.

The *gable dormer* (Figure 13–8) requires a plate on three sides, across the outer corner posts, and from the outer to the inner posts. On this platform the gable timbers are erected. In most cases, 2- by 4-inch timbers will serve here, as the roof areas are all quite small.

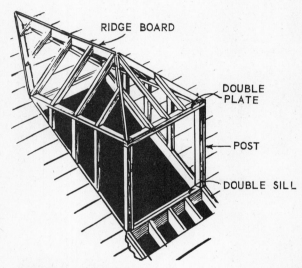

Figure 13–9. Details of a hip dormer.

The *hip dormer* (Figure 13–9) generally allows the use of taller windows than either gable or shed types and extends farther back into the house roof, providing extensive headroom in depth. The collar beams or ceiling joists should be located so as to align the ceiling of the dormer with that of the room.

If it is necessary to build your dormer around a chimney, remember that most building codes specify a 2-inch space between the chimney and any wood framing. So box in the chimney with 2 × 4s, leaving the required space, and then fill the space with metal flashing.

The next step in finishing *any* type of dormer is to frame the window and box it in, covering all sides, including the roof, with tongue-and-groove siding or sheets of exterior-grade plywood. Building

the frame to fit a window of standard size will save trouble. Before the exterior is completed, it is best to put flashing all around the dormer. If you use relatively small sheets of copper flashing and start at the bottom, the necessary 2-inch overlap will be easy to achieve. A minimum overlap of 8 inches on the roof and side walls must be used; 12 inches gives the added assurance of a watertight job. On a gable dormer the flashing is carried right up to the peak, where it joins the main roof; the flashing is slipped

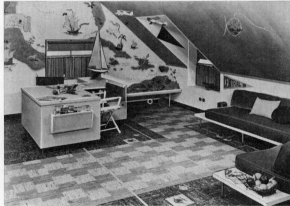

Figure 13–10. Two examples of the interior treatment of a dormer window.

under existing shingles.

For the sake of appearance, try to match the old shingles and the siding materials. In both cases, a layer of siding tar paper or felt is applied beneath the exterior materials. Installing the window, adding shutters to match others on the house, and applying the necessary coats of paint complete the exterior work.

To complete the inside work, you will have to put cross members between studs and rest them on

Figure 13–11. Step-by-step procedure in building a shed dormer.

the side plates to which the ceiling material can be fastened. A peaked ceiling is rarely welcomed.

Enlarging existing windows. If you are considering enlarging an existing window or installing a picture window, make sure that you are not cutting any of the structural members of the framing. Before cutting into your wall to install a larger window, it is necessary to remove the wall covering on both sides, as described in Chapter 8. In the case of the attic this will probably be only the building paper, plywood sheathing, and the siding. Two by fours or heavier lumber are then nailed temporarily across the studs that are to be cut. A precautionary measure, in the event that the wall bears the weight of the roof, is to place shoring under it to hold the weight until the new framing around the opening is in place. Before nailing the temporary cross supports, stand the longer pieces of the new frame against the wall, adjacent to the place where they are to be installed. Then cut off the studs and nail the headers and trimmers around the opening.

SKYLIGHTS

Another method of introducing natural light in an attic is with a skylight. Actually, for the remodeler, a skylight is perhaps the most practical way to get natural light into a room or hall where light has been blocked off by an addition that eliminates an existing window wall. It is often the easiest way to get more daylight into rooms in an older house instead of enlarging the windows.

The need for privacy can also be an important factor in installing a skylight. In a house on a narrow lot, for example, with windows facing a neighbor's house, you may have to draw the curtains even during the day. A skylight will eliminate the perpetual gloom.

Legal restrictions must be checked before installation of a skylight. Most cities have building regulations that apply to skylights, so before going ahead with your remodeling plans, check with the building inspector. Either glass or plastic is permitted in skylights, but you must use wire glass or a code-approved type of plastic. There are also code limits on how much area you can cover with each kind of skylight material. Other restrictions may include distance of the house from the property line and spacing between skylight units.

There are all sorts of skylights, and the homeowner can have his pick of sheet metal (zinc-coated steel) and glass, either custom made or prefabricated, or the ready-made aluminum types with clear plastic domes. To install the last type, which is the most common, the opening at the bottom of the skylight is measured and these dimensions are then marked out on the underside of the roof sheathing between rafters or beams. Then a hole is cut through the sheathing with a saw along the pencil

Figure 13—12. Two treatments of attic skylights.

lines. To strengthen the sheathing around the opening, 2 × 4s are nailed to the underside perimeter of the hole.

After the skylight is placed temporarily over the hole to check it for fit, the roof sheathing is covered with overlapping strips of 15-pound felt (asphalt-impregnated paper) and is fastened with galvanized roofing nails. The skylight is placed over the roof openings and is nailed to the roof deck through their aluminum flanges except for the front flange, which is bent up slightly so that the asphalt roof shingles can be slipped under it. The front flange is then concealed under the next row of shingles and nailed to the deck. The roof shingles are applied so that they overlap the flanges on all sides. However, the rear flange is first covered with a piece of asphalt felt flashing before shingles are nailed over it. The joints where the shingles meet the walls of the skylights are then caulked, and the job is complete.

Figure 13—13. The installation of a skylight.

STAIRS

Some expansion attics are provided with a finished stairway; others are open, resembling basement steps. In the latter case, risers and cove moldings must be cut and fitted under each step for both appearance and safety. A sturdy hand rail is needed also. For full details on stairs, including attic stairs, see Chapter 4.

HEATING

Provision for heating attic rooms varies according to the type of heating system. Generally most home-heating systems will carry up to a 50 percent additional load. It should, therefore, be no great problem to extend the heating system into the newly finished rooms, except that, in the case of a hot-water system equipped with a hot-water expansion tank in the attic, the tank will have to be raised above the radiator level.

If the heating system is hot water or steam, pipes must be run through the walls to the radiators in the attic. Built-in radiators should be backed by a tin or asbestos sheet, concave at the top to throw the heat forward.

If your heat comes from a warm-air furnace, new ducts must be run and registers installed. The ducts should be rectangular in cross section so that they can be installed between wall studs on the lower floor to reach the attic. There, they can be run between the floor joists to reach the desired register positions. You may wish to call in a professional heating man or tinsmith to install the air ducts.

Auxiliary heaters are sometimes easier to install and cheaper than using your regular heating source. There are many types, portable or built-in, operated by electricity and gas.

Insulation. Insulating your attic will do a lot to give your home an even temperature in both summer and winter. In the whole house, the attic is the spot most vulnerable to loss of heat and to the sun's rays, and insulation there gives the highest return in comfort for dollars spent.

Complete instructions for the installation of insulation are given in Chapter 7. Keep in mind that there are two ways of applying insulation to an attic room. One is to apply insulation between the collar beams and all the way down the rafters. The other method is to apply insulation between the collar beams, down the short run of the rafters, and then down the studs. In any attic installation, as previously mentioned, the insulation should *not* go all the way to the peak. It could cause dry rot and retention of heat in the summer. This precaution permits air circulation over the ceiling and behind the walls.

Ventilation should never be omitted when insulation is installed. In hot weather, it prevents excessively high temperatures; in cold weather, it allows water vapor to escape, thereby reducing the possibility of condensation. Attic louvers should be placed as high as possible and, as previously stated,

Figure 13—14. Two treatments of an attic stairway.

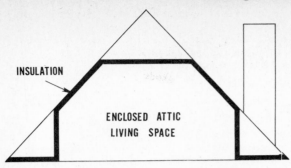

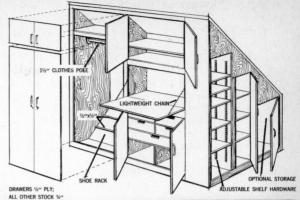

DRAWERS ½″ PLY;
ALL OTHER STOCK ¾″

Figure 13–15. The proper method of insulating an attic.

Figure 13–16. Measurements have been eliminated in the drawing *(top right)* because your attic probably was not constructed like the one for which this unit was built. Your first step, therefore, is to scale the drawing to your attic. Construction should proceed as follows: Cut the panels and enclose the bottom, sides, and back of each space. Cut and edge-nail the shelving (note that the open shelving on the right is mounted on adjustable shelf standards). Mount the drawer shelves and guides. Make the drawers. Then, cut and apply the front paneling, cabinet doors, and desk top, which should be 30 inches above the floor when open.

should be big enough to give at least 30 square inches of vent area for each 100 square feet of attic floor, distributed in at least two louvers. It is advisable to cover the openings. If you use wire screening, to keep out birds and leaves, increase your vent area by 20 percent; if you use insect netting, increase the vent area by 50 percent. These are minimum figures; larger openings are better. Arrangements and types of louvers are shown on page 263.

An attic power roof ventilator is another worthwhile consideration. The newer units offer the advantage of automatic operation, thermostatically controlled within the attic temperature range desired. Automatic control features of earlier units were restricted to the extremes pre-set by the manufacturer, and frequently were not the most efficient for actual climate variations. Installation of a ventilator is well within the capabilities of the average home handyman using the instructions provided. An opening cut through the roofing surface between rafters, mounting of the power unit and vent, a little roofing cement to insure against possible leakage, two jiffy wire connections, setting of the thermostat, and the job is done.

If you are re-surfacing your roof in your home improvement plans (see page 294), consider using a light-colored shingle, as light colors reflect the heat from the sun rather than absorbing it.

BATHROOM AND PLUMBING

Your improvement plans may call for a bathroom in the attic. Usually the bathroom will be more economical if located above the bathroom on the floor below so that the same sewer vent can be used. This also permits extending the pipes between studs up to the attic instead of taking them through studs or joists. When this is impossible, a major installation job is in prospect, since a new sewer line, vent, and water pipes must be run from the basement to the attic, which means tearing out plaster and lath on

floors below. Newer houses with "expansion attics" often have the plumbing roughed in, ready for the installation of fixtures. For complete details on planning a bathroom see Chapter 11; the subject of plumbing is covered in Chapter 6.

LIGHTING

Prior to insulating and closing in the walls, all electrical wiring should be completed. The lighting requirements generally will be the same as in any other room (see Chapter 5), plus a stairway hall light. This stairway light should be controlled by two three-way switches that permit the lights to be turned on and off at either the head or the foot of the stairs.

FINISHING

A hardwood floor may be nailed into place on top of the sub-floor after the building paper is laid, or you may prefer to use resilient flooring materials. If the underfloor is rough, sheets of $1/4$-inch plywood or hardboard will serve as an excellent base or underlayment for resilient sheet material and tiles. The walls and ceiling can be finished with a variety of materials and with different decorative treatments. For installation of floors, walls, and ceilings, see Chapters 3 and 4.

Finishing up the dormer will depend on the type installed. The shed dormer requires a ceiling applied to the underside of the rafters. For a flat ceiling in a gable or hip dormer, you will have to put cross members between the studs, resting on the side plates, to which the ceiling material can be fastened. A peaked ceiling is rarely used.

In this chapter we have discussed several ideas to use in remodeling an attic. Apply them as you wish. Perhaps they may provoke you into developing some original ideas of your own.

Chapter 14

REMODELING IDEAS FOR OTHER AREAS WITHIN THE HOME

Up to this point most of the remodeling projects described have been major jobs. There are, however, some remodeling tasks you can undertake that will add definite value to your home, but will not take too long to accomplish. Closets are a good example of this.

CLOSETS

No matter how big the home, how well it is planned, or even how many closets there are, no homemaker ever seems to have sufficient closet space. Too frequently, however, the reason for this is a lack of proper planning and arrangement rather a lack of available space. That is, most closets are the biggest space wasters in the home. Are you taking advantage of the latest closet fixtures that will store belts, ties, purses, and hats efficiently? Are you putting the closet door to good use? Or the space beneath the clothes? What about other possible storage areas in the home that will help to carry the burden that the closets are bearing alone? Keep in mind that if you are able to store even a few things that are normally kept in the closet elsewhere, your closet will be that much more free and uncluttered.

When planning a remodeling project, do not forget your closets. A well-planned closet will give you more space. Therefore take a careful look at your closets; you are bound to come up with some ideas of your own on how to make them more efficient. Incorporate them with the ideas and suggestions given here and you will be on the road to real closet comfort and efficiency.

Planning closets. There are three things one must consider when planning any closet space, location, size, and equipment. Location is already taken care of in the majority of homes, and unless you are able to relocate storage spaces, you will have to rely on changing their size, or rearranging and modernizing their equipment. However, the interior arrangement and intelligent use of all available space in a closet are often all that is necessary to transform a bad closet into a good one (Figure 14–1).

Closets and other storage arrangements should occupy space that would not be used in other ways whenever such space is of adequate size and in a desirable location. Closets should not interfere with main areas of activity in a house. They should be accessible but inconspicuous.

Modern homemakers are not satisfied with clothes closets that are merely places to hang things. They want closets to be well arranged so that they help keep clothing in good condition and make it easy to get garments out or to put them away.

Ventilation is especially important in clothes closets to help keep the clothing free from odors and, in humid areas, to keep mold from developing on them. Air may be kept in circulation by a window or by openings in the top and bottom of the door.

One clothes closet in the house should have doorways equipped with rubber or felt gaskets and a tread. This makes it possible to shut the door really tight in case it is necessary to fumigate against moths. Shallow "reach-in" closets need doors that are almost as wide as the closet itself. For doorways more than 2 feet 8 inches wide, double or sliding doors are recommended.

In dusty parts of the country a threshold is needed for "walk-in" closets to help keep the contents clean. The floors of "reach-in" closets should be built at least 2 inches higher than the floor of the room so that dust will not seep in so freely.

No matter what the shape of the space available for a clothes closet, one of the six plans shown in Figure 14–2 can be used. Minimum dimensions on the plans may be increased and the arrangement then varied by adding hooks, trays, shelves, drawers, and racks for shoes. Clothing on hangers is indicated by the lines drawn at right angles to the rods.

For a space limited in width but fairly deep, the narrow closet (A) with an extension rod is a good arrangement. The doorway to this closet should be at least 2 feet wide.

The shallow wardrobe closet (B) is a typical reach-in arrangement. This is an excellent closet to use when depth is limited. However, the depth

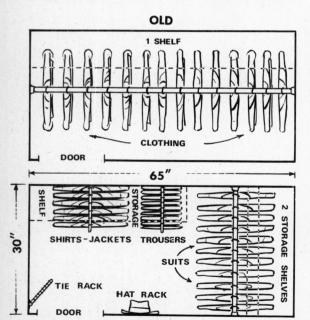

OLD

1 SHELF

CLOTHING

DOOR

65"

30"

SHELF

STORAGE

SHIRTS - JACKETS   TROUSERS

SUITS

2 STORAGE SHELVES

TIE RACK

HAT RACK

DOOR

NEW

Figure 14–1. Remodeling a closet to provide extra storage space.

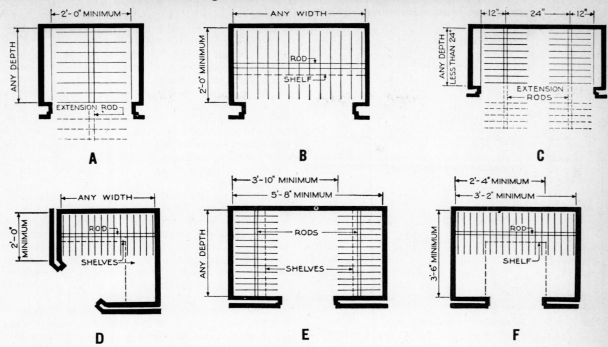

Figure 14–2. How to make the most of various closet sizes.

should be at least 2 feet so that clothes on hangers will not brush against the walls. If this closet is more than 30 inches deep, you will be unable to reach the back of the closet. A shallow wardrobe type of closet requires an opening practically as wide as the closet. Swinging or sliding doors should expose all parts of the closet to your reach. A disadvantage of the wardrobe closet is the amount of wall space needed for the doors.

For space that is too shallow to place hangers crosswise, closet (C) is a good arrangement. Here two extension rods provide the maximum hanging space. The doorway must be practically as wide as the closet.

The corner closet (D) provides considerable hanging space for very little floor area. This closet has no sharp corners that project into the room. Protruding closets that create an offset in a room should be avoided. Often by filling the entire wall between two bedrooms with closet space it is possible to design a square or rectangular room without the use of offsets. Doors on closets should be sufficiently wide to allow easy accessibility. Swing-out doors have the advantage of providing extra storage space on the back of the door. However, space must be allowed for the swing. For this reason, sliding doors are often preferred.

The walk-in closet (E) may be any depth as long as it is large enough to walk into. The area

needed for this type of closet is equal to the amount of space needed for hanging clothes plus enough space to walk and turn. Although some area is wasted in the passage, the use of the walk-in closet does provide more wall area for furniture placement, since only one door is needed. For more shelf space and less hanger space, one side of the closet may be filled with shelves.

Another walk-in closet (F) is similar to the reach-in arrangement shown in (B). This closet may be any width that is wider than the door opening. If you wish, place the door at one end, making the shelf L-shaped.

Fittings for clothes closets. It pays to plan details of closet fittings carefully. Rods, hooks, and trays that are well located make it easier to keep clothing in good condition and to keep the closet in good order. Practically all clothing, dresses, except those for infants, skirts, blouses, trousers, and coats, can be taken care of on hangers.

If the closet is 22 inches or more in depth, and wider than it is deep, the most practical arrangement for hanging garments usually consists of a clothes pole of either metal or wood. Table 14–1 shows the space to allow on the rod and from floor to rod for different types of garments. The space between the wall and the rod should be at least 12 inches, so that clothes may hang freely on the hangers. If there is a shelf above the rod, a minimum of

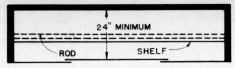

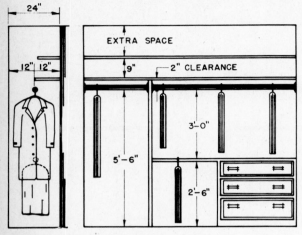

Figure 14–3. Dimensions for a wardrobe closet.

2½ inches should be allowed between the top of the rod and the bottom of the shelf. When attaching equipment, keep these figures in mind.

Table 14–1. Rod allowance for adults' garments

Garment	Space allowance on rod (inches)	Minimum distance from floor to top of rod (inches)
Skirts	2	45
Jackets	3	45
Shirts	1½	45
Suits	3	45
Trousers	3	72
Dresses	1½	63
Men's overcoats	4	63
Women's coats with fur collar	3–6	63
Women's coats without fur collar	2–5	63
Evening gowns	2	72
Garments stored in mothproof bags	3–8	72

For shallower closets, special brackets are available that permit the clothes to be arranged parallel with the back of the closet. These brackets are 8, 10, and 12 inches in length. By spacing them 2 feet apart along the rear closet wall, you can usually put wasted space to use.

If you are dealing with a "hole in the wall" closet (one that is deep and narrow), you should have an extension pole so that the rod can be pulled out into the room. This gadget, consisting of a per-

manent track attached to the underside of the closet shelf, permits a movable arm to slide in and out on ball-bearing rollers. Instead of groping in a dark, narrow closet to find a particular garment, you can bring your wardrobe out into a well-lighted room by a slight pull on the handle.

If only a few garments are kept on hangers, as in closets for work clothes, a long hook may take the place of a rod. Actually, there should be enough hooks in a closet to accommodate nightgowns, pajamas, slips, aprons, overalls, and other garments that do not belong on hangers. Children's play suits and jackets and men's work clothes are also generally kept on hooks.

Hooks should be within easy reach of the doorway, but not any closer than 5 inches. There should be a minimum allowance of 4 inches between the top of a hook and the bottom of the shelf above it. It is better not to place hooks behind a rod. For the clothing of small children, hooks should not be above the child's eye level. Hooks for garments on hangers cannot safely be put on a door that is less than 30 inches wide.

The distance from hook to hook or from hook to corner will vary with the kind of garments hung on them. For clothing ordinarily kept in a bedroom closet there should be a minimum of 7 inches between hooks and 3½ inches from hook to corner. For children's clothing, have hooks spaced about 9 inches from hook to hook, and 4½ inches from hook to corner. For men's bulky work clothes the hooks should be at least 12 inches apart and 6 inches from hook to corner.

Shoe storage. There are several convenient ways to store shoes. The rack shown at left in Figure 14–4 holds shoes vertically, and is a good one to use when wall space is not so limited as floor space; the lower bar may be covered inside with felt to protect the shoes. The tilted racks shown may be used on the floor of the closet, below garments on hangers or hooks. A width of 18 inches will accommodate at least two pairs of shoes and sometimes three, depending on their size.

Horizontal shelves, one above the other, are also satisfactory for storing shoes. They take up more room than the arrangements shown, but they have the advantage of being useful for other purposes. Distance between shelves for storing adults' shoes should be at least 7 inches, for children's shoes 6 inches.

Shelves. Other fittings should supplement the storage space provided in bureaus, chests, and dressers. Clothing shelves for folded clothes are less expensive than trays or drawers and provide enough protection for most articles. The width and distance between shelves (as well as the depth of trays and drawers) vary according to the articles stored. They should be planned to accommodate the largest articles commonly stored in or on them.

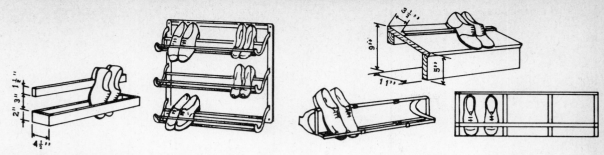

Figure 14—4. Ways to store shoes.

The minimum for shelves for hats, for instance, is 12 inches from front to back; the maximum about 15 inches. The distance between shelves used for hats should be 9 inches from the top of the lower shelf to the bottom of the shelf above.

Door storage units. If your closet is over 2 feet 4 inches deep, there remains an unused space of 6 inches or more between the inside of the door and the clothing. By putting the closet door to work, you gain the equivalent of another wall. Here may be stored umbrellas, even when wet, and here is space for extra hats that will not fit on the shelf. This is also a convenient storage place for shoes and neckties. How much better it is to get the shoes out in the open, instead of on crude racks at the back of the closet, which the victim must approach on his knees while he wades through a wall of clothes!

Storage can be facilitated also by the many types of accessories on the market designed to care for umbrellas, coats, hats, neckties, shoes, trousers, and such items.

Coat closets. The coat or guest closet, generally a hall closet, takes care of every article of outdoor wearing apparel from rubbers to hats. Its efficiency relies a great deal on the arrangement of its equipment. Door storage is particularly useful.

The coat closet should be placed near the main entrance, but not so close to it that doors interfere with access to the closet. When considering the amount of space required, remember that a pole about 26 inches long can easily accommodate 6 overcoats; an overcoat on a hanger needs a 24-inch space (22-inch minimum).

A shelf proportioned to the depth of the closet may be fastened just above the clothes pole on brackets. If possible, two shelves should be installed: an upper shelf, for caps and hats, 14 inches from front to back; and a lower shelf, for gloves and mittens, 12 inches deep and 12 inches below the upper shelf.

Closet lighting. The problem of lighting closets may be solved in several ways. If you are installing a new electrical outlet in a closet, place the outlet in a location just beside or just above the door. A light source in this position illuminates the contents of a closet much better than a ceiling fixture does. The reason, of course, is obvious; the closet shelf cuts off the light from a ceiling fixture and casts a shadow over all the garments hung below it. A fixture just over the door or beside the door jamb at 6 feet above the floor casts its rays both above and below the shelf. An added luxury is a door switch, installed to work automatically as the door is opened and closed. The switch may easily be set into the door jamb just under the top hinge.

If there are no electric outlets in your closets and you wish to save the added cost of wiring, hang a small bracket light just inside the door and stretch an electrical cord to the nearest convenient outlet in the room. Bracket lights can be installed by simply hanging them on a small metal pin placed on the wall.

Bedroom closets. One closet in every bedroom is the minimum for modern homes. Ideally, there should be a separate closet for each person or, if two must share a closet, a separate rod for each. Two feet of rod length is about the minimum to allow for each person.

A basic bedroom closet is shown in Figure 14—3. In this closet a rod provides 24 to 27 inches of hanging space. The tops of both the rod and the hooks on the closet door are 63 inches from the floor, a good height for the garments of most adults. Just above the rod, 65½ inches from the floor, is a shelf 18 inches from front to back. The second shelf above the rod is narrower and may be omitted if height is limited.

On the right-hand side is a section of shelves and drawers, 18 inches wide. The two lowest shelves, used for shoes, are spaced 7 inches apart. The two drawers for ties, handkerchiefs, and toilet articles are 4 inches deep. The four movable shelves, for folded articles, are spaced 9 inches apart and have guards on the front to keep articles from falling off.

One of the closet doors is a handy place to put a full-length mirror. The top of a full-length mirror

Figure 14—5. Ways to use a big closet.

Figure 14—6. A man's storage closet *(top)* and a woman's storage closet *(bottom)*.

for the use of adults should be no less than 5 feet 11 inches from the floor. (See page 100 for mirror installation details.)

It may not be practical to use up good space for a closet just for the clothes of a small child (especially as children do grow up very soon and need a regular-sized closet). But it is a good idea to allot some portion of an adult's closet for the shorter clothes of the youngster, by installing lower rods and perhaps lower shelves as well. These should be temporary installations that allow for removal when they are no longer needed.

Linen closets. The most desirable location for a linen closet is near the bedrooms and opening directly into a hall. In addition to household linens, this closet may accommodate enough surplus supplies of bedclothing to take care of emergency needs. If woolen blankets are stored here during the season of danger from moths, each one should be so wrapped as to be mothproof.

Families that have extra supplies of woolen blankets and comforters should store them in mothproof containers when they are not in constant use. Some families have a large chest or a specially constructed closet for storing woolen clothing and blankets out of season.

The number of shelves needed in a linen closet varies from family to family. Therefore it is a good idea for each woman to determine the amount of storage space needed by measuring her own supplies. It is wise to make shelves adjustable to allow for changes in kind and number of articles to be stored. Drawers or trays add to the convenience of linen closets, but they increase the cost of construction.

Surprisingly little depth is necessary for a successful linen closet. For instance, large bath towels and bath mats will need a shelf no more than 18 inches deep; sheets require 14 inches; pillow cases and hand towels need 8 to 12 inches. Only blankets

Figure 14—7. A built-in storage unit. Details of the plastic drawers are shown in the upper left-hand corner.

demand a greater depth. If your closet is too deep, you will find it very awkward to reach over one or more rows of towels to get at an article tucked away back in the gloom. Any practical homeowner can remedy this situation by putting the door to work and making it support half of the shelving.

Housekeeping closets. It costs very little to make a serviceable closet for cleaning supplies. Such storage space helps to keep the house sightly and prevents the odors of wax, polishes, and soaps from spreading.

The inside walls of the cleaning closet should be smooth and impervious to oil. Plaster walls, enameled or covered with linoleum or oilcloth, or wallboard painted with enamel is a satisfactory surface. If the floor of the closet is raised about 2 inches above the room floor, lint is less likely to come in under the door.

There should be space in a cleaning closet for brooms, brushes, mops, and, if possible, the vacuum cleaner. This closet is also a good place to keep extra table leaves, in a special case with spacers.

In determining the dimensions and the arrangement of a cleaning closet, take into consideration the articles to be stored and the way in which they must be stored. Each article that hangs should have space enough to hang free. And it should be possible to remove any article without first taking out something else. A floor area 18 by 30 inches will be sufficient to accommodate an upright vacuum cleaner with a broom and a mop or two, but an area at least 2 by 2 by 6 feet is preferable.

Locate the closet so that it is convenient to the kitchen and within easy access to the rest of the house. Two good locations are between kitchen and hall and between kitchen and dining room.

The brooms and mops can be stored neatly and efficiently by attaching friction catches about 4 feet from the floor by 1- by 3-inch pieces nailed on the side walls. Here, again, the door may be put to work to hold miscellaneous brushes, dust cloths, and bags.

Allow sufficient clearance between the lowest shelf and the top of the vacuum cleaner or broom, whichever is higher; usually this shelf is about 5 feet from the floor. Here you can store miscellaneous bottles and cans. Allow a 15-inch distance between this shelf and the one above. The top shelf may be used for storage of extra dust cloths and sundry articles seldom used.

Cedar closets. The volatile oils present in cedarwood are a deterrent to moths, and a cedar-lined closet will protect woolens throughout the year without troublesome spraying or other treatment.

Cedar panels. Cedar panels, which are made from thin flakes of aromatic red cedar and fully retain the moth-repelling aroma of the natural wood, come in standard 4- by 8-foot and 16- by 48-inch panels, $\frac{1}{4}$ inch thick, sanded on one side. Either side may be used, but the unsanded surface of compressed flakes gives an unusual and beautiful effect.

The panels are easy to install. Just follow these simple steps:

1. Measure walls and any other surfaces you wish to line with cedar panels. Outline how the panels are to be installed before cutting. Plan to have the edges of panels centered over a wall stud where joints are necessary. (In existing closets, remove shelves, molding, light fixtures, and other items before measuring.)

2. Cut panels to fit with a power or hand saw. Use $1\frac{1}{4}$-inch finishing nails or panel adhesive to fasten panels directly to studs or over existing wall material. The cedar panels will not split, and they have excellent screw- and nail-holding properties.

3. Study the closet space carefully after the walls are completely paneled with the material. Decide how you can increase its usefulness by placing shelves and racks in otherwise wasted space. Use leftover pieces of cedar paneling to cover shelves.

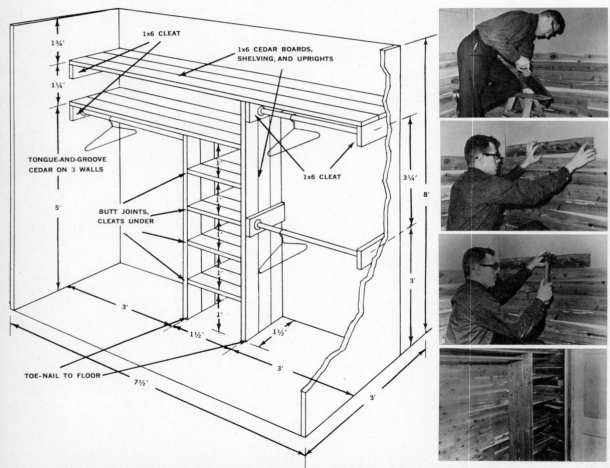

Figure 14—8. Details of a built-in cedar closet.

Figure 14—9. Steps in constructing a cedar closet.

4. Complete your job with corner molding, taking care to miter all joints. Install a baseboard of cedar or any other wood that combines suitably in appearance with the cedar-lined walls.

Solid cedar boards. The solid cedar lining is tongued and grooved at the sides and ends so that pieces join snugly. This not only facilitates application but makes for solid unbroken surfaces. Actually, the aromatic red cedar closet lining is produced in random lengths up to 8 feet. It is $3/8$ inch thick, and comes in a choice of widths from 2 to 4 inches. Manufacturers bundle the material in neat, sturdy packages that protect the wood from weather and make them easy to handle and store. Each bundle of cedar strips will cover at least 30 square feet of closet space.

Table 14–2. *Estimating quantities of cedar boards (8-foot bundles)*

Face size (inches)	Counted as (inches)	Waste (percent)	Board feet per bundle
$3/8 \times 2$	$2\frac{1}{2}$	25	40
$3/8 \times 2\frac{1}{2}$	3	20	40
$3/8 \times 3$	$3\frac{3}{4}$	25	40
$3/8 \times 3\frac{1}{4}$	4	23	40
$3/8 \times 3\frac{1}{2}$	$4\frac{1}{4}$	21	40
$3/8 \times 4$	$4\frac{3}{4}$	19	40

Table 14–3 shows the number of 8-foot bundles required for various size closets. Coverage includes walls, ceiling, floor, and door. For 4-foot bundles double the number shown.

Table 14–3. *Closet size in feet*

Deep	Wide	High	Bundles	Deep	Wide	High	Bundles
$1\frac{1}{2}$	3	7	3	2	$4\frac{1}{2}$	8	5
$1\frac{1}{2}$	3	8	3	2	5	7	4
2	3	7	3	2	5	8	5
2	3	8	4	2	6	7	5
2	$3\frac{1}{2}$	7	4	2	6	8	6
2	$3\frac{1}{2}$	8	4	3	4	7	5
2	4	7	4	3	4	8	5
2	4	8	4	3	5	7	5
2	$4\frac{1}{2}$	7	4				

Where economy is a major consideration in new construction, satisfactory results can be achieved by nailing the cedar directly to the framing. When this is done, it is advisable to close all spaces between studding at the floor and at the ceiling. Cedar strips can be applied to plaster or finished wallboard in remodeling projects.

The cedar strips are applied horizontally on the walls (Figure 14–9), beginning from the bottom. Courses are placed with the groove edges down. Thus the tongue edges of pieces in each course interlock firmly with the groove edges of each succeeding course. Face nailing is recommended, but blind nailing may be employed if desired. Use 4*d* nails and set them just below the surface of the wood. In face nailing, a nail is driven at each bearing point about $3/4$ inch from the top edge of each strip. Blind nailing is done at an angle through the tongue edge. The first course should receive extra nailing. Thus, besides being blind nailed or face nailed near the top edge, pieces in this course should be face nailed at each bearing point approximately $3/4$ inch from the bottom edge.

Joints need not occur over studs. The tongue and grooving serves to "weld" the pieces together firmly. Where the cedar is being placed over plaster or wallboard surfaces, short pieces will remain securely in place even if placed between bearing points.

Cedar molding is available for corner treatments. It can be omitted, however, if extra care is taken to measure strip lengths for snug fitting. Protruding strips at outside corners can be sawed off evenly after nailing. Outside joints require no mitering. The easy workability of cedar makes it possible to form smooth, neat corners by sanding the edges.

The same general directions should be followed, where applicable, in lining the ceiling, the floor, and the door. When the door is lined, the door knob and escutcheon plate must be removed. The finished door, however, need not necessarily be fitted with a key hole from the inside. It usually is sufficient merely to bore a hole for the door knob bar prior to replacing the escutcheon plate. To assure greater airtightness of the closet, a condition which increases its moth-repellency, the door can be weatherstripped.

Panel supports for shelves and hanger rods should be fastened to the wall studs with 2-inch screws. Screw hooks also should penetrate well into the studs for extra strength. Cedar lumber designed especially for use as shelving is available.

All cedar lining, including cedar panels, should be left in its natural state. Application of shellac, varnish, paint, or other finish would seal in the cedarwood oil fumes and prevent their functioning as a moth-repellent. Incidentally, when the solid cedar lining is removed from its package, a white fuzz or frostlike substance may be visible on the surface of the wood. This is merely crystallized cedar oil, an indication of strong oil content. Crystallization sometimes occurs when the cedar has been stored where there is little air circulation or light. The frostlike substance can be brushed or rubbed off easily, leaving the wood clean and bright. It will vanish without wiping if the cedar is aired for a short time.

To keep a cedar closet functioning properly, the following precautions should be followed:

1. Keep the closet as air-tight as possible. Close the door securely after storing or removing articles.

2. Wipe the cedar occasionally with a dry or damp cloth to remove dust and dirt.

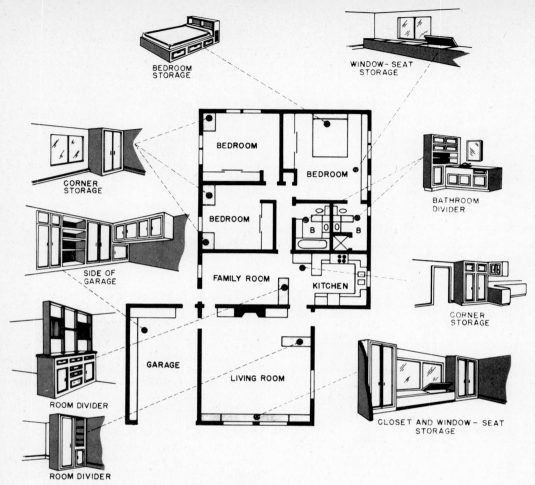

Figure 14—10. Each room in a house should contain some storage space.

3. Sand the wood lightly about once a year to reopen any closed wood pores and thus renew the strength of the cedarwood fumes.

4. Air-dry or dry clean all articles before storing them.

Storage locations. Different types of storage facilities are necessary for the different areas of your home (Figure 14—10), depending on the type of article to be stored. The most appropriate types of storage facilities for each room in the house are as follows:

Living room: Room divider, built-in wall storage units, bookcases, window seats.

Dining room: Room divider, built-in wall storage units.

Kitchen: Wall and floor cabinets, room divider, wall closets.

Bathroom: Room divider, linen closets, cabinets on floor and ceiling.

Bedroom: Wardrobe closet, walk-in closet, built-in wall storage units and shelves, under bed, foot of bed, head of bed, chests, dressers.

Den: Bookcases, room divider, built-in wall storage unit, window seats.

Family room: Built-in wall storage unit, window seats, bookcases.

Recreation room: Built-in wall storage unit.

Entranceway: Room divider, wardrobe, walk-in closet.

Utility room: Cabinets on floor and walls.

Work area: Wall closets, cabinets, open tool board.

Porches: Walk-in closet, under porch stairs.

Patios: Sides of barbecue, separate building.

Outside: Closets built into the side of the house (Figure 14—12).

Figure 14–11. Changing a room from childhood to adolescence without major structural alterations: the three-ring circus be- comes a haven for sportsmen. Because babies grow up, it is important to consider future needs in furnishing a child's room.

Figure 14–12. Ways to store outside equipment.

Chapter 14

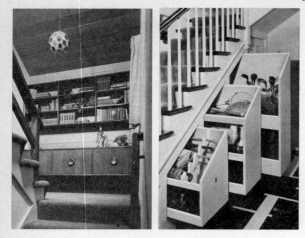

Figure 14—13. Two suggestions for stair storage.

Many of these spaces may call for especially designed storage units since the dimensions may be irregular because of the shapes involved. While converting wasted space into storage areas may take some extra thought and little extra carpentry skill, it is worth all the effort since enough storage is one thing every home seems to lack. It is one remodeling job that costs little, but can add greatly to the value of your home.

BOOKSHELVES

The usual construction of home bookcases merely requires the fitting of boards together at right angles in good and practical proportions. When designing your bookshelves, make them as near as possible to the actual width of the books, because this reduces the amount of exposed shelving to be dusted. For this reason, shelving is generally 1 by 8 or 1 by 10 inches.

Shelves spaced 9 inches apart will accommodate most books, and a shelf or two with 11- or 12-inch clearance will take care of the larger ones. One-inch boards can support spans of about 3 feet without sagging. Two-inch boards can span approximately 5 feet. Longer spans require additional support such as toenailing them into the backing of the bookcase or into the wall studs. Other popular methods of support to a wall are shown in Figure 14—14.

Angle irons or metal shelf brackets can be used successfully, especially where the back wall is painted a dark color. The front edge of the shelf is

A careful inspection of your home will usually reveal several other locations that can be converted quickly and easily into storage spaces. Here are a few spots that you might consider:

1. Under the stairs.
2. Around and over a door.
3. Under the eaves in the attic.
4. Next to a fireplace.
5. By a chimney rising through a room.
6. Under a window.
7. In unused corners.
8. Over stairways.

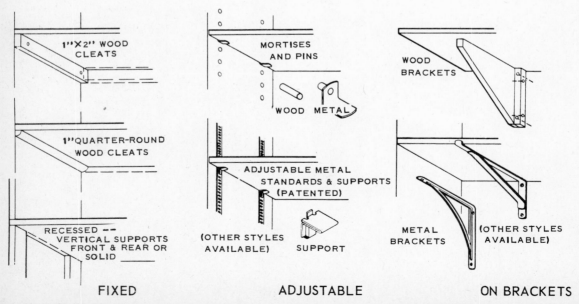

Figure 14—14. Shelf-holding devices.

Remodeling Ideas for Other Areas Within the Home

Figure 14—15. Styles of bookcases.

screwed to the side of the bookcase. If desired, a dado joint may be used in place of screws. Cleats, quarter-round molding, or small metal angle-L brackets can also be used and may be masked from direct view by vertical molding strips along the side edges of the shelves. Perforated metal strips and angle fins that attach to the strips give very good support and are adjustable so that the heights of the shelves may be changed. Another adjustable-type shelf rest sets in ¼-inch holes and may be spaced as desired. Both adjustable types are available from most hardware stores.

As a rule, the standard wall is too thin to permit the installation of built-in or recessed shelves deep enough to hold books. However, if a closet is located behind a wall, the bookshelf can be placed between studs in the wall, with its back extending into the closet. You can put in a matching pair of such bookshelves if the closet is wide enough. The back, sides, and top of the shelf cabinet can be made of plywood. To install a wider set of shelves, you would need to take studs out of the wall. This can be done with little trouble if the wall does not support ceiling joists. When the wall carries a load, however, it will be necessary to install a bracing framework to span the opening and support the load.

Bookshelves can be installed in any recess in a wall, for instance, in the recess beside a fireplace. The problem here is no more complicated than installing shelves in a closet. However, you will probably wish to have side members to which the shelves can be attached, rather than support the shelves on cleats as in a closet. If the shelves are to be several feet wide, they will require support at the back; this means that a back is needed. This back can be made of a single plywood panel. The best method of construction is to build up the shelves complete with sides, back, top, and bottom, and set the unit into the recess. In this way, the nails can be driven through the sides and back into the shelves so that they will not show and no shelf cleats will be required. Apply trim after the installation is complete. The original baseboard, if removed carefully from the recess walls, can be reinstalled to fin-

Figure 14—16. Ready-made shelf units are popular.

ish off the lower edge of the shelves.

Instant shelving systems. With the various shelf and support systems now on the market, it is possible to install shelving in a matter of hours. These shelving kits are available in an abundance of styles to fit any decor from Early American to modern. While the style of the shelves may vary, the support systems made by the various manufacturers are very similar. That is, they usually consist of slotted steel channels, called standards, which are screwed to the wall, and metal shelf brackets that fit into the channel slots. These shelf systems are highly adjustable, making possible a wide number of interesting arrangements.

The shelf brackets come in lengths from 4 to 24 inches, and many systems include ready-made shelves of prefinished wood or hardboard. The shelf brackets may also be used with ordinary wood shelving or plywood. Some of the channel systems are available with decorative surrounds or escutcheons around or behind the standards.

Follow manufacturer's recommendations as to spacing of the standards; as a rule, the heavier the load, the closer the standards should be spaced — 32 to 36 inches apart for light loads, while not over 24 inches for heavier ones. For proper methods of screwing the standards to the wall, see page 24.

To position the channels properly, determine the distance from the floor to the top of the first standard. Put in the top screw loosely to permit the channel to fall plumb. Mark the rest of the screw holes, swing the channel out of the way and drill the holes. Align the tops of the remaining channels from the top of the first one, using a carpenter's level. Of course, if you do not wish to have all the channels of the same length, install the first standard and insert one bracket. Then hold the next channel vertically the proper distance apart and insert the self bracket to align with the first one. Place a shelf on the brackets and level it with a level. Mark the location for the holes of the second and subsequent channels. Then drill all the holes, insert the proper holding device, and run all the screws home. To complete the job, insert all the brackets in their desired locations and place the shelves in their proper positions.

STORAGE WALLS AND ROOM DIVIDERS

A storage wall is a shallow closet built into the wall holding cupboards, shelves, and drawers. Wall closets are normally 18 inches deep, since this size provides access to all stored items without using an excessive amount of floor area. The storage wall unit idea may be used in almost any room in the house. The design and style, of course, will depend completely on your desires and needs. The wall storage units shown in Figure 14–17 will serve as a starting point for your own ideas.

Figure 14–17. Built-in wall storage areas should be planned wherever possible.

Because of the different designs, materials employed, and sizes, it is impossible to give actual construction details. As a rule, however, the first step in constructing a storage wall is to build a frame that will extend from floor to ceiling and extend out from the wall the proper width. When the frame is put in, shelves are placed between the uprights where desired. As described on page 442, there are several ways these shelves may be fixed in place. Once your shelves are in place, the next step will be making doors to fit the openings you have chosen to close. Plywood, solid wood paneling, hardboard, particleboard, as well as other materials can be used

Figure 14–18. A unit of desk and shelves is an excellent room divider.

Figure 14—19. Built-ins make fine room dividers.

as the door materials. Generally the doors are made from the same material used as a facing for the storage wall.

Room dividers. While full wall-to-ceiling storage units can be used as room dividers, the present trend is toward semi-partitioning a room in order to give the illusion of space even though the room is divided.

When you design a room divider, there are few, if any, limitations as to height, width, or style. As has already been mentioned, the room divider may reach the ceiling and could be either a closed storage unit or shelves that have a plywood or hardboard backing in one room with exposed shelves facing into the other room. Or it may be open shelves which allow for viewing through either of

Figure 14—20. Two ways to divide a room.

Figure 14—21. Screens are excellent room dividers.

the two rooms, yet act as a separater between the two areas. A room divider can be just a full or partial screen or even a planter arrangement.

As with the design, the selection of materials that can be employed is almost limitless. Among those commonly used are: plywood, solid wood paneling, hardboard, perforated and filigree hardboard, wood spindles, dowels, perforated metal, glass beads, fine wire mesh, glass, plastic fiberglass, glass blocks—in fact, practically any standard building material. Actually, several companies offer room dividers and screens in kit form, complete with frames and material insets. They can be quickly assembled and finished as preferred. The room dividers come with tension spring plungers at the tops to provide sturdy floor-to-ceiling support.

To make screen room dividers such as those shown in Figure 14–21, cut the vertical frame parts to the proper height. Be sure to measure at the exact location to allow for an uneven floor or ceiling. For a permanent installation, the frame members can be attached to the floor and ceiling. But if you are planning to use spring plungers and floor glides, the frame will have to be shorter to compensate for these hardware pieces. (The exact amount is given in the manufacturer's instruction sheet.) Before raising the divider into position, fasten the hardboard in place and apply the desired finish to the grillwork panels and all frame pieces. Install the plungers and glides as directed by the manufacturer and lift the divider into place, with the spring plungers against the ceiling.

If a divider wider than the width of a single panel is desired, two or more of the panels may be joined by employing a divider molding, which is grooved on two edges. For making the frame and for the installation of the divider, follow the procedure described above.

Before you make any divider, consider all the possibilities and then use the one best suited for your needs. Several different possibilities have been illustrated here.

Chapter 15

ADDING A ROOM OR ROOMS

If you have space problems in your home, if you need more room where there is not any, you may consider obtaining this extra space by adding a new room, or rooms, to the outside of your home. Perhaps the attic has been done over to gain added space, and the basement has been converted into a playroom so that the old first-floor playroom could be made over into a bedroom. But still there is only so much space under a roof, and when that is being fully utilized, the only way to get more space is to build up or out.

Fortunately, almost any home built on an average-size plot of ground can accommodate at least one additional room. Except when the function of an addition, for example, a new or expanded kitchen, more or less dictates where it must be attached to the house, most additions permit a wide variety of location options—usually limited only to the actual design of your home.

PLANNING TO ADD A ROOM OR ROOMS

Once you have selected where the addition is to go, decide on how to make the most of the space available. For exterior additions of any size, an architect's help is indispensable. His technical knowledge and design expertise assure you of getting a sound addition that will harmonize perfectly with the rest of your home. In addition, he knows the local codes and zoning restrictions and will furnish you with a set of plans and specifications that are necessary to obtain a building permit. (More on the services and costs of architect can be found in Chapter 1.)

On smaller jobs, such as converting a garage to living space, or enclosing a porch or breezeway, you can usually handle the job of drawing up the plan to scale. These plans should be submitted to your local building department, and if they meet with the code regulations, you will be issued a building permit. But remember that building codes range from simple ones that set only minimum standards to highly detailed ones that even tell you how large the windows must be. If something in the code is not understood or appears to preclude an important part of your plan, talk it over with the building inspector, since variances are often possible if discussed beforehand.

There are several important details that must be considered before final plans for the addition are made. These include the heating problem, wiring installation, plumbing, and whether or not the wing is to have a basement under it.

Heating. Your heating plant is usually sufficiently large to handle the additional load of the addition (generally most good systems are designed to carry up to 50 percent additional load), but there is a chance that you may require increased heating facilities. This is not a matter ordinarily to be decided by a layman. Discuss it with a heating engineer or the local representative of the company that manufactured your heater. When a heating plant is selected for a house, its size is determined by the size and type of the building. It is often true that the plant will not be capable of adequately heating very much additional space. On the other hand, it may be large enough. A heating engineer, knowing the size of your house, the type of construction, and the amount of insulation, can soon tell you whether or not your heating plant is adequate for the proposed addition.

When a house was not originally insulated, the installation of insulation (pages 255 to 261) often reduces heat loss so much that the original heating unit will be able to take care of considerably more space. If your house is not insulated, you might consider the matter of insulation seriously. It may be that insulating it will enable you to heat a new

Figure 15–1. Adding space to a house can change its style.

wing without robbing the original part of the house and without major alteration of the heating plant.

If you decide that the original plant is not adequate, your solution may be to replace it with one having a greater capacity, or you may purchase an auxiliary heater for the additional room or rooms. Various types of auxiliary heaters are discussed on page 236. In any event, it should be remembered that overloading a heating plant because it is too small is wasteful of fuel and also has an element of danger. An overloaded heating plant may overheat and cause a fire.

Wiring installation. In your original plans, you will have marked out the locations of the various electrical outlets, switches, and fixtures that the new rooms require. Wiring of the new addition should present no special problems. Pages 161 to 163 describe the wiring of new houses. You may have a little difficulty in running the wiring cable from the new addition back to the fuse box or circuit breaker and meter. If you can bring the cables down in the wall to the basement and then run them to the fuse box or circuit breaker, you will probably have less trouble than if you attempt to take them through the attic of the house and then down a wall to the basement. You may find it necessary to install a new fuse box or circuit breaker to handle the additional circuits. It is generally unfeasible to connect the new load to a circuit already in use since overloading is apt to result. Pages 164 to 166 describe the procedures of running cables in a house already built.

Plumbing. You may not require any plumbing in the new addition; on the other hand you may decide to install a bathroom, kitchen, or laundry in it, and this would entail considerable plumbing. Here again, you may wish to do the work yourself, or you may call in plumbers to handle the job for you. Pages 195 to 212 discuss the various details of installing plumbing. It may be found possible to attach the new hot- and cold-water lines to nearby lines in the house, but you may be required to run these lines down into the basement and then across to the water meter or the hot-water heater. Similarly, sewage lines may have to be run a considerable distance before being connected to a main sewer.

Basement. You may decide to have a basement under the addition, or you may feel that this additional basement space is not needed. If you have a basement under the house and plan to have one under the wing, you will not be able to dispense with the foundation wall between the two unless you are prepared to install a series of heavy posts and girders of sufficient strength and size to support the house wall. You could, however, make a doorway between the two basements. Extra support may be required to span the gap where the foundation wall is removed for the doorway.

To keep problems to a minimum, check carefully the existing foundation where the room will be added and the area over which it will be built. Plan any wall openings to avoid the need for relocating major plumbing, such as a soil stack. When making plans, try, if possible, to locate all openings such as doors and windows in the new addition in the same spots where they were in the original plan. That is, turn a window into a doorway, for instance. This ready-made opening makes the task a great deal easier. Keep in mind that it is wise to work your expansion plans around a stairwell. If one exists, use it. If not, attempt to run new stairs along an existing wall.

After the plans have been completed and approved by the building department, figure the materials you need and their costs and what you will do or have done. But when ordering building materials, do not order them all at once because of the storage problems that may come up. It is better to order a little ahead, as you go, and make certain there is a place on the property to properly accommodate what you have received.

THE CONSTRUCTION JOB

There are so many different ways to build an addition onto a house, so many construction methods, and such a variety of designs, that it would be difficult indeed to anticipate all the problems that might arise during the course of construction. However, it might be helpful to consider the main components of the job in a general manner, along with some typ-

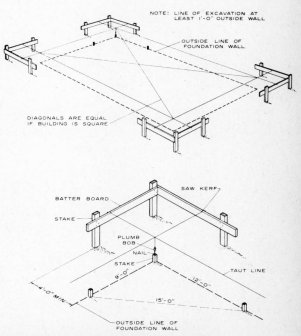

Figure 15—2. Staking and laying out an addition.

ical building procedures. We have discussed in earlier chapters the various trades that enter into the building of a house.

Start construction by laying out the perimeter of the addition as described on page 449. Be very careful with all measurements since a mistake can present serious problems later. Make certain where your sewer lines run. If they are under the addition, they will have to be replaced if they are not made of iron pipe. Also never build any portion of an addition over any part of a septic tank or disposal field or over a working well. This could result in serious problems at a later date, and most building codes restrict it.

Footings and foundation. If there is to be a basement, the first step is to excavate for it and prepare the excavations for the footings (page 32). Next, the footings should be poured, the foundation walls

built or poured, and the concrete floor poured (pages 33 to 35).

Special care should be used to secure a good joint where the new wall abuts against the old. If the walls are poured concrete, reinforcing rods may be set into the old walls and the new walls poured around them to bind the two walls together. With concrete blocks, it may be desirable to remove two or three from the old wall and set in new ones so that they are half in the old and half in the new wall. This ties the two walls together firmly. Reinforcing rods can also be used here. The outside of the joint should be carefully plastered and tarred (page 35) so that it is well sealed and will not allow water to seep through and into the basement.

If there is not to be a basement, the footings need not be set so deeply into the ground. The building code in force in your locality should give you information on how large and how deep they should be. Footings and foundation walls should be prepared as already described. Where there is to be no basement, the ground under the wing can be left undisturbed or paved with concrete. If left undisturbed, shields must be provided to prevent termites from entering the house (page 40). Also, ventilating grilles should be installed in the foundation walls to provide ventilation of the space between the ground and the floor. It is usually a good idea to leave an opening large enough to permit entry into the space under the floor for periodic inspection of the floor and foundations. This opening can be closed off with a door.

One construction method that has had some success has been to pave the ground and then use the space between the floor and the ground as a cold-air return duct for the heating plant. This requires effective sealing of the foundation walls to prevent escape of heat. The advantage claimed for this construction is that the air being returned under the floors to the heater warms the floors so they

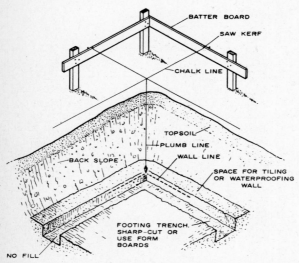
Figure 15-3. Establishing corners for excavation and footing.

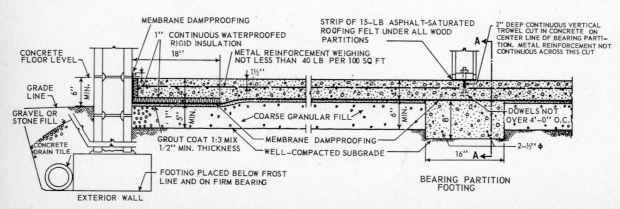
Figure 15-4. Details for slab-on-ground construction.

do not become chilly as they would with the type of construction discussed in the previous paragraph. Also, cold-air return ducts need not be installed, as with ordinary construction.

There is another construction procedure that might be used if the first floor of the wing is not too much above the ground level. By this method the footings, foundation walls, and sub-floor are all poured as a unit. First, a thick layer of gravel is laid, and in this gravel bed the cold-air return ducts are installed. These can be made of vitrified tile or chimney liners. The concrete is then poured on top of the gravel to form, in one solid mass, the footings, walls, and floor. On top of this concrete floor the inside and outside walls can be constructed, and a wood flooring laid. Other types of flooring material can be used (pages 115 to 134). The floor is kept warm, it is said, by the air returning to the heating unit from the house through the cold-air ducts under the floor.

It has been reported that this construction is being used without a wooden or any other type of top flooring. Carpets are placed directly on the concrete itself. If the concrete remains thoroughly dry and warm, this should occasion no difficulty.

Framing. As described in Chapter 2, a box sill goes on top of the foundation after it hardens; this usually takes about two or three days. Once the sills are in place, cut and install the joists. The size of the joists depends, of course, on the span between support points and usually is specified by the local building code. For instance, the typical code detailed here permits the use of 2×8 joists spaced 16 inches apart on centers for spans up to 11 feet 4 inches, 2×10 joists for spans up to 14 feet. The box sill material is, of course, the same size as the joists.

Table 15–1

Joist and rafter sizes	Maximum span, floors with 40 pounds per square foot load	Maximum span, roofs with 30 pounds per square foot load
2×4		7 feet (also may be used as ceiling joists, no load, up to 9 feet)
2×6	8 feet 6 inches	9 feet
2×8	11 feet 4 inches	12 feet
2×10	14 feet	15 feet
2×12	16 feet 6 inches	18 feet
2×14	19 feet 6 inches	21 feet

Note: This chart was taken from a typical building code, for usual framing lumber species used on single-pitch roofs and on floors, and was based on 16-inch joist spacing. Some codes permit 24-inch spacing.

Figure 15–5. Step-by-step procedure for roofing an addition.

The sub-floor may be either plywood or wood strips, and it should be installed as directed on page 42. Remember, when using plywood sub-flooring, the panel seams that run parallel to the joists must be located on the joists and nailed to them.

The next step is to lay out the wall framing flat on the sub-floor; then tilt it up and nail through the sub-floor into the box sill. Temporary diagonal braces may be nailed to the wall and sub-floor to hold up the wall until two wall frames join at the corner. Most wall frames are made up entirely of 2×4s, except for headers above windows and other openings. Lumber sizes for these openings are given on pages 45–46.

Different types of house wall construction are discussed on pages 43 to 51. Regardless of the type of construction and the materials used, the walls of a new addition should be tied in well with the original walls. This requires removal of the siding (on houses so constructed) and at least part of the sheathing from the original walls so the new one can be firmly attached and cross braced. Ordinarily, the outside wall of a house is framed with sufficient strength to carry the added load of the new wing roof and ceiling joists. It may be desirable, however, to install additional supporting members. If you employ a panel type, use its square corners to square up the framing when you nail on the first panel of each wall. All vertical seams should come along the centers of studs. The siding should match that on the rest of the house in most cases.

Roof rafters are usually about the same size as the floor joists, although the smaller sizes are frequently employed in areas where little or no snow load is encountered. The span of a rafter, however, is figured on the horizontal distance between supports, not along the slant of the rafter. They are usually spaced 16 inches on centers, but some codes permit 24-inch spacing if slightly heavier rafters are used.

The rafters are decked over with sheathing, and a finished roof of the same type and color as the remaining portion of the house is applied, as described on page 51. Be sure to use flashing between the old and new structures to keep the weather out.

Windows and doors should also be selected according to style. If windows are large, use double-glazed or insulated types to keep heat losses down. To save work and avoid fitting problems, it is a good idea to purchase pre-hung doors which come in a matching frame and with all hardware installed. They cost a little more but speed up the job.

The heating, any plumbing, and all electric wiring should be installed before the insulation is put up. The flooring, ceiling, and walls are then applied and the room is finished as desired. As the work progresses, remember to clean up as you go.

THE PORCH OR BREEZEWAY

Lounging, reading, or eating out-of-doors is fun on a porch or breezeway. Also a porch or breezeway can easily be turned into an extra year-round room.

Building a porch. While adding a porch increases the living space of your home, it also alters the outward appearance of your home. It can transform the dull, flat-wall look of a box-style house into an attractive, inviting home. Because the addition of a porch changes the character of the outside, it is necessary to plan it carefully.

There are three major phases in building a porch: laying a foundation, building supporting posts, and adding a roof. Presented here are procedures for building two major types of porches, with a concrete or wood floor; the sidewalls and wood posts; and two major types of roofs, the shed or lean-to and the flat roof or sun deck. Since the porch best suited for your home is almost certain to differ from those shown here, it is simply a matter of adapting standard construction techniques covered in detail in Chapter 2. One of the basic ways to build a porch or breezeway is as follows:

1. A concrete slab makes a fine, low-cost porch floor that is easy to care for (Figure 15–6). Lay out edges of slab with string lines; check squareness by measuring across the diagonals. The sides of the porch should line up with a stud on the house. Level the edge of the slab against the house 12 to $12\frac{1}{2}$ inches below the siding or top of the foundation wall. Slope the sides of the form down and away from the house for drainage, 2 inches for each 10 feet. Excavate 6 inches below the bottom edge of the form and fill with pit-run gravel or crushed rock. In areas where the ground freezes, reinforce the concrete with 6×6 welded steel mesh or $\frac{3}{8}$-inch reinforcing bars criss-crossed on 12-inch centers. Fill the form with concrete (1 part portland cement, 3

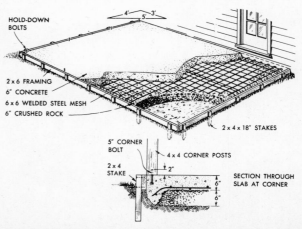

Figure 15–6. Details of a concrete porch slab.

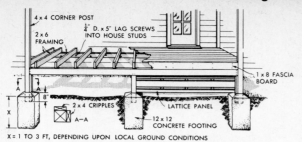

Figure 15—7. Details of a wood-floored porch.

footings away from the posts and caulk the joint between the post and concrete to keep out the water. On seams over 10 feet set the center post midway between the corners. As shown in Figure 15–7, the flooring is 1×4 tongue-and-groove fir or pine, end-matched. Around the sides and end, build hinged latticework panels to keep out debris and animals. Let the porch remain unpainted for one week after it is finished to allow the wood to dry. If any cracks develop between the flooring boards, fill them with lead paste or lead paint sediment and allow it to dry before paint is applied as directed in Chapter 9.

3. Sloping roof rafters (Figure 15–8) bear on the 2×6 beam lag-screwed to the house studs, as does the wood floor. Support the eave end of the rafters with the beam of double 2×4s on edge over 2×4 studs. If the area beyond the end of the eave is to be a clear span without studs, use doubled 2×6s or 2×8s for the beam to support the rafters. At the side of the house, lag-screw through the 2×4 and into the siding stud every 2 feet. Line up the edge of this 2×4 with the side of the floor and the corner post. If the exterior wall of the house is brick, fasten the 2×4 with lag screws in lead sleeves. Drill the holes for the sleeves into the brick wall with a

parts sand, 4 parts gravel, and minimum water) and strike off level with a straight-edged 2×4 across the top of the form. As soon as the concrete begins to set, finish the surface with a wood float first, then a steel trowel. Work from the plank-bridge across the floor area. Use an edger around the sides and a groover to make a rectangular pattern if desired.

2. Wood flooring over joists may be necessary to meet the high level of the house floor. Fasten a 2×6 over the siding with lag screws into the studs to support the ends of the joists. Set the corner posts into the concrete footings. Slope the top of the

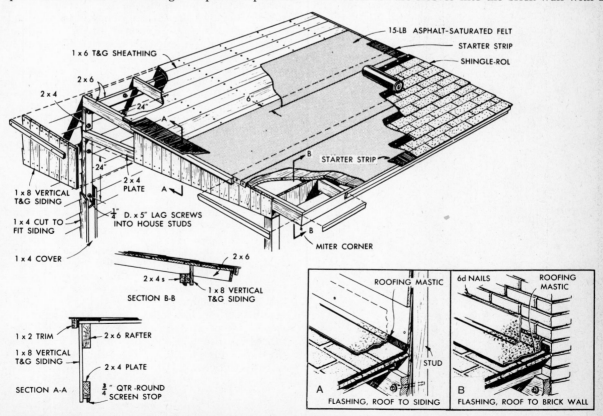

Figure 15—8. Details of shingle construction for a porch roof.

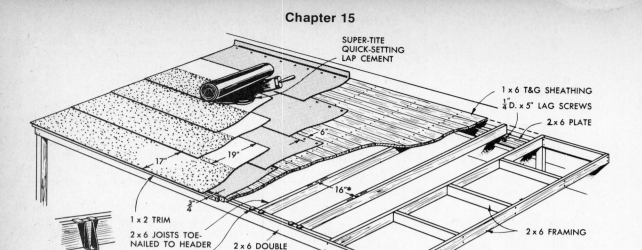

SUPER-TITE
QUICK-SETTING
LAP CEMENT

1 x 6 T&G SHEATHING
¼" D. x 5" LAG SCREWS

2 x 6 PLATE

6"

17"   19"

16"*

¾"

1 x 2 TRIM

2 x 6 JOISTS TOE-
NAILED TO HEADER

METAL HANGERS

2 x 6 DOUBLE
HEADER

4 x 4 CORNER POST

2 x 6 FRAMING

*JOIST SPACING MAY VARY FROM
16" O.C. TO 24" O.C.

Figure 15—9. Details of roll roofing construction.

masonry bit and portable electric drill. Vertical tongue-and-groove siding covers the area between the rafters and side beams and across the end. Cover the roof with 15-pound roofing felt turned over at the edges and covered with a 1 × 2 trim strip. Space ¾-inch footing nails 6 inches apart.

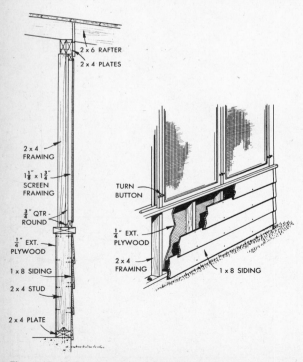

2 x 6 RAFTER
2 x 4 PLATES

2 x 4
FRAMING

1⅛" x 1¾"
SCREEN
FRAMING

¾" QTR-
ROUND

¼" EXT.
PLYWOOD

1 x 8 SIDING

2 x 4 STUD

2 x 4 PLATE

TURN
BUTTON

¼" EXT.
PLYWOOD

2 x 4
FRAMING

1 x 8 SIDING

Figure 15—10. Details of the outside wall of a porch.

Apply the roof by first nailing a 9-inch starter strip along the eave and sides. Brush adhesive cement on the starter strip and apply the first course of shingle roll roofing, overlapping the eave and trim strips at the sides ½ inch all around. Nail through the top selvage. Apply succeeding courses by cementing the lower edge and nailing the top selvage. For flashing, use copper, aluminum, or galvanized steel slipped under the siding (A), or bent into routed-out brick joint (B). Nails through the bent-over flange hold the flashing in the joint. Fill the joint with asphalt mastic. Counterflash the brick walls.

4. Flat roof framing (Figure 15–9) is similar to sloping roof framing, except that here the rafters rest in the metal hangers from a header and 1 × 6 fascia trims both the sides and the end. For the built-up roof, use 30-pound roofing felt overlapped 6 inches and nailed down with ¾-inch galvanized roofing nails spaced 6 inches apart. Mop the surface with a quick-setting lap cement, brush grade. Immediately apply a cover layer of selvage-edge roll roofing with a 19-inch granular surface edge. Apply the first course with the edge of the granular surface ¾ inch over the eave. Press this layer together with underlying felt. Mop the selvage with more quick-setting lap cement and apply the second course, leaving 17 inches of granular surface roll to weather; the edge of the second course laps 2 inches over the granular surface of the first course. Press the courses together to set the cement. Continue with the courses, turning up about 4 inches of the last sheet under the flashing at the house.

5. Walls can be built around the porch base to accommodate stock-size screens in the summer and storm sash in winter. The stub wall also protects

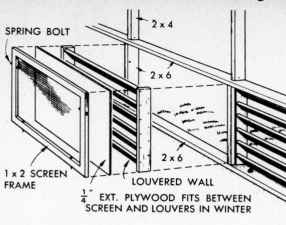

SPRING BOLT

2 x 4

2 x 6

2 x 6

1 x 2 SCREEN FRAME

LOUVERED WALL

¼" EXT. PLYWOOD FITS BETWEEN SCREEN AND LOUVERS IN WINTER

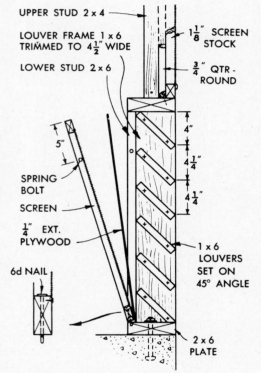

UPPER STUD 2 x 4

LOUVER FRAME 1 x 6 TRIMMED TO 4½" WIDE

LOWER STUD 2 x 6

1⅛" SCREEN STOCK

¾" QTR-ROUND

5"

SPRING BOLT

SCREEN

¼" EXT. PLYWOOD

6d NAIL

4"

4¼"

4¼"

1 x 6 LOUVERS SET ON 45° ANGLE

2 x 6 PLATE

Figure 15–11. Details of louver construction.

the screening from damage. Build the wall up high enough to accommodate stock-size screens and sash ordered from your local dealer. Cover the outside with bevel siding, the inside with exterior-grade plywood (Figure 15–10). Screens and storm sashes slip up under the vertical siding at the top and are held in against the quarter-round mold with turn-buttons. The screens and 2 × 4 studs are flush on the outside.

6. Louvers can be built in the stub walls (Fig-

ure 15–11). Fit the screen frame inside with two nails in loose-holes at the bottom, using one spring bolt at each side. To close the porch for winter, simply slip ¼-inch exterior-grade plywood panels between the louvers and the screen frame.

7. Full-length screen wire that is permanently attached should be copper, bronze, plastic, or aluminum, since it will be exposed to the weather all year round. Keep the studs 3½ or 4 feet apart on centers to match the width of the screen wire (Figure 15–12). One way to stretch the wire tightly is to align the edges along the centerline of the studs and tack the top edge. Temporarily tack the bottom edge to the 1 × 2 below the final line of the bottom of the screen. Cut off the temporary cleat, tack the sides, and cover the edges with half-round molding mitered at the corners.

8. Combination screen and storm doors quickly enclose a porch (Figure 15–13). Inserts in the doors allow you to change from screens to storm sashes. However, the wide stiles of the door decrease the screen or glass area. The clear opening between the floor and beam in such an arrangement should be 6 feet 8 inches to match the standard door height. Both combination doors and screen frames can be installed without a base plate or stud. Nail the doors or screen frames together with a t-astragal strip if they will be left in place (B), or join them

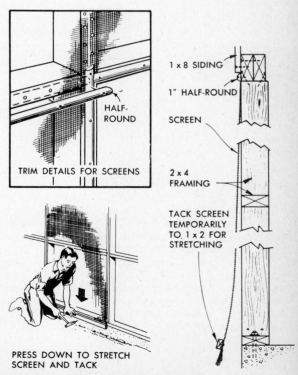

TRIM DETAILS FOR SCREENS

HALF-ROUND

1 x 8 SIDING

1" HALF-ROUND

SCREEN

2 x 4 FRAMING

TACK SCREEN TEMPORARILY TO 1 x 2 FOR STRETCHING

PRESS DOWN TO STRETCH SCREEN AND TACK

Figure 15–12. Details of screen construction.

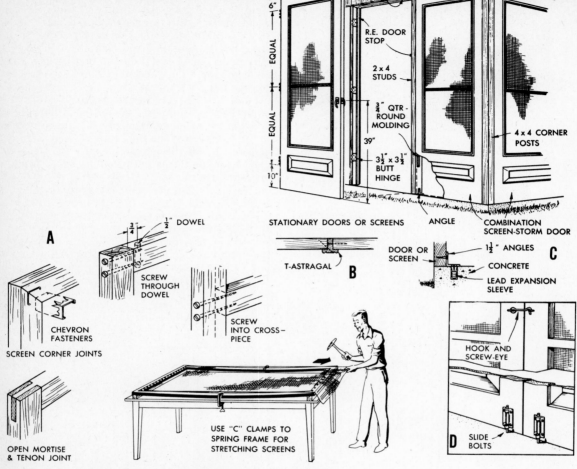

Figure 15–13. Construction details for combination screen and storm doors.

with hooks and screw-eyes if you plan to remove them seasonally (D). Along the bottom, use 1½- by 1½-inch corner irons screwed to door rail and floor (C). In concrete, drill ⅜ inch for a lead sleeve insert to fit a No. 8 × ¾-inch flathead screw. For removable doors or screens, drill a hole in the floor and install a slide bolt on the bottom rail (D).

Screens are not very often available in stock heights up to 6 feet 8 inches or 7 feet, but your lumber dealer can custom-make them to fit your porch, or you can make your own from 1⅛- by 1¾-inch clear pine screen stock.

Enclosing a porch. A porch is fun in warm weather, but useless for living during most of the cold season. For year-round enjoyment, why not enclose your porch?

If you now have a porch, you already have a floor, roof support columns, and an entry to the house. To convert it into a twelve-month room, you need exterior window-walls, insulation-finished interior walls and ceiling, a finished floor, an electrical system, and a heating supply.

The basic carpentry involved is in installing framing to replace the framing holding the screens, in order to accommodate window frames. The framing is not special, just standard window framing (see page 45). Therefore, whether you have a porch with one open side, or two or three, it should be no problem. Actually, at this stage, it is important that your thoughts on windows be set into a plan. Although there is a great heat loss (less insulated glass is used) from the use of multiple windows, many homeowners who convert a porch into an extra room wish to retain the cool porch comfort of

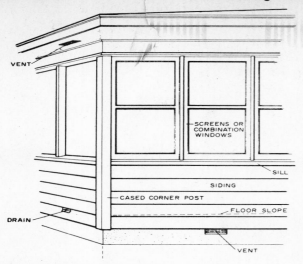

Figure 15–14. An enclosed porch.

summer by an almost continuous framing of windows.

When studs and window frames are completed, you are ready for interior and exterior insulation. Because your converted-porch room usually has no basement, a greater-than-usual window area, and auxiliary heating methods rather than an attachment to the basic home heating, an extra emphasis on insulation is advisable. The money you spend on converting the porch will return poor value if you are not able to use the room year round. Exterior insulation sheathing, insulation batts between studs, and the use of interior finish wallboard with added insulation value are all recommended.

To complete the job, install easy-care resilient floor tiles or indoor-outdoor carpeting over a concrete floor, or, if the porch has a wood deck, install the tile or carpeting over an underlayment. When installing the electric wiring, provide convenient outside lighting, too (see page 173). If extending your heating system is not feasible, consider electric baseboard heating, a wood-burning fireplace, or a space heater.

Enclosing a breezeway. A breezeway between the house and the garage is one of the most useful, convenient, and economical improvements you can make. And by enclosing it, at very little extra cost, you greatly increase its usefulness. Most breezeways already have two walls, formed by the side of the garage and the side of the house, in addition to the floor and roof. In warm weather, cooling breezes are channeled effectively through this area. In inclement weather, a breezeway provides access to the garage or yard. In winter's cold, it is almost useless. But when enclosing your breezeway for full year-round use, remember to still retain the advantage of

cooling summer breezes. Be certain to plan adequate windows in the two new walls that must be built to complete the new enclosure (awning, hopper, or jalousie-type windows are probably best). For really low-maintenance yet good-looking walls, panel the interior with one of today's elegant but budget-priced prefinished panelings. If the walls formed by the house and the garage are shingled, remove the shingles first before installing furring and prefinished panels.

The actual construction techniques and finishing considerations are the same as those for "Enclosing a porch," on page 456.

THE GARAGE

The garage can be more than just a place to put the car. It can be expanded to serve many other useful purposes.

Converting a garage to extra living space. If you need extra living space, your attached garage may

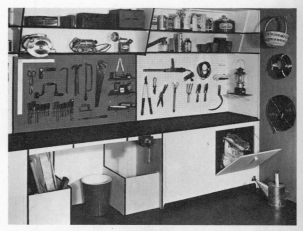

Figure 15–15. Making the most of a garage: *(top)* a workbench – storage area; *(bottom)* a living area.

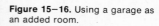
Figure 15–16. Using a garage as an added room.

solve the problem. Actually, there are several advantages for such a conversion. First and most important is the saving that is realized because foundation, walls, and roof are already in existence. This can amount to up to a 50 percent saving in cost where a room would otherwise have to be added by attaching a new extension to the exterior of the house. Another point in its favor is that the room is protected from the elements, and therefore work can be done at your leisure in all kinds of weather. The work can also proceed with the least amount of inconvenience to your family.

The converted room can be utilized as a den, bedroom, family room, or even kitchen if desired. Because a powder room is easily installed, your garage can become an attractive studio apartment. But, preliminary planning is most important in converting a garage into a living space. Take time to orient the new room to the rest of the house and the outdoors so it will best serve its intended purpose. Ask the following questions:

1. How can the extra space fit into what will actually be a larger house than you now have?

2. Where should the room be entered? Should it be a dead end in the house traffic pattern, or will the room's function be such that through traffic will not disturb activities within the room?

3. Are present windows adequate, or should they be enlarged to provide a better view window and to admit more light?

4. Should the garage door be replaced with a bank of windows, view window, floor-to-ceiling glass, or sliding doors?

5. Should there be an outside entrance?

6. Where will you need electrical outlets for reading, TV, projector, etc.?

7. How many and what kind of built-in storage units do you want?

A typical garage conversion addition is shown in Figure 15–16. Most of the work involved is described in Chapters 3 and 8. But, remember that when filling in the garage door space, it is a good idea to plan to have a picture window area or a window and door combination since much work is already done because of the header spanning the existing opening. Rough framing consists of a 2×4 sill or sole plate (a sill rests directly on the foundation; a sole plate on the floor or sub-floor), cripple studs, window sill, and furring. If the header is too high, as with an 8-foot-high garage door, either fur down from it or install a false header below it.

When all the openings in your former garage space have been relocated and rough-framed where you want them in the new room or rooms, you must prepare the sub-flooring, add to heating and wiring, locate plumbing and fixtures (if a bathroom is in your conversion plans), install new windows and a door, insulate the walls and ceiling, panel the walls and apply ceiling material, and put down the finish floor. Details on how to do these various jobs are given in the earlier chapters of this book.

Before finishing the exterior of your new addition, break up and remove the concrete apron or sloped slab at the garage door. Use a cold chisel and heavy hammer to score the concrete in sections small enough to lift and cart away. Break the slab at score marks with a heavier sledge. The job is made easier if you dig under the slab. A carport arrangement may be designed to use the old driveway. The exterior should be finished to match the house.

Chapter 16

HOME IMPROVEMENT AND OUTDOOR LIVING

Home improvement does not stop with the house structure itself. Today, outdoor living is part of modern living, and thus must be considered in any home improvement plans. As with all home improvement work, planning should precede any actual construction. Make an overall plan or sketch of your available outdoor area. You may not be able to do the entire job at once, but make those improvements first that you need the most. A patio is a natural place to start. It can be connected to the house or built as a special area in the lawn.

THE PATIO

A patio adds a great deal to a home. It not only is a place to relax in comfort, but it also improves the property in value and in appearance.

Where you locate the patio will depend on the style of your home, the lot size, and access from the house. Consider also such factors as privacy from the street and neighbors, noise, shade from any existing trees, and how the patio will fit in with your garden plan. Location A (see Figure 16–1), near the front of the lot, increases the width of the house and is handy to the house, but it needs a wide lot for adequate space. Traffic noise from the street or a house nearby may be undesirable. Location B is readily accessible from the garage or carport, and a patio in back of the house is close to the kitchen or dining room for outdoor entertaining. The house itself blocks off the street noises. Outdoor cooking may be a problem at location B if prevailing winds blow from the direction of the house. Location C, at the back of the lot, needs a high fence along the back to provide privacy. A drying yard or vegetable plot blocked off with another fence isolates the patio

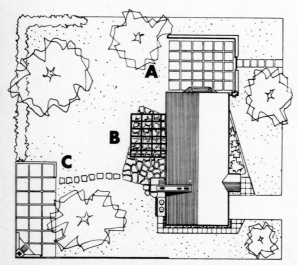

Figure 16–1. Possible sites for a patio or terrace.

from neighbors at one side. An outdoor barbecue in a corner is ideal if prevailing winds blow across the patio. One disadvantage with the location at the back of a lot is the distance dishes and prepared foods must be carried. A sink near the cooking oven is a desirable convenience. With some house designs, it is possible to fit the patio in the pocket of U-shaped or L-shaped homes.

How big a patio you need depends upon you. The patio's primary function will largely determine the size. Activities should also be considered in deciding on the amount of space needed for equipment. Equipment and furnishings normally used on patios include picnic tables and benches, lounge chairs, serving carts, game apparatus, and barbecue pits. The placement of these items and the storage of games, apparatus, and fixtures should determine the size of the patio.

Patios vary more in length than in width since they may extend over the entire length of the house. A patio 12 by 12 feet is considered a minimum-size patio. Patios with dimensions of 20 by 30 feet or more are not uncommon, but are certainly considered large. Make certain, when planning your patio, to check with the local building department to see whether a building permit is necessary to construct a patio. Even if there is no need for a permit, as such, there may be regulations regarding closeness to lot lines, fences, and the like.

Another important consideration is the selection of the patio paving. When doing this, consider: (1) appearance—its color and texture; (2) cost—local materials usually cost least; (3) maintenance—choose a paving for easy upkeep; and (4) application—paving that is easy to apply yourself is usually best. Let us take a look at some of the more popular pavings.

Concrete. For permanent, rugged construction, concrete remains the overwhelming patio favorite. It is easy to pour and can be put down in small sections. It can be colored in many shades and can be finished from a smooth to a pebbly surface depending upon the mix. However, concrete is subject to cracks and sometimes it is difficult to color evenly. But most disadvantages can be overcome easily.

Subgrade preparation and grading. Remove the soil to a depth of about 4 inches below the desired surface elevation and smooth out the area to the approximate grade. The slab should drain quickly after a rain or washing, so it should be built with a slight slope (1/8 inch per foot) away from the house. Avoid low spots or pockets. Remove all black dirt, vegetation, wood, bricks, and large rocks from the soil and level off and compact the loose soil with a tamper or heavy roller. If the soil is clay, the subgrade should be soaked several days before concrete is placed on it.

Forming. Adopt a plan of your choice for the design of your patio. It can be laid out in squares,

Home Improvement and Outdoor Living

Figure 16—2. Concrete is a popular patio flooring material.

diamonds, rectangles, circles or any other design, as determined by your imagination and personal taste. Use 2- by 4-inch boards for side forms, securely nailed to 1- by 2-inch or 2- by 2-inch stakes driven firmly into the ground. The stakes should be no more than 4 feet apart and are needed at every joint in the form lumber. A 1- by 4-inch stake can be used to lap the joints in the 2 × 4s to help hold both ends in alignment. For flat, horizontal curves, use ¼- by 4-inch plywood strips. Cut the strips so that the exterior grain will be vertical when they are in place. Stakes will be needed closer together on curves to hold the forms at the proper grade and curvature.

When the forms are set, smooth the subgrade to accommodate the desired thickness of slab. Pull a template, riding on top of the forms, across the subgrade to get a smooth, uniform depth.

To determine the amount of concrete needed for your patio, use the formula given on page 27.

Figure 16—3. Building a concrete patio: (A) Remove the soil to a depth of about 4 inches. (B) Build the forms in the desired size. (C) Put a thin layer of sand at the bottom of the form. (D) Place concrete in the form and strike it off as described in Chapter 2. (E, F) Give the concrete a float or broom finish.

Figure 16—4. Concrete patio blocks are attractive.

Also given in Chapter 2 are the full instructions for placing the concrete in the forms, and finishing it off, and the method for curing the concrete.

Pre-cast patio stones or slabs. Concrete pre-cast slabs units available from local product plants or dealers make ideal units for building walks and patios. The design, pattern, arrangement, and colors are unlimited, and the ultimate beauty of the fin-ished area is as varied as the individual taste. The following are tips on the construction of walks and patios:

Prepare the area. All soil, sod, and debris must be removed to a depth about twice the thickness of the stone. Where there are soft, spongy areas, remove the soil and replace it with 4 to 6 inches of gravel fill, well tamped.

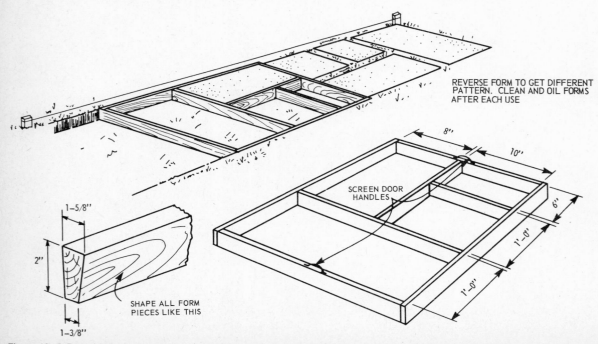

Figure 16—5. Reusable forms for making concrete patio blocks or flagstones. Dividers are leveled for easy removal.

Figure 16—6. Bricks *(left)* and flagstone *(right)* are popular patio paving materials.

Place sand bed. After cleaning the walkway or patio area, place a 2-inch sand bed on it. Wet the sand and tamp it thoroughly in place. Level the sand bed using a 2- by 4-inch straightedge.

Place concrete patio units. Lay the patio units flat in the pattern desired. Leave a ¼- or ½-inch space between the units, which will later be filled with sand. Edge or trim blocks or pre-cast concrete strips may be used to hold the patio in place. Red-wood divider strips may be placed to divide a patio into larger eye-catching units.

Patio units can be pre-cast in forms built to your particular pattern. Such a job can be done at your leisure, and the finished product stacked until you are ready to install it. Or the forms may be put in an area where the sod has been removed to the proper depth, and the concrete patio units can be cast in place. Pre-cast patio units are usually 2 inches thick, an economical size that is easy to handle.

Place concrete of proper mix in forms using the proportion of 1 part cement : 2 parts sand : 2¼ parts water. Level with a straightedge, then wood-float, leaving a textured surface. Fill in the strips between the cast stones with strips of sod.

For quantities, the form illustrated in Figure 16—5 is most successful. Reverse the form when repeating the pattern to get varied effects. Colors and patterns may be varied to suit individual taste by following the suggestions in the section on concrete patterns. For attractive patterns, redwood divider strips may be inserted.

Brick and flagstone. Many kinds of bricks and tiles may be used in the construction of a patio. A good grade of No. 1 hard-burned common bricks or specially burned patio tiles can be used in either simple or elaborate patterns. Flagstone and slate are

available in different colors; the price varies with thickness. Flagstone is the most expensive of all patio materials; colored slate, which is cheaper, is often used instead. It tends to scratch, and dirt gets imbedded in the grooves, but if it is fixed in a bed of concrete, most difficulties can be solved. The basic techniques of constructing a brick and a flagstone (or slate) patio are very similar.

There are two ways of paving a patio: it can be laid either on a sand base with sand-filled joints or on a concrete base with sand or mortar joints. The sand-base method is easier and requires a minimum of experience and equipment. A patio can be laid level on the site or slightly elevated. When a patio is constructed on a slight elevation, a retaining wall consisting of three built-up sides must be constructed. The construction of a low wall of this type, consisting of approximately five or six tiers of bricks, is similar to that described in Chapter 2. The entire area inside the brick enclosure must, of course, be filled with earth before any of the terrace tiles or bricks are laid.

Whether the patio is to be built at ground level or on a built-up elevation, excavate the soil to a depth of about 3½ inches below the surface. With a spirit level, make sure that the ground is fairly even. However, a slight slope away from the house should be made to allow for adequate drainage. If there is unevenness in spots, fill them with fresh earth and tamp these spots smooth before attempting to lay any bricks or tiles.

If the patio is to be laid on a portion of the lawn which is already established, make the excavation the exact width of the finished patio (Figure 16—7). If it is to be laid on newly graded earth that has not yet been seeded, make the excavation approximate-

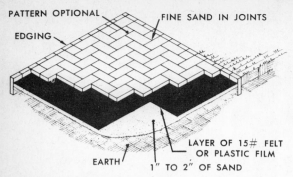

Figure 16–7. Bricks on a sand base.

shovel, sweeping it into the open joints. Tap it firmly with the edge of a thin board and sweep up the surplus so that all the joints are uniformly filled. Water is then applied with the garden hose. Use a spray nozzle and regulate the flow so that it barely trickles with a weak stream. Play this over each brick, washing it clean and settling the joints at the same time. Spray water over the complete area at frequent intervals for a few days to insure penetration and to aid curing. Brushing the bricks with a small brush while applying the spray is helpful in getting a clean-looking job.

Where a more rigid or permanent surface is required, use a 3-inch base of concrete. This con-

ly 1 inch wider all around. Place 1-inch boards on edge along all sides as a guide for leveling and to hold the bricks in place until the new lawn is well sodded. The boards can then be removed and the spaces filled with sand or dirt.

Cover the bottom of the excavation with 1½ inches of sand carefully leveled to form a smooth, even surface. Lay the bricks flat on the sand in the desired pattern and as close together as possible, keeping the courses straight. As soon as all the bricks or tiles are laid, fill the spaces between them by spreading sand on top and sweeping it into all the joints. Spray the entire surface with water to pack the sand firmly and completely fill all the joints.

Another method is to lay the bricks on a cushion of sand (Figure 16–8) with open joints (½-inch space between bricks) in the desired patterns. After the bricks are in place, mix 2 parts of sand to 1 part of cement, and throw this dry mixture on with a

Figure 16–9. Cutting and laying flagstones in patio construction.

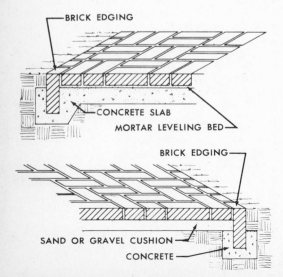

Figure 16–8. Brick patio designs on a concrete base.

crete base can be of a mixture of 1 part cement, 2¾ parts sand, and 4 parts water. Spread the concrete mixture over the area and lay the bricks in the manner described above. The joints may be filled with sand and cement, but a grout fill is preferable for a terrace constructed in this way. A grout fill is made with a ready-mixed cement mortar or may be mixed of 1 part cement to 3 parts of sand.

Mix the mortar with water to the consistency of light cream and pour the fill into the joints until they are completely filled. To avoid mortar stains, brush the brick or tile surface with raw linseed oil before grouting and smooth the fill flush with the surface of the brick. Spray the patio with water twice daily after the grout has set, for two or three days, before using. The mortar or cement stains can then be easily washed off the surface. Flagstones can be laid in the same manner, except that they should be set in with wider mortar joints to give added texture and a more varied pattern to your patio.

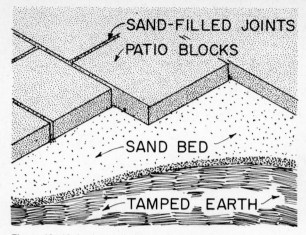

Figure 16—10. Laying patio blocks on sand.

WOOD DECKS

A wood deck is simply a handsome platform or patio, on or above the ground, that can add much to the livability, beauty, and value of a house.

A well-designed wood deck can turn a hilly site into a useful, enjoyable outdoor living area at a fraction of the cost of adding an inside room. And, there is no substitute for the style of living it can provide as an area for sunbathing, entertaining, dining, conversation, container gardening, children's play, and parties. As an aesthetic feature, good wood deck design eases the transition from house to garden and is a part of each. Where the land slopes upward from the house, the deck bridges the space with a usable level floor. Where the land slopes down and away, the deck extends the floor level of the building out into otherwise wasted space. Even on land that is generally flat, the deck can be a floor-level area gently leading to the garden a step or two below.

Redwood is a favorite decking material because of its durability and beauty. Of course, woods other than redwood may be used in deck construction, but they must be treated with pentachlorophenol solution and painted or stained; special care must be taken to treat areas that will be inaccessible after construction.

Structural elements of the deck. The deck structure gathers the weight and load of the deck and transmits it downward to the ground. The top layer is the decking itself, often decorative in pattern, but always designed to support a stated load with a minimum of deflection. The decking rests on joists, which are the primary structural element of the floor. The joists rest upon beams, which gather the load and transmit it to posts or other vertical supports. The posts rest on footings, which bear the

Table 16—1. Typical decking spans* (nonstress-graded redwood lumber with live load of 40 pounds per square foot)

Size	Grade	Span (inches)
1 × 4	Clear all heart	16
2 × 4	Clear all heart, select and construction heart	24
2 × 6	Clear all heart, select and construction heart	32

*The span of the decking depends on the design of the deck and the various loads that will be applied. Under normal conditions the spans shown are adequate.

Table 16—2. Typical beam (lintel) spans* (nonstress-graded redwood lumber with live load of 40 pounds per square foot and dead load of 10 pounds per square foot)

Beam size	Grade	Width of deck			
		6 feet	8 feet	10 feet	12 feet
4 × 6	Clear	Span 8 feet 6 inches	Span 7 feet 6 inches	Span 7 feet	Span 6 feet 6 inches
	Construction heart	5 feet 6 inches	5 feet	4 feet 6 inches	4 feet
4 × 8	Clear	11 feet 6 inches	10 feet 6 inches	9 feet 6 inches	9 feet
		7 feet 6 inches	6 feet 6 inches	6 feet	5 feet 6 inches
4 × 10	Clear	14 feet 6 inches	13 feet	12 feet	11 feet
	Construction heart	10 feet	9 feet	9 feet	7 feet

*Allowable spans for nonstress-graded redwood used in a single span. Abnormal loading such as planter boxes and heavy barbecue grills will require shorter spans or longer beams. Deflection limited to L/360.

Table 16–3. *Typical joist spans (nonstress-graded redwood lumber with live load of 40 pounds per square foot)**

Joist size		Clear all heart and A	Select heart and select	Construction heart and construction
2 × 6	16 inches o.c.	10 feet 6 inches	10 feet	8 feet
	24 inches o.c.	9 feet	8 feet	7 feet
	32 inches o.c.	8 feet	7 feet	6 feet
2 × 8	16 inches o.c.	14 feet	14 feet	12 feet 6 inches
	24 inches o.c.	12 feet 6 inches	12 feet	10 feet
	32 inches o.c.	11 feet	10 feet 6 inches	9 feet
2 × 10	16 inches o.c.	18 feet	18 feet	16 feet
	24 inches o.c.	15 feet 6 inches	15 feet 6 inches	13 feet
	32 inches o.c.	14 feet	13 feet	11 feet

NOTE: o.c. means "on center."

*The joist span and spacing depend upon the design of the deck and the loads that will be applied. This table lists some suggested spans and spacing of various sizes and grades of redwood. They are suitable only for normal use; for unusual loads, such as planter boxes and grilles, the span should be smaller or the joist larger with a narrower spacing. Deflection limited to L/240.

concentrated load of the deck and structure. In extremely low-level decks the beams may rest directly on footings.

Decking. The deck surface is the most visible part of the entire deck structure, and its size, grade, and placement determine the arrangement and size of the framing.

Two-inch nominal redwood is recommended for most decking situations. The most common sizes are 2 × 4s and 2 × 6s, although wider pieces are sometimes used for special effects. Nominal 1-inch-thick material may be used where joists are placed within 16 inches on center. Where a pattern of narrow lines is desired, 2 × 4 material may be used on

Figure 16–11. Suggestions for wood decks.

edge, with longer spans than are possible when the decking is laid flat. The decking spans possible with the common sizes and yard grades of redwood are given in the Table 16–1. In general, use the finish grades for decking and the more economical construction grades for framing.

The general approach in laying out the deck is to decide on the pattern and size of the decking first. Choose the grade of decking desired, then determine the spacing for joists.

Joists. The joists (usually 2-inch dimension lumber) bear the load of the decking and whatever loads are placed upon the deck. The joist span is determined by the joist spacing and the grade of lumber. Typical joist spans for redwood yard grades are given in Table 16–3.

The joists usually rest upon the beam or header and are anchored to it. If the joist must not rise higher than the beam, it may be hung from the beam by a patented joist hanger or be fastened to the beam with a ledger strip under the joist. The joist can overhang slightly beyond the beam for appearance or added space if desired. Overhang depends upon the depth of the joist, but in no case should it exceed one-quarter of the length. Check local building codes to ascertain whether cross-bracing or lateral bracing for joists is required.

Beams. Beams rest upon the posts and support the joists. The size of the beam required depends upon the spacing and span of the beams. However, a general rule is to utilize as large a beam as necessary in order to minimize the number of posts and footings. Beams of 4-inch thickness and greater are often used, and since these thicker members are not always readily available, it is sometimes necessary to construct a "built-up beam" from thinner members by fastening them together with bolts or lag screws.

The beam can be fastened to the tops of posts by a metal post connector or by a wooden cleat bolted or nailed to the post and beam. When the post must extend above the deck level to support a railing, seat, or overhead shelter, the joists may be supported on paired members bolted to the posts. When the beam rests directly on footings, it should be anchored to the footings to prevent the tipping of the beam. This can be achieved by the use of nailing blocks or anchor bolts in the footings.

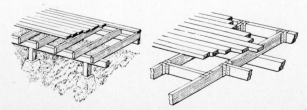

Figure 16–12. Deck beam arrangements.

Where the length of the deck requires splicing the beam, make a butt joint over the post and tie two beams together with cleats on each side. Where doubled 2 × 4s are being used, never splice both at the same place, but try to splice each over posts.

Ledgers. Where one side of the deck meets a house or other buildings, joists can be supported by a ledger attached to the house. Usually a 2-inch-thick ledger is sufficient. But, better bearing and easier toe-nailing are obtained if a thicker ledger is used (Figure 16–13). To prevent a rain or snow from wetting interior floors, the ledger should be located so that the surface of the deck is at least 1 inch below the floor surface of the house.

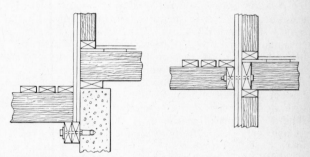

Figure 16–13. Fastening ledgers.

Posts. The posts bear the weight of the deck, transmitting it through the footings to the ground. For most low decks, the 4 × 4 is an adequate post. For steep sites or for heavy loads, such as a large group of people, snow, or heavy plant containers, larger posts will be required to bear the weight. (Consult local building codes for wooden member sizes required.) While supporting the deck, the post can continue upward to support railing, seat, and overhead structure.

Where the beam bears upon the top of the post, the length of the post must be carefully measured and the end precisely trimmed to insure a good seat for the beam. Accurate measurement may be achieved by careful leveling from a reference elevation either to the post held in a standing position or to a 1 × 2 "story pole" held in place of the post. Mark the level position, adjust for the slope of the deck, if any, and trim carefully. The post should be plumb when measured and when installed.

Cross-bracing may be necessary to prevent lateral movement of the deck, particularly if it is elevated high above the ground. Good connections between post and beam will help brace the deck structure, but diagonal bracing across corners or across the understructure may be the only way to achieve the stability required by local building regulations.

Footings. The footing anchors the entire structure to the ground and also transmits the weight of the deck to the ground. Building codes are usually very specific on the subject of footings. Generally they must extend to undisturbed soil or rock, and in cold climates they usually must extend below the frost line. In low-level decks, concrete blocks or pre-cast footings may be used if they are set firmly in the soil. If concrete footings are site-poured, metal post anchors or steel straps may be set in the wet concrete. Drift pins offer a concealed method of connecting the post to the footing when the underside of the deck is to be in open view. While anchors of metal are the most rigid and are recommended for high decks, wood nailing blocks imbedded in concrete usually are adequate for low decks.

Placement of footings. The location and placement of footings are determined by the design of the deck's structural members so that weight is properly transmitted to the ground. Placement points can be ascertained with a tape measure, a string, or a long, straight 2 × 4, and a wooden peg.

If the deck is to extend from a corner of the house, it is a simple matter of projecting a straight line from the non-deck side of the house out to where one corner of the deck will extend. Then measure and mark the points within the line where footings will be desired.

With this right angle (consisting of the line and the deck side of the house) established, two corners of the deck are determined. The length of the deck is then measured along the wall from the corner of the house. With a third corner thus established, the location of the other corner footing can easily be determined with a tape measurement from these other established points.

Accuracy of the four points can be proved by diagonal measurements between the farthest corners. If these diagonal distances are not identical, the deck will not be square. This could be the fault of either a non-square house or an inaccurate measurement. If it is the former, the deck can be designed to match the house.

The following is another method for ascertaining the placement of footings: If the deck is to project from a wall where a corner line projection is not convenient, a right-angle projection can be made by creating a mathematical right-angled trian-

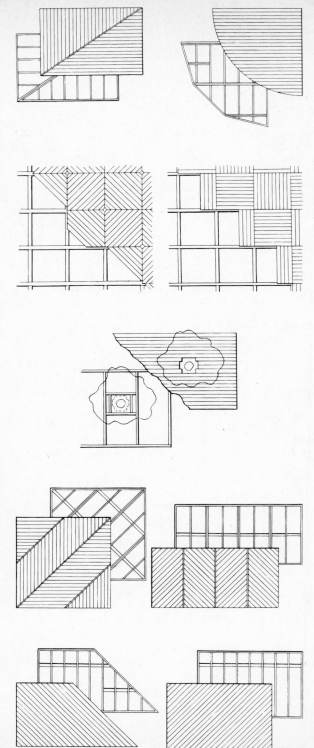

Figure 16–15. Deck patterns.

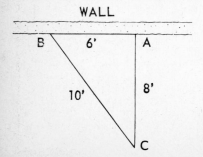

Figure 16–14. Right-angle triangle method of starting a deck layout.

gle of 6 by 8 by 10 feet or proportionally larger. This is done by marking a point (A) on the house wall, which designates one end of the deck.

Measure 6 feet from point A one way or another on the wall to establish point B. To establish the right angle desired between point A and C, see Figure 6 – 14. The mathematical triangle that establishes this right angle can be created using a taut string approximately 2 feet longer than the outside dimension of the deck. This string, nailed to a "batter board," should be pulled out from the wall at an approximate right angle to the wall, anchored, and marked at the 8-foot distance from the wall. Then a long 2 × 4 marked at 10 feet can be extended from point B to point C. The string and the marked 2 × 4 may have to be moved left or right until the marks on each match. When they do, a right angle has been created to use as a reference point for placement of footings where desired inside or outside the triangle. Other footings can be placed by measurements from this reference point and wall reference points.

Laying out the deck. The size and pattern of the decking affect the framing plan of the deck. Determine the decking pattern first. The most common pattern is to have decking in one direction with joists at right angles to the decking. The beams are at right angles to the joists. This arrangement is referred to as *standard* framing. In standard framing, the layout is simply a matter of determining decking spans, choosing joist size and span, and then locating posts or other supports for beams.

Vertical-grain wood is recommended for decking, but when flat-grained lumber is used, it is important to make sure that the bark side of the piece is up before nailing. This minimizes the raising of grain in flat-grain pieces. Either side of a vertical-grain piece may be up when the piece is laid.

Nails. Use only corrosion-resistant nails for secure holding power and to avoid iron stains on the wood. Stainless steel and aluminum never cause staining of redwood. If these are not locally available, hot-dipped, high-quality galvanized nails with a ring or spiral shank are usually adequate. For 2-inch decking, use a 16d nail. Use 8d nails for 1-inch decking.

Nailing. Predrill holes for nails at the end of decking pieces to avoid splitting the wood and to achieve a secure fastening. For most decks, seasoned decking material should be spaced about ⅛ inch apart. This will be sufficient to allow draining of water. At the ends of the deck plank, nail through predrilled holes. Use only one nail per bearing, alternating from one side of the piece to the other. This method is sufficient for retaining kiln-dried redwood, which does not require heavy nailing because of its stability. The nailing on alternate sides overcomes any minor tendency to pull or cup. When the decking rests on only two supports

and each piece completes only a single span, as in herringbone and parquet decking, nail two nails at each end.

Use any handy measuring template to make sure the spacing is uniform between the boards. One common method is to use a nail as a spacer, pulling it out when the decking has been secured. Keeping nails in alignment improves the appearance of the surface of the deck.

Special situations. There are several special locations for decks that you might be concerned about. They include:

Decks on the ground. On level ground it is often desirable to use wood decking as a patio paving surface. The deck on the ground may serve as a complete patio paving, or may be alternated with concrete, brick, grass, or plantings. This provides a quick-draining terrace at ground level and is possible only with a decay- and insect-resistant wood such as heartwood redwood.

First, a 3-inch bed of tamped sand should be laid below the planned surface of the deck. This will promote drainage and keep weeds from growing through the deck. If the soil is poorly drained, a chemical soil conditioner and 3 inches of coarse gravel under the sand will improve drainage of a deck on the ground.

The decking should be nailed to an all-heartwood 2 × 4 cleat, laid flat in the sand. If the decking is laid in the standard parallel pattern, the 2 × 4s should be placed at 2-foot intervals to allow the use of random-length wood in 2-foot multiples.

If the decking is laid in a parquet pattern, the squares should be fabricated first, then laid down as large paving squares. Regular parquet or diamond design can be handled this way. Careful leveling is necessary to lay the parquet deck. When plantings or other materials are to be alternated with the parquet decking, a border strip of 2 × 4 heartwood redwood on edge will suffice to contain the planting and may serve as formwork for concrete or other paving.

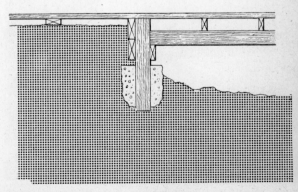

Figure 16–16. A deck on a downhill slope.

Downhill slopes. If the deck is begun on grade and then extends out over a slope, the transition from nailing-strip framing to joist-and-beam framing can be achieved without any interruption of the surface decking (Figure 16–16).

The transition from brick, grass, or other materials as ground cover on a level space to redwood decking over a slope can be made easily. Locate the standard deck framing to bring the surface of the deck up to the edge of the other materials. Swimming pools sometimes use the last available level ground space, but decking can provide a usable area where none would otherwise exist.

Decking over concrete. A wood deck can be laid directly over a concrete patio, and it will provide a better-insulated and faster-draining surface than the concrete. If the decking lays directly on the concrete, the same basic framing can be used as when deck is laid directly on the ground. One modification will be required: Although the ground can be leveled, the slab probably has a slight slope, so the deck framing may have to be shimmed. If the deck is to be elevated above the slab, as in the case of a floor-level deck with a 12- to 18-inch air space below, standard framing should be used.

Roof-top decks. The areas above first-floor rooms, carports, garages, and other flat-roofed areas offer attractive possibilities for outdoor living rooms adjacent to second-floor rooms. But before such a roof area is used as deck area, it must be made "traffic-proof" so that wear will not cause leaks. Since most flat-type roofs that would be used for deck purposes are usually already covered with a webbing of impregnated felt, tar, or asphalt and gravel, or simply a layer of 90-pound felt rolled roofing, an additional built-up arrangement must be provided to withstand the traffic. As a rule, building a wood deck is similar to building a deck over a concrete slab.

Where the roof slope exceeds a ¼ inch per foot pitch, to provide the necessary drainage you can use anything from 2 × 2s up to 2 × 10s cut on a diagonal across the face to form long wedges or shims to level the deck floor. The "shims" should be spaced at 16-inch intervals, the usual spacing for floor joists. The decking boards are then fastened to the shims or the shims may be used to support square decking platforms. The advantage of the latter is that they may be lifted up at will for roof repairs underneath or for recovery of lost items that may have fallen through. In either case, the outer end of the shims is closed with a fascia of the same material used for the flooring boards.

Exterior-grade plywood, special fiberglass deck panels, or fiberglass cloth, as well as specially designed roof decking materials, may also be used as coverings for roof-top decks. These should be installed as directed by their manufacturer. In addition, if your roof is covered with roll roofing, there are several so-called deck coatings that can be painted or sprayed over the surface. While these products will convert the average roof into a suitable deck for sunning, they are not applicable for heavy service.

Changing levels in the garden. While a deck creates level space on a sloping lot, it may also serve as access to the rest of the garden, by providing steps or multi-leveled platforms where garden levels may vary. Stairs can be as simple as two or three deck-wide platforms leading from a low-level deck into the garden, providing broad access and lounging space. They may be as complex as a series of deck platforms, with stairs between, to ease the transition on a steep site. They may be long, straight, or winding stairs whose purpose is purely one of connecting the deck to the ground. Each type of stair has its place, and all are constructed in basically the same way.

Figure 16–17. Two roof-top decks.

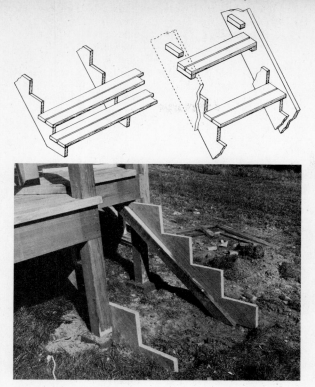

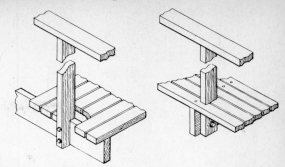

Figure 16—19. Deck railings.

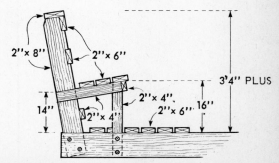

Figure 16—18. Step details.

Constructing stairs. Treads should be a minimum of 11 inches. The risers should not be higher than 7 inches for comfortable climbing, but can be as low as 4 inches. If you are in doubt as to whether to make one step or two, generally two would be preferred to avoid one high step.

When the drop to the next level is just one step, the step can be a simple inverted box. For two steps or more, it is usually best to frame the steps with stringers. For wide stairs, space notched stringers at intervals up to 3 feet 6 inches apart, depending upon the size of material used for treads. If only two steps are planned, a 2 × 12 can usually be laid on edge and notched as a stringer. If more steps are needed, a sloping stringer will be used. If notched stringers are used, they must have a minimum of 3½ inches effective width below the notch, according to most building codes (Figure 16–18).

Stairs can be set inside a boxed stringer, either on cleats or on notched stringers, to an all-heartwood redwood or concrete pad or to the deck at the lower level.

Railings. When the deck is elevated above the ground more than 2 feet, a railing should be provided. In many instances a railing is required by law.

Railing supports should be securely fastened to the framing of the deck in order to have sufficient strength and resistance to outward forces (Figure 16–19). Toenailing to the surface of the deck is *not* satisfactory. Railing supports should be bolted to joists or beams, or may be an extension of the support posts of the deck. The posts and railings can be very decorative and an infinite variety of designs is possible.

When small children are expected to use the deck, it is wise to use either a small-aperture wood grille, expanded metal, or other protective wire screen to insure against their falling through the railing. Any of these protective grilles will provide complete safety while not obstructing the view. For privacy, insert solid panels in the railings or raise full-height screens to close off neighboring homes from view. Screening or expanded metal should be aluminum or galvanized iron.

Seating. Since seating is a necessary element of a deck of any size, a solution to at least part of the seating requirements is a built-in bench or seat as part of the railing structure. Typical details are given in Figure 16–20. As in the railing, the back supports for seating must be well anchored to the framing of the deck, and the post supporting the deck may be extended to form part of the framing for the seating.

Figure 16—20. A built-in deck seat.

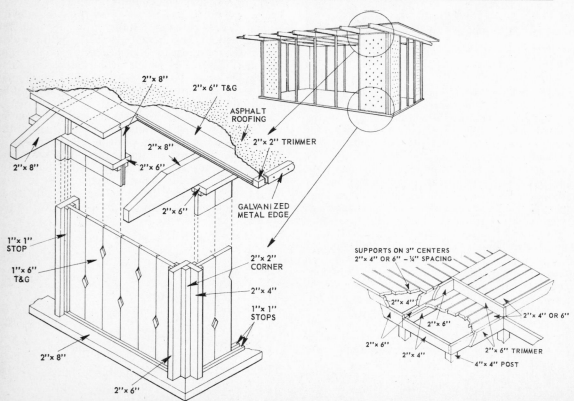

Figure 16–21. A simple garden shelter appropriate in most settings.

PATIO AND GARDEN SHELTERS

The use of a patio or garden shelter determines its design and location. Planning must include decisions as to the need for sun and wind control, plumbing and electricity, and storage. Consideration should also be given to the relation of the shelter to other activity areas, buildings, and natural objects present in the garden.

The basic roof designs (Figure 16–22) used in garden shelters include a flat roof, a sloping or shed roof, a gable roof, and a pyramid roof. The flat and shed roof are by far the most commonly employed in garden shelter design. The gable and pyramid roofs are somewhat more complicated for the average home handyman to undertake, but they are basic roof designs and most building contractors can handle them with ease.

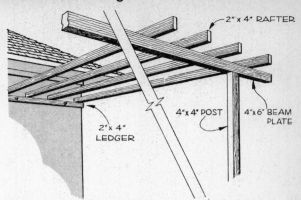

Figure 16–23. Basic post-and-beam construction.

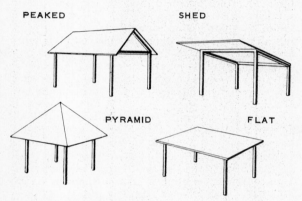

Figure 16–22. Basic roof designs.

Although appearance is often the deciding factor in the design of the roof, if the roof is to be watertight, it should be slightly sloped to allow for moisture runoff. The flat and shed roofs may be cantilevered beyond their normal overhangs. If this design is contemplated, the advice of a building professional should again be sought.

The minimum height of any shelter should be 8 feet. No matter what type of roof, the ceiling should be high enough to allow for head clearance in all areas. The height of the shelter should not interfere with surrounding objects, such as utility poles or wires.

Most garden and patio shelters are of post-and-beam design. Posts, properly spaced to provide adequate support, are set in the ground or securely connected to a firm foundation. The posts support horizontal beams (plates), which in turn support the roof rafters at right angles to the beams. Many patio shelters are attached to existing buildings, and a modification of the basic post-and-beam construc-

tion is used. On the left of the illustration in Figure 16–23 a ledger strip is shown attached to the existing building. The building performs the function of the posts, and the rafters rest directly on the ledger strip. Check with local building authorities before starting construction to find out the local building requirements and restrictions placed on garden structures, both free-standing and attached to dwellings.

Setting posts for support. For most patio and garden shelters, 4 × 4 posts are sufficiently large in size for the job. On larger structures, bigger posts are sometimes necessary to support heavier roof loads and still maintain wide post spacing. The use of 2 × 4s or 2 × 6s in tandem with a spacer block between them to form a column instead of a solid post is sometimes possible.

Posts in the ground. The simplest method of anchoring the redwood post is to set it directly in the ground. For most structures, firmly tamped earth around the post will give sufficient rigidity (Figure 16–24A). If the soil is sandy or unstable, a concrete collar should be poured around the post after it has been placed in the hole and earth tamped around the base (Figure 16–24B). Posts should be carefully plumbed with a level. When they are set in concrete, temporary bracing is often necessary to hold them plumb while the concrete sets. The depth to which posts should be set depends on the soil conditions and wind load. A depth of 36 inches is adequate for most 8- to 10-foot-high structures, but it may be necessary to set the posts deeper for higher shelters.

When posts are set in the ground, the floor of the shelter may be a wood deck, gravel, paving blocks, grass, or earth. Ordinarily, if a concrete slab is to be poured as the shelter floor, the posts are anchored to the slab rather than set in the ground.

Posts in concrete. Three common methods of placing posts in concrete are illustrated in Figure

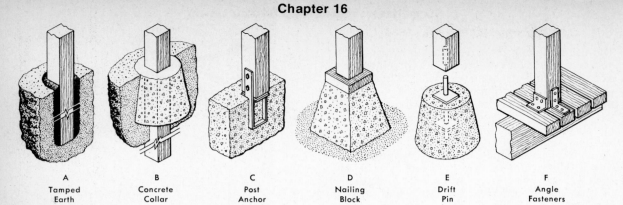

Figure 16—24. Post footings.

16–24. Patented post anchors of many types, available at most local building supply dealers, may be inbedded in concrete, as shown in Figure 16–24C. These provide positive anchorage of the post to the concrete. Figure 16–24D shows the nailing block method, where the post is toenailed to a wood block set in concrete. The nailing block is usually less secure, however, than a metal anchor bolted through the post. When a concealed anchorage is desired, the drift pin (Figure 16–24E) is often used. A small space should be left between the bottom of the post and the concrete surface to avoid the accumulation of moisture and dirt.

Where the shelter is to be built above an existing redwood deck, the posts may be placed over the existing support members of the deck. The posts should be firmly anchored with angle fasteners, as shown in Figure 16–24F. All metal parts used in connection with redwood must be corrosion resistant to avoid iron staining.

Connecting posts and beams. The beams support the roof rafters and tie the posts together, giving rigidity to the structure. To perform these functions properly, the beams must be adequately connected to the posts. Where design permits, the best bearing is achieved when the beam is placed directly on top of the post.

Several methods of connection are possible. A patented post cap (Figure 16–25A) is useful where the beam is the same width as the post. Many models are commercially available. A wood cleat (Figure 16–25B) can also be used in connecting beams to posts. When the beam is smaller than the width of the post, it may be bolted to the post singly (Figure 16–25C), or in pairs (Figure 16–25D). When 2-inch-dimension redwood is used in tandem with a redwood spacer block to form a column, a 2-inch-thick horizontal member may be bolted between the two parts of the column (Figure 16–25E).

Installing the rafters. Rafters support the finished roof or may be used alone without further elements to create a roof pattern. Actually, the method of installing rafters varies with the manner in which they meet the beam. The most common method is to have the rafters resting on top of the supporting member and toenailed or anchored to it by some other conventional method. Rafters may also be

Figure 16—25. Roof support construction.

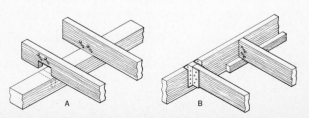

Figure 16—26. Methods of installing rafters.

notched to lower roof height (Figure 16–26A).

Rafters for either a flat or sloping roof, which are to be flush with the top of the beam, may be attached in one of several ways: with a patented metal rafter hanger; with a wood ledger strip nailed under the rafter for support; or with the rafter toe-nailed and nailed from the reverse side of the beam (Figure 16–26B).

When rafters extend from an existing building, they may be attached either flush or on top of a ledger strip fastened to the building. It is important that the ledger strip be bolted or securely fastened to the existing structure if it is to give the necessary support to the rafters.

Some roofing materials or methods require cross supports between rafters. This may be achieved by nailing blocking between the members.

Roofing possibilities. The roof of the patio or garden shelter can be one of its most interesting features. To decide what kind is best, you must determine the function the roof will serve. While in some climates it is not necessary to make a solid roof or to enclose a shelter, in others an open shelter would not give sufficient protection.

A wide variety of materials can be used. Many roofs are wood or a combination of materials with a wood framework. Shingles or shakes, reed fencing, bamboo, window screening, lath, louvers, canvas, glass, or plastic can be used. Recommended application instructions for most products are available from the suppliers. In most instances, only nailing is required for installation. The roofing material should harmonize with the nearby structures. A lath or slat roof of wood creates shadows while letting light penetrate and breaks the wind without stopping vertical air circulation. The lath members might be anything from a slim ½- by 3-inch batten to a 2-inch-thick piece. Generally widths more than 6 inches are not used as roof slats. The roof slats are usually spaced at a distance equal to the width of one of the slats. Sometimes 2-inch-thick material is used as slatting, allowing greater spans between rafters, but requiring stronger rafters because of the greater weight on each rafter.

It may be desirable to make the roof slats removable. In such a situation they can be attached to

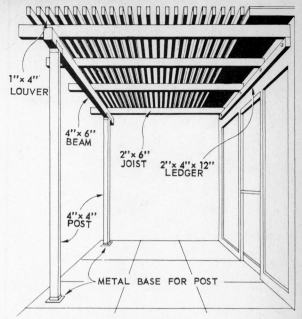

Figure 16–28. A lattice roof design.

a framework that fastens to the rafters in sections.

One very popular type of overhead shelter is the eggcrate. The eggcrate is composed of horizontal roof supports at right angles to one another, with equal spacing in both directions. Normally the rafters in each direction are the same depth and thickness and are flush on the underside. Two methods of constructing the eggcrate are shown in Figure 16–27.

In the blocking method rafters are placed in one direction, and blocking is nailed between them to form a straight line. The best method for proper alignment of the blocking is to measure and mark the spacing desired on the two end rafters. Then stretch a chalk line between the marks, and snap it to mark the rest of the rafters. With a square, draw lines down the vertical faces of the rafters so that they can be seen from below. Blocking can be secured by toenailing or nailing through the ends of the block from the other side of the rafters. Mortising is another method for constructing an eggcrate. This is used where the span is not large or the members are of sufficient size. Members in one direction are notched to fit complementary notches in the cross-members. The resulting joints should be flush on both planes. Both the eggcrate and lath overheads may be covered over with another material, such as canvas, plastic, or matting, for more shade or protection from the elements.

Translucent plastic fiberglass panels are very popular as a patio roofing material. These plastic

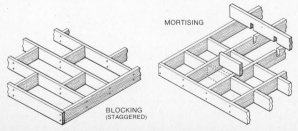

Figure 16–27. Two methods of constructing eggcrates.

Chapter 16

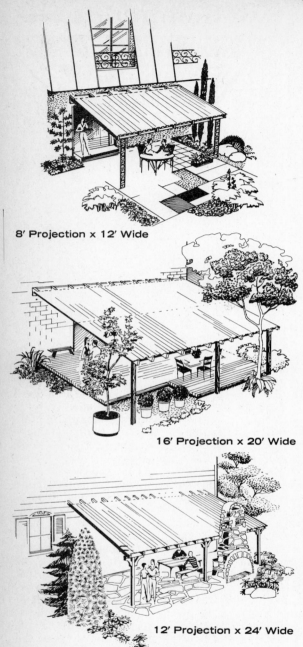

8' Projection x 12' Wide

16' Projection x 20' Wide

12' Projection x 24' Wide

Figure 16—29. Three sizes of plastic panel roofs.

panels generally come corrugated and it is difficult to get a perfect waterproof seal where the end of the panel butts against the flat wall. For a weather-tight seal, you can attach the end of the corrugated panel to wood, insert small pieces of half-round and caulk

the openings. However, there are available matching rubber and asphalt moldings. These moldings are nailed to the wood, and the plastic panel is set over the molding. It is best to use a mastic sealer between the molding and the plastic. Where two panels join, an overlap of corrugation is necessary. The panels come with one end of the corrugations up and the other down, both sides up, or both sides down. Depending upon which you get, you have to overlap from one to two corrugations to produce a weather-tight joint. You will find detailed overlapping information with the instruction sheets issued by the company whose material you purchase. Remember, use the special mastic made by these plastic companies. Although regular caulking compound can be used, this special mastic is translucent and will not stick out like a sore thumb after the job is completed. This is particularly true if you use white plastic panels. In addition most manufacturers recommend that the panels be fastened with aluminum non-rusting nails and neoprene washers. Nails should be driven through the crown of the corrugation. At overlaps the nail should pass through both sheets and the non-drying mastic before it goes into the rafter. Predrilling of nail holes will prevent localized crazing or chipping of the plastic (Figure 16–31).

Some landscaping situations suggest a trellis or colonnade instead of a rectangular shelter. Posts are placed in a single line, either straight or curved, and crossbars to support the trellis are fastened to the posts at right angles in the same way that beams are. In this type of construction it is highly recommended that the posts be set in the ground for the stability that this method of anchoring offers. Diagonal bracing of the crossbars to the posts is recommended for added stability. The connecting rafters or trellis are nailed to the crossbars parallel to a line between the posts. Additional layers of lath or treillage may be added as desired.

Walls for the shelter. Most shelters have at least one wall, either solid or louvered, for privacy and protection against weather and insects. The climate will determine whether or not to completely enclose a shelter. In areas where winds are strong, walls in a shelter will provide strength against racking, and diagonal bracing may not be needed. If walls are not desired in spite of prevalent winds, diagonal bracing or shear panels should be used at corners.

BARBECUE GRILL OR OUTDOOR FIREPLACE

Pleasant evenings and outdoor cooking mean fun for all. You will enjoy the exciting experience of entertaining family and friends at meals cooked in your own backyard. Inexpensive, serviceable fireplaces for outdoor cooking can be built with minimum labor and time.

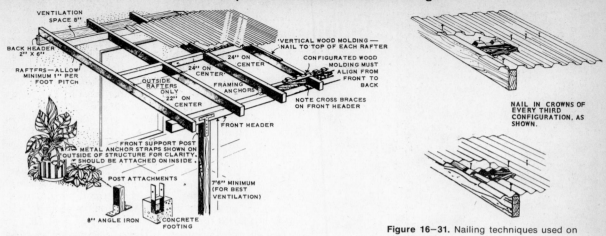

VENTILATION SPACE 8"

BACK HEADER 2" X 6"

RAFTERS—ALLOW MINIMUM 1" PER FOOT PITCH

OUTSIDE RAFTERS ONLY 22" ON CENTER

24" ON CENTER

24" ON CENTER

FRAMING ANCHORS

VERTICAL WOOD MOLDING — NAIL TO TOP OF EACH RAFTER

CONFIGURATED WOOD MOLDING MUST ALIGN FROM FRONT TO BACK

NOTE CROSS BRACES ON FRONT HEADER

FRONT HEADER

FRONT SUPPORT POST METAL ANCHOR STRAPS SHOWN ON OUTSIDE OF STRUCTURE FOR CLARITY. SHOULD BE ATTACHED ON INSIDE.

POST ATTACHMENTS

8" ANGLE IRON

CONCRETE FOOTING

7'6" MINIMUM (FOR BEST VENTILATION)

Figure 16–30. Construction details of a fiberglass plastic roof.

NAIL IN CROWNS OF EVERY THIRD CONFIGURATION, AS SHOWN.

Figure 16–31. Nailing techniques used on plastic roofs.

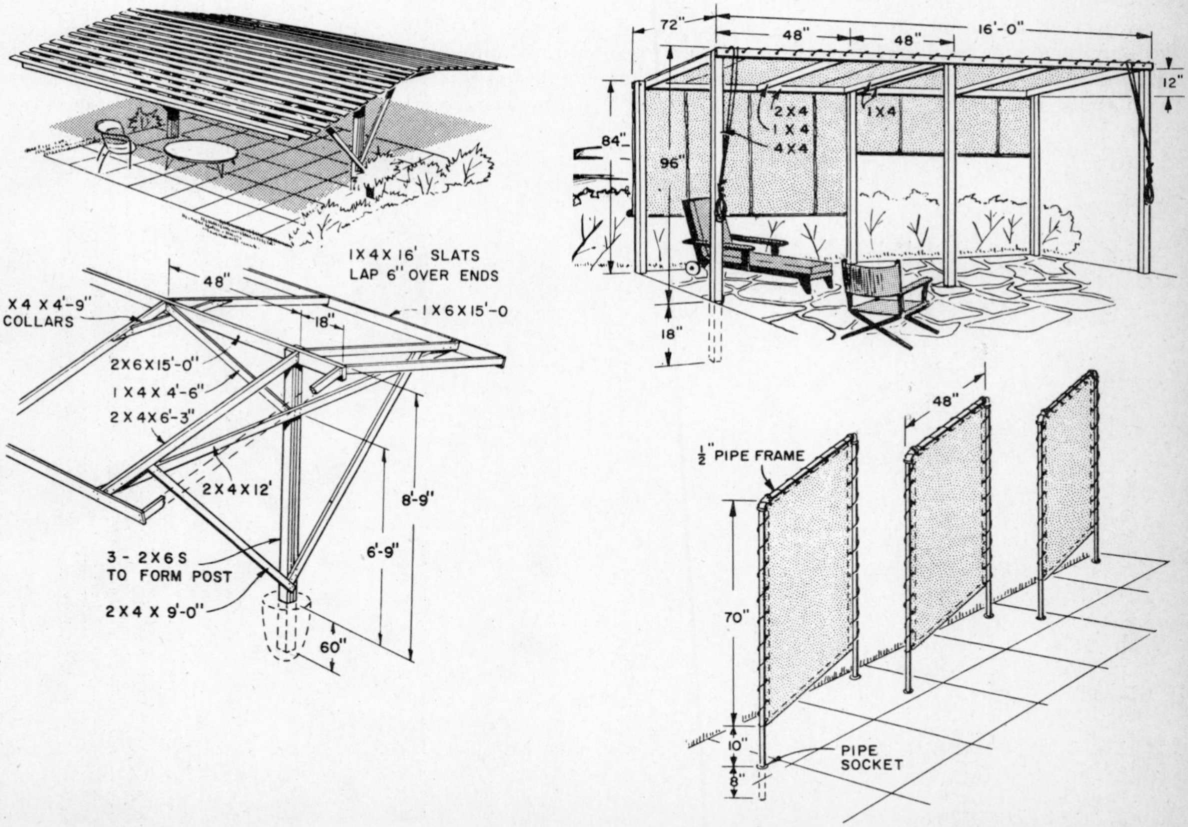

1 X 4 X 16' SLATS LAP 6" OVER ENDS

1 X 4 X 4'-9" COLLARS

48"

18"

1 X 6 X 15'-0

2 X 6 X 15'-0"

1 X 4 X 4'-6"

2 X 4 X 6'-3"

2 X 4 X 12'

3 - 2 X 6 S TO FORM POST

2 X 4 X 9'-0"

8'-9"

6'-9"

60"

72"

48"

48"

16'-0"

12"

84"

96"

2 X 4
1 X 4
4 X 4

1 X 4

18"

½" PIPE FRAME

48"

70"

10"

8"

PIPE SOCKET

Figure 16–32. Slat and canvas shelters.

Figure 16—33. A built-in patio storage unit.

it with a 2- to 3-inch concrete backing.

Where landscaping layout permits, select a secluded spot for the open-hearth type of fireplace. If there are tall trees and heavy shrubbery in the garden area, a fireplace with a tall chimney will be quite appropriate. For more open spaces a higher degree of decoration is desirable, and in this case a rustic type of fireplace, faced with cobblestones, would be appropriate. Whenever possible the fireplace should be placed so that the opening will face the prevailing wind. This will assure good draft and keep the smoke out of the eyes of both the cook and others. The two most common types of fuel used are wood and charcoal briquets. Those who live in urban areas prefer briquets as they burn without creating annoying smoke. If wood is used as fuel, do not build the fireplace beneath a tree or close to any shrubs, because smoke will damage foliage. On the other hand, if charcoal is used the fireplace can be set anywhere. Gas and electric-fired outdoor barbecue grills are also available, and these can be located almost anywhere on the patio, too.

In the construction of an outdoor fireplace a proper foundation or base is essential. For a simple slab foundation used in areas free from severe frost damage, excavate sod, loose earth, and other materials to a depth slightly below ground surface. Level and tamp the earth. Place 2- by 4-inch form boards so that the final surface of the slab will be at least 1 inch above ground level. Make the slab base at least

The outdoor fireplace can be as simple or as elaborate as individual taste prescribes. A patio need not be large to set off effectively any type of open-air fireplace. It can be made of concrete blocks or masonry, reinforced poured concrete, a combination of brick and concrete, or even concrete faced with cobblestones, and can be finished with stucco or painted with cement paint. If a facing of either cobblestones or brick is applied, be sure to provide

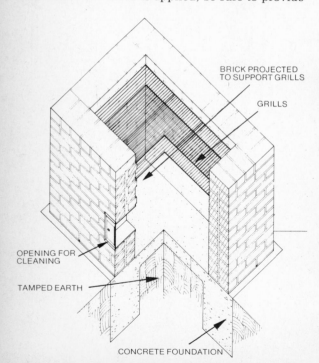

BRICK PROJECTED
TO SUPPORT GRILLS

GRILLS

OPENING FOR
CLEANING

TAMPED EARTH

CONCRETE FOUNDATION

Figure 16—34. A simple brick fireplace.

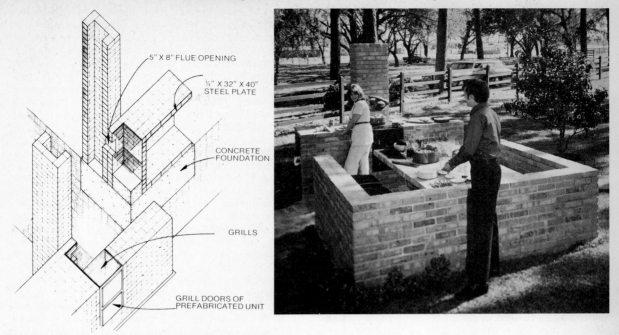

5" X 8" FLUE OPENING

¼" X 32" X 40" STEEL PLATE

CONCRETE FOUNDATION

GRILLS

GRILL DOORS OF PREFABRICATED UNIT

Figure 16–35. A brick barbecue fireplace with a prefabricated unit.

2 inches wider on all sides than the fireplace. If the soil in your yard does not have good drainage or is subject to frost heave, the slab should be placed on a 4-inch layer of gravel or crushed stone.

The masonry fireplace shown in Figure 16–34 is lined with standard fire bricks for increased durability. The bricks measure 9 by 4½ by 2½ inches and are laid so that the wide face is exposed to the flame. Four bricks will cover approximately 1 square foot. For best results, use air-setting, high-temperature cement mortar. Thirty-five pounds will be needed for 100 bricks.

To help insure a good fire-box and draft, it is often wise to purchase a prebuilt fireplace unit. Such a unit is available for inclusion in almost any type of outdoor fireplace design. It certainly simplifies building and reduces construction time by half.

If you do not want an upright fireplace, a fire pit can be a welcome addition to your patio. Youngsters and adults enjoy an evening of fun around the fire. In winter, too, this handy pit can be used as a warming area.

STEPS

When slopes to the house are greater than a 5 percent grade, stairs or steps should be used. This may be accomplished with a ramp sidewalk, a flight of stairs at a terrace, or a continuing sidewalk. These stairs have 11-inch treads and 7-inch risers when the stair is 30 inches or less in height. When the total rise is more than 30 inches, the tread is 12 inches and the riser 6 inches. For a moderately uniform slope, a stepped ramp may be satisfactory. Generally, the rise should be about 6 to 6½ inches, and the length between risers sufficient for two or three normal paces.

Exterior steps may also be required to rise from the ground to a door sill or a patio or porch. In calculating these riser-tread figures, measure first the distance from ground level to door sill (or other point of arrival when climbing). Divide by units of 6, 7, and 8 (or fractions of these) to decide how many equal risers will be needed. Then count the number of needed treads (calling the ground level one tread and the sill another) and lay out the plot of the whole stairs.

Concrete steps. Concrete porches and steps are attractive, safe, nonslippery in wet weather, and will last indefinitely. They are easy to keep clean, and will not rot or burn.

Porch steps. The first step in making a small stoop and stair arrangement is the excavation. This should be 2 feet deep, and its other dimensions are roughly those of the entire area to be covered by the steps. Before pouring, make sure that no dirt or stones have fallen into the excavation, because these earthen sides act as your form in retaining the concrete. Therefore, no forms are necessary below grade. The foundation of the building forms one

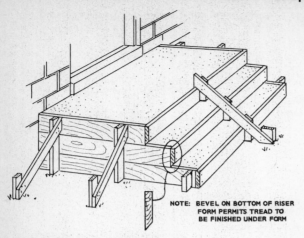

NOTE: BEVEL ON BOTTOM OF RISER
FORM PERMITS TREAD TO
BE FINISHED UNDER FORM

Figure 16–36. Forms for concrete steps.

end of the hole, and must be well cleaned of all dirt so that the new concrete can adhere to it. Tamp the earth in the bottom of the hole, unless it is already firm, to produce a sound base for the concrete.

When the excavation is completed, start building the form for the steps. Remember that the safest and easiest steps to climb have a tread 11 to 12 inches deep and a step height or rise of 6 to 7 inches between treads. Side forms are usually 1-inch boards backed (Figure 16–36) up with 2×4 form studs braced and tied. Riser forms for steps not more than about 3 feet wide may be 1- by 8-inch boards; wider steps require 2- by 8-inch riser forms to prevent bending or bulging when the forms are filled with concrete.

If 1- by 8- or 2- by 8-inch riser forms are used, an actual step height or rise of about $7\frac{1}{2}$ inches is obtained, resulting in steps that are easy to climb. If one low riser is needed to complete a set of steps, the small step, for safety's sake, should always be the bottom step, not the top. To make steps that afford maximum comfort in climbing, the riser form boards may be tilted in at the bottom about 1 inch. This provides additional toe space on the treads. Edges of steps may be rounded by finishing with an edging tool after the concrete has become quite stiff.

First the foundation must be poured, the part below ground level. Let it set for at least one day before doing the work above grade. Then the form is set in place, and the job is finished. To mix the concrete for the foundation, use a $1:2\frac{3}{4}:4$ formula. Remember that thorough mixing is most important for achieving durable concrete.

After this foundation has set for at least one day, set up the form on it. The form must be placed so that it is level and square with the house before it is fastened and braced firmly into place. It is se-

cured by means of the 2×4 stakes, and also by two or four diagonal braces (not shown) running from the top edge of the sides to stakes in the ground outside. Put these wherever the form needs support to prevent moving or spreading under the weight of the concrete. As a final check on the form after it has been placed in position, but before the stakes and braces are secured, measure the diagonals across the square that will form the steps. If both are the same length, the sides are square, parallel, and ready to be fastened into position.

When the form has been properly placed, spread a thick cement paste over the base and house foundation. This will bond the new concrete to the old. To make such a paste, mix $\frac{1}{2}$ bag of cement with 3 gallons of water. Then spread the paste evenly over the top foundation. This is done immediately before pouring the final batch of concrete, which is made in a $1:2\frac{1}{4}:3$ ratio. The pouring must be done very carefully to avoid jarring the form out of position.

After the concrete has set for a few hours, the platform and steps may be finished with a wood float. This produces an even but gritty surface that will not be slippery in wet weather. A small trowel or dull knife blade should be run along the inside edge of the form between the boards and concrete to make a smooth and slightly rounded edge on all surfaces that will be exposed.

Leave the form in position for a week. Then remove it, and cure the concrete by covering it with straw or burlap bags. Keep it damp for a week or ten days. After this curing, the form can be removed and the steps are ready for use.

Patio steps. Before setting up a form for patio steps, prepare the ground over which the steps are to be placed. If the soil is well drained and contains gravel and sand in relatively small amounts, all you will have to do is to level and tamp the area thor-

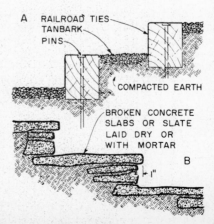

Figure 16–37. Types of patio steps.

oughly to compact the soil. If, however, the soil is a heavy, tight clay through which drainage of surface water is slow in wet seasons, it will be necessary to excavate to a depth of 6 to 10 inches below the grade and put in a tamped gravel fill. Thorough tamping of the fill is very important. However, never use cinders as a fill because they will eventually disintegrate under the heavy concrete casting. After the forms are set, the concrete is mixed and poured in the same manner as described for porch steps above.

Pre-cast concrete steps. Pre-cast concrete tread and riser units are available at your local masonry supply dealer. They are very easy to install, are durable, and will require no maintenance.

When pre-cast concrete steps are installed, concrete-block support walls must be placed on a concrete footing poured on firm soil below the frost line. These footings should be at least 6 inches thick and 12 inches wide. Mortar is used in setting pre-cast support walls, tread and riser units, platform units, pre-cast stair stringers, and block support walls. The mortar should be made in the proportions of 1 volume of masonry cement and between 2 and 3 volumes of mortar sand. One volume of portland cement and between 1 and 1¼ volumes of hydrated lime or lime putty and between 4 and 6 volumes of mortar sand may also be used. The sand should be in a damp, loose condition. Mortar joints should be thin and should be pointed up by tooling after the mortar has partially set. Mortar droppings should be wiped clean immediately with a wet cloth.

If desired, an additional finish may be applied by troweling a thick cement paste onto the blocks and pre-cast concrete steps. To make this, mix ½ bag of cement with 3 gallons of water. Wet the surfaces thoroughly before applying the paste. After this finish has had time to harden, the work is cured in the usual manner.

Brick steps. Making brick steps is a bit more difficult than construction of concrete units, but can nevertheless be mastered by the novice. Steps are generally laid in a bed of mortar or concrete. To do this, excavate to a depth of 9 inches and put in a foundation of gravel or cinders well tamped down. The concrete base requires the building of a form. A workable formula to use for steps is: twice the height of the riser plus the width of the tread equals 25. In general, steps should be at least 3 feet wide.

A light concrete mixture consisting of 1 part cement, 2¾ parts sand, and 4 parts pebbles is poured into the form. The concrete base can be eliminated entirely, and the solid brick bed can be used as a form if the steps are attached to the foundation walls with steel reinforcing. The excavation should be deep enough to accommodate a base of cinders or gravel and the thickness of two bricks laid flat. Bricks should be wet before they are laid; dry porous bricks absorb too much moisture. Sprinkle them with a hose for five minutes before using.

Starting at one corner, place a bed of mortar on the foundation with a trowel and edge each brick into position. Sufficient mortar must be used to fill the space completely between the brick and the foundation, and the brick should be tapped down into the mortar bed. Excess mortar that oozes out of the joints should be scraped off the outside edge with the trowel. After the first course is laid in this fashion, the second layer is started and proceeds in the same manner. Frequent use of the level and a straightedge will assure a good job.

In step wall construction it is a good practice to finish the joints on the exterior face. The weather joint is preferred because of its water-shedding ability. All jointing should be done after the mortar has stiffened slightly.

The inside cavity between the side brick wall, the steps, and main body of the house now should be filled in with a mix consisting of 1 part cement, 2 parts sand, and 4 parts gravel. Steel reinforcing rods, ½ inch in diameter, may be placed in the mixture.

Concrete porch floors. If a new concrete porch floor is to be 2 feet or less above the general ground level, a simple slab built on a fill makes an excellent floor. The fill of gravel, crushed rock, or cinders that supports the floor should be well tamped before placing concrete. The concrete floor is usually built 4 to 5 inches thick and should be reinforced as a protection against possible cracking due to uneven settlement. It is also important that the thickened edges of the concrete slab be reinforced with two ½-inch round reinforcing bars. This construction makes a reinforced concrete beam that spans the distance between supporting piers. The piers are made by filling 8-inch post holes with concrete. At laps the ends of the ½-inch round bars should extend past each other about 2 feet. The porch floor should be sloped about ¼ inch in 1 foot to provide adequate drainage. The surface of a porch may be finished in the same manner as patios.

SIDEWALKS

Like patios, the three most popular paving materials for sidewalks are concrete, brick, and flagstone. Sidewalks are constructed in the same manner as patios. See pages 460 to 463.

ILLUSTRATION CREDITS

ILLUSTRATION CREDITS

Adams Co.: Fig. 4–49
American General Products, Inc.: Figs. 4–50, 4–51
American Plywood Assoc.: Figs. 13–2, 13–16, 14–12 (bottom), 14–19 (right)
American Standard, Inc.: Figs. 11–1, 11–5 (top), 11–11, 11–18
Andersen Corp.: Fig. 8–12
Armstrong Cork Co.: Figs. 3–1, 3–6, 3–7, 3–8, 3–11, 3–12, 3–13, 4–17, 4–19, 4–20, 4–22, 4–23, 4–24, 4–25, 4–26, 4–27, 10–12, 12–1, 12–15 (right), 13–10, 13–12, 14–11, 14–13 (right)
Asphalt Roofing Mfg. Assoc.: Figs. 8–29, 8–30, 8–31, 8–33, 8–35, 8–36, 8–37, 15–5

Baker Brush Co.: Fig. 9–3
Benjamin Moore & Co.: Figs. 9–8, 9–9, 9–10, 9–11, 9–13, 9–14, 9–17, 9–21, 9–22, 9–23, 9–24, 9–25, 9–26, 9–27, 9–28, 9–29, 9–30, 9–31, 9–32, 9–34

Better Heating-Cooling Council: Figs. 7–1, 7–3
Bilco Co.: Figs. 12–2, 12–16, 12–17, 12–18
Bird & Son: Figs. 8–14, 15–1
Brick Institute of America: Figs. 2–15, 2–16, 2–17, 8–28, 16–6, 16–7, 16–8, 16–34, 16–35

California Redwood Assoc.: Figs. 3–18, 16–12, 16–13, 16–14, 16–15, 16–16, 16–18, 16–19, 16–20, 16–21, 16–22, 16–23, 16–24, 16–25, 16–26, 16–27, 16–28
Cedar Closet Assoc.: Figs. 14–8, 14–9
Certain-Teed Products Corp.: Fig. 8–26
Connor Forest Industries, Inc.: Figs. 10–1, 10–2
Conweld Corp.: Figs. 3–14, 14–32
Crane Mfg. Co.: Fig. 6–40

Decro-Wall Corp.: Figs. 3–45, 3–36, 3–54

E. I. du Pont de Nemours & Co.: Fig. 9–1

Dura-a-Flex, Inc.: Fig. 4–35

E. L. Bruce Co.: Figs. 3–20, 4–4, 4–6, 4–7, 4–8, 4–11, 4–16
E. L. Mustee & Sons, Inc.: Fig. 6–39
Eljer Corp.: Fig. 11–17

Family Handyman magazine: Figs. 2–10, 6–13, 7–36, 12–10, 12–11, 13–3, 13–4, 13–5, 13–6, 13–11, 16–9, 16–10, 16–37
Formica Corp.: Fig. 10–21

General Tire & Rubber Co.: Figs. 9–38, 11–2
Georgia-Pacific Corp.: Figs. 3–23, 3–26, 3–64

Hardwood Plywood Assoc.: Fig. 2–3
Homasote Co.: Figs. 3–35, 15–15 (bottom), 15–16

Ideal Co.: Fig. 3–68

INDEX

INDEX

Index

Index

Index